How to access the supplemental web resource

We are pleased to provide access to a web resource that supplements your textbook, *Introduction to Recreation and Leisure, Second Edition.* This resource offers chapter summaries, vocabulary lists with and without definitions, learning activities, and web links.

Accessing the web resource is easy!
Follow these steps if you purchased a new book:

1. Visit **www.HumanKinetics.com/IntroductionToRecreationAndLeisure**.

2. Click the <u>second edition</u> link next to the book cover.

3. Click the Sign in link on the left or top of the page. If you do not have an account with Human Kinetics, you will be prompted to create one.

4. If the online product you purchased does not appear in the Ancillary Items box on the left of the page, click the Enter Key Code option in that box. Enter the key code that is printed at the right, including all hyphens. Click the Submit button to unlock your online product.

5. After you have entered your key code the first time, you will never have to enter it again to access this product. Once unlocked, a link to your product will permanently appear in the menu on the left. For future visits, all you need to do is sign in to the textbook's website and follow the link that appears in the left menu!

→ Click the Need Help? button on the textbook's website if you need assistance along the way.

How to access the web resource if you purchased a used book:

You may purchase access to the web resource by visiting the text's website, **www.HumanKinetics.com/IntroductionToRecreationAndLeisure**, or by calling the following:

800-747-4457 . . . . .U.S. customers
800-465-7301 . . . . .Canadian customers
+44 (0) 113 255 5665 . . . . European customers
08 8372 0999 . . . . Australian customers
0800 222 062 . . . . .New Zealand customers
217-351-5076 . . . . .International customers

For technical support, send an e-mail to:
support@hkusa.com . . . . U.S. and international customers
info@hkcanada.com . . . . Canadian customers
academic@hkeurope.com . . . . European customers
keycodesupport@hkaustralia.com . . . . . Australian and New Zealand customers

HUMAN KINETICS
The Information Leader in Physical Activity & Health

07-2012

Product: Introduction to Recreation and Leisure, Second Edition, web resource

Key code: HK-PRSRKZ-OSG

This unique code allows you access to the web resource.

Access is provided if you have purchased a new book. Once submitted, the code may not be entered for any other user.

Second Edition

Introduction to Recreation and Leisure

Human Kinetics

Editor

Human Kinetics

Library of Congress Cataloging-in-Publication Data

Introduction to recreation and leisure. -- 2nd ed.
  p. cm.
Includes bibliographical references and index.
ISBN 978-1-4504-2417-2 (hard cover) -- ISBN 1-4504-2417-1 (hard cover) 1. Recreation. 2. Leisure. I. Human Kinetics (Organization)
GV14.I68 2012
790--dc23
                2012003985

ISBN-10: 1-4504-2417-1 (print)
ISBN-13: 978-1-4504-2417-2 (print)

The web addresses cited in this text were current as of February 23, 2012, unless otherwise noted.

Acquisitions Editor: Gayle Kassing, PhD; **Developmental Editor:** Melissa Feld; **Assistant Editor:** Rachel Brito; **Copyeditor:** Bob Replinger; **Indexer:** Dan Connolly; **Permissions Manager:** Dalene Reeder; **Graphic Designer:** Joe Buck; **Graphic Artist:** Kathleen Boudreau-Fuoss; **Cover Designer:** Keith Blomberg; **Photographer (cover):** Top: amridesign/fotolia.com; Bottom: © Human Kinetics; **Photographer (interior):** see Photo Credits page; **Photo Asset Manager:** Laura Fitch; **Visual Production Assistant:** Jason Allen; **Photo Production Manager:** Joyce Brumfield; **Art Manager:** Kelly Hendren; **Associate Art Manager:** Alan L. Wilborn; **Illustrations:** © Human Kinetics; **Printer:** Sheridan Books

Printed in the United States of America   10   9   8   7   6   5   4   3

The paper in this book is certified under a sustainable forestry program.

Human Kinetics
Website: www.HumanKinetics.com

United States: Human Kinetics
P.O. Box 5076
Champaign, IL 61825-5076
800-747-4457
e-mail: humank@hkusa.com

Canada: Human Kinetics
475 Devonshire Road Unit 100
Windsor, ON N8Y 2L5
800-465-7301 (in Canada only)
e-mail: info@hkcanada.com

Europe: Human Kinetics
107 Bradford Road
Stanningley
Leeds LS28 6AT, United Kingdom
+44 (0) 113 255 5665
e-mail: hk@hkeurope.com

Australia: Human Kinetics
57A Price Avenue
Lower Mitcham, South Australia 5062
08 8372 0999
e-mail: info@hkaustralia.com

New Zealand: Human Kinetics
P.O. Box 80
Torrens Park, South Australia 5062
0800 222 062
e-mail: info@hknewzealand.com

Contents

Chapter 4   Leisure and Recreation for Individuals in Society 61

Daniel G. Yoder and Juan Tortosa Martínez

Part II   Leisure and Recreation as a Multifaceted Delivery System   77

Chapter 5   Leisure Service Delivery Systems 79

David N. Emanuelson

Chapter 6   Parks and Protected Areas in Canada and the United States. 93

Paul F.J. Eagles and Jeffrey C. Hallo

Chapter 12   Leisure and Recreation Across the Life Span 251

Lynn A. Barnett and Joel A. Blanco

Part III   Delivering Recreation and Leisure Services   275

Chapter 13   Program Delivery System. 277

Diane C. Blankenship

Chapter 14   Recreational Sport Management. . . . 289

Craig M. Ross and H. Joey Gray

Chapter 15   Health, Wellness, and Quality of Life . .305

Terrance Robertson, Matthew Symonds, Michael Muehlenbein, and Clifford Robertson

Chapter 16   Outdoor and Adventure Recreation . . 321

Alan Ewert and Franklin Vernon

Chapter 17   Arts and Culture 341

Gaylene Carpenter

Chapter 18   The Nature of Recreation and Leisure as a Profession. 365

Denise M. Anderson

Chapter 19 International Perspectives on Recreation and Leisure 385

Holly Donohoe, Arianne C. Reis, Alcyane Marinho, Jinyang Deng, and Huimei Liu

Preface

Welcome to recreation and leisure studies. This introductory course textbook provides you with a broad view of one of the top industries for the 21st century. Recreation and leisure programs serve people 24/7/365 and are part of a global economy. These services are vital to the lives of individuals, families, and communities and can provide you with a challenging career path.

This book invites you to take an amazing journey as you explore the world of recreation and leisure. Your escorts are 43 professors and professionals in the field from the United States, Canada, Brazil, and China. Their careers and passions mirror the various aspects of this profession. As rising stars, experts, leading thinkers, and icons in the field, the contributing authors serve as your personal guides as you begin your undergraduate studies of this exciting field. Their unique viewpoints provide a foundation for understanding the field on which your undergraduate studies will build.

Introduction to Recreation and Leisure, Second Edition, showcases the authors who have made incredible contributions in providing this unprecedented view of recreation and leisure. The goal of this book is to illustrate the wealth of opportunities within this diverse profession.

For students pursuing a career in recreation and leisure or considering the field as a career choice, this book offers vital information that will help in making informed choices. We want to provide you with a big picture of this diverse profession so that in your later studies you can explore specific areas in depth to gain an understanding of recreation and leisure as the following:

- A profession that offers lifetime career satisfaction or perhaps an entry-level start on a career path with many options
- A contemporary industry that provides employment opportunities in a wide variety of fields and associated fields
- A worldwide phenomenon that drives most of the world's economies

ORGANIZATION

Introduction to Recreation and Leisure is divided into three parts. Part I, Foundations of Recreation and Leisure, provides the foundation of this industry, including an introduction, history, and philosophical concepts. Part II, Leisure and Recreation as a Multifaceted Delivery System, introduces you to various sectors and areas of the field. Part III, Delivering Recreation and Leisure Services, presents the different types of programming found in recreation and leisure services. These interest areas include recreational sport; health, wellness, and quality of life; outdoor and adventure recreation; and culture and the arts. This part ends with a chapter that addresses the nature of the profession and what it takes to become a professional and another chapter that provides an international perspective on recreation and leisure.

FEATURES

Several unique and useful features are included in the book.

- **Learning outcomes**. Each chapter lists the many important concepts that you will learn and understand.
- **Outstanding graduates**. Students who have graduated from recreation and leisure programs and gone on to successful careers have been highlighted. They share insights and advice on recreation and leisure as a career.
- **Glossary**. Important terms are printed in boldface in the text, and the definitions are included in the web resource and instructor guide available online at www. HumanKinetics.com/IntroductionToRecreationAndLeisure.

ANCILLARIES

Four types of ancillaries are available to supplement the information presented in the textbook:

- **Instructor guide**. The instructor guide includes chapter summaries, learning outcomes, learning activities, reflective questions, websites, and glossary terms for each chapter.
- **Test package**. The test package includes a variety of questions: true–false, multiple-choice, matching, and short answer. Instructors can create their own tests.
- **Presentation package**. A Microsoft PowerPoint presentation package covers the major topics and key points from the chapters. Instructors may use the presentation package to supplement their lectures. The presentation package may be adapted to suit each instructor's lecture content and style.
- **Web resource**. New to this edition is a web resource for students. Access is available to students by following the instructions on the key code page at the front of the book. Students will find chapter summaries, learning experiences, a glossary, and web links to explore more about recreation and leisure.

Introduction to Recreation and Leisure, Second Edition, presents a comprehensive view of the multifaceted, expansive field of recreation and leisure. Enjoy learning about recreation and leisure, reading what the principal thinkers and leaders have to say about the field, and meeting outstanding graduates from universities across the United States, Canada, and the world who share their career experiences. Let's enter the world of recreation and leisure.

Photo Credits

Chapter and Part Openers

Part I: © Jade Lee/Asia Images Group/age fotostock; **Chapter 1:** © Human Kinetics; **Chapter 2:** Library of Congress/George Grantham Bain Collection; **Chapter 3:** iStockphoto/Kenneth C. Zirkel; **Chapter 4:** © Human Kinetics; **Part II:** © Joseph Sohm/ Visions of America, LLC/age fotostock; **Chapter 5:** © Don Mason/Lithium/age fotostock; **Chapter 6:** Photo courtesy of Paul F.J. Eagles; **Chapter 7:** Galina Barskaya/fotolia.com; **Chapter 8:** Bold Stock/age fotostock; **Chapter 9:** Alexey Stiop/fotolia.com; **Chapter 10:** © Jochem Wijnands/ Picture Contact Bv/age fotostock; **Chapter 11:** © Sharon Simonson/age fotostock; **Chapter 12:** Stewart Cohen/Digital Vision; **Part III:** © Bettina Strenske/Image Broker/age fotostock; **Chapter 13:** © Human Kinetics; **Chapter 14:** Michael Pettigrew/fotolia.com; **Chapter 15:** © Human Kinetics; **Chapter 16:** Photo courtesy of Alastair Rose; **Chapter 17:** Dragan Trifunovic/fotolia.com; **Chapter 18:** Brand X Pictures; **Chapter 19:** © Florian Kopp/Image Broker/age fotostock

Contributor Photos

All photos courtesy of each individual contributor except for Jinyang Deng photo courtesy of Yi Deng and Daniel Yoder photo courtesy of Leann R. Shryack.

Outstanding Graduate Photos

All photos courtesy of each graduate.

Additional Photos

Photo on p. 6: © Brian Summers/First Light/age fotostock; **photo on p. 12:** © Jim West/age fotostock; **photo on p. 13:** Doug Olson/fotolia.com; **photo on p. 24:** © Michael Weber/Image Broker/age fotostock; **photo on p. 26:** "Ball Players." Artist: George Catlin; **photo on p. 29:** Library of Congress/Detroit Publishing Co.; **photo on p. 33:** © John E Marriott/All Canada Photos/age fotostock; **photo on p. 46:** Photodisc/Getty Images; **photo on p. 50:** Ludovisi Collection; **photo on p. 52:** © Robert Ginn/Index Stock/age fotostock; **photo on p. 54:** Jeff Greenberg/age fotostock; **photo on p. 57:** © Michael A. Keller/age fotostock; **photo on p. 64:** © Image Source/easyFotostock; **photo on p. 65:** Getty Images/DAJ; **photo on p. 67:** © Igor Gonzalo Sanz/age fotostock; **photo on p. 71:** © Dennis MacDonald/age fotostock; **photo on p. 83:** © Walter Bibikow/Agency Jon Arnold Images/age fotostock; **photo on p. 86:** © Human Kinetics; **photo on p. 88:** Felix Mizioznikov/fotolia.com; **photo on p. 95:** Photo courtesy of Paul F.J. Eagles; **photo on p. 96:** Photo courtesy of Paul F.J. Eagles; **photo on p. 98:** Photo courtesy of Paul F.J. Eagles; **photo on p. 105:** Photo courtesy of Paul F.J. Eagles; **photo on p. 107:** Photo courtesy of Paul F.J. Eagles; **photo on p. 111:** Photo courtesy of Paul F.J. Eagles; **photo on p. 114:** Photo courtesy of Paul F.J. Eagles; **photo on p. 117:** Photo courtesy of Paul F.J. Eagles; **photo on p. 131:** John Joseph Kelso / Library and Archives Canada / PA-120557; **photo on p. 132:** © Human Kinetics; **photo on p. 134:** © Human Kinetics; **photo on p. 136:** © Human Kinetics; **photo on p. 153:** Photo courtesy of Western DuPage Special Recreation Association (WDSRA); **photo on p. 154:** Photo courtesy of Western DuPage Special Recreation Association (WDSRA); **photo on p. 156:** Photo courtesy of Western DuPage Special Recreation Association (WDSRA); **photo on p. 170:** © The Bakersfield Californian/ ZUMAPRESS.com; **photo on p. 172:** © Michael Owen Baker/Los Angeles Daily News/ZUMAPRESS.com; **photo on p. 175:** © Human Kinetics; **photos on p. 183 (left to right):** Photos courtesy of Patrick Tierney, © Human Kinetics, and © Ron Buskirk/ age fotostock; **photo on p. 186:** © Ron Buskirk/age fotostock; **photo on p. 190:** © Martin Siepmann/Image Broker/age fotostock; **photo on p. 201:** © Human Kinetics; **photo on p. 206:** Thomas Perkins/fotolia.com; **photo on p. 210:** Bold Stock/age fotostock; **photo on p. 220:** © Human Kinetics; **photo on p. 227:** © Joseph Sohm/Visions of America, LLC/age fotostock; **photo on p. 233:** © Ton Koene/age fotostock; **photo on p. 247:** © Kit R. Roane/age fotostock; **photo on p. 254:** © Human Kinetics; **photo on p. 256:** © Human Kinetics; **photo on p. 259:** © Jeff Greenberg/age fotostock; **photo on p. 262:** Photodisc; **photo on p. 266:** iStockphoto/ Mark Rose; **photo on p. 268:** © Human Kinetics; **photo on p. 272:** © Keith Morris/age fotostock; **photo on p. 279:** © Human Kinetics; **photos on p. 282 (left to right):** Peter Fox/fotolia.com and Fabio Barni/fotolia.com; **photos on p. 296 (left to right):** © Human Kinetics and Sorbotrol/fotolia.com; **photos on p. 298 (left to right):** Stockbyte and © Human Kinetics; **photo on p. 307:** Galina Barskaya/fotolia.com; **photo on p. 311:** Tomasz Trojanowski/fotolia.com; **photo on p. 314:** © Human Kinetics; **photo on p. 323:** Danny Warren/fotolia.com; **photo on p. 327:** Denis Pepin/fotolia.com; **photo on p. 331:** Adryn/fotolia.com; **photo on p. 336:** Oleg Kozlov/fotolia.com; **photo on p. 344:** Photo courtesy of Mele 'Ohana of Oregon; **photo on p. 348:** Photo courtesy of Gaylene Carpenter; **photo on p. 349:** Photo courtesy of Gaylene Carpenter; **photo on p. 352:** Jules Abbott, University of Oregon Museum of Natural & Cultural History; **photo on p. 354:** Photo courtesy of Gaylene Carpenter; **photo on p. 357:** Photo courtesy of Patty Prather; **photo on p. 363:** Photo courtesy of Gaylene Carpenter; **photo on p. 368:** © Human Kinetics; **photo on p. 372:** © Jeff Greenberg/age fotostock; **photo on p. 375:** © Human Kinetics; **photo on p. 381:** Stockbyte; **figure 19.2:** Photo courtesy of Holly Donohoe; **photo on p. 394:** © Karsten Kramer/Image Broker/age fotostock; **photo on p. 396:** © SuperStock/age fotostock; **photo on p. 400:** Photo courtesy of Ling Ping; **photo on p. 402:** Photo courtesy of Jinyang Deng.

PART I

Foundations of Recreation and Leisure

CHAPTER 1

Power, Promise, Potential, and Possibilities of Parks, Recreation, and Leisure

Ellen O'Sullivan

> Play for adults is recreation—the renewal of life; for children it is growth—the gaining of life.
>
> Joseph Lee, father of the American playground movement

LEARNING OUTCOMES

After reading this chapter, you should be able to do the following:

> Identify the role that parks, recreation, and leisure play in all facets of life for all people
> Define the terms play, recreation, leisure, and flow
> Identify the different types of benefits associated with parks, recreation, and leisure
> Identify ways in which changes in the world influence trends in parks and recreation
> List the unique qualities and opportunities afforded by this professional field

WHAT IF?

What if there were an aspect of life with promise and potential to empower people to grow and thrive; provide communities with facilities and services that enhance quality of life; connect people both locally and globally; preserve and protect our natural, historic, and cultural heritage; and contribute to a prosperous economy? What if there was an aspect of life so central to human existence that people spent more time engaged in this critical life pursuit than working or attending school combined? What if there was a category of the economy that accounted for substantial expenditures and appeared to be an ever-growing economic force? What if there were a variety of career opportunities associated with this essential aspect of behavior and major component of the economy that created opportunities for personal growth, professional flexibility, sense of purpose, and resourcefulness on the part of the professionals in that field?

WELCOME TO THE WORLD OF PARKS, RECREATION, AND LEISURE

Welcome to the opportunities, options, pursuits, and possibilities of parks and recreation. The shortened term for this profession, which encompasses myriad pursuits and passions such as sports, events, tourism, health and wellness, adventure recreation, environmental preservation and management, is generally parks, recreation, leisure, and tourism.

The challenge in learning more about this field as a personal pursuit, professional career, or a combination of both is to grasp the size and significance of the world known as parks, recreation, and leisure.

This field is powerful because its activities and pursuits are truly everywhere, touching the lives of all human beings, and occur 24 hours a day, seven days a week, for the 52 weeks of a year. The potential and promise of parks, recreation, and leisure are simultaneously challenging to grasp and critical to the well-being of individuals, communities, societies, and the world. The benefits of this field ensure that we have sufficient clean air and water to sustain life, opportunities to live purposeful and pleasurable lives, memories of happy times with friends and family, and options and opportunities for health and well-being throughout our lives.

DEFINITIONS OF PLAY, RECREATION, LEISURE, AND FLOW

People often use four terms interchangeably—play, recreation, leisure, and flow—but they do not refer to the same actions or conditions. We often hear people speak about children going out to play or adults looking forward to the weekend and the leisure time that it promises. People who meet for the first time ask one another what they do for recreation. Even within the field of parks, recreation, and leisure, experts offer differing definitions or explanations of these four terms.

Play

Definitions for **play** date back to previous centuries. These descriptions cite a number of related purposes including biological, physical, cognitive, and social development of children. Theories abound around play; self-expression, surplus energy, arousal, and recapitulation are some of the desired outcomes cited.

By the late 20th century people understood that a better and more comprehensive definition of play included a set of circumstances rather than one specific definition. For *play* to be a true play experience, it must be voluntary, spontaneous, intrinsically rewarding, and absorbing.

Now at the beginning of the 21st century, renewed interest and attention is focused on play and the effect of the lack of unstructured play on the positive development of today's children. Contemporary psychologists have raised the critical need for children to play, and both parents and professionals in the field have been listening. Health officials have suggested that growing levels of childhood obesity and the epidemic of adult onset diabetes among children can be related to lack of play in contemporary life.

Recreation

Another relevant term is **recreation**. Aren't play and recreation the same thing? Not if we adhere to the more accepted definitions of the two terms. It is widely accepted that recreation refers to activity, as in participation in recreation or a recreation activity. Although participation in a recreation activity can be play, not all recreation is play. A recreation activity that has a structured timeframe or lacks true voluntary participation may or may not be play.

Leisure

The term **leisure** has a myriad of meanings. Leisure can refer to any or all of the following: unobligated time, state of being, and consumption patterns. One widely accepted element of leisure is that it is not work but rather an antidote to a person's working life. The irony of the leisure definition is that when Cziksentmihalyi studied flow, he found that most people reach flow while at work rather than while at leisure.

Flow

For much of his academic career Mihaly Csikszentmihalyi has studied **flow**, a state of being in which a person is fully engaged in an activity that results in feelings of energy, focus, and success that often turn out to be the optimal life experiences for that individual.

Through his studies Csikszentmihalyi has identified eight conditions needed to reach flow, the optimal human experience (Csikszentmihalyi, 1991). For flow to occur, the undertaking must

1. require skill,
2. merge action and awareness,
3. provide clear goals and feedback,
4. require concentration and absorption of attention,
5. provide an individual with personal control over the act,
6. create a loss of self-consciousness,
7. cause a person to lose all track of time, and
8. provide intrinsic rewards.

Why Do These Differences Matter?

Although the variations among the definitions of these terms might seem relatively small or inconsequential, that assessment is not accurate. A person working in the field of parks, recreation, leisure, and tourism will be called on to implement a number of activities and provide various experiences for people. At that point the variations of these terms become clearer. An organized soccer league for 10- and 11-year-olds is definitely recreation, but it is not likely to be a play experience. Adults have time available for leisure, but they don't necessarily pursue recreation activities during that time. Consider the differences between a tourist and a traveler; tourists are generally interested in the activity of going to new places, whereas travelers are most often seeking to become immersed in a culture through travel.

PARKS, RECREATION, AND LEISURE: EVERYWHERE, EVERYONE, ALL THE TIME

Well-worn soccer balls skirt the streets of villages around the world, whether the villages are wracked with strife or disaster or support manicured fields and youth and adult teams in matching uniforms. The five rings of the Olympic Games burn brightly every four years as tens of thousands of athletes representing hundreds of countries from around the world gather in the spirit of competition and unity. Street merchants in Bangkok play a checker-like board game hastily constructed of cardboard and discarded bottle caps. Visitors from around the world marvel at the migration of wildlife across the plains of the Serengeti while other visitors admire the exceptional beauty and unique geological features of Gros Morne National Park in Newfoundland. People travel great distances to snorkel in Belize, fish in New Zealand, explore the Louvre, or observe the changing of the guard in Ottawa or at the Tomb of the Unknown Soldier in Washington, DC. Historic sites and natural areas around the world are preserved and protected so that people can engage firsthand in a natural, cultural, or historic awareness and appreciation.

Parks, recreation, and leisure is everywhere—in the far reaches of the Sahara, the crowded seashores of California, the Broadway theaters and museums of New York City, the Hell's Gate Airtram, and the Classic Chinese Garden of Vancouver. Leisure pursuits take place in cities and towns, small villages, the countryside, and mega-urban centers. Leisure experiences occur inside buildings or outside and sometimes in either location. For example, basketball is played either indoors or out, and band concerts, too, take place in buildings or in parks. The array of places is extensive, including auditoriums, zoos, churches, and casinos. There are even health clubs and spas located in airports, rock-climbing walls in retail establishments, and, of course, play areas at fast-food restaurants and even some furniture stores. Parks and recreation can be and is found everywhere—all the places and spaces in which people gather to play, enjoy, and relax.

Another dimension of the "everywhere" quality of parks and recreation is illustrated in the fact that a variety of organizations provide park, recreation, and leisure services. The delivery of services is not limited to just one type of organization. For example, one golf course might be under the governance of a city or state, and another similar course might be a private country club for members only, while a third course might be managed by a corporation. Organizations offering adventure pursuits can run the gamut from outdoor leadership training by a nonprofit organization such as a local YMCA to travel companies designing and offering adventure experiences around the globe. Parks and recreation services and facilities are provided by all types of organizations and businesses.

Recreation can take place indoors or outdoors, at home or in a park, and at any time of day.

It's for Everyone

Consider the ways in which parks, recreation, and leisure touches the lives of everyone, all ages, life stages, cultures, social classes, and genders. Recall personal experiences or observations and identify the people participating in a recreation activity or spending time in a natural setting. These might include the following:

- College students playing coed volleyball in the school's intramural league
- A 10-year-old taking beginning drawing lessons at the community center
- A parent and toddler enrolled in the movement class at the local YMCA
- Female friends spending time together at a day spa
- Families picnicking while enjoying an outdoor band concert
- A 12-year-old going away to camp for the first time
- Guys playing pickup basketball at the local park
- An adolescent testing self-sufficiency on an Outward Bound trip
- Grandparents taking grandchildren on a trip to the Grand Canyon
- A teen group teaching retirees how to surf the net
- A stressed-out adult watching the sunset
- Employees attending the annual company outing to a theme park
- Special Olympic athletes crossing the finish line with elation that brings smiles to the faces of participants and spectators alike
- The over-60 softball team exhibiting a desire to win similar to that of the youth soccer league players
- Both fledgling and gifted artists displaying work in the same community art show

An adage often used by park and recreation professionals employed in the community sector is that parks and recreation takes people "from the cradle to the grave," and while that is not the most appealing description, it does reinforce the presence of parks, recreation, and leisure in everyone's life.

All the Time

Although the pursuits of open space, physical activity, and social outings happen all the time—any month of the year, any day of the week, and throughout all the life stages of human existence. Some recreation activities are associated mainly with the summer or the winter, and holidays sometimes serve as an impetus. For example, the New Year with its emphasis on resolutions motivates people to become more physically active or seek out new experiences. Independence Day celebrations are commonly accompanied by picnics, concerts, fireworks, trips, and other outings, and Halloween brings out the childlike spirit in young and old alike with parties and parades.

The physical characteristics of different seasons provide opportunities for year-round activity. The first thaw finds people tending lawns and starting gardens. Summer draws people to mountains, lakes, streams, or seashores. Winter gives way to skiing, skating, curling, and snowboarding. People's passions for certain activities have influenced the "all the time" approach to parks and recreation. At one time, tennis or soccer could only be played in warm weather, just as ice-skating and hockey once required cold weather. Indoor facilities and lighted playing fields and trails expand the opportunity for parks and recreation services to "all the time."

Recreation is pursued 24 hours a day as well. Ski areas open at first light to give would-be lift ticket purchasers the chance to check out snow conditions. Health clubs open at 4:30 a.m. enabling early risers to work out before heading to work. Heavily industrialized communities offer adult leagues and activities to accommodate the traditional three shifts of factory work. The city of Las Vegas with its "Beyond the Neon" slogan offers unusual times for programs and activities because many residents work shifts in the casinos, which, of course, operate around the clock. YMCAs and community centers offer sleepovers, which provide not only fun and excitement for children but also leisure time for parents. Midnight basketball continues to put recreation on the 24-hour timetable.

Parks, recreation, and leisure is "all the time" in an additional way. Play is essential for children. From infancy and through adolescence, they acquire important life skills through recreation and leisure activities and experiences. The peekaboo games so popular with babies and the Duck, Duck, Goose of almost everyone's early childhood teach important social connections and interactions. The same holds true at the other end of the life cycle, as recreation provides stress reduction for overworked adults and social support for older people living on their own.

Parks and Recreation: It Makes Up Most of Our Time

People sometimes discount the role and the importance of unobligated, or discretionary, time and the role it plays in their quality of life. They focus on attending school, getting a good night's sleep, and going to work, but those activities don't take up all of their time.

If people living in industrialized nations sleep between six and eight hours every day and work or go to school for another eight hours during the week, how much unobligated time do they have? Although the number of hours consumed by sleep, work, and the requirements of daily living such as housework, commuting, and so on varies from person to person, one thing is certain. Unobligated time accounts for well over one-third of most people's lives. To see how this can be true consider the following:

- **Life span.** People born today in the United States or Canada can expect to live at least 77 years, and school attendance and work do not occur during all 70 of those years.
- **Sleep.** Approximately one-third, or 8 hours, of every day is spent sleeping.
- **Infants and toddlers.** Children from birth to 4 years old spend a minimum of 6 hours per day exploring, learning, and growing through play.
- **Formal schooling.** Young people start school at 5 years of age and complete formal schooling between the ages of 18 and 25; therefore, only 13 to 20 of their 70-plus years are occupied with school. School and related activities such as homework might consume 8 hours per day, and a school year lasts 30 to 36 weeks. This leaves a substantial amount of time for nonacademic and nonsleeping activities.
- **Working world.** Full-time work will claim the years from 18 or 25 to 55 or 65. Most people work 40 hours per week, whether it is 8 hours for five days or 10 hours for four days per week, and have a minimum of two weeks of vacation plus holidays.
- **Third age.** Retirement, when every day is a Saturday and people are not restricted to two weeks of vacation, typically lasts at least five years and could be longer depending on longevity.
- **New age of employment.** Because of factors leading to a situation referred to as the "new normal," particularly as it relates to work life in the United States and Canada, recreation and leisure may play differing roles. Because of a myriad of economic circumstances, our society now includes people who are chronically unemployed, underemployed (meaning that job responsibilities do not match their higher levels of skill), and overemployed (referring to those who must hold down two or three jobs or work in an organization in which severe cutbacks result in an increased work load and longer working hours).

Play around with the years and hours cited in the previous list to see how much time in a person's life is available after you account for sleeping, eating, schooling, and working. The remaining hours available for leisure, or unobligated time, just might surprise you. Depending on individual variations, leisure time could amount to more than one-third of a person's life.

Beyond Everywhere and Everyone

Although we know that parks, recreation, and leisure facilities and services are everywhere and available to everyone most of the time, their presence alone isn't enough to prove their value to the lives of individuals, families, work groups, neighborhoods, communities, and society. Just being everywhere all the time is not necessarily a valuable or positive attribute.

The obesity epidemic or an outbreak of the flu may be everywhere, but that doesn't make these occurrences positive for individuals or society. Cable television operates 24 hours a day, 365 days a year, but that does not mean that the programs or offerings are positive or of value or interest to the viewer. So we need to explore the depth of values and benefits that lie beneath the surface of parks and recreation. A review of the "everyone" list of people participating in recreation activities included earlier in this chapter begins to uncover the values of parks and recreation.

- Why would a university student choose to join the intramural coed volleyball team? Is it a chance to be physically active, a time to hang out with friends, an opportunity to meet new people, a change of pace from classes and study time, or all of these reasons or a combination of them?
- Why would a 12-year-old look forward to leaving family and friends behind venturing to a residential camp for a month? Could it be the chance to acquire new skills, practice being independent, and make new friends, or is it a way to be recognized as self-reliant?
- What motivates a single mother with a very long day ahead of her to rise at 5:30 a.m. to sit with a cup of tea and watch the sun rise? Might it be the opportunity to relax, reflect, and regroup before the nonstop demands of her day?

It is these values and benefits that an individual or a family or a community derives from the park setting, the recreation activity, or the leisure experience that imbues parks and recreation with its inherent value. Incorporating parks and recreation into people's lives, whether it was the Olympics of ancient Greece or is the sand gardens of Boston, Massachusetts, or the 39 national parks in Canada, reflects those benefits. The unusual list of questions titled "Guess Who I Am?" (figure 1.1) from an issue of *Parks & Recreation* published by the

GUESS WHO I AM

1. I keep you in good health and prevent you from heart disease, but I'm not a doctor or cardiologist.
2. I host parties and events of all sizes, but I'm not a meeting planner.
3. I put a smile on your face, but I'm not a dentist or orthodontist.
4. I often raise lots of money for charity, but I'm not a professional fund-raiser.
5. I provide an outstanding forum for you to learn about many things, but I'm not a teacher or professor.
6. I have often introduced couples who meet and begin long-term relationships, but I'm not a matchmaker.
7. I often bring music to your ears, but I'm not a musician or singer.
8. I have lots of friends in the animal world, but I'm not a veterinarian.
9. I have tons of friends in the insect world, but I'm not an entomologist.
10. I am often surrounded by birds of many types, but I'm not an ornithologist.
11. I enjoy the company of trees and shrubs, but I'm not a nursery manager.
12. I am very photogenic, but I'm not a fashion model.
13. My brethren and I have been in many movies, but I'm not a movie star.
14. I'm often on your local television news, but I'm not a news anchor.
15. I often appear in your local newspaper, but I'm not a reporter or photographer.
16. I work around lots of sneakers, but I'm not an athletic shoe salesperson.
17. I'm a good friend to many of you on the Fourth of July, but I'm not a fireworks technician.
18. I make the value of your house as great as possible, but I'm not a real estate agent.
19. I often entertain children, but I'm not a babysitter.
20. I often prevent crime, but I'm not a police officer.

OK, that's 20 clues. Can you guess who I am?

Figure 1.1 The answer, of course, is parks and recreation.

Reprinted courtesy of *Parks & Recreation*, National Recreation and Park Association.

National Recreation and Park Association can serve as a springboard for the various ways parks and recreation can be viewed and the diverse roles it can play (Corwin, 2001).

VALUES AND BENEFITS OF PARKS, RECREATION, AND LEISURE

When you start to develop a list of the range of benefits that can be attributed to state and provincial parks, community centers, historic sites, and fitness clubs, just to cite a few alternatives within the greater parks and recreation family, the list can become cumbersome. A more organized way to consider these benefits is to incorporate two different levels. A broader, more general, category consists of three different types of benefits as identified by Bev Driver (1998), an early proponent of this approach. These three types of benefits are improved condition, prevention of a worse condition, and realization of a psychological experience. Originally, the benefits consisted of improving or preventing conditions, but the benefit attributed to psychological experiences was added when it became apparent that important benefits could be gained in more internal, and certainly less tangible, ways such as awareness, appreciation, and sense of self. The three conditions incorporate the following:

1. Improved condition. If a human, natural, or economic factor is not functioning at full capacity or is functioning in a deleterious manner, the benefit of recreation would be to ameliorate this condition.

2. Prevention of a worse condition. Not every instance of poor performance or threatening conditions can be improved, so in this case, the value of parks and recreation would be to stem further erosion or deterioration of a human, natural, or economic condition.

3. Realization of a psychological experience. This category represents the leisure pursuits that people select for the intrinsic values they gain through the experience. Stress reduction, sense of control, and spirituality are examples of these benefits.

Each of the three types of benefits can be further divided into four different categories of values and benefits: individual, social, environmental, and economic.

Individual and Personal Benefits of Parks and Recreation

The first category is individual and personal benefits of parks and recreation. This category encompasses the many different avenues in which a person's life can be enriched and enhanced or even extended by various leisure pursuits. The various individual benefits and the range of outcomes associated with these benefits are extraordinary as is the potential impact they have on one's life (see figure 1.2).

INDIVIDUAL AND PERSONAL BENEFITS OF PARKS AND RECREATION

Broad Benefits
- Full and meaningful life
- Balance between work and play
- Life satisfaction
- Quality of life

More-Specific Benefits
Physical health
- Muscle strength
- Flexibility
- Cardiovascular conditioning
- Weight control

Emotional well-being
- Sense of self
- Sense of control
- Problem-solving ability

Lifelong learning
- Independent living
- Personal growth
- Adaptation to change

Quality of life
- Awareness and appreciation of the arts, history, and nature

---

Figure 1.2 There are many benefits of parks and recreation and the outcomes associated with these benefits and the potential impact are extraordinary.

The benefits attributed to parks and recreation can be observed in people at play and in pursuits such as the following:

- An overstressed adult sitting on a beach quietly enjoying the serenity of the sunset
- A child the first time he or she manages to ride a bicycle without external support
- A 78-year-old who learns to use the Internet at the community center as a way of keeping pace with the changes in the world around him

In more recent years, parks and recreation professionals have collected data and statistics that better document the role their services play in a person's well-being as well as conducting specific studies. Some of the studies that reveal the benefits of parks and recreation include the following:

- Children with a park playground within 1 kilometer were almost five times more likely to be classified as being of a healthy weight rather than at risk or overweight compared with those children who do not have playgrounds in nearby parks (Potwarka, Kaczynski, & Flack, 2008).
- Participants in green exercise activities showed significantly greater improvement in self-esteem than those who participated in other activities. The combination of exercise, nature, and social activities could play an important role in mental health treatment (Barton, Griffin, & Pretty, 2011).
- Those who were regular exercisers had lower levels of risk factors related to cardiovascular disease and type 2 diabetes. Those who did not exercise had higher levels of risk factors related to cardiovascular disease and type 2 diabetes (Buchholz, Martin, Bray, et al., 2009).

Social and Community Benefits of Parks and Recreation

The second category is social and community benefits of parks and recreation (see figure 1.3). This subset of values and benefits is characterized by the many opportunities for success and enjoyment that are afforded by interacting with others; these encounters can be positive and enriching for individuals, small groups, and society overall.

SOCIAL AND COMMUNITY BENEFITS OF PARKS AND RECREATION

Broad Benefits
- Social bonds and sense of belonging
- Strong, vitally involved groups and communities
- Ethnic and cultural understanding and goodwill

More-Specific Benefits
Sense of community
- Community pride
- Community cohesiveness
- Reduced alienation
- Involvement in issues

Awareness and appreciation
- Tolerance and understanding
- Outlets for conflict resolution
- Cooperation

Social support
- Lifeline for elderly
- Support for youth
- Cultural identity

Figure 1.3 Parks and recreation offer many social and community benefits that bring about opportunities for success and enjoyment with others.

The social and community benefits attributed to parks and recreation can be exhibited through the following:

- A newly widowed gentleman who receives a hot meal and the social support of others through his daily visit to the senior center
- A young Latino child experiencing firsthand the art, food, and songs of his parents' homeland at the community Latino festival
- The sense of belonging and community that envelops the crowd gathered at the annual Fourth of July picnic and fireworks display

Similar to the data and statistics presented for the individual benefits of parks, recreation, and leisure, there is evidence of the value human contact and

Recreation and leisure bring social and community benefits. Seniors can play bingo and enjoy a meal together at a community center.

group interactions can contribute to the social and community well-being of all. Some of the community benefits that can be attributed to parks and recreation include the following:

• Organized sport programs that engage at-risk youth by empowering them and providing opportunities for positive peer mentoring will foster reductions in youth crime. Young offenders in organized sport programs have demonstrated significant increases in ratings in perceived competence in sport skills and increased self-esteem (Carmichael, 2008).

• One study shows that time spent at a community playground is valuable to American families; 77 percent of parents agreed that spending more time at a playground increases a family's sense of well-being. Almost unanimously (95 percent), parents agreed that the more time a family spends together being active, the better is their sense of family well-being. Three-quarters also wish that their family had time to visit a playground more often (Harris Interactive, 2011).

• Community arts researchers have found direct connections between culture and revitalization. In a study of 10 Chicago neighborhoods, social networks were identified as a key mechanism by which com-

munity arts contribute to neighborhood improvement. By developing social networks, low-budget arts programs leverage local and nonlocal assets that result in direct economic benefits for the neighborhood—new markets, new uses of existing facilities, new jobs for local artists—as well as broader community engagement (Stern & Seifert, 2008).

Environmental Benefits of Parks and Recreation

The third category, environmental benefits of parks and recreation, addresses the wide-ranging and critical role of the environment in quality of life (see figure 1.4). An interesting difference between this category and the others is that the environmental benefits sustain human life by protecting the ecosystem in addition to providing other more pleasurable benefits.

The environmental benefits attributed to parks and recreation can be exhibited through the following:

• Setting aside public lands as natural watersheds for preservation allows local residents to pay less for drinking water and provides them access to hiking trails.

- Urban dwellers flock to the city parks to reconnect with nature.
- Fourth graders calculate the speed of the water in the streambed during outdoor classroom sessions.

Some of the studies that reveal the benefits of environmental activities conducted through parks and recreation include the following:

• The trees in the urban forest of Lethbridge, Alberta, capture over 8.4 million kilograms of carbon dioxide per year. When considering the distance that an average car owner drives each year, public trees capture the annual carbon dioxide emissions of more than 1,600 cars throughout the city. In economic terms, the net benefit of the urban forest to the city is over $3.9 million annually (City of Lethbridge, 2011).

• Drinking water is another positive outcome associated with preservation of open space. New York City recently purchased 1,655 acres (670 ha) outside of the city in an ongoing effort to protect and maintain the watershed required to ensure quality drinking water for the city (New York City Department of Environmental Protection, 2011).

ENVIRONMENTAL BENEFITS OF PARKS AND RECREATION

Broad Benefits
- Clean air and water
- Environmental protection
- Preservation of natural and historic areas

More-Specific Benefits

Health and well-being
- Reduced stress
- Venues for physical activity

Education
- Improved science and math skills
- Natural life cycle knowledge
- Environmental ethic

Economic impact
- Catalyst for relocation
- Reduced cost of utilities
- Increased tourism

Figure 1.4 The environmental benefits of parks and recreation sustain human life by protecting the ecosystem.

By setting aside land for recreation, governments benefit individuals and the environment.

Economic Benefits of Parks and Recreation

The fourth and final category is economic benefits of parks and recreation (see figure 1.5). While other values and benefits are often under-recognized, this category of benefits tends to be more visible and seemingly more important. The adage "money talks" certainly comes into play in this instance.

The economic benefits attributed to parks and recreation can be exhibited through the following:

- The owners of small stores and restaurants adjacent to national parks who make a living providing services to park visitors
- The corporations that increase productivity through fewer sick days by implementing recreation and wellness programs
- The older adults who lower their cholesterol levels by exchanging costly medications for daily walks

---

ECONOMIC BENEFITS OF PARKS AND RECREATION

Broad Benefits
- Cost reduction
- Funds generation
- Catalyst for development

More-Specific Benefits

Cost reduction
- Health care
- Decreased vandalism and crime
- Less stress

Increased financial resources
- Enhanced land values
- Neighborhood revitalization
- Increased worker productivity

Catalyst for economic growth
- Favorable business climate
- Increased tourism

Figure 1.5 The economic benefits of parks and recreation include improved finances, health, safety, and growth.

Some of the information and studies that reveal the economic benefits of parks and recreation include the following:

- Treed urban parks provide numerous social, environmental, and economic services of measurable value to a city. In Allan Gardens, trees provided $26,326 in annual benefits ($16,665 environmental; $9,661 aesthetic) during 2008, and delivered a benefit-to-cost ratio of 3.4:1 (Millward & Sabir, 2011).

- The national bicycling industry contributes an estimated $133 billion a year to the U.S. economy. It supports nearly 1.1 million jobs and generates $17.7 billion in federal, state, and local taxes. Another $46.9 billion is spent on meals, transportation, lodging, gifts, and entertainment during bike trips and tours (Flusche, 2009).

- World-class festivals and events have been a driving force in the Canadian economy through the recession. Research, data, and economic modeling for this report were compiled from 11 of Canada's top tourism research organizations. Data from this report include an estimated 12.6 million visitors at the 15 largest events, an estimated $780 million spent by tourists, and an additional $300 million spent for local event operations. This new spending contributed $650 million to local economies, created the equivalent of 15,600 full year-jobs, and generated $283 million in tax revenue at all three levels of government (Enigma Research Corporation, 2010).

Another way of looking at the economic relationship between supporting the health, safety, and growth of a child is succinctly presented in the sidebar "What Recreators Can Do" by Bob Jennings, a naturalist in Oklahoma.

RECREATION AND LEISURE: THE LESS DESIRABLE SIDE

Although the benefits and values garnered through play, park visits, recreation activities, travel, and constructive use of leisure time are nearly limitless, some less desirable experiences can be categorized as recreation and use of leisure time. The vast array of actions and activities that fall within this category have been called purple leisure, immoral leisure, or taboo leisure. The reality is that numerous activities that may be pleasurable and exciting for people

What Recreators Can Do

It costs approximately $30,000 to incarcerate a juvenile offender for one year. If that money were available to Parks and Recreation, we could do the following:

Take him swimming twice a week for 24 weeks,

And give him four tours of the zoo, plus lunch,

And enroll him in 50 community center programs,

And visit the nature center twice,

And let him play league softball for a season,

And tour the gardens at the park twice,

And give him two weeks of tennis lessons,

And enroll him in two weeks of day camp,

And let him play three rounds of golf,

And act in one play,

And participate in one fishing clinic,

And take a four-week pottery class,

And play basketball eight hours a week for 40 weeks,

After which we could return to you: $29,125 and one much happier kid.

Reprinted courtesy of *Parks & Recreation*, National Recreation and Park Association.

are not beneficial for the individual or positive for society overall.

Jay B. Nash, an early American theorist on recreation and leisure, is well known for his pyramid model of recreation that features various levels of recreation ranging from detrimental to positive. The lowest levels of his pyramid include activities detrimental to self or society. Recreational drug use or gang membership would be found in the base of his pyramid. Most people accept that drug usage and gang membership are deleterious for the individual and erode overall societal well-being.

The next level up on Nash's pyramid includes passive forms of recreation in which the participant is a spectator, as would be the case with amusement and entertainment. Higher up the scale are those recreation pursuits deemed more positive for the individual participant or society overall. These may inspire greater involvement and participation by the individual. Involvement in either physical or emotional levels is considered good recreation, and the pinnacle, great recreation, is designated by Nash as creative participation.

What are some of these actions and activities that fall within this less than desirable side of recreation? Some of these activities are legal, and some are illegal. Others are defined by the norms of society and by various religious groups. Gambling involves many people and considerable sums of money, and some gambling is legal through the auspices of government. Dancing and contact among single people of the opposite sex is considered taboo in some religions and societies. The list of less desirable recreation can include horse and dog racing, recreational drug use, binge drinking, pornography, prostitution, vandalism, and the sex tourism trade to countries outside North America, just to name a few.

The factors that immoral or taboo recreation have in common are likely to include one or more of the following conditions:

1. Is the action or activity detrimental to the person him- or herself?

2. Is the action or activity demeaning or harmful to others (i.e., to human beings or animals)?

3. Does the action or activity cause harm to the overall well-being of society?

Admittedly, these lines are blurring as government and society provide greater leeway, often in return for increased tax revenues, to such pursuits as gambling and tobacco smoking, among others.

TRENDS IN PARKS, RECREATION, AND LEISURE ALTERNATIVES

Many people think that the popularity of Pilates and pickle ball or increased interest in travel to Guatemala can be considered **trends**, although these developments are more likely to be temporary changes in behavior and preferences. The reality is, however, that changes and trends in leisure result from overall changes in society. These more encompassing societal changes may eventually result in variations in participation patterns or interest levels in various forms of recreation, which some people refer to as trends. For instance, increased participation in women's volleyball and softball actually represents an overarching trend of increased participation by girls and women in team sports.

True trend tracking in recreation, leisure, parks, and travel requires close attention to factors through an environmental scan. In this case, the term *environmental* refers to conditions outside the control of individuals and organizations. Awareness of these factors is useful in staying ahead of changing behaviors and preferences related to recreation and leisure. A number of factors specifically influence trends and emerging directions in parks, recreation, and leisure alternatives. Included among those factors are economics, demographics, legal issues, politics, science and technology, environmental factors, and competition. Another layer that could be added to these factors is whether elements within them have a global, national, regional, or local effect.

So rather than create a list of activities that may or may not be popular at any given time, the following list reflects the more general, overarching changes that can be referred to as trends:

Blurring of Life Stages

- Older adults consider themselves young and don't let the number of candles on a birthday cake dictate recreation and leisure pursuits appropriate for them.
- Children are being encouraged to participate in activities at earlier ages than ever before as evidenced by soccer for 3- and 4-year-olds and beauty pageants for tots.
- Young adults are taking longer to finish formal education, marrying later, and becoming independent at later ages, thus blurring the life stages of teenager and adulthood.

Disparities

- Growing inequality in the United States will result in the growth of expensive recreation experiences for an ever decreasing group of participants.

- Third-tier economies with close ties to tourism may risk damage to or erosion of the natural and cultural environments of those emerging nations.

Increased Ethnic Diversity

- As white majorities give way to greater ethnic diversity, which brings with it cultural shifts, the variations and popularity of recreational activities such as sport, music, dancing, and dining will continue to change.
- Common interests in play and recreation pursuits hold the potential for bringing people across the globe closer to one another in terms of understanding and appreciation.

Work Redefined

- The increasing pursuit of work and employment that require little or no physical activity will continue to drive both the need for and interest in enjoyable physical activity.
- The amount of leisure time available to people may decrease as people are employed in more than one job or retire at much later ages than did those of previous generations.

Widespread Touch of Technology

- The expansion of affordable technology, most particularly as it relates to communication and interaction, may lead to increased contact with friends and families as well as interactions with people from around the world.
- Chronic conditions resulting from natural or accidental causes may no longer hold people back from fully participating in recreation and leisure experiences.

Going Green

- People's love of the outdoors and the serenity or adventure that it affords could result in legal and political ramifications related to preserving open space.
- The popularity and overuse of open space may result in the destruction of valuable natural assets around the globe.

The list of trends are illustrative of what the future might hold. So if you watch and listen carefully to the changes around you, you will not be shocked if the following were to occur:

- Both Yosemite National Park in California and Mauricie National Park in Quebec are closed to the public for a minimum of 20 years.
- Victims of motorcycle accidents with traumatic brain injuries are snowboarding with joy and abandon.
- People both with and without passports sit around a table discussing their trip to India, and the insights and experiences of those who physically made the trip to India and those who toured the country virtually are difficult to distinguish.
- More than 400 members of the Alberta Skydiving Club are over the age of 85 years.
- Laughing clubs held in public parks are the number one recommendation of physicians for their patients who suffer from complications of serious stress.

A world of surprises lies ahead, and those surprises will not exempt parks, recreation, leisure, and tourism from their effects. In fact, the ongoing evolution of change factors serves as both a challenge and a sense of excitement for this field.

PARKS AND RECREATION: A PASSION, A PURSUIT, A PROFESSION

For the thousands of people who never pass up an opportunity to collect mineral specimens or plan vacations around the Major League baseball schedule or sport bumper stickers that read "backstrokers keep their faces dry," parks, recreation, and leisure is indeed their passion. For those who play golf every couple of weeks or try to catch new exhibits at the local gallery or look forward to planning their various weekend adventures, parks, recreation, and leisure is a life pursuit.

Yes, parks, recreation, and leisure assumes many roles in people's lives. It can be either a passion or a life pursuit or a bit of both. However, you may recall the series of questions at the start of this chapter; one of the queries was this:

What if there were a variety of career opportunities associated with this essential aspect of behavior and major component of the economy that created opportunities for

personal growth, empowerment, sense of purpose, and resourcefulness on the part of the professionals in that field?

There is! It's the profession of parks and recreation. The everywhere, everyone, most-of-the-time characteristics of this field as well as the values and the benefits cited previously transform parks and recreation into a profession with the potential for both making a living and being enriched personally by the many alternatives within careers associated with this field. These career options enable a person to work in the following situations:

- With almost any segment of society—age groups from cradle to grave, rich, not so rich, those with abilities and disabilities, those highly proficient to rank beginners, well and ill, and everything in between
- With a wide range of interest areas such as art, music, dance, drama, sports from Little League up, games, nature, environmental protection, therapeutic settings, fitness, wellness, arts, culture, travel, tourism, and additional areas that are discussed in later chapters
- In a variety of settings such as parks, nature centers, hospitals, correctional facilities, resorts, college campuses, military installations, corporations, hotels, and communities and housed within various organizational patterns such as public, nonprofit, private, commercial, or corporate entities and independent contractors

A Professional Career Choice

The array of career options and opportunities presents a challenge when attempting to share information and insight into a diverse and dynamic field such as parks and recreation. One way in which you can secure greater insight into this field is by engaging in conversations with people employed in the profession. Throughout the book you will find Outstanding Graduates—profiles of graduates of recreation and leisure programs and their career paths.

These interviews are a great beginning for learning about this field; however, you can gain additional insight. In the event that you find yourself with extra time and in the company of professionals working in parks and recreation, ask them how they found themselves in this particular career category. The majority of them will share personal stories about their road to becoming a park and recreation professional. It could be that a passion for swimming, golf, gymnastics, ceramics, the outdoors, or some other leisure activity set them down this path. Or maybe the positive influence that a coach, camp counselor, theater director, park ranger, or recreation therapist had on their life spurred their career choice. Naturally, some professionals are drawn to the field because they want to work with a certain group such as children, dancers, or active adults, just to cite a few.

Qualities and Characteristics of the Profession

If the situation presents itself, try to discover the characteristics of their work world that make the field of parks and recreation particularly worthwhile for them. It is virtually impossible to identify every characteristic of such a diverse field because spas and stadiums don't appear to have a great deal in common. However, it would be enlightening to attempt to discern those attributes of the working world of parks and recreation that might resonate with others exploring career options. Some of those attributes and characteristics include the following:

• **Variety of settings.** Park and recreation activities take place indoors, in the woods, on the sea, close to home, and around the globe; therefore, this profession provides the opportunity to accommodate shifts in your career goals.

• **Burnout prevention.** Often professionals who work with people have a tendency to burn out from the continual challenges of one group or another. The number and diversity of people from cradle to grave, the rich and the poor, and the healthy and less healthy provide ample opportunity to transport your skills and knowledge to a different population.

• **Less formal settings.** Although not true of all parks and recreation career settings, it is true that many activities, programs, and services take place in a less formal setting than in other professional alternatives.

• **Creativity in approaches.** Although parks and recreation professionals must adopt specific practices, consider safety issues, and meet focused

goals, the flexibility to creatively meet these requirements helps many practitioners pursue their own growth and development.

• **Continual change.** Another asset of the parks and recreation field is that no two days are exactly the same. The rain changes the forest, a child learns to float, and a new exhibit opens at the museum. Part of the attraction of this profession is the continual change that keeps professionals alert and retooled.

• **Responsibility.** Many of the entry-level positions in parks and recreation come with the opportunity to assume responsibility almost right from the start. Whether it be responsibility for a park area, tour group, or swimming pool, new parks and recreation professionals often are in charge.

• **Resourcefulness.** The less formal nature of the programs and settings combined with the challenges of working with a variety of participants with individual goals and abilities spells the need to be resourceful. One of the many things that parks and recreation professionals comment on is the ongoing challenges of their positions.

Making a Difference

When you ask several parks and recreation professionals who have spent several years working in this field why they stayed in the profession, you will hear a variety of responses. However, you may find a thread that holds the various responses together. That theme most often reflects "making a difference." These professionals might talk about making a difference in the life of one person or a group. Or they could mean their contribution to the vitality and viability of a community or the far-reaching difference that will result from their effort to protect nature or preserve cultural or historic sites.

The common "making a difference" response will be ever present in conversations with parks and recreation professionals. A quote attributed to Socrates perhaps sums up the essence of a career in parks and recreation: "Leisure is the best of all professions." Socrates was most likely suggesting that being at leisure is the best way to occupy time, but based on some of the attributes and characteristics of the field, the "best" connotation could be applied to the professions within parks, recreation, and leisure as well.

Background Information

Name: Karl Robideau

Education: Bachelor of arts in tourism management, Vancouver Island University.

Credentials: Safety, first aid, and management certificates and awards.

Special awards: Sales awards from Norwegian Cruise Line, Cobra Group, and Park West Gallery.

Career Information

Position: Gallery manager, front-of-house manager, and auctioneer.

Organization: Mossgreen Gallery & Auctions is located in the heart of South Yarra, Melbourne, Australia. Mossgreen is one of the city's most innovative destinations for the arts, antiques, and selling exhibitions of fine design. Mossgreen Gallery & Auctions play an important role in building the perception of Melbourne as the Australian center for the arts.

The company is a privately owned for-profit small business that employs approximately 10 full-time employees and 5 part-time staff. We recently added a hospitality section of the business by opening Mossgreen Café.

Job description: The primary responsibility of the gallery manager is to create and implement successful gallery exhibitions, communicate with clients and artists, and monitor and oversee the marketing and promotions. Day-to-day duties also include gallery presentation, event management, logistics (shipping and packaging), and direct sales. Front-of-house duties involve organizing live bidding on site, telephone and absentee bidding, and business development through partnerships with online auction companies. Administrative duties such as inventory and database management as well as website and social media organization are important daily aspects of the position. As an auctioneer, presentations aim to educate and entertain while maximizing sales in structured settings.

> *I have always followed these rules in my career: Work hard, play harder, laugh loud, and love life.*

Career path: I started my career by working and learning with the Walt Disney Corporation, Norwegian Cruise Line, and Fairmont Hotels and Resorts. In these settings I was able to develop my passion for working with others. These world-class organizations offered training and education that allowed me to excel in sales and marketing.

Through this professional development and the international connections and relationships I cultivated, I was able to combine my passion for the arts and travel by working as an auctioneer and entrepreneur with Plymouth Auctioneering and Park West Gallery. After that, I decided to continue with further education by completing my bachelor's degree. I then joined my wife in Australia and was able to use my skills and experiences to obtain my current position with Mossgreen, which is an industry leader with a successful business model.

Likes and dislikes about the job: I like that my job has diversity in the roles and that no day is the same. It's great to work in an environment that nurtures growth and creativity. It's also exciting to meet some of Australia's best artists and represent them in a world-class exhibition such as the Melbourne Art Fair.

The position has its difficulties due to the nature of working in a private organization that depends on the economy. Reaching sales targets and financial goals sometimes requires long hours and working through weekends.

Advice to Undergraduates

Considering a career in tourism, recreation, and leisure is opening a door to a world of possibilities. Dedicate yourself to your passion and always allow for change and innovation in the workplace and your interests. Take advantage of the opportunities that extracurricular activities offer.

Unique Quality of Parks and Recreation

Aristotle believed that a good life is predicated on engaging in activities that are intrinsically valuable. Recreation activities and leisure pursuits generally fall within this parameter. Other disciplines can create and support activities that are intrinsically valuable, and other employment areas involve working with children or adults or in the outdoors or nonprofit sector. What then makes parks and recreation unique in its own right?

The one quality that makes parks, recreation, and leisure both unique and valuable while setting the field apart from other endeavors is the voluntary nature of participation along with the promise or potential of fun and enjoyment. Our bodies compel us to eat and sleep. There are societal norms that contribute to time spent in schooling and work. However, this is not the case with participation in parks, recreation, and leisure activities. The common elements that draw people to choose from an extensive array of alternative opportunities within their leisure time are the power, promise, potential, and possibility that those choices hold for fun, pleasure, or meaning. That statement may seem a bit misleading when we consider the teenagers who submit to family vacation under duress or the people training to run marathons or even the people involved in less-than-positive activities in their free time. It is important to note that some recreational pursuits such as vandalism and gang activity are usually voluntary choices made during a person's unobligated time and as such can be considered recreation. The common element that enables a teenager to enjoy a family trip and the long-distance runner to venture outside in inclement weather is the power, promise, potential, and possibility that the vacation, the training, or even the vandalism holds for fun, pleasure, or meaning.

Yes, fun is fundamental; fundamental to attracting people to activities and options that will be valuable to them and possibly to friends, families, neighborhoods, communities, or society overall. There are numerous instances when the concept of fun can and is dismissed as having no value, but it is the element of fun that attracts people to particular activities and motivates them to remain committed and involved. A concise explanation of the role that "fun" can and does play might include the following:

> FUN is FUNdamental to valuable life experiences. Fun attracts attention, sparks an interest, engages participation, creates motivation, fuels repeated involvement, and supports results. FUN is FUNdamental = Positive results for individuals and society.

MOVING ON

This chapter begins our discussion of the profession. However, it barely scratches the surface of the unique qualities and characteristics of the profession and only touches on the diverse values and benefits that parks, recreation, and leisure hold for individuals, groups, communities, the environment, and the economy. The rest of the book serves as a road map to guide your journey that starts by exploring the history and background of this field as well as identifying the various organizations that provide leisure-related services for people. Other sections and chapters provide an overview of the variety of settings and populations that make up this unique profession. This book offers you a depth of information about the various career choices in recreation and leisure.

For glossary terms, learning experiences, and more, please visit the web resource at
www.HumanKinetics.com/IntroductionToRecreationAndLeisure

CHAPTER 2

History of Recreation

M. Rebecca Genoe, Douglas Kennedy, and Jerome F. Singleton

“ Those who cannot remember the past are condemned to repeat it. ”

George Santayana, Spanish and American philosopher

LEARNING OUTCOMES

After reading this chapter, you should be able to do the following:

> Identify and explain the historical development of recreation and leisure in prehistoric societies
> Describe the historical development of recreation and leisure in ancient Rome and Greece, Europe, the United States, and Canada
> Explain and describe how government and professional organizations influenced the development of recreation and leisure in Canada and the United States

INTRODUCTION

History shapes what we understand today. To appreciate how recreation and leisure services are delivered in the United States and Canada today, you must understand the historical periods and their societal expectations that have influenced the development of these services. North American societies have been affected by the generations of immigrants that have landed, settled, and influenced recreation and leisure. By understanding how leisure has emerged, it is possible to see how history often repeats itself, and what we see today is similar to what happened long ago. Whether lessons can be learned from the past undoubtedly requires an appreciation and understanding of our history.

TRACING THE ROOTS OF LEISURE IN CANADA AND THE UNITED STATES

As past definitions of leisure influence our understanding of leisure today, we will trace the development of leisure from prehistoric societies to the Protestant Reformation.

Prehistoric Societies

People in prehistoric societies were primarily concerned with survival (Shivers & deLisle, 1997). Hunting and gathering were the primary activities and provided resources to maintain life. There was little "free time" as we know it today. Work, survival, and rest melded to become one life-sustaining activity. Once prehistoric people could create tools and were able to store information in a larger brain, more free time became available. This free time was used for ritualization, or ceremonial acts (Ibrahim, 1991). These acts often focused on celebrations of successful hunts, offerings for bountiful harvests, and beseeching the gods for their favor. It is believed that playlike activities were also critical to the needs of emerging tribes. These activities depicted historical events, transportation practices, war games, and the use of farm tools. Play prepared children for their responsibilities as youth and adults and became a way of achieving solidarity and morality. It also became a healing experience and a means of communication and provided pleasure and entertainment. As societies emerged, playlike activities were also a means to relax, recover, and replenish strength after working (Kraus, 1971). These emerging societies also developed structures that allowed people an opportunity to focus on specific work roles. One person could focus on being a hunter, while another could be a builder. With these roles established, greater cooperation provided people with the resources for activities that did not relate to sustaining life. Thus, for the first time, greater opportunities for leisure were experienced. This is no different from today when people "specialize" in a particular vocation needed by society, while relying on the specialties of others for their own well-being.

Ancient Greece

Ancient Greece (1200-500 B.C.) is an excellent example of how societal structure influenced the development of leisure. Greek citizens, who could vote and participate in state affairs, sought to become the well-rounded ideal of that era. They embraced what was known as the **Athenian ideal**, which was a combination of soldier, athlete, artist, statesman, and philosopher. Rather than focusing on one area of expertise as is valued today, developing all areas was valued. This was only possible because the tasks of everyday living were provided by laborers or slaves (Shivers & deLisle, 1997) who outnumbered the citizens approximately three to one. Those who were freed from everyday activities had the opportunity to pursue the range of activities necessary to become the Athenian ideal.

Leisure was very important in Greek society. The Greek philosopher Plato and his student, Aristotle, supported this in their beliefs that virtuous and constructive leisure activities were the route to happiness and fulfillment. Contemplation, which involved the pursuit of truth and understanding, was thought to be the highest form of leisure (Dare, Welton, & Coe, 1987). Athenian philosophers strongly believed in the unity of mind and body and valued each. Play was perceived to be essential to the healthy growth of children from both a physical and social perspective (Ibrahim, 1979). Citizens regarded leisure as an opportunity for intellectual cultivation, music, theater, and poetry as well as political and philosophical discussions. The concept *schole* meant to cease and have quiet or peace. It meant having time for oneself and being occupied in something for its own sake, such as music, poetry, the company of friends, or the exercise of speculative faculties (Ibrahim, 1991). *Schole* embraced the experience and not the outcome. How different this is from today where the pursuit of an activity is often valued only if something tangible like a victory, mastery of a skill, or a specific expectation is gained.

An important part of ancient Greek culture, and perhaps at odds with the notion of *schole*, was its passion for games. Athletic games were held to celebrate religious rites and heroes, for entertainment, and for pleasure. Only men played sport, and women were often excluded from public life (Shivers & deLisle, 1997). Four Panhellenic games were very popular among the spectators and athletes. These included the Olympic Games, the Pythian Games, the Nemian Games, and the Isthmian Games and are thought to be held in honor of the gods, although others suggest that they commemorated the death of mythic mortals and monsters (Ibrahim, 1979; Mendelsohn, 2004). When athletic games were held, wars often ceased so that participants could compete (Poliakoff, 1993). The early Olympic Games, honoring Zeus, included chariot races, combat events, boxing, wrestling, footraces, and the pentathlon—a five-sport event embracing the Athenian ideal. Athletes also competed individually, not on teams, and represented their home villages (Ibrahim, 1991). This is similar to the modern Olympic Games, in which participants represent their countries. The early Olympics were an extremely serious event as well. It was not uncommon for participants in aggressive sports such as pankration (a combination of boxing and wrestling) to be encouraged to fight to the death. This fate was seen as especially noble because it would immortalize the competitor in story for generations to come as having sacrificed his life in the pursuit of victory. So important were the Olympics that Athenians would place an olive wreath on their door when a boy was born, thus signaling the hope that he would become an Olympian (Mendelsohn, 2004). This seriousness of purpose and the use of leisure time to develop sport-specific skills are still found today. We "work" at getting better so we can "play" a sport well. Like the ancient Greeks, we claim to value well-rounded people, yet parents increasingly encourage their children to specialize in one particular sport, often played year-round, so that they have the greatest opportunity to become better than their peers. It should be of no surprise then that at a time when success in sports rivals that of the adulation shown to the earliest Olympic victors, the world finds itself facing an epidemic of cases in which competitors turn to illegal performance-enhancing drugs to assure victory.

Ancient Rome

The emergence of Rome as a dominant society influenced how leisure was perceived at that time. Rome conquered the majority of Europe and Asia after about 265 B.C. and emerged as a dominant power in the Mediterranean (Shivers & deLisle, 1997). The Roman Empire influenced the judicial systems and societies it conquered by attempting to overwrite with its own culture what had come before. The Roman government was based on distinct classifications of citizens. These included senators, who were the richest and owned most of the land and power; curiales, who owned 25 or more acres (10 ha) of land and were office holders or tax collectors; plebes, or free common men, who owned small properties or were tradesmen or artisans; coloni, who were lower-class tenants on land; and finally, indentured slaves. Early Roman slaves were captured in war and served as agricultural laborers. Much later, large numbers of captives from Asia, Greece, and central Europe became slaves and were exploited by their owners (Shivers & deLisle, 1997). As in societies that came before it, the opportunity to participate in leisure during the Roman era was limited to those who had the appropriate resources. The greater one's standing at this time, the greater the opportunity for freedom from the daily requirements necessary to live a comfortable life. Senators enjoyed almost unlimited leisure, while colonies struggled to make a comfortable life. This is not unlike the present day where distinct economic classes enjoy varying degrees and types of leisure.

Different from the ancient Greeks, who saw leisure as an opportunity for well-rounded development, Romans perceived leisure to be primarily rest from work. Considering that the Romans were on an almost constant crusade to dominate foreign cultures, this viewpoint was necessary and allowed recuperation before the next crusade. Play, then, served utilitarian rather than aesthetic or spiritual purposes (Horna, 1994). As the Roman Empire grew and the increasing availability of slaves decreased the amount of daily work people were required to do, leisure time increased and was increasingly used as a way to control the masses. During Emperor Claudius' reign (41-54 A.D.), Rome had 59 public holidays and 95 game days, and by 354 A.D., there were more than 200 public holidays and 175 game days. The reason for this was simple: As Romans became less occupied with work, they became increasingly bored and critical of the government. The government then attempted to pacify unrest by providing pleasurable experiences through spectacle and celebrations of holidays. "Bread and circuses," free food and entertainment, provided the framework for Roman society (Horna, 1994).

To hold people's attention, leisure activities became increasingly hedonistic and shocking. When battles between gladiators became less interesting, animals from foreign lands were brought in to become part of the savagery seen in the great coliseums. When the scale of those battles became ordinary, artificial lakes were created by slaves who were then used to re-create bloody sea battles depicting a successful conquest. This focus on the entertainment of the masses, instead of their participation, has led some historians to argue that one of

Leisure in ancient Rome focused on spectacle and entertainment for the masses instead of participation. Today, some sporting events such as boxing also take on the appearance of spectacle and sometimes the participants are even called gladiators.

the reasons for the fall of the Roman Empire was its inability to deal with mass leisure (McLean, Hurd, & Rogers, 2005). This concern is often heard today in reference to current leisure habits. Increasingly, it appears that people are more content to be spectators than participants. Some sporting events such as football and boxing also take on the appearance of a spectacle similar to that seen in ancient Rome. In fact, it isn't uncommon to hear the participants in these events referred to as "gladiators." Should this be a concern? Well, with the rate of obesity increasing greatly in Canada and the United States, it is worth considering whether the focus on mass leisure seen during the Roman era (and perhaps the eventual outcome) is being repeated.

Middle Ages

When the Roman Empire eventually collapsed, the Catholic Church became the dominant structure in Europe (Shivers & deLisle, 1997). The Catholic Church rejected the activities that the Roman Empire had accepted, including its hedonistic ways (Horna, 1994). One example of this was the fact that people involved in theater could not be baptized. The concept that "idleness is the great enemy of the soul" emerged, and doing nothing was thought to be evil. The church wielded great influence during this time over the social order, consisting of nobility and peasants. The clergy dictated societal values, whose adoption would lead to saving souls, the highest goal at the time. Although the Catholic Church influenced what were acceptable and unacceptable leisure activities, so strict were many rules that during the end of this period the church went through a period of renaissance where individuals within the church developed different perspectives. This renaissance saw a renewed appreciation for a variety of leisure activities.

Renaissance

Spreading from the 14th century in Italy to the 16th century in northern Europe, this era saw power shift from the church to the nobility. Previously ostracized by the church, artists were now supported and encouraged by the nobility to express their art (Horna, 1994). Play was perceived to be an important part of education. During the 16th century, Francois Rabelais (1490-1553) emphasized

the need for physical exercise and games. Michel Eyquem de Montaigne (1533-1592) supported the concept of unity of mind, body, and spirit, opposing the medieval ideal of separation, or dualism, of the mind and body. John Locke (1632-1704) was so concerned with play as a medium of learning that he made the distinction between play and recreation: Recreation was not being idle, it provided a specific benefit by easing and helping to recover the people wearied by their work. Jean-Jacques Rousseau (1712-1778) advocated for the full freedom of physical activity rather than constraint. It was during the Renaissance that an increased interest in play, both as a form of popular entertainment and as a medium of education, developed.

Three types of parks emerged during the late Renaissance under the nobility:

1. royal hunting preserves providing wild-game hunting,
2. formal garden parks where participants viewed their surroundings much as you would experience a museum, and
3. English garden parks with a greater emphasis on interacting with the environment through activities such as picnics and other restful pursuits.

These parks, developed by the nobility for their own use, were often seen as symbols of status. People caught hunting in a royal hunting preserve who were not nobility were often killed. Still, the growth of parks within the nobility provided other classes an understanding of what was possible and led to the first thoughts of parks for the masses.

Protestant Reformation

During the Protestant Reformation (16th century), Martin Luther and others questioned the accepted practices of the Catholic Church and split off into other Protestant religions. Each religious group governed the perception of what was acceptable as leisure. Play was frowned on as evil by certain churches during this transition. The reformer John Calvin believed that success on earth determined your place in heaven. With that in mind, extraordinarily hard work and lack of leisure time were signs of great success. The influence of the Protestant and Catholic churches in Europe was critical to the earliest development of leisure in Canada and the United States because settlers came primarily from Europe, bringing these values and social structure to the New World. This was no different than what we see today with immigrant groups in Canada and the United States participating in different recreation activities, having different perspectives on leisure, and helping to expose others to different beliefs.

DEVELOPMENT OF RECREATION IN THE UNITED STATES AND CANADA

Recreation developed over time in the United States and Canada. Exploration in Canada began in the 11th century and in the United States in the 15th century. It continued to develop as the populations in both colonies grew. By the late 19th century, governments in both countries began to play a role in providing recreation and leisure services. This role changed and developed throughout the early part of the 20th century. Never static, recreation and leisure continued to evolve through wars and the depression, longer and shorter workweeks, and other periods in the United States. In Canada the

post–World War II era brought renewed interest in recreation services, but later declines in resources meant a lack of funding for recreation. One consequence of this ever changing face of recreation and leisure was the emergence of **professional organizations** that addressed the needs of both countries' citizens.

Early Settlement of the United States

To fully understand leisure during the settlement period, it is important to recognize the purpose of the earliest inhabitants and visitors. Christopher Columbus opened up the Americas in a time when exploration for the purposes of trade, profit, and control resulted in circumnavigation of the world (Shivers & deLisle, 1997). Europeans seeking adventure, wealth, or freedom from persecution arrived later in the United States bringing with them their traditions and beliefs. Two early colonies founded in the United States were in Virginia and New England (Shivers & deLisle, 1997). Preceding this period, Native Americans had developed their own unique forms of recreation. Although these activities often celebrated great religious rituals, they were also often highly competitive. One of the most well-known recreation activities, which is

Men of the Choctaw tribe playing lacrosse, which continues to grow in popularity today.

still growing in popularity, is the game of lacrosse. Given its common name by French settlers, this activity was common throughout Native American tribes in the east, Great Lakes region, and south with each having variations of the same activity. The game itself was often filled with great traditions and ceremony, used to release aggression or settle disputes, and often included wagering (Vennum, 2005). Other Native American tribes developed their own unique activities. The Illinois developed a straw game in which wagering revolved around who could guess the correct number of straws after a large pile was divided. Although this was often a male-dominated game, women were known to participate in their own game involving plum stones, which were used like modern dice (Illinois State Museum, 2000).

Virginia

The settlement in Virginia, established in Jamestown in the 17th century, was composed of aristocracy, adventurers, and traders. These people loved sports games, theater, books, music, and exercise and continued to pursue these activities once they arrived. However, with little free time available as they tried to survive, the governors banned recreational activities (Shivers & deLisle, 1997). One of the primary reasons for the strict control over these activities was the harsh conditions the colonists faced and the need for diligence to ensure survival. So difficult were the conditions, that of the 8,000 colonists who arrived in Virginia by 1625, only 1,200 survived an additional 10 years (Edgington, Jordan, DeGraff, & Edgington, 1998). The Virginia Assembly enforced observance of the Sabbath, prohibited gambling, and regulated drinking (Ibrahim, 1991). Penalties for partaking in Sunday amusements or failure to attend church services included imprisonment. Activities common to the weekend, including dancing, fishing, hunting, and card playing, were among those strictly prohibited (Kraus, 2001). However, these restrictions were lifted once survival became easier in Virginia and a "leisure class" began to emerge through the benefit of indentured servants and slaves. This societal arrangement mirrored that of those discussed previously in which the absence of a significant and identifiable middle class suggested the development of a developing leisure class. With laws and social mores relaxing in response to a social class seeking new ways to take advantage of its free time, many activities such as cockfighting, dice games, football, forms of bowling, and tennis (all of which were illegal) became more common among the privileged while still unavailable to the working class (Kraus, 2001).

New England

Although the settlement in New England also had to fight for its survival, its settlers were Calvinists escaping persecution in Europe. All forms of recreation were illegal, and the Puritan ethic restricted social activities. This philosophy valued frugality, hard work, self-discipline, and observance of civil and religious codes. Pleasure was considered to be the devil's work, and time not spent in worship or productive labor was considered wasteful (Shivers & deLisle, 1997). People were expected to behave religiously all of the time, thus work became a holy task. If daily activities belonged to God, then "God's time" should not be wasted in trivial pursuits. This Protestant work ethic often removed pleasure from lives. Leisure was considered a lure to sin and a threat to godliness. Puritans believed that they should avoid pleasures in their own lives and struggle against pleasure in the community (Cross, 1990). New England Puritans banned labor, travel, and recreation on Sundays. However, recreation was tolerated if it could help with work, such as quilting bees and barn raisings (Cross, 1990). The restrictions on Sunday activities continue today with "blue laws" that restrict the sale of items such as liquor that may not be purchased on Sundays.

Eventually, the strict control over the masses could not be sustained. Towns saw construction of meeting houses and taverns. The love of games and sport was rediscovered in these taverns. Later, bees, or working groups, emerged as a form of leisure. These provided a chance for dancing and horseracing (Ibrahim, 1991). Hunting became a popular leisure activity among the men because game was abundant. Training days, where young men learned how to serve in the militia, were held in Boston, and these were celebrated at the local tavern. Taverns were also used for cockfighting, animal baiting, dances, and orchestras. The church during this period of the 18th century, while increasingly concerned with these activities, was content to allow its participation in the relatively controlled setting of these public facilities. On the other hand, acceptable leisure activities included public readings and moral lectures. Amateur musical performances were occasionally tolerated. Plays were eventually accepted in Boston and Philadelphia. New York City had its own theater. The mercantile class enjoyed many leisure activities, including sleigh rides, horse races, balls, and card parties (Ibrahim, 1991). The trend of allowing questionable activities to occur behind closed doors, while encouraging acceptable activities to be held in public is still seen today. Laws often prohibit activities such as drinking in public, while taxes may support community events such as picnics and parades that are seen as more wholesome.

Early Park Development

An important development during the early colonial period was the realization that open space was important to growing communities. The Boston Common, a 48-acre oasis of nature in the middle of the city was established in 1634 and is viewed as the first municipal park (Kraus, 2001). This in turn influenced the creation of laws in Massachusetts requiring that bodies of water larger than 10 acres (4 ha) be open to the public for fishing and hunting (Edgington et al., 1998). As communities grew and the first organized urban planning efforts took shape, further efforts were undertaken to ensure open space was provided. The center of Philadelphia, Pennsylvania, is a prime example. Several north–south streets are intersected by streets named after species of trees. Within each of the resulting quadrants is park area providing a touch of nature within the metropolis. The creation of Central Park in New York City is probably the best-known example of early urban open-space provision.

Frederick Law Olmsted, considered the founder of American landscape architecture, was hired to design New York's Central Park in 1858, as well as municipal parks in Brooklyn, Philadelphia, Detroit, Chicago, and other areas in the late 19th century. He adapted the English style of a natural park to the rectangular restrictions of American parks (Ibrahim, 1991). He also established the initial purpose for city parks throughout the United States: pro-

viding a space for contemplative leisure (Ibrahim, 1991). Organized and structured sports so common in parks today were not permitted. Instead, the parks were initially intended to soothe the minds of newcomers to North America who were facing an increasingly industrial age and limited amount of open space (Kraus, 2001). Olmsted felt that parks should be large enough to shut out the city and that green spaces could inspire courtesy, self-control, and temperance. Olmsted's parks involved walkways, natural vistas, and landscaping to create a feeling of nature in the middle of the city (Cross, 1990). Parks developed by Olmsted were an attempt to regain the countryside in the city. They had artificial lakes, regularly mowed grass, and pathways for carriages. Although the parks existed for passive use, they were full of people enjoying activities such as baseball, cycling, skating, and horseback riding. Refreshment stands and restrooms were included for people spending the day at the park (Goodale & Godbey, 1988).

Playground Movement in the United States

The **playground movement** in the United States was first adopted by New York City when land was allocated for Central Park in 1855 (Ibrahim, 1991). Its purpose was to provide passive rest and aesthetics. In Chicago, however, Washington Park was opened in 1876 for more active sport. In Boston, Dr. Maria Zakrzewska promoted the concept of a "sand garden," which would eventually shape the idea of playgrounds for generations to come. In 1868, city leaders determined that an ever increasing number of children without constructive freetime pursuits needed more constructive outlets, so they developed the first organized playground program. It grew until 1886 when the addition of a pile of sand changed the notion of playgrounds. Started by school leaders and well-meaning citizens, a "sand garden" was created in Boston solely for use by children. Although this may seem commonplace today, it was for most children the first time they had ever played in sand or experienced a space designed for the active use of children only. So successful was the first Boston sand garden that city leaders produced 21 more playgrounds of the type by 1889. The popularity of this effort grew until many more playgrounds were created in New

The sheep meadow in New York City's Central Park in the early 20th century. As you can see, Olmsted was successful in bringing the countryside to the city.

York City, Chicago, and other areas (Kraus, 2001; Edgington et al., 1998).

Government Involvement: United States

As the United States expanded in population and size, the government became increasingly concerned with the national quality of life. In 1880 President James Garfield stated, "We may divide the whole struggle of the human race into two chapters: first, the fight to get leisure; and then the second fight of civilization—what shall we do with our recreation when we get it" (Kraus, 1990, p. 154). One major issue confronting government leaders was the amount of natural resources that would be available for future generations. Forests were being eliminated at breakneck speed to support massive amounts of construction. Out of this concern, the conservation movement was born and was intended to protect the national heritage of America, not to influence specific leisure behavior of Americans

(Ibrahim, 1991). Mindful of what many thought was a perilous decline in available natural resources, the Forest Service was created in 1906, with the creation of the National Park Service following in 1916. Yosemite Valley and the Mariposa Grove were granted to California to protect and preserve for future generations. Yellowstone National Park in Wyoming was the first national park, and Yosemite was taken back by the federal government and became the second (Ibrahim, 1991).

While the conservation movement sought to preserve natural resources typically far from the centers of the population, recreation participation within urban areas steadily increased in number and variety. Perhaps no era of American history so embraced the free-spirited notion of leisure than the Roaring '20s. This era saw the widespread increase in commercial recreation, disposable income, and the use of recreation as a sign of status. However, the economic pendulum of the time swung back quickly and in a shocking reversal of fortune: The crash of the stock market and ensuing Great Depression quickly ended the lifestyle of the Roaring '20s. The stock market crash led to never-before-seen levels of unemployment, poverty, and inadequate housing. With local governments struggling, the federal government assumed a larger role in the provision of parks and recreation (Goodale & Godbey, 1988). Massive unemployment stimulated a growing concern for the mass leisure that was now thrust on the unemployed. This sparked a new discussion of how people defined "free time." Studies showed that people were humiliated by unemployment and that leisure was meaningless without a job (Cross, 1990).

During this period in the United States, the American federal government tried a variety of actions to combat the economic peril that befell many. One effort included an attempt to spread jobs through the population by implementing a 34-hour workweek (Ibrahim, 1991). Making the biggest impact on recreation for generations to follow was the creation of the Works Progress Administration (WPA). This massive organization sought to put citizens back to work through a variety of methods. One of the most important to parks and recreation was the branch of the WPA known as the Civilian Conservation Corps (CCC). The CCC was responsible for countless construction projects providing a variety of recreation areas never before seen, many of which are still in use today. To get an idea of the scale of the CCC's work, consider that it employed enough workers to complete the following: the building of 800 state parks, 46,854 bridges, 28,087 miles (45,200 km) of trails, 46,000 campground facilities, and 204 lodges and museums and the planting of more than three billion trees (Edgington et al., 1998).

The increase in facilities provided by the federal government spurred state and local governments to establish and enhance their own agencies responsible for recreation. After six CCC camps were created in Virginia in 1933, the state created its first state parks from the original camps and opened them all on the same day in 1936 (Virginia State Parks, 2005). In Missouri, after 4,000 men were employed by the CCC to construct facilities, the state developed in 1937 an independent state park board (Missouri State Parks and Historic Sites, 2005). Other states, such as Delaware, Florida, and Georgia, also created state park systems during this

time to address the increasing popularity of the new sites provided by the federal government.

Professional Organizations: United States

Professional organizations emerged early in the United States. In 1906, Jane Addams, Joseph Lee, and Luther Gulick among others organized the Playground Association of America. In 1911, the name was changed to Playground and Recreation Association of America. In 1926, the name was changed again to the National Recreation Association. As employment in leisure-related agencies grew and professional preparation and competence continued to be of interest, additional professional organizations were formed. Initially acting independently, the National Recreation Association, American Institute of Park Executives, National Conference on State Parks, American Association of Zoological Parks and Aquariums, and the American Recreation Society merged in 1965 to become the National Recreation and Park Association (NRPA). With the addition shortly afterward of the National Association of Recreation Therapists and the Armed Forces Section of the American Recreation Society, and even after the American Association of Zoological Parks and Aquariums left to form its own organization, NRPA had become the largest organization in the United States to serve the needs of the general public and professionals in the promotion of parks, recreation, and leisure-related opportunities (Ibrahim, 1991). The mission of the NRPA is "To advance parks, recreation and environmental conservation efforts that enhance the quality of life for all people" (NRPA, n.d., par. 2). Affiliate park and recreation associations within each state further address this mission. These affiliates such as the Virginia Recreation and Park Society, Florida Recreation and Park Association, and Texas Recreation and Park Society serve their members through local outreach that meets the demands of professionals serving unique populations.

American Alliance for Health, Physical Education, Recreation and Dance (AAHPERD) was founded in 1885 when William Gilbert Anderson invited a group of people who were working in the gymnastics field to discuss their profession. AAHPERD is the largest organization for professionals involved in physical education, leisure, recreation, dance, health promotion, fitness, and education. The organization provides resources, support, and education to professionals to enhance their skills and improve the health and well-being of Americans (AAHPERD, n.d.a). It is an alliance of six national organizations and six district organizations. The mission of AAHPERD is to promote and support healthy lifestyles with high-quality programs in health, physical education, recreation, dance, and sport (AAHPERD, n.d.b).

Post–World War II Growth: United States

After World War II, recreation and leisure saw changes, challenges, and growth in several areas. Among those were the following:

• **Therapeutic recreation.** The extraordinary increase in the number of citizens who faced disabling injuries from their wartime fighting provided a challenge. The use of recreation as a therapy and the birth of therapeutic recreation as a distinct discipline occurred largely from its provision in government-sponsored Department of Veteran's Affairs (VA) hospitals. As recreation therapy grew and expanded from VA facilities to services provided in the community, a growing need for training and education evolved. Colleges and universities filled this need by creating a distinct body of knowledge, while professional organizations such as the National Therapeutic Recreation Society and American Association for Therapeutic Recreation were formed in 1966 and 1984, respectively. Lastly, professional certification of recreation therapists was provided by the National Council for Therapeutic Recreation Certification in 1981.

• **Concern for youth fitness.** A critical development in recreation and leisure came about in 1956. A battery of physical fitness tests comparing American youth to their peers in Europe produced shocking results that showed European children to be in much better condition. Having been involved in two world wars within the last half-century, the government, under President Eisenhower, created the President's Council on Youth Fitness in 1956. Eventually changing its name in 1966 to the President's Council on Physical Fitness and Sports, this initiative promotes health and wellness for all ages by first introducing physical skill testing and awards in schools, and also offering Active Lifestyle awards for all ages. In 1983, Congress declared May National Physical Fitness and Sports month. These initiatives mirrored a growth in mandatory physical education classes throughout the school year. Unfortunately, as time passed, the concern for youth fitness and the need for physical education were eclipsed by the concern for academic achievement in other areas. Perhaps it is worth considering whether this decreased emphasis on physical education in schools is just one factor in the sedentary American lifestyle that many see as contributing to a growing obesity epidemic.

• **Economic challenges and the impact on national affluence.** The end of the 20th century saw swift changes in the American economic landscape. The pendulum of affluence swung quickly from the relative comfort in the 1950s and 1960s, to times of great difficulty as the Arab oil embargo and stock market corrections affected the decades that followed. One way in which recreation and leisure addressed decreased government funding during tough times was the reliance on fees and charges. Following a marketing model for the first time to provide recreation programs, many agencies assessed charges to offset program cost or in some cases to produce a profit that would support other programs. These fees and charges, including membership fees, subsidized many programs but have been criticized for potentially excluding those with less income.

While some decades saw economic struggle, others enjoyed relative prosperity. During that time, the American thirst for consumer spending was in evidence as an ever increasing number of opportunities evolved to use recreation and leisure as a method to demonstrate one's social class. Private-club memberships grew, second homes were purchased, and increasingly expensive pieces of recreation equipment were within reach. This was not a new theme. In his 1899 book *The Theory of the Leisure Class*, Thorstein Veblen first introduced the notion that the use of leisure was an important way for people to define who they were. His term "conspicuous consumption" was as true at the beginning of the century as it was at the end. People increasingly embraced recreation activities and their associated equipment and lifestyle as a way to create their identity and compete with others (Veblen, 1998 [1899]). So true was the recurrence of this use of leisure that "shopping fever" became a term used in 2001 to describe other issues such as "mall mania," "home shopping," "cyber shopping," and "shopping as therapy," all of which related to the "dogged pursuit of more," a condition known as "affluenza" (DeGraff, Wann, & Naylor, 2001, p. 2).

How did recreation emerge in Canada? The following sections provide insights into the development of recreation in Canada.

Early Settlement of Canada

Canada, a frontier settlement, consisted of a few homesteads and resource-dependent rural communities (Harrington, 1996). The communities' economic well-being were based on natural resources such as fishing, logging, and agriculture. The first European explorers arrived in Canada in the 11th century. The first permanent European settlements were founded in the 1600s (Francis, Jones, & Smith, 1988). However, before the Europeans began to explore and settle, there were many different nations and languages among Canada's aboriginal peoples (LaPierre, 1992). The origin of Canada's first people is uncertain. Some argue that the aboriginal peoples emerged on the continent, while others argue that they migrated from Siberia. Regardless of their origin, Native Canadians were living in North America at least 10,000 years before the arrival of the Europeans (Francis et al., 1988). The aboriginal peoples in southern Canada enjoyed games, music, and storytelling for entertainment. Games were often based on hunting and fishing skills (Karlis, 2004). The Inuit, who lived in the Arctic, played many games including Nalukatook, involving bouncing on a walrus hide held by others, and Ipirautaqurnia, which involved flipping a whip accurately. Baggataway, played by the Algonquins and Iroquois, involving a curved netted stick, is now referred to as lacrosse (Karlis, 2004).

Colonization

Between 1604 and 1607, the first Acadian settlement was formed when Champlain and his men explored the coastline of the Maritimes and wintered at Port Royal, the first agricultural settlement in Canada. In 1606, Champlain's men took part in Canada's first theatrical production, and in 1607,

Champlain founded the Order of Good Cheer, which was the first social club in Canada. However, the colony was abandoned in 1607 due to lack of money (Francis et al., 1988). In 1608, Champlain constructed a habitation, or wooden buildings forming a quadrangle, which became the center of the first permanent French settlement. The French colony existed only for the purpose of trading fur and grew very slowly. By 1620, there were only 60 people in Quebec. However, by the 1650s, the French colony began growing steadily, and by the late 1700s, the language was altered by settlers to reflect traditions of the emerging country, thus the identity of Canadians emerged.

While the French were settling New France, the British were settling colonies in Newfoundland, Virginia, New York, and Massachusetts. They also sponsored expeditions north of New France, and in 1610 and 1611, Henry Hudson discovered Hudson Bay. Fifty years later, British fur-trading posts were established around the bay (Francis et al., 1988).

Because early settlement in Canada focused on the fur trade, and farming in Canada required a great deal of hard labor and preparation for winter, recreation opportunities were limited for the early settlers (Harrington, 1996). However men and women enjoyed activities such as curling, skating, ice hockey, snowshoeing, and tobogganing in the winter. Drama and music were also popular leisure activities at that time (McFarland, 1970).

Park Development

The first park in Canada, the Halifax Common, was established in 1763. Two hundred forty acres (97 ha) were designated for exercise for the militia in the early years (McFarland, 1970). Later the park was used for skating, lawn tennis, croquet, and archery (Wright, 1983). Municipal parks and public squares were established throughout the 19th century (McFarland, 1970; Searle & Brayley, 1993). For example, 14.9 acres (6 ha) of land in London, Ontario, were deeded from the federal government for Victoria Park in 1869. Also, 200 acres (81 ha) of land on the Halifax peninsula were leased from the federal government for 999 years for Point Pleasant Park, where all members of the community could enjoy exercise and recreation in 1875. However, much like in the United States, games were often prohibited in the parks, as was walking or lying on the grass. Parks were largely used for walking, sitting, horse drawn carriage driving, bird watching, and enjoying the plant life (McFarland, 1970).

As transportation improved in Canada and the railway was built, it became possible to travel for pleasure. This led to the formation of national parks. In 1885, the Canadian Pacific Railway suggested the establishment of Rocky Mountain Park, in Banff (Wetherell & Kmet, 1990). Although the difficult work required of the early settlers to build the country meant that there was little time for leisure, recreation eventually became a part of the lives of Canadians.

Playground Movement in Canada

In Canada, the playground movement developed supervised playgrounds for children. Similar to its development in the United States, the playground movement in Canada was born from an increasing sense that recreation and leisure had an important role to play in the betterment of its citizens' quality of life. In the 1800s, municipal parks were used by the upper classes, and the lower classes did not have

access to open areas. However, concern for those who lived in overcrowded areas with high crime and disease led to the creation of safe places for play (McFarland, 1970). This movement was based on the notion that play was the only appropriate method for physical development for children and was necessary for their health, strength, and moral character (Searle & Brayley, 1993). There was a belief that children required encouragement to play and that the playground could be used to teach health and social customs in a play environment (McFarland, 1970). In 1893, the National Council of Women was formed, and the council and its local groups played a major role in initiating the playground movement (McFarland, 1970).

According to McFarland (1970), there were two different justifications for the playground movement. The first was the prevention of delinquency and drunkenness, and the second was the belief that all people had the right to opportunities for leisure. However, the emphasis on preventing delinquency and drunkenness was necessary for receiving funding and to justify giving time to the playground movement. School grounds were selected for the playgrounds, and in 1908, the Toronto school

The early development of the national park system of Canada was stimulated by political pressure raised by the railway companies. This early linkage of tourism and national parks provided strong stimulus for Canadian travelers to explore these unique places.

board was the first to develop summer playground programs. In general, playground programs were initiated by local branches of the National Women's Council, followed by the formation of a playground association, and finally, a civic department responsible for playgrounds and recreation programming was established. In the beginning, teachers were chosen for playground supervisors, and programs included games, stories, reading, sewing, and music. Eventually, summer and winter programs merged, and indoor programs were developed, which led to the hiring of full-time supervisors for public playgrounds. The playground movement led to the concept of a comprehensive parks system (McFarland, 1970).

Government Involvement: Canada

Federal, provincial, and municipal governments have long been involved in providing recreation opportunities for Canadians. The land for the first parks in Canada was often deeded or leased to municipalities from the federal or provincial governments. For example, the Canadian government authorized Saint John, New Brunswick's horticultural society to establish gardens, a park, and a pleasure resort with 1,700 acres (688 ha) for Rockwood Park (McFarland, 1970). Also, the city of Vancouver received permission from the federal government to establish Stanley Park on part of the local harbor peninsula. In 1865, a Montreal city bylaw designated 13 open spaces for citizens to enjoy, although games and walking on the grass were prohibited (McFarland, 1970).

In 1883, the province of Ontario passed the first legislation that affected the development of provincial parks. The Public Parks Act established parks in cities and towns with the consent or petition of the electors. The local government could appoint park management boards that included the mayor of the municipality and six board members. These park boards could purchase land for parks not more than 1,000 acres (405 ha) in cities and 500 acres (202 ha) in towns. In 1892, the province of Manitoba passed a similar act (McFarland, 1970); thus, the provincial governments played an important role in the development of parks in Canada.

In the 1940s, the federal and provincial governments, under the National Physical Fitness Act, provided recreation services that influenced municipal recreation (McFarland, 1970). In Ontario in 1945, 18 municipalities passed recreation bylaws, and one year later, 70 had passed bylaws (Markham, 1992). The governments focused on leadership development in schools and the community and increased awareness of the possibilities of public recreation programs. The act was repealed in 1954 (Westland, 1979). The Ontario provincial government gave grants to municipalities and encouraged the local provision of recreation opportunities for all. In the 1950s, British Columbia and Alberta supported local governments in developing municipal grant structures suitable for social and economic situations (McFarland, 1970).

All three levels of government continue to be involved in providing recreation services. The Interprovincial Sport and Recreation Council (ISRC) developed the National Recreation Statement in 1987. The statement defines the roles of each level of government. In 1978, the provinces and territories agreed that recreation was within their jurisdiction; thus, their role in recreation became significant. Once local volunteers make decisions about recreation services, provincial governments are responsible for providing the assistance, leadership, and recognition necessary to deliver these services. They provide support to community volunteers who manage recreation clubs and societies and provide leadership and instruction, raise money, and coordinate programs. The interprovincial council agreed that it is the role of the provincial governments to state policy outlining the goals and objectives and stress the importance of recreation as a social service. Some of their other roles include observing and analyzing trends and issues to update policy; providing municipal governments with resources to enhance the quality of life of a community through grants for conferences and training; providing programs and services to build a delivery system that links the three levels of government and voluntary, private, and commercial sectors; and planning and supporting recreation research.

The role of the municipality in providing recreation services is to ensure a wide range of opportunities for all community members. Municipalities are responsible for establishing a recreation authority to provide opportunities, be aware of resources and opportunities and ensure that information is available to the public, provide incentives and services to develop opportunities based on needs, conduct regular assessments of needs and interests that are not being met, and develop a council to determine the best use of community resources (Interprovincial Sport and Recreation Council [ISRC], 1987).

Finally, the Interprovincial Sport and Recreation Council outlined the federal government's role in providing recreation services. The council agreed that the federal government must take action to influence the scope of recreation and work closely with all recreation agents in implementing programs that affect recreation services. The federal government should provide recreation through national organizations and ensure Canadian representation in activities that serve a national purpose. The federal government should contribute to the development of recreation services through provision of resources to support public, voluntary, and commercial sectors. And finally, the federal government should provide promotional materials to encourage recreation participation (ISRC, 1987).

Parks Canada is one federal agency that provides recreation opportunities for Canadians. The mandate of Parks Canada is to protect and present examples of Canada's natural and cultural heritage as well as to foster understanding, appreciation, and enjoyment to ensure this heritage (Parks Canada, n.d.). The agency serves as the guardian of parks, historic sites, and national marine conservation. The agency guides visitors to national parks and serves as partners in building on the traditions of Native Canadians, diverse cultures, and international commitments. Parks Canada recounts the history of the land and people and is committed to protecting heritage, presenting the beauty and significance of the natural world, and to serving Canadians (Parks Canada, 2002).

Professional Organizations: Canada

Professional recreation groups began to emerge in Canada in the first half of the 20th century. Both national and provincial associations serve recreation professionals and volunteers. The Canadian Parks and Recreation Association (CPRA) was founded in 1945 (CPRA, n.d.a). It developed from the expanding mission and influence of the Ontario Parks Association in the later years of the war. During postwar discussions, the Ontario Parks Association called on the government to consider parks, playgrounds, and recreation a separate reconstruction project after the war. On July 11, 1944, in Windsor, Ontario, the CPRA started as a means of broadening the mandate of the Ontario Parks Association for Ontario and Quebec. Formal creation of CPRA occurred one year later (Markham, 1995). At that time it was known as the Parks and Recreation Association of Canada. Its purpose was to deal with changes that occurred after World War II, including the need to provide parks and recreation services. The name was changed in 1970 to the Canadian Parks and Recreation Association, and the society has responded to and will continue to respond to social, economic, and political changes within the country (CPRA, n.d.a). The mission of CPRA is to build healthy communities and enhance the quality of life and environment. The association serves as a national voice for parks and recreation, and it advocates on behalf of parks and recreation as essential for health and well-being of Canadians. CPRA communicates and promotes the values and benefits of parks and recreation, responds to diverse and changing needs, and provides educational opportunities (CPRA, n.d.b).

Another national organization for recreation professionals is the Canadian Association for Health, Physical Education, Recreation and Dance (CAHPERD). CAHPERD is a national, charitable, voluntary organization that focuses on the healthy development of children and youth by advocating for physical and health education. CAPHERD began as the Canadian Physical Education Association in 1933. The name changed in 1948 to the Canadian Association of Health, Physical Education and Recreation, and in 1994, "dance" was added to the name to recognize its value (CAHPERD, n.d.).

Provinces also have recreation associations. For example, the Saskatchewan Parks and Recreation Association (SPRA) is a nonprofit volunteer organization that promotes, develops, and facilitates parks and recreation opportunities throughout the province (SPRA, n.d.a). In the 1940s, 10 communities in Saskatchewan had recreation boards. The Saskatchewan recreation movement was established and later renamed the SPRA. The association converted military units to recreation facilities after the war. The society emphasized physical activity at that time. In the 1950s, the first library was opened and community halls and curling rinks were built (SPRA, n.d.b).

Recreation Nova Scotia, another provincial organization, promotes the values and benefits of recreation toward a healthier future. Recreation Nova Scotia began as the Recreation Association of Nova Scotia in 1972 and in 1998, merged with the Recreation Council on Disabilities in Nova Scotia and Volunteer Nova Scotia (Recreation Nova Scotia, n.d.).

A third provincial organization, Parks and Recreation Ontario (PRO), is a not-for-profit group whose history goes back to 1945 (PRO, n.d.). PRO is open to all who are interested in recreation, parks, fitness, sport and facilities, aquatics, therapeutic recreation, arts, and culture. Membership includes more than 1,000 recreation professionals, volunteers, educators, students, citizens, elected officials, and commercial organizers (see Markham-Starr, 2005, for more information).

Post–World War II Growth: Canada

Like the United States, Canada also experienced a host of challenges related to recreation and leisure after World War II, some similar and some different. Included in these challenges were the following:

• **Concern for fitness.** The 1960s were characterized by renewed concern for physical fitness (Searle & Brayley, 1993). The Fitness and Amateur Sport Act, which was passed in 1961, redefined the role of government in sport, recreation, and leisure. In the 1960s all levels of government became involved in financial assistance to promote recreation development. Much of this money was dedicated to building facilities (Searle & Brayley, 1993). ParticipACTION was established in 1971 as a nonprofit organization to promote a healthy, physically active lifestyle (Canadian Public Health Association [CPHA], 2004). The program was started by Pierre Trudeau in order to battle rising health care costs (Canadian Broadcasting Corporation, 2000). ParticipACTION pioneered the use of social marketing and health communication techniques and produced one of the longest-running (1971-2000) communication campaigns to promote physical activity in the world (CPHA, 2004). The media campaign suggested to Canadians that a 60-year-old Swede was as fit as, or more so, than a 30-year-old Canadian (ParticipACTION, n.d.). The program continued until 2000, when the federal government refused ParticipACTION's funding request (CBC, 2000).

• **Economic challenges.** In 1973, the Arab oil embargo ended the rapid development of recreation resources and opportunities. High energy costs led to empty arenas and poorly maintained parks. The oil embargo also affected pleasure travel when gas was rationed and higher jet fuel costs made flying expensive. Provincial and municipal governments were forced to limit the growth of recreation. They needed to adopt a new style of leadership. Municipal recreation agencies became less involved in directly providing services and started playing a facilitative role instead (Searle & Brayley, 1993).

• **Changing demographic trends.** The changing nature of the family throughout the 1980s and 1990s influenced recreation service delivery, causing service providers to respond to different needs, opportunities, and constraints. Various family structures had to be considered, including blended families, single-parent families, childless families, multiple generation families, and traditional nuclear families, to name a few (Searle & Brayley, 1993). The majority of single-parent families were headed by women in the 1980s, and these families had lower incomes than two-parent families (Harrington, 1996). Common-law relationships became more common throughout the 1980s and 1990s, and marriage rates were lower. The age of first marriage rose during the 80s and 90s, divorce rates also rose, and fertility rates declined (Harrington, 1996). All of these trends have had an impact on leisure services delivery.

People living in poverty also posed a new challenge for service providers. The new poor were of particular concern and included children living in poverty, the working poor, and frail elderly community members. Leisure services were needed to help build self-esteem, develop social support networks, and teach self-reliance skills. Focus was on satisfying needs and delivering programs in the most appropriate way for clients (Searle & Brayley, 1993). Multiculturalism was another issue arising in the 1980s and 1990s and continues today. Canadian public policy defends the idea that differences in a nation are good for it, and the government protects the cultures of new Canadians.

SIMILARITIES BETWEEN CANADA AND THE UNITED STATES

Recreation has developed similarly in the United States and Canada. For example, both countries developed playgrounds in similar ways at about the same time. The following are among the trends that have been identified:

- Expansion of activities for children to activities for all ages
- Expansion of summer programs to yearlong programs
- Provision of indoor and outdoor activities
- Expansion of playgrounds into rural areas
- Shift from philanthropic to community financial support of playground programs
- Increased importance of organized play over unorganized play
- Shifting philosophy to include use of leisure and not just provision of facilities by communities
- Increased importance of community and group activities over individual interests (Rainwater, 1992)
- Creation of play spaces
- More opportunities for child development through play
- Growing belief in the importance of outdoor play for young
- Increased opportunities for public recreation
- Quest for a better balance between work and play
- Appreciation of the value of play in the life of a child

What is clear is that the playground movement in Canada and the United States continued the path of the pendulum that had long before started swinging toward a greater appreciation for recreation

and leisure. Like in ancient Greece, economic class separation in Canada and the United States was a growing reality, class structure in Western society since the industrial revolution has been structured related to economic wealth, and the upper classes were demonstrating a growing concern for those in the lower classes. Recreation and leisure was no longer seen as a privilege, but was increasingly considered an important part of life and a way for those who were well off to help those who were less so. This sense of obligation helped ensure the value of recreation and leisure, and in this case the playground movement, as a way to address life's challenges.

Government has played an important role in providing recreation and leisure opportunities in both the United States and Canada. In the United States, the government began to play a role in providing social services during the Great Depression when the lack of jobs increased the amount of time available (most likely more than was wanted) to pursue leisure activities. The federal government also developed organizations to protect natural resources and preserve them for future generations. This continued a trend of governments tackling societal problems through concern for the leisure-related issues facing their citizens. Changing demographics in Canada and the United States will influence the definition of leisure in the next 20 years.

SUMMARY

Leisure in the United States and Canada has been influenced by past definitions of leisure. Primitive societies had little time for leisure as they fought for survival. However, as their tools became more sophisticated, they gained more free time. Play was used to teach children about their roles as adults, as an opportunity for ritualization, and for rest and relaxation in prehistoric societies. Among the ancient Greeks, contemplation, education, philosophy, and athletics were important leisure activities and helped in reaching the "Athenian ideal." However, only full Greek citizens had opportunities for leisure. In ancient Rome, leisure was considered to be time away from work, and recuperation was of great importance. Leisure was also used as a method of social control. After the fall of the Roman Empire, the Catholic Church, which restricted leisure participation, controlled what people perceived to be leisure by placing values on activities. Further restrictions were placed on leisure and social activity during the Protestant Reformation, as new churches emerged. These strict rules were relaxed during the Renaissance when artists were supported and play was considered important for education.

Early settlers in the United States and Canada brought these perceptions of what was acceptable leisure to their new countries. These views and the environmental conditions they faced have influenced leisure today. The first colonies in the United States restricted leisure as settlers, like members of prehistoric civilizations, fought for survival and had time for little else. However, as restrictions were lifted, work bees, hunting, and going to the tavern became popular pastimes. As time passed, exploration and settlement resulted in increasing recreation opportunities for European settlers. As governments established parks as early as the 1700s, participation started to grow and a concern for the appropriate use of leisure time emerged.

The playground movement in both the United States and Canada began in the late 1800s and early 1900s. The first sand garden was founded in Boston, and more playgrounds followed in New York and Chicago following Boston's success. The movement was started in Canada by the National Council of Women to give children opportunities for supervised play in order to prevent delinquency and promote healthy development.

All levels of government in both countries are involved in recreation. Governments provide facilities, funding, support, policy, information, and training for recreation services. The growth of organizations concerned with recreation program provision and the workers responsible for it emerged in the United States at the same time as the playground movement. These organizations evolved to become the two main national organizations found today: the National Recreation and Park Association and the American Association for Health, Physical Education, Recreation and Dance. In Canada, professional organizations emerged on the national level with the Canadian Parks and Recreation Association and the provincial level in the 1940s with Recreation Nova Scotia. Like in the United States, these agencies provide support for recreation programs and promote the importance of recreation and leisure for health and well-being. In Canada after World War II, leadership styles changed from direct service to facilitative assistance due to decreases in funding for recreation. The ParticipACTION program was developed in the 1970s to encourage Canadians to become fit, and the President's Council on Physical Fitness and Sports was formed in the 1960s to address fitness in the United States. Finally, as the new millennium unfolded, it became clear that many themes of the past including how best to serve a changing society, the appropriate use of mass leisure, government's role, and the importance of professional organizations were again as important as ever.

For glossary terms, learning experiences, and more, please visit the web resource at
www.HumanKinetics.com/IntroductionToRecreationAndLeisure

CHAPTER 3

Philosophy and Leisure

Donald J. McLean

> " Happiness is thought to depend on leisure; for we are busy that we may have leisure, and make war that we may live in peace. "
>
> Aristotle, Greek philosopher

LEARNING OUTCOMES

After reading this chapter, you should be able to do the following:

> Explain the five branches of philosophy, the relevance of each to leisure research, and the effect of each on leisure services delivery

> Compare and evaluate the concepts of leisure as both a state of mind and a state of being and apply these two conceptions of leisure to the provision of recreation services

> Demonstrate a comprehensive understanding of the leisure research literature by comparing theories of leisure based on both empirical research and philosophic analysis

> Explain the importance of being able to justify conclusions and decisions logically in leisure services

> Explain why aesthetics is important to our understanding of leisure and how considerations of aesthetics influence the provision of leisure services

> Apply ethical reasoning to evaluate the worthiness of leisure services

INTRODUCTION

The methods of philosophy can be put to good use in both the study of recreation and leisure phenomena and the delivery of leisure services. Contrary to the popular belief that philosophy provides obscure answers to theoretical issues, philosophical inquiry has many practical implications for and is important to both leisure research and service delivery by helping to focus our attention on important questions and issues related to recreation and leisure. Perhaps the best way to summarize the usefulness of philosophy to the field of recreation and leisure studies and services is that it provides us with guidance in *how* to think rather than *what* to think about issues and problems related to leisure and recreation.

WHY DOES PHILOSOPHY MATTER?

For many people, the subject of **philosophy** appears to have little relevance to recreation and leisure. Our stereotype of philosophers suggests that they are deep thinkers who are uninterested in practical matters relating to relaxation, pleasure, or fun. This "highbrow" image of philosophy is spoofed in the old Monty Python skit of the philosophers' soccer game: Aristotle, Kant, Hegel, and other great thinkers from the past stand like statues deep in thought on a soccer field. The ball just sits there for the whole match until Archimedes suddenly has a revelation and kicks the ball to Socrates who then fires it into the net while the other players look on in bewilderment.

Like the immobilized philosophers in the skit, many recreation students become frozen in their seats, their eyes glazed over, when their instructor announces that the week's topic is the "philosophy of leisure." Typically, students have chosen recreation and leisure studies because they prefer active, hands-on experiences to abstract thinking. What use, students ask, is there in learning what some dead white guy from long ago thought about leisure and recreation? Wouldn't their time be better spent learning how to program activities, create budgets, and market events?

Because the philosophy of leisure is often taught as a history lesson, or as part of the "intellectual foundations" of leisure and recreation, it is understandable that students are doubtful that philosophy has any real application to leisure services. Yet philosophy affects both the study of leisure phenomena and the delivery of recreation services in fundamental ways. It is just that we tend not to recognize the importance of philosophy to recreation and leisure studies because it typically functions in the background of our thinking and practices. But when we understand what philosophical inquiry is, it is not difficult to see the contribution that it makes to both the theory and practice of leisure and recreation. To learn why philosophy does matter to people interested in recreation and leisure, let's begin by first examining why philosophy has gained a reputation for being irrelevant.

The term *philosophy* translates from ancient Greek as "lover of wisdom," and originally it referred to all scholarly inquiry. However, over the last several hundred years, the evolution of modern-day universities has seen the rise of many separate disciplines such as physics, chemistry, sociology, and anthropology as knowledge and methods of inquiry have become increasingly complex. In fact, the discipline of leisure studies follows this pattern of the increasing specialization of knowledge because most recreation curricula and departments did not exist before the 1960s.

The division of knowledge into a variety of specialized fields is an important explanation for why philosophy appears to have lost much of its relevancy. As discipline-based knowledge has grown, the scope of philosophic inquiry has been whittled away. But despite the loss of academic ownership to other disciplines, philosophy is primarily associated with five branches of inquiry: metaphysics, epistemology, logic, aesthetics, and ethics. Each of the five types of philosophical inquiry has relevance to recreation and leisure studies, but as will be explained later, the first two, metaphysics and epistemology, have more importance to leisure researchers, whereas ethics is more relevant to leisure practitioners. The fourth branch of philosophical inquiry, logic, has important implications for both leisure researchers and leisure practitioners, whereas the fifth branch, aesthetics, has received relatively little attention from either practitioners or researchers. To advance our understanding of the relevance of philosophical inquiry, let's now examine the ways in which each of the branches of philosophy has influenced thinking and practice in recreation and leisure.

METAPHYSICS AND LEISURE

Metaphysics concerns questions about the fundamental nature of reality. It is the branch of philosophic inquiry that is most likely to generate amusement and derision from nonphilosophers. Questions such as "Does a tree make a sound when it falls in the forest if no one is around?" or "Is the cup really on the table?" or "Does God exist?" are classic examples of metaphysical inquiries that can seem pointless to more practically minded people. (I remember being in a philosophy seminar in which we once really did discuss whether or not the professor's coffee cup was on the table!) Many people have argued that metaphysical inquiry into the ultimate nature of reality is too speculative to be of any practical use. Even famous philosophers such as David Hume dismissed metaphysics as so much gibberish about nothing.

Although most contemporary philosophers do not subscribe to the view that metaphysical inquiry is meaningless, ironically, it was advanced physics that popularized speculation about the nature of reality. Scientist–media personalities such as Carl Sagan and Stephen Hawking have done much to fuel the public's imagination about such topics as the ultimate nature of the universe and our place in it. Many people today are fascinated by theories of alternate realities as predicted by quantum mechanics, the origins of the universe, and other metaphysical speculations that stretch beyond the boundaries of empirical science.

In recreation and leisure studies, metaphysical inquiry has mainly revolved around more down-to-earth questions of how leisure should be defined. Although the average person may believe that everyone knows what leisure is, scholars and researchers have gone to great lengths debating the essential qualities of leisure. And, as many researchers have noted, the term *leisure* is difficult to define. Unlike phenomena studied in the natural sciences in which the subject matter stays the same no matter the time or place, (e.g., water has the same physical properties that it did 1,000 years ago and does not vary from one society to another), socially constructed phenomena such as leisure are continually in flux (e.g., ideas about leisure vary from culture to culture and at different periods in time). The variability of leisure as a socially evolving phenomenon of human existence makes it much more difficult to determine what the essential qualities of leisure in fact are. Nonetheless, intellectual debates concerning the essence of leisure historically have fallen into two opposing theses about the fundamental nature of leisure. The traditional view is that leisure is a public, objective state of being. The modern view is that leisure is essentially a private, subjective state of mind. Let's first examine the traditional view of leisure as a state of being and then compare it with the modern definition of leisure as a state of mind.

The idea that leisure is a state of being, that is, a set of life circumstances, is attributable to the ancient Greeks. According to Aristotle, having leisure meant being free of the burden of work so that one could engage in more ennobling activities such as music and philosophy. For the ancient Greeks, an essential element of leisure was to possess sufficient material resources so that one could have time for leisure. Thus, if you were a slave in ancient Athens, you were incapable of having leisure because you did not have the resources to engage in it.

The idea that leisure is a state of being is also reflected in contemporary conceptualizations of leisure as unobligated time. Modern economic systems, which formalized the division between work time and leisure time, have helped reinforce the idea that the most fundamental feature of leisure is that it is a time when we are free from work and other obligations of life. As well, the ancient Greek ideal that leisure time should be used to engage in worthwhile activities still resonates with many people, although research indicates that most of us do not devote much of our free time to uplifting activities. Sebastin de Grazia's book *Of Time, Work and Leisure* provides a modern-day justification for the idea that people should use their leisure time performing worthwhile activities. For both ancient and contemporary thinkers who see leisure as a state of being, the critical point is that leisure is defined by the circumstances and actions of people that can be observed by others. Leisure, therefore, is not a private experience, but instead it occurs in a public, social context where others can judge whether we are at leisure or whether the activities that we are engaging in qualify as leisurely. Leisure as a state of being thus depends on a social consensus as to what activities and living conditions qualify as leisure.

In contrast to the notion that leisure is a state of being, many leisure researchers have argued that leisure is primarily a private state of mind. John Neulinger, for example, theorizes that leisure is a psychological state in which the experience of leisure depends on how a person perceives a situation. Neulinger's theory of leisure is based on two variables: perceived freedom and motivation (Neulinger,

1974). According to his theory, perceived freedom means that a person thinks that he or she is free in a particular instance. With Neulinger's theory, perception of freedom does not depend on the individual's actual circumstances. Even for people who are desperately poor or repressed, so long as they *think* that they have freedom, a necessary condition for leisure is satisfied. The other psychological component necessary to having leisure is whether the person perceives that his or her motivation is intrinsic or extrinsic, in other words, whether motivation is generated internally (e.g., one plays music because it is pleasing to oneself) or externally (e.g., one plays music to make money). Thus, when people perceive that they are free to choose to engage in a leisure activity that they find intrinsically motivating, then the resulting outcome is a state of mind whereby they experience pure leisure. According to many modern-day leisure researchers, leisure is therefore a private, subjective state of mind rather than a public, objective state of being.

Although it may seem fine and well that leisure researchers investigate and debate the fundamental characteristics of leisure, students and practitioners may wonder how such discussions could have any relevance to delivery of leisure services. But the choice between thinking that leisure is a state of being or a state of mind can have a profound influence on leisure service delivery choices (Sylvester, 1991). Sylvester states that viewing leisure as a state of mind may encourage practitioners to provide leisure experiences that are inauthentic, illusory, and even immoral:

> Regardless of the actual content, context or consequences, *anything* counts as leisure as long as the individual avows a subjective experience of freedom. Applying to illusions as well as real events, the potential for leisure is virtually boundless. If you experience leisure, then leisure it is, for there is no disputing the truth of subjective states of mind. (Sylvester, 1991, p. 441)

Sylvester argues that viewing leisure as a private state of mind opens the door to all sorts of horrid and depraved activities qualifying as leisure. Less shocking, but still worrisome, he says, is the possibility that leisure service practitioners may chose to provide clients who live in inequitable and

OUTSTANDING GRADUATES

Background Information

Name: Tammy Wright

Education: Bachelor of science in recreation, park, and tourism administration from Western Illinois University.

Credentials: Wildland firefighter type 2 and medical first responder.

Special awards: Distinguished Alumni Award from Western Illinois University, 2011.

Affiliations: Association of National Park Rangers and National Association for Interpretation.

Career Information

Position: Park ranger.

Organization: The Bureau of Land Management (BLM) may best be described as a small agency with a big mission: to sustain the health, productivity, and diversity of America's public lands for the use and enjoyment of present and future generations. It administers more public land—over 245 million surface acres—than any other federal agency in the United States. Most of this land is located in the 12 Western states, including Alaska. The BLM also manages 700 million acres of subsurface mineral estate throughout the nation.

The BLM does its complex and challenging work with an annual budget of more than $1 billion and a workforce of about 10,000 full-time employees. The BLM is one of a handful of federal agencies that generates more revenue for the United States than it spends.

Organization's mission: The BLM's multiple-use mission mandates that we manage public land resources for a variety of uses (such as energy development, livestock grazing, recreation, and timber harvesting) while protecting an array of natural, cultural, and historical resources, many of which are found in the BLM's 27 million-acre National Landscape Conservation System. This system includes 221 wilderness areas totaling 8.7 million acres as well as 16 national monuments in 4.8 million acres.

> *What better field to work in than recreation and leisure services? We, as facilitators of recreation and leisure services, get to plan how people spend their free time. In many cases, it's only hours long, but it's those precious few hours that can lead to a lifetime of memories for anyone.*

Job description: I am responsible for operational and administrative functions of visitor services and visitor interpretation and for the maintenance of the field office's developed and primitive recreation sites. I am responsible for patrolling trails and recreation sites to provide visitor assistance, promote visitor compliance with rules and regulations, evaluate the conditions of facilities and areas, produce and disseminate written information and interpretive materials, issue special-use permits and campfire permits, serve as liaison between community organizations and user groups, assist in analysis of recreation needs for the field office (including the design and layout of hiking trails and campground facilities), maintain facilities in a neat and clean condition, identify maintenance needs, and perform routine repairs and other duties as assigned.

Career path: I began my career as a seasonal park ranger with the National Park Service working summer seasons at Wind Cave National Park and winters at Carlsbad Caverns and Death Valley National Parks. After just two years of working seasonally, I accepted a permanent position with Carlsbad Caverns National Park. After one year, I made my way to working for the Bureau of Land Management in California. While in college, I volunteered for a docent position at a local historical house and for the local convention and visitors' bureau. I also accepted jobs where I worked with the public as much as possible.

(continued)

repressive circumstances with leisure experiences that encourage them to accept their disadvantaged situation. And, even for well-to-do clients, he questions whether practitioners should "engineer" pleasant subjective leisure experiences. Rather than providing impetus for true personal growth, development, and achievement, subjective leisure may deceive people into thinking that their leisure lives are fulfilling and meaningful when, in fact, the leisure activities that they are engaged in lack ennobling qualities.

Although the concerns that Sylvester raises about subjective leisure are well founded, regarding leisure as a state of mind may be beneficial in many situations. For example, some adventure recreation programming, such as high-ropes courses, deliberately uses the perception of risk to facilitate participants' personal growth. Being suspended 40 feet (12 m) off the ground can result in a perception of adventure and risk, although in reality the participants are safe because they are harnessed and belayed. Exposing participants to real danger in this situation would be not only unnecessary for achieving the benefits of the recreation experience but also irresponsible and unethical.

We can readily think of other examples in which approaching leisure as a state of mind is the proper approach. We would be unwise and insensitive to tell an enthusiastic young child that his or her piano playing is not very good. Nor should we disparage those who sometimes seek out artificial leisure environments such as Disney or engage in virtual reality experiences. And what of harmless, idiosyncratic types of leisure, such as eccentric hobbies, that few people other than those engaged find enjoyable? Should these activities not be classified as leisure because other people do not appreciate their merit?

But despite the fact that treating leisure as a state of mind is desirable in many situations, it is equally true in other instances that it is reasonable to conceptualize leisure as an objective state of being. For example, we make the effort to visit a significant natural or cultural resource because we want to experience the authentic object or environment. No replica or simulation will suffice. We join a competitive sport program because we want to see how our skills match up with the skills of others. We set for ourselves challenging goals to exercise, become fit, and lose weight. In these instances our leisure experience is guided by our ability to achieve a particular objectively recognized state of being.

So, in some situations and contexts it is helpful to think of leisure as a state of being, whereas at other times it would be best to treat leisure as a state of mind. Perhaps the lesson here is not that we must define leisure in one way to the exclusion of the other, but instead to be aware of the fundamentally different ways in which leisure can be conceptualized and to understand how our presuppositions about the nature of leisure can influence our assumptions about the kinds of leisure experiences that will be beneficial to people. Thinking about the essential nature of leisure therefore is not simply an academic exercise for researchers. Let's now consider the next branch of philosophic inquiry, epistemology, and its influence on the field of recreation and leisure.

EPISTEMOLOGY AND LEISURE

Epistemology is the study of knowledge itself. The term *epistemology* is derived from the Greek words *episteme* (knowledge) and *logos* (explanation); hence, epistemology is the branch of philosophy that explains knowledge, or provides theories about how it is we know what we know. Epistemology concerns questions of how we can acquire knowledge, what types of things we are capable of knowing (the scope of our knowledge), and how trustworthy the knowledge that we possess is (how certain we can be of what it is we know).

Traditionally, epistemological debate about the source of knowledge divides into two camps: those who think that knowledge is derived from sense perceptions (**empiricists**) and those who believe that knowledge comes from ideas generated by our minds (**rationalists**). Empiricists believe that knowledge ultimately must be based on evidence. Thus, empiricists place a great deal of importance on how observations are collected.

Whether we are leisure researchers or practitioners, we want to have the best information possible for advancing knowledge and making decisions. In North America the study of leisure has predominately been data driven, but debate has been ongoing about whether observations should be collected to produce quantitative or qualitative data. Many leisure researchers believe that the investigation of leisure phenomena should use methods conducive to producing quantitative data; that is, observations of leisure should primarily take the form of numeric scores. Examples of quantitative data include the numbers generated from questionnaires that use Likert scales or the tallies from observational checklists. Researchers can then use such data to perform statistical analysis and test hypotheses about factors that are thought to influence people's leisure experiences. Often, the collection of quantitative data has a narrow focus so that the amassing of information concerning a few variables can be carefully controlled.

Other researchers take the position that observations of leisure should be gathered primarily by interpreting the meaning and significance that people associate with their leisure experiences. To understand the meaning that people attribute to leisure, researchers collect and analyze the words and statements of subjects from interviews or create field notes based on the researchers' interpretations of subjects' behavior and actions. Qualitative analysis emphasizes explaining and understanding the lived leisure experiences of the subjects being studied and tends to have a broader focus than quantitative analysis does.

The fact that there are two schools of thought about how observations should be collected has, not surprisingly, created an epistemological debate between the adherents who favor quantitative data collection and those who favor qualitative data collection. Although we need not trouble ourselves with the details of this lively controversy, generally speaking, the supporters of research that produces quantitative data maintain that it is more trustworthy than qualitative data, whereas those who support the collecting of qualitative data argue that it provides a more comprehensive understanding of people's leisure experiences. The debate is thus largely a disagreement between which epistemic quality of knowledge is more important: the certainty and trust that arise from knowledge derived from observations (quantitative) or the scope and relevancy of the knowledge deriving from gathering data about people's lived leisure experiences (qualitative). But despite these disagreements about the strengths and weaknesses of quantitative and qualitative data, note that both sides agree substantially on one fundamental point: that knowledge about leisure is based on the collection of evidence. Both believe that the source for new knowledge about leisure comes from our ability to collect observations of leisure phenomena. Thus, the debate about quantitative and qualitative data is essentially a quarrel between empiricists.

In contrast to the empiricist belief that knowledge of leisure must derive from observation, rationalist epistemology says that our minds are the primary source for our knowledge about leisure. To those of us who have been trained in empirical research techniques, it might seem inconceivable that any new knowledge about leisure could be produced by simply thinking about it. Yet many of our fundamental ideas about leisure have not been derived from empirical research. It would be absurd to believe that the classical conception of leisure was the result of data collected by questionnaires, interviews, or field notes. Although Aristotle is thought of as an empiricist philosopher for his copious observations of the natural world, his methodology when examining leisure is better classified as philosophic analysis, Similarly, many modern scholars, such as Josef Peiper, have greatly advanced our understanding of leisure without employing empirical research methodologies. The method of inquiry that these nonempiricist leisure scholars use is often referred to as theoretical research. Rather than looking to external sources for knowledge of leisure by collecting observations from research subjects, theoretical research generates knowledge by the internal thought processes of the leisure researcher who applies reason and logic in the form of philosophic analysis of leisure concepts and issues.

Theoretical research is particularly helpful when we are trying to come to conclusions about matters of values rather than matters of fact, as the following example illustrates. Gambling is a popular but controversial leisure activity that has been the subject of considerable empirical research, particularly since the relaxation of gambling restrictions in the latter third of the 20th century. Yet the collection and analysis of data on gambling can provide only partial answers to the practical question of whether it is a desirable leisure activity. Statistics on tax revenues generated, employment and economic multipliers, gambling addiction rates, and so on cannot fully answer the question of whether the vast expansion of the gaming industry has been beneficial. To conclude that the expansion in gambling opportunities has improved people's quality of life requires us to employ nonempirically based reasons as well. Does, for example, the enjoyment that a large number of people gain from visiting casinos outweigh the pain experienced by the relatively few who are addicted to gambling? Should gambling opportunities be expanded because governments find themselves needing more tax revenues? Is it right to try to restrict and control people's access to gaming? Answers to these and other questions about gaming surely help enrich our understanding of gambling as a leisure activity and cannot be wholly determined simply by collecting information. Rather, we also need to employ our ability to reason abstractly, to analyze various value issues relating to gambling, and to construct arguments to justify the conclusions that we draw.

So, our understanding of leisure seems to depend on both empirical data and theoretical or philosophic analysis. Given that leisure is a complex social phenomenon, perhaps we should not be surprised that it cannot be adequately comprehended by a single method of knowing. Although we natu-

Theoretical research can help us come to conclusions about matters of value as opposed to matters of fact. For example, is it right to try to restrict and control people's access to gaming?

rally have our preferred method of comprehending leisure—whether by quantitative or qualitative research, or by theoretical or philosophic analysis—we should be wary of excluding other ways of knowing. Simply being aware that there are multiple ways to gain knowledge and understanding of leisure can help us avoid thinking that our preferred way of understanding leisure is the only way.

LOGIC AND LEISURE

We have learned from our examination of the epistemology of leisure research that both empirical and theoretical or philosophic analysis is needed for comprehensive understanding of complex social phenomena such as leisure. The generation of new knowledge by empirical and theoretical or philosophic analysis is based, in part, on accepted rules of logic. **Logic** is the branch of philosophy concerned with principles and structure of reasoning. It is the study of the rules of inference that we can use to determine whether our reasons (premises) properly support conclusions that we make. Inferences (reasoning from premises to conclusions) can take the form of being either deductive or inductive. Deductive inferences are constructed so that if it is the case that our premises are true, then our conclusion *has* to be true as well. In contrast, the premises of inductive inferences are structured so that if our premises are true, then it is *likely* that our conclusion is true. Because research aims at finding out new things that we think are true, logic plays an important role in our inquiries by making sure that the conclusions we draw are properly supported. Both empirical research and theoretical or philosophical analysis place a high premium on conformity to accepted rules of logical inference. Leisure research that is deductively invalid or inductively weak is likely to be judged fatally flawed and be rejected.

Although the rules of logical inference are important to leisure researchers, logic is also important to leisure services practitioners. While many day-to-day work tasks of leisure services practitioners can be implemented in a routine manner, other important management functions such as strategic planning, budgeting, policy creation, and evaluation and action research involve systematic processes whereby decisions must be supported by reasons and rationales. Leisure services practitioners can use inductive and deductive reasoning in these formal management processes to help structure and guide their decision making.

Besides using logic to aid their decision making, practitioners often need to be able to justify their decisions to a variety of stakeholder groups. To be effective managers and providers of leisure services, practitioners must have not only some understanding of the formal rules of logic for their own decision-making purposes but also knowledge of rules and principles of informal logic that relate to everyday conversation. Informal logic—also referred to as **critical thinking**—assesses how people use reasoning and language to try to persuade others to accept conclusions. It focuses not only on detecting fallacies of reasoning but also on understanding nonlogical aspects of communication that may influence the acceptance of a conclusion. Thus, we use informal logic to assess both the structure of inferences and the context in which they are made (for example, who is making the argument, what is the situation in which it is being made, and who is the audience to which it is being directed). As philosopher Leo Groarke (2008) notes, informal logic primarily "focuses on the reasoning and argument (in the premise-conclusion sense) one finds in personal exchange, advertising, political debate, legal argument, and the social commentary that characterizes newspapers, television, the World Wide Web and other forms of mass media." Whether leisure services providers work in the public, nonprofit, or commercial sectors, being skilled in the application of informal logic helps them effectively justify their decisions and actions to the many constituencies whom they serve and to whom they are accountable.

AESTHETICS AND LEISURE

Up to this point, we have primarily considered how philosophy relates to leisure in terms of generating scientific knowledge about leisure but have not examined our understanding of the art of leisure. **Aesthetics** is the branch of philosophy that deals with questions of the nature of beauty and value that we associate with art and the natural environment. Our love of beauty is a primary motivation for our interests in the arts, whether it is dance, music, theater, painting, sculpture, or other aesthetically oriented leisure activities in which we delight. As well, aesthetics is an important factor in outdoor recreation, particularly for those who are attracted to wilderness. Issues concerning the aesthetic values of wilderness constitute a significant part of the outdoor recreation literature. For example, Roderick Nash, an environmental historian, argues that the aesthetic values that Western society has associated with wilderness have run the gamut from seeing nature as repugnantly ugly to sublimely beautiful. In his book *Wilderness and the American Mind*, he argues that wilderness is not a physical place so much as a "mood or feeling in a given individual" (Nash, 1982, p. 1). Nash notes that ancient Greek, Western pagan, and Judeo-Christian value systems traditionally regarded wilderness as an alien, threatening environment that was repulsive rather than attractive. The ancient Greeks regarded the wild heath as fit only for barbarians and found beauty instead in the city and rural countryside. The ancient Hebrews saw wilderness as a harsh, forbidding wasteland that was the antithesis of the beautiful, idyllic Garden of Eden. The medieval people of northern Europe thought of wilderness as dark, sinister forests inhabited by pagan beings such as trolls and wood-sprites. When the pioneers came to North America, they brought with them these negative images of wilderness. Combined with the fact that these pioneers were faced with the very real need for survival, wilderness was seen as a forbidding environment to be subdued and civilized.

But Nash notes that as life in North America became more "civilized" by settlement and urban development, people had less reason to see wilderness as an imminent threat to survival. In addition, in the 18th and 19th centuries, a new aesthetic judgment arose toward wilderness based on a philosophic movement called Romanticism. Rather than seeing nature as ugly and evil, the Romantics took the opposite view that wildlands represented the height of divine beauty.

The idea that nature could be aesthetically pleasing was also taken up by the 19th century transcendentalist philosophers and essayists such as Ralph Waldo Emerson and Henry David Thoreau. The New England transcendentalists believed that profound spiritual truths must be discerned using intuition and imagination rather than rational thought, and they believed that the sublime beauty of nature was a primary pathway to understanding reality. For writers like Thoreau, who retreated to his cabin at Walden Pond, civilization rather than nature was what threatened the well-being of humankind.

Interest in the aesthetics of the natural environment waned for the better part of the 20th century as the field of philosophical aesthetics focused primarily on art, which is, of course, the creation of humans rather than nature. But issues concerning aesthetics and the natural environment have been revived recently with the rise of the new field of environmental aesthetics. This renewed interest in the aesthetics of natural environment has been driven by the growth of environmentalism and environmental legislation that can be traced back to the National Environmental Policy Act of 1969, which requires that consideration of aesthetics values be included in environmental impact assessments. Our aesthetic values and judgments concerning nature thus have some practical implications for the management of wilderness. Do we, for example, manage wildlands so that the aesthetic values of the landscape are not altered, much in the way that we try to preserve a fine artwork? Should we determine the aesthetic value of a natural environment by collecting data concerning the aesthetic experiences of visitors? Do we try to optimize the aesthetic appeal of natural environments, say by introducing nonnative species if visitors judge them to be more beautiful than the indigenous ones? Should ecosystems that are aesthetically pleasing receive more management resources and attention than those that are unremarkable in their beauty (or perhaps even ugly) but are ecologically more important? Should we alter the natural environment in ways that make it less aesthetically attractive so that disabled recreationists can have access, say by paving a trail to make it wheelchair accessible? In these and in other instances we find ourselves in situations where we must judge the importance of aesthetic values against other important nonaesthetic values to make practical managerial and policy decisions. Given that society is becoming more sensitive to environmental issues, we can expect that environmental aesthetics will play an increasingly important role in decision making for natural resource management. An awareness and understanding of aesthetics is therefore not an abstract exercise in philosophizing; instead, it can help us make better-informed decisions about our roles as stewards of nature and providers of meaningful leisure experiences.

ETHICS AND LEISURE

Of the five branches of philosophy, **ethics** is the most one most closely allied with leisure. Ironically, we often do not think of ethics being that relevant to leisure and recreation. After all, doesn't leisure services provide nice things in life such as fun, pleasure, and enjoyment? Why would people working in recreation need to worry about ethical issues? (In fact, it has been suggested that both leisure researchers and practitioners themselves have a tendency to associate recreation and leisure activities with the notion that they are intrinsically good.) But leisure services providers are likely to encounter many vexing ethical issues and dilemmas during their careers to which they must devise acceptable solutions. Consider the context in which leisure services occur. Leisure services are a people-oriented business, and when people interact, chances are that things can go awry. Leisure services providers are often put in positions of trust. Park rangers are charged with protecting both the natural environment and the safety of park visitors. Therapeutic recreation specialists are often entrusted with the care of vulnerable populations. Supervisors and program leaders of youth programs are expected to exercise a high degree of responsibility and provide healthful activities for their young charges. And the list goes on. Clearly, the provision of organized leisure services is not simply fun and games; it is a serious undertaking that imposes significant ethical responsibilities on services providers.

Ethics, the philosophical study of morality, is closely allied historically to the Western conception of leisure. The ancient Greeks, whose writings form the basis of the study of morality in Western culture, framed ethical inquiry in terms of how people could find happiness and how society should be organized to facilitate the living of a good life. For philosophers such as Plato and Aristotle, leisure played a critical role in living an optimal style of life.

Let's first see how Plato handled this question of how ethical behavior relates to living a good life.

Then we can compare it to how his student Aristotle refined his master's teachings on the value and ethics of leisure.

PLATO'S PHILOSOPHY OF LEISURE

Plato wrote several dialogues to answer the practical question of how people should best live their lives. His dialogues read like the script of a play. In them, various characters debate with each other about a particular question or issue. Plato's greatest dialogue, *The Republic,* lays out his vision of a utopian society. He reasons that a perfectly ordered society would maximize the happiness of its citizens. To achieve such an ideal state Plato argues that people's thoughts and actions must be strictly controlled. He proposes a harsh censorship of playful leisure activities that he believes would disrupt the order of a perfect society:

> We must begin, then it seems, by a censorship over our story makers, and what they do well we must pass and what not, reject. And the stories on the accepted list we will induce nurses and mothers to tell their children and so shape their souls by these stories. . . . (Plato, Republic II 377c cited in Hamilton and Huntington, 1961, p. 624)

Plato is taking aim at the telling of various Greek myths and the epics of the poet Homer. Anyone familiar with Greek mythology knows that the residents of Mount Olympus were hardly good role models. Their chief god Zeus is depicted as a philandering husband who is taken with the seduction of both mortal and divine females. His jilted wife Hera hatches various plots for revenge on her hapless rivals. The rest of the Olympian gods are no more admirable and are portrayed with all sorts of human failings, vices, and weaknesses. Plato believed that telling these stories of debauched and corrupt gods would harm both individuals and society, so he wanted them banned.

As well as controlling storytelling, Plato believed that other types of leisure activities should be censored. He thought some musical instruments, such as flutes, should not be allowed in his ideal society because their sound would stir the passions of listeners. Similarly, music that was either dirgelike or effeminate should be prohibited because it would make people weak or sad (Plato, Republic II 398e, 399d cited in Hamilton and Huntington, 1961).

Plato carefully separated good leisure activities from bad ones based on his theory of what an ideal society should be like. According to his political philosophy, leisure activities are tools to be used to shape the character of citizens of his utopian society. Only those types of leisure activities that he judged to be virtuous were allowed. He saw many forms of leisure and recreation as threats to his perfectly ordered society. He was most fearful of playful forms of recreation that excited the emotions. Plato thought an ideal society should be ruled by reason alone. The citizens of his ideal Republic were expected to behave as somber, sober rationalists. Perhaps the metaphor of an anthill would best describe his vision of how society should be structured. The workers, soldiers, and rulers who were the citizens of Plato's utopia would all go about doing their assigned **work** with the greatest seriousness. **Leisure, recreation,** and **play** would only be encouraged if it had educational or developmental value (Hunnicutt, 1990).

We can still see a legacy of Plato's political philosophy in present-day leisure services. For example, a lot of recreational programming for youth is based on the notion that activities should contribute to positive character development (Johnson & McLean, 1994). And, like Plato, many adults are concerned about the influence of music and stories on children. Even though modern-day democracies permit many freedoms, V-chips are used in televisions, sales of "adult" books and magazines are restricted, and filters are used on computers to try to prevent young minds from being exposed to the images and ideas that parents and community leaders believe harmful.

Plato's philosophy makes it clear that leisure and recreation is an important tool for influencing individuals and society. He does not regard leisure and recreation as mere fun and games, but instead treats it as a critical component of a properly functioning society. Yet his vision of leisure emphasizes repression and control. Who would really want to live in his dreary, regimented utopia? Where is the notion that freedom is an integral part of experiencing leisure? To put the freedom back into leisure we need to turn to Plato's student, Aristotle.

ARISTOTLE'S PHILOSOPHY OF LEISURE

In many ways Aristotle followed Plato's political teachings. Aristotle was willing to advocate the repression of the majority of people living in his society. Women and slaves were not allowed the luxury of leisure. That privilege was reserved for the male citizenry. But Aristotle did not picture this leisured class as the idle rich. Rather, the leisured elite was expected to strive for self-perfection. For Aristotle, living the ideal lifestyle was a practical matter. It required following those habits of living that were virtuous and avoiding those that were vices (Hemingway, 1988).

Aristotle defined virtue as a midpoint between the vices of excess and deficiency (Aristotle cited in [Nicomachean Ethics 1107a] McKeon, 1941). Take, for example, the virtue of courage. It is an excellence of character that results from neither being cowardly (a deficiency) nor foolhardy (an excess).

Aristotle began his philosophic inquiry by asking himself what an ideal lifestyle for human beings should be like. What do you think?

He recognized that every person's situation varies according to personal circumstances. However, each should live his or her life to maximize virtue—in other words, each person should try to be his or her very best. To excel in one's life requires a continual commitment to self-improvement. Aristotle therefore argues that one needs to develop habits of living that lead to excellence. It is instructive that the Greek word for ethics is derived from the word *ethos,* which means "habit"—a behavior or practice we continually engage in throughout our lifetime.

But what is the ultimate purpose of developing virtuous habits? Aristotle says that happiness results from being the best we can be. The sort of happiness that Aristotle is thinking of should not be equated with simple pleasure. Amusing ourselves can be pleasant, but he says it is childish and has the potential to cause us harm. **Amusement** for sheer pleasure degrades rather than improves us. Aristotle admits that amusement is helpful if it refreshes us from work. But amusement is never as good as true leisure, which provides a life of deep fulfillment rather than fleeting bodily pleasures (Aristotle cited in [Nicomachean Ethics 1176b] McKeon, 1941).

By using leisure to become our best, Aristotle is not simply thinking of moral goodness, but also those characteristics that make us uniquely human. And what did he think was our most noble quality? Aristotle says that it is our capacity for rational thought that distinguishes us from all other forms of life. He argues that the employment of reason in intellectual contemplation leads to perfect happiness. Therefore, he concludes that the person who has the most rewarding lifestyle is the philosopher who is at leisure to develop his intellect to its highest capacity (Aristotle cited in [Nicomachean Ethics 1178a] McKeon, 1941).

We may disagree with Aristotle that being an intellectual is the most rewarding life people can live. It could be plausibly argued that excelling at other human activities such as food preparation, athletics, or art could produce equally satisfying lifestyles. But perhaps it is not important to quibble over which human activity is best. Instead, the important feature of Aristotle's theory of happiness is that it is based on the idea that human fulfillment results from achieving excellence from things we choose to do when we use our leisure appropriately.

Aristotle's philosophy of leisure, which emphasizes discipline and commitment rather than the freedom and choice we associate with our modern-day leisure experiences, may seem demanding. Nonetheless, freedom is an important element of Aristotle's concept of virtuous leisure. First, we need freedom from material wants so that we can have time for leisure. This means that we cannot be enslaved to our work. We need a sufficient level of material comfort (food, shelter, clothing, and so on) so that at least during part of our day we can have time for leisure. Second, we need intellectual freedom to understand why virtuous leisure activities are good. When we are children we can be trained to practice virtuous habits without knowing why those things are desirable. For example, we learn at a very young age not to lie. But it is only when we are older that we fully understand why lying is wrong (e.g., it is hurtful to others). So it is with the practice of virtuous leisure activities. If you are an ancient Greek freeman, you choose certain activities to excel at not because someone has trained you to do them, but because you understand and appreciate that these activities are noble. Third, freedom is the essential characteristic of any virtuous leisure activity. These activities are simply worthy in themselves; we do not do them because they will bring fame, wealth, or other extrinsic rewards. In other words, virtuous leisure activities are intrinsically good.

CONTEMPORARY PHILOSOPHY OF LEISURE

We might ask whether Aristotle's elitist definition of leisure has much relevance to our modern lifestyles. Perhaps we can relate to Aristotle's refined version of leisure when we think of the high level of accomplishment of professional athletes, cordon blue chefs, and concert pianists. These people live lives devoted to perfecting their talents. But these examples are not leisure activities. Instead, they refer to occupations—ways of making a living. It is difficult for us to think of excellence apart from working. Typically, when we are very good at something, we want to find ways to turn it into a career. We tend to value activities that can be made productive. We are very work oriented, whereas the ancient Greeks were work averse. It was not that the Greeks thought that work was something evil, but rather they regarded it only as a necessity of life. They worked so that they could enjoy life. According to their value system, it was leisure that gave meaning and purpose to their life, not work (de Grazia, 1963).

For most of us, it is typically our work, our career, and our occupation that give us our sense of self-worth. If you do not believe this is true, think back to the last time you met someone at a social occasion. When making new acquaintances, was it your leisure activities or your work that you primarily used to describe yourself to others? In our modern culture the question "So what do you do?" implicitly assumes that you will respond by describing your occupation and workplace. Extolling the virtues of work would seem very odd to the ancient Greeks. We, however, with our modern lifestyles appear to have reversed that equation.

Weber's Analysis of the Work Ethic

Have you ever heard someone being praised for having a strong work ethic? The term is derived from Max Weber's influential book *The Protestant Ethic and the Spirit of Capitalism* (Weber, 1958 [1930]). The **Protestant work ethic** refers to a cultural ideal that regards work as *the* most important activity in an individual's life. Weber believed that a new reverence for work arose from the Protestant Reformation, when Christian religious leaders such as Martin Luther and John Calvin rebelled against the Catholic Church. Both Luther and Calvin saw the medieval church as a corrupt institution in which the upper echelons of the clergy lived a life of wealth and leisure. Up until the time of the Reformation, the church had followed Aristotle's teachings concerning leisure and the good life. The clergy and the nobility comprised the leisured class—both educated and wealthy enough to have the free time to engage in refined intellectual and cultural activities. The great mass of ordinary, uneducated peasants were little more than slaves who provided brute labor for the upper classes. In their radical break from the church, Luther and Calvin turned Aristotle's conception of the good life on its head, making work—not leisure—the foundation of a worthy life. Both Luther and Calvin believed in the notion of a "calling" whereby everyone had

Weber's work ethic changed our view of the good life to one that valued hard work over leisure.

been assigned by God a certain task or occupation, which they should perform throughout their life. Answering one's calling in life was considered a virtue because you would be doing the work God intended for you. Conversely, ignoring your calling was a vice and would lead to an empty, directionless life. Thus, since the time of the Reformation, it has been work rather than leisure that culturally defines our conception of the good life.

Russell's Critique of the Work Ethic

Some modern philosophers have taken great exception to the notion that work can make our lives truly happy. Bertram Russell penned a tongue-in-cheek essay in the early 1930s titled "In Praise of Idleness" in which he criticizes the idea that work is virtuous. Russell argues that preindustrial societies were based on a "slave morality" used to justify the subjugation of large numbers of manual laborers so that a privileged aristocracy would have leisure to pursue spiritual, cultural, and intellectual activities. However, with the coming of the industrial revolution, modern technology has created such an abundance of goods that it is now possible for everyone to have sufficient resources for a leisured lifestyle. But rather than using technology to give everyone adequate leisure, Russell says we have continued to support the idea that leisure should be reserved for the upper crust of society and denied to the working class.

Russell argues that it would be more rational to replace the traditional, but outmoded, slave morality with a leisure ethic that distributes work evenly. Rather than having a leisure class that does no work at all and a working class that is either overworked or unemployed, Russell proposes a work-sharing arrangement that would reduce people's working time to four hours per day and still provide the "necessaries and elementary comforts" of life (Russell, 1960, p. 17). Russell believes that with these greatly reduced work hours, humanity would enter a new golden age of leisure, giving people the freedom to pursue cultural and intellectual interests. Perhaps Russell is naive to think that everyone would use their liberation from work for ennobling leisure activities. Would not many people choose to waste their free time engaged in frivolous amusements? Nonetheless, even if many people would not use their leisure wisely, we can still ask if that is a good enough justification for keeping people busy with work. Maybe what is really needed is not only sufficient free time, but also the availability of attractive and meaningful leisure opportunities that professionalized leisure services can provide.

Pieper's Critique of the Work Ethic

Josef Pieper, a Catholic theologian, also strongly criticizes our allegiance to the work ethic in his book *Leisure: The Basis of Culture* (1998). Pieper, who is writing of Europe in the aftermath of World War II, says that we no longer know what leisure is because we live in a totally work-oriented culture. Pieper argues that our fixation on work is

so complete that even liberal arts disciplines such as philosophy are now treated as a type of "intellectual labor" and are only valued for their usefulness for solving practical problems. (And isn't this why many people ridicule philosophy and leisure studies—because these disciplines are thought to be "useless"?) According to Pieper, knowledge for knowledge's sake is devalued by our culture of work, and our leisure time is only thought to be useful if it refreshes us so that we can then resume our work with renewed vigor. Ironically, Pieper observes, our worship of work produces a meaningless, unsatisfying lifestyle. We live to work well, rather than working so that we can live well.

Veblen's Critique of Consumption

Although many people believe that being a success entails working hard to achieve enough financial independence to be able to retire to a life of luxury, could our worship of work actually sabotage our leisure lives? Many critics argue that our economic system actually works against our aspirations for a truly leisured lifestyle.

Modern economies encourage ever expanding growth in the production and consumption of products and services. As individuals, we live in a consumer culture where our success is measured by how much we can purchase. The more luxurious and expensive the goods we can own, the higher our social status. The American economist Thorstein Veblen termed the ostentatious displays of wealth as "conspicuous consumption" (Veblen, 1998 [1899]). Veblen criticized the superrich of his era—the Vanderbilts, Carnegies, and Rockefellers—as status seekers who used the great wealth they had amassed from their 19th-century business empires to give themselves an air of nobility. Their mansions, yachts, and lavish parties were symbols that these American industrialists "had arrived" at the good life.

Of course, most of us are not billionaires. We cannot hope to own executive jets, hand-built sports cars, or vacation homes on private Caribbean islands. Yet compared to the standard of living of ancient Greek freemen, the lifestyle of the average person living in postindustrial societies is opulent. We have at our disposal a vast array of consumer products and services that Aristotle and his compatriots could not have imagined.

Other Critiques of Consumption

Unfortunately, to be able to afford these products and services means that most of us must devote a huge portion of our adult lives to work. The flip side of a highly consumptive lifestyle is that we must also be highly productive to pay for it. During our working lives, many of us find our time for leisure limited. Our careers require us to put in long days at work, leaving little time or energy for family and friends.

The consumerist lifestyle that most of us have adopted encourages us to think of leisure as a basket of commodities from which we pick and choose. Instead of being participants in unique and personal recreation activities, we are consumers of leisure experiences designed and mass produced by others (Hemingway, 1996). In this market-driven context, the concept of freedom is inextricably tied to the act of purchasing: the more leisure products and services there are for sale, the greater our freedom to choose.

This free-market model of leisure services and products is undeniably attractive to most people.

The leisure industry is one of the biggest and fastest growing sectors of the economy. Yet this apparent success masks several drawbacks to our commercialized leisure. As social economist Juliet Schor (1998) argues in her aptly titled book *The Overspent American*, the most obvious problem with the idea that we can buy happiness is that many of us spend more on our leisure than we can afford. In the United States and Canada, personal bankruptcies filings are trending upward. Although the great recession has contributed to the rise in bankruptcies as unemployment has spiked, another reason for the increase in personal financial problems stemmed from the fact that many people were simply living beyond their means by using easy credit to subsidize their spending habits. Using credit to finance otherwise unaffordable spending on vacations, entertainment, and recreational equipment can quickly lead to a buildup of bad debt (in contrast to good debt such as traditional mortgages and student loans, which are investments in future well-being). Although the financial meltdown has encouraged or required many people to curtail their spending, it is yet to be seen whether we have entered a new era of frugality or have simply taken a respite from rampant consumerism that will be revived when economic conditions improve.

The consumerist lifestyle demands that we work more to afford more goods. These shoppers hope to find happiness from the products they can purchase.

Aside from the question of the long-term viability of consumerist lifestyles, the commodification of leisure may discourage our personal growth by making our recreation experiences too convenient. Commercial providers of leisure services typically want to make their offerings as attractive as possible to their potential clientele. Competitive advantage can be gained by making the consumption of leisure services and products as effortless as possible. The examples are many: golf manufacturers advertise that their clubs alone will lower your handicap, therefore, you don't have to improve your swing; resort operators provide familiar fast-food items at exotic destinations so that guests will not have to adjust to the local cuisine; movie and television producers "dumb down" the content of popular entertainment lest audiences be made to think; and the list goes on.

Although our modern leisure services and products may be convenient, we might ask whether most of them are worthy of our time, not to mention our money. Aristotelian leisure is based on the idea that we should devote our free time to being the best we can be. The ancient view of leisure emphasized commitment and accomplishment. In contrast, as philosopher Albert Borgmann notes, commodified leisure appeals to our desire for comfort (Borgmann, 1984). Often, our modern leisure practices do not result in self-improvement. In fact, many of our recreational activities may cause us harm. Watching television, our most popular leisure pastime, has been linked to several modern maladies including obesity, depression, and paranoia (Kubey & Csikzentmihalyi, 1990; Gerbner, 1999). But it is attractive because of its easy access—you simply turn on the TV, then sit back and enjoy. But even our more active forms of recreation tend to cater to our desire for creature comforts. When practical and affordable, we often choose to motorize outdoor recreation activities. Why climb up a slope when you can use a chairlift? Why paddle or row when you can simply twist the throttle on an outboard engine? Why carry your clubs when you can ride in a cart? These uses of machines are said to enhance our leisure experiences, yet they may also disengage us from our environment and each other. Harvard sociologist Robert Putnam (2000) argues in his book *Bowling Alone* that Americans are becoming increasingly isolated socially. He cites a wealth of statistics showing that membership in community organizations dropped dramatically at the end of the 20th century. As a result, Putnam believes that Americans have become less satisfied with their lives because they have experienced a decline in their **social capital**—the social connections that support people in times of difficulty and make life more enjoyable in times of leisure. He attributes diminishing social capital to the changes in society that alter our work and leisure values:

> Over the last three decades a variety of social, economic and technological changes have rendered obsolete a significant stock of America's social capital. Television, two-career families, suburban sprawl, generational changes in values—these and other changes in American society have meant that fewer and fewer of us find that the League of Women Voters, or the United Way, or the Shriners, or the monthly bridge club, or even a Sunday picnic with friends fits the way we have come to live. (Putnam, 2000, p. 365)

A similar decline in social capital may be happening in Canadian society, although the data are more mixed. For example, a study of the "social cohesion" found that Canadians perceived themselves as having a high level of personal social support ("someone they can confide in, count on in a crisis situation, obtain advice from when making important decisions, and someone who makes them feel loved and cared for"), but they had a low level of social involvement ("frequency of participation in associations or voluntary organizations and frequency of attendance at religious services") (Jackson et al., 2000, pp. 66, 68).

Putnam compares the malaise in community involvement to the problems that faced American society at the end of the 19th century when rapid industrialization created a host of social problems in large cities. He notes that people responded to these social ills by becoming more involved in civic activities and voluntary organizations, and he argues that we need to find ways to use our leisure time to be more civically engaged.

Perhaps it is because we are at least subconsciously aware that many of our leisure activities are unworthy experiences that we devise various rationales to justify our modern leisure lifestyles.

We interpret shopping to be an exciting recreational activity rather than a mundane necessity of life. We tell our employees that we value wellness, but what we are really worried about are rising absenteeism and medical expenses. We take mini-vacations that cause the least disruption of our work schedules, taking along our laptop and handheld computers to avoid falling behind. At home, rather than spending unstructured, spontaneous time with our kids, we plan infrequent special activities and call it *quality time*. Unfortunately, this list goes on as well.

What we seem to lack is a sense that our leisure activities can be self-justifying. Our view of leisure as a commodity is based on the implicit premise that our leisure activities are a means to achieving some other goal. Perhaps that is not a surprising mindset, given that we live in a commercialized culture, constantly bombarded with messages about products and services that promise this or that benefit. But this lifestyle is ultimately unsatisfying for many of us because it keeps us focused on our leisure as a means to something else, rather than a worthy end in itself. The ancient Greeks understood very well that leisure should be reserved for activities that were good in and of themselves. Aristotle did not recommend philosophic inquiry as the best leisure activity because it made him more productive at work. Rather, he simply argued that it was the most intrinsically worthy activity that human beings could do.

Aristotle, it must be acknowledged, did not face the challenges to leisure that we do today. His social environment was far less complex than what we must deal with as leisure services providers. Of course, it may seem that there is little we can do to influence the quality of people's lives, given the strong cultural and economic forces that encourage people to be workers and consumers. But we are not completely powerless. As leisure services providers, we can make a difference in the lives of the people and communities that we serve. It all begins with a clear understanding of our own leisure values. For example, if we know that people are stressed by a culture that overvalues work, then we have an obligation as leisure services providers to advocate for the value of leisure. If we see that people are stressed by an economic system that encourages the overconsumption of products, then we can offer alternative leisure activities that encourage social interaction and community building. Surely, if we think of ourselves as quality-of-life specialists, then we need a philosophical understanding of some of the major problems that people and communities face, or else we may unwittingly become part of the problem, rather than part of the solution.

SOLVING ETHICAL DILEMMAS IN LEISURE SERVICES

So far, we have used ethical analysis to help us evaluate our leisure lifestyles. In our role as socially responsible leisure services providers, we need this macro, or big-picture, understanding of the broad social and political issues that affect the quality of people's leisure lives. Essentially, we are using ethical analysis to continue the ancient Greeks' project of determining the role of leisure in a worthwhile life. This sort of analysis is prescriptive rather than descriptive, because it aims not simply to describe our past or current lifestyles but instead to determine how we should live our lives. But we can also use ethical analysis in a micro, or small-picture, way to help us solve problems relating to the delivery of leisure services. Consider the following sidebar, which presents an **ethical dilemma** that narrowly focuses on a particular situation and set of individuals at a public recreation center.

Dealing effectively with the tanning-bed problem mentioned in the sidebar requires more than having a big-picture understanding of the situation. After all, the big picture tells us that skin cancer is a serious health problem, and as socially responsible leisure services providers we shouldn't provide equipment or services that are potentially dangerous. Yet many of the people we serve don't agree with our point of view; therefore, we are left in an uncomfortable position in which a lot of people may be angry or unhappy. What we need is a way to resolve these ethical dilemmas that are common in leisure services. Fortunately, ethical analysis can help us decide the proper course of action in cases where we are confronted with a moral conflict involving particular people at a particular time and place.

To deal effectively with ethical dilemmas we need an ethical decision-making method we can use to justify our decisions. And as responsible leisure services providers we are obligated to provide the people who are affected by our decisions

Tanning-Bed Case

You are the recreation supervisor at a multipurpose community recreation center. The mission of the center is to promote the well-being of the citizens in the local community by providing a wide variety of high-quality recreation activities. Since the center opened, the fitness area has played an important role in satisfying the recreation center's mission. The fitness equipment and programs are popular and benefit participants' physical health and well-being. Recently, however, some of the patrons have asked the recreation center to install tanning beds. Many of these requests are from teenagers and young adults who say they like to work out at the center, but also want to be able to get a deep tan. You have never wanted to install tanning beds, because you have read research that indicates that the exposure to UV rays that these beds produce increases the likelihood of skin cancer, including the most deadly form of the disease, malignant melanoma. You announce that the center will not purchase the beds because of the possible negative health effects. Unfortunately, your decision is met with dismay and even outright hostility. Many of the young people who want the beds installed say they are not worried about cancer. Some say they will drop their membership and join a nearby private health club that has the beds. Several of the middle-aged members have contacted their representatives on city council (to whom you report) to lobby for purchasing the beds. And a few have threatened to go to the local media and "raise a stink" about how adults should be allowed to choose whether they can tan and should not be treated like children by the recreation center staff.

with reasonable explanations for our actions. Not everyone will agree with our decisions, but we need to demonstrate that our decisions are not made arbitrarily. Skepticism about the wisdom of our decisions is likely to be stronger when we are dealing with ethical dilemmas, and emotions tend to run high when moral points of view come into conflict. Although it is a common belief that ethical issues are based on opinion rather than fact, in reality we can nonetheless apply ethical theories to help us create a rationale for our actions.

Ethical Analysis: Three Approaches

Let's consider how we might apply ethical theory to help us determine what to do in the tanning-bed case. Three basic ethical theories can help us decide whether to install the beds: (1) **consequence-based ethics**, (2) **duty-based ethics**, and (3) **virtue-based ethics**. Using the first approach, we weigh the consequences of installing or not installing the tanning beds. If we install the beds we will make many people who use the recreation center happy. We will also not lose members to the private health club because of a lack of tanning beds. We also will not have to deal with client complaints to the city council or the newspapers. From a consequence-based ethics perspective, the only downsides would be

Philosophical analysis can help solve the problem of whether or not tanning beds should be used at a recreation center.

the initial cost of the equipment and the possibility that some recreation center clients might eventually develop skin cancer. Because there seems to be several definite, immediate benefits to installing the beds, based on a review of the likely consequences, it would be reasonable to conclude that we should go ahead and spend the money on the tanning beds.

The second way we can determine the most ethical course of action is to use a duty-based ethics perspective to evaluate our duties and obligations. One important duty we have is to carry out the mission of the recreation center. We are there to serve the public, so we have an obligation to provide services that people want. But we also have an obligation to provide services that benefit people's well-being. Given that public recreation organizations receive tax monies to provide leisure services that serve the public good, it is reasonable to assume that protecting the community's well-being is a more important duty than simply providing services that people want. Therefore, from a duty-based ethics perspective we should not install the tanning beds because that would betray our obligation to provide healthy leisure services.

At this point in our moral deliberations we see that we have come to opposing conclusions. Analysis from consequences-based ethics indicates that we should install the tanning beds, while duty-based ethics argues that we should not install them. How do we break this moral deadlock? Well, we might want to turn to the third way of analyzing ethical dilemmas: virtue-based ethics. With virtue-based ethics, moral decisions are made by reflecting upon one's character. Instead of comparing outcomes or weighing duties, virtue-based ethics resolves ethical dilemmas on the basis of our personal integrity. For example, do we diminish ourselves and become a less noble person if we installed the tanning beds in the fitness center? If the users of the beds are mature adults aware of the dangers of UV exposure, then possibly not. These adults have simply made a choice to engage in an activity that endangers their health. But what about the teenagers who also want to use the beds? Will we find it hard to look at ourselves in the mirror before we go to work knowing we have helped expose teenagers to health risks that they might not be willing to take if they were mature adults? Therefore, from a virtue-ethics perspective we might install the tanning beds only if we had an

effective way to prohibit teens from using the beds and if we could ensure that the adults at the center were well educated about the risks of UV exposure.

We can see from the application of the three ethical theories to the tanning bed scenario that solutions to ethical dilemmas are not always obvious. Some of us may think that tanning beds should be installed, while others may be opposed to placing this type of equipment in a community recreation facility. Furthermore, we may disagree on which ethical theory is best for solving the dilemma. Some people may think consequences should decide the issue, others may believe duties are paramount, while a third group may believe that considerations of our character should dictate what to do. The important point is not that we might disagree about the proper solution to the ethical dilemma, but instead that our moral deliberations help us justify and explain our decision to people who disagree with us. For example, suppose the people who want the tanning beds are thinking in terms of the consequences. They want the beds because they are after certain outcomes such as what they believe to be a healthy look or a sexier body. Now we can talk to them on their wavelength by pointing out negative outcomes such as skin cancer and premature aging. If they still insist that the benefits outweigh the costs, then we can also explain that we have a duty to uphold the mission of the agency to provide healthy recreation, and that according to our own professional standards, we would not feel right about providing equipment that could cause serious health problems. Of course, it is completely possible that people still will not be persuaded that we are making the right decision, but at least we have provided them a reasonable, well-thought-out explanation for our decision. And we have accomplished this very practical task by using ethical analysis to justify our decision!

Serious social and ethical issues are bound to arise as we work to help people improve their leisure lifestyles. If we are unable to assess the worthiness of various leisure activities, then we run the risk of providing leisure opportunities that may not enhance the quality of people's lives. Ethical analysis can give us a macro understanding to judge the worthiness of the various leisure and recreation activities that we might choose to provide. We have seen that most of our current leisure experiences seem to be geared toward the worlds of work and commerce rather than with the provision of opportunities to engage in intrinsically satisfying activities and personal growth. But besides providing us with a big picture of some of the social issues facing leisure services, ethical analysis can also help us deal with micro issues arising from the ethical dilemmas that we will inevitably encounter during our careers as leisure service providers. Without an awareness and understanding of the ethical issues arising from leisure and recreation activities, we run the risk of causing unintended harm to the people whom we serve and the resources that we have been entrusted with. Rather than having to rely solely on our intuition, we can use methods of ethical analysis to help us justify and explain our solutions to difficult moral dilemmas.

SUMMARY

We hope that our examination of the five branches of philosophy—metaphysics, epistemology, logic, aesthetics, and ethics—has persuaded you that philosophic analysis plays a fundamental role in both leisure research and the provision of leisure services. Both philosophy and leisure are often misperceived as being frivolous and of little practical consequence. Yet our examination of the relevance of philosophy to leisure illustrates that neither is trivial. Leisure and recreation, both as an academic discipline and as a service practice, has tremendous potential to affect the quality of people's lives and the natural environment. Leisure and recreation are complex social phenomena and are essential to living a worthwhile life. Philosophical inquiry helps us understand leisure and recreation and guide service practices in many ways. Metaphysics emphasizes understanding of the essential qualities of leisure. Epistemology teaches us that knowledge of leisure needs to be generated by both empirical and rationalist methods. Logic helps leisure services decision makers not only avoid making faulty inferences but also persuasively defend and justify their positions to others. Aesthetics reveals to us the significance of beauty to our leisure experiences and the need to find a proper balance between aesthetic and nonaesthetic values. Finally, ethics helps us deal with larger questions of what constitutes worthwhile, fulfilling leisure and provides us with theories to analyze moral dilemmas that practitioners inevitably face.

So, contrary to popular opinion, leisure services is not a matter of fun and games, and philosophy is not idle speculation. Far from being either impractical or inconsequential, the study of leisure and philosophy is fundamental to helping us think and act in ways that improve the quality of people's lives and protect the natural environment.

For glossary terms, learning experiences, and more, please visit the web resource at
www.HumanKinetics.com/IntroductionToRecreationAndLeisure

CHAPTER 4

Leisure and Recreation for Individuals in Society

Daniel G. Yoder and Juan Tortosa Martínez

" The person and the group are not separable phenomena, but are simply the individual and collective aspects of the same thing. "

Loran David Osborn and
M.H. Neumeyer, sociologists

LEARNING OUTCOMES

After reading this chapter, you should be able to do the following:

> Explain how leisure and recreation is a complex human endeavor that takes place within society
> Describe how leisure and recreation, whether as a solitary activity or undertaken with friends, family, or larger groups, affects and is affected by society
> Describe how gender, ethnicity and race, religion, and socioeconomic class affect leisure and recreation and how leisure and recreation in turn affects those factors
> Demonstrate that the value of "goodness" or "badness" can be applied to leisure and recreation
> Demonstrate the implications of a social perspective for leisure and recreation professionals

INTRODUCTION

Consider the leisure of the individual *in* society, not the leisure of the individual *and* society. Although this distinction may seem trivial, it is important. Individuals and societies do exist as separate entities in concept, but on a practical level, neither can exist independent of the other. Societies are composed of men, women, and children of various ages, races, classes, and so on. Without these essential parts, there could be no whole. Nor do individuals exist isolated from society; human beings are social animals by nature. All human existence (including leisure and recreation) takes place at the intersection of the individual and the diverse social structures that make up our world. Even the act of thinking, seemingly the quintessential individual activity, is impossible without the use of mental cultural symbols. These mental images are possible only within the borders of a common cultural context.

We begin this chapter with a general discussion of how leisure and recreation activities take place against a social backdrop and that even when people are physically alone in their activities, **society** influences them, and their activities may in turn influence society. We also discuss the relationships between leisure and primary groups of family and close friends, secondary groups, and four social institutions: gender, ethnicity, religion, and social class. Throughout this section, we note the similarities and differences in recreation and leisure. Because the moral value of a leisure activity (its goodness or badness) is determined by both leisure participants and the world in which they live, we consider good and bad leisure. Finally, we discuss the implications of leisure and recreation in society for the professional practitioner.

LEISURE AS A COMPLEX SOCIAL PHENOMENON

Leisure is a wonderfully complex social phenomenon, affected by many social institutions including economics, politics, work, technology, and war. But we must be careful in thinking that leisure and recreation is a trivial pastime, influenced and even dictated by these social structures. In fact, leisure and recreation significantly affects the social forces we have just listed. Consider, for example, Las Vegas, Nevada. Without the leisure and tourism industries that pour billions of dollars into Las Vegas each year, the town would be much different, if it even existed at all. Examples like this, while perhaps not as obvious, play out every day in thousands of communities across North America and the globe.

Solitary Leisure and Society

A few leisure activities are entirely solitary, some are purely social, and most can be either private or communal. Reading is almost always undertaken alone, and playing a game of tennis always requires interaction with others. Playing cards is an example of an activity that can be either solitary or social, which characterizes the majority of leisure activities. Some people spend hours playing the classic solo card game, solitaire. On the other hand, you cannot play bridge without other players to compete against.

Although we might be inclined to think that our **solitary leisure** is ours and ours alone, it does not take place in a social vacuum. Indeed, other people and groups of people profoundly affect our solitary leisure activities. Furthermore, the leisure activities we undertake while we are alone have an influence—sometimes significant and sometimes not so significant—on the people and the world around us. The world around us affects our private leisure in many ways: it may support it, infringe on it, prohibit it, or even force us into it.

Let's consider one single act of solitary leisure and its influences. Even if you don't recognize the name, nearly everyone is familiar with the story of Aron Ralston, the young climber who was forced to cut off his arm after it became trapped between two boulders in the Utah backcountry. Thousands of dollars were spent by state and county agencies in the effort to find and save Ralston. Hundreds of volunteers sacrificed days for the search. The tragedy could have been averted if Ralston had hiked with a companion. But Ralston chose to go it alone on this adventure. On the other hand, this story has been a tremendous inspiration to many people—not just outdoor enthusiasts. It is impossible to measure the positive consequences of this single act of courage on a solo hike in the Utah desert.

Leisure and Primary Groups

Although some leisure activities can be solo endeavors, most directly involve others. Moreover, the others involved in the leisure activity are not merely bystanders, but essential components of the activity. Kelly (1987) has noted, "In general, people are more important in leisure than the form of the activity" (p. 158). Especially significant are those who are part of the participant's **primary group**. Sociologists have defined primary groups, as "small groups in which there are face-to-face relations of a fairly intimate and personal nature. Primary groups are of two basic types, families and cliques. In other words, they are organized around ties of either kinship or friendship" (Lenski, Nolan, & Lenski, 1995, p. 48). We examine leisure activities with family and close friends only briefly here because this topic is more thoroughly considered in chapter 12.

Social custom and societal expectations profoundly affect leisure when activities are undertaken with family members and close friends. Defining the term **family** is not as simple as it may seem at first glance. Because different cultures use various forms of kinship groupings, and even the same culture may change its notion of family over time, a definition that all can agree on has been elusive. But no matter how it is defined, the family profoundly influences leisure.

The leisure lifestyle of adolescence clearly shows the effect of two occasionally competing forces—family and friends. Let's consider clothing as an example. Kelsey is a typical 16-year-old from Montreal. Like many teenagers, she considers her parents to be too conservative, especially when it involves how she dresses. As she comes down the stairs on her way out to meet her friends for the evening, her father notices that her blouse is small and very revealing and her jeans are torn in several places. His comment, "There is no way you are going out in public in that shirt and those pants!" is met with, "Oh, Dad! That's the way we dress now. Do you want me to be covered from head to toe?" Most people—certainly older mainstream parents—do not wear such revealing clothing nor do they wear clothing that is badly worn and torn. However, that is the norm for this particular group of young people.

Families typically move through a series of somewhat predictable stages. Not all families go through every stage, but most do or aspire to do so. These stages are not distinct; instead, each stage merges into the one before and after it. Each phase of a family's development includes typical leisure activities, roles, and patterns. For example, many new families without children have a great deal of flexibility. Leisure activities can be spontaneous. Couples may be able to throw a few items together and get away for a weekend vacation in an hour or so. This is not the case for a family with children. Work and school schedules must be coordinated. Perhaps child care must be arranged. Considerably more clothing and equipment must be organized. Child safety must be considered. Even the destination of the vacation is affected. A quick trip to Las Vegas is more common for a family without children, while a trip to visit grandparents is common for families with children.

A clear example of familial influence is found in the area of sport participation. Clark (2008) used data from the General Social Surveys of 1992 and 2005 to study children's participation in sport. He found that the family affects not only children's

A person may participate in various athletic pursuits throughout his life because of childhood experiences playing soccer with his father.

choices in sport but also choices even through adolescence and early adulthood. Other studies support his contention that "sporty parents have sporty kids" (p. 55).

Leisure and Secondary Groups

Secondary groups affect a person's leisure activities, and in turn, the leisure activities of an individual have the potential to affect the secondary group. Henslin (1993) defines a **secondary group**, compared with a primary group, as "a larger, relatively temporary, more anonymous, formal and impersonal group based on some interest or activity, whose members are likely to interact on the basis of specific roles" (p. 150). Some secondary groups, such as a college classroom, a political party, and a labor union, are not related to leisure, but many are. Examples of these include a pottery class, the National Rifle Association, a travel club, and a Texas Hold 'Em poker league.

A few examples show the obvious influence a secondary group can have on its members. Jane

has dedicated Wednesday evenings to attending her pottery class at the local park district. Instead of returning home after work on Wednesdays to spend time with her family, Jane grabs a quick bite to eat and heads straight to the pottery class. Nick is a member of the National Rifle Association (NRA), and with a particularly contentious national election coming up he receives promotional material from this organization nearly every week. Instead of watching his favorite TV shows on Wednesday night, Nick attends NRA meetings each week and decides to vote for a candidate who supports the NRA and opposes gun control. Jim and Margaret, recently retired and fairly affluent, love to travel. They have joined a local group that organizes trips for its members. They benefit from the reduced group rates and the opportunity to interact with people with similar travel interests. Rusty has been involved with a poker league that plays Texas Hold 'Em every Friday night. Not only does he enjoy playing, but he also sees a great deal of potential for this activity as a fund-raiser. When the board of the local food pantry (of which Rusty is a member) discusses fund-raisers, Rusty volunteers to organize a poker tournament for the community.

Although we can see how a secondary group influences the actions of individuals, the influence an individual may have on the group is not quite so obvious. It is nevertheless very real. For example, Jane, the fledgling potter, has had a very bad week. When she attends the week's pottery session, she gets into an argument with the instructor about the schedule for firing her pottery pieces. Their heated conversation is overheard by several other class members, and it casts a pall on the evening's class. Although Nick believes in most of the positions taken by the NRA, he cannot support the right of Americans to own assault rifles. It is one thing to have a rifle or a shotgun for hunting, but assault rifles are just too dangerous, he believes. Thus, he begins to encourage other members to write letters to the national organization to put pressure on it to change its stance on this issue. Jim and Margaret believe that the local travel club has been a little too conservative in planning trips. At a meeting they ask why the club cannot plan a trip to an exotic location such as Tahiti. Although some of the members balk

at the idea, some become convinced that this is a good idea, and they assign a subcommittee to look into the possibility of such a trip. Finally, Rusty has convinced the food pantry's board to take on the poker tournament as its primary fund-raiser. The organization needs to discontinue two other fund-raising events to have enough volunteers for this activity. Moreover, one of the board members has to resign from the board because he has been convicted of a felony and the state will not issue a license for the poker tournament as long as a convicted felon is on the board of directors.

As the examples illustrate, members of secondary leisure groups are not only influenced by the groups, but they can in turn affect the group itself. The possibility of significantly affecting the group is more likely if the secondary group is local, such as the pottery class. Although it is difficult for an individual to change a national organization such as the National Rifle Association, it is possible.

In addition to primary and secondary groups, another type of social structure affects a person's leisure activities: social categories. Lenski and Lenski (1987) note that human beings can be grouped

As a member of a pottery class, the individual has an influence on the group as much as the group influences the individual.

into a variety of societal classifications. We become members of some of these groups voluntarily, and we are born into others. For instance, we can choose to become a member of a cooking and dining club, but our gender is largely predetermined.

SIMILARITY AND DIVERSITY IN RECREATION AND LEISURE

The human race possesses a unique dynamic balance among all the fascinating characteristics that make us different and all the equally fascinating characteristics that make us the same. Over the last three decades, it has become popular to focus on the richness of our differences. Diversity is an incredibly important physiological and social phenomenon, but we dare not forget or minimize our sameness. In truth we are much more alike than we are different. President Bill Clinton said in a 2006 speech at Georgetown University,

> I always try to mention in every speech I give now that when the human genome was sequenced, the most interesting finding to me was that all human beings are genetically more than 99.9 percent the same, yet all of us spend over 90 percent of our lives—I no less than anyone else—thinking about that one tenth of one percent.

Such may be the case with diversity in leisure and recreation. Let's look at four examples.

Nigata is an 18-year-old female member of the Tarahumara tribe in the interior of Mexico. She is looking forward to the upcoming *tesguinado*, a festival that will celebrate the good news that the men of the tribe have won a running race against another tribe of Native Americans. There will be food and much drinking of *tesguino*, a beer made from corn. But to Nigata what is important is not the food or the alcoholic beverage but the chance to spend time with a Juriuaco, a young man from her tribe. Young men and women customarily begin lives together at ceremonies like this (Beauregard, 1996).

Hameed is a 73-year-old Islamic man who lives in Pakistan. Tomorrow he will go to a large community gathering to celebrate the national team's victory in an international cricket match. The huge crowd will consist of men and women of his village of all ages. Hameed is often called on to supply trained horses

for the event. One of the most popular parts of the celebration is a feast of lamb and rice. For Hameed, however, the best thing about this celebration is the opportunity to gather his extended family around him. Nearly 40 of his children, grandchildren, and great grandchildren will gather. Although the year has been difficult because of violence and a terrible drought that has devastated the local crops, Hameed will be able to forget those issues for a couple of days (Countries and Their Cultures, n.d.).

No one has more reason to complain than Mable Johnson does. The 36-year-old Pointe-aux-Chenes, Louisiana, native suffered through hurricane Katrina and a serious economic downturn in which she lost her job. Although it did not seem as if things could get worse, they did when the Gulf oil spill devastated the beaches in her community. But for a couple of days she can forget all that because Mardi Gras is coming up. Many of her friends who moved to Texas after the hurricane will be returning, and they will have a huge Gulf seafood feast. Her brother was just recently able to begin harvesting shrimp again. He will not only supply fresh seafood from his boat but also help pay for the party that will go on for a solid week. Mable is looking forward to reliving the excitement that her entire family felt when her beloved New Orleans Saints football team won the Super Bowl a few months ago.

On July 6 at 12:00 noon in Pamplona, Spain, the *chupinazo* (a firework) indicates the start of the famous celebration of the Running of the Bulls festival. The festival is really called the Sanfermines because it honors a saint, Saint Fermin. Most festivities in Spain have a religious background. Pablo is excited because for the first time he will be attending this well-known, big party, which goes on until July 14. Thousands of people gather around the city hall for the *chupinazo*. Events will be going on all day and all night, most of them involving plenty of food and drinks, lots of drinks. During this week people will set aside work and personal problems to have a good time with family and friends. The most famous event of the week is the running of the bulls, which occurs at eight o'clock every morning. Pablo has decided to run tomorrow morning, but he is already drinking wine and it seems that he is going to party hard. The running of the bulls is dangerous, and in some years people die. Maybe Pablo will change his mind.

Community gatherings serve to create and maintain a shared culture through recreation and leisure. Here the *chupinazo* (a firework) indicates the start of the famous celebration of the Running of the Bulls festival.

On the surface, these four scenarios may seem quite different. The key characters are different in terms of age, race, religion, nationality, gender, abilities, and economic status. In one celebration alcohol is strictly forbidden, but in others it is common. In one setting the game of cricket occupies an important place, whereas in others cricket is virtually unknown. Closer examination, however, reveals that the similarities are profound. Each situation involves a person who is attending or looking forward to attending a community gathering that involves friends, family, and others and serves to create and maintain a shared culture. Each activity involves food, although the food of the southern United States differs markedly from that of Spain. All four events include or allude to some type of sport or physical activity. Moreover, each scenario demonstrates that recreation and leisure can provide a break from the routine of life. In the next few pages we will examine how gender, ethnicity and race, religion, ability, and socioeconomic class influence recreation and leisure.

LEISURE, RECREATION, AND GENDER

Before venturing further into this topic it is important to discuss the difference between gender and sex. **Sex** refers to the biological component of being either male or female. **Gender**, on the other hand, is a social category that includes attitudes, expectations, and expressions of masculinity and femininity. Gender is one of the most defining characteristics human beings possess. Because of that, it is linked to leisure in myriad complex relationships.

Historically, men have enjoyed a privileged position in all Western cultures. Although patriarchy has been most evident in politics, industry, the arts, and many professions, male superiority has also been expressed and fortified in leisure and recreation. In the 1800s many recreation activities were reserved for men only. At that time, no "self-respecting" female would have gone to a tavern. And segregation of the genders for no apparent logical reason was common. For example, men rode bicycles, and women rode tricycles in the early years of cycling in the United States. It simply was not proper to do otherwise.

The traditional roles within the family have also affected the leisure activities and recreation of men and women. Males were assigned the role of the breadwinner who earns the family's financial resources. Women were assigned the tasks of caring for her children and husband and maintaining the home. Thus, many recreation activities for women took place in the home and included a domestic component like cooking, decorating, or supervising activities for children.

The roles and expectations of men and women in Western society have changed significantly over the past century. Robinson and Godbey (1997) have noted, "Perhaps the most important ongoing social revolution in the United States is the change in women's roles" (p. 13). However, many authors and researchers caution that although change has been made, androgyny, the balance of both male and female characteristics, has not yet fully arrived. Sociologists have pointed out that one of the barriers to a more androgynous society is that parents and other people in nurturing roles have a tendency to treat children in a gender-biased fashion. This can be seen in the actions of the father who invites his son to go hunting with him but never considers that his daughter might want to go as well. Teachers may also show similar biases when it comes to recreation activities. They may discourage young boys from playing with dolls and little girls from playing with toy trucks because it is not acceptable in their eyes. Such behaviors, although not intentionally meant to harm children, have long-term effects, in many cases continuing to deny rewarding and self-enhancing activities to millions of Americans (Eschleman, Cashion, & Basirico, 1993).

Today, although men are responsible for more housework than they were in the past, women still endure far more from the disadvantages of the double shift of housework and child care (Roberts, 2010). This circumstance limits the time available for leisure. But the apparent imbalance in leisure time between men and women is somewhat offset by the fact that men, on average, still work more hours outside the home than women do. Women have lower unemployment rates than men do, but they are twice as likely to have part-time jobs.

Furthermore, although the gap is slowly closing, employed women still earn less on average than men do (United States Department of Labor, 2010). Thus, in regard to income, women are still disadvantaged. This condition affects the choices that they are able to make about their leisure time (Roberts, 2010).

As mentioned previously, sport has been almost entirely a male arena. However, progress has been made. No longer is the old adage true that boys perform and girls cheer. One of the most important steps in the process was adoption of **Title IX** in 1972, legislation that directed educational institutions to develop parity between men's and women's sports in the United States. As evidence of its effectiveness, in 1971, 300,000 females took part in high school sports in the United States; in 1994 that number had risen to 2.24 million (Online Newshour, 1997). This increase in sport participation by girls and women shows that the gap in participation rates between men and women is narrowing.

In Canada, progress has also been made to provide gender equity in sports opportunities. However, Beaubier (2004) notes that a policy to govern the process has been only recently enacted. Canadian Interuniversity Sport, the leading national organization to control sports at the university level, developed a policy statement that included 12 goals to achieve gender equity. Some in Canada believe that the policy is incomplete and encourage Canadian sports organizations to look to the Title IX legislation in the United States for further development on this issue. Russell (2002) offers five conclusions about gender, recreation, and leisure:

1. Although the disparity has decreased over the past century, men continue to experience more leisure in terms of its breadth and depth. A greater diversity of recreation activities is available to men and boys, and it is easier for males to devote more time and effort to activities that are especially important to them. (These activities are often referred to as **serious leisure**.)

2. Long-entrenched roles for the different genders significantly affect recreation. Especially in older and more traditional families, women typically assume the complex and time-intensive task of caring for others. It is not uncommon for the mother in the family to plan, purchase, prepare, and serve the food, then clean up after a Saturday evening barbeque with neighbors. The values and benefits

of this leisure activity will likely be different for the mother than for the father in this family. The mother values her ability to provide her neighbors a meal and enjoyable evening, despite the amount of work involved, while the father values spending time with the neighbors in a relaxing atmosphere.

3. Because men tend not to be the primary caregivers in the family, their recreation more often takes place outside the home. Women, on the other hand, more often spend leisure time in the home. Often their leisure activity is blended with, or at least compatible with, caring for the home.

4. The burden of family care has a greater impact on females; thus, women's leisure and recreation are often quite fragmented. Men, as a result, may have more opportunity to block out an entire afternoon or even a few days exclusively for leisure. Although a woman may plan an afternoon of relaxing reading, she may be interrupted by children who need clothes washed or a husband that needs her help.

5. Older women especially might labor under the false belief that leisure must be earned or that they are not entitled to leisure at all. If they do not do work outside the home, they may not feel like they work and therefore are unworthy of leisure.

LEISURE, ETHNICITY, AND RACE

Race and ethnicity are sometimes used interchangeably, but there are important differences. **Race** refers to biological characteristics, whereas **ethnicity** refers to cultural characteristics. Henslin (1993) notes that people of the same ethnicity "identify with one another on the basis of common ancestry and cultural heritage. Their sense of belonging centers on country of origin, distinctive foods, dress, family names and relationships, language, music, religion and other customs" (p. 311). Leisure and recreation is part and parcel of these various cultural qualities. Some social scientists and politicians argue that more equity exists among racial and ethnic groups today, while others contend that stereotyping, prejudice, discrimination, and racial inequality are every bit as prevalent as they ever were, but they simply are more difficult to detect. Others operate under the assumption that, even if race and ethnicity are issues that must be attended to, they have little relation to leisure. Phillip (2000)

however, disputes this line of thinking: "Perhaps, nowhere else does race matter as much as during leisure. While schools and workplaces have been integrated over the past three decades by force of law, no similar laws have been enacted to secure the racial integration of leisure spaces" (p. 121).

Slightly more than 308 million people lived in the United States in the year 2010 (U.S. Census Bureau, 2010). The diversity of the population in terms of race and ethnicity has been increasing exponentially. For instance, the state of California has a population of over 37 million people, including 14 million Hispanics or Latinos (U.S. Census Bureau, 2010). These groups are still considered minority groups, although in California the concept may need to be reconsidered. Minority groups on average still have lower socioeconomic status (U.S. Census Bureau, 2010) and are at greater risk of social exclusion. Not surprisingly, therefore, leisure participation rates vary according to race and ethnicity (Bell & Hurd, 2006). The use of parks is a good example. Park usage varies significantly among various ethnic groups. Most park users are Caucasian (Byrne, 2007). People from minority ethnic groups or races may feel uncomfortable or even unwelcome in some leisure settings where their ethnic group is underrepresented. For example, some Hispanics may not participate in programs because of a perception of discrimination, fear of not being liked, absence of other Hispanics, and language difficulties (McChesney, Gerken, & McDonald, 2005). Besides variations in participation rates, use patterns vary among races and ethnic groups. For example, African Americans may choose not to participate in activities that are stereotyped for Caucasians. Instead, they may choose activities that adhere more to their cultural norms (Shinew et al., 2004).

Beyond recognizing differences, attention has been devoted recently to the issue of *why* leisure is different for racial and ethnic groups. Two general explanations have come to the forefront: the marginality hypothesis and the ethnicity explanation. The marginality hypothesis explains lower participation in some activities as the consequence of a history of discrimination, resulting in fewer socioeconomic resources. To explain why fewer African American children than white children join swim teams, this theory holds that historically African

American children were denied access to quality aquatics facilities and coaches. On the other hand, the ethnicity explanation suggests that different rates and patterns of participation are the result of different norms, beliefs, and social organizations. According to this theory, African Americans would be more inclined to participate in track and field events rather than swimming because black role models are common in track and field and relatively rare in swimming. Floyd (1998) argues that these two approaches to accounting for differences in leisure and recreation may be only a beginning. He suggests that each has serious weaknesses and that leisure researchers must continue to conduct research in this area. Although research in the arena of sport seems to be continuing, little research has been done recently in other types of recreation and leisure activity.

LEISURE, RECREATION, AND RELIGION

Although religion is fundamentally related to ethnicity, it warrants further attention. For our purposes, we must differentiate between two related concepts. **Spirituality** is a personal belief system that may, but most often does not, have a strong social component. **Religion**, on the other hand, is a thoroughly and universally social institution. According to Eschleman, Cashion, and Basirico, "Religion has always been the anchor of identity for human beings. Religious beliefs give meaning to life, and the experiences associated with them provide personal gratification, as well as release from the frustrations and anxieties of daily life" (1993, p. 344). In all of its wonderfully diverse forms, religion pervades nearly every human endeavor, from presidential elections to child rearing, from marriages and funerals to hairstyles and the length of skirts. Even the recreation activities of those who do not consider themselves to be religious are affected by religion. For example, Norman and Arlene are a middle-aged couple who haven't attended church for the past 20 years. One of their favorite leisure activities since their oldest daughter started high school is watching her participate in athletic events. Because of Arlene's work schedule, she has had difficulty getting time off on Saturdays for her daughter's volleyball games. It would be much easier for her if

some of them were played on Sunday afternoons. However, that's not likely because their community, like many others, does not hold school events on Sundays to avoid conflict with the local churches. Also, the mascot for the sports teams was changed a few years ago as a result of vocal and influential Christian parents. No longer do Norman and Arlene cheer for the Fighting Blue Devils. They now cheer for the Lightning. One of the biggest tournaments of the season is held at the local YMCA. Norman and Arlene did not realize however that the Young Men's Christian Association of the United States of America, a national organization with its roots in the Christian faith, was one of the pioneers in developing the sport of volleyball. It is possible that the games they now enjoy watching would not exist if it were not for this Christian-based organization.

We must be careful not to portray religion as simply a constraint on leisure and recreation. In fact, churches use recreation as a method of maintaining its sense of community, to attract new members, and to keep its members from activity it perceives as harmful. For example, instead of promoting traditional Halloween events like trick or treating, churches across the country offer parties that emphasize other types of fun and worship. Many churches and synagogues have athletic teams that participate either in community leagues or in leagues with other churches and synagogues. Moreover, many children attend summer camps operated by religion-related organizations. Even the traditional potluck after Sunday morning service is a leisure activity that serves to maintain the sense of community of the church people.

Nowhere is the relationship with religion in the United States and Canada more complex and intriguing than in the special arena of sports. This should come as no surprise given the fact that these countries not only have the greatest diversity of sports but also have the greatest diversity of religions. Many athletes have had to struggle with the demands of their faith and their desire to participate in sports. One of the classic examples of this struggle is depicted in the 1981 movie, *Chariots of Fire*, in which devout Christian Eric Liddell must choose between the biggest race of his life and honoring his faith's admonition about running on the Sabbath. More recent examples include a girl who could not compete in a state gymnastics event because of her orthodox Jewish family's observance of the Sabbath on Saturday and an Iowa high school wrestler's refusal to wrestle a female competitor because of his Pentecostal religion's prohibition against contact sports between males and females.

Much attention has been given to the theory that sport has replaced religion in the lives of many North Americans. Edwards' seminal work on the topic of sport as religion continues to influence sport sociologists. According to Edwards (1973) sports and religion have 13 important similarities. Four of them follow:

- Just like religion, sports have their saints. These are the great athletes of previous eras that serve as examples for current athletes and fans.

- The world of sports has its "gods," those superstars that transcend time and culture and dominate the lives of individuals and even countries.

- Sport has its hallowed shrines. These range from the widely recognized Hall of Fame sites to the trophy rooms of colleges and high schools.

- Sports have powerful symbols of faith. The bat that Ruth hit his record home run with and the ball that Dwight Clark caught to win the 1982 National Football League playoffs are examples. And who can argue that there is not a certain sacred quality of an Olympic gold medal?

In writing about the similarity between religion and sport, Prebish noted that "religion is the raft that ferries from profane reality to the realm of the sacred, that enables us to transcend ordinary reality and directly apprehend the extraordinary" (1993, p. 3). He goes on to make the case that for some people, sport does the same thing. When we watch the Super Bowl, we make a mental and emotional journey from everyday life to a world of fantasy.

LEISURE, RECREATION, AND SOCIOECONOMIC CLASS

The individuals of nearly all societies are categorized according to some combination of wealth, power, party affiliation, life chances, and prestige. Some systems, like the **caste system** in India, are very rigid. The boundaries are distinct and movement between the different categories is nearly impossible. A **class system**, like that in many developed countries including the United States and Canada, is much more fluid with overlap between classes

One of the similarities between sport and religion can be seen in the hall of fame gallery at the Pro Football Hall of Fame where former players are enshrined each year.

and the possibility of movement up and down among the classes. In many countries, classes are designated according to a combination of income, education, and occupation. This classification system is referred to as socioeconomic status, SES.

Contemporary industrialized societies comprise four classes (Newman, 1999). The upper class consists of owners of vast property and wealth. The middle class is made up of managers, small-business owners, and professionals. The working class is made up predominantly of laborers who earn modest wages and own little property. Finally, the people of the lower class are those who either work for minimum wages, are periodically unemployed, or are unemployable.

Socioeconomic inequalities around the world are significant and have recently increased in many countries. Inequalities in the United States are relatively high, and they too have increased over the last several years. According to the Central Intelligence Agency's *World Factbook* (2004), the United States ranks 39th on the world's inequality scale of average income measured by the Gini index, which measures the degree of inequality in the distribution of family income in each country. In this scale, African countries such as Namibia and South Africa rank as most unequal, followed by most South and Central America countries. On the other end of the spectrum are countries from Northern and Eastern Europe such as Sweden, Hungary, Norway, and the Czech Republic, which have less difference in average family income.

There is general agreement that socioeconomic status affects leisure. There is, however, less agreement on exactly *how* it affects it. Addressing a particular leisure category, Gruneau wrote, "Recent research on sports and social equality in the United States demonstrates a general pattern of underrepresentation of people from the lowest income levels among active participants in organized sports and physical recreation" (1999, pp. 52-53). Recognizing some of the disagreement about the relationship between socioeconomic status and leisure, Kelly noted, "Economic stratification is at least a filter, with low incomes simply eliminating the majority of the population from cost-intensive activity" (1996, p. 78).

Research supports the notion that class affects travel and tourism. Mill (1986) determined that economic standing, one of the key elements of SES, affected several aspects of tourism. Not surprisingly, people in the upper and middle classes traveled more often through commercial providers, while the working class tended to travel by some form of public transportation. The destinations for travel were also different. The upper classes tended to travel internationally more often than other classes. The higher on the SES scale, the longer the time spent at a destination. And as might be expected, the upper and middle classes spent more money when they traveled for leisure purposes.

We should not overlook the fact that although class affects leisure, the reverse may also be true—leisure may affect class. Thorstein Veblen, in his classic 1899 treatise, *The Theory of the Leisure Class*, argued that the upper class, which he called the leisure class, used leisure as a way to display and maintain their prized position in society (1998 [1899]). Elegant and exclusive social gatherings and highly consumptive activities sent a clear message to those in lower social positions that class did indeed matter. At the same time, many of the lower classes emulated the upper classes and tried to match their leisure styles. When a sufficiently large group from the middle class was able to participate in activities that resembled those of the rich, the upper class found even more expensive and elaborate leisure activities to maintain their status.

BENEFITS AND CONSTRAINTS IN LEISURE

Only with difficulty can we imagine a leisure activity that does not offer some benefit. If nothing else, leisure is by definition a voluntarily chosen activity. Thus, one of the benefits of all leisure activities is that they provide the participant with an opportunity to express free will. At the same time, it is difficult to imagine any leisure activity that does not have at least some constraints. Few activities (leisure or otherwise) are totally free. The following example will illustrate the mixed nature of leisure.

Nicole is an active 21-year-old college student at a Midwestern university. When interviewed about her leisure activities she states,

> I am mostly into leisure activities with my friends. Like during last spring break my best friend and I went to Panama City in Florida.

Lying on the beach for three days and doing pretty much nothing was pretty nice. I seriously needed a break from school and work. I just wish my boyfriend could have gone with us, but he had to work. I probably should not have gone because I really didn't have the money. But I decided that I could do it if we traveled by car and stayed in a cheaper motel a few blocks from the beach. One of the things I have always wanted to do was parasail, but on the day I was going to do it, the wind came up. The people who ran the company said they could not do it if the wind was over 20 miles per hour. It was the last day, and I couldn't go. I was disappointed, but then I saw some people surfing. I rented a board and spent the rest of the day surfing. I had a great time and a wonderful workout.

One night my best friend and I wanted to go to a really great bar, but she got a little sick and could not go. I really wanted to go but didn't want to go alone. I had heard the place was a little bit wilder than I am used to. It would have been fun, but my parents always told me to be careful when I am by myself in a strange place, so I just stayed in our room that night. All in all, it was a really wonderful time, and I hope to have another spring break trip but with my boyfriend.

Benefits of Leisure and Recreation

Nicole obviously got more out of her spring break trip than a nice tan. She mentioned that she got to relax on the beach and got some exercise while surfing. She was also able to share these experiences with her best friend. The individual benefits of recreation and leisure are easy to observe, but many less obvious leisure and recreation contributions occurred as well. Nicole and her friend spent money on transportation, lodging, and food. This spending contributed to the economies in communities along the way and in Florida. The beaches are a main attraction to the area; thus, a great deal of effort is made to keep the beaches clean and attractive for locals and tourists. Finally, consider that Nicole alluded to the trip being recuperative. After a week of fun and sun, she was revitalized and ready to go

back to school and her part-time job. In turn, her increased productivity at work was valuable to her, to the community in which she lived, and to the field in which she was employed.

The National Recreation and Park Association (NRPA) recognized that many people take recreation for granted and do not understand the contribution of this field. Thus, NRPA developed a program called Parks and Recreation: The Benefits Are Endless to promote the role of recreation and parks to the public. Even if the benefits are not truly endless, they are certainly numerous and varied. The benefits are classified as individual and social (Henderson, 2010). Within the individual benefits category are physiological benefits and psychological benefits. Subcategories of the social value of recreation include economic, environmental, and recuperation for other activities including productive work.

Constraints in Leisure and Recreation

Let's also consider what this tells us about leisure and the constraints inherent to it. Although Nicole had a generally good time on her spring break, she is certainly not operating without constraints on what she wanted to do for leisure. She was limited by

- whom she could go with on spring break,
- how much money she could spend on her vacation,
- the weather,
- a company's unwillingness to provide a particular activity,
- her parents' values of what leisure activity is appropriate, and
- her apprehension about going to a bar alone.

Another lesson that we can learn from this scenario is that most of these constraints did not fully prevent Nicole from participating. She negotiated most of them and was able to have an enjoyable time regardless.

The great variety of constraints poses a challenge for categorizing. Therefore, researchers have developed multiple models for grouping these phenomena. Structural constraints include time, money, health, and equipment; intrapersonal constraints include fear, low self-esteem, and attitudes; and interpersonal constraints include family responsibilities and a lack of partners with whom to share the leisure activity (Crawford, Jackson, & Godbey, 1991). Henderson (1997) grouped constraints as antecedent limitations such as attitudes and lack of skill and intervening constraints such as weather and resources.

GOOD AND BAD LEISURE AND RECREATION

If we're not careful, we may assume that leisure and recreation is unequivocally good. Who can argue that an exercise program for seniors or making parks available for picnics are not admirable and decent efforts? Certainly no one could be opposed to arts and crafts classes and family vacations. But some activities are not wholesome, and some seem to be just downright wrong. We could list the bad activities, but that wouldn't be especially helpful because the list would be in a constant state of flux with leisure activities being struck from the list and new ones being added all the time. It may be more productive for us to consider how to determine the goodness or badness of an activity.

Participation in recreation cannot be forced upon us. We decide to participate because we think it will be fun and possibly rewarding. In fact, the defining quality of leisure and recreation is the freedom to participate or not. But the same freedom in leisure and recreation can be problematic when considering the moral value of an activity. We might think that our leisure is just that—entirely and completely *our* leisure. How dare anyone tell us that our chosen activity is wrong and then try to stop us from doing it! Although that may be our initial reaction to placing moral value on recreation and leisure, we must go beyond that if we are to truly understand our society and ourselves. Let's take a moment and consider how we determine good and bad in contemporary culture.

Goodness has been discussed by every culture since the ancient Greeks. Today we have several different and competing theories about what is good and bad, right and wrong. Although there are a lot of diverse ideas, nearly all agree that goodness is not a concept simply left up to the individual to determine. Even proponents of **hedonism**, a

philosophy in which individual pleasure is the chief good, recognizes that our consequences have actions that affect our pleasure seeking; thus we have to consider our behaviors in light of those around us. Other ethical theories place concerns for others at the middle of the debate about good and evil. The point is that the individual actor and the various societies of which he or she is a part of jointly determine goodness in all things, including leisure and recreation.

Let's briefly consider a couple of contemporary theories about good and bad leisure. Nash (1953) was one of the first to tackle the issue. His model of good and bad recreation resembled a pyramid with the very best activities at the peak. These activities not only provided satisfaction to the actor but also contributed to making a better society. In the middle of the pyramid were activities that were merely entertaining to the participants. They were not harmful to anyone, but they did not affect society either. Near the bottom were activities that, although freely chosen, were harmful to the individual. Finally, at the bottom of the diagram, were activities that not only hurt the participant but damaged society as well. Curtis (1979) devised an even simpler continuum with "good" recreation activities on one end and "bad" recreation activities on the other end. Curtis labeled bad activities as "**purple leisure**" and defined them as activities that might bring pleasure to the individual but would cause harm to society.

Let's look at various recreation activities in light of this discussion of goodness and badness. Activities at the top and bottom of Nash's model and at either end of Curtis' continuum are pretty easy to understand. Most of us would agree that writing and performing a beautiful song would be good and vandalizing a playground would be bad. But it is much more difficult to reach consensus on the goodness of many other activities. Where would we put hunting? How about alcohol use? Marijuana use? Cocaine? Television viewing? Playing violent video games? Or how about ultimate fighting? Is it wrong or bad to go to a strip club? Then there is the thorny issue of gambling. At one time in the United States almost every type of gambling was banned. Then it became available only in certain states and locations like Nevada and American Indian reservations. Now, some form of gambling is available in

OUTSTANDING GRADUATES

Background Information

Name: Michael J. Bradley

Education: Doctor of philosophy in health, leisure, and human performance, Oklahoma State University; master of science in recreation, park, and tourism administration, Western Illinois University; bachelor of science in leisure studies, Oklahoma State University.

Special awards: 2011 Outstanding Graduate Student Award (National Recreation and Park Association), National Graduate Student Service and Leadership Award (Rho Phi Lambda), 2012 Student Conference Scholarship Award (National Association of Recreation Resource Planners).

Affiliations: National Recreation and Park Association, Oklahoma Recreation and Park Society, National Intramural-Recreational Sports Association, National Parks Conservation Association, National Association of Recreation Resource Planners.

Career Information

Position: Assistant professor of recreation and park administration.

Organization: Eastern Kentucky University. The department offers nationally accredited BS and MS degrees in recreation and park administration. Students and faculty are engaged in classroom instruction, service-learning projects, grant writing, and research. The faculty is committed to providing a combination of theory and experience to prepare and motivate students for successful employment in the field. A career in park, recreation, and leisure services enables students to have an impact in their work, in their communities, on the environment, and on the lives of others.

Job description: As an assistant professor, I teach undergraduate- and graduate-level courses in the parks and recreation field of study. I conduct relevant research in the field and pursue avenues to aid in education about the environment and conservation.

"Whether preserving natural areas, providing open play areas, programming for children and adults, or simply volunteering, our field has numerous people who care about others."

Career path: My dream is to teach, research, and interact with students, children, and adults. I'm hoping to help create and conserve our recreation areas so that we may enjoy them today, tomorrow, and into the future. I love academics because I have the opportunity to educate future professionals and conduct research to influence the decision processes throughout various agencies.

My work has focused on working with students, children, and adults as a Boys and Girls Club assistant unit director and teen coordinator and recreation supervisor for a parks department. I also did research in the Oklahoma state park system and as a research assistant for the leisure studies program at Oklahoma State University.

Likes and dislikes about the job: I enjoy meeting and understanding people, aiding in the education process, and learning new things myself. Being in academics means being constantly busy, and I hope that I can continue to find the time to enjoy my own leisure and recreation. It is an earnest interest in overcoming obstacles in order to prevail over the ills of society. I really believe that if you want to make a difference, this is a great field for building that foundation.

Advice to Undergraduates

While pursuing a degree is important, experience is also a vital part of your portfolio and resume. If you want to excel, seek out experiences that enhance, broaden, and strengthen your marketability. Begin and continue active involvement in state and national professional associations. Your experiences and commitment to the profession will prove just as valuable as your education.

just about every state and county. Many states have horse and dog races to bet on. Casinos are floating on almost every major body of water in the United States, and there are only three or four states that do not have a legal lottery. In Canada, gambling is legal to anyone over the age of 18. Options include scratch tickets (similar to the lotteries in the United States), horse races, bingo, betting on sports events, and gambling at one of the 106 casinos scattered across Canada. So, is gambling good or bad? It's legal and widespread, provides jobs and resources for schools and (whatever else governments do with the money), and provides entertainment for many. But it is also associated with addiction, corruption, and other negative aspects—possibly the diminution of the work ethic. As you can see, determining whether a leisure activity is good or bad is not easy. But as a society, we must attempt to because leisure activities affect us all.

IMPLICATIONS FOR PROFESSIONALS

Charged with the task of providing leisure and recreation opportunities, leisure and recreation professionals must first understand how leisure and recreation takes place. Who participates? How do they participate? What are their motivations? What are their constraints and limitations? What are the benefits of recreation? Are there direct consequences or indirect consequences that will not be evident for years? Armed with the answers to these questions, we can design programs, facilities, and open spaces that make it possible for human beings to flourish.

For example, knowing the demands and limitations placed on single mothers, recreation and parks professionals must offer programs that allow them the opportunity to participate. Perhaps that means that some fitness programs take place in the middle of the morning and the agency offers a toddler play period at the same time. Given the fact that money is in short supply for this population, the agency must also subsidize the program so that the mothers do not have to choose between their own physical fitness and paying the utility bills. This must all be accomplished without perpetuating the stigma that single-parent households are inferior and a societal burden that must be dealt with as conveniently as possible.

But even these efforts, as challenging as they are, are not enough. On another level, leisure and recreation professionals must be educators. They must continue to drive home the point that leisure and recreation is essential—so important that people, regardless of their lot in life, have it by right, not because they are of a particular color, age, ethnicity, gender, religion, or class. Showing the current benefits and extolling the future benefits of leisure and recreation for all will strengthen the case. The world really can be better today and tomorrow for all of us through equal leisure and recreation opportunity.

SUMMARY

As we have seen, leisure is a wonderfully complex human phenomenon that is never undertaken in a social vacuum—it is absolutely inseparable from society. A multitude of social institutions including stratification, religion, ethnicity, gender, family, and friendships thoroughly influence leisure. But the causation arrow goes both ways. Leisure often profoundly affects the society in which it takes place. Thus, contrary to the thinking of previous eras, leisure is not a trivial pursuit relegated to the realm of leftover time and energy. Rather, it is an essential ingredient of the lives of individuals, communities, nations, and humankind. Into this rich boiling stew of the human experience venture leisure and recreation professionals.

For glossary terms, learning experiences, and more, please visit the web resource at **www.HumanKinetics.com/IntroductionToRecreationAndLeisure**

PART II

Leisure and Recreation as a Multifaceted Delivery System

CHAPTER 5

Leisure Service Delivery Systems

David N. Emanuelson

> " In every real man a child is hidden that wants to play. "
>
> Friedrich Nietzsche,
> German philosopher

LEARNING OUTCOMES

After reading this chapter, you should be able to do the following:

> Identify the three sectors that deliver leisure services to the public and the way in which they operate

> Compare and contrast the challenges facing leisure service professionals in the three sectors

> Explain how various challenges require leisure service professionals to possess diverse technical skills

> Describe the educational courses that leisure service professionals should take to prepare for the opportunities that await them

INTRODUCTION

Most people, including leisure service professionals, equate leisure with recreation. But leisure is not a precise synonym for recreation; leisure is defined only as time not spent working. Therefore, leisure services are the services provided to fill time not spent working. Not all leisure services are recreation, however. Some leisure services are tasks that are essential for human existence, such as thinking and planning, which are necessary for human beings to do before they actually do work. On the other hand, all recreation is a form of play, an activity that everyone needs to do to recharge their batteries and to refresh them so that they can get back to the essential work of their lives.

According to the U.S. Department of Labor and the Canadian government, Americans and Canadians spend about 38.5 hours per week working. Because a week is 168 hours long (7 days times 24 hours), the average time that most people spend working is less than 25 percent of that total, suggesting that Americans and Canadians have nearly 130 hours of week to do things other than working.

Considering that the average person sleeps 8 hours a night, the total hours spent sleeping should be 56 hours a week, leaving 74 hours for other things. Estimates are that people use half of the remaining time in a week to do things essential for existence, such as cooking, cleaning, and personal maintenance, leaving about 30 hours a week for recreation, which in this chapter will be used interchangeably with the phrase *leisure service industry*.

So it should be no surprise that a major portion of the national economies of Canada and the United States is dedicated to satisfying their citizens' desires for recreation. In fact, leisure services are the largest segment of the **gross domestic national product** in both countries. Gross domestic national product is the sum of total goods and services manufactured or provided by all businesses, nonprofit organizations, and government entities in a country.

The definition of the leisure service industry is broad, including travel and tourism, amusement and theme park operations, hospitality and restaurant management, sport and entertainment, and community parks and recreation—practically anything that people do when they are not working. This definition means that the leisure service industry is diverse. Because it is a diverse field, unlike professional fields such as accounting, finance, and economics, leisure service professionals need to be trained in more than one discipline.

This chapter reviews the leisure service field and the delivery systems and sectors in which they exist. The chapter also considers challenges that leisure service professionals face and the range of management skills needed to be successful in one sector or another. During the course of the discussion, the chapter identifies technical skills common to all sectors, determines which ones are specific to a sector, and suggests a course of education that will prepare professionals for success in the leisure service industry.

As part of the review process, this chapter considers leisure service delivery systems in both Canada and the United States, largely because they are similar but also because they have important differences. The differences are particularly true at the governmental levels. Canada is a federation called a **constitutional monarchy**, part of the British Commonwealth with allegiance to the queen of

England. In Canada the Crown is the foundation of the executive and judicial branches of government. By contrast, the United States is a **constitutional republic**, in which the executive branch is elected and the judicial branch is appointed by the chief executive.

In the United States leisure services provided by the National Park System in the Department of Interior are considered both administrative and legislative functions of the national government. The department head is a cabinet-level position and is appointed by the president, but the department was created through legislative action and its funding comes from Congress. Understanding the distinctions is important. In the 1980s President Ronald Reagan appointed cabinet members and instructed them to reduce their funding requests, but Congress insisted on maintaining the funding levels. The Supreme Court sided with Congress, causing departments such as Interior to continue their operations above and beyond the wishes of the president.

The United States also differs from Canada because it has a different form of federalism. In the U.S. federal system, states have substantial power. They charter businesses, nonprofit organizations, and local **governmental units**. A governmental unit is a generic term that describes a government group at any level: national, state, county, city, or other local unit. The term can be used to refer to one large unit such as the state or subdivisions within the unit such as departments. In Canada chartering of these entities is done at the national level. Yet by most other appearances, businesses, nonprofits, and local governments deliver leisure services in a similar way in Canada and the United States.

Leisure services are provided by three sectors of the economy: the private, or commercial, sector; the nonprofit sector; and the public, or government, sector. The private sector was the first historically to provide leisure services, so this chapter begins with an overview of private-sector delivery systems and the way in which they function. Discussion then moves to the nonprofit sector because it was the second one to deliver services. Last discussed is the public sector, which provides a unique array of services that businesses and nonprofit organizations are not in a position to offer.

For instance, government provides parks and open space, which the public can enjoy without paying fees. This free use of parks and open space is possible because governments collect taxes to support these services. In Canada and the United States, parks and open space are provided in that way, but government also provides other services that businesses and nonprofits cannot. The chapter touches on these services as well.

PRIVATE SECTOR

The commercial recreation sector is the largest of the sectors, about 100 times larger than the public sector, and it provides students with the greatest career opportunities. More than 22.5 million businesses operate in the United States, and 2 million are found in Canada. Estimates are that the leisure service sector comprises more than 8 percent of the gross domestic product of the United States and nearly 2 million commercial recreation businesses. In Canada the leisure service sector comprises more than 12 percent of the gross domestic product and more than 200,000 businesses.

Leisure services are part of the service industry segment of national economies, called the "soft" sector. Although the service industry contains other subparts including insurance, banking, retail, education, and health care, its largest segment in the United States and Canada is the leisure service industry. The service industry is not thought to produce any "hard" products such as appliances or furniture. For the most part, the leisure service industry buys and sells hard products, but doesn't actually produce them. Exceptions are the sports retail, recreational vehicle, and souvenir industries, which manufacture hard products and sell them in retail outlets. Officially, the leisure service industry is composed of a number of industries, including

- travel and tourism,
- hospitality,
- resort,
- gaming,
- amusement park,
- restaurant,
- professional sport,
- sporting goods manufacturers and retailers,

- movie and entertainment industry,
- camping and outdoor recreation, and
- video games.

In 2008 these industries provided an estimated 6.7 million jobs in the United States and generated $91 billion in annual national and state tax revenue. Today those numbers are even higher. Economists have estimated that $1 of every $12 in the U.S. economy is from leisure service industry spending. The total gross national product of the United States is estimated to exceed $14 trillion, so the amount of money spent on leisure services exceeds $1.17 trillion annually.

What makes the leisure service industry unique, and therefore leisure service delivery systems unique, is its diversity. Other than health care, a sector in which hospitals can be operated for profit, as not-for-profit, or by governmental units, no other profession spans all three sectors. And no other profession except health care requires the diversity of management skills required in the leisure service profession.

What also makes the leisure service industry unique is that it goes beyond just the service industry. Because the leisure industry also includes the sporting goods retail industry, recreation vehicle industry, and souvenir industry, which manufacture hard products, the leisure service industry is not limited to the service industry alone, often defying definition.

An example of how difficult it has become to define the leisure service industry is the cruise industry. As a subcomponent of the travel and tourism industry, the cruise industry provides destination voyages to the four corners of the world. For as little as $500 a person, cruisers can live on a ship for a week, be fed gourmet meals, see Las Vegas quality shows, purchase jewelry and other retail goods, and visit exotic ports of call that may offer adventure excursions.

As a growing industry that seeks to keep up with the need of Canadians and Americans to travel in comfort and at affordable cost, the cruise ship industry serves as an example of what has been taking place in the leisure service industry worldwide. Since the year 2000 the industry has been growing by leaps and bounds. Cruise lines are introducing new ships regularly. One cruise ship company, Royal Caribbean Cruise Line, recently launched a massive ship that cost over $1.2 billion and holds in excess of 5,000 passengers and 1,500 crew members. This ship, the size of a small city, is a business that serves the needs of its passengers, exchanging services for money and doing so in a way that passengers are willing to pay for those services.

Innovation has become the hallmark of the private-sector leisure service industry. Las Vegas, founded as a place where gamblers could make wagers with no fear of breaking the law, is now a major convention center and family vacation destination. It has amusement parks, restaurants, entertainment venues, luxury resorts, and, of course, gambling casinos. New hotels are regularly added to the market, which boasts 90,000 hotel rooms.

The important point is that the private-sector leisure service industry is big and getting bigger. The leisure service industry has been predicted to grow as the middle classes grow worldwide. As a burgeoning international middle class with disposable income seeks leisure services throughout every stage of their lives, from their youth through their golden years, the leisure service industry has the potential to be a growth industry worldwide over the long haul, just as it has been in Canada and the United States.

Private-Sector Leisure Service Delivery Systems

Private-sector delivery systems are called **businesses**. In both the United States and Canada, businesses are organizations created to provide a service or product. They charge a higher price than the cost of producing that product or service, and the difference between the cost and the price is the profit. Businesses can be as small as a single person who sharpens and waxes skis near a ski resort or as large as the resort operation itself, which provides lift services, food, accommodations, and transportation.

Making a profit changes the power dynamic of leisure service businesses. Managers of leisure service businesses must possess a level of power that exceeds that of government and nonprofit managers. All leisure service managers need some power; it's just that leisure service private sector managers need more than their counterparts do.

The additional power that leisure service private sector managers need is the power to focus on their customers, meaning that customers become more important than the employees.

Because leisure service businesses are always looking for ways of making a profit, they are motivated to identify unmet customer needs and meet them—for a fair price, of course. In some ways, that challenge makes the private sector more exciting than the nonprofit or government sectors. Those who work for businesses always have something to do because there is always more money to be made. People who find that type of career exciting tend to gravitate to the private sector. Leisure

The Louisville Slugger Museum and Factory crosses different segments of the leisure service industry. It is a tourist destination, a sporting goods manufacturer, and a retail establishment.

service students need to decide whether that type of life is for them.

All leisure service organizations focus on their customers at some level. But leisure service businesses are different from delivery systems in other sectors because they focus on customers who are willing and able to pay for services. Being focused on profitability means that businesses cannot afford to waste their time on people who will not pay them for services. On the other hand, nonprofit and government leisure service delivery systems cannot ignore those who cannot pay.

Business authors have developed a theory of the firm that suggests that everyone working for the business will act in the best interest of the business, focusing on the customer and helping it make a profit, which is, in effect, acting in their own best interest. The theory suggests that if the business prospers, employees will retain their jobs or even share in the profits. Therefore, managers need not worry about being overbearing in their attempts to motivate employees to work hard. Employees will work hard on their own because it's in their own best interest to do so.

Challenges of Managing Leisure Service Businesses

Managing a leisure service, regardless of the sector—commercial, nonprofit, or public—requires understanding of the rules for management, some of them formal and others informal. Each sector has its own traditions, rules, and standard operating procedures that make it different not only from the others but also from other services in their sector.

The private sector is where businesses operate. Because businesses exist to make a profit, they need to be able to identify human needs and offer services to meet those needs, for a price to be sure. Businesses focus on the customer because the transaction between the business and the customer provides the business its lifeblood. This focus is called taking a **marketing approach**.

The singular focus on the customer provides private sector managers a challenge that doesn't exist in the public and nonprofit sectors of the leisure service industry. With no taxes or donations to sustain them, they have no safety net. Managers walk a tightrope, particularly those who manage start-up businesses rather than existing businesses. Because of their dependence on revenues, commercial recreation managers confront challenges that managers in the other two sectors don't face. Businesses are susceptible to economic downturns and must comply with government regulations. Stockholders and owners expect a return on their capital. Lenders need to be repaid with interest. Customer needs change, and competition is a constant threat.

Leisure service managers in the commercial sector also have advantages compared with their counterparts in nonprofit and government organizations. The level of transparency required of businesses is not as great as that required of government and nonprofit agencies. The media has no access to financial records of privately owned companies and limited access to those of publicly traded companies.

Another advantage is that private-sector employees have fewer rights than public-sector employees do. The salaries and wages of business employees can be kept secret from other employees. In some cases, business employees can be terminated for divulging their pay, allowing managers to use pay as a motivational tool.

Unlike governmental units, privately held businesses do not have public board meetings. No state open meetings act requires businesses to make decisions in public. To do so would provide competitors with strategic information. Therefore, setting prices for services is not open to debate in the private sector as it is in the public sector. And board members of companies in the private sector, unlike their counterparts in the public sector, can be paid substantial sums of money for attending meetings.

Corporate board members in privately held companies are themselves the owners. Any discussion about corporate strategy occurs within that group. For publicly traded companies, corporate board members can be appointed by senior management, tantamount to allowing the senior executive to select his or her own bosses, or they can be elected by the stockholders, although the major stockholders control most of the votes.

Skills Required for Managing Leisure Service Businesses

The skills that business managers need to possess are economics, business accounting, finance, mar-

keting, and organizational leadership. These skills are taught as academic courses in leisure studies and business programs at the university level. These subjects have principles and formulae for success.

Other advantages of being a manager in the private sector include generally higher compensation. If a manager is the owner of the company, she or he is entitled to all the profits. If the manager works for a corporation that she or he does not own, pay may be commensurate with performance. It has been said that there are only three ways of acquiring wealth in America: marrying into money, investing well, and owning or being the senior manager of a business. An employee of a business, nonprofit, or governmental unit will find it difficult, although not impossible, to become rich. About the only way that most people earn a great deal more than they spend is to operate a business in which employees are paid less than what they actually produce.

A person must be business minded to manage in the private sector. With a focus on the needs of the customer and the art of the deal, managing in the commercial recreation sector can be rewarding. But like walking a high wire without a net, being an entrepreneur has its risks.

NONPROFIT SECTOR

The nonprofit sector of the leisure service industry consists of organizations chartered or permitted to provide services by the national government in Canada and state and federal governments in the United States. In the United States most nonprofits are chartered by the individual states, but some are nationally chartered, such as Boy Scouts of America. All U.S. nonprofits must follow the codes of the Internal Revenue Service of the U.S. government. In Canada the national government takes a more vigilant approach, making sure that nonprofit organizations do charitable work.

In the United States nonprofit organizations are exempt from paying federal taxes under section 501(c) of the Internal Revenue Code and file annual reports with the IRS to substantiate their tax exemption. Numerous categories are identified under this section, but the most pertinent for leisure services are social and recreational clubs allowed under IRS Code 501(c)(7) and charitable organizations allowed under IRS Code 501(c)(3).

According to the IRS Code, to receive exempt status, a social club must be organized for pleasure, recreation, and other similar purposes and cannot discriminate against any person based on race, color, or religion. "A club may, however, in good faith, limit its membership to members of a particular religion in order to further the teachings or principles of that religion and not to exclude individuals of a particular race or color."

The other category, charitable organizations, is for the purposes of religion, education, scientific, literary, testing for public safety, fostering national or international amateur sport competition, and preventing cruelty to children or animals.

Further, the tax code defines *charitable* as including

> relief of the poor, the distressed, or the underprivileged; advancement of religion; advancement of education or science; erecting or maintaining public buildings, monuments, or works; lessening the burdens of government; lessening neighborhood tensions; eliminating prejudice and discrimination; defending human and civil rights secured by law; and combating community deterioration and juvenile delinquency. (www.irs.gov/charities/charitable/article/0,,id=175418,00.html)

In the nonprofit sector, although meeting the needs of clients is important, doing it for a price or making a profit is not always important. Whereas business organizations exist to earn and distribute taxable wealth to owners and shareholders, nonprofit corporations cannot distribute excess revenues to shareholders because there are no shareholders. Businesses are able to retain surplus revenues called profits and use those profits as capital for expansion of the businesses. Nonprofits strive for excess revenue over expenditures so that they can reinvest into their organizations.

On the other side of the coin, if revenues fall short of covering expenses, nonprofit organizations face survival issues. They are like businesses in that way, and governmental units for that matter. In none of the sectors can organizations lose money and expect to be in existence over the long run.

As mentioned earlier, the IRS allows various kinds of nonprofit leisure service organizations. Some nonprofit leisure service providers do chari-

table work, such as Boys and Girls Clubs, and they rely on donations rather than fees for existence. Other nonprofit leisure service organizations, such as country clubs, don't do charitable work at all and charge substantial fees for their leisure services. Both of these examples have nonprofit status approved by the Internal Revenue Service, permitting them to exist with the understanding that, over the long run, they will stay true to their purpose and reinvest excess revenue into the organization. Their profitability is closely monitored by the IRS because nonprofit organizations have to file tax reports just as private corporations do.

Today, tens of thousands of youth sport organizations are organized as nonprofits in America. They are organized as nonprofits to accept revenue, and their short-term profits are not taxed.

Nonprofit organizations often compete against businesses and governmental units for clients. For instance, the local YMCA might compete with a private fitness club or the local parks and recreation department by selling memberships to their fitness clubs. A local youth club athletic team might compete with the local park district for youth baseball players.

Nonprofit leisure service providers exist in many communities to fill a void because a governmental or private leisure service provider is not available. A charitable organization may be needed to meet the needs of children or adults who have low incomes or are disabled. Even where a governmental provider is available, some nonprofits exist because people want their leisure services needs met in different ways. Country clubs, tennis clubs, swimming clubs, and other athletic clubs exist because of their exclusiveness, but to maintain their tax-exempt status they cannot discriminate by race, color, or religion.

Leisure service nonprofit organizations face a unique challenge from other nonprofit organizations. The primary management responsibility of the charitable ones, such as the Boys and Girls Clubs, is to seek donations so that they can continue to exist, knowing that fees from clients, who are mostly low income, do not generate sufficient operating revenues. The primary management responsibility of less charitable ones, such as country clubs, is to ensure the happiness of their members so that they will continue to pay membership fees.

Nonprofit leisure service providers, such as a private swim club, exist either because those services aren't available in the community or they meet users' leisure needs in other ways.

Nonprofit Leisure Service Delivery Systems

Like the business sector, the nonprofit sector of the field offers many opportunities for leisure service professionals. Among the 1.8 million nonprofit organizations in the United States today, approximately 20 percent deliver leisure services, so almost 360,000 nonprofit leisure service organizations are delivering services to Americans.

These nonprofit organizations range from such well-known organizations as the YMCA and Boys and Girls Clubs to nonprofit resident and day camps, local youth baseball and girls' softball programs, and hospitals that provide wellness centers. Not every nonprofit provider employs full-time staff. Local youth baseball programs don't. On the other hand, larger ones like Boys and Girls Clubs and YMCAs employ full-time leisure service professionals.

Nonprofit leisure service delivery systems differ from leisure service businesses in that the nonprofit leisure service sector has boundaries that businesses do not. For instance, in search of revenue, businesses can venture into markets that are off limits to nonprofit organizations. The cruising industry, the hospitality industry, and gaming are examples. State governments will not issue charters for nonprofit organizations to provide these leisure services. Businesses are permitted in these industries because state governments recognize that these industries are profitable but are not appropriate for nonprofit leisure service organizations.

Nonprofit leisure service delivery systems are, therefore, more limited in the range of services that they can provide. Athletics programs are within that scope. So are fitness services, such as the operation of YMCA fitness programs and fitness centers. Camping, both residential and day camping, are within the scope of nonprofit leisure service organization services as well.

Challenges of Managing Nonprofit Leisure Service Agencies

Because fees and donations are their primary sources of revenue, nonprofit organizations, like businesses, need to focus on their revenues to remain financially viable. Like businesses, nonprofits must be creative in the services that they provide to their clients. Transparency is another way that nonprofits are similar. Like businesses, the records of nonprofit organizations are not readily available to the media or public, although they are required to submit reports to the IRS.

The boards of directors for nonprofits are similar to those of private-sector companies in that they can be self-appointed. When an opening on a board of directors occurs, the remaining board members select the replacement. Also, board meetings are not open to the public or regulated by state open meetings acts, so replacing board members can be done without public scrutiny. Nonprofit board members are rarely compensated for their service to the organization. In fact, their primary responsibility is to bring money into the agency through their fund-raising efforts.

Managing the nonprofit organization can be different as well. Because employees are generally not rewarded by the sharing of profits, managing nonprofit employees is similar to managing public employees. Management is generally done on a group basis using sociological principles of group motivation.

Nonprofit managers do not share in the surplus revenues of the organization. Big salaries or other perks are absent. Nonprofit managers focus on how much revenue the agency generates from services, which clients receive free services, how judiciously the agency spends its money, and how the agency can maintain an environment in which clients can be donors and employees will say complimentary things about the organization.

The good news is that nonprofit organizations usually succeed. Of the new nonprofit organizations created each year, less than 20 percent fail, partly because a safety net is present. When nonprofits are chartered by states, the people who charter them usually have established a need for their services and sources of revenue for their operations. Initially, these organizations have volunteers performing the work, and eventually donors provide a stable base of revenue. Therefore, the risk that the agency will fail is smaller, although the financial reward to management is also less.

Skills Required for Managing Nonprofit Leisure Service Agencies

Nonprofit leisure service managers need to have a blend of skills in business and public administra-
tion. Managers need to understand economics, business accounting, finance, marketing, and business leadership. But they also need to understand fund accounting, organizational theory, and fundraising. Several universities have emerging academic programs in public service, focusing on nonprofit agency management. These programs blend business and public administration classes.

People who pursue careers in nonprofit leisure service are not necessarily doing it for personal enrichment. They are typically intrinsically motivated people who want the security of a stable environment as they perform a service for the community. Like for-profit managers, they need financial skills.

PUBLIC SECTOR

Government spending in the leisure service industry makes up about 1 percent of the entire amount of money spent. Even so, leisure service governmental services are a cornerstone of employment in the leisure service field. Many graduates from academic programs in leisure service are drawn to the public sector, particularly at the county and municipal levels. State and federal leisure service professionals attain their positions by political appointment or competitive testing.

Federal and State Agencies

The federal government is primarily in the business of maintaining national forests, parks, and recreation areas. Most recreation services are park and nature conservation oriented, and most of the user fees charged are for admissions, parking, and use of camping, food, and accommodation facilities. The federal government provides outdoor services through a number of agencies in various departments.

The 50 state governments provide services similar to those of the National Park Service. State departments of natural resources primarily manage their state park systems, some of which have restaurants, hotels, campgrounds, boat rentals, and other supplemental services. Some parks charge fees for admission and parking, whereas others are free of charge.

For the most part, federal, state, and county agencies are not considered entrepreneurial. They exist to conserve land and in some cases to block access by the public to maintain land in its natural state.

State governments have created special taxing districts that own athletic stadiums and convention centers. These sports authorities can be funded by property, sales, excise, and hotel room taxes to construct and maintain facilities. These facilities can be rented to professional and university sport programs, generating millions of dollars in revenue.

Municipal Public-Sector Leisure Service Delivery Systems

At the local level the United States has more than 25,000 municipalities. At the municipal level a multitude of structures of government provide parks and recreation services. The most common are parks and recreation departments of cities, villages, and towns.

Special districts are another way of delivering public parks and recreation services. Some states have provisions within state law to create park districts at the local level, as occurs in Illinois, Ohio, Colorado, Utah, California, Oregon, Washington, and North Dakota. Of the states that provide park districts, the option of providing parks and recreation services as municipal departments is still available. Only in Illinois and North Dakota

do park districts outnumber parks and recreation departments. Although California has more than 175 park districts, in the other states that permit park districts, municipalities and voters have been reluctant to create them.

Challenges of Managing Government Leisure Service Agencies

It has been said that public administration is like managing in a fishbowl because nothing is private. The main reason for public scrutiny of government is the relationship between taxation and responsibility. Unlike businesses or nonprofit organizations in which revenues are exchanged through transactions that both parties agree on, taxation is not voluntary. Because the public is required to pay taxes, government officials bear a greater burden to explain how the taxes are spent. This principle is called **transparency**, meaning clear and open. To assure that government dealings are transparent, laws adopted at the federal, state, and local levels require that all information, with a few exceptions, be public, that meetings be announced and take place in public, and that individuals or companies doing business with governmental units bid competitively for that business.

A park district, a public-sector leisure delivery provider, maintains and provides playground equipment for children, among its many duties.

Another challenge in managing governmental units is that public employees have greater rights than do business and nonprofit employees. In most states, public employees cannot be hired and fired by the managers without consent of the elected board. Thus, every employee who is terminated has the right to a board hearing before termination. Like the private sector, the public sector may have employee unions to deal with, which mean another set of rules for hiring and firing employees and giving pay increases.

Boards in the public sector are different, too. The governing boards that levy taxes and approve budget expenditures must be elected. Appointed parks and recreation department boards may have advisory authority with leisure service managers, but only the elected boards have the power to decide. Directors of parks and recreation departments therefore have two boards as their bosses—the city council and their appointed advisory boards. Sometimes leisure service managers have three bosses (city council, park board, and city manager), depending on whether the municipality has a strong mayor–council system or a council–manager system. This arrangement can make managing a public leisure service agency an extremely difficult assignment.

Working for an elected board in an environment where everything that a leisure service manager does is public information adds a dimension of politics to the management process. Although nonprofit leisure service managers might worry about offending potential donors, a governmental leisure service manager who offends a member of the public may find the offended party seeking election to the manager's governing board. Disgruntled employees can run for election as well, and many of each group do.

Another challenge of managing a governmental leisure service agency is that managers need to possess two types of financial management skills. One is the management of tax-supported services, typically the parks, which usually do not have admission fees and are supported entirely by tax revenues. The other is the operation of recreation programs and facilities, which usually generate self-sustaining revenues from user fees. Public-sector managers are therefore running governmental units that provide both tax-supported and fee-supported services in a transparent arena in which disgruntled employees or members of the public can run for their boards.

Skills Required for Managing Government Leisure Service Agencies

The skills required of leisure service public administrators are somewhat different from those required of business or nonprofit managers. Leisure service public administrators have less need to understand economics because governmental units rely heavily on relatively stable tax revenues. Financial management is less important because state governments are stringent about how governmental units handle public funds.

Government accounting is different from business or nonprofit accounting. To maintain the required levels of transparency, governmental units have much more complex accounting rules than do business and nonprofit agencies, which report to the IRS and state departments of revenue and are not required to produce detailed reports. Governmental units report directly to the people, so their reports are more detailed. Such is not always the case in Canada, where public officials often report directly to the Crown or representatives of the Crown.

The skills required of public leisure services managers need to include government accounting, organizational theory, and political science. If the manager oversees the operation of parks only, her or his skills need to include those related to park maintenance and conservation. If the leisure service manager manages recreation programs or facilities, the skills need to be more diverse, including marketing and financial management, as well as skills related to the recreation facility or program.

Managing a leisure service agency in the public sector may seem to be more difficult than managing in the other sectors, so why would someone choose to do it? The answer is that working in the public sector is just as rewarding as working for a nonprofit organization. Serving the public has its intrinsic rewards.

PROFESSIONAL PREPARATION FOR LEISURE SERVICE DELIVERY

Regardless of whether a student seeks a career in the private, nonprofit, or public sector of the leisure service industry, all students should pursue proficiency in certain areas. Previous discussion of the

OUTSTANDING GRADUATES

Background Information

Name: Phil W. Gardner II

Education: Pennsylvania State University, Environmental Interpretation–Outdoor Adventure.

Credentials: Search and rescue field team member and leader (Pennsylvania DCNR); disaster assistance response training; wilderness first responder (WFR); wilderness first aid (WFA) instructor (Red Cross); adult, infant, and child CPR/AED (Red Cross); standard first aid (Red Cross); master educator for Leave No Trace; open water diver (PADI); ACA kayak level 1 instructor.

Special awards: Eagle Scout.

Affiliations: Center for Wilderness Safety, Boy Scouts of America, Leave No Trace, American Canoe Association, Kairos.

Career Information

Position: Recreational specialist.

Organization: Institute of the Great Outdoors is part of the outdoor education division of the Cleveland Metroparks. Our focus is providing not only recreational opportunities to the public but also skill building and education for nearly every outdoor pursuit. Our participants include school-aged kids learning about geocaching, families learning how to prepare for an emergency, and people of all ages taking ACA instructor classes. We also provide these activities to people with disabilities through adaptations to our kayaks and canoes and by providing hand cycles. The current goal is to bring more outdoor recreation to the heart of Cleveland and especially to its youth by leading trips down the Cuyahoga River, which runs right through the city and out into Lake Erie and by creating our new youth watersports camp. Institute of the Great Outdoors (IGO) is at Garfield Park in Garfield Heights, Ohio, and serves as a portion of the recreational component of the Cleveland Metroparks mission.

> *In many ways, we are caretakers and we must take care of those who entrust their time with us and reach those who need a little time away from the stress they put on themselves.*

Job description: I plan, prepare, lead, and evaluate outdoor recreational opportunities, trips, and classes. I listen to the public and gauge their interests, and I offer the opportunity to learn skills. For those who are more adventurous, we take them on overnight tours and provide advanced-level courses. Activities include backpacking, mountain biking, canoeing, kayaking, stand-up paddleboarding, geocaching, survival skills, medical training, and photography. My job also involves maintaining equipment and communicating with people who show interest in doing a program with us and places that wish to host an activity. I also need to look at the bigger picture and see if we are meeting our goals, expectations, and quality of programming and make changes where needed.

Career path: I grew up in the Boy Scouts and eventually found myself working at scout camp. After one year of doing so, it was clear that I had found my calling. After four years of college learning how to teach and lead in the outdoors and three summers of camp, I took a National Outdoor Leadership School's Semester in the Rockies course in Wyoming for three months. That gave me the chance to compare my skills with those of professionals while learning from them directly in the field as we thrived in the mountain snow, canyoneered in Utah, caved in Montana, and climbed in Wyoming. NOLS provided an excellent educational experience to build from and allowed me to set my sites on raising the bar in the activities I was involved in. I returned to complete two more summers of camp as the director of High Adventure, where I was able to promote scouting and outdoor fun and safety to the older scouts who would normally run out of challenges facing leisure service professionals and the skills required of them suggest that every leisure service professional needs to understand how to manage money and people and how government works.

Understanding how to manage money means that leisure service professionals need to understand accounting, so that they can read financial reports. They need to understand financial management, so that they can take appropriate action when their financial reports are not in order. Students seeking to prepare themselves to manage finances should take courses in financial accounting if they seek careers in business or nonprofit leisure service management, or governmental accounting if they seek careers in governmental leisure service management. And all students need to take courses in finance to understand how to manage their budgets.

To prepare for leisure service delivery in all three sectors, students need to take courses in marketing. Marketing teaches how focusing on product (service), price, place, and promotion leads to understanding what the customer needs, how much the customer is willing to pay, where and how the service ought to be provided, and how to communicate its availability to the customer. Understanding these essentials of marketing is crucial not just to leisure for-profit managers but also to nonprofit and government managers.

Political science and public administration courses are essential to students pursuing careers in public-sector leisure service delivery and are useful to those seeking careers in nonprofit and business leisure service delivery. Public-sector managers need to understand how government works if they intend to be successful working in government. But because government creates and regulates business and nonprofit entities, managers in those sectors need to understand what they will face. Government taxes businesses and forces some nonprofit organizations to provide a certain portion of their services as charitable work, suggesting that business and nonprofit leisure service managers would benefit by understanding what makes government tick.

PROFESSIONAL ACCREDITATION

All leisure service professionals need to consider professional accreditation, not only because many agencies require it but also because accreditation teaches some of the skills required for successful careers in the field. The National Recreation and Park Association (NRPA) in the United States, in conjunction with state associations, has developed an accreditation program called the certified park and recreation professional (CPRP) program. Undergraduate students who complete an accredited NRPA curriculum, with the NRPA-prescribed learning outcomes, are eligible to take the accreditation test.

The NRPA also has an accreditation program for agencies provided by the Commission for Accreditation of Park and Recreation Agencies (CAPRA). The CAPRA process is based on 144 standards for national accreditation, which can be awarded only after CAPRA members make an onsite visit to verify eligibility.

If an undergraduate student completes a program that is not NRPA accredited, he or she is required to take continuing education units (CEUs) before taking the exam. After a leisure service professional has obtained a CPRP, he or she is required to take CEUs on a regular basis to maintain accreditation. Continuing education units need to be approved by the NRPA.

SUMMARY

Leisure service delivery systems exist in the private, nonprofit, and governmental sectors of the economy, and they account for a substantial proportion of the national economies of Canada and the United States. As subunits of the leisure service industry, the private sector operates businesses that serve the leisure needs of people by charging fees for services that exceed the costs, nonprofit organizations provide services for fees to some people and waive fees to others, and governmental units levy taxes for services where it is not practical to charge fees and charge fees for leisure services where doing so is practical.

The private leisure service business sector is characterized by innovation. In pursuit of profits, entrepreneurs are alert to new and changing leisure service needs of their customers. Nonprofit sector organizations have other challenges, including fund-raising, as they seek donations to support operations that in many cases serve low-income people who cannot afford to pay fees or make donations. Governmental units provide leisure services that are necessary but cannot be provided by the private and nonprofit sectors, such as parks and open space.

Students who desire to prepare themselves for a leisure service professional career in any of the three sectors need to consider taking business courses, such as accounting, finance, economics, and marketing. They also need to understand government and should study political science and public administration. NRPA-accredited undergrad curricula that teach these learning outcomes allow students to become CPRPs without the necessity of meeting postgraduate continuing education requirements.

For glossary terms, learning experiences, and more, please visit the web resource at **www.HumanKinetics.com/IntroductionToRecreationAndLeisure**

CHAPTER 6

Parks and Protected Areas in Canada and the United States

Paul F.J. Eagles and Jeffrey C. Hallo

"There is nothing so American as our national parks. . . . The fundamental idea behind the parks . . . is that the country belongs to the people, that it is in process of making for the enrichment of the lives of all of us."

Franklin D. Roosevelt,
U.S. president, 1933-1945

"The day will come when the population of Canada will be ten times as great as it is now but the national parks ensure that every Canadian . . . will still have free access to vast areas possessing some of the finest scenery in Canada, in which the beauty of the landscape is protected from profanation, the natural wild animals, plants and forests preserved, and the peace and solitude of primeval nature retained."

James Harkin, Dominion Parks Commission for Canada, director of the first national park agency in the world, 1911-1936

LEARNING OUTCOMES

After reading this chapter, you should be able to do the following:

> Describe the history and development of Canadian and American park systems, as well as their similarities and differences
> Differentiate and discuss various types of parks and other protected areas
> Name and describe the accomplishments of a few of the most prominent people who promoted and created parks through history
> Summarize current issues and trends in park resources management
> Define the terms *preservation*, *wilderness*, *conservation*, *multiple use*, and *wise use of natural resources and parks*
> Explain a few career opportunities in park settings

INTRODUCTION

Parks and other protected areas are important parts of the cultures of Canada and the United States. Just mentioning a national park, **wildlife refuge**, or wilderness evokes strong feelings among many citizens and foreign tourists. This chapter presents the history and a current description of the major park systems and other protected areas in the United States and Canada.

The term *park* is derived from the Old French and Middle English term *parc*, which means "an enclosed piece of ground stocked with beasts of the chase, held by prescription or by the king's grant" (Runte, 2010). One of the first parklike areas was the Greek *agora*, which were plazas established and used for public assembly. Today, however, parks and other protected areas may be defined as places set aside to protect and provide for the use and enjoyment of natural, cultural, historic, or recreational resources. The movement to create parks and protected areas that emerged in the late 1800s and continues strongly to this day was driven by society's need to reconnect with nature after having been removed from it because of industrialization and technological advancement.

Modern parks in the United States and Canada reflect our ideals of democracy and are managed for public use and enjoyment. Parks provide a place for the public to escape the stresses of life, to rejuvenate, and to connect with nature and history. Parks in one form or another exist in every country in the world, which indicates their critical role in society.

Their purpose may be particularly crucial in the United States and Canada, where well over a billion visits occur annually to local, state, provincial, and national parks. A substantial body of research has shown that parks and other protected areas aid substantially in child development, public health, economic growth, and quality of life. Parks also serve a critical function in protecting and ensuring the long-term sustainability of plants, wildlife, fish, historic or cultural sites, geology, and natural processes (e.g., bird migration routes and the filtration of water).

This chapter contains two major discussions. First is an outline of the situation in Canada. Second is a similar outline for the United States. Those sections are followed by a summary and comparison between the two countries.

HISTORY OF PARKS IN CANADA

Canada is a large country composed of 10 provinces and 3 territories. The nation was created when four British colonies came together to form a country through confederation in 1867. Over time, other colonies joined to create new provinces, and other provinces were created from territories. Starting in 1885 the national government started to create a national park system in Canada with the creation of a park in the Rocky Mountains. This park ultimately became Canada's most famous national park, Banff National Park. Also starting in 1885 the province of Ontario, Canada's most populous province, purchased land near Niagara Falls for the creation of a park and tourist destination. This site was the first major park created by a province in Canada. These two parks were the start of the development of the national and **provincial park** systems in Canada.

As the country grew, the provinces retained considerable land management responsibility. One important power was the ownership and management of all crown land, or public land as it is called in the United States. Because the provinces owned the crown land within the provincial boundaries, creating parks was relatively easy for them. Conversely, the federal government could not easily create parks within provinces because provincial cooperation was required. Therefore, some of the provincial park systems in Canada are as large and prominent as the **national park** systems in many other countries.

First Parks in Canada

The first parks created in Canada were in cities. The movement to form city parks was strongly influenced by the British experience in England. The large, green central parks of London, for example,

were well known to the early populace of Canada and became a model for park creation in British North America.

In 1763 the lieutenant governor of the British Colony of Nova Scotia granted the Halifax Common, former military land, to the city of Halifax. It was first used as community pasture and for military exercises. The Halifax Common later became city parkland and is now located in the heart of the city. It is recognized as the first park to be created in Canada.

Toronto was the first city in British North America to formally create urban parks and a public agency to manage those parks. After eight years of operation, Toronto's Committee on Public Walks and Gardens, the name of Canada's first park management agency, took political action in front of the elected city council to forward the idea of urban parks. The chairman of the committee spoke at a Toronto City Council meeting in 1859 and stated the following:

In the first place, they furnish to the wealthy places of agreeable resort, either for driving or walking, and free from exposure

The creation of Banff National Park, the first national park in Canada, was influenced by the Canadian Pacific Railway, which saw the promise of tourism.

to the heat and dust of an ordinary road . . . thus enabling them to enjoy the inestimable blessing of the free open air of the Country—so conducive to the promotion of health and morality.

In the second place, to the mechanic and working classes, Public Grounds are of incalculable advantage. How much better it is for the families of such to have these places of recreation and healthful exercise, than to have them exposed on the crowded streets of the city? (as cited in McFarland, 1982, p. 258)

As seen in this speech, the committee assumed the responsibility for providing "public grounds" for all classes of society, especially for the working class who badly needed access to "places of agreeable resort," free of charge. This public-spirited and socialistic approach to parks—public use subsidized by community taxes—became a fundamental aspect of park management in Canada.

Over the next 150 years, virtually every city and town in Canada created parks for the welfare, use, and health of its citizens. The municipalities funded these parks from income earned by **land taxes** and provided most of the parks and their facilities free to local citizens who wished to use them.

In the initial days, city parks were managed by volunteers working on parks boards. Starting in the early decades of the 20th century, some staff members were hired to manage special facilities, such as agricultural fairs and sports grounds. Not until the 1960s did universities and colleges in Canada start to train people specifically for working in parks and recreation in cities. The first program of this type in Canada was the Department of Recreation at the University of Waterloo, which took in its first students in 1968.

Provincial and National Parks

The origin of provincial and national parks can be traced to the 1880s and occurred simultaneously

Niagara Falls parks in Ontario were created in 1885 to manage a major international tourism activity.

in Niagara Falls in Ontario and on the remote mountain pass of the Bow Valley in the Northwest Territories of western Canada.

From the beginning of European settlement, Niagara Falls attracted tourists. Because the Niagara River and Niagara Falls are located in both the United States (New York) and Canada (Ontario), cross-border discussions were necessary to determine how to manage this rapidly developing tourism development. The Canadian side of the river had the best view of the falls, and by 1885 every possible view was privately owned. Entrepreneurs charged fees for visitors to enter their premises to look out windows at the magnificent waterfalls and cataracts. One planning idea proposed by people in New York in the early 1880s was to create reserves and organize tourism management institutions to develop public parks and foster cooperation between the two countries. Ontario adopted the idea and asked the Canadian government to fund and operate the Canadian portion of a park and tourism reserve. The idea was to create a national park on the Canadian side of the river by buying out all the private properties and replacing them with a properly designed park and tourism facility. The vast expense of the proposed land purchase and park development incited opposition from members of the national Parliament from the province of Quebec and the Maritime provinces. They objected to large amounts of federal money being spent in Ontario on this development. In 1885 Ontario moved alone to create a major park and tourism facility along the Niagara River and Niagara Falls. This action involved the purchase and removal of thousands of buildings on the lip of the falls and the gorge and the creation of a green parkway available for all to use. The Ontario Parliament also passed legislation for the creation of the Niagara Parks Commission, a park and tourism management body (Seibel, 1995).

The Ontario provincial government actions at Niagara set precedents in three important areas. First, Niagara was the first park created by a provincial government in Canada and had the first stand-alone park management agency with its own legislation and mandate. Second, the park stimulated the creation of future parks in Ontario by the provincial government, not the national government. It also set a tone of American–Canadian cooperation in park

management. All three movements continued and strengthened in subsequent years. This textbook is an example of the ongoing sharing of ideas and cooperation in park management.

Simultaneous to the debates over Niagara in Ontario, the government of Canada pushed the first national cross-country railway through the Rocky Mountains. When hot springs were discovered near the railway tracks in the Bow Valley in the eastern Rocky Mountains, the potential for tourism was quickly recognized. The national government acted through a cabinet order in 1885 to reserve the hot springs for public use. This action was followed in 1887 by formal federal legislation to create Rocky Mountain Park, Canada's first national park, later renamed Banff National Park. This national government activity started the federal government of Canada in the parks business. Rocky Mountain Park in Canada became the third national park in the world, after Yellowstone National Park in the United States, created in 1872, and Royal National Park in the British Colony of New South Wales, now a state of Australia, created in 1879 (Marty, 1984).

In 1887 Canada's federal government created North American's first wildlife conservation reserve at Last Mountain Lake in the Northwest Territories, now Saskatchewan. This small reserve was established to protect the nesting and migration habitat of wildlife in the Canadian prairies (Foster, 1978). This reserve became the first of many national wildlife areas and migratory bird sanctuaries created by the national government in Canada.

In 1893 Ontario made the next important move by creating Algonquin National Park. This huge area of forested and rocky hills, lakes, and rivers became a forest conservation area and park. The government wanted to manage the logging industry in this area, protect the headwaters of five important rivers, and stop farmers from clearing the Algonquin highland forests. This creation of a large conservation park along the American national park model by a provincial government was a first for Canada. It set a precedent for Ontario and other provinces (Killan, 1993; Saunders, 1998). The name was changed to Algonquin Provincial Park in 1913, giving notice that the parks operated by provinces were unique and separate from those operated by the national government (i.e., national parks).

Algonquin Provincial Park in Ontario became a model for provincial park creation across Canada.

By 1900 the die was cast in Canada. The initial debates and decisions coalesced into precedents that would guide future park creation and management across the country. After this date, cities and towns throughout the country saw park creation as a normal and expected activity. Provincial governments created regional parks for specific tourism and resource management concerns in regional geographical areas. Provincial parks were increasingly created for **conservation** and tourism purposes. Two types of federal reserves were established: national parks and national wildlife areas. The signing of the Migratory Bird Treaty with the United States in 1916 gave the federal government a powerful tool to regulate waterfowl and bird hunting. This action also gave this government the power to deal with wildlife management all over the country.

Over the next century, these emerging approaches strengthened and deepened. Many more parks and reserves were created. Management institutions were created. Canadians used and appreciated these areas in increasing numbers. In the 20th century, parks became a central part of the life of all Canadians and were to become a major part of the culture of the country. After World War II a massive expansion in auto ownership and increasing prosperity lead to a vast increase in outdoor recreation, spurring increased park creation across the country.

Long-Distance Hiking Trails

In Canada the provincial governments do not have a formal role in the creation or management of long-distance hiking trails. Nevertheless, Canada has a large number of long-distance hiking trails, all of which are operated by nongovernmental organizations, typically called trail clubs. The oldest trail is the Bruce Trail in southern Ontario, which runs along the Niagara Escarpment from Niagara Falls in the south to Tobermory in the north on the Bruce Peninsula. This trail was opened in 1967, Canada's centennial. Initially, the trail was almost entirely on private land, but over time many landowners stopped giving permission for public use of their land, so the trail is now on a combination of private land, parkland, and land owned by trail clubs. The Canadian long-distance trail movement was heavily influenced by earlier trail activities in the United States, especially the Appalachian Trail.

The most ambitious trail effort in Canada is that of the Trans Canada Trail. The creation of this trail is ongoing, and the goal is a national trail from Newfoundland across Canada to the west coast, and including a branch north to the Yukon, for a total length of 22,500 kilometers (14,000 mi). The trail also involves a water route from central Alberta to the Arctic Ocean. The trail was 73 percent complete by 2010 (Trans Canada Trail, 2011).

National Heritage Rivers System

Canada has a national heritage rivers system that is cooperatively managed by the provinces and the federal government. The system contains 41 rivers. The goal of the system is to promote, protect, and enhance Canada's river heritage and ensure that Canada's leading rivers are managed in a sustainable manner (Leduc, 2009). The system has no legal mandate and is entirely cooperative among governments.

Wilderness in Canada (1600-2005)

In Canada, the concept of establishing large areas of uninhabited lands as designated wilderness is largely restricted to national and provincial parks. This situation is markedly different from that in the United States, and reasons for the differences are important. In summary, in Canada aboriginal land rights are respected, meaning that the creation of parks or wilderness sites involves negotiation with aboriginal peoples who have land rights according to the Canadian constitution. In Canada outside of some parks, all land is influenced by the land rights of aboriginal people. Very little land is considered vacant. A brief summary of the history of this situation follows.

After the American Revolution the British government formed alliances with many of the aboriginal groups, for political and military reasons, that lived in the area that is now Canada. One of the major reasons for these alliances was the shared concern of the British government and the aboriginal peoples of the expansionist nature of the aggressive United States to the south. Shared actions were in both their interests to preserve independence. Because the British needed the military prowess of the many aboriginal people, their land rights were recognized and supported.

Therefore, the wilderness in Canada contains aboriginal people. It was a living landscape composed of forests, rivers, wildlife, and native people. In the United States the situation was much different. Native people were removed from the land and placed into reservations, thereby creating the mythology that the area was wilderness, land without people. Therefore, widespread support never arose in Canada for the classical American view of wilderness, large expanses of land without people. Canada's wilderness contains people. These are the substantive reasons why the American wilderness concept, outside of national parks, has never gained much traction in Canada.

Important People in Canadian Parks

During the 1870s and 1880s Sir Sandford Fleming was the engineer in charge of the construction of the Canadian Pacific Railway, which was built to link the industrial eastern provinces through the open prairies to the west coast province of British Columbia. In an attempt to increase the use of his developing railway, Fleming proposed a series of national parks across Canada for the purpose of creating tourism demand and railway use. The discovery of thermal springs in the Bow Valley in the Rocky Mountains in 1883 provided an opportunity for the national government of Prime Minister John A. Macdonald to create the first of Fleming's proposed parks. Therefore, Fleming, a railway engineer, and Macdonald, a powerful politician, were central figures in the creation of Canada's first national park in 1885, now known as Banff National Park.

In 1887 the federal government of Canada created the first bird sanctuary in North America. Areas around Last Mountain Lake in the Northwest Territories, now Saskatchewan, were withdrawn from settlement and set aside for the breeding of waterfowl. The creation of this reserve was the work of Edgar Dewdney, then the lieutenant governor of the Northwest Territories. He feared that the extension of the railway into this area would destroy the wildlife habitat. The creation of this wildlife reserve set the precedent for the national government to set aside areas for wildlife conservation.

Starting in 1885 Alexander Kirkwood, a clerk in the Ontario Department of Crown Lands, lobbied for the creation of a national forest and park in the Algonquin Highlands of southern Ontario. His idea slowly gained the support of other government officials, influential members of the community, and ultimately elected officials. In 1893 the government of Ontario created Algonquin National Park, later renamed Algonquin Provincial Park. This action created the first large provincial park in Canada based on the emerging American model of large, uninhabited wilderness reserves. The Algonquin Indian people retained hunting rights in the park, but never lived there because of its inhospitable environment in winter. This action set in motion events that resulted in the creation of thousands of provincial parks in all Canadian provinces.

In 1911 the government of Canada created the Parks Branch, the first national park management agency in the world, and appointed James Harkin as the Dominion Parks commissioner. Harkin was an aggressive supporter of park creation and management. He was a strong supporter of parks, wilderness values, and tourism. He set out to attract Canadians to national parks and to ensure that national parks became cultural icons that rivaled the historic sites and art in Europe. He was famously successful in his goals, and as a result, he is recognized as the person who started the movement to make national parks the cultural icons that they are today.

These five people, Fleming, Macdonald, Dewdney, Kirkwood, and Harkin, set in motion ideas that resulted in Canada's national and provincial park systems. Two of these people were politicians, and three were government employees. Although many of their ideas can be traced to England and the United States, they adapted them to Canadian reality. Note the influence of politicians and government employees in this movement, which reflects that the Canadian style of government, largely borrowed from Britain, involves a powerful and professional civil service reporting to elected politicians. Notably absent from the Canadian experience (unlike the American park movement described later) are writers, artists, and scholars. A possible exception to this rule is Sir Sandford Fleming, the railroad engineer, who was also a planner, author, and civil servant.

PARK SYSTEMS OF CANADA

By 1900 the form of the emerging park systems in Canada was set with four types of parks: city parks, regional parks, provincial parks, and federal national parks and federal wildlife areas. All over the country, towns and cities made park creation and management a normal role of government. In some provinces special regional park agencies were set up to manage parks, usually around geographical features such as rivers or lakes. All provincial governments moved forward in creating provincial park systems, often in active competition with the emerging national park system. Over the years successive Canadian governments worked slowly but diligently to add to the two major federal systems, the national parks and the national wildlife areas.

City Parks

Parks are located in virtually every village, town, and city in Canada. They fulfill many functions—sport, recreation, and health being particularly important. In the 1980s some cities added conservation of natural lands to these functions. Today, city parks are a mixture of recreation, parks, and green space.

Most city parks are managed by a parks and recreation department, part of the municipal government. This department is responsible for facility construction, park maintenance, and recreation programs. Advisory groups, sports organizations, and volunteers are hallmarks of municipal parks and recreation management. Park management at the municipal level is operated by professional managers, specialized part-time employees, and many volunteers.

Land taxes pay for most municipal park management. Some recreation service fees are used for special-purpose activities, such as renting a community hall or paying for sport lessons. Therefore, city park management is funded from a combination of land taxes and use fees.

No national inventory of the number and size of municipal parks exists in Canada. The amount of land used for parks in cities varies from a small percentage of the city land area to nearly 40 percent. Examples include Stanley Park in Vancouver, a large natural park on the ocean near the downtown of the city; Victoria Park in Kitchener, a traditional city park of trees, lawns, gardens and statues located downtown in the city; and Pleasant Point Park in Halifax, a park with impressive lawns and gardens.

Regional Parks

In Canada provincial governments often create regional park agencies to fulfill both conservation and recreation mandates. The province of Ontario has the most extensive system of regional parks in the country. Over many decades the Parliament of Ontario passed legislation to create regional park agencies to establish and manage park systems in specific areas of the province. The Niagara Parks Commission manages parks in the Niagara River and Falls area, the St. Lawrence Parks Commission in the St. Lawrence River area, and the Lake St. Clair Parks Commission in the St. Clair Parks area. The Niagara Parks has one of the highest park visitation rates in the world, as many as 16 million visitors per year. The Ontario Parliament also passed legislation to create regional planning bodies that coordinate the conservation and management of specific landscape features. The best example of this is the Niagara Escarpment Commission, which coordinates planning and conservation over the Niagara Escarpment that runs through southern Ontario from Niagara Falls in the south to the Bruce Peninsula in the mid-north. The creation of this commission was strongly influenced by users of the Bruce Hiking Trail, which weaves throughout the Niagara Escarpment lands.

Unique in Canada, Ontario provincial legislation encourages and provides for the creation of 36 conservation authorities that manage watersheds in the populated areas of the province. Each of these local government authorities oversees a park system, largely composed of water management projects such as dams, river valley protection areas, and wetlands. Many of these conservation areas are close to large cities and are therefore important for providing outdoor recreation near urban areas. Ontario conservation authorities serve about five million **visitor days** of outdoor recreation each year on 250 conservation areas. These parks are typically located close to urban areas and serve a valuable near-urban outdoor recreation function. They also have a major role in providing environmental education sites for local schools.

Provincial Parks

Every province and territory in Canada has a provincial or territorial park system, but the size and use of the systems vary considerably. Some provinces, for example, British Columbia, Alberta, and Ontario, developed large and well-used provincial park systems. Other provinces, such as New Brunswick, Newfoundland, and Prince Edward Island, oversee small systems. These differences result from the history and political cultures of each province.

The wealthier and more heavily populated provinces created large provincial park systems for the public, predominantly for the middle- and upper-middle-class members of their societies, while concurrently discouraging federal efforts to create parks in their provinces. The poorer provinces encouraged the national government to meet the demand for parks by funding, creating, and managing national parks in their provinces. This approach ensured that federal tax dollars rather than provincial tax dollars were spent on parks.

National Parks and Wildlife Areas

The national park system in Canada is large, popular, well funded, and growing. Because most Canadians have grown up visiting Canada's national parks or at least hearing about them and seeing them in the media, national parks in Canada became national cultural icons. In the 1930s and 1940s the mountain parks were backdrops for many popular Hollywood movies. This exposure created a positive profile in the minds of both Canadians and Americans that helped create a boom in tourism that continues today. The national parks are one of Canada's premier international tourism destinations.

As of 2011 Canada had 42 national parks and national park reserves. More national parks are proposed and under land-claim discussions with aboriginal groups; therefore, more parks will be created in the coming years (Parks Canada, 2011a). Parks Canada, the federal park management agency, is responsible for four park and reserve systems: national parks and reserves, national historic parks and sites, national canals, and national marine conservation areas. The Canadian Wildlife Service with Environment Canada is responsible for two park and reserve systems: national wildlife areas and migratory bird sanctuaries.

National parks in Canada are created according to a system plan that calls for at least one national park in each major biogeographic regions of the country (see figure 6.1). This plan divides the entire country into 39 easily recognizable biogeographic regions, such as the Pacific Coast Mountains, the Prairie Grasslands, and the Hudson-James Bay Lowlands. This approach is ecologically sound in that the park creation is based on the existing biogeography of the country. This approach ensures that national parks are created in all regions of the country. Parks Canada was one of the first park agencies in the world to develop such a system plan, and the system plan idea subsequently spread all over the world.

The number of national parks continues to increase in Canada as the demands of the system plan are fulfilled. Most of these new national parks are in the arctic and subarctic, but substantial new parks have been created in the populated southern areas of British Columbia and Ontario.

The national parks attract approximately 26 million **person visits** per year. Because national park visitors tend to stay for more than two days each visit, the total number of visitor days is more than 50 million per year. The highly popular mountain parks of Banff, Jasper, Kootenay, and Yoho attract the most visitors. Those four parks combined serve approximately 7 million person visits per year, or more than 15 million visitor days. Some of the remote northern parks receive fewer than 1,000 visitors per year.

Canada also has an extensive system of national historic parks and sites. Historic sites are chosen according to a national historic sites system plan. The goal of this plan is to represent the country's important historic and cultural themes within the park and site system. The plan has five themes:

1. Peopling the land
2. Developing economies
3. Building social and community life
4. Expressing intellectual and cultural life
5. Governing Canada

All historic sites and parks are commemorated within one of those broad themes. To be recommended for designation, a site, person, or event must have had a nationally significant effect on, or illustrate a nationally important aspect of, the history of Canada. Places designated as national historic sites are occasionally acquired by the federal government for protection and interpretation. Of the 849 national historic sites, Parks Canada administers 140 and contributes money to others managed by other governments or organizations. Parks Canada serves approximately 10 million visitors per year at the 140 sites that it manages. The number of yearly visitors to these sites varies dramatically, from 3.6 million person visits to the historic fortifications of Quebec City to a few hundred person visits to historic sites in the far north of the country.

Parks Canada also manages a series of historic canals. These canals were original built for military purposes but are now used for recreation and are extremely popular with boaters. The Trent-Severn Waterway in southern Ontario serves approximately 1.5 million person visits per year.

Parks Canada has the responsibility, shared with the Fisheries and Oceans Canada and the Canadian Wildlife Service, to create a system of national marine conservation areas. These areas are found off the Atlantic, Arctic, and Pacific coasts of Canada. Major reserves are also planned in the Great Lakes area. As of 2011 Parks Canada has created only four such reserves, but many more are planned.

The Canadian Wildlife Service manages two large national systems: national wildlife areas and national migratory bird sanctuaries. The national wildlife area system in Canada is large, poorly funded, and not well known by the Canadian public. Fifty-one national wildlife areas are scattered across Canada (Nature Canada, 2011). These sites are important for migratory birds, both for nesting and migratory stopover. The national wildlife areas have just 100,000 visitor days of use per year. The visitation rates at the 92 sites in Canada's national migratory bird sanctuary system are not documented and therefore cannot be reported. The very low visitation and tourism profile of these wildlife areas leads to a low political profile in Canada.

Canada's National Parks System Plan

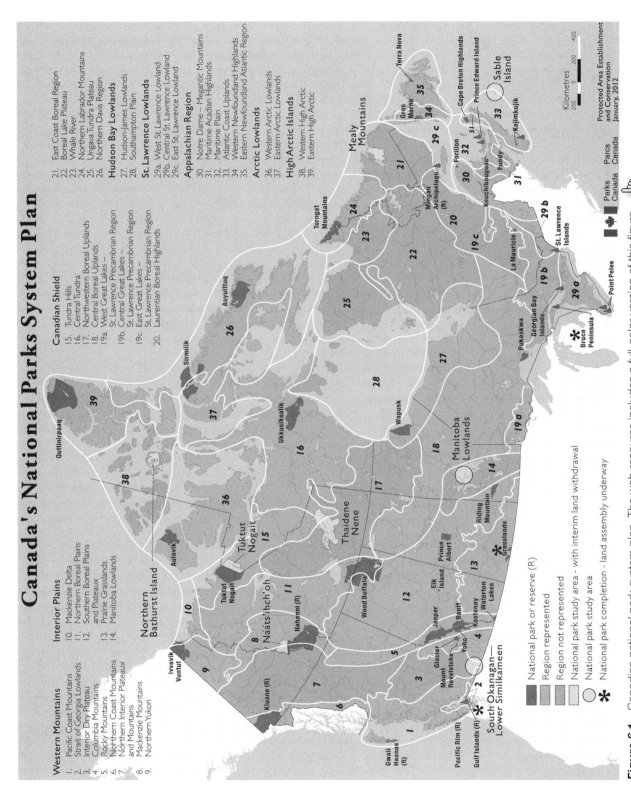

Western Mountains
1. Pacific Coast Mountains
2. Strait of Georgia Lowlands
3. Interior Dry Plateau
4. Columbia Mountains
5. Rocky Mountains
6. Northern Coast Mountains and Mountains
7. Northern Interior Plateaux and Mountains
8. Mackenzie Mountains
9. Northern Yukon

Interior Plains
10. Mackenzie Delta
11. Northern Boreal Plains
12. Southern Boreal Plains and Plateaux
13. Prairie Grasslands
14. Manitoba Lowlands

Canadian Shield
15. Tundra Hills
16. Central Tundra
17. Northwestern Boreal Uplands
18. Central Boreal Uplands
19a. West Great Lakes – St. Lawrence Precambrian Region
19b. Central Great Lakes – St. Lawrence Precambrian Region
19c. East Great Lakes – St. Lawrence Precambrian Region
20. Laurentian Boreal Highlands
21. East Coast Boreal Region
22. Boreal Lake Plateau
23. Whale River
24. Northern Labrador Mountains
25. Ungava Tundra Plateau
26. Northern Davis Region

Hudson Bay Lowlands
27. Hudson-James Lowlands
28. Southampton Plain

St. Lawrence Lowlands
29a. West St. Lawrence Lowland
29b. Central St. Lawrence Lowland
29c. East St. Lawrence Lowland

Appalachian Region
30. Notre Dame – Megantic Mountains
31. Maritime Acadian Highlands
32. Maritime Plain
33. Atlantic Coast Uplands
34. Western Newfoundland Highlands
35. Eastern Newfoundland Atlantic Region

Arctic Lowlands
36. Western Arctic Lowlands
37. Eastern Arctic Lowlands

High Arctic Islands
38. Western High Arctic
39. Eastern High Arctic

National park or reserve (R)
Region represented
Region not represented
National park study area - with interim land withdrawal
National park study area
National park completion - land assembly underway

Figure 6.1 Canadian national park system plan. The web resource includes a full-color version of this figure.

Reprinted, by permission, from The Canadian National Park System plan. Available: www.pc.gc.ca/eng/docs/v-g/nation/index.aspx.

103

Summary

The differences between the Parks Canada systems and the Wildlife Service systems are vast. The national parks, national historic parks, and heritage canals focus on both conservation and tourism. Canadians are encouraged to visit through excellent information sources, tourism facilities, and programs. As a result, the public profile is high, visitation is high, and the government responds with substantial funds. The wildlife areas, in contrast, focus on wildlife conservation. Recreation is not encouraged, with the exception of some hunting and fishing. As a result, the public profile is low, visitation is low, and the government provides limited management funds. This situation suggests that for a park system to obtain sufficient government funds to be managed effectively, it must have a positive public profile and a clientele that is mobilized to support the parks politically. Many people argue that a park or reserve with low visitation has fewer management stresses and therefore has more effective conservation. This position ignores the many stresses that occur in such a reserve besides recreation, including poaching, nearby resource extraction, illegal logging, destructive farming, all-terrain vehicle use, and many other resource-damaging activities. Such stresses can be effectively curtailed only if the reserve has sufficient funds, staff, and political support. This example from Canada shows that without tourism, political support does not exist and therefore government funds are not allocated, resulting in few or no management staff.

Canada has a tremendous range of diversity in the management approaches used in park management. The institutions used include (1) a government agency largely funded from taxes (e.g., Parks Canada), (2) a stand-alone government agency that functions like a private corporation (e.g., the Niagara Parks Commission), (3) a government agency that has a few supervisory staff but uses private corporations to provide most of the public services (e.g., British Columbia Provincial Parks), (4) a nonprofit organization that functions like a private corporation and provides all park services (two national historic parks and some provincial parks in Ontario are operated using this approach), and (5) a mixture of public agencies and private operations that uses both public funding and tourism fees and charges. This range of management approaches is an important area of park management that needs further investigation by scholars in the parks and recreation field. This diversity of activity reveals that park managers of the future in Canada need to have a broad background in business as well as cultural and natural resource management.

Over the last decade, park funding has varied among jurisdictions. For example, major reductions occurred in the provincial parks' budgets in Alberta and British Columbia. The large system in Ontario saw budget increases in accordance with large increases in parkland area and visitation (Eagles, 2005). The national parks saw major increases in budget along with substantial growth in the numbers of national parks. In all jurisdictions, the trend was toward increased use of tourism fees and charges to fund part of parkland management. The Canadian provincial parks did not suffer the massive budget cuts that were experienced by the American state parks in the same period.

Parks, reserves, and other types of protected areas exist because of the acceptance and approval of society and therefore of government. For the sites to exist and be effectively managed, political support must be sufficient to counter the many societal forces that would see these lands used for other purposes. Parks need to be used and appreciated by substantial numbers of citizens.

HISTORY OF PARKS IN THE UNITED STATES

The history of parks in the United States illustrates a combination of concern for the social and psychological well-being of children and adults, the conservation and **preservation** of natural areas as the country developed and resource extraction and urbanization accelerated, and the evolution of natural areas as attractions that spurred tourism business opportunities. Improvements in transportation, the rise of the middle class, the recognition of the need for workers to renew and refresh themselves, and the fascination with the natural world increased the demand for parks and protected natural areas (Sears, 1980).

City Parks and Playgrounds

As early American cities began to grow with an influx of immigrants and prosperity brought on by the industrial movement, awareness grew of a need for public parks in the bustling, increasingly congested, and hygienically challenged cities such as Boston, New York, Chicago, and Philadelphia. Thus began a period from about 1850 to the 1930s when American cities built city parks and playgrounds for the public (Cavallo, 1981; Young, 2004). Most notable among these was Frederick Law Olmsted and Calvin Vaux's plan to landscape Central Park in New York City. Olmsted felt strongly about the concept of park access for people as a demonstration of democratic principles. Olmsted believed that parks could serve as meeting grounds for people of different backgrounds and classes, unlike other developed spaces in cities that were highly stratified by social class. He also believed that great parks and open space in cities were evidence of the progressiveness of American democracy (Rybczynski, 1999). Olmsted went on to play a role in designing, planning, and building major city parks in or around Boston; Atlanta; Riverside, Illinois; Chicago; Buffalo; and Niagara Falls, New York.

Federal Conservation Initiatives

Early federal protection of natural areas dates back to 1832 when the federal government created the Hot Springs Reservation in Arkansas as a protected area for the use of Native Americans, people traveling through on their way west, and local residents. The site was later redesignated as a national park in 1921. The first national park in the world, Yellowstone, designated by President Grant in 1872 in the territories of Montana and Wyoming, was clearly an idea ahead of its time, made possible by the incredible confluence of natural features present at Yellowstone and the prescience of prominent citizens and scientists who led expeditions into the area in 1869 through 1871 and proposed the creation of a park. The idea also received considerable support from the corporate leaders of the Northern Pacific Railroad, who understood the potential of the park to attract tourists (Runte, 2010). Progress at creating federal parks and protected areas was

Yellowstone National Park in Wyoming contains significant geothermal features that are viewed by millions of people each year.

at first slow; by the turn of the century, only five national parks had been designated and three of those were related to California redwood or sequoia forests. Among them was Yosemite National Park, designated by the U.S. Congress in 1890. The seed of the idea for national parks had been sown in the 1800s but needed time and leadership to grow.

Although national parks were created in the 1800s and early 1900s, no federal park agency was in place to lead the charge for preservation of parklands or outdoor recreation. After years of advocating for such an agency by people such as Frederick Law Olmsted, Horace McFarland, Henry Barker, and Stephen Mather, Congress passed the law creating the National Park Service (NPS) in August 1916 (National Park Service, 2003). Stephen Mather, a Chicago businessman, was named the first director of the NPS. Congress transferred the management of historic sites, army forts, battlefields, cemeteries, and monuments to the newly created NPS as well as the existing national parks and national monuments. Substantial growth in the number of national park sites occurred, but use waned during the Great Depression (1929-1939) and U.S. involvement in World War II (1941-1945). The Civilian Conservation Corps (CCC) (1933-1941) employed about 3 million young men in many public works projects and was instrumental in building hundreds of roads, trails, campgrounds, visitor centers, and water systems that exist today in national and state parks.

Strong leadership for national government involvement in conservation came from President Theodore Roosevelt. In less than eight years as president he created six national parks and supported the passage of the Antiquities Act of 1906, which created 16 national monuments (including the Grand Canyon). Over the years presidents have used this act to take bold and often controversial conservation action by creating national monuments without congressional approval. Two major figures were advisors to President Roosevelt: Gifford Pinchot, scientific conservationist and head of what became the USDA Forest Service and founder of the Society of American Foresters, and John Muir, ardent preservationist, Sierra Club founder, writer, and lobbyist for wilderness and parks (Ehrlich, 2000; Keene, 1994; Miller, 2004; Zaslowsky & Watkins, 1994).

Two other realms of conservation, wildlife and forests, also benefited from federal action during Roosevelt's time. Teddy Roosevelt used executive orders to create 51 bird reservations during his presidency, and he established the Pelican Island National Wildlife Refuge in 1903. This was the beginning of a system of national wildlife refuges. Their primary function is to preserve habitat and migration routes for wildlife (particularly waterfowl), but they also allow wildlife-related recreation such as hunting, fishing, and bird watching. Roosevelt also created the U.S. Forest Service in 1905 and set aside 148 million acres (60 million ha) as national forests. Although national forests were at the time primarily viewed as a place to manage timber resource, they are now heavily used and managed for outdoor recreation.

All these efforts at creating protected natural areas, along with the increasing urbanization of the country, the increasing popularity of automobiles, and the expansion of the roads associated with them, starting in about 1910, gradually increased the pressure on national park and national forest managers to provide access, accommodations, campgrounds, and information for an increasing number of visitors (Belasco, 1979). The "See America First" patriotic movement generated public interest in America's natural wonders (Shaffer, 2001), and rangers began to expand their focus from protecting resources to accommodating and educating larger numbers of recreationists and visitors. This activity foreshadowed a massive expansion in travel and outdoor recreation that took place following the end of World War II.

State Park Initiatives

Several states initiated efforts to protect natural areas for public use such as Massachusetts' Great Pond Act (1641); Georgia's Indian Springs (1825); New York's off-and-on attempts to protect the scenic attributes of Niagara Falls, culminating in state acquisition in 1885; and California's failed attempt to support a Yosemite State Park, starting in 1864. According to Landrum (2004), in addition to Niagara Falls, other early **state parks** that have remained successful include Texas' San Jacinto Battleground State Historic Site (1883), Minnehaha Falls Park (1885) and Itasca State Park in Minnesota (1891), Miller State Park in New Hampshire (1891), and New York's Adirondack State Park (1892). Each park's story typically involved local proponents who were persistent and creative in garnering support. Stephen Mather saw one of his challenges to be maintaining the quality of the national park system. He was concerned about attempts to designate parks of little national significance as national parks, and he became a prime sponsor of a national conference in 1920 that promoted the idea of a system of parks that would come under the domain of each state. Although it is unclear who proposed it, the idea of creating a park every 100 miles (160 km) (the distance that automobiles at that time typically traveled in a day) for the public to enjoy and camp in appeared, and it was suggested that this goal was clearly more appropriate for state parks to fulfill (Landrum, 2004). The idea developed that state parks should preserve representative environments, preferably scenic or historical and cultural sites, typical of each state to provide outdoor recreation areas closer to home for local residents and for tourists.

Trail Initiatives

In 1921 Benton MacKaye, a forester and planner, proposed a foot trail along the Appalachian ridges from the highest mountain in the north,

Mount Katahdin in Maine, to the highest peak at the southern end, Springer Mountain in Georgia, passing through 12 other states along the way. The approximately 2,150-mile (3,460 km) Appalachian Trail was completed in 1937. The National Trails Systems Act of 1968, which gave the NPS the responsibility of overseeing the Appalachian Trail, provided funds to start the process of purchasing the entire trail and buffering it where possible with federal land. The act also designated three types of trails: national recreation trails; national scenic trails; and connecting, or side, trails. The act designated the Appalachian Trail and the Pacific Crest Trail (stretching from the Mexican border to the Canadian border along the mountain ranges of the Pacific Coast states) as national scenic trails. As of 2011, amendments to the act have created 30 national scenic trails and national historic trails, and over 1,000 national recreation trails in all of the 50 states, most in or near urban areas. National park systems maps can be viewed at www.nps.gov/hfc/cfm/carto-detail.cfm?Alpha=nps#.

Another form of trail parks is located along rivers. In 1968 the Wild and Scenic Rivers Act was passed to protect free-flowing (not dammed) rivers, thereby

Adirondack State Park in New York State, one of the oldest state parks in the United States, contains a mixture of public and private land.

assuring that white-water recreational opportunities such as kayaking and rafting could be protected. Three categories of rivers were established: wild rivers, scenic rivers, and recreational rivers. The differences were based on different levels of access, primitiveness, and shoreline development; wild rivers were the most pristine. On the 40th anniversary of this act in 2008, 11,000 miles (17,700 km) of 166 rivers in 38 states and Puerto Rico were protected. Most rivers are managed by the agency that manages the land through which the river flows, usually the USDA Forest Service, NPS, Bureau of Land Management, or U.S. Fish and Wildlife Service (National Park Service, 2005).

Wilderness

In the 1930s forward-thinking preservationists saw that the American **wilderness** was a rapidly diminishing resource. A paradox was becoming apparent. Protecting an area by declaring it a national park virtually assured that roads would be built to and within that park. Eventually thousands of people would visit it, and the characteristics of "wilderness" would be diminished or lost. In the 1960s an oft-repeated phrase was that "Americans were loving their parks to death" as congested roads and campgrounds became the norm, at least in the summer vacation season or autumn leaf-color season. Early proponents of creating protected wilderness areas included Aldo Leopold, U.S. Forest Service scientist and the father of wildlife ecology; Robert Marshall, an environmental lawyer; Howard Zahniser, president of the Wilderness Society; and Hubert Humphrey, senator from Minnesota who sponsored four versions of the Wilderness Act over eight years. The fourth amended version eventually passed Congress and was signed into law by President Lyndon Johnson in 1964 (Nash, 1982).

Because wilderness designation would permanently prohibit development, roads, timber removal, and motorized activities, this bill caused considerable concern among lumber interests, some outdoor recreationists, and real estate developers. But Congress passed the Wilderness Act anyway. The process of designating new wilderness areas has provided some of the most heated environmental battles in the second half of the 20th century and the first decade of the 21st century. Especially controversial were the USDA Forest Service Roadless Area Review and Evaluation (RARE) process, the Endangered American Wilderness Act of 1978, and the 1980 Alaska National Interest Lands Conservation Act. The two acts were signed and engineered by President Jimmy Carter, doubling the size of the NPS and National Wildlife Refuge lands and tripling the size of designated wilderness. Recently, in the greatest expansion of wilderness areas in 15 years, President Barack Obama signed the Omnibus Public Lands Management Act of 2009, which protected 2 million acres (800,000 ha) of wilderness. In 2011 there were about 757 wilderness areas. Designated federal wilderness comprises about 110 million acres (45 million ha); 57 million of those acres (23 million ha) are in Alaska. California, Arizona, Idaho, and Washington have the next largest amount of wilderness area.

Era of Fiscal Restraint

Starting in the 1970s, after the rapid growth in participation in outdoor recreation and the expansion of federal programs to accommodate this growth, a series of developments led to a leveling off and even decline of federal actions. A few initiatives were associated with the nation's bicentennial celebration in 1976: the creation of bicentennial parks around the country and the Urban Park and Recreation Recovery (UPARR) program, which provided federal assistance to counteract the decline in many urban areas by rehabilitating critically needed recreation and park facilities. The increase in oil prices in 1973 and 1979 caused many park agencies to experience tight budgets when dollars appropriated for conservation or visitor services needed to be spent on more costly utilities and fuel. In addition, because fuel costs were increasing across the entire federal budget (e.g., military, agriculture, airline ticket prices, and so on), monies that might have been allocated to parks were shifted to higher-priority agencies. Hiring freezes and program cuts were the result. With more of their budgets going to pay for energy and educational efforts focusing on conservation, parks had less money for traditional environmental educational programs or visitor recreation programs.

In the 1980s the practice of hiring private companies to perform some park jobs once done by park employees (privatizing), such as trash collection, vehicle maintenance, lawn care, and even staffing visitor centers or gift shops, became popular. Under President Reagan, James Watt, secretary of the interior, eliminated the Bureau of Outdoor Recreation, reduced the rate at which new federal lands were purchased for parks, and supported mining and drilling for oil on federal lands. During this time, a grassroots backlash, the Sagebrush Rebellion, began. Local proponents of private land rights and public access performed actions of civil (and occasionally criminal) disobedience in opposition to various conservation actions on federal lands. The Reagan administration (1980-1988) instituted staff reductions in the land agencies and advocated state and local conservation initiatives, many of which were suggested by the 1987 President's Commission on Americans Outdoors report.

In the late 20th and early 21st century, few federal conservation initiatives were launched and new park acquisitions were limited because federal budgets were tight. One bright spot was the Transportation Efficiency Act of 1991 and its successors the Transportation Equity Act for the 21st Century (1998) and the Safe, Accountable, Flexible, Efficient Transportation Equity Act of 2005, which designated that 10 percent of the allocations for highway construction be set aside for alternative transportation options such as mass transit and walking, biking, and horse trails. Many localities used these funds for rails-to-trails initiatives to develop corridor park trail systems. In the 1990s many federal agencies became better connected to and appreciated by local and state tourism promoters, and now partnerships abound between what used to be separate entities. Local tourism businesses began to understand better how their livelihood in ecotourism was based on quality parks (because they attracted tourists and their money) and became partners in supporting parks in Congress or state legislatures and in volunteering labor and services to assist parks. Congress authorized the Recreation Fee Demonstration Program in 1996 and the Recreation Enhancement Act in 2004 to allow federal lands that charged entrance fees to increase their fees and retain funds from fees collected to improve their recreation facilities and services.

After the September 11, 2001, terrorist attacks in New York City, most federal parks had to divert a segment of their tight budgets to homeland security efforts, especially the National Park Service, which manages many high-profile monuments that could present symbolic targets for possible future attacks. The cost of extra security patrols and the addition of law enforcement officers and metal detectors to the entrances of many park buildings put a strain on other operations. Another area of concern is parks on national borders, such as Big Bend National Park in Texas and Organ Pipe Cactus National Monument in Arizona. Some believe that illegal aliens or terrorists could sneak into the country through these areas. Because of these concerns, some visitors stay away, park rangers have to be trained in law enforcement and border patrol strategies for 24-hour guarding, and time and money are spent more on security and less on visitor services or programs (National Geographic News, 2004). By 2005, with federal budget deficits growing and gasoline prices remaining higher than in the past, funding for park agencies and programs had decreased or remained level. President George W. Bush proposed not providing grants from the Land and Water Conservation Fund to individual states. These funds have been used since 1965 to purchase parklands and develop facilities such as campgrounds, playgrounds, trails, and visitor centers (National Park Service, 2005).

Since 2005 a national and global recession has further strained parks. Many local, state, and national parks have seen additional cuts to funding available for their operation and maintenance. Some parks, such as state parks in New York and California, have reduced their services or been closed as a cost-savings strategy. Making such problems worse is a long history of underfunding parks that had created a backlog of needed maintenance, facility upgrades, and staff even before the recession hit. For example, the national parks have a maintenance backlog of approximately $8 billion, which is more than twice their annual budget (NPCA, 2006). Currently, park leaders and managers are attempting to address these funding issues by reducing costs, by partnering with private industries and nongovernmental organizations, and by turning toward a more revenue-focused business model. Many parks use volunteers and friends groups (advocacy groups affiliated with a park that raise funds through donations) to ease constraints related to funding. In 2006 the National Park Centennial Initiative was undertaken by creating a matching fund for government and philanthropic contributions to benefit the parks in the years approaching the system's centennial in 2016. In addition, in 2009 the NPS invested $750 million in nearly 800 projects to stimulate the economy through the American Recovery and Reinvestment Act.

PARK SYSTEMS OF THE UNITED STATES

Most parks have been created on undeveloped lands and waters and reserved for public use and enjoyment; therefore, most publicly owned parks are managed by some level of the government. Similar to schools, public water supplies, and airports, parks are services that local, state, and federal governments provide their citizens for their benefit and enjoyment. Most parks have **frontcountry** areas with facilities, roads, and primary visitor attractions, but many parks also have **backcountry** areas where nature predominates.

City Parks

Historically, city parks were created to address social needs by providing safe areas for children to play and soothing islands of green in which to escape from urban crowding, congestion, and concrete. Most city parks are smaller, closer to home, and more sport oriented than other kinds of parks. City parks, by definition, are owned, managed, and staffed by city government. City parks are used in more varied ways than traditional resource-based state or federal parks. For example, city parks often provide swimming pools, concerts in the park, and food stands. Some even have small zoos, botanical gardens, or carnival-type rides. City parks usually are less concerned with maintaining natural resources in an undisturbed state; in most cases, the natural environment has already been heavily altered and the area artificially landscaped or designed. Therefore, the grounds are often heavily modified to provide amenities such as tennis courts, golf courses, swimming pools, fountains, paved walkways, ice-skating rinks, skateboard ramps, soccer fields, and playgrounds. Despite the less-than-pristine environment, city parks often provide inner-city children their first taste of a "natural" area (American Planning Association, 2003; Har-

nick, 2000; Taylor, Kuo, & Sullivan, 2001; Wals, 1994).

City parks vary greatly depending on the size of the city. Some New England towns, such as Burlington, Vermont, and New Haven, Connecticut, have classic "greens," which are only a few acres or less in size. Larger and more well-known or unique city parks are Central Park in New York City; Boston Commons; Jackson Square in New Orleans; the Riverwalk in San Antonio, Texas; the town squares of Savannah, Georgia; Grant Park in Chicago; Phoenix's unusual mountain parks (including the largest city park in the United States, South Mountain Park and Reserve); and Water Gardens Park, in Ft. Worth, Texas. It has been said that there are no great cities without great parks, and when you think of these large cities, this does seem to be true (Tate, 2001). But even the smallest cities and towns in the United States have parks that are often the centerpiece of local pride.

County Parks

County parks are usually larger, more natural, less congested, and quieter. They are typically oriented to activities such as swimming, hiking, boating, fishing, and camping that require a more natural setting than city parks can provide. They are owned and managed by county governments and usually operated by county employees, although a recent trend for some counties is to subcontract park operations to a private operator or group such as the YMCA. County parks are larger and less oriented to urban uses than city parks but are often not as environmentally sensitive, as restrictive in uses, or as large as most state parks. Some county parks have larger facilities than those found in city parks, such as multiple playing fields or arenas for sports tournaments and events. Local school systems often conduct lessons in environmental education at county parks because they are typically close by, are easily accessible, and have parking. Fishing, sailing, canoeing, or water safety lessons are also conducted in county parks. In coastal states, many beach parks, especially the more developed ones, are county parks.

State Parks

State parks are typically more focused on preserving the natural or historic characteristics of an area and providing compatible outdoor recreation. Usually, they are more distant from urban population centers than most city or county parks, although in a few cases, population centers have grown around state parks. In general, state parks are larger than most city or county parks. In 2011 there were 6,624 state parks in the United States (NASPD, 2011). Often state parks are associated with water bodies, have substantial wildlife populations, and are representative of key environmental ecosystems that characterize the state, such as beaches in Florida, deserts in Arizona, prairie in Illinois and Kansas, and mountains in California, Colorado, and New Hampshire. But most state parks are not unique enough, scenic enough, large enough, or filled with enough features to qualify as national parks. Besides highlighting natural areas, many state parks promote the state's important historical figures or events.

The character of state parks varies substantially. Some are similar to large city parks in a more natural setting, and others are as wild or wilder than some national parks or forests. Adirondack State Park and Forest Preserve in New York is the largest park in the lower 48 states (6 million acres [2.4 million ha]), larger than even Yellowstone National Park (Adirondack State Park Agency, 2011). Most state parks are of modest size, usually ranging from a hundred to a few thousand acres, and they provide basic facilities such as campgrounds, picnic areas, trails, visitor centers, and environmental education programs. In contrast, the variety of amenities in Eugene T. Mahoney State Park, in a rural area south of Omaha, Nebraska, is more typical of a city park. It has an outdoor swimming pool with water slides, a large playground area with play equipment, and an ice-skating rink (Nebraska Game and Parks Commission, 2011).

Several states have created what are called resort state parks to increase both visitation and self-generated revenues. These parks provide services like those of a resort, but they are located on state parklands and are managed and funded by the state park service or a corollary association, often with subcontracts to concessionaires. Lake Barkley State Resort Park in Kentucky has a golf course, aerobic fitness center, swimming pool, tennis courts, small airport, cabins, lodge hotel, restaurant, and marina (Kentucky State Parks, 2005). Seyon Lodge State Park in Vermont provides overnight stays in bed

Point Lobos State Park in California protects valuable shoreline habitat and provides opportunities for nature-based recreation.

and breakfast style accommodations and guided fishing. The resort state park idea has expanded to at least 12 states, many of them in the South (Alabama State Parks, 2012; West Virginia Division of Natural Resources, 2005).

Besides having state parks, most states, especially those in the East, also have state forests. Many of the forest areas have camping areas, hiking trails, and hunting areas. Many states, mostly in the Midwest and West, operate state fish and game or state wildlife management areas, which are usually available for various forms of outdoor recreation.

Federal Parks, Forests, and Refuges

Before 1700 most of what became the United States of America was the domain of millions of native Americans who were later largely exterminated by war, killed by disease, evicted from their natural territories and moved onto reservations, or forced to seek refuge in Canada (Brown, 1970; Nash, 1982). Their lands became available to European immigrants who had to apply for ownership from the federal General Land Office, which claimed to have the original title to the land. Tracts of land not delegated to the states or claimed by private owners were retained in federal ownership since the creation of the United States government in 1776. Much of this land was not suitable for agriculture or residential development or was eventually recognized as land that the public should have access to (public domain land). Growing societal needs for recreation and the preservation of dwindling natural resources prompted Congress to establish national parks, national forests, national wildlife refuges, and other federal protected areas. A variety of agencies were created to manage these places (Zaslowsky & Watkins, 1994; Zinser, 1995). Although most of these areas were initially conserved for reasons other than recreation, recreational opportunities were often a side benefit.

National Parks

The National Park Service (NPS) has been a world leader in establishing and managing national parks. The NPS operates under a principle of preservation and is funded by the U.S. Department of the Interior. Its mission is to "conserve the scenery and the natural and historic objects and the wildlife therein and to provide for the enjoyment of the same in such manner and by such means as will leave them unimpaired for the enjoyment of future generations." Maintaining a balance between allowing use and protecting and preserving resources is a constant challenge. Providing recreational opportunities that do little or no permanent harm to the park or its wildlife is one of NPS's prime missions. Many believe that the national park idea is one of the best ideas that the United States has contributed to the world (National Park Service, Office of International Affairs, 2005; Sellars, 1999). Containing 394 units, the national park system encompasses approximately 84 million acres (34 million ha) and manages many categories of parks (see table 6.1).

With such diversity of areas, almost any imaginable form of outdoor recreation occurs in the national park system. Activities include mountain climbing, horseback riding, boating, camping, history reenactments at the sites where they occurred, hiking, white-water rafting, and driving and "windshield" sightseeing, especially during spring wildflower or fall leaf-changing seasons. The 286 million visitor days of activity annually to the national parks make a significant contribution to the economy of the nation and especially to rural areas that depend on the tourism that the national parks attract. Considerable adaptability and creativity are needed to manage these diverse areas, and expertise from many disciplines is needed across the system of parks. These disciplines include ecology, geology, archeology, military history, national history, fisheries, wildlife and resource management, forestry, outdoor recreation management, interpretation, business management, marketing, public relations, urban recreation programming, environmental education, alternative energy, public works, transportation management, tourism, law, and political science. The NPS also coordinates the Land and Water Conservation Fund, which is a program in which federal funds are distributed to the states and federal agencies for new or continuing park or conservation projects.

National Forests and Grasslands

The Forest Service was created in 1905 and is an agency of the Department of Agriculture (USDA). The USDA Forest Service manages large forests

Table 6.1   U.S. National Park Service Categories and Examples

Categories	Total number	Examples
National parks	58	Yellowstone, Grand Teton, Yosemite, Smoky Mountains, Grand Canyon, Rocky Mountain, Shenandoah
National monuments	74	Grand Portage, Bandelier, Craters of the Moon, Coronado, Fort Sumter
National preserves	18	Big Thicket, Big Cypress, Timucuan, Gates of the Arctic
National historic sites	78	First Ladies, Fort Davis, McLoughlin House, Carl Sandburg Home, Lincoln Home
National historical parks	45	Minute Man, Women's Rights, Valley Forge, Chaco Culture, Cumberland Gap
National memorials	28	Chamizal, African American Civil War, USS Arizona, Mount Rushmore, World War II, Flight 93
National military parks	9	Shiloh, Gettysburg, Horseshoe Bend, Pea Ridge
National battlefields	16	Manassas, Fort Donelson, Cowpens, Antietam
National recreation areas	18	Gateway, Santa Monica Mountains, Golden Gate
National reserves	2	New Jersey Pinelands, City of Rocks
National seashores	10	Gulf Islands, Padre Island, Canaveral, Cape Cod, Point Reyes
National lakeshores	4	Pictured Rocks, Sleeping Bear, Apostle Islands, Indiana Dunes
National rivers	5	Buffalo, Big South Fork, New River Gorge, Mississippi
Wild and scenic rivers	10	Obed, Ozark, Rio Grande, Farmington, Salmon
National parkways	4	Baltimore–Washington, George Washington
National scenic trails	3	Natchez Trace, Potomac Heritage, Appalachian
International historic site	1	Saint Croix Island
No designation	11	National Mall, Rock Creek Park, Catoctin Mountain, Wolf Trap National Park for the Performing Arts

and grasslands and follows a basic conservation and **wise-use philosophy**. The agency's mission is to achieve quality land management under the sustainable multiple-use concept to meet the diverse needs of people. Gifford Pinchot, the first chief of the Forest Service, described conservation and wise use as providing "the greatest good to the greatest number for the longest time." **Multiple-use management** means that USDA Forest Service areas should be used for outdoor recreation, livestock grazing, timber production, watershed management, and wildlife and fish habitat. Providing recreational opportunities, which the agency tries to balance with the other uses, is a major focus of the Forest Service. The 175 USDA Forest Service units (155 national forests and 20 national grasslands) include 192 million acres (78 million ha) in 42 states (USDA Forest Service, 2011). National forests constitute 98 percent of USDA Forest Service lands. These lands contain designated wilderness areas, recreation areas, national monuments and preserves,

and national scenic areas. The Forest Service also manages scenic byways, wild and scenic rivers, campgrounds, alpine ski areas, boating areas, picnic areas, and over 100,000 miles (160,000 km) of trail (USDA Forest Service, 2011; Zinser, 1995).

Historically, the Forest Service gave priority to timber management but was induced over time through court cases, political pressure, and debates on wilderness to increase the outdoor recreation opportunities in the forests, especially since the 1960s. Today recreation is a primary focus and use of the national forests. From 2005 to 2009, an average of 178 million people visited USDA Forest Service lands, waters, and recreation sites per year (USDA Forest Service, 2011). Common recreation activities on national forests and grasslands include hiking, camping, wildlife watching, hunting, fishing, mountain biking, horse trail riding, skiing, and off-highway vehicle (**OHV**; e.g., all-terrain vehicle, snowmobile) use. In general, more consumptive, higher-impact forms of recreation are permitted and deemed appropriate on national forests and other federal lands as compared with state and national parks.

Wildlife Refuges

The U.S. Fish and Wildlife Service (USFWS) is part of the U.S. Department of the Interior. Its mission is to work with others to conserve, protect, and enhance fish, wildlife, and plants and their habitats for the continuing benefit of the American people. Its programs (including administering the U.S. Endangered Species Act and other federal wildlife laws) are among the oldest in the world dedicated to scientific wildlife conservation, although Canada had a wildlife conservation reserve in 1887. As of 2011 the service manages a 150-million-acre (60-million ha) national system of more than 553 national wildlife refuges and thousands of small wetlands and other special management areas. Under the fisheries program it operates national fish hatcheries, fishery resource offices, and ecological services field stations (U.S. Fish and Wildlife Service, 2011).

Most wildlife refuge areas are water related, either freshwater or saltwater, and therefore are often found along rivers, lakes, marshlands, or coastal areas. The primary focus of refuges and fish hatcheries is wildlife and fish habitat protection, promotion of breeding, and provision of safe refuge to animals. Refuges permit secondary recreational activity as long as it is compatible with the primary purpose of the refuge and funds are available to administer it. The primary recreational uses in wildlife refuges are hunting, fishing, wildlife observation, nature photography, environmental education and interpretation, hiking, and motorized and nonmotorized boating. Hunting or fishing is permitted in wildlife refuges because much of the funding and support of wildlife refuges came from hunters and anglers when Congress expressed little interest in spending money on wildlife, birds, and fish. The hunting and fishing is regulated and in some areas controls the populations of animals whose natural predators have been long removed. About 30 percent of refuges are not open to recreation; these are mostly in Alaska.

Other Areas Managed by Federal Agencies

Several other federal protected areas exist that are less well known, but many are found only in certain regions of the United States and they usually provide fewer recreation programs and facilities. The Bureau of Land Management, U.S. Army Corps of Engineers, Tennessee Valley Authority, Bureau of

Aransas National Wildlife Refuge in Texas provides winter habitat for the endangered whooping crane.

Reclamation, and American Indian reservations manage these areas. In addition, wilderness areas are specially designated lands owned by the federal government.

National Resource Lands

The Bureau of Land Management (BLM) manages 245 million acres (99 million ha) of land, about one-eighth of the land in the United States, more than any other federal agency (Bureau of Land Management, 2011). Most of the lands that the BLM manages are located in the western United States, including Alaska, which contains about a third of all of BLM-managed land. Most BLM lands are dominated by extensive grasslands, forests, high mountains, arctic tundra, and deserts. The BLM manages a variety of resources and uses, including energy and mineral mining; timber; grazing; wild horse and burro habitats; fish and wildlife habitat; wilderness areas; and archaeological, paleontological, and historical sites.

BLM recreation management areas include backcountry areas with minimal development of recreation facilities and special recreation areas that provide specific recreation facilities such as campgrounds, boat launch ramps, cabins, and environmental education centers. BLM reports about 59 million visits per year (Bureau of Land Management, n.d.). Most of the land managed by BLM is desert and barren, but some of the land contains lakes, rivers, and mountains, and some of it is extremely scenic. BLM lands contain trails, campgrounds, picnic areas, boating areas, visitor centers, horse-riding trails, and OHV sites, sustaining a variety of recreational pursuits.

Wilderness Areas

Areas designated under the 1964 Wilderness Act and the 1973 Eastern Wilderness Act are managed by the four federal agencies discussed earlier: Bureau of Land Management, U.S. Fish and Wildlife Service, USDA Forest Service, and National Park Service. The Wilderness Act defined wilderness "as an area where the earth and its community of life are untrammeled by man, where man himself is a visitor who does not remain." Wilderness areas are generally open to the public for nonmotorized and nonmechanized (i.e., no bikes) recreation. Road, buildings, and other manmade structures

are typically not found in wilderness areas. Permits are often required. These areas are truly wild and contain only a minimum of facilities. Following is a summary of the federal wilderness areas:

- National Park Service—44.4 million acres (18.0 million ha) and many other areas managed as wilderness but awaiting formal designation
- USDA Forest Service—36.7 million acres (14.9 million ha)
- U.S. Fish and Wildlife Service—20.7 million acres (8.4 million ha)
- Bureau of Land Management—8.8 million acres (3.6 million ha)
- Total national wilderness—757 sites, approximately 110 million acres (44.5 million ha) (www.wilderness.net)

These national wilderness areas are subareas designated from existing national parks, national monuments, national preserves, national forests, national grasslands, natural resource lands, and fish and wildlife refuges. For example, 86 percent of Everglades National Park is designated wilderness. Some states have state-designated wilderness areas that are smaller than federal wilderness areas and tend to follow the same principles of "no development or motorized access."

U.S. Army Corps of Engineers Waterways and Sites

The Army Corps of Engineers is the steward of the lands and waters at thousands of federal water resource sites like dams, reservoirs, and flood-control projects. This agency is part of the Department of Defense, but most of its employees are civilians. Its natural resources management mission is to manage and conserve natural resources consistent with principles of ecosystem management while providing public outdoor recreation experiences to serve the needs of current and future generations (U.S. Army Corps of Engineers, 2011).

The Army Corps of Engineers is the nation's largest provider of outdoor recreation. It manages more than 4,254 recreation areas at 422 projects (mostly lakes and reservoirs). A substantial number of these sites are leased to state or local park and recreation authorities or private interests. The Corps hosts about 370 million visitors a year at its lakes, beaches, and other areas, and estimates that 1 in 10 Americans visit a Corps project at least once a year. Recreationally, the Corps manages campgrounds, boat launch ramps, fishing piers, marinas, bathrooms, and swimming areas. In total, the Corps manages 12 million acres (5 million ha) of land and water for recreation, including 33 percent of all freshwater fishing opportunities in the United States. The Corps also manages the intracoastal waterway and reservoirs that provides substantial boating opportunities in many states (U.S. Army Corps of Engineers, 2011).

Tennessee River Valley

The Tennessee Valley Authority (TVA) is a federal agency that operates in a limited service area encompassing only seven states: Tennessee, Alabama, Georgia, Kentucky, Mississippi, North Carolina, and Virginia. President Franklin Roosevelt created the TVA during the Depression in 1933 to create electricity, flood control, and economic development in an underdeveloped region. TVA is the United States' largest public power company, and because it manages a major river (650 miles [1,050 km] long), many recreation opportunities are available on TVA-managed areas. Millions of people enjoy recreational activities on TVA reservoirs or rivers and adjacent land each year. The reservoirs and the 290,000 acres (117,000 ha) of land surrounding them offer opportunities for recreational activities, including waterskiing, canoeing, sailing, windsurfing, fishing, swimming, hiking, nature photography, picnicking, bird watching, and camping. Recreation management has not been a priority of TVA, and recently it has begun minimizing the amount of active recreation management that it does (TVA, n.d.). But because of its water-related resources, millions of people still engage in recreational activities on areas managed by TVA.

Large Western Reservoirs

Across the arid western states, water management became a critical focus as the population in those areas grew. In 1902 Teddy Roosevelt established the Bureau of Reclamation (BOR). This agency is part of the U.S. Department of the Interior and is best known for the dams, power plants, and canals that it has constructed in 17 western states. These water projects led to homesteading and promoted the economic development of the West. The mission of BOR is to manage water and water-related resources in the western United States in an economically and environmentally sound manner for the American people. As a recreation provider, BOR serves a major role in providing water recreation opportunities to the rapidly growing western states. In otherwise dry western states BOR reservoirs make possible water-based recreational activities such as boating, waterskiing, bird watching, fishing, waterside camping, and swimming in natural areas. Over 90 million visitors make use of 7.1 million acres (2.9 million ha) of BOR recreational land and waters each year (BOR, 2011).

American Indian Reservations

The Bureau of Indian Affairs (BIA) is responsible for administering and managing 55.7 million acres (22.5 million ha) of land held in trust by the United States for American Indians, Indian tribes, and Alaska natives. Most of the land is in Arizona, New Mexico, Montana, and South Dakota, although 31 states have some Native American lands. The BIA is an agency within the U.S. Department of the Interior. Developing forestlands, leasing assets on those lands, directing agricultural programs, protecting water and land rights, developing and maintaining infrastructure, and promoting economic development are among the agency's responsibilities. As part of their economic development efforts, many tribes attract tourists to their lands by offering guided tours, camping, hunting, fishing, museums, lodges, and alpine skiing. Since the passage of the Indian Gaming Act (1988), many tribes have opened casinos and associated resorts, hotels, shopping areas, and restaurants that attract visitors to American Indian lands (U.S. Department of the Interior, n.d.).

National Marine Sanctuaries

Two federal agencies, both part of the U.S. Department of Commerce's National Oceanic and Atmospheric Administration (NOAA), manage ocean area "parks": the National Marine Sanctuary Program and the National Marine Fisheries Service. During the 1970s, when many environmental acts were passed, the Marine Protection, Research, and Sanctuaries Act of 1972 created the sanctuaries program, partially in response to oil spills and reports of toxic dumping in the ocean. Today, 13 national marine sanctuaries protect 18,618 square miles (48,221 sq km) of ocean and coasts (National Marine Sanctuaries, 2011).

The act to create these underwater sanctuaries was passed 100 years after the legislation to create the first national park on land. The primary purpose of the sanctuaries is to conserve natural and cultural marine features. These sanctuaries also provide underwater environmental education and opportunities for snorkeling and scuba sightseeing, fish and coral watching, and photography.

INTERNATIONAL TREATIES AND PROTECTED AREA DESIGNATIONS AND PARKS

Protected natural areas that transcend national borders are known as transboundary protected areas. Because the world's natural resources and parks are best managed on an ecosystem scale, some believe that the programs should be developed so that national borders do not interfere with good conservation practice.

Transboundary protected areas, which are normally found in two adjacent countries, have been created around the world. Typically, these areas were created to facilitate conservation on biological diversity across national boundaries. By 2007 there were 227 transboundary complexes involving 3,043 individual parks or protected areas in a large number of countries (Lysenko, Besançon, & Savy, 2007). North America's first international transboundary cooperation was founded in 1932, involving the Waterton–Glacier International Peace Park World Heritage site in Alberta and Montana. Another major U.S.–Canadian transboundary protected area includes a vast complex in the northwestern Yukon and northeastern Alaska involving the Ivvavik and Vuntut National Parks in Canada and the Arctic National Wildlife Refuge in the United States. A world-renowned wilderness canoeing area is also a transboundary unit. This area comprises Quetico

Dinosaur Provincial Park in Alberta is a World Heritage site that protects significant dinosaur fossils.

Provincial Park in Ontario and the Boundary Waters Canoe Area in Minnesota. In total, Canada and the United States have nine transboundary protected-area complexes. Canada also has a transboundary area with Greenland (Denmark), and the United States has two with Mexico (Lysenko, Besançon, & Savy, 2007).

In addition, the United Nations Educational, Scientific and Cultural Organization (UNESCO) designates international **biosphere reserves**, which are terrestrial and coastal areas representing the main ecosystems of the planet in which plants and animals are to be protected and where research, monitoring, and training on ecosystems are carried out. These reserves are designed to operate as examples of sustainable land use. Many of the larger national parks and adjacent areas in the United States and Canada have been designated as international biosphere reserves. Canada has 13 biosphere reserves and the United States has 47 (UNESCO, 2011a, 2011b). Examples of biosphere reserves in Canada are Long Point in Ontario and Waterton in Alberta. Examples in the United States are the Mammoth Cave Area in Kentucky and the California Coast Ranges.

Similarly, UNESCO designates **World Heritage sites** to encourage countries to protect natural and cultural heritage sites that are of universal significance. Many of the nature sites are major national parks. In 2011, 911 World Heritage sites were designated globally (UNESCO, 2011a). Canada contains 15 World Heritage sites (Parks Canada, 2011b), and the United States contains 21 sites (UNESCO, 2011b). Some sites were designated for world-class natural features, such as Dinosaur Provincial Park in Alberta, the Rocky Mountain Parks in Alberta and British Columbia, Nahanni National Park in the Northwest Territories, Redwood National Park in California, and Everglades National Park in Florida. Other sites were designated for world-class cultural and historic values, such as L'Anse aux Meadows National Historic Site in Newfoundland, the Old Town of Lunenburg in Nova Scotia, the Statue of Liberty in New York, and Independence Hall in Philadelphia.

Another international designation for wetland areas is the **Ramsar Convention**, which designates internationally important wetlands for conservation (Wetlands International, 2005). In 2011 there were 1,913 Ramsar wetlands designated worldwide within 160 countries. Canada had designated 37

sites, and the United States had 29 sites (Ramsar, 2011).

The World Heritage sites and the Ramsar wetlands are designated through international conventions. Once designated, each site must be managed according to international law as outlined in the convention. The biosphere reserve designation is simply a cooperative arrangement among countries that has no international legal structure and thus requires much less conservation commitment.

COMPARING CANADA AND THE UNITED STATES

Table 6.2 shows the status as of 2002 of the parks and protected areas in Canada and the United States according to the United Nations List of Protected Areas (Chape, Blyth, Fish, Fox, & Spalding, 2003). Urban parks are not included in the list because of their small size, and historic parks are not included because of their cultural focus.

Similarities Between Canada and the United States

The park systems in the countries are similar and often designate the same types of lands for protection. This resemblance is not surprising because both countries developed their park systems with constant communication and friendly competition over two hundred years. The United States and Canada are similar in geographic size, so directly comparing the area dedicated to various types of parks and protected areas is possible (see table 6.2). Both countries have similar amounts of area designated as nature reserves and habitat and species management areas. Canada has much more national parkland, in part because the large provincial parks are of national-park stature and size and are recognized as such in the international classification of parks. The data in table 6.2 comes from the 2003 version of the United Nations List of National Parks and Protected Areas. The data on this list are presented according to the **International Union for Conservation of Nature and Natural Resources (IUCN)** categories of protected areas, not according to the official titles of the parks. For example, many provincial parks in Canada are classified in the UN list as category II parks, or national parks.

Table 6.2 Parks and Protected Areas in Canada and the United States

IUCN* category	Number in Canada	Number in the United States	Area in Canada in million acres	Area in United States in million acres
Ia: Nature reserve	724	74	5.7 (2.3 ha)	9.1 (3.7 ha)
Ib: Wilderness	112	586	25.9 (10.5 ha)	89 (36 ha)
II: National park	1,110	210	106 (43 ha)	64 (26 ha)
III: Natural monument	287	277	0.310 (0.125 ha)	17.5 (7.1 ha)
IV: Habitat and species management area	571	788	77 (31 ha)	106 (43 ha)
V: Protected landscape	765	1,319	3 (1.2 ha)	30 (12 ha)
VI: Managed-resource protected area	941	287	18 (7.3 ha)	272 (110 ha)
Unclassified	789	4,442	8.4 (3.4 ha)	5.9 (2.4 ha)
Total	5,299	7,983	245 (99 ha)	593 (240 ha)

*Founded on October 5, 1948, as the International Union for the Protection of Nature (IUPN) following an international conference in Fontainebleau, France, the organization changed its name to International Union for Conservation of Nature and Natural Resources (IUCN) in 1956. In 1990 it was shortened to IUCN–The World Conservation Union.

Therefore, table 6.2 shows 1,100 national parks in Canada, although only 42 of them are owned and operated by the national government; provincial governments own and manage the rest. Additionally, neither national historic sites nor historic canals are included in the database used for the table. The IUCN does not recognize cultural or historic sites in its classification system, and historic sites are discussed only briefly in this chapter.

The similarity in the form and function of parks in Canada and the United States is caused by several factors. The government structures are similar, including cities, towns, counties, provinces or states, and a federal government. Each of these levels of government develops and manages parks. Both countries have cultural roots in England, which transferred to North America the English love of nature, outdoor recreation, and the use of specialized reserves for conservation and recreation (Glendening 1997; Hudson, 2001; Jones & Wills, 2005; Ritvo, 2003). The green parks in the central areas of English cities were a model widely emulated across the various British colonies in North America (Sheail, 2010). As the park movement in Canada and the United States deepened and strengthened through increasing activities by cities, provinces or states, and national governments, communication of ideas between the two countries was ongoing. Many government precedents, numerous management details, and much wording in legislation

moved back and forth between agencies in the two countries over a 200-year period. Therefore, both countries have national parks, national historic sites and parks, national wildlife reserves and areas, provincial and state parks, regional parks, and municipal parks. And it is not surprising that parks in both countries have been created for everyone's use and are funded primarily by taxes.

After the parks were established, their management was done first by volunteers and later largely by professionals. Starting in the United States in the 1930s and followed by Canada in the 1960s, specialized college and university programs developed to provide training for leisure, parks, recreation, and resource management professionals. Park managers in both countries are now viewed as professionals who have received training appropriate to the challenging tasks of conservation and recreation.

Canada and the United States both played a large role in park management internationally. Both countries have influenced the types and forms of park management that has developed around the world. United States government officials and academic scholars were particularly influential in spreading the concept of the United States model of national parks worldwide. The U.S. model is typically seen as consisting of extremely large areas from which aboriginal people have been removed. Management is by a government agency that concentrates on conservation and outdoor recreation. Canadian officials have been influential in international activities such creating biosphere reserves and management of the World Heritage Convention. Scholars in both countries have written abundant literature that has widely disseminated the concepts of park planning and management, as well as outdoor recreation planning and management. The United States and Canada have consistently shown international leadership in park planning and management.

Differences Between Canada and the United States

Although the park systems in both countries are similar, there are important differences (Eagles, McLean, & Stabler, 2000). The wilderness concept is more popular in the United States than in Canada; therefore, the United States has much more designated wilderness. Through the power of the presidential executive order, the United States has a national monument designation that is not used in Canadian park law. But the biggest differences occur in the amount of land making up protected landscape and managed resource-protected areas. In the United States the federal government manages these lands and has designated large areas as national forests and Bureau of Land Management protected areas. In Canada the provinces manage the forestlands, and Canada does not include all undesignated crown lands managed by the provinces, territories, and the national government in its tabulation of protected areas. Therefore, formal lists of protected areas create the impression that the United States has much more protected land. This conclusion is misleading because massive amounts of crown and aboriginal land in Canada are available for outdoor recreation but are not formally designated as some form of protected area.

A major difference between Canada and the United States is the constitutional structure of land ownership. In the United States the federal government owns most of the public land. Therefore, the national government of the United States has the capacity to create parks and reserves on this land. As a result, a large number of land management agencies have been created to manage the variety of reserves created on federal land. The United States has more diverse management institutions and reserves than Canada does. For example, the following systems exist in the United States but not in Canada: national forests, national parkways, national scenic rivers, national wilderness areas, U.S. Army Corps of Engineer waterways, and BLM national resource lands.

Another difference between the two countries is that in Canada the provincial parks are much larger and are part of more fully developed park systems than the state park systems in the United States. For example, the provincial park system in just one province, Ontario, is larger in land area than all 50 of the U.S. state park systems combined. In essence, many provincial park systems in Canada are of national park stature, largely because the provincial governments control most of the crown land within their borders. Therefore, the provincial governments found it relatively easy to create provincial parks on land that they already owned and managed. Some of the richer provinces blocked national park creation while putting the best lands into their own provincial park systems. A few provinces, however, have gone a different direction. Some of the poorer provinces, for example, the Maritime provinces in the East, welcomed national park creation because the federal government would then pay the cost of land management. In these provinces the national parks are prominent and the provincial park systems are smaller and less developed.

In Canada within the territories, the federal government holds crown land, taking into account aboriginal land rights. Therefore, national parks and wildlife areas were most easily created by the national government in territories. For that reason, the major concentration of national parks occurs in the western mountains and in the High North. In the Canadian West, the national parks were created before the provinces had been created. In the North, park creation is ongoing. Canadian parks have been managed more as a system of parks with national planning, whereas in the United States, although there have been several attempts at national plans, they rarely last long (often because of changes in presidential or congressional priorities) and the difficulties in coordinating 50 states.

CAREER OPPORTUNITIES

Traditionally, the operation of most public natural areas occurs within the federal, state or provincial, or municipal levels of government. City parks and recreation departments offer countless opportunities to parks and recreation specialists. Thus, employment opportunities are available with agencies such as the national park agencies, the national wildlife agencies, the forest services, and the many regional, local, and municipal parks and recreation agencies. In the United States opportunities are also available with the AmeriCorps program, with the Student Conservation Corps (SCA), and within many state and local nonprofit groups such as the Vermont Youth Conservation Corps. Many different job positions are available at parks, forests, and refuges (administrative, financial, clerical, secretarial, maintenance, law enforcement, biologists, historians, lifeguards, and so on).

Park rangers carry out various tasks associated with the following:

- Forest or structural fire control
- Protection of property
- Gathering and dissemination of natural, historical, or scientific information
- Development of interpretive material for the natural, historical, or cultural features of an era
- Demonstration of folk art and crafts
- Enforcement of laws and regulations
- Investigation of violations, complaints, trespass and encroachment, and accidents
- Search and rescue
- Management of historical, cultural, and natural resources, such as wildlife, forests, lakeshores, seashores, historic buildings, battlefields, archaeological properties, and recreation areas

They also operate campgrounds, including such tasks as assigning sites, replenishing firewood, performing safety inspections, providing information to visitors, and leading guided tours. Differences in the exact nature of duties depend on the grade of the position, the size of the site, and specific needs (National Park Service, 2004).

Educational requirements vary depending on the position, but a university degree is preferred for most permanent positions. Seasonal employment is available in most areas to gain experience while the employee is in college or has recently graduated.

Educational training should relate to the position sought (e.g., history degree for historians; parks, recreation, and tourism degree for visitor management; biology, ecology, forestry, geology, or wildlife management degree for natural resource management positions). Except for some maintenance positions (electricians, plumbers, and so on), law enforcement jobs, or lifeguard positions, certifications are generally not required, although some positions may prefer or give preference to candidates who have certified park and recreation professional (CPRP) status. Information on obtaining that certification is available from the National Recreation and Park Association in Ashburn, Virginia, United States. Canada does not have a national recreation accreditation system.

Many professional organizations are relevant to those interested in a park-related career. Most have student membership rates and hold annual conferences that offer good opportunities to network and find out about internship or employment opportunities. Some of the better known ones include the National Recreation and Park Association (especially the National Society for Park Resources branch), the Canadian Parks and Recreation Association, the National Parks and Conservation Association, the Society of American Foresters, the National Association of Recreation Resource Planners, the National Association for Interpretation, state and provincial park and recreation associations, the George Wright Society, and the Wilderness Society.

Recreation employment opportunities are also available in the private sector, both the profit-making sector and the nonprofit sector. A range of jobs is available including program planning, direct program delivery, resort-park concessionaire or lodging operations, and the sale of specialized recreation merchandise. Growing opportunities in small businesses are available for people interested in providing outdoor programs and services for activities such as rafting, birding, bicycling, and canoeing. Some resorts recognize the need for a staff naturalist or recreation employee to answer guests' questions and offer tours and sightseeing trips. Summer camps, ski resorts, tour boat companies, bed and breakfasts, park and beach concessionaires, park lodges, watercraft and bicycle rental companies, water parks, marinas, and outdoor equipment stores are a few more examples of potential job sites. Increasingly, nongovernment organizations that assist with park management, such as friends groups, have become important sources of employment for parks and recreation graduates.

A glance at websites such as Cool Works, Eco-Jobs, the NRPA careers webpage, state parks job pages, and federal job pages will show that the number and diversity of career opportunities related to parks and protected areas are immense. Perhaps the best part of these careers is the intangible benefits that a person receives from living and working in places, and often doing things, that others pay to see and experience.

CHALLENGES AND TRENDS FOR THE 21ST CENTURY

Parks are a product and reflection of our society, its needs, and its culture. Most citizens use, know about, and support the creation and management of parks. Over time public demand has resulted in increasing amounts of land being reserved for parks and removed from other types of land use. Park usage is increasing in some regions but decreasing in others. Park tourism leads to two complicated problems. First, how can the cultural and ecological values of the parks be conserved and interpreted while at the same time be actively used by large numbers of tourists? Second, how can the management of all this parkland and visitor use be financed? We are fortunate to have thousands of park resources available because of the farsightedness, willingness to sacrifice, and preservation ethos of previous generations. But those resources face challenges and trends that current generations must respond to.

• **Carrying capacity** is a primary issue associated with parks because of the inherent conflict between the role of these places to provide for use and enjoyment by the public while at the same time protecting the resources that make them special. This dual mandate requires that a balance be achieved among the number and types of users allowed and the impacts that use creates. The point at which this balance is made is the carrying capacity of a park. Carrying capacity is inherently a subjective decision, but it can be informed by strong empirical science. For example, social

scientists have in a number of parks determined public opinion regarding the acceptable level of crowds, traffic, noise, or environmental impacts caused by visitors (Manning, 2007). Likewise, experts can evaluate visitor-created impacts to resources such as wildlife or plants. These opinions (both public and expert) can help inform standards for managing parks within a carrying capacity; if standards are violated then the carrying capacity of a park has been reached and park managers should take action. These actions could include redistributing visitors to lesser used areas of the park, reducing visitor impacts, or limiting the number of visitors. The concept of carrying capacity and practices to assess and manage it help to ensure the sustainability of parks and their resources for future generation.

• **International tourism**. In both countries the impact of international tourists is becoming increasingly important as large numbers of people from other countries, especially from Europe, Japan, and other Asian countries, visit high-profile parks. The increase in visits to national parks by international tourists can be attributed to greater awareness of environmental concerns, scarcity of natural land at home, and higher levels of travel. As international tourism increases, so does the demand for a higher quality of service management and park staff with advanced education in tourism management, cultural sensitivity, and language skills.

• **Funding**. Over the years, government funding for public parks has become increasingly limited, and the number of park agencies that compete for these funds has grown. Some of the causes of the funding shortage include rising land prices and energy and fuel costs, as well as a trend toward reducing taxes. Insufficient funding hinders the provision of environmental and historical interpretation programs and the retention of sufficient park rangers or staff to maintain facilities, manage resources, and serve the public. Parks must compete for funding not only with each other but also with other large and valued public institutions such as education and health care organizations.

Innovative responses to this problem include increasing the use of tourism fees and charges, relying more on volunteer efforts such as friends groups (nonprofit advocacy groups affiliated with a park that raise funds through donations), and encouraging park agencies to function like businesses, tapping all possible streams of income. Many park agencies are aggressively moving into a business model of management in which they have the ability to set prices, retain funds, hire staff, and operate programs with flexibility similar to that of a private business. Traditional income sources continue to include government appropriations and grants, campsite rentals, and day-use fees. Innovative income sources used include souvenir sales, grocery sales, recreation equipment rental, specialized clothing and equipment sales, specialized accommodation rental, fees for using parks as movie-filming sites, art sales, interpretive program charges, corporate sponsorships, leases to private companies, and corporate advertising. Friends groups are also entrepreneurial; examples of fundraising activities include providing specialized festivals; developing aboriginal-themed activities; encouraging film, art, and cultural development; and staffing book or gift stores and donating a portion of sales income to the park and encouraging donations of time and money. Advanced training in the business of leisure and tourism is now needed in all park agencies.

Major park management debates revolve around the types of activities that should be encouraged and allowed, the management structures used, and the source of the funding. The proportion of funding that should come from taxes or from user fees also produces heated debate. In recent years a trend has developed toward increasing the use of various types of fees and charges to fund park management. There is an urgent need for park managers with specialized training in finance and business management. Many universities train resource managers, but only a few train business managers for parks.

• **Market specialization**. Over the years various park agencies have increasingly specialized in providing services to a particular segment of the population. For example, youth and people without much discretionary income heavily use city parks. Conversely, well-educated and wealthy older people who have the time and money to travel heavily use national parks. The baby boom generation is now a key target market. Today's park managers must plan and manage for the needs of this largest, healthiest, wealthiest cadre of retirees in world history. For example, the picturesque landscapes of North American parks attract older travelers, but the services and facilities are usually more appropriate for young, physically active visitors. Aging baby boomers seem to be shifting to a preference for what has been labeled soft ecotourism in which they hike and sightsee in the parks in the daytime but retire to nearby lodges, bed and breakfasts, restaurants, and cabins at night. The boom in the development of eco-lodges near parks is based on this trend of visiting parks for a nature experience but spending the evenings with good food and innovative accommodations. Resolving this competition poses a challenge to parks.

• **Changing demand**. Recently the national park agencies of both Canada and the United States have seen a slight but steady decline in national park use (Balmford et al., 2009; Pergams, Czech, Haney, & Nyberg, 2004). Several key reasons account for this decline. One is the increasing cost of fuel, which makes long-distance travel by car to remote parks more challenging. We are now seeing a move away from travel to distant wilderness parks and a shift to more use of near-urban parks. Another reason is a decline in outdoor activities by young people as electronic gadgets, information technology, and social media increasingly take more leisure time, a phenomena called videophilia (Pergams & Zaradic, 2006). A third reason is massive immigration to both countries of people who do not have a cultural background in nature-based outdoor recreation. One of the biggest problems on the horizon for parks is adapting to and reversing this change in demand. More fuel-efficient vehicles, alternative fuels, and emergence from the economic recession might help reverse the decreases in demand associated with high fuel prices. The other key factors, videophilia and cultural influences, might be reversed through outdoor education programs (e.g., Parks as Classrooms), by actively and thoughtfully integrating information technology and social media with parks, or by changing the focus or operations of parks to be more relevant to young and culturally diverse people.

• **Encroachment**. As private-land development encroaches on park borders, wildlife lose some of their ability to move across natural areas. Development of power plants, housing, and large retail stores adjacent to parks threatens aesthetics and air quality. Development pressures also increase the temptation for government to use public parklands for public services such as roads, power lines, cell phone towers, and pipelines. A major management focus of many agencies now is to stop illegal encroachments by adjacent landowners on parklands, such as homeowners who extend their activities into parkland (McWilliam, Eagles, Seasons, & Brown, 2010).

• **Environmental threats from outside the park**. Problems originating elsewhere can affect park resources. For example, polluted river water originates in a populated area but flows through a park, or air pollution from outside a park can spoil the fresh air and views within the park. Exotic plant species seeds are dispersed by wildlife or wind and cause non-native plants to flourish inside park boundaries, possibly crowding out native species. Historically, park management focused on factors within a park's boundaries. Many park managers (particularly at the regional and national level) are beginning to recognize, plan for, and respond to these transboundary issues through partnerships and collaboration with governmental officials, nonprofit organizations, scientists, and other stakeholders.

• **Climate change**. All global environments are facing increasing threats from a climate that is affected by human forces. While once debated, climate change is now widely recognized among leaders and managers as a primary influence in the future of parks and protected areas. In fact, both the NPS and the USDA Forest Service have made understanding and responding to climate change a primary focus of their efforts. This threat is of great concern because it is pervasive and has the potential to cause significant alterations in current parks and protected areas. For example, climate change threatens glaciers that are a centerpiece of several U.S. national parks (e.g., Kenai Fjords National Park, Glacier Bay National Park, Glacier National Park), and it may cause the loss of Joshua trees from Joshua Tree National Park. Within the western United States and Canada, a warming climate has resulted in a population explosion of native bark beetles, thereby damaging and killing millions of trees. These trees are now dying and creating a major forest fire threat. This change is an example of the types of ecosystem transformations now underway.

• **Antisocial and illegal behavior**. In urban parks, vandalism, drug use, public sexual behavior, crime, and gang activity have made many people afraid to visit parks. Approaches to addressing these problems include establishing zero-tolerance zones for crimes committed within 100 yards (meters) of a park, adding special fines or sentences for doing so, and monitoring parks with cameras. Another strategy is national night-out events to encourage large numbers of people to use the parks, which usually discourages crime. In state parks, national parks, and other protected areas, the production of drugs (particularly marijuana) in remote regions has been a growing concern for managers and visitors. Likewise, illegal immigration, border security, and related human trafficking at parks that share an international border (particularly with Mexico) are an increasing problem. Law enforcement is an important activity in all parks. No conservation or recreation programs can be successful if the laws underpinning these programs are not enforced.

• **Motorized vehicles**. Off-highway vehicle (OHV) use is one of the most prevalent and fastest growing leisure activities on public lands in the United States. From 1999 to 2005 the estimated number of OHV users in the United States grew from 36 to 51 million people (Cordell et al., 2005). This figure indicates that nearly one in every five U.S. residents uses an OHV. National forests and BLM lands are frequently used as places to ride OHVs, and many of these places have trails that cater to OHV recreationists. But OHV use, particularly when not intensively managed, may lead to substantial resource impacts and controversy in these places. The USDA Forest Service in 2006 labeled unmanaged recreation in the form of OHV use as one of the four leading threats to the health of the nation's forests and grasslands in the 21st century. Also, inappropriate and illegal use of motorized vehicles in parks and protected areas is a concern for managers.

• **Coastal development**. On many coastlines, condominiums and high-rise buildings with thousands of residents are being built, greatly increasing the use of nearby coastal parks. Coastal lands have become so expensive that existing coastal parks cannot be expanded. In addition, the high density creates large human-use pressure in the parks.

• **Multiethnic cultural changes**. Projections are that an amalgam of minorities will make up more than 50 percent of the U.S. population by 2050. Because of immigration from a diverse set of countries, the Canadian and American populations are becoming more diverse in cultures and ideas. This transformation creates an issue of concern for park managers because some cultures have little tradition of visiting parks or participating in traditional outdoor recreational activities (Chavez, 2002; Johnson, Bowker, English, & Worthen, 1997; Virden & Walker, 1999). As the ethnic balance in North America shifts, park, forest, and refuge agencies at all levels must understand the preferences and outdoor recreational behaviors of minority groups and work to introduce them to activities that they may have little experience with or adapt facilities or programs to their cultures. This approach will be necessary to continue the legacy of public service that makes park resources available to all citizens and guests in the United States and Canada.

• **Workforce changes**. Many parks and protected areas are staffed and managed by a large cohort of people who are nearing retirement age. Almost half of all U.S. federal employees are within five years of retirement age, although the recent economic downturn may delay some of those retirements. Having such a large percentage of experienced park staff leaving brings with it challenges of retaining knowledge within the organization, providing adequate training, and finding qualified replacements. This change in the workforce also indicates that substantial opportunities will be available to those looking for a career in parks and protected areas.

• **Seasonality**. Most parks in Canada and the United States deal successfully with large fluctuations in visitation resulting from changes in the seasons. In northern areas visitation is largely concentrated in the warmer months, so many parks are staffed by short-term employees, often university students. A few parks in northern areas have snow-based recreational activities, typically downhill skiing, that enable year-round employment. But many parks in northern areas are staffed at very low levels or not all in the colder winter months, especially in Canada. In southern Canada warmer weather in the last decade in September, October, and November has caused a surge in visitation.

SUMMARY

The parks in Canada and the United States contain some of the most significant and attractive natural landscapes in North America. Each year, they illustrate for millions of people the ecological and cultural values of both countries. The parks of Canada and the United States are highly valued not only by their citizens but also by an increasing number of international visitors. These parks have become icons that represent the strong political, social, and cultural ideas that formed each country. Although European countries have many castles and cathedrals that mark centuries of cultural history, in North America the beauty of the wild lands—the mountains, deserts, prairies, rivers, and lakes—celebrates a major aspect of this continent and its people.

Those who work in park settings feel strongly about the value of their role, and many consider their job a positive lifelong endeavor. In an increasingly urbanized, technology-filled, overstimulated, and fast-paced culture, people seek opportunities to connect with nature. Public parks, forests, rivers, mountains, beaches, lakes, deserts, and oceans can provide inspiration, fascination, and education. These natural resources, gifts from earlier generations, can provide escape from work and social challenges, peace and relaxation, and a place to spend quiet times with family and friends or alone. They are living schools for ecology, wildlife, nature, and self-discovery.

Not many places endure unchanged over a lifetime. Over the past 150 years, North America has lost many farms and natural areas to development. Yet most parks remain more or less unchanged over the years: places for swinging or sliding as a child on the first visit to a local park; for swimming or camping with family as an adolescent; for strolling hand in hand or sharing a kiss on a park bench; for celebrating anniversaries in park lodges; for taking children hiking, fishing, canoeing, or camping; and for watching sunsets and moonrises across a scenic natural landscape during the retirement years. Parks are invaluable for creating personal memories as well as maintaining national heritage and culture. All citizens should visit parks, make memories in them, celebrate natural roots and connections to the animal and plant kingdoms, and play a role in protecting and sharing existing parks and creating new ones.

> For glossary terms, learning experiences, and more, please visit the web resource at
> **www.HumanKinetics.com/IntroductionToRecreationAndLeisure**

CHAPTER 7

Public Recreation

Tod Stanton, Susan Markham-Starr, and Jane Hodgkinson

" My friends, love is better than anger. Hope is better than fear. Optimism is better than despair. So let us be loving, hopeful and optimistic. And we'll change the world. "

Jack Layton, leader of the opposition of the government of Canada, 2011

LEARNING OUTCOMES

After reading this chapter, you should be able to do the following:

> Identify the groups that helped create public recreation services in Canada and the United States

> Describe the basic types of recreation programs found in Canada and the United States

> Demonstrate an understanding of why partnerships are important in public recreation

> Recognize the trends in the changing profession of public recreation and the leadership skills needed to advance a professional career

> List and describe the various certifications available in public recreation

> Display how community-based recreation for people with disabilities came about

> Explain factors that led to the deinstitutionalization of people with disabilities

> Cite significant American legislation that has led to services in the community

> Describe the philosophy of community-based recreation approaches

> Demonstrate the continuum of special recreation

> List and describe three types of community-based recreation programs for people with disabilities

Public Parks and Recreation in the United States and Canada

Tod Stanton and Susan Markham-Starr

" I am not concerned with our inability to nail down the specifics of what we do in parks and recreation. As I see it, our strength lies in our diversity. We can do anything. More specifically, I believe our job is to help people improve their quality of life through recreation and parks. "

Robert F. Toalson, Champaign, Illinois, Park District

Public recreation today is facing changes like never before. Many public agencies that provide these valuable services are seeing budgets cut, resources shifted, and priorities redefined. Public recreation is no longer considered a staple for a high quality of life within a community. Required today are new ideas, new leadership methods, and most important, a constant dedication to educate people about the benefits of recreation. A paradigm shift has been underway in the past few years regarding the future of public recreation as many of us have felt the effects of the great recession. But throughout history, one undeniable fact is that public recreation is needed to provide fun and exciting leisure opportunities for people of all ages. The need to embrace 21st century thinking and advance the future is upon us. The question now to our profession is how to relate to a changing environment in a modern world.

In the past, public recreation has been dependent on costly physical features such as playgrounds, trails, swimming pools, and recreation centers. These types of facilities provide valuable recreation opportunities and tend to be focused on providing something for everyone. But recreation programs are now becoming more specialized for target user groups. Does this approach make sense for the public today? The public in today's world is plugged into constant information streams that are available on their terms. The use of technology in our everyday lives has quickened our information-based lifestyle. Knowledge is available instantly. Interacting on social technology networks is becoming a major form of leisure for multiple generations. How we spend our leisure time is changing. New leadership in our field is needed to reach the public in ways not considered just a few years ago.

This section explores the realm of public recreation as a possible career path. The world of public recreation has a focus different from that used by that of our colleagues in the private sector. Public recreation is focused on traditional cultural values that stress the quality of the leisure experiences over profit and, in some cases, the customer. This section examines the pulse of public recreation and leisure services in Canada and the United States, the social and political environments in which public recreation professionals operate, the primary role of park and recreation professionals, and the constantly changing face of public recreation.

HISTORICAL OVERVIEW OF PUBLIC RECREATION IN THE UNITED STATES

The roots of public recreation can be traced to the northeast part of the United States at the turn of the 20th century. The first organized groups at this time focused on the development of playgrounds within park spaces. The need for parks was not new at this time, but traditional park planning of the time was geared to gardens, walkways, swimming areas, performing areas, and other types of passive recreation experiences. With the development of playgrounds, public recreation was able to provide structured active spaces that would lead into a shift in planning that stressed the need for active play in public recreation.

Some of the first groups to pioneer playgrounds were the Massachusetts Emergency and Hygiene Association in Boston with their sand gardens in 1885 and Outdoor Recreation League formed by Charles Stover and Lillian Wald in New York City

in 1898. In October 1903 Seward Park in New York City became the first municipal park in the country to be equipped with a permanent playground. In 1906 the Playground Association of America was founded, and by the late 1920s it would become the National Recreation Association. A separate organization, the Society of Recreation Workers, was formed in 1938. It later changed its name to the American Recreation Society. The current National Recreation and Park Association became a reality in 1956 with the merger of the National Recreation Association, the American Recreation Society, and several other prominent organizations.

HISTORICAL OVERVIEW OF PUBLIC RECREATION IN CANADA

In considering the development of public recreation in Canada, people often turn attention to the services that are closest to its citizens—those at the local level, primarily at the municipal level. In the early 21st century, these municipal services are supported by and driven by provincial and federal programs operating in a system propelled by professional, community, and political initiatives. Local public recreation began as a set of independent initiatives aimed at solving problems (real or perceived) or creating opportunities for local residents. The roots of today's integrated public recreation system come from parks, from playgrounds, from fitness, and from employment initiatives; from those who wanted to reform the "sorry condition of Canada's big cities" (Rutherford, 1974, p. xv); from those who wanted to enhance the physical, mental, and moral health of all; and from those who wanted to enhance investment growth and prosperity in cities. The results were parks established to create civic beauty and promote a healthy environment, playgrounds established to provide wholesome play opportunities for children, and physical activity programs to build the fitness levels of young people so that they would be fit for work or war. The system has been advanced by those who wanted to create a better environment, although each proponent of recreation might define *better* in a different fashion.

Influences on recreation in Canada came from Great Britain, Europe, and the United States. Readily identifiable links are those between British and

Scandinavian proponents of physical fitness such as the Young Men's Christian Association (YMCA) from England; the British Columbia Provincial Recreation (BC Pro-Rec) program, whose first director was from Denmark; and the American advocates of supervised playgrounds and urban recreation programs. Each of these groups helped plant ideas and provide information to Canadians, but the version of each idea evolved according to the social, economic, and political influences in Canada. The expansion of eastern Canadian cities in the mid- and late-19th century, the rapid expansion of the West in the early 20th century, the depression of the 1930s, the post–World War II urban growth, and the role of government as the provider of a social safety net all contributed to the Canadian solution.

Playgrounds Came First, Then Recreation

Municipal recreation in Canada can trace its roots to the National Council of Women's Vacation Schools and Supervised Playgrounds Committee in 1901 after lobbying from the Saint John Local Council of Women led by Miss Mabel Peters (McFarland, 1970, pp. 19-20). The Council focused on "'prevention' as its guiding principle" (Strong-Boag, 1976, p. 268), and by 1913 the NCW's Committee on Vacation Schools and Supervised Playgrounds was able to state firmly its mission and successes, using ideas familiar to us today:

> Its work is formative as opposed to reformative. It seeks to eventually dispense with the curfew, the juvenile court, the jail and the reform school for the young of our land. Educationists are now agreed that the public supervised playground and recreational Social Center stimulates and guides a child's life in a way which no other factor of modern living can do. (Peters, 1913, p. 48)

We no longer have reform schools and seldom have curfews, but we now speak of at-risk youth. The ideas of a century ago are still with us.

Although the National Council of Women and its local councils were advocates for playgrounds and the catalysts for their development, they were not committed to their long-term operation. They wanted to hand off responsibility to other groups such as local playgrounds associations and municipal govern-

ments. The photo shows the publicity efforts of one playgrounds association as they urged visitors to try to get a playground in their neighborhood.

Recreation departments became the norm in Canadian cities in the early to mid-20th century and often merged with parks departments. Through the last decades further mergers occurred between municipal parks and recreation and other units with similar mandates or client groups. For example, agencies that provided recreation, parks, and other social services and culture or tourism services merged into a local department of community services.

Federal and Provincial Governments

The involvement of provincial governments and the federal government in recreation can be attributed primarily to the search for antidotes to unemployment during the depression of the 1930s. Two intertwined threads were involved. One developed in British Columbia, and the other included the efforts of the federal government.

In British Columbia the government began its Provincial Recreation Program, Pro-Rec, to provide physical recreation for unemployed young men and women in 1934 as it tried to deal with "the large number of unemployed youth . . . who are exposed to the demoralizing influences of enforced idleness" (Schrodt, 1979, appendix A). The first director was Ian Eisenhardt, a Vancouver Parks Board staff member who had been trained in Denmark. When the federal government established the National Employment Commission in 1936 to investigate the needs of the unemployed, it was searching for solutions to address not only employment but also leisure needs. The commission consulted experts such as Eisenhardt and devised programs to alleviate the problems of unemployment, and programs similar to the British Columbia program emerged. Through the Federal Unemployment and Agricultural Assistance Act of 1938 and the Youth Training Act of 1939, the provinces were given assistance to create training programs that would prepare young people to work in physical training and health education in local communities and then provide recreation opportunities for trainees in other programs such as forestry, agriculture,

A local playgrounds association's advocacy work to promote playground development in the early 20th century. The sign reads, "Try and secure one for your neighbourhood."

mining, industrial apprenticeships, and domestic and household work (Canada, 1938). Responsibility for these training programs, including recreation workers, was delegated to the various provincial governments. Provinces that established training programs frequently relied on expert advice from Eisenhardt and staff from British Columbia.

Federal involvement in recreation had an influence on the municipal level through its programs of assistance in partnerships with most of the provinces. In 1943 the National Physical Fitness Program was established. This program was to "encourage, develop and correlate all activities related to physical development of the people through sports, athletics, and similar pursuits" (Canada, 1943). The program ended in 1954. Seven years later it was succeeded by the Fitness and Amateur Sport Act (Canada, 1961) and later by the Physical Activity and Sport Act (Canada, 2003). As the federal government's involvement in recreation and leisure services evolved, various government programs came and went, such as Recreation

Canada, which was established in 1971 and dissolved in 1980 (Westland, 1979, p. 30; MacIntosh, Bedecki, & Franks, 1988, p. 81). The role of the federal government in recreation in Canada is to support sport governing bodies, health concerns, the provinces, recreation-related associations, and ParticipACTION, a private initiative to promote fitness through physical activity.

DELIVERY SYSTEMS IN PUBLIC RECREATION

The public recreation system as we know it today has a variety of delivery systems in place within the various forms of governmental units. Public recreation must provide inclusive recreation and leisure services to all, including disadvantaged and disabled patrons. Inclusion is the practice of putting together people with and without disabilities in the same recreation programs. This integrated approach reflects the spirit of the Americans with Disabilities Act. Inclusion addresses the need to provide integration of leisure services for people of all ages, abilities, cultures, ethnicity, gender, race, and religion. This nondiscrimination approach goes beyond the placement of special needs participants in separate recreation program settings.

In the most basic form, recreation programs found in public recreation fall into two classes of activities. The first is active recreation, which includes all types of sports, swimming, and most physical exercise recreation opportunities. The second is passive recreation, which includes low-impact exercise and creative-based recreation programs that could include walking, arts and crafts, and trips and excursions.

American Delivery Systems

In the United States many recreation providers offer a wide range of programs in services. Public recreation services are offered through local, state, and federal agencies. Each of these governmental agencies has a different purpose. The backbone of the public recreation systems in the United States is the local recreation leisure service provider. There are more than 2,100 community park and recreation providers in the United States (www.ncpad.org/fun/fact_sheet.php?sheet=319&section=1967).

Local Recreation Leisure Services

Local park and recreation leisure service providers make up the majority of delivery systems found in the United States. Many local providers are municipal departments that provide structured programs as well as drop-in recreation opportunities. The other two systems that can be found in the United States are counties and special-use districts. Programs include recreation classes, summer camps, aquatics, sports, trips, special events, golf course operations, airport operations, cemeteries, parks, playgrounds, and trails. When most people think of parks and recreation in their daily lives, they typically think of a local recreation leisure service provider.

State Recreation Leisure Services

As we move away from a local presence, the state level of recreation and leisure is becoming less broad. Many states have state parks and state forests. The leisure activities associated with state recreation leisure services typically are passively based. At this level, programming is less emphasized. Recreation sites include golf courses, skiing areas, beaches, marinas, trails, and campgrounds. One of the primary reasons that state parks exist is to promote tourism.

Municipal departments offer programs such as sports camps, day camps, and track meets.

Federal Recreation Leisure Services

Federal recreation leisure services encompass numerous federal agencies that include the USDA Forest Service, National Park Service, Bureau of Land Management, U.S. Fish and Wildlife Service, and U.S. Army Corp of Engineers, to name a few. The primary focus of the federal delivery system is to manage outdoor resources including outdoor education in passive-based recreation methods. Many national parks have interpretative centers, trails, and campgrounds. One of the main goals of this delivery system is to let the public experience be the true power of nature.

Canadian Delivery Systems

The issue of the various levels of government jurisdiction over matters of recreation and leisure services has often been a source of debate. As a result, the National Recreation Statement of 1987 jointly signed by the Canadian federal, provincial, and territorial governments laid out the following broad principles to guide the respective responsibilities of the three levels of government:

1. The federal government will do the following:
   - "Primarily involve itself in those activities that are national in scope."
   - "Provide for the development and maintenance of recreation programs and services appropriate to those facilities and institutions under the jurisdiction of the federal government." (Interprovincial Sport and Recreation Council [ISRC], 1987, p. 11)

2. The provincial and territorial governments have substantial responsibilities related to recreation. These responsibilities are primarily at the level of coordinating programs, providing information and financial resources to program delivery agencies, planning and supporting research. They are very rarely the direct delivery agent for recreation and leisure services (ISRC, 1987, pp. 8-9).

3. Municipal governments are deemed to be the suppliers of services:
   - "Municipal governments are closest to the people; they are likely to respond more flexibly, more quickly and more effectively to the needs of the community in matters of recreation. For this reason the municipality is the primary supplier of direct recreation services." (ISRC, 1987, p. 9)
   - The basic role of the municipality is to ensure the availability of the broadest range of recreation opportunities for every individual and group consistent with available community resources (ISRC, 1987, p. 10).

But, what does this division mean? Who does what? Who has legislative authority? At first glance it might appear that the federal government has overall constitutional responsibility for recreation and leisure, but it does not. Nowhere in the Canadian Constitution Act (Canada, 1982) is there mention of federal responsibility for recreation or leisure. The closest that the Constitution Act of 1982 comes is to guarantee the following through the Charter of Rights and Freedoms:

Everyone has the following fundamental freedoms:

- Freedom of conscience and religion
- Freedom of thought, belief, opinion, and expression, including freedom of the press and other communication media
- Freedom of peaceful assembly
- Freedom of association

Thus, although the Constitution Act does not allocate legislative responsibility for recreation and leisure or state how recreation and leisure services are delivered, it does guarantee the freedoms that are considered to be essential elements of leisure. Individual professionals and the agencies in which they operate must uphold the Charter of Rights and Freedoms.

In keeping with the emphasis on "activities that are national in scope," the federal responsibility for recreation-related matters is governed by the Physical Activity and Sport Act of 2003. This act is under the jurisdiction of two departments, not one. The responsibility for physical activity is allocated to the minister of health, and the responsibility for sport is under the minister of Canadian heritage (Canada, 2011). That latter assignment is in keeping with that department's mandate for programs that "promote Canadian content, foster cultural participation, active citizenship and participation in Canada's civic life, and strengthen connections among Canadians" (Canadian Heritage, 2010). Sport is viewed as part of several programs that contribute to Canadian identity through high-performance sport and international sport. To the Canadian federal government, recreation is a physical activity that enhances health, and international sport solidifies Canada's identity. This focus often seems far removed from the day-to-day responsibilities of recreation professionals.

The various provinces and territories have different views of recreation. All have some type of government unit responsible for recreation, but the labels differ. Over the past half century, provincial governments have committed themselves to assisting recreation and leisure services through various government departments such as education and health and public welfare (McFarland, 1970, p. 60). Yet not until 1972 did a provincial government, Nova Scotia, establish a department whose sole mandate was recreation. Most provinces carried out similar actions in the 1970s. But just as a province can establish a recreation department, it also can change it. Provincial recreation agencies went through amalgamations and disintegrations with partners that now include departments for community services, health, seniors, sport, tourism, culture, parks, and so on, all in the interest of efficiency, effectiveness, and political expediency. Table 7.1 in the web resource shows the names of provincial and territorial departments responsible for recreation.

The previous discussion looked at the legislation and labels for the government agencies responsible for some form of recreation. But how do government departments carry out their responsibility? Tim Burton, former University of Alberta professor, created an explanatory model that explains the five roles that governments can take in delivering public services:

1. Direct provider
2. Enabler and coordinator
3. Supporter and patron
4. Arm's length provider
5. Legislator and regulator (Burton & Glover, 1999)

As we move down the list of the five roles, the amount of direct involvement on the part of govern-

ment agencies decreases. Many recreation students will be most familiar with the **direct provider** role, which "describes the situation in which a government department or agency develops and maintains leisure facilities, operates programs, and delivers services using public funds and public employees" (Burton & Glover, 1999, p. 373). If you have been a town playground supervisor or a city swimming pool instructor, you have been part of the direct provider role. The municipality that developed the program owned the facility, ran the program, and paid you.

The next three roles involve decreasing amounts of direct involvement by the government. When a government department acts as an **enabler and coordinator**, it will "identify organizations and agencies which produce leisure services for the public and help coordinate their efforts, resources

Various delivery systems exist for providing public recreation. In this photo we can see the direct provider role.

and activities" (Burton & Glover, 1999, p. 374). If you have worked for a local community group that received funds and services such as leadership training from a recreation department, you have seen a government unit acting as an enabler and coordinator. When a government department acts as a **supporter and patron**, it "recognizes that existing organizations already produce valuable public leisure services and can be encouraged to do so through specialized support" (Burton & Glover, 1999, p. 374). If your local community festival received a government grant to assist in the production of a special event or to develop a facility, the government would have been acting as a supporter and patron. Furthest away from government's direct influence is the role of **arm's length provider**, which "requires the creation of a . . . special purpose agency which operates outside the regular apparatus of government" (Burton & Glover, 1999, p. 373). Arts and culture organizations such as museums or galleries operate in this relationship. In theory the government unit does not interfere with the internal operation of such an organization, but theory and practice occasionally conflict when political decision makers object to an organization's decisions to acquire a controversial piece of art or mount a controversial play using public funds to do so.

The last role of government, **legislator and regulator**, affects many of our actions as both providers and consumers of recreation opportunities. This role operates in the background of many parts of our work and leisure lives because we must abide by laws passed by various levels of government. When a government agency requires you to obtain a permit to put on an event or have a fireworks display, it is acting in this role. When you as a consumer must get a fishing license or be of a certain age to enter a facility that serves alcohol, you are also experiencing these powers of government.

The municipal, provincial and territorial, and federal levels of government do not all engage in each of these five roles to the same degree. Municipal governments traditionally have operated using a direct provider role, but as cities and towns have faced financial stresses, many have shifted to a model in which they have transferred services to community groups while providing financial or in-kind support to those groups, thus moving toward an enabler and coordinator or a supporter and patron model. Provincial and federal government departments have historically used the latter two models. Provincial and federal governments have also created arm's length agencies to carry out cultural programs. Many provincial agencies' mandates require that they operate in a legislator and regulator model.

PARTNERSHIPS: CONNECTIONS TO THE COMMUNITY

Forming partnerships, cooperative ventures, and collaborative agreements or alliances has long been practiced by recreation and leisure professionals in the public sector. But today the emphasis on reviewing, revising, and renewing partnering efforts is more critical than ever. No agency or entity can thrive alone. Seeking new, inclusive, innovative, flexible, and commonly focused opportunities is imperative. Why? Because in forming partnerships, recreation and leisure professionals may be able to reduce the duplication of existing services, save money, and streamline organizations. Inevitably, they will increase the visibility of the organization, gain a better network, and develop a more viable resource pool. In addition, personnel will have the opportunity to grow along with the community.

Any governmental unit can form a partnership with another governmental unit, with a nonprofit organization, or with a private entity. All these organizations can bring useful resources to the table to advance an opportunity, often producing better results than going it alone. One of the most useful partnerships for a public recreation agency to develop is one with the local school district. A goal for many communities is an indoor pool. This type of facility can be cost prohibitive for most in the public environment. If the school district wanted to upgrade its existing pool but did not have sufficient capital funds and the local park and recreation agency identified the need for an indoor pool but had limited funds as well, a partnership could be explored. This partnership would allow the park and recreation agency use of the school's indoor pool in return for the investment of capital dollars, and the school district would get the upgraded pool. In this win–win solution the community would recognize the benefit of the partnership. These partnerships can work wonders if the parties can produce a win–win outcome.

Most partnerships take the form of an intergovernmental agreement that outlines the benefits received by the parties involved. Parks and recreation departments work with police and fire departments on safety protocol, camps, and programs such as bicycle or fire safety. Ongoing partnerships with the public works department can address building needs and general maintenance operations.

Local neighborhood groups work with parks departments to provide events, develop facilities, and carry out cleanup programs. These partnerships not only benefit the parks and recreation department but also bring families and friends closer together because they are working toward a common goal. What better way is there to share facilities that are funded by taxpayers?

Every community can provide examples of successful partnerships. Look for examples of the following in your community:

- Programs that strengthen families such as Big Brothers and Big Sisters

- Business relationships such as public and private partnerships that develop or operate a facility

- Justice departments involved in community crime prevention programs

- Volunteer groups such as community leagues or neighborhood recreation associations that are advocates for their community and deliver programs

The future of partnerships is bright. As agencies and communities realize the many benefits of working together, more opportunities to develop partnerships will arise.

FACES OF PUBLIC RECREATION

Most people who have chosen a career in public recreation find that they enjoy working with people through providing an essential governmental service. The need to provide recreation programs, facilities, parks, and open space for community enjoyment is a powerful mission that provides

Public recreation departments can cooperate with outside groups to construct playgrounds. As you discover the various aspects of recreation and leisure, community involvement with a variety of interest groups will be one of your most frustrating, and perhaps one of your most rewarding, experiences.

direct quality of life benefits. The diversity of activity types, civil servant calling, and the thrill of a variety of work environments leads to a profession measuring high in self-fulfillment.

Public Recreation Professionals

In the field of public recreation, many career paths include specialized areas of knowledge, such as recreation programming, facilities management, parks, outdoor education, therapeutic recreation, and recreation administration. Professionals within the field of public recreation use a variety of skills obtained from both academic study and on-the-job training. The core skills used at any level include

- ability to navigate the political environment;
- effective communication techniques;
- excellent customer service;
- ability to plan and implement programs, events, and activities;
- demonstrated leadership;
- fiscal forecasting and effective budgeting control; and
- conflict resolution.

Because recreation and leisure professionals need to be well rounded, professional training and preparation are detailed yet practical. Besides taking program development classes, recreation and leisure students take courses in environmental design and planning, leadership, and management.

The opportunity to grow professionally in public recreation will be based on a variety of internal and external forces. A recent topic is diversification, the ability to develop a wide range of job skills through on-the-job training and advancement, in the workplace. The ability to achieve job satisfaction can be linked to job diversification with an organization. An enhanced skill set will provide value to the organization and professional advancement opportunities for the individual. The variety of jobs within the public recreation realm sets up the opportunity for diversity within the workforce that few other careers can match.

Most people today still believe that the field of parks and recreation encompasses sport, fun, and games. Although these elements are certainly part of the profession, they do not begin to cover the diverse areas and links to other professions.

Public Recreation Management

Managers and leaders in recreation and leisure services plan, organize, direct, and control various areas of the agency. Managers fall into three categories: top, or executive, managers; middle managers; and frontline, or supervisory, managers. Within these categories other positions may report to them.

Managers must possess three types of skills:

1. Technical skills require specialized knowledge in operations, techniques, and procedures.
2. Human skills require understanding people and the ability to motivate and work with employees.
3. Conceptual skills allow the development and organization of a philosophy, mission, goals, and objectives.

Besides performing organizational and administrative functions within an organization, managers are also involved in strategic planning, which encompasses community involvement and coordination with municipalities and other agencies. Managers need to work with community members to plan the many activities and facilities that are needed. By working with the community, managers help community members buy in to the activities and develop a sense of ownership. Successful collaboration draws on all the skills required of recreation and leisure professionals.

Professionals must ask themselves the following: What do we do as professionals in public recreation? Whom do we serve? Do we serve our career? Do we serve the public? Do we serve the politicians? Whom do the politicians serve? Coming to your own answers to those questions is a major step in your professional career.

American Professional Organizations

Professional organizations within a career field are an invaluable resource for people who practice that profession. In the field of public recreation, the largest and most recognized association in the United States is the National Recreation and Park

Background Information

Name: Laura Thomas Barron

Education: Associate of applied science in recreation leadership, College of DuPage, 1979. Bachelor of science in recreation and park administration, Western Illinois University, 1981. Master of science in recreation administration, George Williams College of Aurora University, 2004.

Credentials: Certified park and recreation professional (CPRP), certified aquatic facility operator (AFO).

Special awards: College of DuPage Outstanding Sigma College Graduate, Western Illinois University. Distinguished Alumni Award, Department of Recreation, Park and Tourism Administration, Western Illinois University. Jim Berousek Alumni Award for Outstanding Service to Western Illinois University, Department of Recreation, Park and Tourism Administration.

Affiliations: National Recreation and Park Association (NRPA), Illinois Park and Recreation Association (IPRA), Suburban Park and Recreation Association (SPRA).

Career Information

Position: Director of parks and recreation, Oakbrook Terrace Park District, Oakbrook Terrace, Illinois.

Organization: The Oakbrook Terrace Park District, which includes portions of Oakbrook Terrace and unincorporated Villa Park, serves approximately 10,000 residents. Additionally, the Oakbrook Terrace Park District provides services to a number of nonresidents who work in Oakbrook Terrace's large corporate sector. Eight full-time and 40 part-time employees operate three parks and four facilities.

Organization's mission: The Oakbrook Terrace Park District was established to serve the local community and public in seeking recreational and leisure needs that are not only a right but a necessity to the welfare of the public. Park district programs and services are designed to establish the opportunity for everyone to enjoy and participate in varied activities. Programs and services are constantly reviewed and assessed for relevance to public needs. The park district is also dedicated to maintaining the financial balance necessary to establish, maintain, and protect future needs for community leisure. The park district views all its facilities and programs as a whole, and maintenance and implementation is done for the greater good of the entire community and public. The park district is dedicated to maintaining the highest quality of professional staff to serve the public. The park district believes in the ongoing process of providing recreational services for people with special needs throughout the Northeast DuPage Special Recreation Association and accessibility for its facilities whenever and wherever possible. Continued input from the public will be constantly encouraged for the purpose of providing relevant and successful programs.

Job description: Responsible for the overall management of the park district's operations, which includes the Nature Center, Fitness Center, Parks Department, Recreation Department, and Business Department. Additionally responsible for preparing and managing the annual budget and reporting to the Board of Commissioners, as well as acting as a representative of the park district in meeting with intergovernmental agencies and community groups.

Career path: I started out when I was 15 years old at the Wheaton Park District in the Youth Conservation Corp, which was a federally funded project that focused on parks beautification. In following years I worked as recreation program leader and later decided to pursue a degree in leisure services, which would assist me in reaching my goal of a career in public recreation. I have held the positions of activity director and recreation therapist, cultural arts supervisor, recreation supervisor, and superintendent of recreation before becoming director of parks and recreation.

Outstanding Graduates *(continued)*

Likes and dislikes about the job: There are many things that I love about my job. It truly is a calling for me to be able to provide the best possible recreational services and open spaces for our community to enjoy. There is nothing better than observing participants having a wonderful time because of something that new and creative program staff conjured up, or adding amenities to a park that allow someone to lose themselves in a moment of uninterrupted play that can provide them with a positive outlet mentally and physically. We are here to make a difference in a special way, and I try to keep it a mission of ours. Those moments where I witness that enjoyment, I say, "That is why we do what we do." It reinforces to me that my career selection was one of the best decisions I have ever made. What do I dislike? There's nothing I really dislike, but I would say sometimes there are challenges. The most challenging area of my job would be dealing with the struggling economy and doing more with less. It is hard to do things on a grand scale as they were here before the downturn of the economy. Through the loss of funds, we have learned to focus on even more creative ways of providing quality services and well-maintained parks for the community while staying within our budgetary means. We have developed a keener eye for what the current leisure trends are and have strived to keep offerings affordable to encourage continued participation.

Advice to Undergraduates

Stay active in the leisure service field in a variety of areas, whether it is at a park district, a YMCA, a forest preserve district, or a special recreation association. All those areas are not only resume builders but also experience builders that you will draw on time and time again during your professional career. Those experiences may be as simple as assisting at a special event or coaching a youth sport team, but by staying involved you demonstrate your passion for the leisure service field. Make an effort to be part of professional organizations and committees and to network with other professionals and students. Have fun, work hard, and build positive relationships along the way. Have a great attitude and a sense of humor and be loyal to your staff, supervisor, and the agency that you work for. By giving back to the field much more than you expect to receive, you will excel and succeed in more ways than you could ever imagine.

Association (NRPA). This organization provides many opportunities for the park and recreation professional to obtain knowledge within the ever-changing field. In addition to the national organization, numerous affiliates as well as state and local organizations provide resources for the public recreation profession (see table 7.2 in the web resource).

Certifications

Certification is a process in which individuals are examined to determine whether they meet or exceed a defined standard. Certification of leisure professionals was developed by concerned leisure professionals who wished to improve the quality of personnel employed in the field. One of its core strengths is that certification was developed and approved by the professionals in the field itself. Certification is not required to work in the profession.

Several certifications in the field of public parks and recreation signify a demonstrated commitment to being a top professional. The National Recreation and Park Association certification programs are governed by the National Certification Board. Three certifications are currently offered:

- **Certified park and recreation professional** (**CPRP**) certification is granted to people employed in the recreation, park resources, and leisure services profession who meet high standards of performance.
- **Aquatic facility operator** (**AFO**) is a state-of-the-art certification for pool operators and aquatic facility managers.
- **Certified playground safety inspector** (**CPSI**) provides the credentials to inspect playgrounds for safety ensuring that each playground meets the current national standards

set by the American Society for Testing and Materials (ASTM) and U.S. Consumer Product Safety Commission (CPSC).

The Commission for Accreditation of Park and Recreation Agencies (CAPRA) provides assurance that an agency meets national standards best practice for recreation programs and services.

All these certifications are gained through examination that demonstrates that the applicant meets the criteria for basic knowledge and material understanding. Certifications are important in public recreation to signify the potential for advancement, to demonstrate professional commitment to the profession, to develop further skills through continuing education, and to recognize professional accomplishment.

Canadian Professional Organizations

The previous section showed the structure and mandate of the various sectors of the public recreation delivery system. Many recreation and leisure service professionals work within this framework of public and governmental jurisdictions. Just as these professionals have established or worked in organizations to deliver services, they have also joined associations to promote the cause of recreation and leisure services. From the roots of the Ontario Parks Association grew the Parks and Recreation Association of Canada (PRAC) in 1945. PRAC's mandate was "the Dominion-wide stimulation of recreation, [and] the Dominion-wide extension of parks including municipal, provincial and national parks and recreation activities" (Parks and Recreation Association of Canada, 1947). As the organization adapted to changes in the environment in the 1960s, it changed its name first to the Canadian Parks/Recreation Association (CP/RA) in 1969 and later refined it to the Canadian Parks and Recreation Association (CPRA). CPRA promotes itself as an organization of both professionals and volunteers who are involved in parks and recreation. Today CPRA provides services through its partnership with provincial or territorial organizations, each of which is autonomous and offers services in keeping with its local requirements. It is also developing partnerships with organizations such as Canadian Sport for Life (CS4L). CPRA was a key player in the creation and delivery of the

2011 National Recreation Summit which brought over 200 delegates together to focus on recreation community and quality of life (National Recreation Summit, 2011). Other key players and allies in the municipal and recreation arena are the Federation of Canadian Municipalities (FCM) and the Canadian Council on Social Development (CCSD). Table 7.3 in the web resource lists the national, provincial, and territorial associations.

As part of CPRA's 1969 changes, the Recreation Institute of Canada was formed because of pressure to form an organization that reflected the needs and interests of professionals in the field. The institute had a short life. Interest by professionals was not as high as expected, and the institute ceased operation after four years, in 1973. Therein lies one of the essential, enduring debates in the recreation and leisure services field: Is it a profession? If it is, how does it deal with the thousands of volunteers who guide policy and deliver services? If it is not, how does it attain the status and profile that it needs both to ensure the competence of those leading the field and to endure in the face of policy and funding-priority debates with other professions?

CHAMELEON PROFESSION: EVER CHANGING SOCIETAL ISSUES AND NEEDS

Being a chameleon is often viewed in a negative sense, perhaps considered selling out to external influences, but in the case of the public recreation profession, it is not. We must be adaptable. We must respond to changes in the environment, whether those changes are in the physical, economic, political, or social parts of the environment. But we must not lose sight of our founding roots, our reasons for being, and our desire to contribute to the public good. What is the future of public-sector recreation and leisure? To discover where we are headed, we must understand the current reality.

Current Themes

Recent labor, leisure, and longevity trends affect how much unobligated time people have and how they use it. These trends in turn affect recreation and leisure services and professionals who provide them. Most workers today do not work a standard workday from 9 to 5 (Godbey, 1997). About 40 percent of North Americans report always feeling rushed, yet they average approximately 40 hours of free time per week. Our aging, retired population is growing, and people older than 50 have more free time today than they did in 1965. People are working mixed schedules that vary based on the needs of the various communities.

As leisure patterns in North America continue to change, one of the best predictors of change is our aging citizens, who are more active than ever before. In addition, our urban areas are becoming more diverse. More people are pursuing higher levels of formal education, and women are taking on increasingly diverse roles. The gap between the haves and have-nots is widening. Citizens expect government to do more, but they want to pay less. People are obsessed with health, but citizens of the United States and Canada are now more obese than ever, especially the young. All this means that recreation and leisure service professionals must deal with a wide set of issues when creating programs, making plans, and obtaining resources and funding.

Statistics Canada's 2011 census yields the following insights into the current population and the trends that affect employees of Canadian recreation agencies and the people whom they serve:

- The number of seniors (those aged 65 and over) increased 14.1 percent between 2006 and 2011 to nearly 5 million. This rate of growth was higher than that of children aged 14 and under (0.5 percent) and people aged 15 to 64 (5.7 percent).

- Seniors accounted for a record high of 14.8 percent of the population in Canada in 2011, up from 13.7 percent five years earlier.

- The population of children aged 4 and under increased 11 percent between 2006 and 2011. This was the highest growth rate for this age group since the years spanning 1956 to 1961 during the baby boom (Statistics Canada, 2012).

- In 2011, the working-age population (those aged 15 to 64) represented 68.5 percent of the Canadian population. This proportion was higher than in any other G8 country, except Russia.

- Among the working-age population, 42.4 percent were in the age group 45 to 64, a record-high proportion. Almost all people aged 45 to 64 in 2011 were baby boomers.

- In 2011, census data showed for the first time that there were more people aged 55 to 64, typically the age group in which people leave the labor force, than aged 15 to 24, typically the age group in which people enter it.

- In 2011, the proportion of seniors was the highest in the Atlantic provinces, Quebec, and British Columbia.

In 2006, the aboriginal population (First Nations, Métis, Inuit) reached 1,172,790—a growth of 45 percent since 1996, or nearly 6 times greater than the 8 percent increase for the non-Aboriginal population (Statistics Canada, 2008).

But what do these insights tell us about how recreation services will have to change to accommodate the changing population? David Foot's 1998 analysis of population growth or lack of it in *Boom, Bust and Echo* provides us with insights on how Canadian demographics affect many social, economic, and political issues such as real estate, investing, jobs, retail, leisure, urban development, education, health care, and family structure. Foot identified and projected several trends about leisure activities for the declining younger population and the increasing older population. His detailed projections may be subject to debate as the interests of individuals and specific communities are taken into account, but his macro-level analyses such as the population pyramids shown at www.footwork.com/pyramids.html give us a stunning view of the future.

Besides affecting the type of leisure services that must be provided, an aging population also affects funding for recreation services. Many key questions come out of Foot's analyses. For example, in a 2002 *Globe and Mail* article, Foot noted that as population growth slows and the population ages, the capacity for funding public services through taxation declines. This circumstance will have a substantial effect on public recreation. In the same article Foot addressed population growth caused by immigration and noted that immigration has become the main source of population growth in Canada.

The 2006 census noted that immigration had increased since 2001 and that "at 19.8 percent,

Canada had a higher proportion of foreign born than the United States of America" (Statistics Canada, 2007, p. 5). What does this statistic mean to the multicultural makeup of Canada? Where do these immigrants settle? They settle mostly in the major urban centers such as Montreal, Toronto, and Vancouver. What does that influx of immigrants mean for public recreation services in those cities? Are we in recreation prepared to serve this diverse mosaic of traditions, needs, interests, and expectations? There are numerous examples of diverse recreation programs in cities with a substantial multicultural makeup. One example is the Sunset Community Centre in Vancouver, which "serves a multi-cultural population of over 33,000 with a high proportion of Chinese and Punjabi residents, young families and children" (Vancouver Profile, 2011).

Much attention in both Canada and the United States has focused on immigration and the life experiences of immigrants. In many Canadian cities, the life experiences of the aboriginal population are a major social and political issue as agencies and governments struggle to address the issues of a growing, young aboriginal population. As noted earlier, the aboriginal population is growing faster than the nonaboriginal population. Fifty-four percent live in urban areas such as Winnipeg, Edmonton, Vancouver, Toronto, Calgary, Saskatoon, and Regina. "The Aboriginal population is younger than the non-Aboriginal population. Almost half (48 percent) of the Aboriginal population consists of children and youth aged 24 and under, compared with 31 percent of the non-Aboriginal population" (Statistics Canada, 2008, p. 6).

In the United States the attention in recreation and leisure services is slowly shifting toward the aging baby boomer population as well as the immigrant population. For example, during the period from 2000 to 2009, 1,029,943 legal immigrants gained America citizenship. The greatest number, 41 percent, came from Latin America, and the second largest group, 34 percent, came from Asia (Martin & Midgely, 2010).

Park and recreation professionals in America need to understand these new demographics. The traditional ways of providing park and leisure services need to change to match the ever changing face of the public.

Trends in Public Recreation

The pace of change in today's world is accelerating. Our leisure patterns will continue to change, and our recreation needs will change as well. If the public sector does not embrace the changes within recreation, nonprofits and the private sector will become the dominant providers. In some markets, such as fitness, they already are.

The future of public recreation needs to be based on a new breed of professional. This person will need to be technologically well informed, committed to advancing ongoing community-based research, and able to develop strategies to communicate quicker with groups that seek leisure activities. The tools available will only improve as time goes on. The leadership skills needed to be successful in designing strategies to provide solutions to these trends will be based on advanced academic studies and a commitment to continuing education. The need to take the best of private business models for both finances and operations and develop better public recreation models is here to stay. Many of the most successful public recreation providers have embraced this shift. The public does not wish for continued tax increases to fund leisure services.

The biggest trends facing the United States today in leisure services center on a changing population. The challenge within the profession is to develop a new breed of programs that can meet these needs. Much work needs to be done not only in program development but also in operations and facilities to prepare for these challenges. To date, public recreation agencies have identified the need to adjust core thinking, but little real headway has been made.

Public sector agencies will need to address several critical trends in the 21st century:

- The general population is becoming more culturally and racially diverse.
- Seniors are becoming a significant group that needs innovative programming ideas that can provide a rewarding leisure experience.
- Young adults are seeking new ways to recreate.
- Children's programs are geared for active recreation activities to keep them fit.
- Agencies will need to embrace private-sector product models and respond quicker to market changes.

Community Schools

The introduction to and instruction in recreation activities have long been considered essential elements of a well-rounded kindergarten through grade 12 (K-12) curriculum. Recreation activities have been vital not only to nurturing strength, flexibility, and self-esteem in young people but also to furthering educational achievement. Also responding to a need to provide young people with constructive activities is the concept of **community education**. Through participation in community education—after-school and evening classes and activities and programs at the local school—students can further enhance their strength, flexibility, self-esteem, and academic performance.

Six components make up the philosophy of community education. Each component is vital to an effective, comprehensive community school.

1. **Community involvement**: Building a feeling of inclusion among community members by providing encouragement and opportunities for involvement and leadership in the development of community school activities

2. **Facility use**: Making use of existing school facilities, which are owned by the taxpayers

3. **Adult programming**: Organizing and implementing classes and activities that are requested and designed by adults in the community and that appeal to their needs

4. **Youth programming**: Organizing and implementing classes and activities that are requested and designed by young people in the community and that appeal to their needs

5. **Classroom enrichment through community resources**: Augmenting and enriching classroom curriculum and lessons by requesting the expertise and passion of knowledgeable speakers who live in the community and scheduling hands-on learning opportunities during the school day through field trips to community sites

6. **Coordination and cooperation in the delivery of community services**: Bringing people to the table who are involved in similar pursuits to benefit the entire community, thus avoiding duplication of effort and resolving issues

The community education concept was originally grounded in involvement and participation, and that tenet has been the hallmark of its extended success. The practice of community education invited a new, collaborative spirit to the old model of program development. It promoted a process in which people could become involved rather than simply an event in which they could participate. This application in the development of community school services offered a seat at the table for all members of the community, including adults, youth, senior citizens, people with disabilities, males, females, and citizens of all cultural backgrounds and faiths.

Current Conditions of Community Education

Over the years, community education has continued to provide programs and activities that are driven by expressed community need and involve community members in meaningful leadership roles that enrich community living. Community school advisory councils and advisory boards have become important components of successful community schools, providing the foundation, voice, and representation for community members and community organizations—individuals, schools, businesses, and public and private organizations—to become partners in addressing community needs.

Community education advisory councils and boards became incubators for site-based leadership, a model used across the country in school reform efforts. And the influence did not end there. Community participation in education issues and school reform has been embraced by school districts from shore to shore and become part of the institutional culture of those organizations. In the United States, the influence of education reform has been seen in federally funded programs such as Immigration Goals 2000, Education 2000 (see www.ed.gov/G2K/index.html for more information), 21st Century Community Learning Centers, and the

(continued)

Community Schools *(continued)*

No Child Left Behind Act, all of which highlight activities that enhance academic achievement, literacy, and the unique needs of urban and rural communities.

The original community education model was founded on components that provide for the delivery of quality programs, activities, and services; the development of leadership; the shared use of school and community facilities; the integration of resources into the K-12 classroom curriculum;

and the conversations necessary to achieve collaborative and inclusive relationships, all driven by the desire to respond to identified needs. When all these components are given equal voice in a community school, the result is a balanced program that invites participation and welcomes diverse activities that meet the comprehensive needs of the community. When attention is cast on just one or two of these elements, a threat to the full capacity of the model arises.

Careers in Community Education

Skills needed for professional entry-level positions in community schools: Volunteer management; publicity, promotion, and marketing; programming; funding and resource development; demonstrated leadership ability; group-process skills; customer service skills; positive attitude; sense of humor; and ability to build, maintain, and deepen relationships with community members, businesses, and organizations

Types of community education positions available: Community college continuing education coordinator or director, community school coordinator or director, community education agent, school business partnership director, service learning coordinator, volunteer manager, facilities scheduling manager, community resources center manager or director, community school or community learning center grant manager

- Governments will need to invest into replacing deteriorating park and recreation infrastructure.

- Strategies need to be developed to combat shrinking budgets relative to increasing costs.

- Parks and recreation can become economic engines by wise investment in increasing tourism and providing a higher quality of life.

Tomorrow's Leadership Skills

The changing profession and the trends facing public recreation require new leadership skills to lead public recreation into the future. What does the new breed of professional entering the public sector look like? Can they make a difference? New leaders need to innovate as the pioneers of park and recreation did a century ago. With that being said, now is the time for strong leadership to act. Public recreation has grown steadily because advances in technology have given people more free time. The real quest is to use ongoing research to define what public recreation will become. Making tough

decisions will be easier when research is used to validate the direction on a given topic.

The ability to grow leisure services offerings by understanding the needs of the population has led many public agencies to find untapped markets. Capital construction costs have been at near record lows in the great recession. Projects are delivered under budget and ahead of schedule. All this is made possible by the valor to act. Now more than ever is the time to build on our ability to deliver quality of life by practicing what we do best.

The Changing Profession

The future of public leisure and recreation seems to lead to a decline in most forms of sport participation and greater interest in the environment. People now seem to be more interested in the quality of the experience and a sense of place. More diversity of leisure expression is likely to occur because our population is becoming more diverse.

The types of programs needed to meet the demands of the public are becoming more diverse based on several factors. The standard focus on youth and athletics programs is still popular, but seniors, adult-only, families, and fitness-based recreation are becoming more requested. New ideas need to be created to address these new and growing populations. The communities in which services are provided are becoming more polarized. Recreation services that fall in the middle of the general population are less able to meet all needs.

Because state and federal funding of recreation and leisure services is declining, these services will be more locally focused. Citizens want local assistance in enhancing their quality of life. Providing parks and recreation services for all ages and diverse populations is critical. For example, citizens want the local parks and recreation agency to provide parks, various programs, and facilities. Therefore, recreation agencies need to be flexible and innovative in their work efforts, including staff assignments; decision making; training programs; and the knowledge, skills, and abilities needed to do the job.

Finally, outsourcing may become the norm instead of the exception. Recreation and leisure service agencies may become more enterprising than they have been in the past. The customization of leisure programs, in which people are treated appropriately, not equally, will be necessary to retain community consumers. For instance, additional strategic planning will be necessary to place appropriate, applicable facilities and programs in a community, based on numbers and needs. This means that the squeaky wheel may not get the grease. In the past, different areas of a community were often treated as though their needs were all the same. This effort created more amenities but was not necessarily a strategic approach that addressed real needs.

As the members of diverse communities request more and different services, recreation and leisure professionals need to address emerging trends and issues to meet the ever changing needs and expectations of their clientele. As services continue to evolve, parks and recreation professionals will create the future.

The Changing Professional

The profession of public recreation is at a crossroads. As with all careers, the growth of the profession is fueled by economics. Unfortunately, many public recreation agencies have had a hard time during the recent great recession keeping budgets in pace with the demand for recreation services. The amount of professional skill needed for those within the field is different from in years past. The baseline standard of education within the field is moving past a bachelor's degree into a master's degree. The public is also more sophisticated by being armed with knowledge obtained from the Internet.

The new frontier in public recreation is building an organization that can be adaptable in a changing landscape. This is a contradiction in the public recreation realm. Governments are historically slow to react and are set in a traditional hierarchical operational model. The future professional can monitor the public in ways not thought of in the past and can communicate quickly using new technology applications, such as social media. Research will allow professionals to understand the will of the public and produce better decisions. Public recreation professionals need to invest in continuing education to keep skills sharp and learn about new tools that will allow then to work smarter. All agencies are being asked to do more with fewer resources. Professionals in the field today face several major issues:

- How to secure financing for major capital initiatives including parks, facilities, and open spaces
- How to set spending priorities with shrinking budgets
- How to make parks safe while maintaining visitor enjoyment
- How public parks and recreation can strengthen its political position by shaping community quality of life

Park and recreation professionals will need to understand finances and budget better than they did in years past. The ability to execute two critical activities, leading and managing, will be important. The distinction is that management is doing things right, whereas leadership is doing the right things. The ability to provide strong leadership for the organization will be a necessary trait for professional success.

POLITICAL REALITIES: NO PAIN, NO GAIN

One of the most telling comments on the realities of working in public recreation is the title of George Cuff's article "First on the Agenda: Last on the Budget" that appeared in *Recreation Canada* (1990). Based on his personal experiences as a recreation director and later as a mayor, he describes the "challenges, difficulties and competing influences which Council members face the moment they assume public office" (p. 34). Not much has changed in two decades.

To many novices in recreation, the words *politics* and *politicians* are incredibly negative. Why? What would make people think that? The reality of public recreation is that the ultimate decision makers are often elected officials. Who elects them? We do— we, the public! In the abstract, the challenge and the role of public recreation are to serve all of us. But does this really happen? And who is "us"? Is it realistic to believe that the public recreation system can serve all? Who takes up the challenge to try to serve all? Can they succeed? Is recreation really a public good?

Public recreation is about creating a sense of inclusion. Are you prepared to listen to and assist everyone in your community? You should be. How will you deal with competing interests? Think about a small community park. How many groups with competing interests can you imagine want to use that park? How about young soccer players and their parents, older aggressive soccer players, baseball players of all ages, parents of small children, dog walkers, neighbors who want peace and quiet, neighbors who want a pretty park to enhance their property values, kids who want a place to splash in the hot summer, teenagers who want a place to hang out, musicians who want a place to jam, skateboarders who want a place to practice stunts, pacifists who want a place to protest against a war, a theater group that wants a place to perform, a religious group that wants to perform a religious play, or homeless people who want a place to hunker down at night?

Balance will always be needed between the requests of communities and the other desires or actions that political powers believe need attention. Somewhere in the middle of the issue are the parks and recreation staff members who will try to resolve the situation or create the win–win scenario. It is what we do.

Leaders in the recreation profession need to realize that political responsiveness becomes more difficult and complex as the size and diversity of the population that they serve increase. Problems of political responsiveness are most likely found in one of two types of settings. The first, and most widely recognized, is the scenario in which a new group either moves into a community or rapidly increases its percentage of the community's members. One example of this is the growth of youth soccer and parents' desire for more fields and amenities. Difficulties are frequently encountered in accommodating the views and attitudes of the new group in policy-making processes. The second setting is one in which the community experiences rapid population growth that outpaces the ability to provide resources and facilities. This setting further identifies the city with the haves and the have-nots.

What role can interest groups play in obtaining recreation services? Interest groups can be powerful, vocal advocates for recreation services, or they can be adversaries. They can publicly address issues that a recreation staff member cannot. They can provide a public face for those who need services. They can provide the political face for the agency. Recreation professionals must decide how they will work with interest groups. That brings us right back to the question "Whom do we serve?"

The public recreation profession in the United States began with the advocacy work of Joseph Lee, the father of the playground movement. In the late 1800s he helped to create the first model playground in a dejected Boston neighborhood. Lee was convinced that all young people needed a place to play. He promoted a bill in the Massachusetts state legislature that required towns and cities with populations of more than 10,000 to develop playgrounds. Joseph Lee's actions set the stage for future actions by other state and local governments. This example illustrates how powerful a citizen with a cause can be and what a difference a committed person can make.

When we think about developing the work that we do, we must begin with our community members. We work with many members of diverse communities to help them experience, in some form or fashion, a better quality of life. That is why we provide services, activities, and events. That is why we build facilities. That is the very reason that we exist as a profession.

BENEFITS OF RECREATION

Since the foundation work of Joseph Lee in the United States and the National Council of Women in Canada more than a century ago, we have intuitively known that recreation benefits people and their communities. But we must go beyond intuition to research. The Benefits Project collected past research about how parks and recreation helps people, their communities, and the environment. The product of this collecting is the online National Benefits Hub (2011), which moves the exercise from collecting research studies to packaging them into a form that can be used in the political arena. The National Benefits Hub presents benefits in four main categories and eight subcategories: personal (health, human development, individual quality of life), social (community quality of life, antisocial behavior, families and communities), economic (prevention, economic impact), and environmental benefits of recreation.

The Benefits Project was created to address a substantial political issue—the perception, more real than imagined, that recreation services, although important to our communities, are not considered essential by decision makers. This is our biggest challenge as we strive to contribute to the public good.

Strong public recreation delivery systems that provide the core benefits of recreation are crucial to helping people lead healthier lives and to protecting natural resources and quality of life in the communities in which we live. As park and recreation professionals, we must educate the public about why we provide one of the most cost effective and essential quality of life services around. Research is continuing to advance in this area. As noted earlier, the technology available to us is continuing to influence many facets of our lives. The natural human desire to play outside is still evident even though technology has changed the way in which

we think about recreation. Public recreation allows us to reconnect with the outdoors. In 2007 the Outdoor Recreation Research and Education strategic plan conducted by the USDA Forest Service noted that outdoor recreation has increased in the United States. The opportunities to experience nature are becoming more valued in the 21st century.

Three core benefits should be noted and continually explored through both research and practical practice:

- Public recreation should provide access to recreation for all.
- Public recreation should provide opportunities to live a healthy lifestyle through physical activity. Parks and recreation agencies have the parks and facilities to support physical activity.
- Public recreation is essential to lifelong learning through the inherent nature of its diverse programs.

SUMMARY

Most parks, open spaces, facilities, and recreation activities that people can participate in are from the public sector. Several powerful trends are affecting public recreation. New leadership is needed to meet the future needs of the public. Special interest groups are more vocal than ever, seeking partnerships that can advance leisure services. The political realm is not to be understated. The challenge in seeking adequate funding in tight budget cycles in severe economic downturns is causing stress in the public recreation system.

Public recreation provides an exhilarating opportunity for public service, offering challenges, benefits, and opportunities to make a difference. The profession can touch many segments of the community and provide quality moments of career satisfaction. Finally, the opportunity to become a pioneer within the industry by trailblazing new frontiers is certainly available. The countless opportunities available to make a difference mean that today is a wonderful time to be in the field of public recreation.

Special Recreation

Jane Hodgkinson

" A person who is severely impaired never knows his hidden sources of strength until he is treated like a normal human being and encouraged to shape his own life. "

Helen Keller, American author, activist, and lecturer

Special recreation is a recreational service that takes place in a public community setting to provide enjoyment and to challenge and enrich people with disabilities rather than to serve strictly as a treatment modality. Unlike therapeutic recreation services that occur in a hospital or clinical setting, special recreation services seek to provide and enhance opportunities for community recreation by providing resources to a person to participate in a program or activity. For example, an inclusion aide may help a young child with a developmental delay participate in a community preschool, and a special recreation social club may help adults with autism gather with others for a dance in a public location. Program guides may be printed in various formats. All these tools help persons with special needs and their caregivers have options for involvement. Special recreation services seek to break down all obstacles to a person's community participation in a recreation event.

Organized efforts extend beyond parks and recreation departments to schools, YWCAs, YMCAs, libraries, service clubs, national park systems, veterans affairs, branches of the military, scouts, and nonprofit organizations. According to various sources (U.S. Census in 2010), 5 percent of children between the ages of 5 and 17, 10 percent of those between the ages of 18 and 64, and 38 percent of those over age 65 have a disability. Overall, 12.4 percent of females and 11.7 percent of males have a disability. Most of them live within communities.

Programs may focus on a particular recreational interest such as sports, like Special Olympics and Paralympic programs, or on a specific region, such as special recreation associations. Programs such as United Cerebral Palsy or Easter Seals focus on a specific type of condition and offer recreation services bundled with other therapies. Some programs have government support through taxes, and others rely on private pay and donations to fund programs. Regardless, graduates in therapeutic recreation and general recreation should be able to find employment providing community-based recreation services for children and adults with special needs.

Recreational activities offer the person with a special need an opportunity to learn about the world in a fun, supportive environment. A young person can learn about being part of a group, cooperating with others, having fun with friends, improving communication, and gaining social skills. The environment is more relaxed, pleasant, and fun than traditional therapy settings. The person wants to practice the skill because it includes a positive incentive, whether it is riding horses, swimming, or performing a play. These services were not always available because attitudes about people with disabilities have changed over time.

SPECIAL RECREATION HISTORY

In the United States before World War II, people with disabilities were placed in institutions and orphanages, where they resided in large numbers. Parents who gave birth to children with intellectual challenges, such as those with Down syndrome, were encouraged to give their child to the state. The child would then be sent to a facility to live. These institutions did not resemble their predecessors in Europe in the 1700s and 1800s, where patients were bled, purged, and blistered as part of their treatment. U.S. state hospitals were more humane in their treatment but carried large patient loads of both mentally ill and developmentally delayed patients.

By the second half of the 20th century, most people with disabilities in the United States and Canada no longer resided in large institutions such as mental hospitals. Developments in medications and technology, changes in public school funding and practices, acceptance by the general public, and passage of enabling legislation helped people return to their homes and live with their families or in independent-living apartments or homes. President John F. Kennedy, who had a sister with intellectual disabilities in a psychiatric facility, actively championed the movement of children out of large state institutions with the Mental Health Act of 1962. This was the beginning of **deinstitutionalization**, in which people moved from large hospital or institutional settings back to their home communities. During this time, large institutions that had held as many as 25,000 residents with mental disabilities released them to live with their families and community settings. Parents, who had been encouraged to place children with severe disabilities into institutions, began to keep them at home.

As the number of people with disabilities living in homes and community apartments increased, schools, parks, and recreation agencies began receiving requests to provide recreational services. When communities recognized a void in recreational programming focused on the interests of people with special needs, the special recreation movement was started.

ACCESSIBILITY AND UNIVERSAL DESIGN IN SPECIAL RECREATION SERVICES

Depending on geographic area, these organized groups may have some special services that incorporate universal design or special recreation concepts. Providers of special recreation services must always be aware of the accessibility of the location of the programs to allow all to use them. Accessibility as an issue of national concern is not new. See figure 7.1 for a history of the accessibility and universal design movement in Unites States.

The Americans with Disabilities Act (ADA) of 1990 required governmental entities to make their services available to people with disabilities by removing architectural barriers, providing aids to include people in recreational programs, providing communication devices if necessary, helping people with physical disabilities use public transportation, and prohibiting employers from discriminating against people with disabilities based on the disability. This act was so significant that it was sometimes referred to as the Civil Rights Act for the Disabled. Under this legislation all American governmental units (except for congressional exceptions such as the U.S. Capitol) are required to make their facilities and services available to all, regardless of disability, and to offer accommodations for program access. The standards for accessibility under this act are updated as advances are made in standards. In 2010 new guidelines for outdoor areas, golf clubs, swimming pools, beaches, fishing piers, and other sites were released.

The ADA does not just provide support for people who have mobility challenges; it also states requirements for improving access for people with visual, hearing, and other challenges. Access tools such as raised lettering, Braille, and flashing lights for fire detection improve both the safety and opportunities for involvement. Patrons with visual impairments can request audio descriptions of program materials. Rounded door knobs are replaced with hardware that will allow a person who cannot apply pressure to the hardware to open doors and lockers. In historic buildings where renovation of a second floor is difficult, booklets and pictures are made available of areas that cannot be made accessible. Recreation planners must make efforts to consider universal design for all public areas to enhance the experience for everyone.

SPECIAL RECREATION AND ACCESSIBILITY

Varying from state to state and province to province, a wide range of arts, sports, camping, and day-camping experiences exist. Improving access to these facilities can make each recreational event more enjoyable for multiple populations. For example, accessible camps provide residential camping opportunities to people with disabilities. Camp accessibility may be enhanced by including paved walkways for those who use wheelchairs, zero-depth entry into swimming areas, and curb cuts and

---

ACCESSIBILITY AND UNIVERSAL DESIGN MOVEMENT
IN THE UNITED STATES

1919—Congress authorizes a vocational rehabilitation program for veterans returning from World War I. One year later this program is extended to all disabled Americans.

1932—Franklin D. Roosevelt is elected to the first of four terms as president. Roosevelt, the first U.S. president with a disability, had polio.

1946—Rehabilitation services are expanded to serve veterans returning from World War II.

1950s—Polio outbreaks leave 400,000 victims of the disease.

1959—Dr. Dwight York publishes "Tentative Guide—Facilities in Public Buildings for Persons with Ambulatory Impairments."

1961—American National Standards Institute (ANSI) publishes "Making Buildings Accessible to and Usable by the Physically Handicapped."

1968—Congress passes the Architectural Barriers Act (ABA), which required physical accessibility in all new or renovated buildings funded in whole or part by the federal government.

1973—Congress passes the Rehabilitation Act, which established the Architectural and Transportation Barriers Compliance Board as the regulatory agency with authority to enforce the 1968 ABA.

1990—Congress passes the Americans with Disabilities Act (ADA), known as the Civil Rights Act for the Disabled. The ADA addresses discrimination against people with disabilities in employment, public services, public accommodations, and telecommunications. In 1991 the ADA's accessibility guidelines (ADAAG) were published.

Figure 7.1 Accessibility as a national concern began in 1919 and continued through the passage of the ADA in 1990. Those effects are still being felt today.

ramps to increase use of fishing piers or boat launch areas. Initial design of a park, recreational facility, or recreational area may be the first step to allowing access by those who use mobility aids. Many times the accommodations made for access improve usability for everyone, not just those with special needs. For example, curb cuts increase access not only for people who use wheelchairs but also for parents pushing baby strollers and senior citizens who prefer ramped entries rather than stairs. Special recreation managers and planners must always take accessibility into consideration when planning events. People who cannot gain access to a facility will not be able to participate and may decline to participate again.

Special recreation staff have to learn how to use equipment that increases accessibility. Several types of swimming pool lifts allow a person with a physical challenge to enter a swim area. One piece of equipment is a Hoyer lift. The lift sits on the edge of a swimming pool and can swivel from the deck side to the water. A person who has a mobility challenge can transfer from a wheelchair onto

the lift seat and then lower him- or herself into the water. Other types of lifts allow a person with a mobility challenge to walk on a treadmill. Many buses and vans have lifts that allow a person who cannot climb steps to be lifted from ground level to passenger seat level of a vehicle. The person can then transfer to a vehicle seat or have his or her wheelchair secured by a tie down for the ride. People can also use lifts to get from ground level areas to performance areas on stages. Golf carts can provide golfers with ways to pull up directly to their golf ball to play the game.

Many people with autism have difficulty communicating their thoughts. Use of technology tools like I-pads or communication boards can facilitate this process. As new forms of technology are developed that enhance communication, therapeutic recreation staff in special recreation programs need to keep learning new techniques.

The drive to develop accessible play structures on playgrounds has led to the development of cushioned firm playground surfaces, sensory play equipment, and the use of ramps and bermed earth to lead to upper and lower levels of play equipment. Playgrounds can now be used by children with differing needs. The obvious benefit of these types of play areas is that children can play next to their nondisabled peers. Likewise, adults with disabilities can take their nondisabled children to play areas. Many communities are designing baseball, softball, and soccer fields and basketball courts that are made of accessible materials to support team play for those with mobility and developmental impairments. These fields are sometimes supported by donations from professional sports teams.

ACCESSIBILITY AND INCLUSION

No discussion of accessibility would be complete without defining other methods of promoting inclusion of people with disabilities into nondisabled groups. Young children with disabilities benefit from exposure to other children, thus enhancing their language and play development. Special recreation services frequently provide an aide to work with a child in a general recreation program. The aide may provide general assistance to the program instructor, facilitate play, and offer adaptive devices. For example, a child with a cognitive delay may be unable to keep up with classmates in a preschool program. An aide helps the child complete the craft or play the game, encourages the child to interact with others, and assists the child in breaking down activities to small steps. The program becomes successful for both the children with disabilities and those without, who become more aware that people with disabilities are everywhere.

Special recreation staff can also help promote inclusion by organizing events that bring children (both with and without disabilities) together, such as offering face painting on a playground, providing volunteer opportunities for children to serve as "buddies" for other children, or having older children serve as team managers, providing services that teach other children about awareness of disabilities. A number of programs (Special Olympics' Unified Sports, Shane's Inspiration, the Miracle League) help create inclusive settings where inclusion with nondisabled children is promoted.

SPECIAL RECREATION ASSOCIATIONS

When communities seek to provide special recreation services by joining other communities, they form **special recreation associations**, an intergovernmental agreement between two or more communities or park districts, established to provide recreational services to people with special needs. In 1969, Illinois park districts took the lead in forming special recreation associations (SRA).

History of Special Recreation Associations

Communities with park districts and city recreation departments recognized that few if any programs were available for children and adults with disabilities. Summer day camps for children with cognitive or mental disabilities were the first to be recognized and offered. Twelve communities outside Chicago formed the first Special Recreation Association, Northern Suburban Special Recreation Association (NSSRA), in 1969. Illinois passed legislation that allowed communities to form intergovernmental agreements for special recreation, levy a property tax to fund the programs, provide transportation, and share special recreation staff. The benefits for the consumers were immediate. Families were offered as wide a range of recreation programs as those offered to people without disabilities. The participating communities shared staff, adapted equipment, and accessible vehicles. These early programs typically included day camps, social clubs, bowling, and swimming. Later programs expanded to offer trips, scouting, wheelchair sports, nature activities, dramatics, and social programs. During these programs, the participants would learn the skills needed for the program as well as communicating, sharing, being part of a team, being dependable, and other life skills. Illinois now has 30 special recreation associations (specialrecreation.org) serving more than 200 communities. Other states such as Minnesota, Missouri, and North Carolina have services in which communities band together.

After the passage of the United States Education for All Children Act of 1975, schools and special recreation associations took a more directed approach to including children with special needs into classrooms and then later into transition programs to help prepare some students for jobs and adulthood. Working in partnerships, many of the associations provide the schools with leisure education and transition life skills programs such as cooking, exercise, and fitness. Special recreation associations also provide inclusion services.

Benefits of Special Recreation Associations to Communities

The greatest benefits to communities that provide services through SRAs are the efficiencies and economies gained by sharing facilities and staff. For example, rather than each community hiring and training staff and purchasing accessible vehicles, communities pool their resources to create a central group that serves all the communities with services. A second benefit is the ability to share facilities. For example, a community without a swimming pool can obtain swimming services for its residents from a neighboring community. A third benefit of the cooperative approach is the ability to combine the relatively small number of people with disabilities in each community to create a population large enough to make programming feasible. For example, if a community wants to offer tandem bicycle riding for its residents who are visually impaired, there may be too few participants to make the program worthwhile. However, if residents from four or five communities register for the program, it stands a better chance of being successful. Many communities are not large enough to offer sport teams for people with mobility challenges, but by banning together, these coalitions of communities can identify and offer team sports. Another benefit is in the area of staff training. Certain disability groups require staff with extensive training: People with hearing impairments require staff who use sign language, or some people with physical disabilities require staff who can lift or move them safely. People with autism benefit from working with staff who are trained in behavioral management programs. Most people with special needs can participate in public programming in the community but staff training may be the element that differentiates a successful experience from a disappointing one. By pooling staff, an SRA can provide staff trained in diverse specialties.

SPECIAL RECREATION CONTINUUM OF SERVICES

High-quality special recreation services should provide people the opportunity to participate in a variety of activities on a continuum from most restrictive to least restrictive settings (table 7.1). As medical advances help to prolong life and technology makes it easier for people to live in the community, opportunities continue to increase for full participation in community life. The extent to which this process of **inclusion** can be achieved depends on the needs and choices of the person with a disability.

Table 7.1 Continuum of Special Recreational Services

Segregated programs	Parallel inclusion	Supported inclusion	Independent inclusion
Residential settings, hospitals, workshops, prisons	Separate schools; Special Olympics; special recreation association; leisure education	Special Olympics unified sports; park and recreation inclusion programs; school inclusion	Paralympics; senior programs
People live in sheltered settings away from communities and natural families	People reside in home and community and participate in programs with other people with special needs	People reside in home and community and participate in programs with others without disabilities but with support	People independently register and participate

*Segregated recreation programs describe programs that take place inside institutional settings. These programs may help ready a person for life in the community (such as a prison or a hospital) or help develop their recreational interests in the institution.

*Parallel inclusion takes place in a community setting with a group of people with disabilities. Staff or volunteer support is available to people so that they can participate.

*Supported inclusion takes place in the community where the person with a disability is included with others who do not have a disability or special need. Staff or volunteer support is available to help the inclusion take place.

*Independent inclusion takes place in the community. The individual registers and participates in programs with little or no support from family, staff, or volunteers.

Special recreation associations offer recreation opportunities in all four of the areas of the recreation continuum. Services are sometimes provided in specific residential facilities solely for the enjoyment of their residents; segregated programs in a prison or hospital might help ready a person for life in the community. Parallel programs such as Special Olympics are offered to groups with special needs, and staff or volunteers support the participants. Special recreation associations offer inclusion services such as providing adaptive equipment so that people with disabilities can use community services. Special recreation associations also help families pursue independent recreation opportunities.

Some communities offer programs exclusively in a supported-inclusion setting. They make all of their programs available through services such as sign language interpreters, adaptive equipment, or hiring of inclusion aides. Inclusion aides are staff who assist the individual in "fitting in" with the group. Other supported inclusion strategies are to build accessible parks and playgrounds, translate written materials such as brochures into alternate formats, provide program buddies, and train staff in how to integrate people into programs. However, how extensively a person can take advantage of supported-inclusion services depends on the nature of his or her disability. For example, it can be more difficult to provide supported-inclusion services to adults with cognitive disabilities, autism, developmental delays than to children or adults with physical disabilities and challenges.

SPECIALIZED RECREATION PROGRAMS

Many types of recreational programs are available to people with disabilities. Some of these programs are specific to a disability and programming area; for instance, Special Olympics provides sport opportunities to people with intellectual disabilities (and autism), and the Paralympics provides sport opportunities to people with physical challenges. Very Special Arts is an art program offered to people with intellectual disabilities (a disability and a skill area such as the Paralympics). Still others, like Outward Bound, are offered to people with and without disabilities. These programs are generally provided or supported by nonprofit agencies that rely on fund-raising to carry out programs.

Special Olympics

Perhaps no special recreation programming is more known and practiced than Special Olympics. Championed by Mrs. Eunice Kennedy Shriver, Special Olympics offers sport training and competition to those with intellectual challenges and autism. This international program is available in most areas around the world, and more than 3 million people participate worldwide. It is the largest sport program in the world for people with disabilities and includes more than 25 sports.

In 1968 the first Special Olympics were held in Chicago's Soldier Field. Sponsored by the Chicago Park District and the Joseph P. Kennedy Jr. Foundation, these games were the first organized sporting opportunities for people with developmental disabilities. Special Olympics is an international organization dedicated to helping people with intellectual disabilities and autism to become physically fit through sport training and competition. Modeled after the Olympics, competition includes standard track and field events, swimming, winter and team sports, as well as wheelchair events. Led by the athlete oath, "Let me win, but if I cannot win, let me be brave in the attempt," Special Olympics

Special Olympics is one of the most well-known types of special recreation programming. It provides people with disabilities the chance to participate and enjoy the unique joy of sport.

has spread through many countries of the world. In many areas, it is the only recreation or sport program available to people with developmental disabilities (www.specialolympics.org).

Paralympics

The Paralympic Games are the largest sporting event in the world for people with physical disabilities. The multisport competition showcases the talents and abilities of the world's most elite athletes with physical disabilities. Currently, Paralympics features 21 sports, 18 of which are also included in the Olympics. Athletes are divided into six classifications depending on their disability: visual impairments, intellectual disabilities, amputation, spinal-cord injuries, cerebral palsy, and a group that includes all those that do not fit into one of the aforementioned groups, les autres.

Wheelchair games started in 1948. Today wheelchair basketball is played at the Paralympics and at your local special recreation association.

Before the Paralympic Games, however, were the wheelchair games started in 1948 by Dr. Ludwig Guttmann and held in Stoke Mandeville, England. Dr. Guttmann, a neurologist at Stoke Mandeville Hospital, hoped to help the thousands of people injured in World War II to return to sports. By the early 1950s, many wheelchair basketball teams had been organized. The first Paralympics were held in 1960 in Rome, Italy, with 400 wheelchair athletes competing. By 1976 other athletes besides those using wheelchairs were added. At the 1988 Paralympics in Seoul, Korea, the practice of the Olympic host also hosting the Paralympics began. Today more than 5,000 athletes compete in the Summer and Winter Paralympics. The Paralympics offers disabled veterans an area of sport to develop after wartime injuries, and the military has become more active in supporting Paralympic training and events. As technology and medical developments aid injured athletes, some speculate that Paralympic athletes may ultimately become more "accomplished" than their nondisabled peers.

Special Recreation Camping and Adventure Programs

Special recreation camping is now available in most American states and Canadian provinces. Camping opportunities include accessible day camps offered by local parks and recreation agencies, specialty camps (camps geared to a specific disability), and camps located in the natural environment. Accessibility varies in each of these settings. One of the earliest camping programs for people with special needs was Camp Riley in Bradford Woods, 25 miles (40 km) southwest of Indianapolis, Indiana. Bradford Woods, owned by Indiana University, has 250,000 acres (100,000 ha) and was started in 1935 as an outdoor laboratory for IU students. In 1955 a grant from the Riley Foundation established Camp Riley for physically disabled children. The camp became nationally recognized for pioneering universal design in camp facilities and now is host to the National Center on Accessibility. Camp Riley has an accessible amphitheater, switchback trail, climbing tower, universal high ropes, and a therapeutic riding program known as Horseshoes for Hope (rileykids.org).

Another notable program is the National Sports Center for the Disabled (NSCD.org). The NSCD was

OUTSTANDING GRADUATES

Background Information

Name: Jorie Meyer

Education: Bachelor's degree in recreation management with an emphasis on therapeutic recreation from Indiana Wesleyan University; minor in psychology.

Credentials: Certified therapeutic recreation specialist.

Special awards: Illinois Therapeutic Recreation Section (ITRS) New Professional of the Year, 2007; ITRS Outstanding Program, 2009—Video Ventures; ITRS Outstanding Special Event of the Year, 2010—SRA'S Got Talent.

Affiliations: Illinois Park and Recreation Association (IPRA), Illinois Therapeutic Recreation Section (ITRS), National Recreation and Park Association (NRPA), Cambridge Who's Who.

Career Information

Position: Manager of therapeutic recreation programs, Western DuPage Special Recreation Association (WDSRA), Carol Stream, Illinois.

Organization: WDSRA is a cooperative extension of nine park districts and serves more than 4,500 children and adults with special needs in over 1,500 recreation programs, trips, and special events annually. Additionally, WDSRA reaches in excess of 13,000 people through services and events. Twenty-four full-time staff, 9 part-time office employees, and over 400 part-time staff and volunteers operate this nationally acclaimed not-for-profit organization.

Organization's mission: WDSRA's mission is to promote the development of all people through recreational opportunities and to provide equal fun for everyone. WDSRA staff are dedicated to enhancing the quality of life for all WDSRA people.

Job description: Supervise three recreation supervisors responsible for planning, developing, implementing, and evaluating therapeutic recreation programs on a year-round basis. Schedule, design, implement, and oversee WDSRA brochure production. Act as the initial liaison for all new participants and families. Responsible for implementing and coordinating the WDSRA parent group.

Career path: I have held the positions of program coordinator, coordinator of special events and day camps, manager of special events and day camps, and manager of therapeutic recreation programs.

Likes and dislikes about the job: I love serving people with special needs because it is truly my passion. I enjoy watching WDSRA participants mature and grow into their disability, tackling challenges that they first thought impossible. I enjoy mentoring young professionals and watching their accomplishments unfold year after year. I dislike it when parents hold their children back because of their disability.

> *Therapeutic recreation is a fulfilling career. I am always affecting the lives of those around me and cannot think of a better way to spend a majority of my time!*

I continually seek new opportunities within my organization that will challenge me and get me ready for the next step. My career goal is to take on the position of superintendent of recreation and ultimately executive director.

Advice to Undergraduates

Get experience in many different organizations as an underclassman. Doing this will help you decide where you fit in best. Research and find a good internship, because it may ultimately lead you to your first job (it did for me!). After you have chosen your career path, get involved in as many organizations as you can to get your name out there. This will help when you are looking for a new job. Most important, have fun and remain true to yourself.

founded in 1970 in Winter Park, Colorado, when children with amputations were brought from the Children's Hospital in Denver to ski. The NSCD now offers a wide range of winter sports, traveling on mountain trails, and golf links. The center provides trained staff and adaptive equipment.

Wilderness Inquiry, an organization based in Minneapolis, Minnesota, that helps people experience the natural world, started in 1977 with a trip to Minnesota's Boundary Waters Canoe Area Wilderness by two people who used wheelchairs and two who were deaf. Today the backcountry trips are available to people of all abilities. Participants use canoes, kayaks, dogsleds, and horse packs or hike. Trip locations included the Rocky Mountains, Grand Canyon, Yukon's Big Salmon River, Yellowstone National Park, and Alaska's Queen Charlotte's Island (www.wildernessinquiry.org).

The Outward Bound School, developed by Kurt Hahn and Lawrence Holt, opened in 1941 in Wales after earlier programs in Germany, Britain, and Scotland were discontinued. The core mission of Outward Bound is the education of the youth of the world, ages 16 to 24. Outward Bound International (OBI) believes that young men and women must face increasingly complex situations in which self-esteem and confidence are at a premium. OBI trains and prepares people to face difficult natural environments by focusing on four pillars: physical fitness, an expedition that provides challenge and adventure, a project that develops self-reliance and self-discipline, and a sense of compassion through service. In the 1950s, Outward Bound programs expanded in the United Kingdom, Asia, Germany, and Australia. By the 1960s, Outward Bound Schools had spread to the United States and Canada. Programs for those with special needs have been developed in 1970 with increasing focus on helping those with physical and mental challenges discover their strengths and build their confidence (www.outward-bound.org).

Recreational programming in the arts provides a creative outlet for people with disabilities.

In addition to organized camping and adventure programs, people with disabilities can also use parks on their own. Most public and private parks publish the accessible features of their park areas so that potential users can make travel and usage plans. These are often included on local websites. Travel agencies, airlines, and railway companies can provide extensive resources for people with disabilities.

Arts

Perhaps no area of recreational programming offers more opportunities for people with disabilities than the arts. Unlike sports that have winners and losers, art represents how the artist feels or views life and is not measured by points, time, or distance. There is no right or wrong ways to create art opportunities. Many communities offer creative outlets, and individual agencies encourage participation in the arts. Two national programs provide art opportunities.

- **VSA arts**. VSA arts is an international non-profit organization founded in 1974 by Jean Kennedy Smith. VSA arts is dedicated to creating a society in which people with disabilities can learn through, participate in, and enjoy the arts. VSA arts offers diverse programs and events and innovative lifelong learning opportunities at the international, national, and local levels. These range from training institutes and artist-in-residence projects to arts camps and emerging-artist award programs (www.vsarts.org).

- **National Theater for the Deaf**. David Hays in Waterford, Connecticut, founded the National Theater for the Deaf (NTD). The mission of the NTD is to produce theatrically challenging work at a world-class level, drawing from as wide a range of the world's literature as possible; to perform these original works in a style that links American Sign Language with the spoken word; to seek, train, and employ deaf artists to offer their work to as culturally diverse audiences as possible; and to provide community outreach activities that educate and enlighten the general public (ntd.org).

FUTURE OF SPECIAL RECREATION ASSOCIATIONS

As more communities recognize the need to provide recreational opportunities to people with disabilities, as medical developments continue to expand the life expectancies of people who are seriously ill, and as the baby boomer generation ages, increasing the number of people who need assistance with their recreation, the special recreation association movement will continue to grow. The development of accessible recreational facilities will aid involvement. Populations that remain unserved or underserved by recreational opportunities include the homeless and people with conditions such as cancer, diabetes, arthritis, and multiple sclerosis and people undergoing dialysis. Funding for programs to serve these people provides a major challenge, but as those hurdles are cleared, program opportunities will increase through partnerships between agencies.

SUMMARY

Public recreation programs continue to recognize that a well-rounded diverse offering of programs means that niche programs will be more successful than a "one size fits all" approach. In every group of people, there are wide ranges of abilities and skills. Programs that are revenue driven must still take this range into consideration. In the United States, the Americans with Disabilities Act requires that public services be made available to people with disabilities by removing physical barriers to participation and supplying assistance where needed. Medical science developments continue to help people to live longer, and better diagnostic tests keep identifying more people who will need help to recreate in the community.

For glossary terms, learning experiences, and more, please visit the web resource at
www.HumanKinetics.com/IntroductionToRecreationAndLeisure

CHAPTER 8

Nonprofit Sector

Robert F. Ashcraft

" Nonprofit activity is everywhere. It is hard to find a neighborhood without visible nonprofit presence . . . and impossible to find a neighborhood untouched by nonprofit work . . . **"**

Michael O'Neill, professor of nonprofit management, founder and former director of the Institute for Nonprofit Organization Management, University of San Francisco

LEARNING OUTCOMES

After reading this chapter you should be able to do the following:

> Describe the overall role and characteristics of the nonprofit sector in society
> Identify the types of national and community-based nonprofit recreation organizations
> Explain the role of the professional in nonprofit organizations
> Describe challenges and opportunities for the future

INTRODUCTION

An understanding of recreation and leisure services is incomplete without examining the role of **nonprofit sector** organizations. In neighborhoods and communities across North America, millions of people are served by, and give service to, entities that are organized for public and **quasi-public** purposes.

It is hard to imagine that anyone goes through life without being touched by a **nonprofit organization**. Yet only in recent years have nonprofits received the attention expected for an organizational form with such a large societal impact. Historian and scholar David Mason notes the evidence of the influence of nonprofits. On receiving the Distinguished Lifetime Achievement Award from the Association for Research on Nonprofit Organizations and Voluntary Action, Mason made the following remarks to the luncheon group assembled in his honor:

> My values, attitudes, and behaviors, like most of yours, have been profoundly influenced by nonprofits . . . My parents met when they were students in a nonprofit. I was born in one. I learned about God in one, my ABCs in another, how to play ball and be a team player in another, and met my first girlfriend in another. I prepared for my career at a nonprofit university, met my wife in a nonprofit church, went on to several nonprofit graduate schools, joined numerous nonprofit professional groups, brought two newly born sons home from nonprofit hospitals, and on and on it goes, including what I read, how I vote and my avocations. It weaves its way like a golden thread through the tapestry of my life (Mason, 1999).

Similar stories can be told by millions of citizens who have been affected in comparable ways. The nonprofit sector is ubiquitous, so it is often taken for granted. Yet an examination of the sector reveals countless examples of how nonprofit organizations affect human lives. While both complementing and contrasting recreation and leisure services provided by business (the economic/market sector) and by government (the political sector), the nonprofit form (the social sector) is growing in numbers as part of a **three-sector model** of service delivery. Whether people organize to serve their personal self-interests or to promote a broader public good, nonprofits are one way in which citizens often operate along with and sometimes outside the government and business sectors to improve the quality of life in communities. In addition, as a growing career field, the nonprofit sector has emerged as a vocational choice for increasing numbers of recreation professionals.

This chapter reveals the characteristics of nonprofit organizations in the United States and Canada, including their goals and functions, size and scope, and resource base. The significance of the nonprofit sector is considered in ways that differentiate service delivery approaches from those found within government or business recreation providers. A variety of types of nonprofit organizations are discussed, as are the professional opportunities that exist within such entities. Finally, the factors that influence the future of nonprofit organizations is addressed, providing insight into collaborative ventures developing among organizations, the impact of the nonprofit sector in the United States and Canada, and the challenges and opportunities ahead for this important dimension of recreation and leisure service delivery systems.

NONPROFIT SECTOR IN THE UNITED STATES AND CANADA

Although examples of nonprofit sector activities exist across all regions and countries of North America, it is difficult to make direct comparisons from one country to another. There are enormous variations in how nonprofit organizations are structured, how they are registered, and how they operate within the cultural, political, civic, and economic contexts of community life. There are also major differences in the terms used to describe entities that comprise the nonprofit sector. Different terms are found in nonprofit literature such as "voluntary sector," "charitable sector," "quasi-public sector," "independent sector," "third sector," "civil society sector," "social sector," "nongovernmental organization sector," "tax-exempt sector" and "nonprofit sector." The terms underscore why understanding the nonprofit sector is a challenging task, given the variety of interpretations noted. However, these variations also suggest a robust and vibrant sector that accommodates diverse forms and expressions. In this chapter, the term "nonprofit" is used, while fully acknowledging the diversity of terms available.

Nanus and Dobbs (1999) identify three primary sectors of society: economic (commerce, private and publicly held businesses), political (public and government at all levels), and social (nonprofits). As noted in figure 8.1, these sectors are inextricably linked, and together they represent the variety of ways to organize and deliver recreation and leisure services. The sectors exist within a milieu of forces and forms that shape society.

Some nonprofits are widely recognized and provide ready access to their programs, financial statements, governance policies, and so on. However, thousands of small, grassroots, and community-based organizations are lesser known and go largely unexamined. So to fully appreciate the nonprofit sector's role one must consider this segment of recreation and leisure services in all of its vastness and vagueness. One way to understand the range of the nonprofit form is to review what nonprofit organizations hold in common.

Common Characteristics of Nonprofit Organizations

Despite enormous variations, several characteristics apply generally to nonprofit organizations whether found in Canada, the United States, or other countries around the world. According to nonprofit scholars such as Lester Salamon (1999), Michael O'Neill (2002), and others, nonprofit entities share six common features:

1. **Organized**. They have an institutional presence and structure; there is an identifiable entity.

2. **Private**. They are separate from the state. While following laws established by legislative bodies, these entities determine their own policies, programs, and services.

3. **Nonprofit distributing**. They do not return profits to their managers or to a set of "owners." Whereas publicly traded corporations have shareholders, and government entities have voting constituents, nonprofit organizations consider a range of stakeholders when making decisions and providing services.

4. **Self-governing**. They are fundamentally in control of their own affairs.

5. **Voluntary**. Membership in them is not legally required, and they attract some level of voluntary contribution of time and money.

6. **Beneficial to the public**. They contribute to the public purpose and public good.

These characteristics apply to a wide range of recreation and leisure entities found within the nonprofit sector. Therefore, a small running club organized and financed by and for its members in a remote New England community in the United States is as much a part of the nonprofit sector as is the Red Cross, a large multiservice, social service agency with operating units in Canada and the United States. Nonprofit organizations, therefore, are organized to serve public purposes or mutual-benefit purposes that improve the quality of life in communities.

The nonprofit organizational form is found throughout the recreation field, from sports clubs to professional associations, to direct service providers. Interestingly, nonprofit organizations and

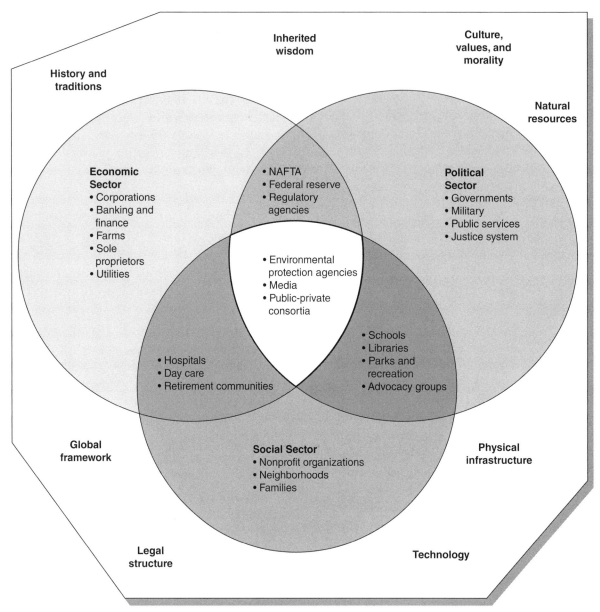

Figure 8.1 Three main sectors of society.

Adapted from B. Nanus and S.M. Dobbs, 1999, *Leaders who make a difference: Essential strategies for meeting the nonprofit challenge* (San Francisco: Jossey-Bass). By permission of S.M. Dobbs.

their activities affect people across the range of individual life-span development from "cradle to grave." Often the introduction to nonprofit organizations occurs through recreation programs, as children and youth become involved in Boy Scout and Girl Scout programs, YMCAs, Boys and Girls Clubs, Little League, and other recreation-based programs. As interests and skills are developed through outlets such as camping programs, appreciation often grows for the outdoors. The Sierra Club, The Nature Conservancy, and The Trust for Public Land, among other environmental organizations, are nonprofit entities that advance specific mission-driven purposes that often appeal to those concerned about outdoor recreation. These youth development and environmental entities are just two examples of recreation-based nonprofits that are part of a much larger collection of hundreds of thousands of organizations operating throughout North America to advance both special-purpose and broadly based public benefit goals.

Goals and Functions

Given the vast array of activities and people that comprise the sector, it is not surprising that the goals and functions of nonprofit organizations are also varied. Such organizations often serve widely different needs and at times conflicting values. For example, one nonprofit may organize to protect a wilderness area by calling for the elimination of off-road vehicle use, while another organizes to open the same area to such activity. Often, however, nonprofit recreation and leisure services organizations share similar values between themselves and among government and business entities. After-school child care programs offer examples where overall goals regarding the education, safety, and recreation needs of children are similar even though their delivery systems (programs, clientele, fee structure, and so on) are organized in different ways for various reasons.

Despite these variations, Salamon (1999) and others suggest that the following two primary goals frame the orientation of most nonprofits:

1. **Public benefit.** Some nonprofits are organized specifically for social outcomes that appeal across a wide spectrum of population groups. Educational organizations, hospitals, museums, and community recreation centers are examples of public benefit nonprofits.

2. **Mutual benefit.** These nonprofits exist primarily to provide services exclusively to a limited number of members with common interests. Examples include business and professional associations, social clubs, and some golf clubs.

Nonprofits, therefore, are organized to serve both individual needs and broader community goals. Some are organized to conserve and preserve historical, cultural, environmental, and other traditions. Others are developed to advance social change with a focus on improving the condition of disadvantaged and disenfranchised people who do not feel a part of mainstream community life. Figure 8.2 shows examples of nonprofit organizations across these various domains.

Organizing Framework

Because the nonprofit sector is so diverse and it encompasses such a wide array of types and sizes of organizations, studying its structure and impact can be difficult. A typology developed by researchers at Johns Hopkins University, known as the International Classification of Nonprofit Organizations (ICNPO) facilitates understanding of the sector (Salamon & Anheier, 1996). ICNPO divides nonprofits into 12 major activity groups and 24 subgroups according to the primary type of goods or services each one provides (e.g., recreation, environment, health). The following are the major activity groups:

1. **Culture and recreation.** Includes organizations and activities in general and specialized fields of culture and recreation

2. **Education and research.** Includes organizations and activities administering, providing, promoting, conducting, supporting, and servicing education and research

3. **Health.** Includes organizations that engage in health-related activities, providing health care, both general and specialized services, administration of health care services, and health support services

4. **Social services.** Includes organizations and institutions providing human and social services to a community or target population

5. **Environment.** Includes organizations promoting and providing services in environmental conservation, pollution control and prevention, environmental education and health, and animal protection

6. **Development and housing.** Includes organizations promoting programs and providing services to help improve communities and promote the economic and social well-being of society

7. **Law, advocacy, and politics.** Includes organizations and groups that work to protect and promote civil and other rights, advocate the social and political interests of general or special constituencies, offer legal services, and promote public safety

8. **Philanthropic intermediaries and voluntarism.** Includes philanthropic organizations and those promoting charity and charitable activities including grant-making foundations, voluntarism promotion and support, and fundraising entities

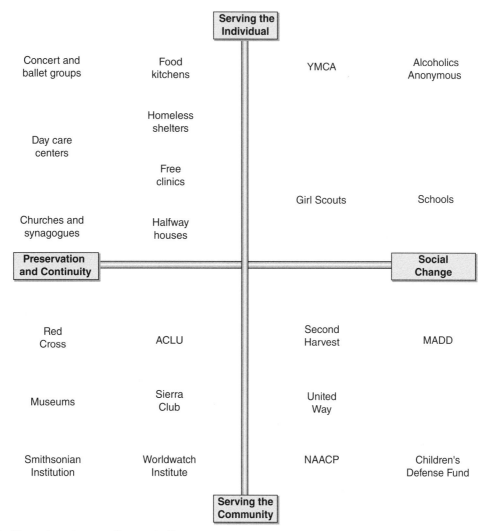

Figure 8.2 Examples of nonprofit organizations.

Adapted from B. Nanus and S.M. Dobbs, 1999, *Leaders who make a difference: Essential strategies for meeting the nonprofit challenge* (San Francisco: Jossey-Bass). By permission of S.M. Dobbs.

9. **International**. Includes organizations promoting cultural understanding between peoples of various countries and historical backgrounds and also those providing relief during emergencies and promoting development and welfare abroad

10. **Religion**. Organizations promoting religious beliefs and administering religious services and rituals; includes churches, mosques, synagogues, temples, shrines, seminaries, monasteries, and similar religious institutions, in addition to related organizations and auxiliaries of these organizations

11. **Business and professional associations and unions**. Includes organizations promoting, regulating, and safeguarding business, professional, and labor interests

12. **Groups not classified elsewhere**.

Size and Scope

Determining the size and scope of the nonprofit sector in North America is difficult for several reasons as previously noted. However, what is known suggests that nonprofits have played a larger role in the United States than in Canada or other countries. This fact in no way minimizes the importance of nonprofits outside the United States. However, given the size and scope of the sector in the United States, spawned from a nation whose laws and culture have encouraged such activity, it is not surprising that nonprofit literature on recreation and leisure organizations frequently accentuates U.S. examples when examining nonprofit organizations and their purposes and approaches to service delivery.

Nonprofit Sector in Canada

Despite an increasing number of studies on the topic, there is still a great deal that is not known about the nonprofit sector and the role it plays in Canada (Hall & Banting, 2000). Canada has no central registry for nonprofits, so what is known comes from those charities, as a subset of the overall nonprofit sector, that register with Revenue Canada (the government agency similar to the Internal Revenue Service in the United States). According to the 2003 National Survey of Nonprofit and Voluntary Organizations, an estimated 161,000 nonprofit and voluntary organizations operated in Canada, and 80,000 of them were registered as official charities (Hall, de Wit, Lasby, McIver, Evers, Johnston, et al., 2005). According to Revenue Canada, a nonprofit organization (NPO) is, "an association [that] must be both organized and operated exclusively for social welfare, civic improvement, pleasure or recreation or for any other purpose except profit" (Revenue Canada, 2011, paragraph 5 at www.cra-arc.gc.ca/E/pub/tp/it496r/it496r-e.html). Revenue Canada details these four categories as follows:

1. Social welfare nonprofits assist disadvantaged groups for the common good and for the general welfare of the community.

2. Civic improvement nonprofits are organized to enhance the value or quality of community or civic life.

3. Pleasure or recreation nonprofits are organized to provide a state of gratification or a means of refreshment or diversion.

4. The final category, which can serve any purpose except profit, is a generic grouping of associations that are organized for other non-commercial reasons.

As noted in the previous list, several categories account for the array of Canadian nonprofits that work to advance community life by providing services that address core social needs while advancing overall community well-being. They range from nonprofits that organize parks and museums for general community betterment to sport clubs involving special interests such as golf, curling, and badminton that are organized and operated to provide recreational facilities for the enjoyment of members and their families.

One emerging source of information about the Canadian nonprofit sector is Imagine Canada, a nonprofit launched in 2005 from a strategic alliance of the Canadian Centre for Philanthropy and the Coalition of National Voluntary Organizations. Imagine Canada seeks to fill the knowledge gap by working with charities, governments, and corporations to advance the role and interests of the charitable sector for the benefit of Canadian communities. The organization conducts and disseminates research, develops public policy, promotes public awareness, shares tools and standards, and encourages businesses to be more community-minded.

Nonprofit Sector in the United States

As previously noted, the nonprofit sector in the United States is pervasive and robust. According to the National Center for Charitable Statistics (2009), there are approximately 1.6 million nonprofits in the United States (http://nccsdataweb.urban.org/PubApps/profile1.php). Of those, nearly 1 million are public charities. The U.S. Internal Revenue Service provides 27 types of tax-exempt organizations under Section 501(c) of the federal tax code. The organization BoardSource (2011) examines the major subcategories of the U.S. nonprofit sector as follows:

• **Charities**. Perhaps the most readily identifiable form of nonprofits are those known as **charities**. The majority of nonprofits in the United States (approximately 1 million) are classified as public charities and are exempt under **Section 501(c)(3)** of the U.S. Internal Revenue Service tax code. They represent diverse organizations from those that provide free services in soup kitchens and homeless shelters to vulnerable populations to those that provide wide community development and cultural enhancement activities such as hospitals, museums, and recreation centers. Many "friends" organizations are organized within this category to support parks and recreation efforts. For example, the Friends of Buford Park and Mt. Pisgah in Eugene,

Oregon, was founded in 1989 to support the ecological integrity of the nearly 2,400 acres (971 ha) that comprise the Howard Buford Recreation Area. Although working in conjunction with the Lane County Parks Department, this friends group is organized separately. Thousands of such friends groups exist across the United States.

• **Foundations**. One way that individuals, organizations, and communities support causes that benefit society is through private, corporate, operating, or community **foundations**. These also operate as 501(c)(3) nonprofits, and their purposes and operating systems are as varied as those of public charities. Some foundations make grants to a range of community causes. These types of foundations encourage grant proposals from many different areas of the community, including recreation and cultural causes. Other types of foundations, however, serve as a conduit for amassing resources to support their own programs and activities. Creating an operating foundation is one way that government parks and recreation programs generate private support for their public goals. There are several other structural variations of this complex nonprofit form.

• **Social welfare organizations**. Some nonprofits advocate for specific issues by lobbying legislators to advance social causes and by actively campaigning for political candidates. These nonprofits, known as **social welfare organizations**, are recognized in the Internal Revenue Service code as 501(c)(4) organizations. They are exempt under the tax code, but donations to these causes are not tax deductible. The National Rifle Association and the National Organization for Women are two examples of such organizations.

• **Professional and trade associations**. Nonprofits that promote business or professional interests comprise a collection of nonprofits known as **professional and trade associations**. They usually qualify for tax exemption under Section 501(c)(6) of the tax code, and they focus on the interests of specific industries or professions. They also may have broader community interests such as chambers of commerce or business leagues. Similar to advocacy organizations, donations to these associations are not tax deductible.

Hundreds of thousands of nonprofits are registered as associations in the United States and,

depending on their specific mission, they fall within one of the 501(c) categories listed earlier. Nonprofits formed as associations are of particular interest to the recreation professional and are worthy of expanded discussion in this chapter for two reasons. The first is that some professional associations such as the National Recreation and Park Association benefit the recreation professional by providing training, certifications, and a network of colleagues that assist in career success and advancement. The second is that the association format is one way citizens organize around mutual interests. Frequently, these interests involve recreation, leisure, and sport pursuits.

According to the American Society of Association Executives (2004), more than 86,000 associations exist in the United States. Five of the largest membership associations are the following (total number of members in parentheses):

1. American Automobile Association (43,000,000)
2. American Association of Retired Persons (35,700,000)
3. YMCA of the USA (16,900,000)
4. The National Geographic Society (9,500,000)
5. National Parent-Teacher Association (6,500,000)

Several of these associations are directly applicable to recreation, sport, and leisure pursuits. Figure 8.3 in the WR provides examples of associations with direct recreation ties.

Resource Base

The resource base of a nonprofit includes all the sources of support that make offering its programs and services possible. Nonprofits derive their revenue from a combination of one or more sources. The following are the most common sources:

• **Membership fees**. These are fees charged to members, usually annually, in return for programs provided by the nonprofit in service to its members.

• **Program fees**. Participants pay fees for participating in specific programs. Depending on the nonprofit, program participants may or may not be members of the organization.

• **Private philanthropy**. Fund-raising from individuals, corporations, and foundations provides revenue to nonprofit organizations. The skills associated with cultivating donors, developing proposals, and securing gifts from a range of philanthropic stakeholders require increased sophistication because contributed income has grown to become an essential revenue source for many nonprofits.

- **Government grants**. Many nonprofits compete for and receive government grants from local, state, and federal agencies to provide services based on targeted community needs and priorities.

- **Interest income**. Nonprofits receive income from cash reserves and other unspent monies that are actively managed to maximize earnings until used for expense purposes. Some nonprofits have developed endowment funds that build assets so that the mission of the organization may continue into perpetuity.

- **Earned income**. For nonprofits that own facilities, earned income can occur through rental arrangements, admission fees, and other agreements that turn physical assets into revenue streams.

- **Sales income**. For many youth development organizations, sales from cookies, candy, and other products provide a dual benefit to the organization: a program in which young people learn to organize, implement a plan, and reach goals and revenue for the organization.

- **Social enterprise**. A new and growing trend for some nonprofits is the creation of for-profit companies that channel profits back into their social cause.

Philanthropy in Nonprofit Organizations

Nonprofit organizations often intersect with our lives in deep and abiding ways through philanthropy. **Philanthropy** is the promotion of common good through voluntary action, voluntary association, and voluntary giving (Payton, 1988). Philanthropy is expressed in a variety of forms by people who freely give their money and time to the causes of their choice.

One way in which our sense of belonging and identification of feelings are attached to nonprofit organizations is through acts of philanthropy. Mason (1999), whose quote introduced this chapter, notes that, "when people describe their relationship to their employer, they state, 'I work for Exxon. I am with Intel.'" However, he continues, "We reserve the 'belonging' for our voluntary enterprises," the nonprofit organizations that we intersect within our lives. Consider the following statements:

> I *belong* to the YMCA.
>
> I *am* a Boy Scout.
>
> I *belong* to the Camelback Mountain Hiking Club.
>
> I *am* a volunteer at the teen center.

The philanthropic tradition in the United States has been well documented. According to research by the Corporation for National and Community Service (2011), in 2010, 62.8 million American adults (26.3 percent of the population) volunteered, giving 8.1 billion hours of volunteer service worth US$173 billion. The amount of money given is no less impressive; more than 80 percent of all U.S. households contributed to charities (individual giving and bequests), contributing an average of US$2,213 annually. More than $300 billion was contributed through private philanthropy in 2009.

In recent years the growing philanthropic tradition in Canada has been studied as well. According to a 2009 research report released by Statistics Canada, 12.5 million Canadians (46 percent of the population) volunteered through a charitable or nonprofit organization. This number is the equivalent of almost 1.1 million full-time jobs. Almost 23 million Canadians made direct financial donations to a charitable or other nonprofit, representing approximately 84 percent of the population aged 15 or over. The average annual donation amount was nearly C$450.

Contributors of time (volunteers) and money (financial donors) provide important human and financial resources that nurture, sustain, and bolster nonprofit recreation organizations. For example, in many nonprofit youth development organizations, volunteers serve as coaches, mentors, teachers, camp counselors, troop leaders, and board members. As financial donors they support cookie sales, donate to annual support campaigns, organize special events, and otherwise contribute income that is a vital part of organizational budgets.

Given the importance of philanthropy to nonprofit organizations, the recreation professional in the United States with responsibility for coordinating volunteer programs or raising funds can benefit from a nationwide network of volunteer action centers. HandsOn Network operates action centers in the United States as part of the Points of Light Institute. The centers help connect interested volunteers with organizations and activities. The nearly 250 action centers across the United States are a resource useful to any recreation professional interested in developing or expanding his or her volunteer program capacity.

In addition, two professional organizations advance competencies for volunteer management and fund-raising. The Council for Certification in Volunteer Administration (www.cvacert.org) articulates competencies, advances ethical practice, and promotes professional development and education to support volunteer managers. CCVA sponsored the certificated in volunteer administration (CVA) credential intended for those who lead and direct volunteer engagement in all types of organizations and settings. Similarly, the Association of Fundraising Professionals (AFP) (www.afpnet.org) is a national association that provides training, research, and other support to those involved in fund-raising. Through AFP's credentialing program, qualified fund-raisers can earn the designation of certified fund-raising executive (CFRE), which attests to a development professional's knowledge, skill, and achievements.

TYPES OF NATIONAL AND COMMUNITY-BASED NONPROFIT RECREATION ORGANIZATIONS

As previously noted, more than a million organizations—large and small, formal and informal—exist within the U.S. and Canadian nonprofit sector. Nonprofit organizations play a critical role in the recreational and cultural life of the United States. Salamon notes that, "Many of the central recreational institutions of local communities—swimming clubs, tennis clubs, Little Leagues, country clubs—are nonprofit in form. Even more importantly, nonprofit organizations form the backbone of the nation's cultural life, producing most of the live theater, symphonic music, and opera, and providing venues for art and for cultural artifacts" (1999, p. 131).

Interestingly, the nonprofit form is often most potent when it is organized around individual special interests in collaboration with government and business to advance mutually agreed-on goals. Instances of these occurrences in the recreation field abound. One example is that of Kartchner Caverns State Park located outside Benson, Arizona. First discovered in 1974 by Gary Tenen and Randy Tufts, the cave was kept secret for years in order to protect its natural and fragile beauty. The discoverers worked through several people and organizations to realize their dream of preserving forever their unique geological find. In particular, they worked through a nonprofit, The Nature Conservancy, and with a government entity, the Arizona State Parks Department, along with the private land owner on whose property the caverns were discovered, to preserve the site. Following years of study and design, Kartchner Caverns opened in 1999 as a state park. Today, three sectors work together to sustain the caverns including *government* (Arizona State Parks, which owns the land and administers the park), *business* (Aramark Sports and Entertainment Services, which holds the contract for concessions at the park), and *nonprofit* (Friends of Kartchner Caverns State Park, which raises funds to support educational, scientific, and conservation programs). Thousands of examples exist whereby nonprofit organizations help to nurture and sustain recreation settings in collaboration with government agencies and business enterprises.

Whether organized in direct collaboration with government and business or as largely independent entities, various types of national and community-based nonprofit recreation organizations produce significant social benefits. Some of these organizations are identified clearly by their mission, purpose, logo, and other features, and they have a history as a successful entity. Many are part of the essential delivery system of the recreation movement.

Nonprofits that are part of the recreation and leisure services arena can be generally organized as follows:

- Voluntary youth-serving organizations
- Religious and faith-based organizations
- Social service and relief organizations
- Special populations–serving organizations
- Environmental and conservation organizations
- Associations

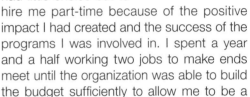

Background Information

Name: Amanda Petru

Education: Bachelor of science in nonprofit leadership and management from Arizona State University.

Career Information

Position: Youth and events manager.

Organization: The Phoenix Regional Sports Commission is a 501(c)(3) nonprofit organization located in downtown Phoenix. The organization is responsible for several million dollars of economic impact through sport-based tourism. Through tribute events, youth sport programs, and events that are bid on and created by the organization, the Sports Commission helps to enrich the community through sports. The day-to-day operations are managed by a staff of four full-time individuals and a handful of interns. Additionally, the board of directors is composed of more than 50 of the valley's most prominent leaders.

Job description: I am responsible for youth and event management. I also handle all the human resources and IT tasks associated with the Sports Commission. Every day is unique in the tourism and nonprofit industry. I spend the majority of my time coordinating events by working with community partners in developing programs that support our mission of enriching the community through sports. I am responsible for executing the organization's largest annual fund-raiser, the Arizona Sports Hall of Fame, as well as all our youth programming. I work diligently throughout the year to recognize and honor the young athletes, contributors, and coaches who are pillars of our community not only on the playing field but in other aspects as well. I am currently working to develop the largest volunteer youth sport coaches' training program in Arizona. Throughout the day I am reaching out to various youth programs to secure their involvement in these community partnerships.

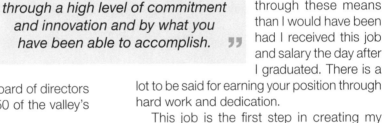

Prove that you are invaluable through a high level of commitment and innovation and by what you have been able to accomplish.

Career path: I started with the Sports Commission as an intern. I worked a full-time job in addition to the unpaid internship with the Sports Commission. At the end of my internship period, the president had little choice but to hire me part-time because of the positive impact I had created and the success of the programs I was involved in. I spent a year and a half working two jobs to make ends meet until the organization was able to build the budget sufficiently to allow me to be a salaried employee. I am prouder of having achieved this position through these means than I would have been had I received this job and salary the day after I graduated. There is a lot to be said for earning your position through hard work and dedication.

This job is the first step in creating my legacy. I cannot imagine leaving until I have helped to establish the Sports Commission as a highly respected and well-recognized community organization. However, I know that this will not be my final stop on my career path.

Advice for Undergraduates

Here is my most pressing advice to any student looking into the field of sports, recreation, nonprofit organizations, and tourism: Apply for internships. Start as young as freshman year and tackle as many as you can, even if you are only volunteering for random events. Get your name out there and start learning the way things operate. It honestly *is* about whom you know. A strong letter of recommendation or a good word from the right person is the best and fastest way to land a position that you really want. Today, no one feels comfortable hiring a complete stranger and hoping for the best. Employers want assurance that the people they are investing in will be able to perform their various tasks at a high level.

(continued)

- Membership or service clubs and fraternal organizations

The mission and programs of some nonprofits cut across more than one category. The Salvation Army, for example, serves youth, is faith based, provides wide-ranging social services, and often serves special populations. In some communities, the local affiliate of Boys and Girls Clubs of America resides inside a Salvation Army unit. It is helpful to consider these varied categorizations when thinking about the core mission of organizations and their targeted client or customer populations. A sampling of these organizations follows. Descriptions are derived directly from organization websites and materials provided by these organizations.

Voluntary Youth-Serving Organizations

More than 50 leading nonprofit youth and human services organizations across the United States belong to the National Collaboration for Youth, an affinity group of the National Assembly of Health and Human Service Organizations. Collectively, they serve more than 40 million young people. These organizations enlist more than 6 million volunteers to provide services and employ more than 100,000 paid staff. Many of the organizations use sport and recreation activities, community service, youth and adult partnerships, and other program-ming features as a means to instill core values in their youth members. Some of these organizations

Some Boys and Girls Clubs of America reside inside a Salvation Army unit. When thinking about the core mission of orga-nizations and their targeted populations it is helpful to consider how many nonprofits cut across more than one category.

are also organized with affiliates in Canada. A sampling of nonprofits with specific youth development goals include the following:

• **Big Brothers Big Sisters of America**. Founded in 1904, Big Brothers Big Sisters of America is the oldest and largest youth-mentoring organization in the United States. In 2010 the organization served nearly 250,000 youth ages 5 through 18, through a network of 370 agencies. Big Brothers Big Sisters promotes one-on-one mentoring relationships between capable adult volunteers and youth. Research studies show that mentoring relationships between positive adult role models and youth have a lasting effect on children's lives. Big Brothers Big Sisters of Canada was organized in 1921 and, similar to its U.S. counterpart, is organized to provide high-quality volunteer-based mentoring programs to more than 1,000 Canadian communities.

• **Boy Scouts of America**. The Boy Scouts of America was founded in the United States in 1910 with the mission of preparing young people to make ethical and moral choices during their lifetimes by instilling important values. Ranging from 7-year-old Tiger Cubs to teenage Varsity Scouts, Boy Scouts of America strives to build character; foster citizenship; and develop mental, moral, and physical fitness in young people. In 2010 the Boy Scouts of America had more than 2.7 million youth members and 1.1 million adult volunteer members in addition to paid staff. The Boy Scouts organization serves more than 300 councils geographically distributed across the United States. Scouts Canada shares a similar purpose—forming the character of boys and imparting patriotic and civic values among members.

• **Boys and Girls Clubs of America**. Founded in 1906, Boys and Girls Clubs of America served 4.2 million children in 2010, particularly boys and girls from disadvantaged circumstances, encouraging them to realize their full potential as productive, responsible, and caring citizens. In facilities that include game rooms, learning centers, and gymnasiums, trained professionals help young people learn to solve conflicts, develop study skills, and work as part of a team. Boys and Girls Clubs also offers programs aimed at developing leadership, career, health, and overall life skills. The organization planted strong roots in Canada in 1929 and

served nearly 200,000 children and youth in 104 clubs in 2010.

• **Camp Fire USA**. Founded in 1910, Camp Fire USA is committed to building caring, confident youth and future leaders through its educational programs. The organization serves over 650,000 children and youth annually with the help of volunteers and paid staff. Camp Fire is organized primarily as a club and offers age-appropriate programs for younger children. For older children, Camp Fire offers self-reliance classes aimed at building the skills necessary to resist peer pressure and cultivate healthy relationships. It also offers service-learning courses intended to instill the importance of community service and offers camping and environmental education programs for children of all ages.

• **Girl Scouts of the USA**. Girl Scouts of the USA was founded in 1912 with the purpose of helping today's girls become tomorrow's leaders. For nearly 100 years, the Girl Scouts program has served girls locally, nationally, and internationally and encouraged them to develop integrity, good conduct, financial literacy, and health so that they can become fulfilled and responsible citizens. Besides emphasizing expression through the arts, Girl Scouts encourages girls to explore their potential in math, science, and technology. Through more than 110 councils throughout the United States, Girl Scouts of the USA has more than 2.3 million youth members in addition to 880,000 adult volunteer members and paid staff. Girl Scouts has a strong North American presence through the Canadian organization, Girl Guides.

• **Girls Incorporated**. Girls Incorporated was founded as Girls Clubs of America in 1945. There is formal history and informal history of many of these organizations. Technically, the first organization of its kind in the United States that was a precursor operated in the 1860s. But the national Girls Clubs of America was founded in 1945. The organization changed its name to Girls Incorporated in 1990. Its goal is to inspire all girls to be strong, smart, and bold. Local affiliates of Girls Incorporated work to help girls and young women overcome the effects of discrimination and develop their capacity to be self-sufficient, responsible citizens, and they serve as vigorous advocates for girls. The organization also works to build girls' skills and interest in

Girl Scouts of the USA is an example of a voluntary youth-serving organization.

science, math, and technology and works to prevent girls from falling victim to peer pressure. Girls Incorporated reaches over 900,000 girls through its affiliates in the United States and Canada and though its website and educational publications. Most Girls Incorporated centers are located in low-income areas and provide a weekly average of 30 hours of after-school, weekend, and summer activities.

• **Little League Baseball**. The Little League program owes its history to the 1880s when leagues for preteen children were formed in New York. In the 1920s and 1930s an organization began to emerge, and in 1939 the first Little League game was played. Little League baseball stakes a claim to being the largest organized youth sports program in the world with over 6,000 leagues in all 50 U.S. states and scores of countries. Through proper guidance and exemplary leadership, the Little League program assists youth in developing the qualities of citizenship, discipline, teamwork, and physical well-being. By espousing the virtues of character, courage, and loyalty, the Little League Baseball program develops superior citizens rather than superior athletes.

Religious and Faith-Based Organizations

Some nonprofits have grown to become nonsectarian organizations with historical roots in faith-based communities. The YMCA and YWCA are two examples. Other nonprofits are created and administered by faith-based or church communities. The Catholic Youth Organization (CYO), Young Men's Hebrew Association (YMHA), and Young Women's Hebrew Association (YWHA) are examples.

• **YMCA of the USA (The Y)**. The first Young Men's Christian Association (YMCA) of the USA was established in 1851. Its initial purpose was to meet the spiritual needs of young men. Today, that philosophy has expanded to include multiple services directed toward a much broader cross section of the population, with an emphasis on families. The mission statement, "To put Christian principles into practice through programs that build healthy spirit, mind and body for all," reflects the organization's commitment to its Christian roots and its global perspective. YMCA programs are family based. Purchased memberships for individuals and families cover the use of basic services such as gymnasiums, game rooms, swimming pools, locker rooms, and lounges. Members are also eligible for reduced fees on other programs such as resident and day camp programs for children and youth sports. The Y's program offerings are virtually endless and serve members nationwide in 2,600 YMCAs and camps. The YMCA has a strong volunteer program that includes more than 500,000 volunteer program leaders and more than 20,000 full-time staff.

• **YMCA Canada**. YMCA Canada was founded in 1851 and is dedicated to the growth of all people in spirit, mind, and body and in a sense of responsibility to each other and the global community. YMCA Canada provides health, fitness, and recreation programs that encourage people of all abilities to pursue healthy lifestyles. Disease prevention and health promotion continue to be mainstays of the YMCA. Program offerings are similar to those in the United States. There are 45 YMCAs and 8 joint YMCA–YWCAs across Canada.

• **YWCA of the USA**. The Young Women's Christian Association (YWCA) of the USA was established in 1858, and now has 2.6 million members and more than 300 associations. The program, rooted in Christianity, is a women's membership movement sustained by the richness of many beliefs and values. Strengthened by diversity, the YWCA draws together members who strive to create opportunities for women's growth, leadership, and power in order to attain a common vision: peace, justice, freedom, and dignity for all people. The YWCA seeks to empower women and eliminate racism. Programs include services for women in crisis, refugee women, single parents, homeless women, women in prison, women coping with substance abuse, and other women in the general population.

• **YWCA Canada**. The YWCA in Canada was established in 1870 with the tagline "A voice for equality—a strong voice for women." The YWCA movement in Canada has provided many of the same services as the YWCA of the USA, emphasizing women's shelters and camping programs. YWCA Canada consists of 33 member associations serving 1 million women, teen girls, and their families through operations in more than 9 provinces and 1 territory across Canada.

Social Service and Relief Organizations

Some of the most recognizable names and logos in the nonprofit sector belong to organizations that provide social and relief services. These organizations are difficult to categorize because some are nonsectarian and others are part of faith-based communities. Each has a mission to improve the quality of individual lives in communities, and they intersect in ways that bolster the goals of recreation service providers or they provide direct recreation services themselves by either joining forces with recreation service providers to meet mutual goals or by providing direct recreation services themselves. The American Red Cross is perhaps one of the best known of any organization in this category.

• **American Red Cross**. The Red Cross was organized internationally in 1863, and the American Red Cross was founded in 1881 as a humanitarian organization to provide relief to victims of disasters and help people prevent, prepare for, and respond to emergencies. Through a network of nearly 700 chapters in the United States, the American Red Cross provides numerous services to meet its mission, including disaster relief services; international services; blood, tissue, and plasma services; services to military members and families; community services; and health and safety services. Red Cross is served by more than a half million volunteers and 35,000 paid employees. Local Red Cross chapters assist recreation professionals by providing water safety, CPR, and first aid training and certification.

• **Canadian Red Cross**. The Canadian Red Cross was founded in 1909. Its work is organized into 4 zones and 22 regions and is supported by more than 30,000 volunteers and 6,000 paid staff. Services of the Canadian Red Cross include disaster relief, international services, first aid and water safety education, and home-care services in some communities (e.g., meals and general assistance for seniors).

Special Populations–Serving Organizations

Although similar in structure to other types, some nonprofits are organized to meet the needs of specific population groups. For example, the United Service Organization (USO) was created in 1941 to support the needs of enlisted military personnel. Many services provided by the USO are oriented toward the leisure and recreation pursuits of its clientele. Other nonprofits work with people with specific disabilities. The Arc of the United States and Special Olympics are two examples.

• **The Arc of the United States**. The Arc of the United States works to include all children and adults with cognitive, intellectual, and developmental disabilities in every community through more than 700 chapters nationwide. Founded in 1950, the Arc is the national organization of and for people with mental retardation and related developmental disabilities and their families. It is devoted to promoting and improving support and services for this group. The association also supports research into and education about the prevention of mental retardation in infants and young children.

• **Special Olympics**. Special Olympics was founded in 1968 to provide year-round sport training and athletic competition in 30 Olympic-type sports for children and adults with intellectual disabilities. With the help of its strong volunteer corps, Special Olympics gives athletes ages 8 years or older opportunities to develop physical fitness, demonstrate courage, experience joy, and participate in a sharing of gifts, skills, and friendship with their families, other Special Olympics athletes, and the community. Through the Family Leadership and Support initiative, Special Olympics offers families not just opportunities for sport, social interaction, and fun but also a much-needed support system. Special Olympics served more than 3.5 million athletes in 2009 worldwide.

Environmental and Conservation Organizations

Environmental organizations are primarily involved in lobbying and education activities for specific concerns such as wildlife protection, global warming, and safe water. They are worthy of consideration because their efforts often make possible the places and spaces in which recreational activities occur. The Sierra Club and The Trust for Public Land are two examples.

• **Sierra Club**. Founded in 1892, the Sierra Club's purpose is to explore, enjoy, and protect the wild places of the earth; to practice and promote the responsible use of the earth's ecosystem and resources; to educate and enlist humanity to protect and restore the quality of the natural and human environment; and to use all lawful means to carry out these objectives. From grassroots campaigns to environmental law programs, the Sierra Club seeks to spread the word about the importance of protecting the planet. The Sierra Club claims more than 1.4 million members and has over 800 field staff throughout 28 field offices and 64 chapters in the United States. The U.S. Sierra Club has created the Mexico Project to help support and strengthen Mexican grassroots environmental and community organizations. The Sierra Club of Canada was founded in 1963 to develop a diverse, well-trained network to protect the integrity of the global ecosystems.

• **The Trust for Public Land**. The Trust for Public Land (TPL) uses its more than 300 paid staff and supporting volunteers to accomplish its mission of conserving land for people to enjoy as parks, gardens, and other natural places, ensuring livable communities for generations to come. Operating in 30 offices across the United States since its inception in 1972, TPL runs several national programs, such as the Working Lands Program (WLP) and Parks for People (PFP). The WLP protects farms, ranches, and forests that support local economies, and the PFP strives to ensure that every American enjoys close access to a park, playground, or other natural area.

Associations

Several nonprofit professional associations concern the recreation field and are a resource to students and practitioners in the field.

• **American Alliance for Health, Physical Education, Recreation and Dance**. The American Alliance for Health, Physical Education, Recreation and Dance (AAHPERD) is the largest organization of professionals, supporting and assisting those involved in physical education, leisure, fitness, dance, health promotion, education, and all specialties related to achieving a healthy lifestyle. Founded in 1885, the association represents an alliance of five national associations and enjoys a membership of more than 22,000.

• **American Camp Association**. The American Camp Association (ACA) is a diverse community

The Trust for Public Land works to conserve land to ensure livable communities and natural places for generations to come.

of camp professionals dedicated to enriching the lives of children and adults through the camp experience. For nearly 100 years, the ACA has used camp programs to impart powerful lessons in community, character building, and skill development. ACA works to preserve, promote, and improve the camp experience, annually impacting 6.9 million campers and learners.

• **American Therapeutic Recreation Association**. With approximately 1,900 members, the American Therapeutic Recreation Association (ATRA) is the largest membership organization representing the interests and needs of health care providers who use recreational therapy to improve the functioning of people with illness or disabling conditions.

• **Canadian Association for Health, Physical Education, Recreation and Dance**. Canadian Association for Health, Physical Education, Recreation and Dance (CAHPERD) is a national, charitable, voluntary-sector organization whose primary concern is to influence the healthy development of children and youth by advocating for quality, school-based physical and health education.

• **Canadian Parks and Recreation Association**. Canadian Parks and Recreation Association (CPRA) is "the national voice for the parks and recreation field." CPRA provides a national network of 2,500 members and advances its belief that parks and recreation is essential to the well-being of individual and community life. There are also provincial and territorial parks and recreation associations operating across Canada.

• **National Recreation and Park Association**. For more than 100 years, the National Recreation and Park Association (NRPA) has advocated the importance of thriving, local park systems; the opportunity for all Americans to lead healthy, active lifestyles; and the preservation of great community places. Its mission is "to advance parks, recreation and environmental conservation efforts that enhance the quality of life for all people." NRPA enhances professional advancement and provides services that contribute to the development of its 18,000 members. Competency guidelines form the curricular content of NRPA-accredited colleges and universities that offer degrees in parks and recreation.

Membership or Service Clubs and Fraternal Organizations

Although we do not always think of service clubs and fraternal organizations as a part of the recreation and leisure services community, we should consider them for two reasons. The first is that many of these organizations support parks and recreation programs through their donations of time and money. The second is that they provide a personal and professional development networking opportunity for the recreation professional who becomes a member. Two of the better-known service clubs are Kiwanis International and Rotary International.

• **Kiwanis International**. Founded in 1915, Kiwanis International has a membership of professional business people dedicated to serving their communities. The organization has nearly 600,000 members and 116 paid staff in 8,700 adult clubs throughout the world. The organization evaluates both children's issues and community needs and conducts service projects that respond to those identified needs.

• **Rotary International**. Rotary is a worldwide organization of business and professional leaders who provide humanitarian service, encourage high ethical standards in all vocations, and help build goodwill and peace in the world. The organization was founded in 1905. Members become actively involved in hands-on projects in which their vocational skills are put to use. Rotary has 1.2 million members worldwide in more than 32,000 clubs in over 200 countries who are served by 740 staff members.

Differences and Similarities Among Organizations

Organizations share differences and similarities according to several distinguishing variables (Hansmann, 1987). These variables include (1) the beneficiaries of their services, such as youth, seniors, or animals; (2) their function, such as service delivery or political advocacy; and (3) their primary source of revenues, distinguishing between nonprofits that rely primarily on sales of goods or services and those that rely largely on donations. Two additional distinctions regarding service delivery are evident within nonprofit recreation organizations. They are (4) whether the organization is facility or nonfacility based and (5) the extent to which volunteers deliver services.

Facility-based recreation organizations attract participants to programs that occur at specific locations. These include Boys and Girls Clubs, YMCAs, and similar organizations. Other nonprofits, such as Big Brothers Big Sisters, are not facility based and therefore rely on community-based facilities for their program delivery. Still other nonprofits, such as Camp Fire USA, Boy Scouts, and Girl Scouts, rely in part on their own place-based facilities, such as summer camps owned by these agencies. However, for other programming they rely on community-based facilities, such as schools, churches, and neighborhood centers.

Another distinction is the role of volunteers in service delivery. Volunteers provide an essential human resource to many nonprofits. In fact, in organizations such as Big Brothers Big Sisters and in Boy Scouts and Girl Scouts programs, volunteers are the delivery system. Without them, there would be no services delivered, and the mission of each organization could not be carried out. Other organizations such as Boys and Girls Clubs rely more on paid staff to deliver their core programs. However, in every case, volunteers serve in a variety of governance roles, such as boards of directors and task groups, and in support roles, such as fund-raising.

THE PROFESSIONAL IN NONPROFIT ORGANIZATIONS

According to the Bureau of Labor Statistics, in 1994 the nonprofit sector employed about 5.4 million people in the United States, representing 4.4 percent of all workers. By 2007, however, nonprofits employed 8.7 million workers, or approximately 6 percent of all workers in the United States (Bureau of Labor Statistics, 2009). Career opportunities for nonprofit professionals are growing rapidly across all subsectors, including recreation and leisure services providers. Nonprofits hire people with diverse skills, just as business or government entities do, because there are as many different job functions as those found in other industries. However, many recreation and leisure nonprofits have relatively small numbers of paid staff in relation to their number of volunteers. Thus, the professional is often given broad responsibility for a variety of duties within the organization.

Given the unique nature of philanthropy in many nonprofits, staff members who demonstrate skills in raising financial resources and working with and through volunteers to accomplish organizational goals are particularly successful. In youth development nonprofits, some practitioners work directly with children. More likely, however, they are responsible for a geographic territory with responsibility for assuring that financial and human resources are acquired and deployed within the mission of the organization.

A variety of job and career resources are available for those interested in pursuing careers in nonprofit recreation and leisure organizations. The national organization Action Without Borders (www.idealist.org) is one of several entities that provides career guidance and posts job openings. Trade publications such as *The NonProfit Times* and *The Chronicle of Philanthropy* are also helpful tools.

Students pursuing degree programs in recreation who have an interest in nonprofit careers may benefit from earning national certification through the Nonprofit Leadership Alliance (formerly American Humanics, Inc.) (www.humanics.org). NLA is a national alliance of colleges, universities, and nonprofit partners preparing undergraduate students for careers in nonprofit organizations. Campus affiliates of NLA offer curricular and cocurricular offerings leading to the Certified Nonprofit Professional (CNP) credential for students pursuing nonprofit professional careers. The program was founded in 1948 and is offered in the United States at nearly 70 colleges and universities nationwide.

CHALLENGES AND OPPORTUNITIES FOR THE FUTURE

Based on research commissioned and released in 2009 by the James Irvine Foundation, as conducted by La Piana Consulting, several trends serve as both challenges and opportunities for the nonprofit sector (http://irvine.org/images/stories/pdf/eval/convergencereport.pdf). These trends include demographic shifts, technological advances, networks

enabling work to be organized in new ways, rising interest in civic engagement and volunteerism, and blurring of sector boundaries. In addition, issues of trust and accountability remain an ongoing trend that requires the attention of nonprofit leaders and managers.

Each of these trends has direct implications for nonprofit recreation and leisure services providers. For example, as communities change and grow, many will find that the majority of their citizens are from ethnic minorities. Sweeping demographic changes also mean that nonprofit providers must make adjustments to stay relevant if they want to make a broad-based impact. This trend also speaks to the need for managing staff across generations in the workplace if organizations are to be successful. Honoring their historic traditions as they change structures, processes, and programs to welcome new and diverse populations to their organizations presents both challenges and opportunities. This tension between exclusion and inclusion cuts across many demographics including race, ethnicity, culture, sexual orientation, and physical abilities. Using history as a predictor of the future, the nonprofit sector in North America will be composed of organizations that change, some that remain static, and some that are created anew.

The use of social media, online giving approaches, and other technological advances presents nonprofits with new ways to reach stakeholders, tell their stories, and engage citizens in their efforts. The opportunity for collaboration in response to marketplace challenges addresses the need for networks that enable work to be organized in new ways. Only the rare nonprofit can afford to operate its programs without regard for other providers of similar services, be they government, nonprofit, or business providers. Issues of pricing, marketing, and consumer choice suggest that the successful nonprofit of the future must use businesslike principles without abandoning the core public service mission that earns its tax-exempt privilege. A call for greater civic engagement and volunteerism among citizens to engage actively in the process of citizenship is prevalent across many communities. It is through nonprofits that people will frequently find their place to engage by focusing their time, money, and know-how on causes that they care about.

Blurring of the lines that demarcate the sectors is a trend that directly affects the recreation field. For example, during the economic downturn of the latter years of the century's first decade (2005-2010), nonprofits were called on like never before to assume responsibilities previously provided by government. For example, in Phoenix, Arizona, the Parks and Recreation Department issued proposal requests to area nonprofits interested in operating and maintaining more than a dozen city facilities that had been closed because of budget reductions. Increasingly, networks of organizations across sectors (government, business, and nonprofit) are called on to work together to provide a common good.

At least one final trend worth amplifying concerns the issue of trust and accountability. If nonprofits depend on the charitable giving of time and money to assure the success of their missions, then such organizations must be led and managed effectively. Although other sectors also face accountability issues, the special trust held by nonprofits as stewards of philanthropy makes this issue especially important.

SUMMARY

Understanding the role of nonprofit organizations is important if recreation and leisure services are to be thoroughly understood. The nonprofit form is one way in which services are organized and delivered. There are enormous variations in how nonprofits are organized across North America. The extent to which the nonprofit form is used in one country compared to another is largely based on the economic, social, and political differences found among different nations.

The career field for graduates of recreation and related degree programs who seek professional opportunities is growing. A number of trends are influencing the organizations of society that deliver recreation services as a blurring of the lines of the three sectors (business, government, and nonprofit) occurs. Successful nonprofit managers will be those who are skillful across a range of competencies and who can span boundaries across sectors. In particular, the ability to raise philanthropic resources and to work with and through volunteers to achieve organizational goals are hallmarks of the successful nonprofit professional.

For glossary terms, learning experiences, and more, please visit the web resource at
www.HumanKinetics.com/IntroductionToRecreationAndLeisure

CHAPTER 9

For-Profit Sector: Recreation, Event, and Tourism Enterprises

Robert E. Pfister and Patrick T. Tierney

> " I wanted to be an editor or a journalist. I wasn't really interested in being an entrepreneur, but I soon found I had to become an entrepreneur in order to keep my magazine going. "
>
> Richard Branson, entrepreneur and founder of the Virgin Group

LEARNING OUTCOMES

After reading this chapter, you should be able to do the following:

> Contrast the characteristics of for-profit service providers with other service providers in the leisure and the tourism industry
> Describe the role of activities of small and medium for-profit enterprises (SME) together with larger corporations in providing services in the recreation, event, and tourism (RET) industry
> Identify strategies for success in acquiring business skills central to the delivery of valued goods, services, and experiences by for-profit enterprises
> Describe trends influencing the management, marketing, and use of technology by SME owners and operators

INTRODUCTION

For-profit organizations that provide recreation, special event, and tourism services are at the center of the commercial recreation sector. The term **commercial recreation** refers to any enterprise that provides recreation or leisure experiences with the intent of making a profit. The scope of a commercial enterprise products or services may be local, national, or multinational. Such enterprises are one of many service providers that allow us, as consumers, to choose opportunities that add to our quality of life and improve our productivity at work. Influenced by diverse interests and expectations, each of us can rely on a wide array of recreation, travel, event, and tourism enterprises when it comes to our leisure choices. Consider, for example, the following scenario:

Reflecting on the past 12 months, you and your long-term partner recognize that it was a memorable year. As outdoor enthusiasts, the two of you were able to enjoy all your favorite outdoor activities together—downhill skiing, mountain biking, kayaking, windsurfing, and even an unexpected Caribbean cruise. It's December, and you are comfortably relaxed in an Aspen lodge, ready to celebrate the joy and rewards associated with a series of well-organized vacations.

You first remember the surprise Caribbean cruise coming as a rewards certificate from your favorite ski equipment retail outlet that you have been going to for over a decade. Their letter stated that they held a drawing and that you had won first prize in a customer loyalty contest. First prize was an all-expenses-paid, four-day Royal Caribbean cruise sailing from Miami.

You discovered that the vacation package was prepared by an incentive travel company that works with commercial enterprises to reward either loyal customers or productive employees. The timing of the trip even allowed you to take in a professional NBA game because the Miami Heat were playing at home before the trip departure. In late spring, you had a kayak trip on the Green River in your home state of Colorado. Then later in the summer, it was off on a California holiday for a multiday mountain bike experience put together by the Downieville Adventure Company. You had the opportunity to bike the course of one of the best-known mountain bike races in the country. Your guide urged you to stay on designated trails and demonstrated how to practice low-impact recreation. In fall, you went back to your favorite retail outlet store to equip yourself for the upcoming ski season. So now you find yourself at Aspen, thinking about how great it was for you to do what you enjoy most with the support of a variety of key service providers.

In this chapter we'll discuss three common attributes of the for-profit industry as illustrated in this scenario as well as how small service providers work with and within the larger service industry. After covering these topics, we'll help you explore the skills that you need for success in this industry and the trends that you need to be aware of.

THREE COMMON ATTRIBUTES

The key service providers identified in the scenario depicted some of the diverse range of goods, services, products, and experiences delivered by for-profit enterprises. Although these service providers may differ in size of their operations, commercial enterprises tend to share a set of attributes and functions that clearly distinguish the for-profit sector from the nonprofit and public sector. In addition, such business enterprises enjoy a standardized statistical category under the provision of the North American Free Trade Agreement.

Attributes of For-Profit Services

When you look closely at the memorable experiences in the scenario, you'll see that some were delivered by large corporate resort properties and others by small businesses. But all share some attributes that distinguish them in at least five ways from noncommercial providers. See the following explanation and table 9.1 for a summary.

• The pricing of services can be the same for domestic and international customers, but this is rarely the case for tax-based (e.g., public) or membership-based (e.g., nonprofit) service providers. Moreover, variable pricing, such as higher prices during peak demand times, is a marketing feature that can be designed to appeal to a targeted market and to maximize revenue.

• Commercial enterprises commonly create travel packages because they appeal to certain market segments and can increase the length of stay for travelers who are looking for a combination involving food, accommodation, and attractions. These packages can serve other purposes, as in the case of incentive travel whereby companies specialize in such activities as a service to the RET industry.

• The ability to buy and sell an enterprise is unique to the commercial sector. In many cases, legal ownership of a business is one of the reasons why diligent and hard-working entrepreneurs invest considerable effort in building the reputation, assets, and customer base of their business. This type of commitment represents value that can be appraised if the time comes to sell the business.

• The need to be responsive to changes in the marketplace is central to maintaining a competitive edge in the commercial sector. This attribute reflects an inherent capacity in the design of the business to respond quickly to customer preferences so as to remain profitable and even capture new and evolving markets.

• Some commercial recreation businesses may choose to be seasonal operations, an arrangement that may reflect their ability to be entirely profitable on a seasonal basis or to shift their services and products in response to cyclical patterns in certain regions.

• All commercial recreation businesses must develop and abide by green or eco-friendly practices in order to minimize adverse impacts on the environment. In their quest to become environmentally and socially **sustainable**, their services must benefit not just themselves but also the resources and communities they rely on. This is in their best

Table 9.1 Five Characteristics That Distinguish For-Profit Enterprises From Other Service Providers

	For-profit	Public	Nonprofit
Pricing of services	Single competitive price	Based on resident fees	Limited to members
Tour packaging	Commonplace	Rarely undertaken	Done for members
Can be sold	Yes	No	No
Ability to respond quickly to changes in the market	High capability	Limited capability	Some capability
Seasonal products or programs	Outdoor operators shift between geographic regions	If facility based, programs often change	Shift based on member preferences

Reprinted, by permission, from R.E. Pfister and P. Tierney, 2009, *Recreation, event, and tourism businesses: Start-up and sustainable operations* (Champaign, IL: Human Kinetics), 11.

long-term business interest and—in many cases—is a legal requirement.

Legal Status, Business Name, and Operational Practices

The legal status of an enterprise is indicative to its choice of a name, and it is fundamental to its ability to be bought, sold, or transferred. For small and medium business, the most common forms of ownership are sole proprietorship and general partnership. In such cases the venture commonly carries the name of those involved in the formation of the enterprise or its owners. An alternative would be for the business to carry a name that reflects its base of operation or its service territory (e.g., Downieville Adventure Company). The third legal status is to incorporate or form a limited liability company (LLC). These forms of doing business are evident in destination resorts,

corporate properties, cruise ship lines, and so forth. With incorporation or an LLC, companies often invest substantially in branding and trademarks for the business because its identity is vital to name recognition in the market place. Naming conventions refer to the choices available to a business given its legal status, displayed in table 9.2.

For-profit service providers carry out a set of operational practices and systematic decisions to ensure that their advertised range of goods and services are available to the people whom they serve. Their operational practices involve the following integrated steps:

1. Planning that goes into assessment of demand and the creation of value-added products and programs (e.g., goods and services) for the consumer
2. Marketing of the products, goods, services, and programs in a well-designed communication plan

Table 9.2 For-Profit Legal Status and Implications for Naming Conventions

Legal status	Implications	Process
Sole proprietorship	No formalities are necessary if a person named John Gow wants to be called John Gow Guide Service. Using a surname alone is possible too.	If a business name does not show the owner's surname or implies the existence of additional owners, many states require the owner to file a fictitious business name statement and publish notice. See DBA.
General partnership, joint venture, limited liability partnership	This option generally takes the path of having two names appear in the business name.	If surnames are not used in the partnership, the owners most likely will file for a fictitious business name. See DBA.
Corporation, limited liability corporation, S corporation	When the owners create a recognized legal entity, the naming process is more involved. Laws and fees governing corporations vary from state to state. Most owners incorporate in the state in which they will conduct business. Some other considerations may be important. Nevada does not charge a state corporate income tax or personal income tax, and it allows a higher level of privacy for businesses. Business-friendly states do this to attract corporations to have offices in their jurisdiction.	Although the owners may have considerable choice for a name, guidelines for naming conventions are established by the laws of incorporation, which will vary by federal and state statute. Some words will be restricted because they are reserved for nonprofit societies or associations. More important, owners will have to research the availability of the name selected because it may not be available to be registered if an existing business has filed for it.
Doing business as, or DBA*	Of course, the owners may choose a name that simply sounds good such as Aardvark Adventures, Dianne's Dance Studio, Frank's Fly Fishing Shop, or Bertha's Restaurant. And the owner's name does not have to be Aardvark, Dianne, Frank, or Bertha.	A business name that is not the owner's name is known as an assumed or fictitious name. The owner will have to complete the DBA process, which varies from one jurisdiction to another. DBA advertisements appear in the business section under DBA, which is the acronym for this process. Several states have online services that make the search process considerably easier.

*https://filedba.com/?r=overturead&OVRAW=Dba&OVKEY=dba&OVMTC=standard

Reprinted, by permission, from R.E. Pfister and P. Tierney, 2009, *Recreation, event, and tourism businesses: Start-up and sustainable operations* (Champaign, IL: Human Kinetics), 66.

3. Delivery of the goods and services in a timely manner to the market

4. Monitoring of the results of their effort after the consumer has purchased the goods or services

All successful businesses have a vital interest in monitoring consumer satisfaction in one form or another. If services that RET businesses provide are not valued by customers and do not meet their expectations, competitors are likely to capture the unsatisfied market. This topic of consumer satisfaction is reflected in the earlier scenario in which a retail outlet implemented a customer loyalty reward and provided a Caribbean cruise to a loyal customer. In other cases, incentives might involve discount coupons, a cash prize, air miles, or gift cards. In figure 9.1 the operational practices are displayed as a set of integrated steps performed by an enterprise, often as part of their business plan.

NAFTA and Recreation, Event, and Tourism Activity

The nature and attributes of the for-profit sector becomes even more differentiated as we look at a variety of recreation, event, and tourism enterprises in the context of their services to the consumer. The adoption of the RET label, or acronym, originates from a monitoring or data-collection need to standardize the coding of industry sectors for statistical purposes combined with the approach contained in the North American Free Trade Agreement (NAFTA). Within NAFTA the new **North American Industry Classification System** (NAICS) recognizes arts, entertainment, and recreation, as well as event, meeting, and convention planning sectors of the economy in a uniform way. Thus, when professionals now describe recreation, event, and tourism businesses, the acronym encompasses a diverse set of businesses responsible for a wide range of commercial leisure services in urban, rural, and even remote locations that attract persons to participate in leisure or a combination of business and leisure activities and to travel to new destinations. An RET enterprise featured herein refers generally to business operations that provide a set of leisure-oriented goods or services and intend to be profitable within a reasonable time.

For-profit leisure enterprises vary from those that provide indoor batting cages in urban areas to those that rent outdoor equipment in remote barrier islands off the coast. Event businesses might arrange large spectator festival events in urban venues or small family weddings in rural communities. Small tourism businesses may offer special services to large time-share resort destinations or offer dogsled trips in the Yukon Territory. Any new term seeking to capture the diversity of commercial activities evident today is likely to meet with some resistance if for no other reason than it is a departure from previous terminology

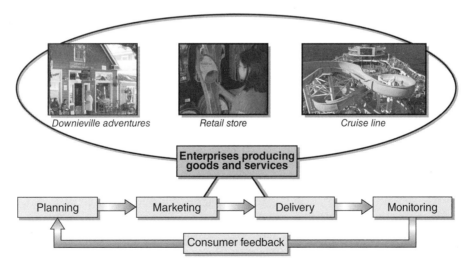

Figure 9.1 The four basic operational practices (planning, marketing, delivery, monitoring) of a recreation, event, and tourism (RET) business are represented in the RET operations model.

and typologies. The following section addresses the rationale for recognizing this category of businesses and provides a description of how previous models or typologies chose to group types of businesses.

RET INDUSTRY MODEL

Travel is said to require simply a motive for travel, information about opportunities, an affordable means of travel, destination attractions, something to do, and a place to eat and sleep. Using this idea as an organizing principle for a travel-commerce model, we can examine the primary function of each business, agency, or organization within the overall tourism industry. Synthesizing earlier theories and numerous research studies on the recreation, event, and tourism industry, we have developed the **recreation, event, and tourism (RET) industry model** shown in figure 9.2. The three basic functional areas are (1) attractions, (2) support and facilitation, and (3) hosting functions. The model also contains two integrated functional groups that merge elements of the attraction and hosting functions.

Attractions

At the top of the pyramid, attraction businesses, as well as public-sector facilities, provide the motive and stimulation for travel and attract people to specific destinations. A basic premise is that the tourism industry attractions function provides the services and products that are the reasons why people travel. They power the demand for businesses in the other two functional areas by creating memorable visitor experiences. Attractions consist of three subcomponents:

1. Tourist attractions primarily lure nonresident tourists. They range from natural and cultural attractions to theme parks, gaming casinos, and seeing family and friends.

2. Event experiences are short-duration activities that are not generally repeated frequently and that attract both residents and visitors. They include special events, conventions and conferences, festivals, exhibitions, and reunions.

3. Local recreation consists of facilities and activities that provide residents with frequently

repeated, nearby leisure experiences. Examples of local recreation organizations include clubs; city recreation departments; sport organizations; day spas; arts, craft, and music suppliers; and movie theatres.

Figure 9.2 clearly illustrates the importance of the private and public recreation and event attractions because without them transportation services or hospitability elements, such as accommodations and food services, would be unnecessary. Length of stay at a destination is also directly related to the number and quality of attractions. The model also shows the wide range of businesses and organizations found in the RET industry, which illustrates how vital, essential, and valuable RET is to our economy and lifestyle, and the wide range of job providers within it.

Support and Facilitation

The support and facilitation function contains two components: transportation and tourist services. Transportation providers, such as airlines, taxis, railroads, recreational vehicles (RVs), and rental cars, deliver tourists to the destination. Without reasonable prices and safe transportation, people would not get to the desired destination and use other elements of the system. Countless services are geared toward assisting visitors, including travel facilitators (e.g., travel management agencies), convention and visitors bureaus, event planners, government land management agencies (e.g., National Park Service and Parks Canada), university tourism programs, research consultants, equipment rental firms, rental and retail businesses, and the travel media. Without these support services, other businesses would function less effectively, and the person might choose another destination or be less satisfied with the experience.

Hosting Function

The hosting function consists of accommodations and food and beverage services. Overnight lodging is provided to visitors by hotels and motels, vacation homes, campgrounds, recreational vehicles, bed and breakfasts, and family and friends. Lodging is a basic visitor necessity, and its quality can greatly influence the visitor's experience. A variety

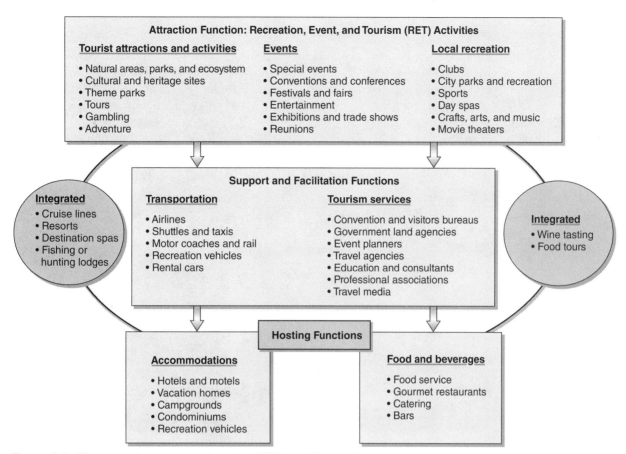

Figure 9.2 The recreation, event, and tourism (RET) model shows businesses of all sizes that represent the three functional areas of the RET industry: attraction, support and facilitation, and hosting.

Reprinted, by permission, from R.E. Pfister and P. Tierney, 2009, *Recreation, event, and tourism businesses: Start-up and sustainable operations* (Champaign, IL: Human Kinetics), 15.

of accommodation options are available, some of which are free (homes of friends and relatives) or low cost (hostels and campgrounds).

The food and beverages functional area includes restaurant, fast food, event catering, bars, and coffee shops. Like accommodations, food and beverage services are a necessity and vary greatly in cost and quality. They too can have a large effect on visitor satisfaction.

Integrated Functions

A growing number of RET businesses integrate or combine attractions and hosting functions at one site. Examples of the integrated function in accommodations include resorts, cruise lines, destination spas, and hunting and fishing lodges. Most integrated accommodations also provide food and beverage products.

An array of food and beverage businesses have an integrated function within RET, in which food and beverage service is a primary attraction for travel, not just a supporting service. Food and beverage services integrated with attractions include activities such as wine-tasting tours, food tours, catering for events, and gourmet restaurants for "foodies," or people who travel specifically to eat at a particular restaurant. A wide variety of travel packages are created around wine-tasting tours and food experiences, such as the Taste of Chicago or the San Francisco Crab Festival.

A cruise ship is a great example of a fully integrated RET business. Clients buy a cruise vacation because of the activities and events on board and ashore. Passengers use a variety of tourism services, stay in cabins, and eat most meals on board while the ship transports them to new destinations.

You can use the recreation, event, and tourism model shown in figure 9.2 to identify links and understand how various types of recreation, event, and tourism businesses fit together. By doing so, you

A cruise ship illustrates a fully integrated RET business that offers accommodation, transportation, and attractions. Clients are attracted to buy a cruise vacation because of the appealing route, activities and events on board, and often the food services.

can better your understanding of the RET industry and start to envision in which part of the RET businesses you might consider working.

CONSIDERING AN RET CAREER

Many people follow their leisure passion, be it travel or recreation, and find a career in the RET field. Some look at the potential to earn a reasonable living while living in a desirable area; for others it is strictly a financial decision. Regardless of your motivation, RET presents a wide variety of career choices. The following sections offer considerations for developing a career, such as entrepreneurship, preparation, and leadership.

Entrepreneur or Intrapreneur?

Preparing for a career in the business field will certainly include developing some skills that differ

based on a position title and your status within an enterprise. Within the RET industry model (figure 9.2), you might choose to be a proactive, self-employed person who operates a small or medium business (e.g., entrepreneur), or you might choose to be a proactive, forward-thinking employee (e.g., intrapreneur) within a larger enterprise or corporation. The term **intrapreneur** was coined and advocated in a book by Pinchot and Pellman (1999, p. ix) in which they stated the word comes from two words, *intra*-corporate and entre-*preneur*. Whether you are an entrepreneur or intrapreneur, you will need personal leadership skills that contribute to success. In addition, if you are employed in a corporate setting, you will need to mimic entrepreneurial attributes such as being mindful of major changes occurring in the industry and having an innovative perspective to respond to the change. In both employment situations, knowledge about managing change will be a springboard for success, as discussed in subsequent paragraphs.

OUTSTANDING GRADUATES

Background Information

Name: Shantel Genest

Education: Bachelor of tourism management, recreation and sport management diploma.

Credentials: Volunteer and event management certificate, first aid and CPRC, class 4 driver's license.

Career Information

Position: Community relations and women's team manager, Victoria Highlanders FC.

Organization: The Victoria Highlanders FC is a semiprofessional soccer club that operates under the United Soccer League (USL). This USL franchise has been in operation for three years.

The club consists of two first teams, the men's Premier Development League (PDL) team and the women's W-League team, and six developmental teams, including two U18 and two U20 teams. The organization also operates youth development academies, spring break training sessions, and other soccer training opportunities for minors.

Apart from the operation of a variety of competitive teams, the club aims to provide an exceptional game-day fan experience to the community of greater Victoria. This aspect includes the operation of a storefront that sells a varied line of team-associated merchandise.

Organization's mission: To further develop the game of soccer within the community by creating opportunities for local players to advance to higher levels of competition (local and international). The club also aims to provide an exceptional fan experience.

Job description: I play two main roles within the business—women's team manager and community relations representative. The management role involves a lot of administrative duties including registration, travel preparation, and liaising between the franchise and other organizations, coaches, and management. As the community events coordinator I look after recruiting and retaining volunteers, planning community-related events, developing our mascot program, and building relationships with charities in the area. Other tasks include developing our merchandise program (ordering, receiving, tracking, selling, and so on) and seeking corporate sponsorships and partnerships.

Career path: Throughout my life I have been involved in sport, playing a wide range of sports including soccer and fastball. I entered the recreation and sport management diploma program knowing that I wanted to work in the sports field and hoped that my position would enable me to help develop sporting opportunities for youth. During my co-op experiences I found myself working at the Gorge Rowing and Paddling Center as a kayak guide and as a tour guide at Club ESL, a specialized tour company based in Vancouver, British Columbia. I first became involved with the Highlanders organization when I was introduced to the GM through networking. The Highlanders were a brand new franchise and a paid position with the club was not available, so I began volunteering on my days off and offered assistance whenever possible. This volunteer work led to a third-year co-op position as the volunteer coordinator and event planner for the club. Upon graduation I was offered a full-time permanent job in community relations with the Highlanders and was later promoted to manage the women's team as they entered the W-League.

Likes and dislikes about the job: I love the excitement of game day. We treat each home game as if it were a standalone event. It is really exciting to facilitate a positive fan experience. I also thrive on the unpredictable nature of the sports industry; there are many external factors that we have little control over, so we have to be quick on our feet.

Working in the professional sports industry can be stressful at times. Different times of year put very different demands on our office staff. The tasks that we must complete in

(continued)

Career Preparation

Many postsecondary curriculums focus on preparing graduates to start as employees. Beginning in such a capacity offers notable benefits. Several common characteristics are found across the various RET employment opportunities. Areas of emphasis that are foundations in both entrepreneurship and intraprenueurship pertain to leadership skills and appreciating the language of business (a combination of accounting, business law, and practice related to contingency planning).

A logical first step is to identify personal opportunities that will strengthen knowledge of leadership and its practice in the industry. Formal education combined with practical, progressive, and innovative work experiences provides a time-tested and sensible combination of activities. The content and focus of any formal or informal work experience program can occur at various points in time. If we were to reflect on Richard Branson's quote at the beginning of this chapter, we could note that his career goal to become a journalist at a young age started him on an educational journey to understand what is required to become a successful entrepreneur. His experiences are instructional.

Foremost among the leadership skills revealed in Branson's autobiography (2006) is the mind-set exhibited in dealing with a changing and challenging business environment. Many authorities stress the importance of visionary leadership qualities in business (Covey, 1992; Kotter, 1996 and 1999; Nahavandi, 2009; Rickards and Clark, 2006). The authors uniformly identify the need to look at challenges with a particular perspective and to adopt skills that ensure flexibility and adaptability to a changing environment. The point is that entrepreneurial skills associated with success in a business are anchored in understanding and applying leadership practices. Moreover, these qualities and practices are portable to each of the diverse RET work environments described in figure 9.2.

The Leadership Factor

In the distinctly service-oriented RET industry covered herein, the ability to discover, adopt, and excel at acquiring basic attributes of leadership should be a priority. Covey (1992) along with Ramsey (2011) set out fundamental and notable principles in this regard. Covey (1992) states that principle-center leaders are (1) continually educated by their experiences and that such people (2) see life as an adventure in which they chart new territory with confidence. Thus, principle-centered entrepreneurs often say that they learned more from their mistakes than from their successes. Their outlook is that life is an adventure and that all experiences are learning opportunities.

Two other valuable principles for people choosing to work in this field are the commitment to be (3) service oriented and (4) believe in other people. Leadership, in Covey's view, is about service to others and recognizing the unseen potential in those whom the leader works with. These principles focus on the people skills linked to effective communication and call for each of us to build capacity to see the best in everyone.

Additional leadership principles include (5) embracing the attitude of optimism and (6) being productive in creative ways, which is described as being synergistic. Without doubt, a positive and hopeful spirit when tackling the things that need to be done lays the foundation for successful leadership. This optimism can be revealed by possessing a sense of humor. When the need arises to negotiate win–win solutions or create change, the capacity to demonstrate synergy is invaluable. It begins with exploring options and expands into seeing new alternatives. It is an asset to every leader.

Finally, a leader needs (7) to demonstrate a balanced lifestyle and (8) to commit to some form of a regular exercise program. The balanced lifestyle is linked to seeing life as an adventure and savoring life experiences. Leaders are commonly active in many ways outside work, and they recognize the need to exercise the mind, body, and spirit.

These principles for acquiring leadership qualities can be experienced in both formal and informal education programs. These eight items are preparatory commitments that will serve those seeking to be either entrepreneurs or intrapreneurs working in the RET industry.

Investing in Professional Networks

Volunteering or obtaining membership in professional associations expands a person's knowledge and skills and is part of building a professional network. In general, choices will be available to network with nonprofit industry organizations as well as specific career-related associations. One type of nonprofit industry association facilitates the exchange of information, educates the travel public, and develops programs to promote professionalism within the industry. Professional and **tourism associations** have been around for a long time and exist for nearly every sector of the industry. The same can be said for **entrepreneurial associations**.

Tourism industry associations provide great opportunities for both students entering the field and established entrepreneurs to network, attend educational sessions, earn certification, meet other professionals, and possibly find a job or a mentor. Tourism associations also conduct research on the industry. These benefits are extremely helpful for people starting out in a career. Some groups operate under the umbrella of a national organization, such as the Commercial Recreation and Tourism Section of the National Recreation and Park Association. See the web resource for a listing of tourism industry associations.

Numerous professional associations have been created to support young entrepreneurs in general, and a number of associations for entrepreneurs are presented in the web resource. Members are challenged to address real-world businesses and economic issues in their own ventures as well as in their communities. Involvement in one or more of these associations would certainly help the aspiring business-minded person obtain timely information and build a valuable network.

Destination Marketing Organizations (DMO)

Regions, states, provinces, and even countries create organizations to promote themselves as preferred tourism destinations. Because membership in these organizations often includes small and medium businesses as well as national corporations, it is instructive to observe how businesses collaborate with visitor service bureaus. It is worthwhile to investigate in a directed studies course how they work, the career options associated with them, and their influence in creating destination images. In the United States and Canada, states and provinces commit funds to tourism offices, welcome centers, visitor information centers, and their corresponding DMOs. They often provide members opportunities for cooperative marketing by displaying company brochures in racks at visitor information centers, placing company information on the DMO website, and providing educational opportunities to attend tourism outlook meetings for the region. Exploring websites will provide an overview of how destination marketing targets the traveler directly, the nature of the relationships with the tourism partners, and ways in which events and attractions are positioned to build a travel itinerary. Some websites have sections on how to start a business within the state or provincial jurisdiction being examined. In addition, many state and provincial DMOs have regular electronic newsletters that keep subscribers up to date on new initiatives, changes in the programs, funding initiatives, and scheduled meetings of professional groups. Their websites tend to keep up with the latest in website technology because the marketing environment is competitive. Going online and searching local websites for information is worth the effort. A search of the diverse websites will reveal the many benefits of an RET career.

Benefits Are Global and Diverse

Examination of for-profit RET opportunities shows that an exciting array of global and diverse settings are open to entrepreneurs or intrapreneurs of all backgrounds. The commercial sector includes a set of businesses and corporations that contribute significantly to the world economy. These businesses are ever changing and technology dependent. What do these special features mean to a business owner? The following paragraphs offer a partial answer.

• **Global.** For the business-minded person, the opportunity exists to explore many places around the world where your idea for a commercial enterprise might be a good fit. The World Trade Organization (WTO) reports that tourism is now the world's largest employer. Leisure travel accounts for 75 percent of all international travel, and domestic travel (i.e., within one's own country) is likely to be four times larger than the number of international arrivals associated with a particular country.

Domestic travel and commercial recreation have been important for a long time. Corporate, sport, and private events are held in worldwide destinations and bring together global participants, as in the case of the Olympics. Although economists began talking about the emergence of a global economy about a decade ago, leisure travel, special events, and domestic tourism have been worldwide activities for more than three centuries.

• **Diverse.** Leisure interests and tourism trends are continuing to expand, and new markets are becoming evident every year. The numerous small businesses providing diverse products and services to society are vital to leisure experiences. If societal demand is present, an opportunity is available for an entrepreneur to fill it. Although no classification can reveal all the commercial enterprises that are encompassed by the leisure or tourism industry, figure 9.2 reveals components of the tourism industry. Entrepreneurship is critical to tourism and travel. Gunn and Var (2002) state the case well:

Because of the dynamics of tourism, opportunities for innovative service businesses continue to appear. . . . There needs to be a

Leisure travel accounts for 75 percent of all international travel and tourism is now the world's largest employer.

volume of business people interested in and able to see opportunity, obtain a site, gather the financial support, plan, build and operate a new business. Small business continues to offer the greatest opportunities in spite of the many risks and obstacles. (p. 68)

• **Economic impact.** The economic benefits associated with commercial and tourism services are extremely important. Tourism is the fastest growing economic sector in terms of foreign exchange and job creation. This growth can stimulate public and private investment in the economy and improve local living conditions for residents. Every year new projects are undertaken by the business council of the World Tourism Organization to strengthen public–private cooperation and partnerships. The small and medium enterprises (SMEs) that dominate the commercial sector occupy a vital role in the recreation, event, and tourism industry. Small and medium enterprises are vital to a nation's economy, and the services provided by SMEs represent 50 to 55 percent of the tourism industry within North America. The National Federation of Small Businesses found that 75 percent of all jobs in the United States are generated by small business enterprises.

• **Technology dependent.** The influence of new technology is evident in all aspects of commerce, and this influence applies particularly to the commercial sector of the recreation, event, and tourism industry. Although many recreation services are not themselves high tech, the business of providing services frequently uses technology. Technology provides a means to disseminate and obtain information quickly from many sources and allows consumers to make better-informed decisions. The changes observed in information and communication systems have profound influence on reservation systems, multimedia distribution of promotional material and special programs, the educational component of events, the nature of e-commerce, and even the capacity to support highly mobile office space for travel and home-based businesses. Tourism applications and Internet sites already have a dominant position on the World Wide Web, and the small business sector of leisure and tourism continues to occupy more sites with the creation and sale of more Internet domains. Technology has created more opportunities than

ever before for the consumer to select among tourism products.

• **Open.** The public marketplace is open to anyone who is willing to acquire the knowledge and skills necessary to participate in the leisure and tourism industry. The free enterprise system is the cornerstone of the open economy and is one of the reasons that the commercial sector thrives in the leisure and tourism field. The global trend toward privatization of public services has also opened new opportunities for RET businesses. You may have interpersonal abilities in dealing with people based on family history, personal travel experiences, language training, recreational lifestyle preferences, or even cultural heritage that will be an asset in a particular aspect of the industry.

TRENDS AND CHALLENGES

Local, regional, and global trends are constantly changing and will affect recreation, event, and businesses and employment prospects in the future. The following are a few of the key current trends and the challenges and opportunities that they present.

Economic Downturn and Staying Close to Home

The economic recession experienced between 2008 through 2010 knocked the travel industry off its feet just as it did other economic sectors in the United States and Canada. A trend to reduce personal travel, referred to as **staycations** (Brown, 2008), came into the vocabulary as families sought to take vacations by staying at, or close to, home. Reduced leisure travel and the reduced travel budgets of government agencies and corporations resulting from the meetings industry being seen as a scapegoat (Hotelier.com, 2010) led to foreclosures and forced sales of some iconic businesses. Declines in personal income and recreation and travel purchases have resulted in losses for investors and staff layoffs. During this time business found ways to do with less travel, and price reduction or value continues to be the key concept to attracting leisure travelers. The economic recovery is fragile, and despite increasing occupancy rates, average ticket prices and profits are depressed and may be for some time. But the recovery has started, led by surging pent-up demand for leisure travel. Bookings for business travel and events are also starting to rebound. With steadily expanding demand, RET business profitability will increase and hiring will start again. New entrants into the RET job market will have to be creative, develop a network, and exhibit entrepreneurial or intrapreneurial skills to find the job that best matches their potential and capability. But they will be well positioned to fill vacancies because of their lower employment cost and the up-to-date training that they have received.

Increasing Requirements for Specialized Skills and Certifications

Today the RET industry is demanding greater professionalism and higher skill levels of workers in the field than ever before. Until recently most professionals did not have specialized RET college degrees. Likewise, few universities offered specialized RET degree programs, and almost none offered master's degree RET specializations. In addition, managers frequently came from other industries besides RET. This situation is changing rapidly because the industry is becoming more competitive and demanding specialized skills from its workers (except for some frontline and entry-level positions). Being trained on the job for two weeks does not provide sufficient preparation to perform professional job functions. Job announcements for professional positions now have minimum degree requirements and a long list of skills and experiences, often highly specialized to the RET industry, such as hospitality accounting or legal issues in the RET field. An array of university undergraduate and graduate degrees are now available to provide appropriate RET training, not just hotel management. An increasingly common way to demonstrate competency in the RET field in addition to a general RET degree is through specialized certificates. These assure potential employers that the holder has met minimum skill and experience requirements. Examples of RET-related certifications include the following:

- Certified special events professional (CSEP), available through the International Special Events Society (see http://isesew.vtcus.com/CSEP/index.aspx)

- Certified lodging manager (CLM), available through American Hotel and Lodging Educational Institute (see www.ahlei.org/content.aspx?id=29293)

- Certified recreation and park professional (CRPP), available through the National Recreation and Park Association (see www.nrpa.org/CPRP)

An RET-related degree or a certification is not a guarantee of a job in the field, but along with industry experience it often provides an advantage over a person who lacks one or both of these and may qualify the applicant for additional job interviews. In addition, RET graduates frequently advance more quickly than nongraduates after they are hired.

Work–Life Balance and Wellness

Along with the trend toward specialized skills and professional certifications is the expectation, especially during tougher economic times, for a salaried professional to put in whatever time it takes to get results. Although professionals have some flexibility about when they start and end their day, layoffs and consolidations have often pushed each remaining staff to be doing the job of two people. Communication technology innovations now permit supervisors and coworkers to contact an employee and allow the employee access to work files almost anywhere and anytime. These trends have resulted in more short-term productivity but also longer hours put in at work, whether these occur at the workplace, at home, or during business travel. The push for more work hours is ubiquitous in American and Canadian societies and certainly not limited to the RET industry, but work in some segments of RET is focused on nights, weekends, and holidays, which can further isolate workers and affect wellness. The combination of all these can place extra stress on the worker's physical and mental health, family and partner relationships, and quality of life. Therefore, a new professional in the RET industry must take proactive steps to achieve a work–life balance. These moves could include selecting an employer and supervisor who do not have unrealistic work expectations and do not push salaried staff to put in large amounts of uncompensated overtime. Workers

OUTSTANDING GRADUATES

Background Information

Name: Stephen Hohener II

Education: Bachelor of arts in recreation, parks and tourism administration, San Francisco State University.

Career Information

Position: Activities coordinator and spa front desk supervisor, Cavallo Point: The Lodge at the Golden Gate (CPL), Sausalito, California.

Organization: CPL is a luxury resort lodge situated in Golden Gate National Recreation Area at the foot of the Golden Gate Bridge across from the city of San Francisco. It was named one of the Top 10 New American Landmarks by *Travel+Leisure* magazine. CPL is both kid friendly and dog friendly and has an extensive Healing Arts Center and activity menu. Other activities offered at the resort include hikes and walks, guided Cavallo Point walks to learn the history of Fort Baker, guided nature walks within the Marin Headlands and under the Golden Gate Bridge, a cooking school, and morning yoga. The resort is a Leadership in Energy and Environmental Design (LEED) gold-certified eco-resort. It was created by the Fort Baker Retreat Group, working with the National Park Service and the Golden Gate National Parks Conservancy in a successful private, public, nonprofit alliance to restore, enhance, and preserve historic Fort Baker, a former U.S. Army post. Guests can stay in one of the carefully restored historical guestrooms, formerly officers' residences, or in a contemporary room that was built to green architecture standards. To achieve LEED gold certification, the resort undertook many activities, including reuse of historical materials, landscape restoration with native plants, and use of green building elements. The resort also hosts the Institute at the Golden Gate, created by the Golden Gate National Parks Conservancy in partnership with the National Park Service, which promotes dialogue, collaboration, shared problem solving, and action for a sustainable world.

Organization's mission: The CPL mission is to provide the highest quality experience for guests while operating in an eco-friendly, sustainable, and community-supportive manner. The resort offers accommodations, award-winning food, a healing arts program, and activities, and it supports the National Park Service mission.

Job description: My current position is activities coordinator and supervisor of the Healing Arts Center front desk. In the activities coordinator position I manage and lead guided hikes and facilitate activities and games for leisure guests as well as team-building programs and meetings for corporate groups. As one of the supervisors of the Healing Arts Center front desk, I manage front-desk operations and staff and encourage guests to participate in CPL spa services and activities.

Career path: After finishing my AA degree I backpacked through Europe and worked various jobs abroad and in the Unites States for the next few years. I came back to finish my college degree in a program that I hoped would allow me to travel and work in the commercial recreation field. I started at San Francisco State University in the Department of Recreation, Parks and Tourism, and during an ecotourism class the teacher mentioned Cavallo Point Lodge as an outstanding eco-resort. A relative heard amazing things about CPL and recommended that I apply for a job with the new lodge. I had hiked in the national park surrounding the lodge and knew of its beauty and uniqueness. In my senior year I applied for an internship at CPL and was lucky to be hired in the Activity Department. My internship special project was to help develop and implement the Integrated Health Program with Dr. Brad Jacobs. At the end of the internship I was hired on full time as the activities coordinator in the Healing Arts Center and spa. Clearly, the internship was

(continued)

Outstanding Graduates *(continued)*

key to starting my career at CPL. Within a year I was promoted to the joint position of activities coordinator and the spa–Healing Arts Center front-desk supervisor.

Likes and dislikes about the job: At CPL I am able to work with corporate and social groups, coordinating onsite activities that provide them with both memorable and pleasurable experiences at CPL. As someone who is fond of the outdoors, I am fortunate that my position at CPL allows me to facilitate certain activities. I still enjoy leading guests on nature hikes underneath the Golden Gate Bridge and through parts of the Marin Headlands for the sheer beauty of the guest's experience.

Advice to Undergraduates

When enrolling within SFSU's Department of Recreation, Parks and Tourism Administration, I initially did not know exactly in what direction this major would take me. By taking the various classes that ranged from the nonprofit to commercial sides of recreation, I was able to discover the specific segments of the field that personally spoke to me and what I wanted in a career. I recommend to all students of recreation, parks, and tourism administration that they get a taste from all the various areas of recreation and tourism so that they can discover their own personal niche within the field.

and employers must realize that staff members need time to be physically and socially active if long-term health and productivity are to be maintained.

Likewise, the RET industry is in a unique position to offer services that greatly improve the health and long-term wellness of its clients. Significant growth has been occurring in health-promoting services in the RET industry. Whether the business is an obvious one like a spa or a less overt RET enterprise like an event-planning company, professionals should be considering facility, food, scheduling, and activity alternatives that promote wellness. Health is a basic demand that is nearly recession proof. Spas have experienced this during the recent 2008 to 2010 recession when spas that focused primarily on pampering lost out to those that offered programs that fostered health as well as personal service. Professionals need to evaluate their services and products to ascertain how they can be modified or how new ones can be developed to enhance client health.

Sustainability and Stewardship

Today, growing concern about the dire environmental impacts of human activities, such as global climate change, has caused many citizens to call for significant changes in businesses operations so that they become more environmentally and socially sustainable. Federal, state or provincial, and local government agencies now require companies that they permit to operate in public facilities and on public lands to have a comprehensive environmental management system and to report their performance on moving toward sustainable operations. Resorts and other businesses will need to be better stewards of natural resources and enlist their clients in these efforts. In this modern time, more than ever, the consumer is well educated and will select a provider based not just on price, value, and quality of the services but also on the company's record of ethical behavior as well as its efforts at reducing environmental impacts and helping the local community. A recent survey of travelers found that 48 percent were willing to pay 10 percent more for services that employ green practices in the travel industry (Tierney, Hunt, & Latkova, 2011). But in the study only 12 percent could identify a green product or service that they had recently purchased or used in the last year, and most of those were low in cost and commitment. Support for green practices is broad, but RET companies need to educate the consumer about their genuine efforts toward environmental and social responsibility. Some firms have used green business certification as a way to distinguish themselves and verify their commitment to potential users. Companies with a strong environmental and community record and certifications in these areas have competitive advantages, stronger growth, and higher profitability than firms that do not. Therefore, ethics, green practices, and sustainability are bottom-line considerations for how a business plans and operates. Workers in the RET industry who have passion as well as hard skills in delivering green practices will be in demand by employers.

Adventure and Entertainment

Large segments of the population are sedentary, and their daily routines are rather mundane. Many persons, from seniors and families to millennials, are increasingly looking toward RET activities to compensate for inactivity and boredom by providing adventure and excitement, but with safety. Others are looking to be entertained while in the care of an RET company. No longer satisfied to lie around the pool for three days, many people require resorts and other RET providers to offer active, educational alternatives and entertainment. So RET providers must offer participatory alternatives, despite potentially greater initial costs, risks, and legal liability. The need is growing for highly trained recreation leaders who are not only technically skilled in delivery of a specific adventure or entertainment activity but also service oriented with the ability to create a quality experience for the customer.

SUMMARY

The for-profit, or commercial, sector of the tourism and travel industry encompasses a diversity of small, medium-sized, and large enterprises largely focused on attractions, hosting, and support functions for domestic and international travelers. In addition, many small and medium-sized enterprises depend on serving the leisure needs of residents in the communities in which they are located. The structure and key elements of this industry are identified in the model presented in this chapter. By the nature of their financial structure, the business enterprises described in this chapter differ in a variety of ways from public and nonprofit organizations. The fact that recreation, event, and tourism business ventures can be sold, bought, and transferred from one owner to another is one distinguishing characteristic.

Preparation for employment in the for-profit sector can come in the form of work experience and formal education. Cooperative education and internship programs allow a student to be placed in a work setting where it is possible to gain valuable experience. Entrepreneurs will say that good judgment in business comes from experience, and most admit that valuable experience comes from prior bad judgment. In other words, working in a business setting allows a person to learn the lessons acquired by the owner over time. In addition, knowing and applying the language of business practices (topics such as accounting, law, leadership, and contingency planning) permit a potential entrepreneur or intrapreneur to contribute to an informed business decision and, at the very least, to be an astute observer of successful practices in the industry. Working in the commercial for-profit sector of the recreation, event, and tourism (RET) industry offers numerous benefits, such as travel during employment and working in the "business of fun." Most important, knowledge and experience is certainly portable across the work setting among the small, medium, and large enterprises that make up the RET industry.

For glossary terms, learning experiences, and more, please visit the web resource at
www.HumanKinetics.com/IntroductionToRecreationAndLeisure

CHAPTER 10

Therapeutic Recreation

Frances Stavola Daly and Robin Kunstler

> " How can the *quality of life* of those who are ill or disabled be enhanced through recreation, or when indicated, through the relating of recreative experience to the therapeutic process? "
>
> Virginia Frye and Martha Peters, authors, *Therapeutic Recreation: Its Theory, Philosophy, and Practice*

LEARNING OUTCOMES

After reading this chapter, you should be able to do the following:

❭ Describe the scope of therapeutic recreation services, including settings, programs, interventions, and clientele

❭ Describe therapeutic recreation and its benefits

❭ Interpret the history of therapeutic recreation for its influence on contemporary therapeutic recreation services

❭ Explain key laws affecting therapeutic recreation services

❭ Identify the building blocks, barriers, and facilitators of inclusion

❭ Describe societal changes that affect therapeutic recreation services in the 21st century

❭ Evaluate therapeutic recreation practice models

❭ Analyze the steps in the therapeutic recreation process

❭ Evaluate the components of professionalism and their significance for the therapeutic recreation profession

❭ Describe future opportunities for the therapeutic recreation specialist

INTRODUCTION

People with illnesses, disabilities, or limiting conditions have the same rights to healthy and satisfying recreation participation as anyone else. **Therapeutic recreation** helps to improve functioning, health and well-being, and quality of life. We will discuss the way in which the field developed; key concepts related to providing therapeutic recreation (TR) services; and the scope of TR settings, programs, interventions, and populations. A discussion of the therapeutic recreation process outlines the daily duties of a **therapeutic recreation specialist** (**TRS**). Important professional issues, trends, and future challenges are examined to provide concrete information that will help you understand TR and evaluate its suitability as a career choice.

Additionally, recreation activities can be powerful tools to help improve aspects of people's functional abilities and health status. One way to understand the value of recreation participation is to recognize that human beings are drawn to activities through which they may attain an optimal experience, which is also known as the zone, a natural high, a peak experience, "flow," or what some call the leisure experience. During an optimal experience, people may express their identity and feel a sense of control over their actions, a heightened sense of awareness, and perceptions of competence and mastery. Recreation activities are a major vehicle to attaining this optimal state because they involve challenge, excitement, rewards, choices, concentration, and pure fun. Because recreation activities are pleasurable and satisfying, freely chosen, and autotelic (the satisfaction is gained from actually doing the activity), people are highly motivated to engage in recreation. Therefore, recreation can motivate people to change, grow, and improve their health. Recreation has "re-creative" powers; in other words, people can renew, restore, and refresh themselves and develop their abilities and skills through participation. Because conditions such as disease or disability may impose barriers on people's ability to engage in recreation, professional assistance such as therapeutic recreation (TR) may be required. In fact, most of us can probably recall a situation in which our ability to participate in the things we love to do was impaired by a physical, emotional, or social condition or situation. At these times, TR specialists can provide programs and **interventions** to facilitate a person's ability to engage in enjoyable recreation. Therapeutic recreation participation also can help people to

- cope with their health problem or disability,
- restore impaired functional abilities,

- "be themselves" in a difficult situation,
- continue to feel a sense of control and make choices, and
- experiment with newly learned behaviors in a safe and supportive environment.

Learning about how therapeutic recreation can help people is relevant to students and professionals working in any area of recreation and leisure services. People with disabilities and health conditions participate in recreation programs in all types of settings, and knowledge of how to support their successful participation is significant for all recreation majors.

You may be wondering how big the field of TR is. Estimates are that 50 million Americans, or approximately one out of every six, have at least one disability. Although only half of the people with a disability consider some aspect of their functioning to be impaired, we can see that huge numbers of people could potentially benefit from TR services. The proportion of Canadians with a disability is considered to be about the same as that in the United States (Bullock, Mahon, & Killingsworth, 2010). Approximately 30,000 people are employed in TR in the United States and Canada (NCTRC, 2009). TR professionals work mostly in hospitals and long-term care facilities. Employment of TR professionals is expected to increase 15 percent from 2008 to 2018 because of the growing population of older people and the increasing number of schoolchildren with disabilities (Bureau of Labor Statistics, U.S. Department of Labor, 2010). More jobs may also develop in community-based settings, as opposed to hospital and inpatient treatment facilities, as services develop for people in their local communities. The Bureau of Labor Statistics also reported that the average salary for 22,000 recreational therapists in the United States was $41,270. The latest TR salary survey of certified therapeutic recreation specialists (CTRSs), conducted by the National Council for Therapeutic Recreation Certification in 2009, found that the average annual salary of 12,000 CTRSs was US$46,500 per year. Although entry-level salaries may be less than $30,000 per year for new graduates, earning potential can go as high as $100,000 per year for directors of departments who have advanced degrees and extensive experience, depending on setting and location.

WHAT IS THERAPEUTIC RECREATION?

What exactly is therapeutic recreation? This question may be the hardest one that you as a student have to answer when family and friends ask, "What is your major?" For TR students, the answer is not simple. Many definitions of therapeutic recreation have been put forth over the years, each with slight variations in language and emphasis, leading to a lively debate about what the true definition of TR is. But all definitions include common core components that capture the essence of TR (Negley, 2010):

- Purposeful selection of recreation activities to reach a goal or **outcome**
- Enhancement of independent **functioning** through recreation participation
- **Quality of life**, wellness, and optimal **health** as core concerns
- Focus on the individual in the context of his or her own environment including supports and resources to be provided by the family and community

A composite definition of TR that brings together these core components has been developed and is stated as "engaging individuals in planned recreation and related experiences in order to improve functioning, health and well-being, and quality of life, while focusing on the whole person and the needed changes in the optimal living environment" (Kunstler & Stavola Daly, 2010, p. 4).

For TR students and professionals, essential elements to informed practice include understanding human beings and their development throughout the life span; variations in human development and experience; the effect of these variations on lifestyle; and the potential contributions of leisure, recreation, and play to healthy human development. TR has strong roots in humanistic philosophy, which asserts that people are capable of growth and change, that they strive to meet their needs and goals, and that they are autonomous (capable of making their own decisions and choices and directing their own lives) and inherently altruistic (desiring to do good). This means that therapeutic recreation specialists believe that, with the help of TR service, people can improve their lives, be it physically, emotionally, mentally, or even spiritually. Interaction with others in recreation activities is a strength of TR. For some clients, TR may be their most successful therapy because it is enjoyable and provides opportunities to make choices, set their own goals, and develop feelings of competence and self-confidence in their abilities.

TR Activities and Interventions

Therapeutic recreation specialists (TRSs), also known as recreation or recreational therapists, use a range of modalities, including traditional recreation activities such as the arts, sport, fitness and exercise, games, crafts, social activities, outdoor recreation, aquatics, and community outings. They also use nontraditional activities such as leisure education, horticulture, volunteering, adult education, and animal-assisted (pet) therapy. TRSs may also implement therapeutic interventions such as cognitive stimulation, sensory awareness, assertiveness training, anger management, pain management, stress management, and leisure counseling, depending on the mission and goals of the agency and the needs of the population being served. Complementary and alternative medicine (CAM) is also becoming an area for TR practice. Interventions such as relaxation, aromatherapy, yoga, and tai chi are popular. TR also addresses the clients' family, environment, or community, advocating for resources and support systems that facilitate successful recreation participation. Depending on the particular setting in which the TRS is employed and the philosophical approach of the agency or TR department, the role of the TRS may be more clinically oriented toward using recreation activities as treatment for functional limitations, known primarily as recreation therapy or recreational therapy (RT), or more broad based, incorporating varying degrees of clinical services as well as educational and recreational components, known as TR. Choosing which approach should be the primary focus of all services has been a topic of ongoing discussion in the profession.

Benefits

To succeed as a TR professional, you must be prepared to answer not only the question "What is TR?" but also the questions "What are the benefits of TR?" and "Why is TR a valuable service to offer our clients?" TR has many **benefits** and is valuable for many reasons. Understanding the benefits of participation in TR programs helps us select appropriate TR activities to enable clients to reach their desired goals. An important TR practice is to have clients be involved as much as possible in planning the TR services that they will receive. This is known as a person-centered approach. By making choices during the planning process, with the assistance of the TRS, clients are at the center of their services. This approach increases their feelings of control over decisions affecting their care and treatment and enhances their motivation to participate, thereby maximizing the benefits of TR. TRSs also use a person's strengths in programming both to overcome their limitations and to reinforce their abilities and perceived competence, which is called the strengths-based approach. We are also required to document the benefits that clients achieve because of TR participation. Research on recreation experiences has found that participation provides physical, cognitive, social, and expressive benefits; promotes growth and development; and contributes to life satisfaction and well-being. For the health care system and society, successful outcomes of TR services can lead to lower health care costs and decreased demand for valuable resources (Ross & Ashton-Shaeffer, 2003).

HISTORY OF THERAPEUTIC RECREATION

How many of you are thinking that history is boring? Maybe you haven't considered the reasons for studying history. Studying history can help us understand how our profession evolved to its current state and prepare us for future challenges. Most students are fascinated to learn that although the therapeutic recreation profession is less than 100 years old, the benefits of participation in recreational activities for people with illnesses and disabilities were recognized thousands of years ago. The ancient Greeks, who believed in a sound mind in a sound body, built curative temples where activities such as walking, gardening, exercise, boating, and music were offered. The Egyptians created a positive environment using music and dance to treat mood disorders. In India,

Charaka, a surgeon, had patients play games and drink wine while he operated on them because he knew that those activities would distract them from the pain. But these enlightened approaches to incorporating recreation often shifted over the centuries to cruel treatment of people with certain illnesses and disabilities. The word *handicap* comes from the image of a person with a disability holding a cap in his or her hand to beg for money or food. History provides few examples of compassionate care for those with disabilities.

In Europe the Renaissance (1400-1600) and the Age of Enlightenment (1700s) brought a greater concern for the rights of all people. The first schools for the deaf and the blind were established in Paris in the late 18th century. In the United States, in the early 19th century hospitals were built to serve people with mental illness. These hospitals provided recreation activities as part of more humane treatment. During the mid-19th century Florence Nightingale, an English woman considered the founder of modern nursing practice, wrote that wounded soldiers should be in beautiful environments or "recreation huts," listen to music, and have visits from family and pets to comfort them

and speed their recovery. During the same period, Dorothea Dix in the United States advocated for better treatment of people with disabilities and illnesses in asylums and prisons. The latter half of the 19th century brought many immigrants to North America, contributing to the growth of cities and social problems of overcrowding, increased stress, juvenile crime, and inadequate health care and sanitation. In response to these conditions, settlement houses, which were community centers that provided social services, education, and recreation were established. The growth of organized recreation, known as the playground movement, gathered momentum in response to a growing awareness of the role of recreation in the health and well-being of citizens, including the less fortunate who may have been poor, ill, or disabled.

Recreation services in the 20th century were extended to a variety of populations. The American Red Cross was one of the first large-scale organizations to promote recreation services to wounded soldiers during and after wartime. During the 1920s research was conducted in Illinois that demonstrated the value of recreation participation for people with intellectual disabilities. Dr. Karl

A traditional recreational activity such as aquatics is one modality that a therapeutic recreation specialist uses with a client.

Menninger, the noted psychiatrist, recognized the vital role of recreation activities in the treatment of psychiatric patients. World War II was a significant event in the history of TR because hundreds of thousands of wounded soldiers returned to the United States and Canada. These young men, who had given so much to their country, also had lost physical functioning because of their war injuries. Dr. Howard Rusk, considered the founder of the rehabilitation movement, promoted the value of individual and group recreation in physical rehabilitation. Wheelchair sports were created as a healthy recreation activity for wounded veterans.

The growing prosperity of postwar America and Canada enabled society to pay more attention to the rights of people who were unable to participate fully in the mainstream of everyday life. Public awareness of the importance of recreation for all people increased with the creation of Special Olympics, new services for senior citizens, the effects of the civil rights movement, and the youth movement of the 1960s with its emphasis on quality of life. Deinstitutionalization, which involved the movement of people with mental illness and cognitive disabilities from large institutions to community-based residences such as group homes, supported residences, and independent apartments, was under way. The first organizations for TR professionals were established during this period to advance recognition of the TR profession, develop standards for practice and personnel qualifications, publish books and journals about TR, and design professional preparation curricula. An era of great accomplishments for people with disabilities and of increased recognition of TR was beginning as demonstrated by the passage of a number of local and national laws.

Legislation

As a result of effective lobbying by people with disabilities and their advocates and supporters, landmark legislation was passed in the United States that not only broadened opportunities for people with disabilities but also reflected and promoted a change to more positive attitudes toward people with disabilities by society as a whole. During the 1970s in the United States, the federal government mandated accessibility of buildings and facilities for ease of use by people with disabilities. The U.S.

Congress passed Section 504 of the Rehabilitation Act of 1973, which guaranteed equal access to programs funded all or in part by the federal government, and PL 94-142, the Education of All Handicapped Children Act, which promised free and appropriate public education for all children. This law was the first piece of federal education legislation to mention recreation. These laws expanded recreation opportunities and services for people of all ages with disabilities and had a huge effect as people with disabilities became more visible in communities because of increased accessibility, mainstreaming of children from special schools into the least restrictive environment, and the normalization movement (Austin & Crawford, 2001). Normalization means giving people with disabilities the opportunity to live a life as close as possible to the patterns and habits of "normal" living. In Canada the provincial governments have been more active than the Canadian national government in passing laws related to the rights of people with disabilities. But the Canadian Charter of Rights and Freedoms, passed in 1982, guaranteed the rights of people with disabilities to equal protection and benefit of the law without discrimination. This measure has served as the blueprint for the Canadian policy of access to all areas of society, including recreation, for people with disabilities. Table 10.1 identifies key U.S. and Canadian laws that have significantly affected the lives of people with disabilities, their rights, and their access to recreation services.

Society's attitudes toward active participation by people with disabilities in everyday life were changing because of the effect of these laws, the effects of the civil rights movement, and the expansion of programs and services. One indicator of the shift in attitudes toward people with disabilities has been the use of person-first language, or sensitive terminology. How we use language reflects our attitudes. By saying "the person with a **disability**," instead of "the blind person" or "the mentally retarded person," we emphasize that the person happens to have a disability as one of his or her characteristics but that he or she is not defined solely by the disability. Using person-first language denotes a positive attitude toward people with disabilities and further promotes their rights to participate fully in the lives of their communities.

Table 10.1 Key Laws of the United States and Canada

UNITED STATES	
Law	**Description**
PL 90-480 Architectural Barriers Act, 1968	Mandated physical accessibility and usability of buildings and facilities
Section 504 of the Rehabilitation Act, 1973	Mandated program accessibility for people with disabilities
PL 94-142 Education for All Handicapped Children Act, 1975	Stated that all handicapped children were entitled to a free and appropriate public education in the least restrictive environment and may receive recreation as a related service
PL 101-476 Individuals with Disabilities Education Act, 1990	Reauthorization of PL 94-142 that emphasized family involvement, required transition planning, and provided for assistive technology
PL 101-336 Americans with Disabilities Act, 1990	A comprehensive civil rights law intended to eliminate discrimination against people with disabilities in all aspects of American life, including employment, government services, public transportation, public accommodations, and telecommunications; required that reasonable accommodation be made to facilitate participation by people with disabilities in these five areas by removing barriers and providing auxiliary aids and services as necessary
CANADA	
Law	**Description**
Vocational Rehabilitation for Disabled Persons Act, 1962	Provided rehabilitation services for people with disabilities
Canadian Charter of Rights and Freedoms, 1982	Stated that all people have the right to equal protection and benefit of the law without discrimination based on mental and physical disability
In Unison: A Canadian Approach to Disability Issues (government report, not a law), 1998	Provided the basis for asserting equal rights for people with disabilities to achieve full integration and access to supports, services, employment, and income

The Reagan-era cutbacks in funding for social services in the United States led to the 1980s being known as the age of **accountability**. Cost containment became the buzzword of health care. Health professions had to be accountable, or responsible, for documenting that their services produced a desired outcome in a cost-effective manner. This requirement prompted a renewed emphasis on the need for efficacy research in TR, which is research that demonstrates that TR can produce the outcomes it claims to produce, and a refinement of TR interventions targeted to specific health care problems and goals. Concurrent with this imperative to demonstrate the value of TR in health care was the passage of the Americans with Disabilities Act (ADA) in the United States in 1990, which was the catalyst for the inclusion movement. The ADA protects the civil rights of people with disabilities in all aspects of American life, including employment, government services, public transit, public accommodation, and telecommunications. Reasonable accommodation must be made to facilitate participation by people with disabilities by removing barriers and providing auxiliary aids and services as necessary.

Inclusion

One effect of the inclusion movement has been to broaden the traditional view of TR from focusing solely on the person to serving the person in the context of the total environment and settings that he or she inhabits throughout his or her life. Inclusion refers to empowering people with disabilities to become valued and active members of their communities through involvement in socially valued life activities. A key tenet of inclusion is that the community offers supports, friendship, and resources to facilitate equal participation in everyday life by all its members. A growing realization is that as health status fluctuates, people require a continuum of treatment, disease prevention, **health promotion**, and opportunities to enhance wellness and improve quality of life. Inclusion philosophy and practices evolved from the core principles and concepts identified in table 10.2. The role of TRSs in facilitating inclusion is to help clients achieve their goal of living in the most inclusive environment possible through minimizing and removing barriers to inclusion. The barriers to inclusion and best practices to facilitate inclusion are presented in table 10.3.

Table 10.2 Building Blocks of Inclusion

Building blocks	Definitions
Deinstitutionalization	The move away from large-scale, institution-based care to small-scale, community-based facilities; began in the late 1960s
Accessibility	Equal entry into, and participation in, physical facilities and programs by all people; accomplished through the elimination of architectural, administrative, and attitudinal barriers to create a usable environment
Normalization	Making available to people with disabilities the patterns and conditions of everyday life that are as culturally normative as possible
Integration	Physical presence and social interaction of people with and without disabilities in the same setting
Mainstreaming	Movement of people into the activities and settings of the wider community
Least restrictive environment	The environment that imposes the fewest restrictions and barriers on a person's growth, development, and participation in a full life
Supports	Friendships, social networks, assistance, and resources that enable a person to participate in the full life of his or her community
Person-first language	Language that puts the word *person* or *people* first in the sequence of a phrase or sentence to emphasize a positive attitude toward the individual, as in "a person with a disability" rather than "a disabled person"
Inclusion	Empowering people who have disabilities to be valued and active members of their communities by making choices, being supported in daily life, and having opportunities to grow and develop to their fullest potential

Table 10.3 Barriers to and Facilitators of Inclusion

BARRIERS TO INCLUSION	
Internal	**External**
Skill limitations	Financial limitations
Dependency	Lack of qualified staff
Health and fitness impairments	Lack of transportation
Lack of knowledge	Inaccessible facilities
	Poor communication supports
	Negative attitudes
	Ineffective service systems
PRACTICES THAT FACILITATE INCLUSION	
Programmatic	**Administrative**
Equipment adaptations	Inclusive agency mission and goal statements
Assistive technology	Hiring qualified professionals
Task analysis	Collaborative planning
Peer partners	Advocacy
Skill-level progression	Marketing
Social opportunities	Transportation assistance
Behavioral techniques	Updated facility accessibility

In summary, the sociopolitical movements of the latter half of the 20th century have led to the broader acceptance of people with disabilities. Their rights are guaranteed by federal laws, and their opportunities have expanded in all venues. TR, like all professions, responded to these forces by developing new approaches and services.

Twenty-First Century Direction

As the 21st century progresses, the following trends will continue to shape discussions about health policies and human services, including TR:

- Increasing cultural diversity in North America representing varied values and interests

- An expanding aging population composed of active and recreation-oriented seniors as well as older and frailer people living into their 90s and beyond

- The growing number of people with disabilities living in communities and the continued effect of the ADA in the United States and the 1998 report of Canadian governments on disability issues

- Complex needs of the wounded warriors returning from Iraq and Afghanistan with severe and involved injuries and conditions, such as traumatic brain injury, post-traumatic stress disorder, and amputations, who will be served in Veterans Administration hospitals and facilities as well as community-based programs

- Millions of people taking personal responsibility for their health and well-being, and recognition of the relationship of leisure and recreation to health and wellness

- The obesity crisis; declining levels of physical activity and fitness; and increases in diabetes, hypertension, and other lifestyle-associated conditions

- Billions of dollars spent on complementary and alternative medicine

- Spiraling cost of health care and the enormous demands placed on the health care system

- Technological innovations as well as increased reliance on technology and the high costs associated with their use

The populations served by TRSs and the settings in which TRSs work will continue to multiply, and the purposes and role of TR will continue to evolve. To organize and deliver TR services systematically, practice models have been developed that explain the relationships between philosophy and practice. Philosophy is a system of beliefs that guides practice. You might be surprised to learn that recreation students study philosophy. But philosophy helps us understand why we do what we do. Therapeutic recreation is based on a system of beliefs about human nature, needs, and behaviors as well as about the meaning and purpose of leisure, recreation, and play in human lives. Each of us is responsible for developing a philosophy of professional practice based on our readings, reflections, and values that will support our efforts and deepen our understanding of and commitment to our chosen field. A philosophy gives meaning and value to our interactions with our clients. Our practice can be explained and organized by a practice model.

THERAPEUTIC RECREATION PRACTICE MODELS

A model is a visual representation that describes the relationships between philosophy and theory and the real world. A model serves as a guide for practice. The benefits of providing TR services according to an appropriate practice model are that a model directs the types of programs and services offered, communicates the purposes and services of TR to other disciplines, and ensures that clients are provided the services and interventions best suited to their needs and goals. Practice models often reflect the political and social realities of the period in which they were developed.

Leisure Ability Model

For many years the primary model of TR services was the leisure ability model, originally developed by Gunn and Peterson. This model was based on earlier work in the field by Edith Ball, Virginia Frye, and Martha Peters, among others. According to this model, TR is provided along a continuum encompassing three types of services: functional intervention (previously known as treatment), leisure education, and recreation participation. The recipient of services, known as the client, moves along the continuum of services, gaining more control over his or her decision-making ability and choices as he or she learns new skills, becomes more independent, and participates in a repertoire of healthy recreation activities. The purpose of TR, according to this model, is for clients to develop an appropriate leisure lifestyle. Carol Peterson, in 1981, defined leisure lifestyle as "the day-to-day behavioral expression of one's leisure-related attitudes, awareness and activities revealed in the context and composite of the total life experience" (Stumbo & Peterson, 2009, p. 14). Stumbo and Peterson go on to explain that "leisure lifestyle implies that an individual has sufficient skills, knowledge, attitudes and abilities to participate successfully in and be satisfied with leisure and recreation experiences that are incorporated into his or her individual life pattern" (p. 14).

An art class is one type of intervention that a therapeutic recreation specialist might use to improve functional skills, develop a new leisure interest, or contribute to overall well-being.

Health Protection and Health Promotion Model

Beginning in the 1980s the movement to control health care costs prompted the development of new models that more clearly positioned TR in the health care arena. One of the first of these models was the health protection and health promotion model (Austin, 1998). Although similar to the leisure ability model in having three components of services, described by Austin as prescriptive activity, recreation, and leisure, the purpose of TR in this model is to achieve optimal health in a favorable environment. This purpose reflects the heightened emphasis on the role of TR in health care as a treatment modality, using recreation activities as interventions to address specific health problems as part of the work of the treatment team. For example, the TR specialist could engage a client with depression in an exercise group or sport program for the mood-elevating benefits of physical activity.

TR Service Model and TR Outcome Model

Austin's model was followed closely by the TR service model and TR outcome model, both presented by Carter, Van Andel, and Robb (1996). In designing these models, Van Andel recognized the need for the TR profession to describe the scope and outcomes of TR services. He legitimized leisure experience and quality of life as viable TR goals in the health care arena in addition to the more accepted treatment goals of improving functional abilities and enhancing health status.

Service Model

The service model presents TR as having a potential role in four types of services: diagnosis and needs assessment, treatment and rehabilitation, education, and prevention and health promotion. Similar to the leisure ability model and the health protection and health promotion model, the TR service model provides services along a continuum based on the client's needs and interests, level of functioning and degree of control, and type of setting in which services are received. The TRS may prescribe a single activity that can serve as both a treatment intervention during rehabilitation and as a leisure experience in the health promotion phase, thereby working on both goals simultaneously.

Outcome Model

In the outcome model, Van Andel hypothesized that as functioning and health status improved with the help of TR, so would quality of life. Even if a person had an impairment in one domain, he or she could experience quality of life (Sylvester, Voelkl, & Ellis, 2001). For example, a person with a terminal illness cannot make gains in physical health but can achieve quality of life as a meaningful outcome through improvements in spiritual and emotional health. This model emphasizes the whole person when providing services, not just one aspect of functioning or health status.

Five Core Themes in the Models

Just as definitions of TR have common themes, the various models share core themes, which have been identified as follows (Bullock & Mahon, 2000):

1. Services are provided along a continuum of growth and intervention.
2. Services are based on a strong belief in the abilities and strengths of the individual.
3. The client's freedom and self-determination increase over the course of services.
4. Therapist control decreases as the client progresses along the continuum.
5. The client's involvement and participation in the natural community increase.

Other Therapeutic Recreation Practice Models

Many of the trends in the 1990s such as the increasingly complex world of health care, the inclusion movement, decreased length of stays in hospitals, more services provided in outpatient and day care settings, recognition of the chronic nature of disability over the life span, and people living longer with severe medical problems and disabilities have led to the development of additional models. These include the self-determination and enjoyment enhancement model (Dattilo, Kleiber, & Williams, 1998), the optimizing lifelong health

through therapeutic recreation model (Wilhite, Keller, & Caldwell, 1999), the leisure and well-being model (Hood & Carruthers, 2007), and the leisure-spiritual coping model (Heintzman, 2008). The growing cultural and lifestyle diversity of North American society has also brought about a rethinking of the models in light of varying cultural beliefs and practices related to health care and individual responsibility (Sylvester, Voelkl, & Ellis, 2001; Deiser, 2002).

In all models, TR emphasizes the abilities and strengths of the client to overcome or alleviate the limitations imposed by disability or illness. People have the right to live in the optimal environment of their choice with appropriate supports. These supports may be provided by the person, his or her family, friends, community agencies, and other sectors of the environment as needed. This ecological perspective recognizes that the person's family, friends, and community are significant factors in his or her health and well-being.

Selecting a TR Practice Model

"How do I know which model is right for me or my clients or my setting?" This is the right question to ask! Having multiple models is a strength of the TR profession because of the range of settings for TR and the diversity of populations served. Choosing the appropriate model is based on several factors, including

- agency philosophy, mission, and goals;
- the needs of the clients;
- the regulations of accrediting bodies and government oversight agencies; and
- your professional philosophy.

Over the course of your career, you should be prepared to adopt the model that best suits your workplace. In Canada the primary model is the leisure ability model, which reflects that nation's longstanding commitment to integration of people with disabilities into all aspects of society and its recognition that recreation is a part of the vision of full citizenship for all Canadians. Practitioners in the United States also follow the leisure ability model, as well as the health protection and health promotion model, which is becoming more widely used in clinical settings.

SETTINGS FOR THERAPEUTIC RECREATION SERVICES

By now you're probably wondering where you can work as a TRS. One of the exciting aspects of the TR profession is the range of settings and populations served by TR specialists. People of all ages, with all types of disabilities, health conditions, or social challenges, are potential recipients of TR services, which can include seemingly infinite types of recreation activities. Students contemplating this profession can consider many possibilities ranging from acute treatment in the hospital setting to residential facilities to in-home TR services. TR is offered in any setting where people live or receive services, including hospitals and institutions, nursing homes, hospice programs, rehabilitation centers, military bases, prisons, assisted-living facilities, adult day care, partial hospitalization and outpatient programs, drug treatment programs, homeless shelters, group homes, schools, early intervention programs, community recreation centers, camps, and people's homes.

Job Duties and Responsibilities

The majority of TRSs spend most of their time fulfilling the TR leadership role by planning and leading group therapeutic recreation programs. Depending on the setting, the TRS may also provide one-to-one TR activities. To implement an appropriate TR program of activities, the TRS conducts individual assessments, develops treatment plans, plans a schedule of TR programming, motivates clients to participate in TR activities, observes and documents their participation and progress, and attends treatment team meetings (also known as comprehensive care-planning meetings or by a similar name) and in-service training. Other duties include maintaining equipment and supplies, supervising volunteers and interns, providing support to family members, advocating for the rights of clients, and organizing special events and community outings. Management responsibilities may include budgeting, risk management, marketing, and participating in strategic planning and performance improvement projects.

TR Process

Many of these functions are related to carrying out the TR process, a series of four steps that help fulfill the purposes of TR. A handy acronym for the four steps is APIE—assessment, planning, implementation, and evaluation. The TR process can be applied in any setting where recreation is used with therapeutic intent to help a person achieve specific outcomes. Let's examine the four steps more closely.

Assessment

The first step is **assessment**, a systematic process of gathering and synthesizing information about the individual client and his or her environment using a variety of methods, including interviews, observation, standardized tests, and input from other disciplines and significant others, in order to devise an individualized treatment or service plan. The information that the TRS seeks includes the client's level and ability of physical, social, emotional, and cognitive functioning related to two areas: (1) capability to participate in different types of TR programs and (2) aspects that can be improved through TR participation. The TRS also obtains information related to the client's leisure functioning, including interests, needs, perceived problems with leisure, patterns of participation, available leisure partners, planning and decision-making skills, and knowledge of and ability to use leisure resources. Obtaining input from the client, to the best of the client's ability, is an essential part of the assessment process. Based on the assessment, the TRS specifies goals or outcomes that the client will work toward during intervention. These goals can be related to changing leisure-related behaviors, reducing health concerns, and improving functional ability.

Planning

Planning refers to the development of the client's individual treatment or program plan. This plan is placed in the client's chart as the official record of the TR services that the client will receive. The plan generally includes an assessment summary; the client's goals, specific objectives, or steps to reach the goals; a schedule of the client's planned participation in the TR program; and a discharge plan if required.

Goals and Objectives Goals are statements that provide direction for the client's services. Client goals may be identified by the team for appropriate intervention by one or more disciplines. For example, goals could be to increase range of motion,

Illustration of the TR Process:
The Case of Mr. Jones

As part of the TR process, the TRS may design a specific intervention targeting a client's functional limitations. For example, Mr. Jones has had a stroke resulting in muscle weakness and stiffness. The team has identified his goals as strengthening his muscles and increasing his range of motion. During the TR assessment, Mr. Jones stated that he enjoyed swimming and spending time with his grandchildren. The TRS worked in conjunction with the physical therapist to plan the interventions to help reach the goals. Based on Mr. Jones' previous enjoyment of swimming, he agrees to participate in adapted aquatics three times a week (the frequency of the intervention) for half an hour each time (intensity), for a total of four weeks (duration). He also needs to learn how to use a flotation device that will support him in the pool. The expectation is that at the end of the four weeks he will have made predetermined improvements in his muscle strength, range of motion, and ability to use the flotation device.

The TRS can also identify and indicate in the written plan specific leadership and therapeutic approaches to use with the client. Mr. Jones may require frequent positive reinforcement, physical assistance, or a demonstration of the appropriate use of the adapted equipment to promote his progress. Mr. Jones' discharge plan could include information and scheduling about an adapted swim program for senior citizens at the local YMCA.

During the implementation phase, the TRS evaluates Mr. Jones' progress in the adapted aquatics. Formative evaluation reveals that Mr. Jones was scheduled for aquatics in the morning, but it became apparent that he was too tired at that time, so the program was moved to the afternoon. He stated he was a little fearful about entering the pool because of his muscle weakness and stiffness, and he required assistance from two staff members rather than one, as was originally planned. This change was made as soon as the need was recognized. At the end of the four weeks the summative evaluation identified that Mr. Jones had made a 25 percent increase in his range of motion and minimal improvement in muscle strength. He also expressed feelings of relaxation because of the aquatics and a desire to invite his grandson to participate with him, thereby gaining the benefits of family recreation. Mr. Jones was successful in making progress toward his functional goals and gained additional qualitative benefits from the TR experience.

---

attention span, or social interaction. As a member of the treatment team, the TRS contributes to addressing team-specified goals and is responsible for developing the goals for the client related to leisure-related behaviors. These goals could include acquiring knowledge of community resources for recreation participation or learning how to use adapted equipment to enable participation in a particular recreation activity. The TRS then specifies a series of behavioral objectives, also known as measurable goals, which are steps toward achieving the overall goal. The successful accomplishment of each behavioral objective or measurable goal, in a progression, will lead to meeting the overall client goal or goals. The terms used to describe goals and objectives may differ from setting to setting. Some settings use the phrase *measurable goals* in place of *behavioral objectives*, or *outcomes* instead of *goals*. The intent and purpose are the same, regardless of the exact terminology.

Selection and Scheduling of Activities

A major component of the planning step is the selection and scheduling of specific TR interventions or activities. Recreation activities are the primary means through which TRSs serve clients, so we need to understand which specific recreation activities produce which outcomes. Just as a doctor knows which medications to prescribe to treat a specific illness, we want to work together with our clients to select the recreation activities that offer the best chance of producing results. The TRS should work with the client to choose activities that he or she is interested in and is willing to participate in. Through the method of activity analysis, the TRS analyzes the components and behaviors that go into doing an activity. The TRS then may prescribe a specific activity or group of activities in the **individual treatment plan**, or care plan. A given activity may help a client progress toward more than one goal, or several activities may address a single goal. For an older nursing home resident with dementia, playing computer games can help increase attention span, improve eye–hand coordination, stimulate cognitive functioning, and promote feelings of accomplishment. This resident may participate in a sewing group as well as, or instead of, the computer games, and be working toward the same goals. Collaboration among disciplines at team meetings can help develop the optimal plan for the client. When setting up the TR program, the TRS may need to coordinate with other disciplines to schedule use of facilities and avoid conflicts in scheduling services such as a physical therapy or occupational therapy activity, a meeting with a social worker, or a consultation with a dietitian.

Implementation

The third step in the TR process is implementation. To implement the program, the TRS puts into action the client's individual TR plan. This step involves client participation in individual and group TR activities. Implementation takes into account the overall facility schedule, available space and resources, needed equipment and supplies, needs of the client, and staffing requirements of programs. Successful implementation may require adjustments to the plan to maximize the benefits to the client.

Evaluation

Evaluation is the final step in the TR process. Evaluation is both formative and summative. Formative evaluation is ongoing during the implementation phase and leads to immediate changes and improvements in the treatment plan. Summative evaluation occurs at the completion of the program to see whether the client's goals were met and whether program changes need to be made when implementing it in the future with other clients. A plan may not produce the desired results because of changes in the client's condition, use of new medications, lack of support from family, failure to obtain important information during the assessment, lack of skill on the part of the TRS, inappropriate leadership approaches, or inconsistency on the part of the team. Determining the factors that may

A therapeutic recreation specialist may have a goal for her client to ride an adapted tricycle.

have impeded the client's progress is an important evaluation task.

As the client participates, he or she will probably achieve the planned outcomes according to the treatment plan. Planned health care outcomes are generally measured in quantitative terms, such as the amount of time spent in activity or improvement in the ability to perform a certain task. A client may experience some unintended benefits as well, such as feelings of relaxation or pleasure in social opportunities. These unplanned benefits may be just as significant and are often more subjective, meaning that they are unique to the participant and relate to the quality, enjoyment, and personal meaning of the experience for the client. They should not be overlooked when reporting a client's progress in TR because they may provide a fuller picture of the client's accomplishments.

A critical responsibility of the TRS is to document the client's progress. TR **documentation** is the written or electronic recording of a client's participation and progress in the TR program. Documenting this information supplies evidence of the TR services provided and the outcomes of participation for the client. This information is recorded in the client's record or medical chart, which is considered a legal document. Therefore, the accuracy of the TRS' documentation should be above reproach. Documentation occurs at regularly scheduled intervals and is reviewed by auditors, surveyors, and regulators of accrediting bodies and governmental agencies. Every TRS must be well informed of agency policies regarding documentation.

Concluding Comments on the TR Process

As you may recall from our discussion of TR models, a TR specialist may begin working with a person at any point along the continuum of services, depending on the person's needs and the department or agency's mission and goals. But all services begin with an individual assessment and reflect the TRS' knowledge of the TR process. In some settings, particularly community recreation programs that serve people with disabilities, TRSs may not be required to develop written individualized plans with specific desired behavioral outcomes. General goals of having a positive recreation experience, learning and refining new activity skills, and increasing opportunities for social interaction are typical in community settings. TRSs may serve as inclusion specialists in community-based programs using their knowledge of disability, accessibility, assessment, and activity analysis to facilitate the participation of people with disabilities in these programs. Thoughtful planning and evaluation of services are also considered best practices in community settings.

THERAPEUTIC RECREATION SPECIALIST

You may be wondering whether you have what it takes to be a TRS. Although no one personality type is best suited to being a TRS, people who enter helping professions, such as TR, often possess certain attributes. These attributes are at the heart of being a TR professional. Being self-aware, having the desire to learn new things and to communicate with people, being comfortable with taking the initiative, being flexible and able to adapt to change and unexpected events, and having creative ideas, energy, enthusiasm, and compassion for people are highly desirable qualities that facilitate a helping relationship focused on helping the client achieve his or her goals.

Professionalism

What does it mean to be a professional? Being a professional in any field means obtaining an education, possessing the credentials recognized by your profession, adhering to a code of ethical behavior, providing services based on professional standards of practice, continuing your education, updating your professional knowledge through reading and research, and being an active member of professional organizations from the local to the international level. Being a professional entails more than just carrying out your job duties and responsibilities.

Education

The first step in becoming a TR professional is to obtain an education in TR, which provides a philosophical and theoretical foundation related to TR service provision and extensive knowledge in areas essential to TR practice. Knowledge areas include the nature of illness and disability, the effects of disability on functioning, the role of TR in addressing the limitations imposed by disability, and the procedures and methods used by TRSs in developing treatment plans and implementing TR services. TR curricula may be an option or specialization in a recreation degree program or a separate degree program, ranging from the associate degree to bachelor's, master's, and doctoral degrees. College programs may apply for accreditation, a process by which the program is evaluated according to a set of standards for curriculum content. Although accreditation of curricula is not required by law, accreditation ensures that the content areas cover essential information for college students. The Council on Accreditation of Parks, Recreation, Tourism, and Related Professions (COAPRT) has developed and issued outcomes for curriculum content areas to be included in recreation degree programs that

OUTSTANDING GRADUATES

Background Information

Name: Cathy Ann Branker-Diamond

Education: Bachelor of science in therapeutic recreation from Lehman College of the City University of New York, Department of Health Sciences, Therapeutic Recreation Program.

Credentials: CTRS.

Special awards: Presidential Citation, NYS Therapeutic Recreation Association, 2011; Outstanding Therapeutic Recreation Graduate, Lehman College, 2011.

Affiliations: NYS Therapeutic Recreation Association; featured dancer, Something Positive Performing Arts Company; certified Zumba instructor.

Career Information

Position: Therapeutic recreation specialist.

Organization: Isabella Geriatric Center is a 701-bed facility located in Manhattan, New York City, that has 1,100 employees serving adults of all ages in long-term care, short-term rehabilitation, adult day health programs, and related services.

> *TR is a field in which we don't treat the disease; we treat the whole person. That's what makes us unique and special to our clients and why TR is such a powerful and meaningful profession.*

Organization's mission: Isabella's mission is "to provide quality care through diverse programs designed to promote health and independence within and beyond our walls."

Job description: As a therapeutic recreation specialist, I carry out the TR process by conducting individual assessments; designing and conducting TR programs including poetry, men's club, Zumba gold, arts and crafts, cognitive games, and special events; evaluating and documenting programs; completing the MDS 3.0; care planning; attending meetings with staff, residents, and families; and working with other professionals and direct care staff.

Career path: I was a professional dancer in my home country of Trinidad and Tobago and came to the United States at age 20 to pursue a career in dance. As a dancer I traveled and performed all over the world. When I sought a career change in New York City, I was drawn to working in geriatric settings. A friend told me that TR would be the perfect field for me because of my love for the arts, creativity, and working with the elderly (which I first did with my mother in Trinidad when she worked at an assisted living facility for seniors). After working for two years in both a nursing home and an adult day care setting, I took off three years to complete my BS in TR at Lehman. I also had the privilege of serving for one year as the NYSTRA student liaison and created a NYSTRA student Facebook page and a resource guide to NYS TR internship sites. My goal is to be a director of TR one day.

Likes and dislikes about the job: What I like about my job are the opportunities to be creative, to perform for residents, and to learn more about the field each day.

Advice for Undergraduates

Do not stop with your degree. Get your CTRS certification. Bring your creativity and unique talent to the job. Join your professional organizations to network, to keep current, and to make lifelong friends.

can be applied to therapeutic recreation. In 2010 an accreditation process exclusively for TR and RT college programs, the Committee on Accreditation of Recreational Therapy Education (CARTE), was formally initiated with the Commission on Accreditation of Allied Health Education Programs (CAAHEP). Regardless of the accreditation status of a college program, the value of a sound education in TR cannot be overstated and is a component of requirements for obtaining appropriate professional credentials.

Credentialing

Credentialing is the process by which a profession or government certifies that a professional has met the established minimum standards of competency required for practice. Credentialing is intended to protect consumers as they receive services. The three types of credentialing programs are registration, certification, and **licensure**. Registration is a voluntary listing of people who practice in a profession, according to established criteria. Certification also requires meeting a set of predetermined criteria and usually includes a written examination. Licensure is a process by which state governments mandate qualifications for practice and administer a licensing program. In therapeutic recreation the largest credentialing program is administered by the National Council for Therapeutic Recreation Certification (NCTRC). To be eligible for certification as a **certified therapeutic recreation specialist** (**CTRS**), according to NCTRC, applicants must meet a combination of education and experience requirements and pass the certification examination. In 2010 NCTRC established a specialty certification program to recognize advanced level of practice in five areas: physical medicine and rehabilitation, geriatrics, developmental disabilities, behavioral health, and community inclusion services. Four states, Utah, North Carolina, New Hampshire, and Oklahoma, have passed licensure laws, and several others, including New York, are actively pursuing this legislation.

The credentialing process attests that you have met the standards to practice your profession and that your judgment and decision-making skills as a professional are to be trusted. To maintain your credentials, most credentialing programs require TR professionals to participate in continuing education activities to update their knowledge and skills for practice. Workshops and conferences that cover a wide range of topics are offered by professional organizations at the local, state, regional, national, and international levels.

Professional Organizations

By becoming a member of a professional TR organization or association, you are joining your peers to promote the value of TR; participate in education, communication, and advocacy; and establish and maintain standards of professional practice and behavior. The national TR professional organizations are the American Therapeutic Recreation Association (ATRA) in the United States and the Canadian Therapeutic Recreation Association (CTRA) in Canada. Almost every state and province has either a TR organization or a TR branch of the state or provincial recreation association. Examples include the New York State Therapeutic Recreation Association (NYSTRA) and Therapeutic Recreation Ontario (TRO). Joining professional organizations demonstrates your commitment to advancing the profession. Many TRSs agree that one of the most valued benefits of membership is the interaction with peers through networking, sharing ideas, and forging lasting friendships based on common interests and needs.

Standards of Practice

Standards of practice define the scope of services provided by TR professionals and state a minimal, acceptable level of service delivery. Adherence to these standards ensures consistent practice across service settings and helps establish the credibility of the profession. ATRA and CTRA have both developed sets of standards that cover the following core practices: assessment, treatment planning, documentation, and management. You will find these standards a valuable guide to designing and implementing quality services and helping to ensure ethical practice and behavior.

Ethics

A hallmark of a true profession is a **code of ethics**, which is a written description of the established duties and obligations of the professional to protect the human rights of recipients of services. ATRA, as well as the provincial Canadian TR associations, have issued codes of ethics for TR professionals. All codes cover the four major bioethical principles:

1. Autonomy—the client has the right to self-determination, which may conflict with what you, the family, other staff members, or the agency thinks is best for the client.
2. Beneficence—we only do good for our clients.
3. Nonmalfeasance—we use care and skill in service so that we prevent or do not cause harm.
4. Justice—we allocate resources in a fair and equitable manner.

Other ethical concerns include confidentiality (the client has the right to control access to information about himself or herself and know who will have access to that information), maintaining a professional relationship with clients (not overstepping boundaries into friendships or personal relationships), and cultural competence (understanding and respecting diverse beliefs and values and how they influence clients' behaviors).

Keeping Current in the Profession

The foundation of a profession is a body of knowledge derived from research. Professionals have the obligation to read and apply relevant research findings and contribute to the body of knowledge in the field by conducting research themselves. Reading research helps practitioners become more reflective and thoughtful in their work and can enrich their practice as they apply proven techniques. Therapeutic recreation research is published in professional journals such as *Therapeutic Recreation Journal*, *Annual in Therapeutic Recreation*, and *American Journal of Recreation Therapy*. Professionals can also contribute to the body of knowledge by writing books, chapters, and magazine articles for the TR field as well as for publications geared to other professions and the public.

Besides reading and applying research, professionals can actively participate in the research process. You may not think at this time that you are interested in conducting research. But a new trend in health care, which started in Canada, uses practitioners' expertise and research findings to select the best programs and services to achieve outcomes. This trend, known as **evidence-based practice** (**EBP**), enables practitioners and researchers to collaborate on systematically collecting data to provide evidence of the optimal type of care for clients. Practitioners can write up the results of their research and publish it in appropriate journals, as well as present their findings at professional conferences. Increasing the body of knowledge of TR through research continues to be a major objective of the TR profession.

Being a professional implies a sense of calling to do more than just go to work every day and carry out assigned responsibilities and duties. Professionalism implies dedication to the beliefs and values of your chosen field, lifelong learning, and commitment to the highest standards of practice. As you explore the TR profession and meet TR practitioners, observe the demeanor and behaviors of people who demonstrate admirable qualities. Can they articulate the meaning and value of TR? Are they enthusiastic and positive about the work they do? Do they demonstrate their love of TR through professional activities outside work and keep up to date with the latest developments? To have a rewarding and fulfilling career, you may wish to emulate these professional qualities.

Your Future in TR

You may now be asking yourself whether TR is right for you and what you can look forward to if you decide to become a TRS. Students are often attracted to therapeutic recreation as a major because of their interest in being part of a helping profession that works with people in health or human service settings. Sensitivity, compassion, patience, communication skills, and the desire to help people are essential to working as a TRS. Many students also are attracted to recreation as a major because of their interest in particular recreation activities such as sport, fitness, outdoor pursuits, music, or art and then discover TR. Whatever has led you to the TR field, essential elements to continued professional success and satisfaction are knowledge of a wide range of traditional recreation activities, the ability to implement credible programs, and the motivation to learn new activities. Although TRSs must have general knowledge of recreation opportunities, also important is being skilled in nontraditional facilitation techniques as well as the increasingly popular wellness and health promotion modalities described at the beginning of the chapter. These methods may include stress management, assertiveness training, sensory stimulation, and a variety of wellness and relaxation techniques. You will learn about many recreation activities as part of your TR curriculum. Attending workshops and conferences is a valuable way to gain exposure to and learn about innovative programs and techniques. Taking noncredit, continuing education or adult education courses helps you keep up to date on fresh program ideas. Certifications are offered in specialty areas such as adapted aquatics, horticulture therapy, fitness training, aromatherapy, and yoga. Some jobs may require a driver's license or certification in first aid, CPR, or lifeguard and water safety instruction. Obtaining specialized training and credentials will enhance your qualifications as a TRS and enrich your job performance. One of the wonderful features of TR is that your personal interests can be incorporated into professional practice. You should strive to keep your work interesting and participate with your clients with a sense of joy and fun. If *you* are bored by the programs that you lead, think how your clients will feel!

Students will benefit from learning not only new interventions and therapeutic methods but also management techniques and administrative processes. Skills in budgeting, grant writing, marketing, public relations, oral and written communication, and the use of technology are essential for TRSs who become supervisors and administrators of TR services. Collaboration skills are needed to work with other disciplines, departments, and agencies to maximize resources and reduce duplication of services. Cross-cultural competence, which refers to the ability to understand, respect, and communicate with diverse people, is essential in the culturally diverse nations of Canada and the United States. Cross-cultural competence is essential for successful interactions with other staff members, clients, and their families.

Future Challenges

What does the future hold for the TR profession? As you have read, TR is a broad and varied field that operates in numerous settings and with people with all types of disabilities and health condi-tions. Changes in health care, economic pressures, social trends, demographic characteristics, and technological advances are influencing society to focus on health promotion, independent functioning, quality of life, and quality and effectiveness of services. These concerns present both challenges and opportunities for growth and innovation in the therapeutic recreation field. Health promotion and disease prevention, particularly in the areas of obesity and stress-related illness, can be achieved by participation in recreation activities such as exercise, dance, gardening, and sport. Wellness practices such as tai chi, yoga, and aromatherapy are being incorporated into many TR programs. Encouraging people to take responsibility for their health can improve health status and lead to independent functioning.

Leisure education refers to the process by which people explore their own attitudes toward leisure and recreation, understand the influence of leisure on society and in their own lives, and develop the skills to participate in the recreation activities of their choice. Leisure education may be seen as the unique contribution of TR to health care because TR is the only health-related discipline with leisure as a component of its philosophy and practice. Research into leisure education has documented its effectiveness in achieving the valued outcomes of improved health, better functioning, enhanced quality of life, and successful community reintegration.

The shift from the institution to the community as the primary residential setting for people with disabilities has opened the doors for TR practice in day programs, group homes, community centers, military bases, schools, and people's homes. Emphasis in these settings is on promoting independent functioning and finding joy and meaning in life through recreation participation in the optimal living environment. TRSs have responded to these changes by offering retirement planning, early intervention, family leisure counseling, and community reintegration. The inclusion movement will continue to expand, offering opportunities for TRSs to function as community inclusion specialists, accessibility consultants, and trainers in leadership techniques and adaptations for people with disabilities. In the political arena TR organizations have lobbied to include TR in legislation and regulations concerning health care, education, and disability.

Many states are pursuing government-sponsored licensure to strengthen the value of the credentialing process for TR practitioners.

Those who enter the profession will confront several challenges. Although many professionals participate in professional organizations, obtain their credentials, keep current with the latest developments, and continually improve their programs and services, greater involvement in these professional activities is vital for the full recognition of TR as an essential service. Membership in professional organizations at every level does not reflect the number of people who identify themselves as working in TR. Many who are eligible to obtain professional credentials have chosen not to do so. Employers continue to hire people to work in TR positions who do not have a college education in TR. Curricula in college and university TR programs vary. Inconsistency in using the best practices of the field still exists across TR settings. These challenges need to be addressed by all professionals to ensure the most effective and meaningful services for the people we serve.

SUMMARY

This chapter has described the scope and range of clients, settings, and services that make up the TR profession. Studying the TR definitions, models, philosophy, and benefits is essential to fulfilling a role as a therapeutic recreation professional. Understanding the TR process and the components of professionalism will help prepare you to make your professional choices and plan for a satisfying and meaningful career. As TR faces the challenges of the future, well-educated and credentialed practitioners will hold the key to ensuring that the benefits of therapeutic recreation are experienced by people with disabilities, health conditions, and social limitations.

For glossary terms, learning experiences, and more, please visit the web resource at
www.HumanKinetics.com/IntroductionToRecreationAndLeisure

CHAPTER 11

Unique Groups

Julia Wallace Carr, Brenda Robertson, Rebecca Lesnik,
John Byl, Jeffrey Ferguson, Carol J. Potter, and Laurie Ogilvie

> " If bread is the first necessity of life, recreation is a close second. "
>
> Edward Bellamy, American author

LEARNING OUTCOMES

After reading this chapter you should be able to do the following:

> Define campus recreation
> Identify the users of campus recreation programs and services
> Summarize the historical progression of campus recreation
> Explain the benefits of participation in campus recreation programs and services
> Discuss the links between trends in campus recreation and commercial fitness facilities
> Describe the general structure and history of correctional systems in Canada and the United States
> Explain the philosophical shifts in the role of recreation in corrections throughout history
> Describe the goals and types of correctional recreation programming
> Identify current trends and issues affecting correctional recreation
> Describe the differences within and among faith traditions
> List the employment requirements in faith-based recreation
> Describe the history, benefits, programs, services, and trends of worksite recreation and health promotion
> Identify the steps necessary to begin a career in worksite recreation and health promotion
> Explain the principles governing the provision of recreational services within military communities
> Compare the differences between military and civilian environments and explain why the uniqueness of military community needs requires a tailored approach to recreation program delivery
> Appreciate the value of recreational opportunities within the military community
> List career opportunities in military recreation

Campus Recreation

Julia Wallace Carr

❝ Every recreational building, whether multiuse or strictly recreational, is only a structure until someone begins to program it for people. Then it becomes a vibrant scene of action, excitement, competition, and exploration. It becomes a magnet to attract thousands of members of the campus community to be part of the phenomenon called campus recreation. ❞

T.R. Jones

Campus recreation—a magnet, a vibrant scene of action, excitement, and exploration—these are wonderful ways to describe what goes on inside the walls of the state of the art recreational facilities housed on campuses all over the country. Campus recreation is unique. The sheer volume of potential participants and the diversity of the facilities make this an exciting and challenging area in which to work and different from most facilities and programs in parks and recreation and commercial settings.

Campus recreation can be defined as a program that provides facilities and activities all along the spectrum from very large to those for just a few participants. Facilities and activities are intended to promote the various components of wellness and encourage the development of lifelong skills and positive attitudes through activity (Mittelstaedt, 2006). The participant base for campus recreation typically includes students, faculty, and staff on a given campus (Franklin & Hardin, 2008). Many centers also serve the local community through special memberships, activities, and facility rentals.

The professional staff for a campus recreation facility is charged with the responsibility of bringing together thousands of campus community members with varying skill levels, needs, and interests. The staff's task is to influence choices related to wellness, recreation, spare time, and lifestyle habits. The primary aspect that makes campus recreation unique is that the main user group of all campus recreation facilities across the country is the **traditional college-aged student**. People from 18 to 24 years of age are typically the target market, and the relationship with this demographic group is relatively short term, anywhere from a few months to four years. Compounding this aspect is that thousands of new participants enter the mix each fall as the freshman class arrives, and they have access to the facilities, programs, and services each year.

Although most recreation and commercial fitness centers have a stable membership base, the participant group for campus recreation is ever changing. The **Council for the Advancement of Standards for Higher Education (CAS)** provides standards and guidelines that give specific operational direction to institutions of higher education. The standards and guidelines state that campus recreation programs must not only provide diverse participation opportunities for diverse populations but also incorporate **student learning** and **student development** in the mission and day-to-day offerings. These programs and services need to enhance the overall educational experience of the student (Dean, 2009; Franklin & Hardin, 2008).

Participants in campus recreation are involved in diverse activities such as adventure trips, individual fitness and group fitness activities, intramurals, aquatics, sport clubs, and informal recreation. Some of these constituents are competitive, whereas others are interested only in maintaining or enhancing basic fitness. Across the United States, about 11 million college students use campus recreation facilities (NIRSA, 2011).

HISTORY OF CAMPUS RECREATION

Campus recreation professionals have served this unique segment of the recreation industry population since the first intramural departments were instituted at the University of Michigan and Ohio State University in 1913 (Wilson, 2008). Preceding this development was a rich history of participation in athletics and recreational activity on college campuses, and more students began to play for play's sake rather than competition. Following the lead of these two institutions, colleges and universities across the country began to incorporate intramurals into campus life.

In 1950 Dr. William Wasson, director of health, physical education, and recreation at Dillard University, developed the idea of holding an intramural institute and workshop for black colleges and universities. A group of 22 African American male and female intramural directors from 11 historically black institutions attended the workshop, and from this meeting the National Intramural Association (NIA) was formed (NIRSA, 2011).

In 1975 the NIA changed its name to the **National Intramural-Recreational Sports Association**. This decision resulted from the fact that the scope of campus recreation was changing. A movement across programs developed to expand the offerings to increase participation opportunities beyond the competitive play of intramurals. In the 1980s and 1990s, this growth helped to position campus recreation as a player on many campuses, and departments began to be recognized as places where significant interventions could take place in the areas of wellness and student learning.

Today, NIRSA is cooperating with other higher education organizations to focus on the entire college experience and to enhance the quality of learning outside the classroom. These organizations include the following:

- Council for the Advancement of Standards in Higher Education (CAS)

Intramural sports are just one aspect of a comprehensive campus recreation program.

- Council of Higher Education Management Associations (CHEMA)
- Inter-Association Task Force on Alcohol and Other Substance Abuse Issues (IATF)
- Student Affairs in Higher Education Consortium (SAHEC)
- Higher Education Association's Sustainability Consortium (HEASC)

NIRSA has evolved from an organization centered on one competitive aspect of recreation, intramurals, to being considered a "cornerstone of students' overall collegiate education and experience" (Wilson, 2008, p. 27). This shift in mind-set has allowed the organization's professionals to be a part of what Dungy (2006) referred to as a shared responsibility for student learning.

BENEFITS OF A CAMPUS RECREATION PROGRAM

Participation in campus recreation programs can have a significant influence on the environment on campus because of the high involvement rate of the student body. About 75 percent of college students participate in campus recreation programs (NIRSA, 2004). The many reports about the ben-efits of participation in campus recreation offer evidence that these departments are valued and important parts of the collegiate community. Some of these benefits are related to the bigger picture of the organization and include retention, recruitment, and satisfaction indicators for the general student body. Other benefits are directly related to the participant and include enhanced GPA and overall wellness.

Campus recreation has received increased attention as recruitment, retention, and satisfaction have become priorities for the administration of institutions of higher education (Lindsey & Sessoms, 2006). Many campuses strategically place the campus recreation center on the orientation tour for students and potential faculty and staff members. Participant interest in campus recreation often results from this tour and has an influence on future participation. In one study, 75 percent of the males considered the availability of recreation facilities and programs very important in deciding to attend college (Haines, 2001). Among females, 62 percent reported that the availability of facilities and programs was somewhat to very important in determining continuance at the university.

Involvement in campus recreation results in satisfaction with academics and a sense of belonging with the campus community (Moffitt, 2010). A Kerr and Down research study (NIRSA, 2004) reported that out of 21 factors for college satisfaction and success, recreational sports programs and services were ranked 5th by heavy users (participated in campus recreation activities at least 25 times per month). In regard to direct participant benefits, campus recreation center visitations show positive associations with academic success and health and wellness (Todd, Czyszczon, Wallace Carr, & Pratt, 2009). High users had better GPAs, higher IPAQ scores, and lower fat intake than all other groups. This group also had lower BMIs than moderate users and nonusers and lower electronic media use than nonusers. Individual involvement in campus recreation programs and services has been reported to produce three major benefits: improved overall emotional well-being, reduced stress, and improved happiness (NIRSA, 2004).

TRENDS IN CAMPUS RECREATION

Trends often occur in two specific areas in campus recreation, facilities, and programming. According to the Collegiate Recreation Facilities Construction Report (NIRSA, 2010), 82 colleges and universities are currently involved in 129 facility construction, expansion, or renovation projects, and 25 projects for outdoor facilities or fields, at an average size of 19.2 acres (7.8 ha), are underway. The costs of these **capital projects** in total are over $1.7 billion; the average project expenditure is $13.2 million. In the *State of the Industry Report* (Recreation Management, 2010), 32.2 percent of the respondents reported that they had synthetic turf fields and were likely to add another synthetic turf field in the future. Sustainability efforts and **LEED** (Leadership in Energy and Environmental Design) facility certifications are other recent trends in the facility side of the house for campus recreation centers.

The programs being offered in campus recreation facilities tend to be directly related to traditionally aged college students. These offerings tend to match up closely with the trends in commercial fitness facilities. These programs include the following:

- Fitness programs
- Mind–body balance programs, such as yoga, tai chi, and Pilates
- Educational programs
- Sport tournaments and races
- Adult sport teams
- Individual sport activities, such as running clubs and swim clubs
- Personal training
- Swimming programming
- Day camps and summer camps
- Aquatic exercise programs

Of the campus recreation professionals surveyed, 29 percent indicated they had plans to add more programming in the next three years. These offerings would be in the areas just listed as well as nutrition and diet counseling, active older adult programs, climbing programs, and sport training (Recreation Management, 2010).

Campus recreation professionals as well as other college student personnel professionals are also seeing emphasis placed on student learning and student development (Keeling, 2006). These professionals need to become educated in outcome development and assessment as well as college student development theory to keep up with this growing trend.

CAREER OPPORTUNITIES

Because of the diverse nature of the facilities and programs offered in campus recreation, career opportunities are numerous. NIRSA boasts more than 4,000 professional members at 700 institutional member sites (NIRSA, 2011). Although these numbers are high, they do not include every campus recreation program in the country. Because of the large number of campuses (both NIRSA and non-NIRSA schools) that have campus recreation as a programming offering, job prospects are positive.

The career path of campus recreation professionals in the past has been as varied as the types of positions in the field. Many institutions offer academic programs that are directly related to campus recreation. Degrees are available in sport management, recreation management, exercise science, and health promotion. Although many schools offer courses that cover the areas involved in programming and operating a center, James Madison University is one of the few, if not the only one, that has a program of study in campus recreation leadership (see www.jmu.edu/recreation/URECTeam/Assistantships.html).

Typically, careers in campus recreation begin when college students accept employment positions at the recreation center. Many start by looking for a way to earn some fun money, and then they fall in love with the environment. They soon develop a passion for campus recreation. The best way to move into the profession following graduation as an undergraduate is through the route of a graduate assistant. In this type of position, graduate students are put into the role of a paraprofessional. They are paid a stipend for their work at the recreation center, and the organization covers their tuition. In

OUTSTANDING GRADUATES

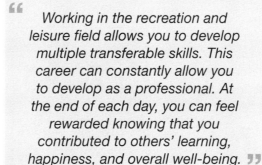

Background Information

Name: Rachael Finley

Education: Master of science, campus recreation leadership at James Madison University, Department of Kinesiology.

Special awards: William Wasson Student Leadership Award, National Intramural-Recreational Sports Association (NIRSA), 2010; AORE Conference Student Scholarship, 2009; National Outdoor Leadership School Student Scholarship, 2009; Marilyn Crawford Graduate Student Scholarship, James Madison University, Department of Kinesiology, 2009; Virginia Recreational Sports Association Student Award of Merit and Scholarship, 2009; NIRSA Foundation Scholarship, Gartenburg Award, 2008; Dr. Tom R. Jones Outstanding Leadership Award, 2006.

Affiliations: National Intramural-Recreational Sports Association (NIRSA), Association of Outdoor Recreation and Education (AORE), National Outdoor Leadership School (NOLS) Alumni.

Career Information

Position: Assistant director of recreational sports—facilities and special events.

Organization: Department of Recreational Sports, a component of the Division of Student Development at Loyola University Maryland. We have 11 full-time staff and over 150 student employees who serve approximately 28,000 students, faculty, staff, and Loyola community members monthly.

Organization's mission: The Department of Recreational Sports is an essential component of the Division of Student Development and the overall mission of Loyola University Maryland. The primary emphasis is grounded in the Jesuit ideal of *cura personalis* (care of the whole person). The department is committed to cultivating the whole person by providing an array of recreation opportunities in an educational, social, and supportive environment. To this end, we offer quality programs and service-oriented facility operations that foster healthy lifestyles for the Loyola University Maryland community.

> *Working in the recreation and leisure field allows you to develop multiple transferable skills. This career can constantly allow you to develop as a professional. At the end of each day, you can feel rewarded knowing that you contributed to others' learning, happiness, and overall well-being.*

Job description: I work on all reservations, including approving or declining reservation requests, contracts, insurance, and collection of payment. I also work on all logistics for reservations and events that take place in our building. I coordinate large-scale special events, oversee the equipment room and 17 student employee equipment room staff, oversee informal recreation budgets, procure all facility equipment, oversee all department apparel, and coordinate the student employee council.

Career path: My career in recreational sports began as a student employee at Central Michigan University. I worked in five different areas of university recreation. I was the first national student intern at the NIRSA National Center. I was also a graduate assistant at James Madison University for the university recreation department for informal recreation, sports clubs, and youth programs for a year and for adventure for two years. I was an independent contractor for outdoor education at Green Mountain College, James Madison University, and Princeton University. Then I started at my current position.

Likes and dislikes about the job: I like supervising students; it gives me an opportunity to contribute to their development. I also like building relationships with people across

Outstanding Graduates *(continued)*

campus and within the Loyola community. The job is robust and dynamic; there's something different every day. I also like collaborating with people in my department. There are many professional development opportunities, and I like the support for student development. I also like the mission and values of the university and the actions that are taken to support it. I like my coworkers and the way in which diversity is valued and supported.

As for dislikes, I don't like my 45-minute commute to work or the lack of windows in my office.

This is an intermediate stop on my career ladder, but I cannot see leaving this position anytime in the near future. I am really enjoying it and would definitely be interested in a vertical movement within the

university or department. I am also contemplating going back for a PhD in the future.

Advice to Undergraduates

Get as much experience as possible in areas that interest you. Push your limits but respect them. Seek out ways to grow; don't wait for them to come to you. Make things happen. Stay true to your values, but figure out what those are first! Figure out what you need to succeed and then find out where and how to get it. Lead yourself.

Ultimately, this career is competitive. Those who are passionate and willing to learn from every experience, both in and out of the classroom, will have no problem finding a job that fits really well.

short, they work part-time in a professional capacity for the organization while they are taking a full graduate load. This experience is valuable to future employers who want to fill positions within their campus recreation departments.

Figure 11.1 represents an organizational chart of a midsized university. The chart illustrates the employment possibilities in one of the many campus recreation departments across the country. This department employs students, part-time and full-time employees, and graduate assistants. The positions require knowledge, skills, and abilities in facility operations, programming, and administration.

SUMMARY

Campus recreation serves a niche on college campuses that other departments do not have the resources, facilities, and staff to provide. Although academics serve to shape the mind, campus recreation rounds out the college experience by developing wellness-related lifestyle habits that can stick with people throughout a lifetime. This unique segment of the recreation industry has moved from rolling out the ball for a friendly competitive game to offering a valued out-of-classroom experience that contributes to the participant's overall quality of life.

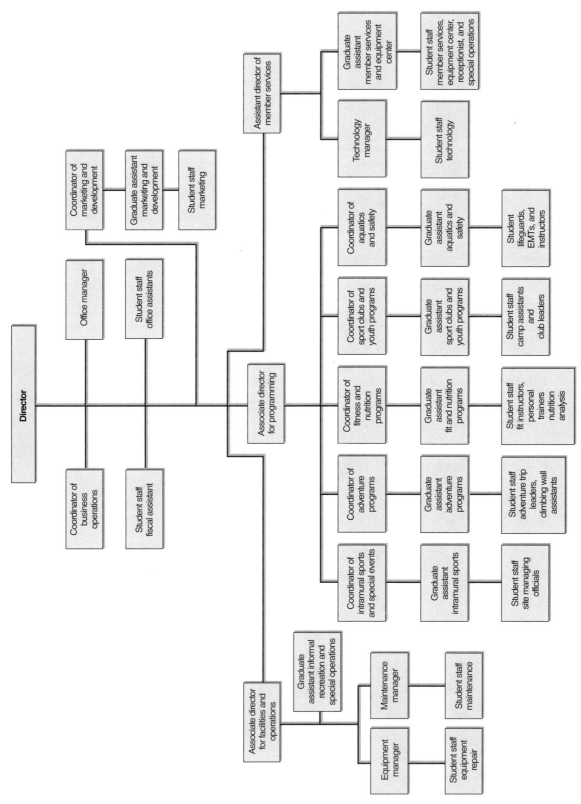

Figure 11.1 An organizational chart for a midsized university representing three fundamental components of the campus recreation department: administration, programming, and facility operations.

Correctional Recreation

Brenda Robertson and Rebecca Lesnik

" It is as if our cities had not yet developed a sense of responsibility in regard to the life of the streets, and continually forget that recreation is stronger than vice, and that recreation alone can stifle the lust for vice. "

Jane Addams, founder of Hull House, *The Spirit of Youth and the City Streets*

Groups within society that are unique in terms of recreation are those actively **incarcerated**. Freedom is one of the underlying tenants of leisure, yet this group experiences a significant loss in freedom due to the nature of their actions. The standard operating procedures of a facility and that institution's staff decide when, where, and how this segment of the population will spend their "free" time. For many, the inability to manage free time in a socially acceptable way has led to their incarceration. But a significant portion of the public does not support correctional recreation despite the fact that these programs can expose those incarcerated to more socially acceptable means of spending their free time. As this section illustrates, correctional recreation can also instill within offenders appropriate outlets for expression spanning the functional domains.

INTRODUCTION TO THE CORRECTIONAL SYSTEM

Both the United States and Canada provide a system of facilities to house **offenders**. These include local, county, state or provincial facilities, as well as federally run facilities. The **correctional system** in both countries state similar missions: to protect society and help offenders become law-abiding citizens.

It is the mission of the [United States] Federal Bureau of Prisons to protect society by confining offenders in the controlled environments of prisons and community-based facilities that are safe, humane, cost-efficient, and appropriately secure, and that provide work and other self-improvement opportunities to assist offenders in becoming law-abiding citizens. (Federal Bureau of Prisons, n.d.)

The Correctional Service of Canada, as part of the criminal justice system and respecting the rule of law, contributes to the protection of society by actively encouraging and assisting offenders to become law-abiding citizens while exercising reasonable, safe, secure, and humane care. (Correctional Services of Canada, 2004)

A system of state- or provincial-level institutions is found in both countries. Each state or province typically runs its institutions differently, but a general concept of care and control is common to all. Detention centers are located in cities, counties, or territories and are often used as holding facilities for offenders until adjudication by the courts. The type and length of sentence handed down by a court of law determine where offenders will serve their time. A juvenile, or youth, detention center is a secure facility for housing offenders under the age of 18. In some cases, however, high-risk **juvenile offenders** may be housed in adult facilities. Staff members, often referred to as probation or parole officers, provide correctional services in settings such as halfway houses or field service units where they manage offenders serving their sentences within the community at large. This living situation is often part of the offender's probation, parole, or conditional-sentence orders. Residents are often expected to obtain employment, pay room and board, and comply with specific treatment orders. The exact number of those housed at state and local levels is difficult to say because it changes daily. The nature of the facility determines how or to what extent recreation services are provided. Local facilities where those awaiting trial or sentencing are housed generally provide few if any recreation opportunities. In facilities that house sentenced people, the nature of recreation programs is based on various risk factors and is often considered an approach to population management rather than treatment. In facilities or units where rehabilitation of the offender is deemed possible, recreation can play an active role in the treatment process.

According to 2009 data, there were 39,132 people incarcerated in Canada and 2,292,133 in the United States. Those numbers represent a rate 117 per 100,000 people in Canada and 743 per 100,000 people in the United States. This number may also rise and fall on a daily basis. The security required in these institutions is determined by a combination of risk factors, which is often reflected by the amount of direct staff supervision. Inmates are sentenced to a specific level of security based on the nature of their crime and several other factors. For example, those who have committed low-level or nonviolent crimes; are able to function with relatively little supervision; and do not disrupt the institution's operations or threaten the safety of the staff, other inmates, or the public can be housed in lower-security institutions. People housed in a formal correctional facility are charged with a wide range of crimes. These people represent all races, backgrounds, origins, physical conditions, and age groups. Some have never been incarcerated, whereas others are repeat offenders. Those factors in addition to the size of the facility, the staff-to-inmate ratio, and the current political climate regarding staff training and administrative expectation present the biggest challenges to providing recreation programming.

HISTORICAL AND PHILOSOPHICAL FOUNDATIONS OF CORRECTIONAL RECREATION

During colonial times in Canada and the United States, the response to inappropriate behavior was influenced by the British practices of capital and corporal punishment (physical chastisement of an offender such as flogging, mutilation, and branding). Institutionalization was generally only employed to hold offenders awaiting punishment. In the colonies, the community accepted respon-sibility for both punishing offenders and helping to strengthen community institutions such as the family and churches as a defense against crime. As communities grew in size, it became more difficult to accept responsibility for the care and control of deviant people (Ekstedt & Griffiths, 1988).

During the 19th century, there was a belief that rather than being able to eliminate negative behaviors, community disorder was in fact contributing to them and that offenders were often products of unstable community life. In response, Americans sought to establish a system of **penitentiaries** in which offenders, after being removed from corrupt and unstable communities, were housed and made into useful citizens (Rothman, 1971). In contrast, popular thinking in Canada at the time held that offenders were a dangerous class who posed a threat to the stability and morality of communities and as such must be removed. Penitentiaries were built as a means of segregating these people (Beattie, 1977).

During the 1930s, interest in exploring the causes of criminal behavior emerged. It was discovered that many people committed crimes leading to incarceration because they did not have the skills to manage their free time appropriately. Prevention was considered preferable to treatment, and this became an issue for both correctional officials and the recreation community. Some believed that the root problem was a community's failure to provide adequate recreation facilities and programs.

The contemporary role of corrections is to provide the degree of custody necessary to contain the risk presented by an offender, to provide an environment conducive to personal reformation, and to encourage offenders to adopt acceptable behavior patterns through participation in education, social development, and work-experience programs.

The function of correctional institutions in Canada and the United States has undergone various philosophical shifts in response to societal changes over time. The role that recreation has played within the institutions has taken various forms reflective of the dominant paradigms of the day. The following are philosophical approaches that have been used at various times in both Canada and the United States.

- Given the lack of activity within institutions, labor is considered to be recreation and those most deserving are granted opportunities to work and therefore opportunities for recreation.

- Participation in most recreation programs is a privilege, and those who earn it have access to opportunities that will serve as an incentive for positive behavior by others.

- Idle minds are susceptible to negative impulses; therefore, active engagement is required to awaken undeveloped and dormant faculties thus occupying the mind.

- Recreation can serve as a mechanism to control the behavior of inmates by granting or denying access to pleasurable pursuits.

- Offenders are incarcerated as their punishment and not for their punishment, and so access to appropriate forms of recreation should not be denied.

- The goal of incarceration is to prepare offenders for release, and because recreation is part of a normal balanced lifestyle, it must be incorporated into the institutional program.

- Because offenders are completely within their care, institutions have a responsibility to work with the whole person, and that involves providing for their cognitive, physical, social, emotional, and spiritual needs.

The role of recreation within corrections continues to be a topic of debate within the justice system today.

RECREATION PROGRAMMING

It is the responsibility of the many correctional recreation professionals located throughout the United States and Canada to provide the most effective and safe activities possible. Recreation therapists working in a correctional environment provide direct service to offenders in state or provincial facilities, federal correctional institutions and facilities, and in private treatment agencies that serve both juvenile and adult offenders. Their role is most often to engage the population in recreation experiences meant to assist the offenders in developing leisure skills and attitudes that will optimize their quality of life within the institution and prepare them to use their leisure time appropriately upon rejoining the community.

Programming Goals

Many positive outcomes can be realized through recreation programs offered in correctional institutions. According to the Federal Bureau of Prisons, correctional recreation programs are expected in large part to keep inmates constructively occupied, to reduce idleness, and to enhance the physical, emotional, and social well-being of inmates. These programs will encourage and help inmates to adopt healthy lifestyle habits through participation in physical fitness and health education programs and will decrease the need for inmate medical treatment (Federal Bureau of Prisons, n.d.). These positive outcomes are also realized when **leisure education** principles

Correctional recreation programs are expected to keep inmates constructively occupied, to reduce idleness, and to enhance the physical, emotional, and social well-being of inmates.

are applied. Leisure education sets out to develop the attitudes, skills, and knowledge required for optimal leisure functioning. The components of a typical program include developing the physical, cognitive, social, emotional, and spiritual skills necessary for participation in recreation activities as well as gaining a knowledge of leisure opportunities and how to use the required equipment and supplies. Other components include developing an understanding of and an appreciation for leisure and its role in quality of life, in addition to providing opportunities to explore and experience a variety of appropriate leisure activities.

The following are goals of correctional recreation programming:

• **Develop acceptable outlets for stress**. Correctional facilities are extremely stressful environments. To survive, inmates must learn to identify and practice socially acceptable ways to relieve stress. For many this is through physical exertion, but for others, cultural pursuits such as music, art, drama, and writing provide positive outlets.

• **Identify activities that serve as alternatives to addictions**. Many people sentenced to correctional facilities experience addictions. Those who participate in treatment programs to address their addictive behaviors often find that they have significantly more free time than they used to. Therefore, replacing recreational pursuits during time previously devoted to the addiction becomes a key approach in the rehabilitation process.

• **Foster interpersonal skills such as cooperation and teamwork**. Lack of the basic skills that enable people to live effectively in a community may cause some people to participate in activities generally considered socially unacceptable. Certain forms of recreation can help people identify and develop interpersonal skills.

• **Develop a new sense of purpose**. A person's sense of purpose is pivotal in the decision-making process and therefore is an important piece of making lifestyle change. Through active participation in therapeutic recreation, a person can explore a variety of pro-social roles. Participants who have this type of opportunity are able to develop a clearly defined sense of purpose that will help to guide their thinking and behavior.

• **Enhance self-esteem through success**. High self-esteem is a critical component of personal accountability and respect for others, which are important goals of the correctional process. Self-esteem is also at the root of inner confidence that enables people to cope effectively with the challenges of life. Positive recreation experiences can enhance self-esteem.

• **Increase access to new social environments**. People are products of their environment to a large extent and often lack the motivation to alter negative social environments. Adopting new recreation interests can serve as a catalyst to seeking new and potentially more positive social environments.

• **Foster new interests**. Offenders often have a limited leisure-activity repertoire caused in part by a negative attitude toward activities even though they have not experienced the activities firsthand (Robertson, 1993). Recreation programs can help identify the source of the negative attitudes and foster a more positive attitude toward a broader range of leisure pursuits.

• **Negotiate constraints**. Many people encounter self-imposed social, psychological, and structural constraints attempting to participate in recreation opportunities such as no one with whom to participate, low self-esteem, and lack of skill or money. Learning how to overcome these constraints can facilitate access to a broader range of activity options, which is desirable when all perceived options have negative consequences.

• **Develop awareness of personal needs and appropriate avenues to satisfy them**. Human behavior is motivated by thought, which is prompted by people's interpretation of personal experience and their relationship with the world around them. Delinquent behavior can become a means for satisfying both real and perceived needs. Recreation can provide appropriate ways to satisfy specific needs.

• **Develop decision-making and problem-solving skills**. Offenders often have not learned the skills necessary to assess situations and to make decisions that will not harm themselves or others. These skills can be developed and practiced in recreational settings, allowing participants to experience and process the impact of their decisions.

• **Develop new interests that could evolve into a career**. Certain offenders are highly creative and talented, yet traditional approaches to education and vocational programs often fail to recognize or develop these skills. Through recreation, creative skills can be identified and channeled into pursuits such as music, writing, drama, and crafts, which could lead to meaningful employment opportunities.

Types of Programming

Recreation programs in correctional settings vary greatly depending on the nature of the institution and the resources available. When planning an activity for people who are incarcerated, the number one concern is the safety of both participants and staff. Before allowing inmates to participate, staff must carefully examine each activity to identify potential hazards. Even a board game could present a dangerous situation for inmates and staff if the game pieces could be used for inappropriate purposes. Careful supervision when conducting these activities is required, including accounting for all equipment. Staff need to recognize that although correctional institutions are meant to serve as rehabilitation facilities, they can be aggressive and hostile settings. Recreation in a correctional setting should focus on the positive aspects of participation: teamwork, cooperation, stress management, and pro-social leadership techniques. Teaching offenders to redirect their negative energy in positive ways not only serves them while they are incarcerated but also can help them lead more positive, productive lives in the community at large.

Some institutions have extensive recreation facilities, while others are limited. Much of this depends on the type and size of the facility as well as funds that are available and allocated to recreation activities. For example, some institutions are equipped with facilities such as a baseball field, full-length basketball court, weight room, crafts shop, and theater, while others may have only a small multipurpose room.

Active recreation programs offered in institutions include basketball, volleyball, aerobics, handball, hockey, curling, table tennis, pool, baseball, flag football, track and field, shuffleboard, soccer, canoeing, orienteering, and rock climbing. Sports are popular in most institutions. Examples of more passive forms of recreation include drawing, painting, sculpting, crafts, music, journal writing, pet therapy, board games, drama, quilting, knitting, singing, and holiday events.

Although certain programs primarily serve to occupy the minds of inmates during down time within the institution, others have therapeutic outcomes. For example, pet therapy is an innovative recreation program offered in some locations that may be made available to juveniles, men, and women at varying levels of incarceration. This type of program typically sets out to foster a sense of responsibility and nurturing toward the animal, which in turn promotes self-esteem and has the potential to provide other therapeutic benefits that can be identified and included in treatment planning for that offender. Many pet therapy programs also incorporate instruction that allows the inmate to train the animal for specialized purposes such as service or assistance to those who have physical disabilities. This type of program promotes ties to the community by providing a valuable service.

CORRECTIONAL RECREATION PROFESSIONAL

Due to the nature and business of correctional facilities, ensuring that recreation programming is more than an approach to managing the population can prove a challenge to the recreational professional. One must work diligently at educating, maintaining programmatic integrity, and exercising the skills of creative problem solving. These three points become part of the mission for recreation professionals who choose to provide service within the correctional environment. Staff members can be sworn law enforcement officers or civilian personnel trained to provide service in a correctional facility. Most facilities require correctional recreation staff to hold some type of advanced degree. Other credentials, such as certified personal trainer, therapeutic recreation specialist, or certified leisure professional, are helpful. All correctional recreation personnel should be certified in first aid and CPR and trained in, or at least familiar with, the duties of 24/7 staff. Being fluent in a second language is helpful. Candidates interested in applying for work in a correctional institution may be subject to polygraph testing, urinalysis, and background checks.

Although the specific job titles may vary from facility to facility—recreation officer, recreation therapist, recreation specialist, program manager, or program supervisor—the role of correctional recreation personnel is virtually the same throughout the United States and Canada. And these professionals play important roles in the lives of offenders while they are incarcerated. Those with a physical education or recreation background provide valuable experience to the population they serve. People hired for this type of position receive training related to their specific job as well as the operations of the facility. Much of the focus is geared toward safety and security, the priority when working in a corrections setting, and one must understand that this profession carries with it an inherent risk because of the work environment. But it can also hold great opportunities for learning and understanding. Being part of a correctional setting and working with offenders will not only help someone to develop a strong sense of their own personal safety and boundaries, but it will also help to develop a sense of appreciation for human thinking and behavior.

TRENDS AND ISSUES

Although often viewed as a large and inflexible governmental machine, correctional institutions are very much affected by societal trends both from the client and administrative perspective. Because of this, they face ever changing and challenging issues such as incarceration rates, budget cuts, philosophical shifts, aging infrastructure, and meeting the needs of the various segments of the incarcerated population based on factors such as age, sex, race, social economics, and societal norms.

A current issue in correctional recreation is how the role of recreation is viewed within the correctional settings. Some correctional administrations and staff understand that participation in positive forms of recreation can be a constructive way for offenders to spend their time relieving stress, countering boredom, and improving health. But some institutions are reluctant to dedicate resources to such programs because of state or local administrative viewpoints or for fear of recourse from a public that supports more punitive approaches to offender treatment. In these cases, basic recreation programs are offered as a means of satisfying legal requirements but lack the developmental or therapeutic components that could aid in offender rehabilitation. But awareness of the relationship between a lack of pro-social recreation and delinquent behavior appears to be increasing. Many people engage in criminal activity as a form of recreation, reflecting lifestyle choices that they have made to satisfy their needs, both real and perceived. Research has shown that many of these people lack the knowledge, attitude, and skills to participate in personally satisfying and socially acceptable pursuits (Robertson, 1998). As such, the way to rehabilitate them so that they can become law-abiding citizens is to help them develop the appropriate knowledge and skills to pursue alternatives through leisure education-based programs that have a strong developmental component.

SUMMARY

Recreation holds the potential to assist correctional institutions, their incarcerated populations, and their staff members achieve the goals of the correctional system. If properly administered, correctional recreation can help foster an institutional environment in which offenders can develop knowledge and skills that will enable them to live more productive lives while incarcerated and after they return to the community at large.

Faith-Based Recreation

John Byl

❝ The city streets will be filled with boys and girls playing there.   **❞**

Zechariah 8:5

People of faith often engage in recreational activities through their religious institutions. In the United States in 2001, 81 percent of those 18 and older identified with a religious group (Kosmin, Mayer, & Keysar, 2001). Therefore, we can see why "religious organizations should be recognized as legitimate providers of recreation activities in the leisure service delivery system" (Emard, 1990, p. 146). Religious institutions play an important role in providing satisfying recreational opportunities within their communities. We examine the differences within and among faith traditions and then explore employment in faith-based recreation.

DIFFERENCES WITHIN FAITH TRADITIONS

Religious groups are not one homogeneous unit. Some of the differences are fostered because of different ways of thinking about beliefs, and some are fostered because of different ethnic roots. For example, compare two protestant Christian groups: the Christian Reformed Church (CRC), which was started by Calvinists of Dutch background, and the Canadian Mennonite Brethren (MB), which was started by Anabaptists of Germanic background. A study of the main journals for each group determined that for the CRC, "enjoying one's leisure time was highly encouraged, especially if the recreation called for a combination of active, stewardly, and playful participation in God's creation" (Byl, 1999, pp. 318-319). But they had little interest in organized church camps for evangelistic purposes. In contrast, the Mennonites valued church camps for two purposes: "One, showing young Christians how to live a Christian life, and two, leading people to Christ" (Byl, 1999, p. 320). The CRC sees recreation primarily as a way to experience God's creation,

whereas the MB views recreation primarily as a teaching and evangelistic tool.

The study demonstrates that two Christian groups can hold significantly different views about the purpose of recreation; the study also indicates that within each denomination members hold different views (Byl, 1999). Some of the differences between religious groups relate to individual commitments and ethnic backgrounds. Some people's religious beliefs intentionally and fully shape their recreation choices, whereas others express beliefs that unintentionally and partially shape their recreation choices. Nationality also shapes unique differences between religious groups. The intersection of nationality and religious beliefs encourages some to recreate with people with similar interests, background, religious affiliation, and language. Being in this comfort zone within a subculture and being shaped by the subcultural values are referred to as **selective acculturation** in leisure (Shaull & Gramann, 1998).

DIFFERENCES AMONG FAITH TRADITIONS

North America is home to many religious groups, but looking at three faith groups provides insight into how various traditions value and engage in recreation. We look at Muslims as an emerging faith group in North America, Christians as a group with a longstanding history, and Jews as the second largest faith group in the United States.

Islam

Nearly 20 percent of the world's population follows **Islam**, a way of life led by the teachings of Muhammad. Muslims are the fastest growing religious group in the United States (Kosmin, Mayer,

& Keysar, 2001). Their numbers doubled in the United States from 1990 to 2000. Because many of these Muslims are recent immigrants to North America, because they immigrated from a variety of countries, and because they live in various socio-economic groups, all Muslims cannot be considered the same.

According to Islamic teachings, both men and women should learn to ride horses, shoot a bow and arrow, swim safely, fence, run, and wrestle. In part these sports are encouraged as a means to personal well-being, and in part they are a means to being well prepared in case of war (Anahar, Becker, & Messing, 1992). Because participation in sport must comply with Islamic teaching, a Muslim may not participate in sport for personal financial benefit or for personal fame, nor can he or she ignore religious practices concerning prayer, modest clothing, and men spectating at sporting events for women or women watching men (Fleming & Khan, 1994; Kamiyole, 1993). Opportunity must be available for prayer in the morning, at 7:30 in the evening, as well as at three other times during the day. The Ramadan requirement of daily fasting from dawn until sunset during the ninth month of the Muslim year must be considered (Taylor & Toohey, 2001/2002). Recreation also must not interfere with family responsibilities such as watching over siblings, performing household duties, or doing school work (Carrington, Chivers, & Williams, 1987; De Knop, Theeboom, Wittock, & De Martelaer, 1996; Fleming, 1993).

Clothing can present Muslim women (and consequently recreation providers) a major barrier to becoming involved in active recreation. In strict Muslim circles, a woman is not permitted to show publicly more of her body than her face and hands. Typically, women cover their heads with a hijab in public (Jalili, 1994), but all this clothing does not encourage active participation in sport. Some Muslim women join private health and fitness facilities for women only so that they can meet their religious mandates (Taylor & Toohey, 2001/2002).

Certainly, a key to helping Muslims become more physically active is to understand their religious customs (Benn, 1996). Here are eight suggestions for providing a more inviting physical activity culture that respects Islamic boundaries (Kahan, 2003a).

1. Muslims must have more opportunities to voice their concerns about combining religious customs with physical activity.

2. Physical education and recreation providers must engage in dialogue with Muslim clergy and parents to attain advice for advancing participation. These providers should also speak with their participants about sensitivity to Muslim needs.

3. Young people need more Muslim role models who excel in physical education and sport as instructors, organizers, and elite athletes.

4. Physical activity providers must ask more questions from and about Muslims to gain better understanding of their faith tradition.

5. Recreation providers need to be aware of prayer times, daylong fasts during Ramadan, and other important holidays such as Id al-Fitr and Id al-Adha and be aware that these holidays occur at different times each year because the Muslim calendar is based on a lunar cycle.

6. Those responsible for program design must realize that Muslims come from a tradition rich in activities such as badminton, field hockey, and folk games. But coed activities in which there is a potential for body contact, such as basketball or touch football, or activities that require exposing large amounts of the body, such as swimming or gymnastics, cannot be considered. Ways to deal with minor physical contact include separating females and males during games or letting females guard females and males guard males, as in a sport like korfball (a version of basketball played with a soccer ball that is popular in Europe).

7. Legal rulings have consistently supported people from specific religious groups who wear clothing required by their religious convictions (Kahan, 2003b). In the case of Muslims, this means that females must wear clothing that covers all but their faces and hands and males must wear clothing that covers the area between the navel and the knees. Public nudity is also forbidden in Islam. Showers must be made optional or shower stalls must be provided for showering and changing.

8. Muslims should encourage the development of Muslim-specific clubs and organizations.

Camps are a popular activity for faith-based organizations.

Christianity

The largest and most popular religion in the United States is **Christianity**. Since the beginning of the Christian church, living in community with fellow believers has been valued. During the past 100 years, togetherness as a congregation has been enjoyed in church fellowship halls through coffee socials, boys and girls clubs, annual church picnics, dances, and competitive leagues with teams from similar congregations. The purpose of this recreation is to enhance a sense of community between people of the same faith.

Typically, church programs, particularly those for kids, include a refreshment break that provides an opportunity for leaders to speak briefly about following Christian principles of living or to share a personal testimony and to invite participants to accept Jesus as savior of their life. Special kids' programs like KidsGames are modeled after the Olympics and take place during church summer camps during the years when the Summer Olympics and World Cup of soccer occur. Competitions are held in various sport events, Bible knowledge,

poster design, and answering an essay question. KidsGames began in Barcelona in 1985 as an evangelical Christian program in preparation for the Olympic Games in that city and is now worldwide (Bynum, 2003).

Besides offering kids' programs, many Christian churches organize adult church sport leagues. These leagues generally do not permit alcohol use at games, and they include time for prayer, fellowship, and talking with others about their relationship with God. These leagues try not to overemphasize the importance of sport by limiting the number of weekly practices and games (Popke, 2001a). In Canada, at least in small-town churches in Ontario, sport is one of the activities ranked lowest in current offerings. Many churches in the United States have built large fitness centers to serve their members as well as to serve and reach out to others in the community. In these fitness centers Christian music is often played, and during breaks in the activity people can share a personal testimony and pray.

Several for-profit companies have organized to fill a niche in the fitness market for Christian fitness centers that train both the body and soul. The Lord's

Gym was founded in Florida in 1997 and now has more than 21 locations. Its membership is open to all people regardless of religious background, but a dress code is enforced, Christian music and television stations are played, and 10 percent of all member fees are given to charities (Popke, 2001b). Another company is Angel City Fitness, which offers classes in yoga, Pilates, kick fit, stretching, and self-defense. Other amenities include personal trainers and a cafe.

An organization that helps churches use sport and recreation programs to reach out to their communities is the Association of Church Sports and Recreation Ministers (CSRM). CSRM provides "a way for these church leaders to come together as a profession to learn from each other, to find support for their chosen ministry field, to meet others working in churches, and to share resources" (Association of Church Sports website: www.csrm. org). CSRM's motto is "Helping churches use sport and recreation programs to reach out to their communities."

Judaism

People of Jewish background are discussed here for two reasons. First, those who identify themselves as Jewish form the second largest religious group in the United States (Kosmin, Mayer, & Keysar, 2001). And second, although Christians and Muslims see all of life as affected by their religious commitments, Jews distinguish between sacred and secular activities, thereby providing an alternative perspective on faithful living in one's recreation.

For Jews, religion affects what happens in the synagogue and in personal and family devotional life but not what happens on the soccer pitch or in the boxing ring. But something that binds Jews together, regardless of religious affiliation, is their nation, Israel. Therefore, some recreation activities are based more on national commitments than on Jewish faith commitments. For example, the quadrennial Maccabiah Games is held in Israel the year following the Olympic Games. According to Maccabi Canada, the purpose of the Maccabiah Games is "to promote the Jewish identity and traditions through athletic, cultural, social and educational activities for both youth and adults alike and to promote a bond with the State of Israel, both domestically and abroad" (Maccabi Canada, 2005).

The Maccabi World Union was set up in 1921 at the Zionist Congress to coordinate the activities of the various Jewish sport clubs and sport organizations operating around the world. The Zionist Congress first met in 1896 for purposes of establishing a Jewish state. The term *Maccabi* is a name to remember Judah Maccabi, who led a band of Jewish patriots against the Syrian invaders. The Maccabi World Union developed the idea of holding a sort of Jewish Olympiad every four years in Israel. The first Maccabiah Games was held in 1932. In addition, the Pan American Maccabi Games is held every four years in various South American cities. The JCC Maccabi Games, sponsored by the Jewish Community Centers, is held annually in the United States. These Olympic-style sporting competitions are held each summer in North America and are the largest organized sport program in the world for Jewish teenagers (Jewish Community Centers Maccabi Games, 2005).

Another important influence on the recreation habits of Jews in the United States and Canada was the establishment of organizations to help recent immigrants adapt to their new surroundings. During the late 1800s and early to mid-1900s Jewish settlement houses, immigrant aid institutions, and Young Men's and Young Women's Hebrew Associations were established in cities like Boston, New York, and Chicago. The Young Women's Associations offered programs in calisthenics, basketball, baseball, track and field, tennis, physical culture, domestic education, aquatics, "religious work, gymnastics, social work, and educational work to promote social and physical welfare for Jewish families" (Borish, 1999, p. 248). These centers were concerned with the Americanization of Eastern European immigrants (Borish, 1999). These organizations provided places where Jews could participate in new activities and learn about North American culture without losing their Jewish culture.

The Jewish Community Centers Association of North America guides the Jewish Community Centers across North America. This organization states that it is a movement

> leading the way to a vibrant future by establishing cooperative ventures with local and national Jewish organizations, by supporting Jewish culture, community, and education, and by encouraging and enabling Jews of all ages and backgrounds to engage in the joys

of Jewish living. (Jewish Community Centers Maccabi Games, 2005)

These centers, like the Maccabiah Games, are concerned with "Jewish living," not **Judaism** as a religion.

EMPLOYMENT IN FAITH-BASED RECREATION

Professionals in faith-based recreation must meet three requirements. First, a passionate commitment to the faith is central and is the first entry point into any position, although for Jewish leaders faith is not critical, but a positive disposition to Jewish culture is important. Second, although some people with ecclesiastical training are hired, most of those hired have training in recreation and leadership. Academic training may consist of a recreation diploma from a college, or a recreation, physical education, or leadership degree from a university. Third, a faith-based recreation leader must nurture the faith, or the culture in the case of Jewish leaders, through recreation in people of various backgrounds. Although some of this nurturing involves specific spiritual instruction, the nurturing may also be primarily focused on encouraging friendships within the group.

SUMMARY

Most North Americans identify with some form of religion. Each ideology presents clear and unique ramifications on the way in which followers engage in recreation. Religious institutions play an important role in advising their members on the importance of recreation and, in many cases, in providing opportunities for their members and those from the broader community to take advantage of recreational activities.

Worksite Recreation and Health Promotion

Jeffrey Ferguson

" The greatest wealth is health. "

Virgil

Worksite recreation and health promotion entails the provision of recreation programs, facilities, and programs that enhance the health and **wellness** of employees. Many models exist for the provision and management of these services, but generally these services are offered at the worksite. The services offered often include opportunities for sport participation, social events, fitness, and health and wellness education.

HISTORY OF WORKSITE RECREATION AND HEALTH PROMOTION

Some employers have been providing recreation and health promotion for better than 150 years.

Two of the first documented programs offered were library resources and singing classes. These program services were offered by the Peacedale Manufacturing Company, Peacedale, Rhode Island, in the 1850s (MacLean, Peterson, & Martin, 1985). As the United States continued to industrialize during the latter decades of the 1800s and early decades of the 1900s, many more companies began offering a variety of employee recreation and fitness programs. In the 1860s the YMCA became one of the first private agencies to work with business and industry to provide positive recreation alternatives to industrial workers (Cross, 1990). One of the things that YMCAs did was build gymnasiums where they could offer fitness-related programs to the young men who were moving to the cities in ever larger numbers to work in the factories. The Playground and Recreation Association of America, now the National Recreation and Park Association, began assisting companies in the provision of employee recreation and wellness programs in the early 1900s. In 1941 the National Industrial Recreation Association was formed to help address concerns related to the provision and management of employee recreation services (Sessoms, Meyer, & Brightbill, 1975). Beginning in the 1930s labor unions began to play an increased role in the provision of employee recreation and health promotion services. The growth of employer-provided recreation and health promotion services has continued since World War II. In 2000 the Employee Services Management (ESM) Association estimated that over 50,000 organizations offered on-site fitness programs (Chenoweth, 2007).

The nature of the services provided has gone through many evolutions and continues to evolve in the 21st century. Company-sponsored picnics, athletic teams, hobby clubs and classes, bowling leagues, aquatics programs, exercise breaks, and group vacations were typical of services offered by employers through the first 100 years of employer-sponsored recreation and health promotion programs. In the decades since World War II, many more companies began providing recreation and fitness facilities. These facilities have included amenities such as gymnasiums, aquatics areas, tennis courts, walking trails, golf courses, athletic fields, aerobic and strength training areas, and child care.

BENEFITS, PROGRAMS, AND SERVICES

Why do employers see a benefit in offering recreation and health promotion services to their employees? As stated by David Chenoweth, "Treating one's employees and fellow workers with respect and care is not just the right thing to do, it is also good business." Employers have learned that the investment they make in employee benefits such as recreation and health promotion services have a positive cost-benefit to their business. Benefits to the employer have included

1. advantages in the recruitment and retention of employees,
2. improved employee morale and loyalty,
3. reduced health care claims and cost,
4. higher levels of employee productivity,
5. better interpersonal relationships in the work setting,
6. reduced absenteeism, and
7. enhanced image in the business community and community at large.

These factors have all been identified as positively affecting the competitive success of an organization.

Employees understand why their employers are motivated to provide recreation and health promotion services, but they have their own motives for desiring these services. Employees tend to seek the following benefits from the recreation and health promotion services provided by their employers: (1) improved wellness, which reduces out of pocket health care cost, (2) improved interpersonal relations with coworkers, (3) reduction of work-related stress, which lessens stress-related health risks and improves home life, and (4) improved physical and emotional well-being, which enhances personal participation in active lifestyles with family and friends.

According to *Healthy People 2010* (U.S. Department of Health and Human Services, 2000), the lifestyle of Americans has contributed to the rising cost of health care in America. A consequence of these lifestyle choices is higher health insurance cost to the employer and employee and the shifting of a greater share of the costs to employees. The result has been growth in employee interest and participation in the services provided by their employers, particularly if participation results in cost savings to the employee.

Generally, employee recreation and health promotion services are organized through human resources (HR) departments as one of the many benefits offered by the employer. The delivery of these services has been handled in a number ways in recent years: (1) retention of this responsibility by the HR department, (2) as a contractual service with an outside company that specializes in employee recreation and health promotion, (3) partnerships with local health care providers, and (4) discounted programs for employees with local park and recreation agencies and commercial fitness providers. Typically, programs run by HR departments and contracted service providers are run at the employee worksite. Companies such as Sprint, Cerner Corporation, Phillips-Conoco, Union Pacific, and Wal-Mart have established "associate" centers on their corporate campuses that serve as the site of service delivery. Programs operated in partnership with local health care providers may include on-site and off-site delivery of various services. Under this model certain health-screening opportunities may be offered only at the site of the health care provider. Employee discount programs are offered by many city park and recreation agencies, YMCAs, and commercial fitness centers. These programs generally require employees to purchase employer-discounted memberships through the agencies. Most of the services are offered at the agency facilities.

Employers that offer recreation services generally have athletic facilities that employees may use for drop-in recreation or for participation in activities such as racquetball, tennis, sport leagues, golf, aquatics, ski and scuba diving trips, and athletic programs for dependents. Health promotion programs that are offered may include drop-in use of aerobic and strength-training equipment, group exercise programs, personal training services, health-screening services, health fairs, wellness education seminars and newsletters, and health-counseling services.

WORKSITE RECREATION AND HEALTH PROMOTION TRENDS

The American College of Sports Medicine has conducted a survey of world fitness trends since 2006 to identify programs that are having an influence on the fitness industry (Thompson, 2010). The top 10 fitness trends identified for 2011 are

1. educated and experienced fitness professionals,
2. special fitness programs for older adults,
3. strength training,
4. children and obesity,
5. personal training,
6. core training,
7. exercise and weight loss,
8. boot camp,
9. functional fitness, and
10. physician referrals.

Some movement has occurred in the ranked importance of the programs and some programs have been replaced in the top 10 by others. The results from these annual surveys indicate that some program offerings thought to represent program trends may have been fads and that the future may hold additional changes in fitness program offerings.

CAREER PREPARATION

People seeking careers in the area of worksite recreation and health promotion are going to need knowledge, skills, and experience in a variety of areas to remain competitive in the job market. Successful job candidates will need to be competent in the areas of public relations, human resource management, budget development and management, facility design and management, risk management, recreation and fitness programming, advocacy, health promotion and exercise science, and recreation sports management. Job candidates can enhance their job prospects by having completed a university-approved internship and by obtaining professional certification through a recognized professional association.

The best place to start the search for worksite recreation and health promotion internships and professional certifications is right on campus with your academic advisor or the office of careers services. These sources will be able to direct you to specific organizations that have internship programs or to organizations that provide internship listings. The following are some organizations that provide worksite recreation and health promotion internship and career information on the Internet.

www.corporatefitnessworks.com

www.acsm.healthjobsplus.com

www.hfit.com/careers.asp

http://phfr.com/jobfinder

www.medifit.com

www.wellnessconnection.com

www.cooperinstitute.org

www.hpcareer.net

Possession of some type of professional certification and a completed internship will increase the marketability of those seeking a career in worksite

OUTSTANDING GRADUATES

Background Information

Name: Jessica Robinson

Education: Bachelor of science in corporate recreation and wellness. Master of science in applied health sciences from the HPERD department.

Credentials: ACSM health fitness specialist, ACSM certified personal trainer, Reebok cycle instructor, CPR American Red Cross, and YMCA healthy lifestyle principles.

Affiliations: ACSM member.

Career Information

Position: Group fitness coordinator–fitness specialist.

Organization: I work for a corporate health company called MountainWest. Corporations in Colorado and surrounding areas hire MountainWest to manage and staff on-site fitness facilities. I work at Level 3 Communications headquarters in Broomfield, Colorado. Level 3 Communications is a nationwide telecommunications company. The Broomfield location is the largest site, having around 3,000 employees. Over 500 Broomfield employees take advantage of the only Level 3 Communications fitness facility, Club Level 3.

Organization's mission: The mission of Club Level 3 is to provide superior customer service to all Level 3 employee owners and to promote total wellness by offering informative fitness assessments and exercise prescriptions, extensive educational wellness programs, and dynamic group fitness classes, all in a friendly, energizing environment.

Job description: I coordinate all group fitness and the monthly schedule. I schedule specialty classes (at least four per year) and any needed subs. I work on attendance tracking and upkeep of the money, deduction spreadsheet, and group fitness binder. I take care of all instructor training and paperwork and all membership paperwork including membership files, enrollment forms, cancellation forms, and referral file upkeep. I also take care of check requests, instructor timesheets, contractor timesheets, miscellaneous earnings, payroll audit, personal training logs, personal training checks, locker spreadsheet tracking and upkeep, and the holiday book. I double-check monies to the home office and evaluate the website schedules. I also work on marketing, request donations, map out courses, and organize three annual 5Ks (St. Patty's Day, Firecracker, and Turkey Trot).

Some of my other duties include putting on one lecture, workshop, and lunch and learn each year; organizing at least one group exercise workshop per year; designing and implementing at least one incentive program per year; attending and observing one group exercise class every two months; completing two evaluations on every instructor each year; and assisting with daily duties of the fitness center, including fitness assessments, personalized exercise plans, machine orientation, group exercise, cleaning, and the equipment safety checklist.

Career path: While working on my master's degree I worked as a graduate assistant in the fitness center on campus. I did personal training with members and taught activity courses. I completed my internship for my master's degree at the Denver Athletic Club (DAC). After working at the DAC I moved to

> *Recreation and leisure is important to individuals' overall wellness. Working in the fitness field is extremely rewarding. Through personal training and group exercise classes, you will have a huge effect on people's lives. Motivation, encouraging words, and education allow people to do more than they ever believed they could and change their lives for the better.*

Outstanding Graduates *(continued)*

Overland Park, Kansas, to work at the Sprint world headquarters fitness center. Sprint has the largest corporate fitness facility in the United States.

After working at Sprint for five months I relocated back to Denver. I accepted the group exercise coordinator–fitness specialist position with MountainWest and have been here for nearly a year and a half.

Likes and dislikes about the job: I absolutely love my job. In addition to the duties listed earlier, I help implement kickball and dodge ball tournaments, communicate with members, and help keep members motivated to achieve their goals. The best part of my job is seeing people meet their goals. Knowing that I helped someone gain confidence and self-esteem is an unbelievable feeling. Another great part of my job is that I have the opportunity to be involved in many activities and aspects of health and wellness. Each day of my job is challenging, and no two days are the same. In one day I may personal-train three clients, teach a group exercise class, referee a kickball tournament, work on marketing for an incentive program, perform a

fitness assessment, and manage group exercise money. I also love having the freedom to implement all my ideas, whether it is starting up a new group exercise class or designing a new program. I have a lot of creative freedom.

The thing I like least about my job is that I really have to put in a lot of extra hours to make a decent salary.

My current position is amazing, but I do look at this position as a stop on my career ladder. I have higher education and certifications than what is required for this position. I see myself in management, education, or a more clinical position in the future.

Advice for Undergraduates

My advice to undergraduate students is to learn as much as possible. Strive to be ahead, earn nationally recognized certifications, and continuously research your field. Fitness is continuously changing, and you need to educate yourself constantly. Take every chance given to gain experience. View every experience as an opportunity to learn and better yourself.

recreation and health promotion. Numerous accredited health promotion and fitness organizations offer a variety of certification programs. These organizations have various requirements that candidates must meet for certification. All these organizations require successful passage of a written exam, and some even require candidates to pass a practical exam to become certified. The programs that have the highest degree of recognition among health promotion professionals also require a college undergraduate degree in exercise science, kinesiology, health education, wellness, corporate recreation and wellness, or a related field of study. Several accredited associations offer certification programs:

American College of Sports Medicine (ACSM): www.acsm.org

National Strength and Conditioning Association (NSCA): www.nsca-cc.org

American Council on Exercise (ACE): www.acefitness.org

Cooper Institute (Cooper): www.cooperinstitute.org

World Instructor Training Schools (WITS): www.witseducation.com

National Exercise Trainers Association (NETA): www.ndeita.com

National Exercise & Sports Trainers Association (NESTA): www.nestacertified.com

Aerobics and Fitness Association of America (AFAA): www.afaa.com

Athletic Trainers Association (NATA): www.nata.org

Outstanding Program

ConocoPhillips Worksite Recreation and Health Promotion

ConocoPhillips has a rich history of wellness, fitness, and recreation that goes back to the 1930s. Today, ConocoPhillips continues to support the health and well-being of employees by providing recreation and wellness facilities, equipment, services, and staff. Currently, recreation and wellness facilities are offered on site at 8 of its international operation sites and 10 of its domestic operation sites. The two major domestic facilities are found at the Bartlesville, Oklahoma, Technology and Research Center and the Houston, Texas, World Headquarters.

Bartlesville Facility

It all started with the Phillips 66ers basketball team, which competed with teams of other oil companies. Phillips needed a gym and locker room for the team, so the facility was built, including a pool and bowling lanes. The fitness center and gymnastics facilities were added later. The locker rooms were expanded, and three group exercise rooms and a testing lab were added as well.

- The facility covers over 90,000 square feet (8,300 sq m) of space.
- The facility opened in 1950.
- The employee population in Bartlesville is approximately 3,500.
- The wellness staff consists of nine full-time employees and several part-time employees.
- More than 30 land and water exercise classes are available.
- Annual programs and events are held at the facility.

Houston Facility

In 2008 new state-of-the-art facilities were built at the headquarters in Houston, Texas. The facility houses a fully equipped fitness center with cardio, free weights, resistance equipment, basketball court, outdoor soccer field, group exercise studios, massage room, testing lab, aquatics center, and conference room.

- The facility covers over 82,000 square feet (7,600 sq m) of space on three levels.
- The facility opened in 2008.
- The employee population in Houston is approximately 6,000.

- The wellness staff consists of six full-time employees and several part-time employees.
- More than 30 land and water exercise classes are available.
- Annual programs and events are held at the facility.

Membership Eligibility

Memberships are available to employees, employee spouses, eligible domestic partners, eligible dependents, retirees and their spouses, as well as their eligible dependents. Only employees can add or remove dependents from their memberships. Eligible dependents can now be up to age 26, even if they are married. But if a dependent is married, his or her spouse is not eligible, nor are their children.

Program Services and Special Events

Wellness–Fitness Services offers a variety of incentive programs for employees. Although programs change from year to year to meet the needs of the employees, a few programs have stood the test of time.

Lean Team

Lean Team is a popular maintain-don't-gain program that runs from mid-November through December. The six-week program starts with teams of three to five employees weighing in as a team on the loading dock scales. The goal of the team is to maintain (or lose) weight throughout the holiday season. Armed with weekly challenge cards and motivation to win incentives, teams start with a six-week challenge. Each week the teams receive information on how to maintain healthy habits through the holidays and encouragement. At the conclusion of the six weeks, teams must face the loading dock scales again. Teams that lose or maintain their preholiday weight within 1 pound (.45 kg) are eligible for prizes.

Health Fairs and Screenings

A health fair is sponsored annually by Wellness–Fitness Services and Human Resource/Benefits. Free health screenings are provided for all employees. Screenings include complete lipid profile, body mass index, blood pressure, and prostate screening for eligible employees. In addition, medical, safety and benefit vendors come on site to answer questions.

Outstanding Program *(continued)*

Family Parties

Family parties such as Spookaroo, Eggstravaganza, and Kid's Night Out are popular recreational activities. These themed-based parties are held on Friday evenings for employees' children of all ages, and their parents are welcomed.

Functional Movement Screening

The functional movement screen is designed to observe basic movement patterns and their effect on functional performance and injury. Research has shown that to maximize movement, the body must function properly. One weak link (joint or muscle) can weaken the entire kinetic chain. The screens include the following:

- Deep squat
- Hurdle step
- In-line lunge
- Shoulder mobility
- Active straight leg raise
- Trunk stability push-up
- Rotary stability

Wellness Screening

The wellness screening consists of basic biometric assessments used to determine wellness or health status: height, weight, body composition, waist-to-hip ratio, and blood pressure. In addition, information regarding nutrition, stress level, and cardiovascular predisposition are gathered. The wellness screening provides a simple snapshot of an employee's health.

Basic Body Age

Basic body age is a noninvasive, low-intensity assessment that can be done in work attire. Cardiovascular $\dot{V}O_2$, muscular strength, flexibility, and body composition are all tested without requiring the participant to break a sweat. This is the perfect assessment to do before beginning a new exercise program.

Fitness Body Age

Fitness body age uses the same biometric screenings as basic body age and adds a jogging treadmill $\dot{V}O_2$ test and two strength field tests (push-ups and sit-ups). Body composition is determined using the three-site skin-fold measurement and requires participants to be in workout clothing. This assessment is perfect for members who want to test and improve their overall fitness. After completing a fitness assessment or movement screen, a personalized fitness program is developed based on individual results and current fitness. Employees are encouraged to have reassessments every three to six months so that they can benchmark their progress. All the fitness assessments and movement screens are designed to help employees and dependents take the essential first step to reaching their fitness goals.

Recreational Leagues and Open Play

A wide variety of recreational leagues and open play opportunities are available to employees and their dependents. Basketball, volleyball, soccer, bowling, ping-pong, water polo, and badminton are a few of the activities. Organized leagues are formed seasonally, and each of the facilities designates times for open play.

SUMMARY

Some employers have been providing recreation and health promotion services for better than 150 years. Through the years these services have been offered directly by employers and through partnerships with organizations such as the YMCA, National Recreation Association, and labor unions. The National Industrial Recreation Association, founded in 1941, was the first organization specifically created to address concerns related to the provision of employee recreation and health services in the workplace. Over the years employers have learned that employer-provided recreation and health services have a positive cost-benefit to their business. Employees have learned that using these services may result in personal saving related to health care and improvement in their quality of life. Services have included the provision of recreation and wellness facilities, company leagues, planned vacations, directed and drop-in exercise programs, health-screening services, health fairs, and wellness education seminars and newsletters. As the demand for these services has grown, so has the need for people who have

education and professional certification specific to the provision of worksite recreation and health promotion.

Recreation in the Armed Forces

Carol J. Potter and Laurie Ogilvie

" "Serving Those Who Serve" is not just a motto; it's a commitment to ensuring that the members of the Canadian Forces are fit, focused and operationally ready. Provision of recreational opportunities for them and their families is a key part of that commitment. "

Major General Langton, Canadian Forces Personnel and Family Support Services

" We are dedicated to providing support and leisure services that are as outstanding as the people we serve. "

United States Army Morale, Welfare and Recreation

Recreation programs in the Canadian and the United States armed forces are based on two basic philosophies: that members of the military and their families are entitled to the same quality of life as is afforded the society that they protect and that quality recreation programs have a direct impact on mission readiness. Recreation programs are designed to maintain a positive quality of life that leads to a sound mind and body, a productive community, and a strong family environment. Recreation programs for the Canadian and U.S. armed forces have unique requirements that set them apart from other public-sector programs. These programs must support military personnel and their families at their home stations as well as in deployed environments at remote sites around the world.

HISTORY

Recreation programs have existed in both Canada and the United States for hundreds of years. In the United States organized programs started on the battlefields of the Revolutionary War where "sutlers" were assigned the responsibility of providing for the personal needs of the soldiers. These itinerant merchants provided many of the services of the

present-day exchange stores, and a portion of their profits were returned to the units. These unit funds were the early structure under which our current recreation program is funded, and the funds were used for a variety of leisure activities, including reading libraries, financial assistance programs, bands, and school projects.

By the Civil War, sutlers had made themselves extinct by pricing themselves out of business, and their roles were assumed by "Canteen Associations," which became the essential social club for the unit and were authorized by Congress in 1893. These activities had naturally become centers for command sponsored social events and were recognized as important for promoting esprit de corps. Organized programs started on the battlefields of World War I, where the Salvation Army and Red Cross members ministered to the needs of soldiers as the forerunners of today's recreation specialists.

In 1940, at the beginning of World War II, the U.S. Morale Division, later named Special Services, was established in the U.S. Army. Between 1946 and 1955, core recreation programs were established and staffed by a combination of active-duty military personnel and civilians. Until the mid-1980s, active-duty personnel held occupational specialties in Special Services at every level of command. As

*The views of the author are her own and do not reflect an official position of the Department of Defense.

those specialties were discontinued, civilians continued to operate programs with military oversight as the program requirements grew and the senior commanders came to understand the value of recreation in mission readiness.

In Canada, it has long been recognized that the success of the Canadian military depends on the physical, emotional, and spiritual well-being of the **military community**. Throughout the history of the Canadian military, **morale and welfare** programs have been available to all serving members and their families with the goal of enhancing the quality of life of the military community and contributing to the **operational readiness and effectiveness** of the armed forces. In 1996, the Canadian Forces Personnel Support Agency (renamed to **Canadian Forces Personnel and Family Support Services**) was created with the mission of providing the military community with morale and welfare programs and services.

Today, in both Canada and the United States, recreation programs within the military environment are broad in scope, evolving constantly to meet the ever changing needs of the military community. The United States' armed forces use the common acronym **MWR** for **morale, welfare, and recreation** to refer to those programs, while in Canada, the **PSP Division**, or the **Personnel Support Division** of the Canadian Forces Personnel and Family Support Services, is the key provider of recreation services within the military environment.

MILITARY VERSUS CIVILIAN RECREATION

Military recreation departments are administered similarly to civilian recreation departments. Many of the programs, such as swimming lessons, leadership certifications, and recreation club activities are conducted in partnership with, or modeled on the products of, civilian agencies. Like their civilian counterparts, military recreation departments also employ many operational tools to more efficiently manage and profile programs and services. From recreation management software to online recreation brochures, military recreation strives to encourage participation, increase patronage, and enhance the benefits of recreation participation.

Although military recreation is modeled after civilian recreation programs, the unique environment and requirements of the military community result in several distinct differences between the two services providers. One of the key differences is the transient nature of the client. Military families relocate frequently. Programs and services based on the expressed need of the military community one year may be quite different the next as the families who make up the community relocate. Recreation professionals must constantly survey the military community, aware of the changing needs and interests of military families.

Secondly, many military communities are located in remote or unstable places around the world. Recreation opportunities are as important to the serving members in isolated or combat environments as they are to members and their families at the home station. Recreation professionals must be prepared and willing to provide services under difficult and sometimes dangerous conditions.

A third difference between civilian and military recreation is the scope of the recreation department. Civilian recreation departments provide service to the residents of their community and other interested users. Military recreation departments are exclusive, providing service to military members, their families, and other members of the military community.

Lastly, volunteer management can be challenging within the military community. Volunteers are a key contributor to the success of the military community recreation program. Without volunteers, many programs would be unsustainable, but with the high turnover of military families, managing volunteers is often difficult. MWR and PSP have developed viable volunteer management programs, striving to develop, support, and nurture the involvement of volunteers in recreation programs.

UNITED STATES ARMED FORCES

The **United States armed forces** provide a variety of recreation programs to maintain individual, family, and mission readiness during peacetime and in time of declared war and other contingencies. The United States armed forces are collectively the U.S. Army, U.S. Marine Corps, U.S. Navy, U.S. Air Force, and U.S. Coast Guard. Although the scope of each MWR program may vary slightly, the mission is to provide quality recreation programs to the United States' fighting forces, both at home and abroad.

Military MWR programs are an integral part of the military benefits package, encourage positive individual values, and build healthy families and communities. They provide consistently high-quality support services that are commonly furnished by other employers or state and local governments to their employees and citizens. MWR programs promote esprit de corps and provide for physical, cultural, and social needs; general well-being; quality of life; and hometown community support of service members and their families. Recreation programs are a vital factor in maintaining each force's ability to fight and win its nation's wars. The fighting forces need a balance of work and leisure to be ready to fight when needed, especially during frequent contingency operations. A contingency operation is a military operation that is either designated by the secretary of defense as a contingency operation in which members of the armed forces are or may become involved in military actions, operations, or hostilities against an enemy of the United States or against an opposing force or becomes a contingency operation as a matter of law. Families left behind during a deployment to a contingency operation must be cared for so that the service member can fight without worrying about those left at home.

Military mission readiness depends largely on the resilience of service members and their families. Resilience is important to the military to help overcome traumatic experiences, such as those encountered in contingency operations, to help family members better cope with deployments, to reduce stress, and to boost energy levels. Resilience is often described as the ability to respond to and cope with difficult or stressful experiences, situations, environments, people, and setbacks common to all in life. Although everything we do involves stress, how we respond to a particular stressor is important. Increasing the ability to handle stress and bounce back from the strains of daily life increases resilience.

MWR provides well-balanced recreation that normalizes behavior after a stressful experience. Participating in exercise and recreation programs reduces stress and builds both mental and physi-

cal resilience. Besides building resilience, MWR enhances mission readiness. This conclusion was demonstrated by findings from the Department of Defense customer satisfaction survey conducted in 2009 and 2011 to assess MWR programs. The survey findings indicated that MWR satisfaction has the greatest effect on mission readiness. This correlation is critical to understanding the importance of MWR recreation in building resilience and influencing military mission readiness throughout the armed forces.

During contingency operations, MWR equipment and deployed personnel provide MWR programs and activities that build unit esprit de corps, increase morale, relieve stress, and provide greatly needed mental diversion during these operations. Internet cafes with computers are operated by MWR at no cost to service members. MWR Internet cafes also offer webcams and headsets for making videos and phone calls using voice over Internet protocol (VOIP), which costs only a few cents per minute. In addition, service members have access to all the popular social network websites to communicate with family and friends. Portable morale satellite units provide free Internet access to remote, forward operating bases. Fitness, recreation, and social activities include cardiovascular and weight equipment, suspension training systems, sports, recreation, games, outdoor recreation equipment, large screen TVs, DVD and CD players, and up-to-date video games. Armed Forces Entertainment, in cooperation with the USO, provides much-welcomed celebrity and professional entertainment. The Department of Defense MWR On-line Library is available through the military services library portals, offering 24/7 one-stop shopping for all library resources in print, electronic, and downloadable formats. Free downloads of thousands of e-books and audio books and free access to comprehensive databases for recreation, lifelong learning, reference, and career transition are available for all ages and all interests. Additionally, monthly shipments of digital books and paperback books are provided to deployed units.

With an increasing number of service members returning from contingency operations with severe injuries, the MWR program provides recreation inclusion training for recreation programmers from all military services. Recognizing that recreation and sport play an important role in the recovery process, training concentrates on posttraumatic stress disorder, limb amputations, traumatic brain injury, spinal cord injuries, adaptive and specialized equipment, accessible design, age-appropriate inclusive recreation programming, and societal and cultural issues. Trained recreation programmers develop or expand inclusive recreation programs at their installations, which enables wounded warriors to develop their abilities and continue their military mission.

The MWR program provides recreation opportunities for people of all abilities to exercise and recreate. With programs ranging from outdoor recreation, fitness classes, team sports, and bowling, just to name a few, MWR helps individuals and units maintain physical fitness, alleviate combat stress, and foster total family fitness. By promoting exercise and recreation, MWR enables service members and families to build physical and mental resilience to stress and affects military mission readiness. The oversight for providing recreation services in the United States is governed by specific agencies within each branch of the military.

- **United States Army**. The U.S. Army Family and Morale, Welfare and Recreation Command (FMWRC) administers the MWR program through its headquarters office in San Antonio, Texas. It is a comprehensive network of quality support and leisure services that enhances the lives of soldiers, civilians, families, military retirees, and other eligible participants. MWR services and activities offer soldiers and their families' opportunities to enrich their lives culturally and creatively. The programs relieve stress, build strength and resilience, and help people stay physically, mentally, and financially fit. The unique challenge to the Army is the requirement to provide the same level of support to troops around the world regardless of the existence of a viable installation (location can vary from a military garrison in the United States to a tent in the desert).

- **United States Marine Corps**. The Marine Corps manages the MWR program through Marine Corps Community Services (MCCS) at its headquarters in Quantico, Virginia. MCCS provides fitness and recreation programs, personal services, and business activities to support individual and family readiness and retention. The vision of the Marine Corps MWR program is to make a difference in the lives of marines, reserves, retirees, and families by doing the right things the right way, in peacetime and in war. The MWR teams strive to provide marines and their families with programs that promote optimal health, quality of life, and mission readiness.

- **United States Navy**. The U.S. Navy Morale, Welfare and Recreation Division, located in Millington, Tennessee, and the Commander, Navy Installations Command, in Washington, DC, administer the MWR program to active-duty, reserve, and retired Navy personnel and their families. The mission is to provide quality support and recreation services that contribute to retention and readiness and the mental, physical, and emotional well-being of sailors. The Navy serves the needs of its members around the world at installations and on board ships at sea. Civilian recreation specialists carry out this mission work on installations in the United States and overseas and are assigned on board most of the Navy's larger ships to manage MWR programs and services.

- **United States Air Force**. The U.S. Air Force operates MWR programs through its headquarters office in San Antonio, Texas, under the title of Services Agency. The mission of the Air Force's MWR program is to contribute to mission readiness and improve productivity through programs that promote fitness, esprit de corps, and quality of life for Air Force people and to provide policy and direction for the worldwide services program to help sustain the Air Force mission. Although not normally considered recreation programs, activities such as mortuary services and wartime feeding are included under the umbrella of MWR services, which makes its program delivery broader than those of the other service branches.

- **United States Coast Guard**. The U.S. Coast Guard in the Department of Homeland Security provides recreation programs to its members worldwide. Although it is the smallest of the service branches, it offers a critical element in the quality-of-life programming for its members and their families. The mission of the Coast Guard Morale, Well-Being, and Recreation (MWR) program, operating out of Chesapeake, Virginia, is to uplift the spirits of the Coast Guard family and be an essential element of Coast Guard mission readiness and retention through customer-owned and customer-driven MWR programs and services.

CANADIAN ARMED FORCES

The mission of the **Canadian armed forces**, or the Department of National Defense, is to protect Canada, defend North America in cooperation with the United States, and to contribute to peace and international security. The Department of National Defense is one of the few Canadian institutions that reside exclusively under the authority of the federal government, with a presence in every Canadian province and territory, and represents the cultural, linguistic, and regional diversity of Canada. The Canadian Department of National Defense represents the many values that unite Canadians, such as helping those at home and abroad, peacekeeping, and protecting Canada.

The Department of National Defense is made up of more than 100,000 Canadians including members of the regular force, the reserve force, the Canadian Rangers, and civilian employees of defense. Within the Canadian Department of National Defense are three Environmental Commands: the Maritime Command, the Land Force, and the Air Command and numerous support divisions.

- **Maritime Command**. The goal of Canada's Navy is to conduct surveillance operations to protect the sovereignty of Canadian coasts and to defend Canadian waters against illegal fishing and ecological damage. The Navy also supports international initiatives for peace and humanitarian assistance.
- **Land Force Command**. The mission of Canada's Army is to perform and support peacekeeping, combat operations, and disaster recovery missions at home and abroad. In times of crises, the army delivers assistance and helps civil authorities restore public order.
- **Air Command**. Canada's Air Force provides surveillance and control of Canada's airspace, provides air transport of Canadian military personnel and equipment throughout the world, and supports army and navy operations. As with the other commands, the Air Force assists with humanitarian relief operations.

- **Military Community**. The Department of National Defense is made up of more than the Navy, Army, and Air Force members. Supporting departments, civilians, and military families contribute to the ongoing operations and continuity of the military community. Today, the military is present in more than 3,000 communities across Canada, with military members and their families representing more than half a million of the Canadian population.

Support for the Canadian armed forces' morale and welfare programs is administered through the Canadian Forces Personnel and Family Support Services headquarters, located in Ottawa, Ontario. The mission of the Canadian Forces Personnel and Family Support Services is "to enhance the quality of life of the military community and contribute to the operational readiness and effectiveness of the Canadian Forces" (www.cfpsa.com/en/corporate/NewsCentre/index.asp, 2010).

Canadian Morale and Welfare Programs

Throughout Canada and locations around the world, the Canadian Forces Personnel and Family Support Services delivers morale and welfare programs, facilities, and instruction to maintain military physical fitness and health. Physical education, leisure, and recreation opportunities are key components of the Canadian military morale and welfare program. Physical education programs are the primary means of ensuring that military personnel maintain required levels of physical fitness, while recreation programs make a positive contribution to a stable military environment and contribute to high levels of morale and operational efficiency.

In each military community, the Canadian Forces Personnel and Family Support Services offers a variety of fitness, recreation, sport, leisure, and special-interest programs and services to military members and their families. Gyms, field houses, swimming pools, golf courses, bowling alleys, meeting places for hobby clubs, sport fields, and arenas make up some of the facilities available in almost all Canadian military communities.

Recreation is a key component of the Canadian Forces Personnel and Family Support Services' mission to enhance the morale and welfare of the Canadian military. A well-balanced recreation program helps maintain total fitness, while reducing mental fatigue, tension, and frustration, all of which can develop within the military operational setting. In addition to the benefits of recreational participation for the military member, the well-being of the military family is a main consideration of the recreation mandate. Because of operational requirements, many military families live in remote communities, relocate frequently, and often live without the military member at home because of operational deployments. A comprehensive, varied, and universal recreation program gives military members assurance that their family is well cared for in their absence, and provides the military family with opportunities to engage in the community while maintaining or enhancing their personal morale and welfare.

Canadian Military Recreation Principles

The military recreation program is founded on seven governing principles, which support numerous recreation program components. The governing principles serve to

1. provide inclusive, creative, and diversified recreation opportunities for the military community;

2. address the physical, emotional, and social characteristics, interests, and needs of all members of the military community equally and consistently;

3. operate according to the needs and interest of the military community, making optimal use of supporting resources;

4. provide opportunities for leadership development;

5. create opportunities for individual and group growth and development through responsibility, accountability, and leadership in the planning and operating of recreational activities;

6. nurture partnerships with recognized recreational agencies for the provision of high-quality, responsive recreational services; and

7. ensure that recreational services are governed in accordance with Canadian military financial, operating, and management policies.

Soldiers take time out to play football. This necessary recreation helps to build physical and mental resilience to stress.

MILITARY RECREATION PROGRAM AREAS

In both Canada and the United States, the recreation mandate operates to serve a variety of MWR and PSP program offerings. These are sports and fitness, skill development, libraries, outdoor recreation, child and youth activities, recreation centers, special events and entertainment, business activities, recreation clubs, and private organizations.

• **Sports and fitness**. At the heart of every recreation program is the sports and fitness program. Because of the need to maintain a strong and healthy force, sports and fitness programs have long been recognized by military leadership as a key to mission readiness and have become the centerpiece of every MWR and PSP organization. These programs offer state-of-the-art gymnasium and fitness facilities as well as organized sports competitions from intramural to competitive levels.

• **Skill development**. A staple of the military recreation program's inventory is skill development through instructional classes. Instructional classes are organized in response to a community's interest in skill development and leadership opportunities. Instructional classes include specialty cardio workouts and aerobics, arts and crafts, camps, swimming lessons, weight training for youth, sport clinics, and leadership development. Programs are available for all ages and interests and are developed and implemented in consultation with members of the military community.

• **Libraries**. Libraries remain a vital part of most MWR programs in areas where the local communities cannot provide adequate or convenient services to the military population. Libraries vary in size and offerings but generally provide standard recreation reading inventories, reading programs, educational studies, research materials, Internet and e-mail services, and support services. Library programs have become especially crucial in supporting troops in deployed locations and on ships at sea around the world where no local civilian resources are available.

• **Outdoor recreation**. Outdoor recreation programs provide outdoor equipment and access to campgrounds, parks, beaches, and lakes as well as adventure programs and other activities that promote the care and protection of our natural resources. Because of the huge land masses placed under the care of military installations, a myriad of outdoor recreation opportunities are available. Military organizations are entrusted with the care and preservation of valuable natural resources and that responsibility provides the opportunity for military personnel to develop new skills while preserving and enjoying natural resources around the world.

• **Child and youth activities**. Child and youth programs and services are offered at all military locations where family support is offered. Programs offer various levels of support that include child development centers, youth centers, and youth activities such as skill development and sports programs. All programs are age appropriate and offer activities that focus on supporting transition, easing the stress of relocation, building and sustaining meaningful relationships, and developing a sense of belonging within the community. Activities that provide universal access to information, tools, resources, and services that support youth; activities that focus on the promotion of healthy and fulfilling life choices; and activities that encourage the development of leadership and assets in youth (40 assets developed by the Search Institute, www.search-institute.org) are also central to the recreation mandate.

• **Recreation centers**. Each military community offers a variety of drop-in opportunities for casual participation in unorganized recreation. Access to facilities and recreation services is available to military members as well as their families and provides a safe and comfortable environment for self-directed activities as well as for designed programs.

• **Special events and entertainment**. Each military community offers a variety of special events annually to profile military community activities and accomplishments, while honoring the contributions of volunteers and community partners. Many services host worldwide concert series tours, which provide live entertainment to troops, while others focus on local events and festivals.

• **Business activities**. A variety of pay-as-you-go activities geared toward leisure and fitness pursuits are available at most military locations. Theaters, golf courses, special-interest clubs, restaurants, night clubs, and bowling centers are popular activities enjoyed by military families. The operation of these types of commercial services is generally offered when no local off-base resources are readily available. These operations provide military members the type of services available in most civilian communities and provide a revenue source to support other morale and welfare activities.

- **Recreation clubs and private organizations**. Recreation clubs or private organizations are self-governing and self-funded entities operated for and by specific-interest groups in accordance with established constitutions and bylaws. Recreation club constitutions and bylaws are military directives that outline club operating principles and member codes of conduct. All recreation clubs are managed by a volunteer executive council and governed by its membership. Examples of recreation club activities include specialty arts, scuba, running, wood hobbies, sailing or marinas, martial arts, gymnastics, swimming, figure skating, and dancing and activities for auto and motorcycle, saddle, and rod and gun enthusiasts. These organizations are authorized when the MWR or PSP program cannot carry out programs in a viable manner because of resource limitations or when a special-interest group is willing and able to operate a self-directed program.

EMPLOYMENT OPPORTUNITIES

Military recreation provides vast employment opportunities because of the thousands of civilian employees around the world that make up the various MWR and PSP organizations. MWR employs more than 100,000 people in the United States and overseas. People entering employment in military recreation programs generally begin in a specialty such as outdoor recreation, club manager, or child development specialist and then move into general management positions within the personnel system. The personnel system may be paid for with federal tax dollars (appropriated funds) or paid for with revenue-generating activity funds (nonappropriated funds); both systems are parallel and considered civil service with portability between each. Careers in MWR are varied but generally start out at the entry level with progressions to the top of the civil service advancement ladder.

MWR assigns people to a variety of locations: from the beaches of California to the sands of the Afghan desert to the icy rivers of Alaska and the high seas of the Atlantic. The variety of both the job and the location means there's little opportunity for boredom in the business of providing recreation programs to the armed forces. MWR employees work hard so that others can have fun and enjoy life, and they do it seven days a week, sometimes 24 hours a day. The benefits of a career in MWR range from the great potential for upward mobility to the opportunity to travel and live abroad. See the web resource for Internet links within United States Armed Forces recreation programs.

In Canada, the Canadian Forces Personnel and Family Support Services is the largest employer of physical education, human kinetics, and leisure study graduates. The variety of positions and the potential for mobility between Canadian military locations contribute to the attractiveness of a career in the Canadian military recreation field. Most recreation positions within the Canadian Forces Personnel and Family Support Services require an undergraduate degree or college diploma plus specific qualifications, such as lifeguarding and first aid certifications or volunteer management certificates to match the position's requirements. Some senior management and director positions require postgraduate degrees and specialty knowledge and experience in the field of military morale and welfare. Furthermore, in recognition of Canada's linguistic diversity, most positions with the Canadian Forces Personnel and Family Support Services require proficiency in both French and English.

Each Canadian military recreation department is composed of a recreation director and various program-specific support staff, for example, an aquatics supervisor, a youth programmer, or an administration coordinator. Part-time staff, such as lifeguards, camp staff, and youth center monitors also provide programs directly to the military family. Throughout Canada, the Canadian Forces Personnel and Family Support Services employs more than 6,000 staff to deliver and support morale and welfare programming. See the web resource for Internet links within Canadian Armed Forces recreation programs.

SUMMARY

Nearly everyone, if not all, in the profession of armed forces recreation would tell you that they feel that they make a valuable contribution to the mission of the armed forces and are very proud to serve those who serve. Armed forces recreation professionals work around the world and strive to improve the quality of life for soldiers, marines, sailors, airmen, and coast guardsmen and their families serving their countries in difficult and challenging times.

Armed forces recreation professionals are proud to support their country's military mission because they believe in the importance of what they do for the armed forces and understand the impact that they have on mission readiness and, ultimately, the defense of their country. Much like their counterparts in the civilian sector, military recreation professionals must strive to ensure that the programs they provide are beneficial.

For glossary terms, learning experiences, and more, please visit the web resource at
www.HumanKinetics.com/IntroductionToRecreationAndLeisure

Leisure and Recreation Across the Life Span

Lynn A. Barnett and Joel A. Blanco

> " People do not cease to play because they grow old; people grow old because they cease to play. "
>
> George Bernard Shaw, playwright

LEARNING OUTCOMES

After reading this chapter, you should be able to do the following:

> Describe the developmental characteristics for each life stage that are the most relevant to the design of leisure and recreation services
> Explain how these developmental characteristics affect the delivery of leisure and recreation programs
> Describe model programs from various leisure and recreation sponsoring sectors that effectively address developmental characteristics through their program content and format

INTRODUCTION

The leisure and recreation industry is one of the largest in the world and increasingly plays a prominent role as a social and behavioral force. The role of leisure and recreation is recognized in national imperatives to improve physical and mental health; decrease risky behaviors such as substance use, sex, delinquency, and vandalism among youth; foster valuable social relationships among community members; and build contributing citizens. As the industry has grown, a corresponding shift has occurred in the overall mission of leisure and recreation services from fun and games to a focus on benefits that can be achieved through leisure and recreation engagement. This philosophical shift emphasizes that the activity itself is not the end point but rather the activity is the vehicle by which outcomes such as challenge, accomplishment, self-efficacy, self-expression, identity development, relationships, and enjoyment are accomplished. When programmers carefully consider how to manage the components of the leisure experience (facility, equipment, staffing, leadership) and appropriately address the developmental characteristics of the target audience, they greatly increase their ability to facilitate a leisure experience among participants. In short, recreation program planners and supervisors need to design programs from the participants' perspective, keeping their characteristics, abilities, needs, and interests in mind.

Life span psychologists generally describe development from three perspectives: **physical abilities** (physical growth, motor development, and sensory and perceptual development), **cognitive abilities** (thinking, reasoning, learning, memory, intelligence, and language), and **socioemotional characteristics** (personality, emotional and moral development, self-concept, identity, and social relationships). These three categories are used to discuss the nature of development within the seven generally accepted **life stages**: **infancy** (birth to 2 years), **early childhood** (3 to 6 years), **middle and late childhood** (7 to 12 years), **adolescence** (13 to 19 years), **early adulthood** (20 to 39 years), **middle adulthood** (40 to 59 years), and **late adulthood** (60 years and older). For each of these stages, developmental highlights are presented, key points for programming are offered, and examples of programs from various service sectors are discussed. This discussion of developmental characteristics and programming considerations is by no means intended to be comprehensive. Instead, we introduce some of the ways in which development shapes leisure engagement, which affords an important perspective from which to generate leisure opportunities and services.

INFANCY: FROM BABY TO TODDLER

Infancy is the time from birth until approximately 2 years of age. Rapid change occurs over this two-year period that affects how infants or toddlers function, move, and interact with the world around them. Physical, cognitive, and socioemotional milestones of this developmental stage are presented, followed by considerations for programming and examples from various leisure service sectors.

Developmental Highlights

During this first stage of life infants make large gains in gross (large-muscle) motor skills such as sitting up, rolling, and crawling. Cognitively, infants begin to grasp the concept of cause and effect, recognition, and memory. The beginning of infancy is also marked by the need to feel secure, and in the second year of life, as motor and cognitive skills develop, toddlers begin to realize their uniqueness, express their individuality, and initiate interactions with toys and peers. The major physical, cognitive, and socioemotional characteristics associated with this life stage are as follows.

Physical Abilities

The infant's physical development in the first two years is extensive and remarkable. New motor skills are the most dramatic and visible changes that occur in the first year of life, and they significantly increase the ability of infants to move and control their bodies. At birth, infants have little ability to coordinate their trunk or arms, but by their first birthday they can typically walk on their own, and they become increasingly independent in the second year. The age at which infants develop **gross motor skills** varies, but the sequence of these accomplishments remains fairly consistent.

Fine motor skills (small body movements) are more difficult for the toddler to master than gross motor skills because they require precise coordination of complex muscle groups. These skills develop in small steps, unlike some gross motor skills that seem to emerge quite suddenly, like standing up. The improvement of fine motor skills over the first two years of life is a reflection of the toddler's increasing eye–hand coordination. The age at which a particular baby first displays a particular motor skill depends on the interaction between inherited and environmental factors. Each infant has a genetic timetable for maturation, which can be faster or slower than that of other infants from other ethnic groups, from the same ethnic group, and even from the same family. The importance of early environmental experiences in the development of motor skills has been demonstrated in several research studies. Child development experts believe that motor activity during this stage is vital to the child's physical and **psychosocial development** and that few restrictions, except for safety reasons, should be placed on their motor escapades.

Cognitive Abilities

It is truly astounding that the infant began life as a single cell and nine months later is born with a brain and nervous system that contains about 100 billion neurons. The newborn's brain at birth is about 25 percent of its adult weight, but by the child's second birthday the brain has grown to be about 75 percent of its adult weight. The areas of the brain do not mature uniformly. Some areas, such as the primary motor areas, develop earlier than others, such as the primary sensory areas. Shortly after birth, a baby's brain produces trillions more connections between neurons than it can possibly use, and the brain eliminates the connections that are seldom or never used throughout the first 10 years of life. Before birth, genetic factors primarily direct how the brain establishes basic wiring patterns, but after birth, environmental experiences are important in the development of the brain.

Cognitive development in the first two years of life is extensive. During their first six months, infants have the ability to recognize the properties of objects and are able to sort them mentally into categories. The ability to understand cause-and-effect relationships develops slowly in the first few months of life, and toward the end of the first year, problem-solving abilities begin to develop. By their first birthday, most infants are able to set simple goals for themselves, and many have the knowledge and ability to achieve them. In their second year, toddlers actively experiment with actions and objects and thus find new ways to accomplish their goals. Toward the end of the second year, they are able to accomplish many new cognitive feats. They can mentally manipulate images of objects and behaviors, they can pretend, and they can remember what they saw several days before and then reenact it. All of these increased abilities broaden the toddler's styles and possibilities for play.

Socioemotional Characteristics

A newborn has a relatively stable and characteristic style of responding to the environment, which can be shaped and modified by later experiences. Research (Kagan, 2002, 2008, 2010) has shown that infants have characteristic temperaments. One infant might be cheerful and happy much of the time, whereas another baby might cry a lot and display a negative mood consistently more often. Infants show their unique personalities by differing from one another in their emotional responses to similar situations. Central to the development of the infant's personality are issues related to trust and independence (Erikson, 1968). The first year of life is characterized by a critical period in which the infant comes to regard the world as a secure place where basic needs will be readily satisfied, or instead as an unpredictable place where needs are met only after much crying, and sometimes not even then. The development of this sense of security inspires infants to have trust and confidence in their world. They can then explore and interact within the world with a minimal amount of fear and apprehension about the future. If infants become attached to an adult who will consistently meet their needs and provide comfort, the subsequent development of their self-concept, conscience, and emotional understanding will be greatly increased (Bowlby, 1989).

In the second year of life, infants are able to recognize themselves and see themselves as having a distinct and unique appearance. Along with this developing sense of self, independence becomes a more central theme in the toddler's life. Because of their developing mental and motor abilities and the sense of pride that they feel in their new accomplishments, toddlers seek autonomy. If their desire to do things themselves is met with encouragement rather than annoyance and constraints, they will develop a sense of confidence in their abilities. The sense of

Toddlers make efforts to communicate with one another, and by their second year they show elementary signs of peer play.

autonomy felt during the toddler years later gives adolescents the courage to be autonomous adults who can choose and guide their own future.

From early in their development, infants are captivated by the social world around them. Babies make efforts to communicate with one another, and by their second year they show elementary signs of peer play. The amount and variety of communication between peers is extensive by the middle of the second year of life. Children show their toys to one another, offer and give one another toys, invite peers to play with them, protest a playmate's actions, and, in general, communicate their feelings effectively to one another. As communication becomes more sophisticated, early signs of cooperative play can be seen.

Considerations for Program Design

Play takes several forms during infancy, and these should be considered when designing programs for even the youngest participants. Much of the play in the first few months of life is **sensorimotor** in nature and meant to stimulate and engage infants' sensory organs because they cannot yet grasp objects or coordinate their movements. Infants enjoy vivid colors, bright pictures, and sounds from rattles, noisemakers, mobiles, and music boxes. Face-to-face play often begins between the infant and her or his caretaker at about 2 to 3 months of age. The focused social interaction of face-to-face play may include vocalization, touch, and gestures. Because of these social interactions with their caregivers, at this age infants respond more positively to people than to objects. This frequency of face-to-face play decreases after 7 to 9 months of age as infants become more mobile. As infants develop the ability to crawl, walk, and run, they are able to explore and expand their world. Play programs for infants should allow physical contact with objects that extends purely visual exploration into opportunities to learn how things work and how the infant's movements can cause changes to toys, such as making things pop up, produce sounds, or move in different ways. Termed *manipulative play*, the infant's newfound ability to grasp, reach, and coordinate movements to make things happen provides for the fun derived from figuring out how to cause things to happen in the infant's world.

An atmosphere conducive to play must be arranged. The primary ingredient is freedom—freedom to make mistakes and messes. Play spaces that carry a lot of rules and restrictions are not conducive to play, nor are those where, for example, adults are constantly monitoring the noise level, trying to prevent the toddler's clothes from being wrinkled or dirtied, or are guiding the toddler to play with a toy in the "correct" way.

Examples From Recreation and Leisure Services Sectors

Public parks and recreation agencies usually offer a variety of programs and services for infants and toddlers, who are typically accompanied by a parent or other adult. Many programs feature music and movement because they are fun and facilitate gross motor skills, language, social development, and sensory stimulation. The following is an example of a program designed specifically for infants and toddlers that offers all of these features and is fun for this age group:

Parent and Child Creative Art Exploration

- Create fingerprint masterpieces, giant crayon artwork, and clay stamped pendants.
- Create art and experience the tactile feel of different materials, and learn new skills such as cutting, folding, rubbing, painting, gluing, and stamping.
- Choose an animal of the week or day, teach children about it, and follow with an art project inspired by how and where the animal lives.

Infancy is a time of rapid change and development that acquaints infants with people and objects in their environment. Gross motor skills develop and recognition of people, places, and objects occurs. Programs should foster development and prepare the infant for the next stage of life: early childhood.

EARLY CHILDHOOD: PRESCHOOL YEARS

Early childhood is the time between the ages of 2 and 6 years. Significant changes occur as toddlers grow taller and stronger and increase their energy level as well as their attention span. Developmental characteristics and programming considerations are presented for preschool children, along with things to consider in designing programs for children of this age.

Developmental Highlights

During this time significant improvement occurs in fine motor skills, and gross motor skills continue to be refined and coordinated. Cognitively, children's attention span increases, and they begin to engage in mental reasoning and symbolic thought. Symbolic thinking means that the child is able to think about objects even when the objects are not physically present. In this stage, they have strong desires to explore, take initiative, and interact with their peers. Pretend play and construction play are the dominant forms of play behavior.

Physical Abilities

During the preschool years, boys and girls slim down as the trunks of their bodies lengthen and body fat decreases. For the first time, sex differences in body type become apparent: Girls have more fatty tissue than boys do, and boys have more muscle tissue. Gross motor development during these years improves dramatically because bodies are becoming slimmer, stronger, and less top heavy and brain maturation permits greater control and coordination of the extremities. Children between the ages of 2 and 6 years move with greater speed and grace, and they become much more capable of directing and fine-tuning their movements.

Fine motor skills also show significant improvement. Although 3-year-old children have had the ability to pick up the tiniest objects for some time, they are still somewhat clumsy at doing so. By the end of this period children can construct buildings with blocks, draw colorful pictures of family members, and use scissors to cut along lines on paper with some accuracy. The difficulty that many preschool children experience with tasks requiring fine motor skills results from the fact that the central nervous system is not yet fully developed.

Cognitive Abilities

The brain continues to grow in early childhood, but it does not grow as rapidly as it did in infancy.

Because of their increased fine motor skills, preschoolers can draw colorful pictures of family members.

Children's emerging cognitive abilities stem from the increasing maturation of the brain combined with enhanced opportunities to experience an increasingly vast and more complicated world. Research has shown that during early childhood, the most rapid growth takes place in the areas of the brain involved in maintaining attention to tasks and in planning and organizing new actions (Anderson, Lorch, Field, Collins, & Nathan, 1985). Children also show an interest in, and begin to understand, the way that the mind works. At the beginning of this stage, they can connect desires to actions and simple emotions. For example, they are able to comprehend that people will seek what they want, and if they get it they will feel happy, but if they don't they will likely keep searching and feel sad and angry (Wellman & Woolley, 1990). One of the major developments at this age is that children come to realize that other children may have different desires and interests than they do (Doherty, 2008).

Preschool children's thoughts are determined more by their subjective views of the world than by reality. For example, at 3 years old, children believe that wishes usually come true and that

inanimate objects have lifelike qualities and are capable of action. This type of imaginative thinking declines by the later preschool years, thus allowing children the ability to take into account the actions and feelings of others in what they do and say. In other words, children begin to see things from others' perspectives and possibly adapt their behavior accordingly. Early childhood is also a time when mental reasoning emerges, reflecting a transition from primitive to more sophisticated use of symbols. The prevalence of pretend play during this age is a good example of the child's newfound ability to engage in symbolic thought.

The child's ability to pay attention changes significantly during the preschool years. Toddlers wander around, shift attention from one activity to another, and seem to spend little time focused on any one object or event. By comparison, the preschool child is able to spend much longer periods on a play episode or watching a video or television program. In addition, as children age, the speed and efficiency with which they can process information increase.

Their language ability continues to grow at a rapid pace. They progress from the ability to produce single sentences to more complex ones, and their knowledge of the elements of language (vocabulary, grammar, syntax, semantics, pragmatics) also increases with vigor. For that reason children at this age can hold intelligible conversations with adults and peers, and they show strong interest in reading books and writing stories.

Socioemotional Characteristics

During early childhood, children combine their increasing perceptual, motor, cognitive, and language skills to make things happen. They have a surplus of energy that allows them to venture in new directions and to take new initiatives—even if they seem dangerous. During these adventures they begin to hear their inner voice guiding and judging their activities. This inner voice is an early indication that young children can regulate their actions by considering possible consequences. Their initiatives and enthusiasm may bring them rewards or punishments. Initiatives are supported when their questions are answered, when they are given the freedom and opportunity to initiate motor play, and when they are not derided or inhibited in their fantasy or play activities. In contrast, if children are made to feel that their motor activity is imperfect, that their questions are a nuisance, or that their play is silly or foolish, they will likely develop a sense of guilt over self-initiated activities that may persist through life's later stages.

As children grow older, peer relationships consume an increasing amount of their time and energy. One of the most important functions of these same-age peer interactions is to provide children with a source of information and comparison. At this stage, children are able to compare themselves to others and thus achieve greater understanding of who they are and where they fit in relation to their peers. Research has shown that play with peers has significant value. It releases tension, advances cognitive development, increases exploration, promotes attachments to others, helps children deal with problems and traumatic events, and provides a safe haven in which to engage in potentially dangerous behavior (Barnett, 1991). The preschool years are generally recognized as the golden years of pretend, or make-believe, play; at no other time in life is a human being so thoroughly involved in the world of fantasy. The ratio of activities involving make-believe to all episodes of free play increases significantly from the age of 3 to the age of 6. Pretend play makes up approximately two-thirds of all play of preschool children.

Considerations for Program Design

Being overweight is a serious health issue in early childhood. The increasing prevalence of childhood obesity in our society has led many to label it a national epidemic. Obesity is of special concern at this age because being overweight in the preschool years carries over into adolescent and adult ages (Sorte, Daeschel, & Amador, 2011) and places the child at risk for developing a number of serious illnesses now and in later life (type 2 diabetes, hypertension, respiratory problems). An important part of warding off childhood obesity is active play, both structured and unstructured. Research shows that few children are getting the recommended one hour of physical activity per day (National Association for Sport and Physical Education, 2012). The recreation professional can play a huge role in designing programs that are fun and help children meet this goal.

Examples From Recreation and Leisure Services Sectors

The rapidly developing coordination of gross motor skills and the development of fine motor skills provide numerous opportunities for physically active play and the use of imagination and symbolism. The provision of raw materials (blocks, clay, drawing supplies, for example) can sustain play for long periods as the child's imagination continually reframes his or her play world. Recreation programs should focus on providing raw materials and maximizing opportunities for creative expression. The following is an example of a program for physically active play.

Overcoming obstacles. Negotiating an obstacle course made up of a variety of materials and a range of age-appropriate challenges is fun for children on their tricycles, Big Wheels, or scooters. Because their gross motor coordination naturally improves during this stage, testing out their newfound skills is naturally fun and stimulating. Providing a colorful series of pathways with various markings, obstructions, and barriers can sustain their attention for a long time as they gleefully try to master the course.

Early childhood is a time when children enjoy undertaking initiatives to test their expanded skills and abilities. Whether they are using gross or fine motor skills, memory, attention, language, construction, or symbolic play, children should be active and exploring at this stage. The promotion of active play opportunities to keep children healthy results in benefits that extend into the next stage and well beyond.

MIDDLE AND LATE CHILDHOOD: ELEMENTARY SCHOOL YEARS

Children 7 to 12 years old are in the stage termed middle and late childhood. The developmental tasks of this stage are more sophisticated because cognitive and motor skills become more complex and refined. Physical, cognitive, and socioemotional tasks associated with this stage of development are discussed and considerations for program planning are presented.

Developmental Highlights

Although physical growth is slower and more consistent during middle and late childhood than it is in other life stages, cognitive and physical changes are dramatic. School age children can skillfully manipulate objects, pay attention for longer periods, and think logically. Friendships and acceptance by peers also become important during this stage.

Physical Abilities

During the elementary school years, physical growth is slow and consistent. Improved muscle tone results as muscle mass gradually increases. Children double their strength capabilities during these years, which allows them to run faster, climb, and move their weight more easily. Lung capacity also expands, so that with each passing year children can play actively for longer periods. During this period, children's motor skills become much smoother and more coordinated than they were in early childhood. As children move through the elementary school years, they gain greater control over their bodies and can sit and attend for longer periods. But children in this age range are far from reaching their physical maturity, and they need to be active.

Fine motor skills continue to improve and are refined during middle and late childhood. Children can use their hands more steadily and more adroitly than they were able to in earlier years. At 10 to 12 years old, children begin to show a level of skillful manipulation similar to the abilities of adults. The intricate, precise, and complex movements needed to produce fine-quality crafts or to play a difficult piece of music can be readily mastered.

Cognitive Abilities

A 9- or 10-year-old has very different thought processes from those of a preschool child. Older children not only know more but also use their minds much more skillfully and effectively when they must solve a problem or remember information. Their thought processes involve considering evidence, planning, thinking logically, and formulating alternative hypotheses, and they try to incorporate these abilities into their reasoning. One of the most important cognitive achievements of middle childhood is the ability to reason logically about things and events. Children acquire an understanding of logical principles, and they know how to apply them in specific, concrete situations. Children's logical thinking, acquisition of knowledge, and ability to communicate clearly and persuasively with others illustrate major developmental differences between children of preschool and elementary school ages.

A major advance related to cognitive development centers on the issue of children's intelligence. For many years, the assessment of intelligence related to the child's ability to solve mathematical problems, comprehend passages of written materials, and memorize words that are presented quickly and appear at random. Recent research has rejected this narrow perspective and instead has put forth the idea that there are multiple types of intelligence and that these collectively constitute a better assessment of the child's competencies and intelligence. The original definition has been broadened to include proficiency in solving practical problems,

Children of elementary school age begin to show a level of skillful manipulation allowing them to play a difficult piece of music.

social skill development, musical aptitude, and self-understanding, among others (Gardner, 1983, 1993, 2002). This new way of thinking about the child is being incorporated into more school curricula and has spawned appreciation of individual differences among children.

Socioemotional Characteristics

Several noted theorists such as Freud and Erikson have posited that middle childhood is a quiet or relatively uneventful period emotionally because changes in emotional development are not as dramatic as those that occur in early childhood or adolescence. During this period, children are interested in learning how things are made and how they work, and they struggle to master cultural values such as social norms. Based on their degree of success, children come to view themselves as either industrious or inferior, competent or incompetent, productive or failing, winners or losers. When adults encourage children in their efforts, a sense of industry increases, but when their efforts are viewed as mischief or making a mess, a sense of inferiority results. Children's social worlds beyond their parents and family also contribute to attaining a self-view of being industrious rather than inferior.

During middle and late childhood, children spend increasingly more time with their peers, which leads to the child's sense of competence. In middle childhood, children tend to become more dependent on each other not only for companionship but also for self-validation and advice. When school-aged children play together, they develop patterns of interaction that are distinct from those of adult society and culture. They have special norms, vocabulary, rituals, and rules of behavior that flourish without the approval, or sometimes even the knowledge, of adults.

Although acceptance by the peer group is valued, personal friendships are even more important. Increases in their emotional understanding lead to the ability to self-regulate emotional responses so that they become more situation appropriate. Children also now have the capacity for genuine empathy so that, for example, they can feel sympathy for a distressed friend. The acquisition of these newfound emotional skills allows intimate friendships to develop and grow. Research has identified six functions of children's friendships at this age and provided evidence of the importance of each to the child's healthy development (Gottman & Parker, 1987). These functions are

- **companionship** (providing a partner and playmate who will spend time and join in collaborative activities),
- **stimulation** (providing interesting information, excitement, and amusement),
- **physical support** (offering time, resources, and assistance),
- **ego support** (providing the expectation of support, encouragement, and feedback, which helps the child maintain an impression of himself or herself as competent, attractive, and worthwhile),
- **social comparison** (providing information about where the child stands in relation to others and whether the child is "OK"), and
- **intimacy and affection** (offering a warm, close, trusting relationship with another in which sharing and self-disclosure take place).

The importance of these functions of friendship in the child's life cannot be overemphasized. Researchers generally agree that during this age, peers play a more central role in socializing the child than the parents do, primarily because of these functions of friendship and the consequences of peer isolation. Recent national studies have shown that children at this age in particular are frequently victimized by bullies (Vernberg & Biggs, 2010). Being the target of a bully can have profound and lasting effects, and can lead to social withdrawal, feelings of isolation, depression, anxiety, and at later ages, drug and alcohol abuse and ideation and actual attempts at suicide. Recognizing the critical value of social interactions for the developing school-aged child thus becomes important in the design and delivery of leisure programs and services.

Considerations for Program Design

School-aged children in the United States and other Western nations on average spend 40 to 50 percent of their waking hours in discretionary activities outside school (Larson and Verma, 1999). How these children use this free time has important consequences for their development. Participation in organized activities is common. For example, 84 percent of 6- to 11-year-olds participated in one or more sports, lessons, or clubs during the past year (Tab, 2006). These organized activities occur outside school and are characterized by adult supervision, a defined structure, and an emphasis on skill building. Unfortunately, the most common out-of-school activities include sedentary activities, such as watching television, playing video games, or just "hanging out." A diversity of active programs should continue to be readily available to children of this age. The findings of a great deal of research consistently show that a significant number of important benefits accrue to children who are regularly engaged in activity during the out-of-school hours (Barnett, 1991; Mahoney, Larson, & Eccles, 2005). Recreation programmers should be aware of these benefits and the importance of designing and providing attractive, fun, and active games and programs for children of this age.

Examples From Recreation and Leisure Services Sectors

Activities that allow children to apply their dramatic improvements in fine motor skills, attention span, and cognitive problem solving should be incorporated into recreation programs for children in this age group. In addition, the desire to be with friends and feel accepted and valued by peers strongly suggests that recreation programs should afford a multiplicity of social opportunities. The example here pertains to the desire to empower children to feel comfortable being individually expressive and to expand their world of fun things to which they have been exposed.

Exposing children to various forms of art and creativity. A continuation of exposure to various artistic mediums and opportunities for creativity and individual composition can be addressed with projects involving melted glass that can be used to make picture frames, light catchers, jewelry, holiday designs, or other concoctions.

This stage of the life span is a relatively easy age group for whom to design recreational activities and programs of both short and long durations. Their natural affinity to be physically active, combined with their advancing cognitive and social skills, motivates them to be curious and want to engage with their surroundings. Besides the traditional sports that peak in popularity at this time for both boys and girls, many other opportunities can be offered by professionals. As cognitive skills continue to increase and the role played by peers climbs to dramatic heights, adolescents seek their own range of testing and enjoyable experiences, as we shall see in the next section.

ADOLESCENCE: TEENAGE YEARS

Adolescence occurs between the ages of 13 and 19 years. Near the beginning of this stage, teenagers experience puberty, which has substantial effects on their physical, emotional, and cognitive development. In American culture, adolescents become more independent from their parents and begin to form intimate friendships and romantic relationships. These and other developments present both implications and challenges for programmers.

Developmental Highlights

Adolescence is highlighted by significant socioemotional change focused on developing self-concept and identity. Moreover, physical maturation occurs as teens experience changes associated with puberty. The cognitive processing and memory of teenagers increase significantly, and they can consider hypothetical situations more effectively than younger children can.

Physical Abilities

A noticeable growth spurt occurs in adolescence—a sudden, uneven, and somewhat unpredictable jump in the size of almost every part of the body. While their bones lengthen, adolescents eat more and gain weight more rapidly than before, primarily to provide energy for the many changes taking place. A height spurt follows soon after the start of the weight increase, burning up some of the stored fat and redistributing some of the rest. In the following one to two years, muscle mass increases, and the pudgy and clumsy appearance typical of early puberty generally disappears.

Adolescence has been regarded as a period of transition from childhood to adulthood. Rapid physical maturation involving hormonal and bodily changes occurs with puberty. This change often plunges adolescents into a preoccupation with their bodies and a perception of what their bodies are and should be like. Early and late maturation, social comparisons with peers, and differing amounts of peer attention contribute to emerging sexual feelings, experimentation, and the formation of sexual identity.

Cognitive Abilities

Adolescent thought is qualitatively different from a child's thought. Cognition is different and more advanced—the result of improvements in cognitive processing and memory as well as exposure to a new type and culture of learning in school. The single most distinguishing feature of adolescent thought is the capacity to think of possibilities, not just reality or practicalities (Keating, 1990). This ability to think in terms of possibility allows adolescents to fantasize, speculate, and hypothesize more readily and on a far grander scale than children, who are still tied to the tangible reality of the here and now.

Although adolescents make great stride in terms of logical capabilities, they remain limited in terms of emotional management. During this phase, teenagers show development in an area of the brain that controls intense emotional output, such as anger. Another area of the brain, which aids in reasoning control over emotion, does not mature until after adolescence. This circumstance can work against teenagers' new logical abilities during times of intense emotion.

Teenagers are in a position to make personal decisions and independent choices that could have far-reaching consequences for their future. They can decide, for example, what and how diligently to study, whether and where to go to college, whom to befriend, what career to pursue, whether to become sexually active, whether to use drugs, and whether to take a part-time job. Because they think about possibilities but are often significantly influenced by emotion, few adolescents decide these issues in a rational manner (Keating, 1990).

Socioemotional Characteristics

This period is primarily the story of developing an identity. Adolescence is a time when teenagers try

During adolescence peer relationships become increasingly important.

to find out who they are, what they are all about, and where they are headed in life. Although identity formation is a gradual process that begins in infancy and lasts into old age, adolescence is the first time that physical, cognitive, and social development is advanced to the point that the person can reflect on experiences and construct a feasible path toward adult maturity. At this age adolescents need to experiment actively with the numerous roles and identities that they draw from the surrounding culture. A person who develops a healthy identity is flexible, adaptive, and open to changes in society, in relationships, and in careers. Adolescents who do not successfully experiment with and commit to an identity can become confused and may withdraw, isolating themselves from peers and family, or they may lose their identity in a crowd (Bosma & Kunnen, 2001).

As adolescents learn to be less reliant on parents, they become increasingly dependent on friends to satisfy several of their basic needs such as secure attachment, playful companionship, social acceptance, intimacy, and sexual relations; thus, their experiences with friends increasingly shape their sense of well-being. In particular, the need for

intimacy intensifies during adolescence, motivating teenagers to seek close friends and significant others. Teenagers with superficial relationships, or no close friendships at all, report feeling lonelier and more depressed, and they have lower self-esteem compared with teenagers who have intimate friendships (Berndt, 2002; Yin, Buhrmester, & Hibbard, 1996). As peers gain in importance and influence, young adolescents conform to peer standards; this conformity to peer pressure in adolescence can be positive, such as doing charity work as part of a group, or negative, such as being part of a group that steals, vandalizes, uses illegal substances, or ridicules others.

Teens spend a considerable amount of time either dating or thinking about dating. In many cultures, dating is a form of recreation, a source of status and achievement, and a setting for learning about close relationships. Early romantic relationships serve as an arena for adolescents to explore how they should romantically interact with someone, how attractive they are, and how all of this appears to their peer group. The **sociocultural** context exerts a powerful influence on the functions of adolescent dating as well as on dating patterns. Values and religious beliefs of people in various cultures often dictate how old adolescents should be before they begin dating, how much freedom in dating is allowed, whether dates must be chaperoned by adults or parents, and what roles males and females should have in dating.

Considerations for Program Design

Recreational professionals involved in adolescent programming face unique challenges, but they also have the potential to create a genuine positive effect on young people. As previously mentioned, teenagers face increased risks for many unhealthy and negative behaviors. Positive recreational experiences, however, can reduce these risks and focus adolescents toward healthier behaviors. One barrier to successful programming can be a generation gap between the programmer and the young people whom he or she is trying to reach. An adolescent generation gap has been part of American culture since the 1950s. Teenagers have their own sense of fashion, language, music, and cultural norms. Programmers who try to mimic this culture often merely look silly and might discourage adolescents from participating.

This issue should not discourage recreational programmers from working with this population. Instead, programmers should provide a structured and safe environment while giving young people the opportunity to take greater control in designing their own recreational experiences. Adolescent programming can harness the new cognitive abilities that were not present in earlier stages of development. With increased cognitive abilities, teenagers can often develop creative programming ideas that appeal to their demographic. Allowing teenagers to have greater responsibility for creating leisure experiences can assist them in further developing these abilities, helping to create a more capable teenage population.

Recreation professionals can model appropriate behaviors and serve in an advisory capacity while leaving many decisions to young people. One of the main roles of the professional will be maintaining an inclusive and safe environment. Although adolescents may have the cognitive tools for creative programming, their tendency to overlook potential

consequences must be scrutinized. In addition to monitoring safety concerns, programmers should ensure that recreational programs are inclusive to all who want to participate. Teenagers can be cliquish, and adults will sometimes have to try to break down social barriers.

Examples From Recreation and Leisure Services Sectors

Continuing advancement in adolescents' physical and cognitive abilities is an important factor that should be taken into account when designing programs for this age group. Along with these considerations, programmers should incorporate teenagers' ability and desire to take increasing levels of control in making their leisure choices. The following suggestion illustrates a programmer's ability to cede some decisions and control to adolescent participants while maintaining a safe and inclusive activity.

Low and high ropes activities. The provision of these types of activities incorporates many of the elements that create a successful teen program. The activity typically begins with elements that are low to the ground but involve problem solving in a group setting. As adolescents become comfortable with this first phase, they are met with increasing challenges by moving to elements that are higher off the ground. Teens will need to rely on teamwork and trust in their fellow group members to accomplish tasks. They will also be able to use their advanced physical abilities in new and exciting activities such as rock climbing and rappelling. Although adolescents will be able to make many decisions on their own, properly trained recreational professionals should be on the scene to monitor safety and other concerns.

Adolescence is a time for teens to explore their identities, experiment with various roles, and explore romantic relationships. During this time, teens become more autonomous and desire more control over their activities and environments. Therefore, recreation programmers need to provide flexible and appealing environments and activities that facilitate this exploration in an active and healthy manner. Although these ideas can each help create a successful program, programmers need to remember that adolescents also enjoy unstructured social experiences that allow them to hang out with their peers. Most times simply providing a safe and supervised environment in which teens can socialize will be highly successful. Recreation professionals will still be accomplishing the goals pertaining to this age group by allowing teens to make individual choices while ensuring a safe and inclusive environment.

EMERGING AND EARLY ADULTHOOD: 20S AND 30S

Early adulthood has traditionally been defined as the ages between 20 and 39 years. Recently, developmental scholars have begun to recognize a separate phase called **emerging adulthood**, which occurs before entrance into early adulthood (Arnett, 2000). Many significant changes occur as young adults begin careers and make important choices about relationships and marriage. The physical, cognitive, and socioemotional characteristics of young adulthood are presented along with considerations for planning recreation programs for this age group.

Developmental Highlights

Early adulthood is focused on developing a career path and looking for a significant other with whom to share the joys and challenges of life. Physical performance and health are at their peak during this time, and much of leisure tends to center on social and physical pursuits.

Physical Abilities

During early adulthood, particularly between the ages of 19 and 26, most people are healthiest and reach their peak physical performance. Young adults have fewer colds and respiratory problems than they did when they were children, and few have chronic health problems. Young adults can draw on these physical resources for a great deal of physical activity and pleasure, often bouncing back easily from physical stress and abuse. The hidden danger is that physical exhilaration can lead them to push their bodies too far. The negative effects of abusing the body may not show up in emerging adulthood, but they will probably surface later in early adulthood or in the middle adulthood years.

Young adults reach peak physical performance during early adulthood but begin to decline in physical performance during the latter half of this age period. About the age of 30 or shortly thereafter, muscle tone and strength usually begin to show signs of decline, the body's fatty tissue increases, the lens of the eye loses some of its elasticity and becomes less able to change shape and focus on near objects, and hearing begins to deteriorate. During emerging adulthood, the body's resiliency has typically been able to compensate for poor health habits. With increasing age, however, these behaviors begin to exert more consequences. Many of these changes can be improved by reducing the incidence of certain health-impairing lifestyles, such as overeating, and by engaging in healthy lifestyles that include good eating habits, regular exercise, and not abusing alcohol or drugs.

Cognitive Abilities

Some developmental psychologists believe that many people do not consolidate their thinking skills until adulthood. Adolescents may begin to plan and hypothesize about intellectual problems, but people become more systematic and sophisticated at this process as young adults. Young adults engage in more reflective judgment when solving problems, and they think deeply about many aspects of politics, their careers and work, relationships, and other areas of life. They also become more skeptical about whether there is a single truth and often are not willing to accept an answer as final. As young adults move into the world of work and begin to face many of the constraints imposed by reality, the idealism that they held as adolescents declines.

Socioemotional Characteristics

In American culture, economic independence is seen as one of the major indicators of achieving adult status. As our economy has shifted to an information model, the age at which individuals first obtain a "real" job has come later. The number of students going to college has increased, and fewer adults are entering the work force immediately after high school. Along with this trend, other social markers of adulthood such as marriage and parenthood are also being delayed.

Several key markers characterize emerging adulthood. Without dependents or social obligations, this group has the ability to be highly focused on their own identity and development. Although adolescents explore their physical identity, emerging adults are preoccupied with their careers and romantic identities as they work toward full adulthood. Many leisure activities will be social gatherings designed for singles to meet one another. But feelings of being in transition and uncertainty in self can also be part of this phase. Emerging adults often change relationships, residences, and jobs. These situations can lead to stress as emerging adults work toward achieving maturity and independence.

As people negotiate these stresses, they will transition into early adulthood through social markers such as permanent employment, marriage, and children. In this phase, recreational interests will change based on life situations. Leisure activities will increasingly take place in a family setting. Social gatherings will become more centered on children's activities, and social groups may be composed of others with children of similar ages.

A wide range of lifestyles can be found in early adulthood. The percentage of adults in their 20s and 30s who choose to remain single has risen dramatically. A growing number of people choose cohabitation before marriage. The past decade has witnessed a significant increase in both the number of adults who engage in this lifestyle and the acceptance of what once was considered an unconventional choice. Progress through development should be based more on life situation than on actual age. Researchers have found that gay and lesbian relationships are similar to heterosexual relationships in their satisfactions, loves, joys, and conflicts (Hyde & DeLamater, 2003; Peplau & Beals, 2002).

Considerations for Program Design

Developmental tasks during young adulthood focus on career development and establishing or enhancing personal relationships. Leisure activities reflect these issues because they are often centered on networking and socializing. Because of the diversity in lifestyles seen during these years, programmers must be sensitive to the needs and interests of various groups. When developing recreational programs for people within this age group, programmers need to recognize the wide range of lifestyles that can be present. In previous developmental phases most people will be in similar situations, typically marked by advancement though primary and secondary education. But as people enter early adulthood, this uniform similarity will disappear as people choose various and diverse paths through life. Recreational professionals can no longer consider only age when designing and implementing programs.

Instead, managers should identify a specific target audience for each program. Programming for college undergraduates will be very different from a program for working professionals, even if those attending the programs are of the same age. Networking and social events are important to young adults as they work to expand and develop friendships beyond those that they made in high school and college. These events and networks can be useful from a professional and personal perspective as people try to further their careers and perhaps find romantic partners. But as early adults enter into marriage and parenthood, their leisure may become more focused on their individual family units. Programming for these people can center on individuals, families, or group of families with children of similar ages.

Additionally, even as people begin moving into traditional adulthood, greater variety in lifestyles now exists than during previous generations. The content, timing, and environmental requirements of recreation programs must be tailored to the lifestyles of the participants, often requiring a range in both how and when programs are offered and staffed. The proportion of traditional heterosexual dual-parent families is on the decline, and both public and private recreation providers must be aware of the changing demographics of their clientele.

Examples From Recreation and Leisure Services Sectors

For this age group, various lifestyle choices will be accompanied by differing goals for leisure time use. Recreation professionals should be aware of these differences and adjust their programs accordingly. While individuals are still in the emerging adulthood stage, much of their leisure will be centered on socialization with others in the same transitioning life stage. Often the goal of these activities will be to find and develop friendly or romantic relationships.

Outdoor recreation activities such as trust activities appeal to adults because in general they desire social opportunities and possess the cognitive and physical skills necessary to engage.

After a person transitions out of emerging adulthood, recreational goals may change. Considering the needs of each group before planning a program can greatly assist in providing and directing a successful program. The following activity uses technology to meet this age group's socialization needs.

Social networking. Today's emerging and young adults are more technologically well informed than those of previous generations. People with specific interests are increasingly using computer networking to locate and contact one another and coordinate leisure activities. Social networks can provide a cost-effective resource for leisure providers to market their programs to a specific audience.

People in emerging and early adulthood have diverse lifestyles, but leisure remains centered on beginning, or further developing, relationships. Whether this occurs between a new friend with a similar interest or among a family unit that is recreating together, a tailor-made leisure program can assist people in forming and maintaining bonds.

MIDDLE ADULTHOOD: 40S AND 50S

Middle adulthood is the time between the ages of 40 and 59. Although physical aging and decline become more noticeable in this stage, middle adults continue to make gains in some aspects of their cognitive abilities. The developmental characteristics of middle adulthood and programming considerations are discussed in the following sections.

Developmental Highlights

During middle adulthood, people begin to show signs of their age, and the risk of developing chronic disease increases significantly. Although these risks increase from previous developmental stages, they can be substantially reduced by healthy lifestyle choices. People in this stage have the benefit of life experience that enhances reasoning and problem solving. During this life stage, adults seek to evaluate the influence that they are having on others and society through work, raising a family, community activities, and so on.

Physical Abilities

Physical changes in middle adulthood are usually gradual. Although everyone experiences physical changes during midlife, the rate of aging varies considerably from one person to another. One of the most noticeable signs of bodily changes in middle adulthood is physical ability. Muscle strength decreases noticeably by the mid-40s, and many people experience joint stiffness and more difficulty in movement because the cushions that surround bones become less efficient. From middle adulthood on, bone loss is progressive; the rate of this bone loss begins slowly but accelerates in the 50s. People also lose inches in height during middle age, and many gain weight. Obesity increases the likelihood of several ailments, among them hypertension, diabetes, and digestive disorders. For people who are 30 percent or more overweight, the probability of dying in middle adulthood increases by about 40 percent.

Changes to the sensory organs and cardiovascular system are also observable in middle adulthood. Hearing may no longer be as acute, and the ability of the eye to focus and maintain an image experiences its sharpest decline during this period. When weight is not controlled, cardiovascular disease increases considerably in middle age. Blood pressure usually rises as people move into their 40s and 50s. The lining of the blood vessels shows increased fatty deposits, and scar tissue slowly accumulates, gradually reducing blood flow to various organs, such as the heart and brain. Regular exercise, weight control, and a diet rich in fruits, vegetables, and whole grains can often help to stave off many cardiovascular problems in middle adulthood.

Although a certain amount of physical deterioration is inevitable, much of this is under a person's control based on lifestyle choices. Some evidence indicates that when healthy choices are made, the current cohort of middle adults is among the healthiest in history. Because of medical advances and greater knowledge of the importance of diet and exercise, current deaths in middle adulthood from cardiovascular disease are low compared with previous decades (Coccheri, 2010; Lewis, 2009). Thus, middle-aged adults have a great deal of influence on their abilities during this time. Many middle adults are able to continue active leisure patterns throughout this developmental phase. It remains to be seen what will happen to the current group of children suffering from the obesity epidemic when they reach middle adulthood, but many people in the current cohort maintain abilities longer than did those of previous generations. The appearance and onset of a chronic illness during middle adulthood are determined largely by genetic makeup and lifestyle factors. At some time during this age range, women usually reach menopause. The changes that women in midlife experience caused by the decline in certain hormones, especially estrogen, progesterone, and testosterone, and cessation of menstruation and ovulation are problematic for only a minority of women.

Cognitive Abilities

Many have wondered whether declines in cognitive abilities mirror the decline in physical character-istics in middle adulthood. Longitudinal research examining people's intellectual abilities through the adult years has found that four of six areas of mental functioning actually reach their highest level during the middle adulthood years (Schaie, 2005, 2010). Vocabulary (understanding ideas expressed in words), verbal memory (encoding and recalling meaningful words), inductive reasoning (recognizing and understanding patterns and relationships in a problem and using this understanding to solve other instances of the problem), and spatial orientation (visualizing and mentally rotating stimuli in two- and three-dimensional space) show peak performance during the middle adulthood years. In only two of the six cognitive areas—numerical ability (performing simple mathematical computations) and perceptual speed (quickly and accurately making simple discriminations in visual stimuli)—do declines occur in middle adulthood.

Practical problem-solving ability often increases through the 40s and 50s as people accumulate experience. People become more adept at handling real-world problems, the result of a history of employing strategies to address those issues. Expertise—having extensive, highly organized knowledge and understanding of a particular topic or domain—often increases in the middle adulthood years.

Socioemotional Characteristics

For middle-aged adults, having a positive identity has been linked with **generativity**—people's desire to leave a legacy of themselves to the next generation, thereby achieving a sense of immortality. People can achieve generativity in a variety of ways. One of these is through birthing and raising children, known as biological and parental generativity. Middle-aged adults can also achieve generativity through their careers, called work generativity. They can achieve cultural generativity by working in their community through volunteering or paid employment in a manner that will be remembered. In contrast, when people sense that they have done nothing for the next generation, a sense of **stagnation** may result.

Middle adulthood has been viewed as a period of life when people question how they should spend their time and often reassess their priorities. Midlife can be a time of evaluation, assessment, and reflection in terms of the work that people do and want

Midlife is a time when adults find that volunteering satisfies an important need to contribute to society and support the development of youth.

to do in the future. One common outcome of this reconsideration of working life is placing additional emphasis on leisure. Leisure can be an especially important aspect of middle adulthood because of the changes that many people experience during this time. For many people, middle adulthood is the first time that they have the opportunity to diversify their interests. By middle adulthood, more money is usually available, and more free time and paid vacations may be available. These changes typically produce expanded opportunities for leisure. Adults at midlife may also begin preparing psychologically for retirement. Constructive and fulfilling leisure activities in middle adulthood have been shown to be an important part of this preparation (Mannell, 2000). If an adult develops leisure activities that can be continued into retirement, the transition from work to retirement can be less stressful.

An important event in a family is the launching of a child into a career or his or her own family. This event typically creates disequilibrium in the family of origin and requires adjustments to be made to the child's absence. The term *empty nest syndrome* has been given to the situation in which the departure of children creates feelings of emptiness or unrest because the satisfaction that the parents felt from their children wanes as the children leave the nest. This circumstance may create a decline in marital

or life satisfaction, particularly for parents who lived vicariously through their children. For many other parents, however, the departure of their children gives them time to pursue career interests and share more time and experiences together.

Considerations for Program Design

Middle adulthood is a time in life when people wrestle with greater health concerns and establishing a sense of generativity. Leisure experiences can be highly effective when recreational professionals design programs that emphasize these areas. Middle adults greatly benefit from sociable leisure activities that include light to moderate physical activity, depending on the abilities of each person. Even light levels of physical activity can provide significant health benefits for members of this age group. Providing physical movement within the setting of a leisure activity can provide encouragement and social support to begin an active lifestyle and continue it into middle age. Generativity can also be fostered through leisure, especially through activities that focus on self-expression and self-exploration and activities that replace roles lost from the empty nest experience or the death of parents or friends.

Examples From Recreation and Leisure Services Sectors

The public, nonprofit, and private for-profit sponsoring sectors all have much to offer those in middle adulthood. From country clubs, to parks and recreation agencies, to specialized athletic clubs, the follow programming idea is relevant to a variety of service sectors.

Physical activity and movement. In middle age, interests may change from more strenuous physical forms of exercise such as aerobics and running to more expressive and social forms of physical activity such as yoga, Pilates, dance, water aerobics, and hiking and walking. Besides being aerobic, these activities often include a social component that fosters the development of social support networks and friendships.

Programming in middle adulthood is focused on self-expression, physical activity, and volunteerism. Expressive activities such as hobbies are popular,

OUTSTANDING GRADUATES

Background Information

Name: Meredith Schwartz

Education: Master's degree in recreation, sport, and tourism from the University of Illinois at Urbana-Champaign.

Credentials: CPRP and CDL (for driving the bus on trips for seniors).

Special awards: Southern Illinois Parks and Recreation Student Scholarship, November 2008; NRPA Society of Park and Recreation Educators Travel Scholarship, July 2008; University City's Department Employee of the Year Award, December 2006.

Affiliations: National Recreation and Park Association, Illinois Parks and Recreation Association, Southern Illinois Parks and Recreation Association.

Career Information

Position: Active adult and special interest supervisor.

Organization: I work for a park district in Oak Park, Illinois, a community of roughly 53,000 people. This park district is incredibly transparent about their values, some of which include thorough planning, evaluation, partnerships, inclusion, and quality customer service. We own seven community centers, a separate fitness center, three historic properties (two mansions and a conservatory), two outdoor swimming facilities, and several neighborhood and community parks. The agency employs 51 full-time staff, 130 part-time staff, and 275 seasonal staff.

Organization's mission: "In partnership with the community, we provide quality parks and recreation experiences for the residents of Oak Park."

Job description: This is a newly created position at the park district. Before my hiring in 2009 the programs that I oversee were supervised by two part-time positions. I create recreation program opportunities in two separate budget areas: active adults (seniors) and special interest programs for people of all ages. Special interest is defined by our park district as any activity that cannot be labeled as art, sport, fitness, or dance (for example, guitar lessons or sewing classes). I am responsible for managing five summer camps each year. I also plan, develop, implement, facilitate, and evaluate all classes, workshops, events, and services for the youth and adult special interest, camp, and active adult program areas. I recruit, screen, hire, train, mentor, and schedule part-time, seasonal, and volunteer staff and independent contractors. I also prepare seasonal brochure information, promotional materials, and a bimonthly newsletter for active adults.

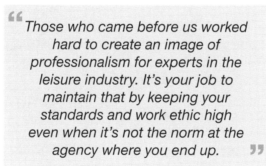

> *Those who came before us worked hard to create an image of professionalism for experts in the leisure industry. It's your job to maintain that by keeping your standards and work ethic high even when it's not the norm at the agency where you end up.*

Career path: From high school through college I held jobs in the recreation industry at golf courses, swimming pools, summer camps, and so on. I graduated from the University of North Carolina with a bachelor's degree in sociology. After graduation I got my first full-time job working for a park and recreation municipality near St. Louis, Missouri. After working there for three years, I decided to return to school for my master's degree in recreation, sport, and tourism at the University of Illinois at Urbana-Champaign so that I could be more competitive in the job market. I value lifelong learning, and I've learned a lot in my current position. As much as I enjoy my job I realize that there is a limit to how much I can grow in the same position. I think

(continued)

269

especially for people who have experienced empty nest syndrome, because they are challenging, fulfilling, and satisfying. Volunteering provides a sense of contribution, and moderate physical activity should be undertaken or continued to maintain health.

LATE ADULTHOOD: SENIOR YEARS

People who are 60 years old or older fall into this last stage of the life span. Because an increasing number of people can now be called centenarians (aged 100 years or older), this stage is the longest and most diverse. Increasing knowledge about how to maintain good health and progress in diagnosing and treating illness and injury are the primary reasons for the steep growth in these numbers. Current literature about aging now focuses on the positive aspects of growing older—a departure from the long-held perception that older adults are in a constant state of decline. Successful aging means that the older adult is satisfied with life, is able to adapt to changing levels of skills and abilities, and maintains relationships that lead an emotionally fulfilling life. One key to aging successfully is to continue to stay engaged physically, cognitively, and socioemotionally. Research shows that successful aging is linked to three main factors: selection, optimization, and compensation (Baltes, 2003; Baltes, Lindenberger, & Staudinger, 2006). Selection is based on the idea that older adults have reduced abilities or loss of

functioning, so they reduce their activities in most domains of their life. Optimization means that it is possible to maintain their activities in some areas through continued practice and the use of technology. Compensation becomes relevant when life tasks require older people to perform beyond their ability. Older adults need to compensate especially in circumstances that have high mental or physical demands, such as when driving a car or when learning or remembering new material. In this section the developmental characteristics of later life are presented and programming considerations are discussed.

Developmental Highlights

As we age, observable declines will inevitably occur in our ability to do activities that we once seemed to do almost automatically. The rate of decline, however, is largely under the individual's control. Our knowledge of how the body functions and what it needs to minimize deterioration has increased significantly. For example, research has clearly shown that engaging in physical activity and good nutritional practices can optimize and sustain health. In addition, as research with older adults continues, myths become dispelled, and studies have shown that some aspects of functioning actually improve with age! Social contact is important to older adults because the support received from others can help mitigate the challenges associated with aging.

Physical Abilities

During late adulthood, functions slow, from speed of walking to speed of thinking, from reaction time to reading time, and from speech rate to heart rate. This overall slowdown is a universal result of aging, and everyone experiences it. Virtually every bodily system becomes less efficient during late adulthood. The heart pumps less blood per beat, the arteries harden, the digestive organs become less efficient, the lungs lose capacity, sleep becomes less sound, and sexual responses become slower. Although many of these changes occur over several decades, the pace speeds up in later life. A general slowing of movement in older adults has been found in everyday tasks such as reaching, grasping, moving from one place to another, and in continuous movement such as walking.

In late adulthood, visible changes in physical appearance become more pronounced, most noticeably in the form of wrinkles and age spots. People also get shorter because of bone loss in the vertebrae. Weight also usually drops after the age of 60, most likely caused by loss of muscle mass, which gives bodies a sagging look. Exercise and appropriate weightlifting can help reduce the loss of muscle mass and improve the appearance of an older person's body.

For many healthy elderly people, the most troubling aspect of aging is not how they appear to others but how they connect with the outside world. This connection depends primarily on their senses, all of which lose sharpness with each passing decade. The decline in vision that began for most people in early or middle adulthood becomes more pronounced in late adulthood. Night driving is especially difficult, and older people take longer to recover their vision when going from well-lit rooms to semidarkness. Although hearing impairment can begin in middle adulthood, it usually does not become an impediment until late adulthood. About 15 percent of the population over the age of 65 is legally deaf, usually because of degeneration of the cochlea, the primary neural receptor for hearing in the inner ear (Olsho, Harkins, & Lenhardt, 1985). Most older adults lose some of their sense of smell or taste or both and often prefer highly seasoned foods (sweeter, spicier, saltier) to compensate for their diminished taste and smell. Change in touch is also associated with aging; people detect touch less

in the lower extremities than in the upper extremities. Older adults are less sensitive to pain and suffer from it less than younger adults do.

Chronic diseases become much more common in late adulthood compared with earlier ages. People's lifestyle choices and social and psychological factors are linked with health status in older adults. Engaging in physical activity, developing good eating habits, and maintaining a network of people who provide emotional and physical support have all been linked to better functioning and recovery from illness in older people (Lee, Manson, Hennekens, & Paffenbarger, 1993; Pruchno & Rosenbaum, 2003; Singh, 2002).

Cognitive Abilities

In late adulthood some dimensions of cognitive functioning decline, but others remain stable or even improve. The "hardware" of the mind is termed **cognitive mechanics** and reflects the **neurophysiological** structure of the brain. Cognitive mechanics refers to the speed and accuracy of the processes involved in many cognitive abilities: sensory input, attention, visual and motor memory, discrimination, comparison, and categorization. Because of the strong influence of biology, heredity, and health on cognitive mechanics, the likelihood is high that these processes will decline with age. In contrast, **cognitive pragmatics** refers to the culturally based "software programs" of the mind. Cognitive pragmatics includes cognitive abilities such as reading and writing skills, language comprehension, educational qualifications, professional skills, and the practical and personal types of knowledge about the self and life skills. Because of the strong influence of culture on cognitive pragmatics, their improvement into old age is possible for many people. Thus, certain types of cognitive abilities may decline during old age, whereas others may improve.

Socioemotional Characteristics

This final stage of development is a time when older adults reflect on the past and review their life experiences and integration within the broader community. If these retrospective glances and reminiscences provide a positive picture of a life well spent, the older adult will be satisfied and feel a sense of integrity. But if he or she finds this retrospective to be negative, despair will result from the belief that time is now too short to attempt to remedy events or try alternative life paths (Erikson, 1968). The individual conducts a life review—looking back at his or her experiences and evaluating and interpreting (and often reinterpreting) them. Sometimes this life review proceeds quietly, but for other people it may be intense, often requiring considerable effort to achieve some sense of reconciliation. As the past marches before him or her, the older adult observes it and reflects on it. The person often reconsiders previous experiences and their meaning, and greater understanding may take place (Cully, LaVoie, & Gfeller, 2001). This reorganization of the past may provide a more meaningful picture for the person and add new and significant meaning to the person's life. This life review may help prepare the person for death and in the process reduce the fear of confronting impending mortality (Butler, 1996).

Research has shown that self-esteem often drops significantly when people reach their 70s and 80s. Several explanations have been suggested, including deteriorating physical health and negative societal attitudes toward older adults, although research has not fully confirmed how strong an influence these factors exert (Robins, Trzesniewski, Tracey, Potter, & Gosling, 2002). Self-esteem is also related to personal control—the extent to which people believe that they control what they do rather than feel controlled by their environment. The term *self-efficacy* has been used to describe perceived control over the environment and the ability to produce positive outcomes (Bandura, 2000). A person who ages successfully believes that he or she is in control of his or her environment and has a feeling of self-efficacy (Bertrand & Lachman, 2003). Researchers have found that many older adults are effective in maintaining a sense of control and having a positive view of themselves. For example, recent studies have found that many centenarians are very happy and that self-efficacy and an optimistic attitude accounted for their happiness (Dunbar, Leventhal, & Leventhal, 2007; Jopp & Rott, 2006). The importance of self-efficacy—the perception of feeling useful well into old age—cannot be overstated. Many older adults continue to work, at least part-

Programming choices for older adults should include more than the traditional activities such as playing cards and bingo. Programmers must also offer fitness activities to optimize health.

time, and a significant number volunteer within their community or religious organizations. Studies have shown that older people who volunteer and engage in altruistic behaviors toward community members are less frail and feel healthier and happier than those who do not (Jung, Gruenewald, Seeman, & Sarkisian, 2010).

Social integration and support are also important to the physical and mental health of older adults. These factors are linked to a reduction in the symptoms of disease and to the ability to meet personal health care needs. Social support also decreases the probability that an older adult will be institutionalized, and it is associated with a lower incidence of depression (Antonucci, 1990; Joiner, 2000). The importance of social integration—maintaining and fostering close ties with others—cannot be overemphasized. Being part of a social network is related to longevity; both women and men who actively participate as members of organizations live longer than their counterparts who participate less (House, Landis, & Umberson, 1988; Mannell & Dupuis, 1996; Tucker, Schwartz, Clark, & Friedman, 1999).

Considerations for Program Design

The biggest challenge to serving the older adult population has just begun with the aging of the baby boomers. This group will be more diverse in terms of abilities and interests. Regardless of their individual needs and constraints, they need to be as active and self-determining in their lifestyle as possible. The challenge to the recreation professional is to capture these principles as fully as possible while remaining mindful of the limitations of the participant. The following are characteristics of effective programming for older adults.

- **Self-determination**. Older adults should be involved in determining program ideas, projects, and trips to the greatest extent possible. Participants who are engaged in all aspects of the planning process will be more involved, happier, and more motivated.

- **Diversity**. Health status and cognitive and physical function vary greatly among people in the 65-to-74, 75-to-84, and 85-and-older age groups, as well as among people within each of these groups. Recreation professionals must remember that individual differences are pronounced, especially for those over the age of 60. The error in assuming that senior programs are appropriate for and enjoyed by everyone within this age group could be substantial.

- **Choice and variety**. The traditional senior activities of long ago—chair exercises, playing cards, and bingo—may be suitable for only a few older adults. Instead, a range of recreational opportunities such as dancing, art, cultural activities, and exercise should be available.

- **Social connectedness**. Intergenerational activities are popular with people of all ages and are important because they help refute the stereotypes associated with ageism and expose younger generations to the wisdom and abilities of older adults. These activities can include social gatherings, senior–junior Olympics, dancing, and arts and crafts. In planning activities, programmers should remember that older adults generally prefer to participate in exercise and physical activity classes with people their own age because they feel more comfortable with people they can relate to in terms of body image, stage of life, and performance. Older adults also tend to prefer not to exercise with children, whom they might consider noisy and unpredictable.

Examples From Recreation and Leisure Services Sectors

Designing programs specifically for older adults is a relatively easy task compared with designing activities for people in many of the other life stages. The declining health and independent mobility of people in this age group provide a strong impetus to incorporate health- and fitness-related aspects into recreation programs. This aspect can come in many forms, as we will see in the next section, but providing a range of recreational opportunities to stave off physical and cognitive deterioration should be at the core.

Health and fitness activities can be fun and at the same time purposeful for older adults. Because of the need and importance of these programs, a diversity of activities have been shown to be both beneficial and enjoyable, so virtually all older adults can find one or more that suit their capabilities and are pleasurable. Some activities that have been shown to improve health and well-being are aerobics,

Pilates, tai chi, restorative or healing forms of yoga, and qi gong. Activities that incorporate elements of balance, strength, and conditioning are preferable and easily administered. These can also be extended to many forms of dance that involve a range of movement, such as tango, ballroom, folk, jazz, line dancing, round dancing, and Zumba.

Older adults are a diverse population in terms of interests and physical and cognitive abilities. Although recreation programmers might be challenged to meet the needs of such a diverse group, the unifying theme is to address health and wellness and provide opportunities for social interaction through recreational activities and programs. As the population ages and the baby boomer generation approaches older age, the sheer numbers of participants and the range in abilities will be both challenging and exciting to the recreation profession.

SUMMARY

The importance of leisure and recreation in the lives of people of all ages is well established. Leisure experiences may serve different functions at different ages and stages and in different circumstances of life, but leisure is a fundamental contributor to happiness and effective functioning. The ways in which people use their discretionary time and the many choices available for individual expression provide glimpses into the ways that people live in their world and the desires and preferences that they have for optimal interaction. Leisure affords people of all ages with unique opportunities for enjoyment, fun, pleasure, affiliation, movement, and skill and personal development.

The leisure professional is thus entrusted with a significant and overwhelming responsibility. Providing opportunities in which people can express themselves through recreation and leisure programs, facilities, and resources is an awesome challenge. As such, recreation professionals must be closely attuned to the developmental characteristics of people at different ages as well as sensitive to the diversity within each of these life stages. The key points of each stage of development across the life span have been presented, and considerations for incorporating these characteristics into leisure programs and services have been offered. We hope that you have gained insight into the process of applying the knowledge of these characteristics to design, program, and implement recreational opportunities for people across the life span.

For glossary terms, learning experiences, and more, please visit the web resource at
www.HumanKinetics.com/IntroductionToRecreationAndLeisure

PART III

Delivering Recreation and Leisure Services

CHAPTER 13

Program Delivery System

Diane C. Blankenship

" Do what you love, love what you do! "

LEARNING OUTCOMES

After reading this chapter, you should be able to do the following:

> ❯ Develop a program delivery system based on leadership
> ❯ Design a program delivery system based on program classifications
> ❯ Revise a program delivery system based on program format and skill sequencing

INTRODUCTION

What is the force that pulls people into the recreation profession? Generally, the magnet is working with people or working within the natural environment through programs and services. Each of us has memories of personal recreational experiences. Do you have fond memories of a camp you attended, a park you visited, a sport you played, a trip you took, or a play or recital that you performed in as a child? I will never forget dogsledding in Wyoming, sailing on Chesapeake Bay, or skiing in the Alps in July. These memories keep us returning for more programs and experiences and seeking new personal challenges. The programming element of recreation draws students to the profession like a moth to a flame. Likewise, it draws people to recreation programs and facilities. The programs, services, and facilities do not just happen without a lot of work and planning. The greatest planning challenge and creative challenge is developing the **program delivery system** of an agency. This chapter reviews the major program delivery systems used within the park and leisure industry. This system requires the recreation professional to plan programs with various leadership involvements, from various classification categories, and through various delivery formats. The challenge is to develop a program delivery system using leadership of various forms, program categories from arts to sport, and various formats from classes to special events. Recreation professionals create and deliver programs using various aspects of the program delivery system to meet the diversified needs of their customers and measure the outcomes of participation, whether the agency is public, private, commercial, or nonprofit.

PROGRAM DELIVERY HISTORY

The modern level of professional program delivery began as something very different and developed along with the progression of society in general from the agricultural era. During the 1800s, Canada and the United States consisted of agricultural communities and a limited number of urban centers. Within rural agricultural communities, recreation was planned and provided by either the family or the church. The isolation of families on their farms demanded that recreation be a family affair conducted at home. The church and local agricultural community planned and coordinated special gatherings around holidays and harvest festivals. These events provided an opportunity for families to socialize with others in the community. In the urban centers recreation was focused on the family but also occurred within local park systems and involved some limited commercial entertainment. Local parks provided space for people to play on their own with little supervision. As time moved on, the necessity for leadership at local playgrounds was realized. Today's process of planning programs and services began on the playgrounds within urban centers during the industrial revolution.

The process of formalizing planning recreational programs and services continued to develop through the 1930s when the process of formally training people for leadership positions began at colleges and universities. The process and art of planning comprehensive recreation delivery systems continued to develop along with the formalizations of community recreation departments, school recreation programs, local parks, and national destinations for vacations. The conclusion of World War II in 1945 was followed by a great expansion of wealth, roadways, and labor-saving devices. Demand grew for trained recreation professionals who could systematically and creatively develop program delivery systems to meet expanding needs, interests, and population segments, such as people with disabilities, seniors, and children.

This developmental process continued for decades and has culminated with the development of program standards that address program leadership, participant outcomes, variety and diversity of programs and services, and diverse communities and experiences. The developmental process of recreation program delivery demands that professionals look broadly across the community at the needs of community members. Agencies must know how to meet those needs, assesses outcomes of the programs and services, and provide a diverse menu of programs and services. Recreational professionals enjoy and embrace these challenges.

MISSION AND OUTCOMES

When you, as a recreation professional, face the task of developing a program delivery system, you may feel overwhelmed. The options and choices for programs and ways to deliver them are endless. The guiding light of every organization's program delivery system is the mission statement of the organization. The mission helps you determine what the program delivery system should contain

in areas such as fitness or health. The outcomes that the programs should achieve must go hand in hand with the mission. The mission focuses the areas to address in terms of programs, and a list of outcomes identifies the benefits that the programs should provide to the participants. Finally, the program **goals** and **objectives** identify the specific outcomes for participants in each program. When you review the outcomes within programs, you can determine whether the general outcomes for the program delivery system have been achieved and whether the organization is achieving its intended mission. The mission, outcomes, and program goals and objectives are related to one another and assist you in developing and evaluating the program delivery system of the organization.

Mission Statement

Every organization, whether public, private, non-profit, or commercial, has a guiding statement such as a mission statement. The **mission statement** is a broad statement that defines the purpose of the organization in regard to the group of people that

Special events that appeal to a broad based audience, such as various mud runs like the Tough Mudder and Warriors Dash, are the newest trend in the recreation industry for program systems. Runners and walkers are looking for new events to try, new races, and common experiences for the average person, and these events combine running or walking with a series of seven or more physical challenges.

the organization serves. It broadly describes why the organization exists, what it is intended to do, and whom it serves. The two mission statements noted in figure 13.1 contain the statement "quality of life" and statements concerning parks or open space. These broad areas provide an abundance of choices and opportunities for the professional but also express large expectations from the people whom the agency serves. The reality of the profession is that the agency cannot be all things to all people. With that in mind, the agency determines the scope, boundaries, and areas for the program delivery system. After these boundaries are determined, the agency develops goals and objectives for the agency as well as for each program. For example, a quality of life area for both Toronto and the Maryland–National Capital Park and Planning Commission is wellness. Both agencies approach this aspect by offering a wide variety of fitness activities and requisite facilities. Both agencies have pools, fitness centers, ice-skating rinks, and a variety of classes for all ages and fitness levels. The boundaries of programs can be naturally determined by the facilities that the agencies manage and operate. An agency does not offer swimming if it does not have a pool or ice-skating if it does not have an ice-skating rink. Each program has goals and objectives that relate back to improving an element of quality of life for participants.

Program Goals and Objectives

The program goals and objectives assess the outcomes for the participants and serve as a means for the agency to determine whether it has achieved its mission. In the case of the City of Toronto, the agency examines the collective outcomes of the programs to determine whether it is improving the quality of life for the residents of the city. All elements within the agency are interrelated and dependent on each other; therefore, the recreation professional must consider all the following elements when developing the program delivery system:

- Mission
- Resources

MISSION STATEMENTS

Toronto, Canada Parks and Recreation Mission Statement

The people in the diverse communities of Toronto will have full and equitable access to high-caliber, locally responsive recreational programs, efficiently operated facilities, and safe, clean, and beautiful parks, open space, ravines, and forest.

Services: Parks, Forestry, and Recreation is engaged in an extensive range of frontline services that contribute to the quality of life of all Torontonians and the overall health of the city's diverse communities.

www.toronto.ca/divisions/parksdiv1.htm

Maryland National Capital Park and Planning Commission Mission Statement

Throughout 80-plus years of service, the Maryland–National Capital Park and Planning Commission has endeavored to improve the quality of life for all of the citizens of the bi-county area it serves and of the communities in which these citizens live, work and raise their families. This mission is embodied in three major program areas. These major program areas respond to the vision of our founders and are incorporated into our charter. The mission of the Maryland–National Capital Park and Planning Commission is to

- manage physical growth and plan communities,
- protect and steward natural, cultural and historic resources, and
- provide leisure and recreational experiences.

www.mncppc.org/About_M-NCPPC/Our_Mission.html

Figure 13.1 A mission statement helps an organization determine what the program delivery system should contain in areas such as fitness or health by keeping the organization focused on why the organization exists, what it is intended to do, and whom it serves.

- Goals
- Objectives

The program delivery system requires recreation professionals to create opportunities that vary in leadership interaction, program area, and format. The leadership options within the program delivery system are the first elements to be examined within the chapter.

LEADERSHIP WITHIN THE PROGRAM DELIVERY SYSTEM

The leadership used within programs and services is the backbone of all program delivery systems within public, private, nonprofit, and commercial agencies. Leadership characteristics vary from program to program and service to service. The leadership used for a class is different from the leadership used at a public park. The leadership used affects the participants' experience; their control over the experience ranges from being highly controlled by the leader to being total independent from the leader. Four options are available for leadership of programs and services: (1) **general leadership** or supervision, (2) **indirect leadership**, (3) **facilitated leadership**, and (4) **structured leadership**. You should view the leadership options on a continuum from general leadership to structured leadership as shown in figure 13.2. As you move from left to right on the continuum, the involvement between the leader and participants increases and the leader assumes more control over the participants' experience.

General Supervision Leadership

General supervision leadership focuses on providing facilities and areas for people to recreate, play, and socialize independently. General supervision is used in facilities or areas such as parks, trails, picnic areas, and beachfronts. The focus is acquiring and maintaining facilities and space to provide opportunities for self-directed leisure experiences. People determine what they will do at these facilities based on their own needs, wants, desires, and personal schedules. Have you been to a local park recently? Think back to that experience and examine why you were there, what you did, and what other people were doing. My most recent trip to a state park was to swim at the lake with my daughter. We met another family there and enjoyed relaxing at the beach area and playing in the water. As I looked around, I saw other people doing many different activities. I saw a man scuba diving in the lake, families enjoying the shade trees and cooking out, people on the hiking trail, people riding bikes, people playing soccer, and others simply reading books.

If you think about the region in which you live, you will likely be able to identify a wealth of facilities or open spaces that are available to the public free of charge or for a small fee. These facilities are generally owned and maintained by local, state, or regional government agencies. Facilities such as playgrounds, athletic fields, trails, and parks all provide seasonal or year-round recreation opportunities. Local trails can be used by hikers, dog walkers, and runners during spring, summer, and fall. During winter, trails may be used for snowmobiling, cross-country skiing, and snowshoeing. The absence of leadership permits individuals, families, and groups to use the facility or outdoor resource to create their own experience based on their personal goals and objectives. This leadership option serves as a vital component in the program delivery system to let people determine and control their own recreational experience. If you look at the leadership continuum in figure 13.2, you will see a leadership option on the opposite end—the structured leadership option.

Structured Leadership

Structured leadership is used in the program delivery system when programs require face-to-face interaction between the leader and the participant in an instructional manner. This approach is used in all types of classes, from swimming and aerobics

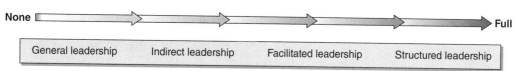

None ▷ Full

| General leadership | Indirect leadership | Facilitated leadership | Structured leadership |

Figure 13.2 The leadership continuum shows four different leadership options available for programs and services.

to pottery and acting. The participant's experience is controlled, guided, and facilitated by the leader. Can you image a fitness class with no leader? Who will move the group through the warm-up, the intense exercises, and the cool-down? What sort of classes have you taken in your life? Didn't the leader tell you what to do, when, how, and for how long? Programs that are instructional in any way require structured leadership from a qualified leader. For example, swimming lessons or fitness classes require a leader with the proper skills, training, and certification to conduct the class. Swimming instructors and fitness instructors go through specific training to learn how to teach in those areas and obtain their certification.

Structured leadership is used to assist people in moving through an experience when they lack the knowledge to do so independently. Participants want to learn to do something, but they need help learning the skills or process. This type of leadership is used throughout the recreation profession within public, private, nonprofit, and commercial recreation. Examples include fitness classes, arthritis exercise, boot camp workouts, and yoga. Each type of agency has skilled leaders and offers a variety of structured leadership programs. If I wanted to find a fitness class in my community, I could go to the local recreation center, private gym, YMCA, or Curves, which serves only women. If you look

within your local community, you will be able to identify numerous agencies that provide structured leadership programs. General leadership and structured leadership meet different needs within a community. Another group of people within every community has highly defined needs and interests. This group requires a different type of leadership called facilitated leadership.

Facilitated Leadership

Facilitated leadership is a point on the leadership continuum that falls between the two extremes and serves a different need within the community. Facilitated leadership is used for a purpose and outcome within communities different from those supported by the structured or general leadership options. This leadership option is used to work with groups to become independent in providing programs and service for the group. An example is working with a group so that it can become a club that operates out of a recreation facility but does so independently. Have you ever been a member of a club or organized group? One of the most common groups within communities is youth sport leagues, such as soccer, football, hockey, lacrosse, and cheerleading. With facilitated leadership, the recreation professional within the community works with the group to set

General supervision leadership (a) provides spaces for people to recreate; structured leadership (b) requires a leader to deliver instruction.

OUTSTANDING GRADUATES

Background Information

Name: Katy Barger

Education: Bachelor's degree in recreation and parks management with a concentration in community programming from Frostburg State University in the Department of Recreation and Management.

Credentials: Nationally certified interpreter guide, Flying Wild certified, Project Wet certified, Project Wild certified, Project Learning Tree certified, solo fundamentals of canoeing.

Career Information

Position: Head naturalist at Rocky Gap State Park (RGSP).

Organization: I work for the Department of Natural Resources, Maryland Park Service, at Rocky Gap State Park. I work in Flintstone, Maryland. The Department of Natural Resources strives to preserve and protect our natural environment. This organization serves the entire state of Maryland and involves the park service, wildlife and fisheries, forest service, and land resources, just to name a few. There are thousands of employees, and every single person in Maryland is served by us. In my park alone, we have 90 seasonals.

Organization's mission: The Department of Natural Resources leads Maryland in securing a sustainable future for our environment, society, and economy by preserving, protecting, restoring, and enhancing the state's natural resources.

Job description: My job entails quite a variety of things. In the off-season, my main job is environmental education. I visit many after-school programs, giving environmental lessons to the children. In April and September, all age groups, kindergarten to high school, visit me at Rocky Gap for a fun-filled day. It's not all fun and games; we are providing environmental education based on recreation. I also help run an outdoor school for sixth-graders of Allegany County. RGSP has partnered with the Alice Ferguson Foundation to run field studies, teaching middle school and high school youth about watersheds. All year long, I run the RGSP Aviary, which holds our birds of prey. Every day we take care of these birds. We feed them and keep their cages in top shape. We use the birds for environmental education, a program we call Scales and Tales. With this program, we teach people about their impact on the environment and how they can help improve the world around us. Over the summer months, when the park is full of guests, my world shifts. I am in charge of the nature center at Rocky Gap. I plan all kinds of fun events for the families every day. Our nature center houses our reptiles (snakes and turtles), which we feed and care for. We use these for programing as well. We teach children to not be afraid but also to not bother the critters that are in the wild. The nature center provides the public with weekly hikes, games, crafts, and educational opportunities. Last year, we had the first-ever day camp. I assisted in the planning of the camp. Every year we have junior rangers. We plan environmental education lessons for a group of children and get them to do hands-on activities to learn more.

> *Take your time, enjoy your surroundings, and everything will work out. Get out there, experience nature, and pursue your dreams!*

Career path: I came to Rocky Gap for my internship my senior year in college. I did not think I would enjoy it, and I always said I would never work in the park service. My professor told me that Rocky Gap would be just the right fit for me. I trusted her and never regretted my decision. I am so thankful for her guidance. Rocky Gap is the best thing that's happened in my career path thus far. They provide me with many opportunities. I'm happy to have found such a good fit!

My career path changes every day. I love to program, and RGSP gives me this opportunity. I hope to continue my journey through the park service so that one day I can become

(continued)

up a place for activities, a process for the league or club, and procedures for operating the group. The recreation professional and the group leadership work hand in hand to formalize the operation of the group. After the operations are established, the recreation professional is not involved with the group and the group operates independently. In our local community, youth soccer is extremely popular. The local recreation department does not have the staff to coordinate and conduct a youth soccer league for the community. To meet this need, parents volunteer and formalize a board of directors that takes over the leadership role for the soccer league. The board works with the local recreation department to schedule field use and field maintenance. Beyond the use of the facilities, the board runs and coordinates the community youth soccer league.

The facilitated leadership option is a useful technique for working with groups who have special interests, manpower, and the necessary skills. These groups can conduct programs and events for the community by representing the agency, but they place few demands on the agency. You can see this in your local community particularly with sport leagues, arts councils for performing and visual arts, and recreational interests such as skiing and book clubs. The final option for service leadership that helps people pursue their leisure independently is indirect leadership.

Indirect Leadership

Indirect leadership is the final leadership option that recreation professionals can use to meet the needs of the people they serve. This form of leadership falls on the continuum between general supervision and facilitated leadership. The indirect leadership option provides the agency with an opportunity to augment programs and services. Indirect leadership focuses on providing people with equipment or services for a fee, such as equipment rental or picnic shelter rental. The only interaction between the participant and the leader occurs during the rental process. The recreation experience is determined by the participant, not the leader. Many agencies have picnic shelters for rent to accommodate people who need a place for large group gatherings. Family reunions, school picnics, birthday parties, and church functions all use picnic shelter rental programs to hold recreation events. Other centers rent bikes, canoes, and paddle boats.

This type of service provides resources for people to pursue activities or have group gathering that would otherwise not occur.

The four leadership options within the program delivery system are generally blended together to provide a variety of programs and services to meet the needs of the people served by the agency. People who lack the skills and knowledge to participate in an activity require a highly supervised experience, whereas those who have the skills, knowledge, and desire to participate in certain activities may need a space, place, or equipment for their recreational experiences. This mixture of leadership helps ensure that the agency meets its mission. The leadership element is not the only element within the program delivery system that recreation professionals need to consider in meeting the mission of the organization. To plan the program delivery system, two other elements must be reviewed—the program classification area and program format.

PROGRAM CLASSIFICATION

The second area of the program delivery system to consider is the **program classification** area. This review process is both creative and challenging. The creative element involves creating program options across the many options listed in table 13.1. The challenge requires escaping the personal box of experiences to plan new things. The field of parks and recreation divides all programs and services into 14 classifications areas. Each classification area includes hundreds of opportunities for programs and services. The program classification list shown in table 13.1 is a tool that can be used with the leadership options to evaluate the current program delivery system and to generate additional ideas for programs and services for any organization.

Let's examine the aquatics area in detail. Within the aquatics area, agencies use all the leadership options to meet a wide spectrum of needs within the community or within the group of people that the agency serves. The type of aquatics program provided helps determine the type of leadership to use for the program. For example, swim teams are common in public, nonprofit, private, and commercial agencies. Because this activity requires face-to-face leadership with swim coaches, the supervision leadership option is used to conduct a swim team

program. Many recreation agencies have one or more indoor or outdoor pools of various sizes under their responsibility. These pools provide open swim or free swim times, swim team practices, pool parties, and adults-only events. Table 13.2 has a sample of activities that could be conducted within pools and the leadership option used for these programs. Recreation professionals ask three specific questions when reviewing a list like the one in table 13.2: (1) Do these programs meet the mission and goals of the agency? In this case, the programs address improving the quality of life or wellness of the community. The answer to the first question is yes. (2) Do these programs serve the various segments of the community in term of age, gender, abilities, or ethnicity? The programs listed in table 13.2 provide opportunities for all ages with the open swim and class options. The lessons, swim team, and parties focus on children, and the masters swim program and water fitness focus on seniors, boomers, athletes, and others. The open swim can meet the needs of people of any age, group, ability, gender, or ethnic origin. The answer to the second question is also yes. (3) Do these programs serve a continuum of skill levels from introductory level to advanced level? The programs, classes, and services provide opportunities for people at a beginner level to advanced level. Swimming lessons are the first step in learning skills. From this experience the staff can recruit children into the swim team and introduce them to a lifetime sport that they can continue as an adult through the master's program. The current aquatics programs listed in table 13.2 provide opportunities for a variety of skill levels. As you review this list, you should recognize that a pool provides great opportunities for programs and services that use each of the leadership options to meet the agency's mission, serve a broad base of consumers, and provide activities for people of various skill levels. The process of developing a program delivery system depends on this creative planning process to generate and evaluate the programs and series within the program delivery system. One more trick of the trade can help professionals stay out of the box as they develop program delivery systems. This technique takes the planning effort from the leadership options and classification options one step further to generate different program formats within the classification areas.

Table 13.1 Program Classifications

Classification	Description	Example
Arts	Creative process of making items	Painting or sculpture
Performing arts	Activities or programs that focus on self-expression in music, dance, or drama	Concert in the park, community play
Craft	Making something of decorative value	Pottery or knitting
New arts	Using technology such as digital cameras or computers	Photography class
Literary	Activities involving books, writing, or speeches	Book club
Self-development	Activities or programs that promote personal development	Stress management class or retirement seminars
Aquatics	Activities or programs done in the water	Swimming lessons, water aerobics, or swim team
Outdoor	Activities or programs done in the outdoor environment	Hiking program, kayaking program, or campground
Wellness	Programs that focus on improving wellness comprehensively	Fitness classes, nutritional seminars, stress management seminars
Hobbies	Activities in which people collect, create, or educate others	Coin collecting, model railroading, garden clubs
Social recreation	Programs and services that promote social interaction	Dances, festivals, teen clubs
Volunteer services	Programs in which people provide services to others	Working the front desk, greeting customers, taking care of roadways and parks
Travel and tourism	Trips that take people to attractions	Ghost tours, biking tours, visiting casinos or national parks
Sports, games, and athletics	Activities with some rules that involve competition	Card games, soccer leagues, swim teams

Table 13.2 Aquatics Classification and Leadership

Leadership option	Aquatic programs
General leadership	Open swim Lap swimming Dive-in movie
Structured leadership	Swim lessons Water fitness Arthritis water fitness Swim team
Facilitated leadership	Triathlon workout club Masters swim club Water walking club
Indirect leadership	Swimming birthday parties Fins and floatation devices

PROGRAM FORMATS

Program formats, the method in which the program is structured for participants, help the recreation professional further develop the program delivery system into a more comprehensive plan. Eight program formats (listed in table 13.3) can be used within any of the classification areas and can be analyzed based on the leadership option needed for the program. This next step in developing the program delivery system helps to determine the scope and variety of programs and services. This step helps the recreation professional determine whether a program should be offered only once or on a continuous basis, whether the program should be leader directed or self-determined, or whether the program should have an element of competition or not.

Let's take a closer look at how the program format, leadership, and classification areas can be used to develop a program and program delivery system using the aquatics and sport classification areas. What programs could be offered in the area of aquatics and soccer using the eight formats? For many of the formats, listing a program is easy, whereas for others, identifying a program is more challenging. For example, what could be done in the formats of interest groups and outreach programs in aquatics and soccer? This task is the challenging and creative part of developing a program delivery system. Look in table 13.4 at the various programs and services that could be offered by recreation agencies in the eight format areas. The programs listed in table 13.4 are just a sample of what could be done with programs in a specific classification area. What other programs or services could be done within each of the format areas?

Table 13.5 pulls together the three major areas of a program delivery system—leadership, classification, and format. This table can be used to

Table 13.3 Program Formats

Format	Explanation	Program example
Competition	Program that involves competition or a contest	Indoor soccer league
Class	Instructional sessions over a series of weeks	Aerobics class
Club	Group that is self-conducted with regular meetings	Running club
Drop in or open	Area in the facility left for people to use freely	Open gym time
Interest group	Similar to a club but organized around an issue or program	Arts council
Outreach	Taking programs to people or reaching people not normally served by the agency	Playground day camp program or mobile arts bus
Special event	One-time large program	Arts and crafts festival
Workshop or conference	Programs that focuses on learning a skill	Digital photography editing

Table 13.4 Program Formats for Aquatics and Soccer

Format	Aquatics	Sports (soccer)
Competition	Dual swim meet	Indoor youth soccer league
Classes	Lifeguard classes	Soccer skills class
Clubs	Masters swim club	Travel team
Drop in or open	Open swim	Area open to practice
Interest groups	Swim team advisory group	Soccer league advisory group
Outreach	Special Olympics training program	Wheelchair soccer
Special event	Pool water carnival	Soccer tournament
Workshops or conference	Stroke and turn judge clinic	Coaching clinic

Table 13.5 Program Formats and Leadership

Leadership	Format	Aquatics	Sports (soccer)
Structured	Competition	Dual swim meet	Indoor youth soccer league
Facilitated	Classes	Lifeguard classes	Soccer skills class
General	Clubs	Masters swim club	Travel team
Indirect	Drop in or open	Open swim	Area open to practice
General or structured	Interest groups	Swim team advisory group	Soccer league advisory group
Indirect or general	Outreach	Special Olympics training program	Wheelchair soccer
Structured	Special event	Pool water carnival	Soccer tournament
Structured	Workshops or conference	Stroke and turn judge clinic	Coaching clinic

generate additional program or service options or evaluate existing programs or services. The items listed in this table comprehensively represent different leadership options for programs to provide choices for people to participate in a leader-directed program or a self-directed activity. The activities go far beyond providing competitive formats, which are not always appealing to beginners. Finally, a review of the activities in this table shows that a logical progression of programs is available to attract new participants and keep them coming back for more programs or services at the agency. This progression provides participants with opportunities to develop their skills and use new skills in new programs. The essence of every program delivery system is to offer diversity in programs, services, leadership, and formats to meet the varied needs of the people who are served by the organization.

SUMMARY

This chapter explores the program delivery system in several ways. First, the programming element is the flame that attracts the moth; it draws into the field of recreation people who enjoy the creative challenge of meeting the needs of those they serve and positively influencing their lives through programs and services. The backbone of the program delivery system is the mission of the organization, which guides all the planning efforts of the organization. The leadership options provide a variety of experiences to the participant from instructional classes to open use of facilities for people to do what they want to do when they want to do it. The next area of consideration in developing a program delivery system is the classification area of the programs and services. This steps ensures that a well-balanced array of programs and services exists for the participant instead of overrepresentation of one classification and underrepresentation of a needed classification area. The final step in developing a program delivery system involves using program format options to develop programs and services for participants. This step also ensures that one format is not overrepresented in the delivery system while others are neglected. All these considerations lead to providing a balanced menu of programs and services to participants. After the program delivery system is developed, planned, and conducted, the professional can examine the outcomes for the participants, determine whether the system is meeting the mission of the organization, and then make the necessary changes to provide quality programs and services to the community or customers.

For glossary terms, learning experiences, and more, please visit the web resource at
www.HumanKinetics.com/IntroductionToRecreationAndLeisure

CHAPTER 14

Recreational Sport Management

Craig M. Ross and H. Joey Gray

" Sports for all means sports for all ages, all racial and ethnic groups, all ability levels, all genders, and all social strata. "

Andre Carvalho, chief of the Programme Development and Operations Group, United Nations

LEARNING OUTCOMES

After reading this chapter, you should be able to do the following:

› Describe the components pertaining to the foundation of recreational sport management
› List the broad scope of recreational sport activities and events
› Describe the trends affecting recreational sport management
› Analyze and evaluate the scope of participation in recreational sport
› List career opportunities in recreational sport management

INTRODUCTION

Recreational sport, or sport for the masses, is a popular and appealing form of leisure and recreation to many American adults. In youth sport programs participation has risen to an all-time high (Cordes & Ibrahim, 2003). Participation in **recreational sports** far surpasses that in all other types of recreational activities (Edginton, Jordan, DeGraaf, & Edginton, 2002; Kraus, 2000). In 2009 more than three-quarters (77 percent) of Americans (217 million people) who were 6 years old or older participated in some type of sport, fitness, or outdoor activity (Physical Activity Council, 2010). Robinson and Godbey (1997) in their book *Time for Life* have even described sport and fitness activities as "mainstays in the lifestyles of large numbers of Americans" (p. 186).

Sport in American society has experienced tremendous change and increased popularity over the past several decades. Today, sport and physical activity are as much a part of American culture as other institutions such as work, marriage, and the family. Sport interest and participation from all sectors of society are reaching unprecedented levels. Once considered simply a diversion from work and a tool for recreation, sport has grown to be a multibillion-dollar industry. For some people, sports like baseball and events like the Super Bowl are like religion (Eitzen, 2009). Avid fans spend thousands of dollars on tickets, paraphernalia, fantasy camps, and the like. In 2010 the average ticket price for the Super Bowl was between $800 and $1,000. Today, sport fans and participants alike possess unfailing devotion to sport with both their discretionary time and their money. Price (2005) further suggests that the best way to understand American sport is to take it as a "contemporary folk religion" (p. 142).

Sport has had a noteworthy influence not only in the United States but also around the globe (Kidd, 2008). Sport and physical activity have become universal phenomena (Ghafouri, Mirzaei, Hums, & Honarvar, 2009). This increased popularity and devotion to sport globally have had a significant impact on the way sport and leisure services have been delivered in the past and will continue to be delivered in the future.

On the one hand, sport has become very entertainment and spectator oriented, and record numbers of people are attending professional sporting events. Professional athletes are considered folk heroes and are paid astronomical salaries. On the other hand, when sport participation is viewed as an "experience," it is considered leisure (Kelly & Freysinger, 2000). In this regard, sport has become participant oriented, involving diverse populations in a variety of programs and activities. The growth of sport in some form in modern society cannot be questioned. "Sport has a major role in modern society as an element of the economy, a spectacle with symbolic meanings, an arena of development for the young, and in the leisure lives of many individuals" (Kelly, 1996, p. 226).

EXAMINING SPORT MANAGEMENT FROM A RECREATIONAL PERSPECTIVE

The discipline that manages sport programs has been referred to by experts in a variety of different terms and titles over the years. Although there is no consensus on the name of the field, the term *sport management* is generally the umbrella term used to identify the administration and management of a large number and variety of sport, fitness and wellness, and recreation programs (Stier, 2001). Henderson (2009) suggests that sport management covers a field of study that mainly focuses on the business side of sport. Supporting Henderson, according to the North American Society of Sport Management (2010), sport management addresses the application of business to the professional side of sport, which includes topics such as sport marketing, employment competencies, management competencies, event management, sport and the law, personnel management, facility management, organizational structures, and fund-raising.

Professional sport management focuses on **sport performance** and often works with elite athletes (e.g., sport agents) or planning, promoting, or managing professional sporting events for spectators (e.g., sport promotion, sport communication, sport equipment sales, ticketing agents). Settings include professional sport, intercollegiate athletics, sport marketing firms, and national sport governing bodies. The primary emphasis or goal in this area is to win championships with elite athletes by increasing revenue and profits for team franchise owners or stakeholders through ticket or sport equipment sales and promotion, stadium and arena facility management, and entertaining spectators.

The major defining characteristic of recreational sport management that separates it from professional sport management is its focus on **sport participation** for the masses. Recreational sport provides diverse sport programs, facilities, equipment, and services that promote and enhance greater appreciation for lifelong involvement in sport and fitness. Over the years a significant increase has occurred in the demand for broad-based recreational sport programming that meets the needs and interests of all participants regardless of age, race, gender, religion, or athletic ability. It is important to identify and understand the components of recreational sport and the role they play in the realm of sport management.

More recently, recreational sport management has begun to emphasize the leadership and management of people and resources in a variety of participatory or recreational settings. In this delivery, the key principle of "active" sport participation is represented by various degrees of competitive activ-

ity within many sectors. These sectors include, but are not limited to collegiate, municipal parks and recreation, commercial, corporate, correctional, and military recreation.

From this perspective, recreational sport is a major component of a person's lifestyle, as either a participant in or spectator of sports during leisure (Mull, Bayless, & Jamieson, 2005). These authors provide a leisure sport management model (see figure 14.1) that illustrates the concepts of participation and being a spectator in sport programming, ranging from **educational sports** at the lowest level to **professional sports** at the highest.

A large number of participants, ranging from youth to seniors, actively participate in sport at the educational or instructional and recreational levels. Then, as participants progress upward in the model toward the apex, participation in the leisure experience shifts from being actively involved in the activity to involvement as a spectator watching the event. For example, at the professional level of sport, the leisure experience of most people consists of watching professional

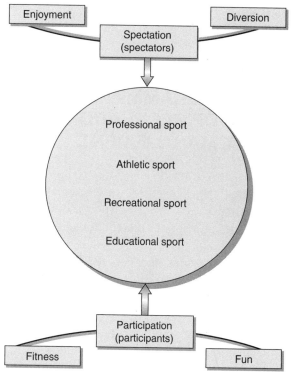

Figure 14.1 A leisure sport management model that focuses on being a spectator and participant.

Reprinted, by permission, from R.F. Mull, K.G. Bayless, and L.M. Jamieson, 2005, *Recreational sport management*, 4th ed. (Champaign, IL: Human Kinetics), 9.

athletes perform and compete rather than being actively involved in the sport.

DEFINING RECREATIONAL SPORT

Traditionally, recreational sport has been described as intramural sport, physical recreation, physical activity, non-varsity athletics, open recreation, intramural athletics, and so on. However, none of these accurately reflects what recreational sport actually is. The basis of recreational sport is the involvement during leisure time either as an active participant or as a spectator at one of the levels of the leisure sport hierarchy. The major characteristic of recreational sport management that separates it from other sport disciplines is its focus on sport participation for the masses. Recreational sport programs are designed to give *everyone* an active role regardless of sport interest, age, race, gender, or athletic ability. It truly is sport for all. Because recreational sport programs are participant driven, sport programmers and managers put significant effort into defining and meeting participants' wants and needs. The increasing complexity and magnitude in recreational sport management are more than likely a result of societal demands for more and better services, targeting mass participation in recreational sport.

FIVE PROGRAMMING AREAS OF RECREATIONAL SPORT MANAGEMENT

Five basic program delivery areas comprise the recreational sport spectrum: instructional sports, informal sports, intramural sports, extramural sports, and club sports. **Instructional sports** are the recreational sport activities that teach skills, rules, and strategies in a noncredit or academic environment; **informal sports** involve self-directed participation with an individualized approach focused on fun and fitness; **intramural sports** involve structured sports in the form of leagues, tournaments, and contests conducted within a particular setting; **extramural sports** consist of structured sport activities between winners of various intramural sport programs; and **club sports** are undertaken by groups of participants that organize because of a common interest in a sport.

Instructional Sport

Most traditional recreational sport programs are based on sport competition, and they appeal primarily to people who are already familiar with a particular sport or have some degree of skill and involvement with sports. The instructional sport program area focuses on an even larger segment of the population that needs to learn basic sport skills and how to incorporate the physical activity and fitness components of sport into daily life. This program area was developed to encourage participants to gain the core skills in various levels of sport activities and to provide a way for people to have fun and enjoy the many benefits of participating in the sport activity. The primary emphasis, then, is on participant skill development, enjoyment, and learning how to play the game.

Years ago, instructional sport was offered only through educational settings, such as physical education classes and varsity athletics. But with the increased interest and popularity in recreational sport participation, instructional sport has expanded into nonacademic settings such as the YMCAs, YWCAs, Boys and Girls Clubs, municipal parks and recreation, commercial recreational sports, and the armed forces recreation sector. Practically every setting (campus, military, municipal, youth, and so on) now offers instructional sports that teach individuals or groups through classes, lessons, clinics, and workshops and usually at three instructional levels: beginning, intermediate, and advanced. Examples of instructional sports include exercise and conditioning, gymnastics, martial arts, swimming, golf, bowling, tennis, racquetball, and squash.

Informal or Self-Directed Sport

Informal sport, probably one of the most misunderstood and misrepresented program delivery areas in recreational sport management, is self-directed sport participation for fun and fitness. This program area is at the other end of the spectrum from structured intramural sports and possesses the least structure. Informal sport activities include backyard volleyball or softball at the family picnic, pickup basketball games at the local park, an early-morning swim or lunchtime run, or lifting weights in the weight room of a fitness facility. This program area emphasizes self-directed participation. The participant designs and develops the specific personal program and goals, and the recreational sport staff facilitates the involvement or experience through appropriate and available facilities and equipment. In most sectors (municipal parks and recreation, armed forces recreation, educational recreation), informal sport involves the largest number of participants. Because informal sports are the least structured, sport takes place whenever there is an available facility or interest in the activity. For recreational sport programmers, many elements go into informal sport programming and management. Because the primary goal is to facilitate sport participation, perhaps the biggest concerns for informal sports programmers are facilities and equipment management and scheduling. Having available and accessible facilities and equipment is essential to creating a satisfying and positive experience for all participants.

Although the benefits of fitness and wellness are part of all of the program delivery components, managing specific fitness and wellness programs has become a special programming area in informal sports over the past decade. Group exercise programs such as step aerobics, trekking, indoor cycling, and mind and body activities such as Pilates, yoga, and tai chi are especially popular with women. These programs help participants enhance or achieve overall well-being through sport and fitness activities and play an integral role in the overall management of recreational sport.

Intramural or Structured Sport

Intramural sport is structured participation *within* a specific setting such as leagues, tournaments, and matches. The word "intramural" is derived from the Latin words "intra" (within) and "mural" (walls). Intramural sports, then, are structured activities between teams and individuals within an agency's limits or boundaries such as city limits, university campus, YMCA branch, and so on. Intramural sports are generally limited to participation among the participants served by a particular agency and should provide opportunities for men, women, and mixed competition with a variety of rule modifications to meet the particular needs and interests of the participants in that setting. Intramural sports can include the following:

- **Individual sports.** Events that generally allow people to participate alone (e.g., fishing, golf, swimming, diving, trap and skeet, cycling, hunting, boxing, and archery)
- **Dual sports.** Events that require at least one opponent (e.g., badminton, table tennis, tennis, squash, handball, and racquetball)
- **Team sports.** Events that require a specific number of players who play as a team of either men, women, or mixed intramural divisions (e.g., baseball, basketball, softball, kickball, lacrosse, field hockey, rowing, soccer, volleyball, wallyball, water polo, and flag football)
- **Meet sports.** Separate events occurring within a larger event and usually conducted over a period of one or two days (e.g., swimming, gymnastics, diving, wrestling, golf, and track and field)
- **Special events.** Nontraditional activities usually not practiced regularly by the participants (e.g., Wacky Olympics, sports all-nighters and festivals, and superstar competitions)

Intramural sports are typically the "signature" program or mainstay of recreational sport agencies. In many instances, they provide the basic sport opportunities from which agencies build and expand their overall program offerings. This is because of the familiarity and high-profile nature of traditional sport programs, the large participation base, a well-organized and highly structured program delivery, competitive (but wholesome!) atmosphere, and the recognition and awards for participants and teams who excel.

Historically, the term *intramural sports* has been associated with recreational sport programs at colleges and universities. However, municipal and community recreation departments, churches, YMCAs, military bases, elementary and secondary schools, industries, and private clubs now offer a variety of sport events that are very similar to collegiate recreational sport but with a different participant than the typical 18- to 22-year-old college student. These events, although not thought of as intramural sports, in fact meet the definition of sport played "within the walls" of a particular agency.

Extramural Sport

Extramural sports refer to structured recreational sport participation that provides participants with an opportunity to compete against participants from other agencies or organizations. Competition takes place between winning teams from several programs. Extramural sports include sport programs and activities in which participants and teams from winning programs are extended an invitation to represent their home agency and compete for an overall championship. The Little League Baseball World Series is an extramural sport event. Other examples are a navy basketball team representing its base Morale, Welfare and Recreation (MWR) department playing in the local municipal parks and recreation tournament or a collegiate intramural flag football championship team from one university playing against other collegiate champions for "national champion" recognition. Many times, the extramural sport program fills the gap between varsity athletics and intramural sports and provides additional opportunities for many higher-skilled athletes to compete.

Club Sport

Club sports involve any group that organizes to further its interest or skill level in a specific sport activity. These interests range from very competitive club teams that travel and play in various high-level competitions to the recreational, social, and instructional clubs that conduct activities such as basic-skill instruction and tournaments among themselves.

The history of club sports is long. It is believed that club sports are the forerunners of college athletics, intramural sports, and formal physical education classes. The main purpose of a club sport program is to provide various degrees of interaction and sport participation to its members. In many instances, a club sport is formed for the social aspects that incorporate practices, informal get-togethers, and philanthropic functions. Other clubs offer instruction and skills development for beginning to advanced skill levels, and others organize for the sole purpose of competition and tournaments. Because clubs are not limited to the college setting, they can be found in the public, military, commercial, private, and correctional settings. Club sport programs have become popular because they generally operate with fewer administrative resource needs such as staffing, facilities, referees, and so on than other types of organized recreational sport

programming. Many clubs are self-sufficient and generate all needed funding.

The nature of club sports allows members to direct their interests both within and outside of the recreational agency. Characteristics that distinguish club sports from intramural sports, informal sports, and extramural sports include the following:

- They are self-administered and regulated to some degree with participant-developed operating policies.
- Members are able to conduct their club sport without substantial administrative support from the agency.
- Members seek opportunities for regular and ongoing year-round participation.
- Club sports offer a more structured design than informal sport participation.
- Unlike the staff-structured intramural sports program, club sport members develop, operate, and administer the club.

SCOPE OF PARTICIPATION IN RECREATIONAL SPORT

Participation in recreational sport has grown steadily over the past several decades. Millions of people participate in team, individual, or dual sports in municipal parks and recreation programs, campus recreational sport programs, nonprofit agencies such as the YMCA and Boys and Girls Clubs, employee recreation programs, private clubs, commercial recreational sport facilities and programs, and armed forces MWR programs around the world. The following brief descriptions of participation in recreational sport programs and facilities provide an overview of the scope of participation that should meet the needs of most people who want to participate in recreational sports.

Active Participation Choices

Active participation, as discussed earlier, is a much more integral part of recreational sport management than it is of varsity **athletic sports** and professional sports. The key principle of active participation is the person's choice to participate in either structured sports (instructional, intramural, extramural, or club) or self-directed sports (informal) and the

OUTSTANDING GRADUATES

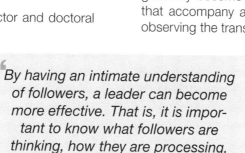

Background Information

Name: Jay Whitacre

Education: Master of science in outdoor recreation, Indiana University.

Credentials: Swiftwater rescue, wilderness first responder, level 1 avalanche, SCUBA advanced open water, professional ski instructor of America (Alpine, telemark, and snowboarding), high and low rope facilitation, Indiana University Outdoor Adventures full instructor.

Special awards: Outdoor Recreation Graduate Student of the Year 2011.

Affiliations: Association for Experiential Education, Wilderness Education Association.

Career Information

Position: Associate instructor and doctoral student, Indiana University.

Organization: Indiana University Outdoor Adventures is an outdoor recreation program that serves the Bloomington campus and surrounding community. This student-run program provides a myriad of experiential learning opportunities, including adventures for first-year students, spring break trips, and outdoor recreation courses.

Job description: I facilitate courses focused on a variety of outdoor recreation pursuits for undergraduate students. The courses follow a nontraditional format; that is, the students learn in an experiential manner. The courses move beyond acquisition of simple skills to personal growth and life management.

> *"By having an intimate understanding of followers, a leader can become more effective. That is, it is important to know what followers are thinking, how they are processing, and when to be a follower yourself."*

Career path: It is my goal to further the adventure recreation field by becoming a professor so that I can continue to expose people to adventures that push them to new levels. I also want to globally revitalize an overall waning passion with the outdoors through scholarship and research.

Likes and dislikes about the job: I like taking people to places that they normally do not have the opportunity to visit, seeing the passion for the outdoors awaken in people during extended trips, witnessing people gradually become self-sufficient in the skills that accompany adventure recreation, and observing the transfer of success in the outdoors to other areas of life. I dislike people's apprehension about becoming involved in adventure recreation endeavors due to unfamiliarity with the activities. I also dislike the lack of incorporating the outdoors into people's daily lives.

Advice to Undergraduates

The field of adventure recreation is one that many continue to explore but fail to pursue as a lifelong endeavor. Adventure recreation offers wonderful resources for personal growth and health. Many people will discount the importance of the outdoors, but do not fall victim to the personal prejudices of others when pursuing your own passions.

---

broad spectrum of degrees of participation. This broad spectrum of recreational sport, which should be afforded to *all*, is the distinguishing feature that differentiates it from athletic and professional sports.

Participants

It is essential for recreational sport programmers to recognize whom they provide service to in order to better meet the needs and interests of the participants. Recreational sport management is intended for the enjoyment of all age groups. These groups include children, youth, adolescents, adults, and senior citizens.

Location

Very simply, participation in recreational sport occurs in both *indoor* and *outdoor* sport facilities. Indoor recreational sports facilities may include bowling centers; handball, racquetball, and squash courts; gymnasiums for volleyball, basketball, badminton, and floor hockey; billiard rooms; roller- and ice-skating rinks; aquatic centers; strength and conditioning weight rooms; and exercise rooms. Outdoor recreational sport facilities may include softball and baseball diamonds; golf courses; trap and skeet ranges; fields for soccer and flag football; tennis courts; and outdoor aquatic centers. Outdoor facilities may also include natural facilities such as white-water rivers and streams, caves, lakes, and mountains.

Sport Settings

Recreational sport management is programmed in a variety of sport settings. These include the following:

- Recreation departments on armed forces installations around the world
- Boys and Girls Clubs
- Churches
- City and community parks and recreation departments
- Commercial recreational facilities such as racket clubs, bowling centers, and roller- and ice-skating rinks
- Correctional institutions (city, county, state, and federal)
- Educational institutions (public and private elementary, secondary, and higher education)
- On-site industrial and corporate recreational sport facilities
- Private clubs (country clubs and fitness and health clubs)
- YMCAs and YWCAs
- Vacation resorts (hotels, motels, and cruise ships)

These settings represent thousands of employment positions in recreational sport programming and open the door to numerous job opportunities for those wanting a career in this field.

Recreational sport can take place indoors in a gymnasium or outdoors on the volleyball court.

Benefits

Recreational sport participation can provide one of the most important sociocultural learning environments in our society, and it provides a substantial range of benefits for participants and the community, organization, or agency that sponsors them. While active participants gain many health and physical benefits, the community or agency can also benefit from an economical or environmental perspective. By providing sport opportunities and by encouraging participation, recreational sport programs can develop participant interests, knowledge, and skills to enable participation in recreational sport and fitness activities that can last a lifetime.

Personal Benefits

For the person who regularly participates in recreational sport activities, improved health, physical fitness, and self-esteem can be gained. However, the benefits from recreational sport are not only physical. Although physical benefits are easy to detect, active participation can also provide positive and enjoyable experiences that can decrease stress and psychological tension. Recreational sport activities provide participants the opportunity to "burn" excess energy and emotional stress not released in other aspects of their lives. These activities also create a positive social environment where people can relax and enjoy the company of others.

Competition and winning and losing help many people learn how to control their emotions and express aggression in a positive way. Cooperation is fostered because people must work together to achieve a goal. By working with others, people gain interpersonal skills, learn to tolerate differences, and learn time management and goal-settings skills. People can develop integrity by establishing their own values and behavior patterns, and then by testing those against the values and behaviors of others.

Community Benefits

By providing opportunities for social interaction, recreational sport programs can help increase community cohesion and encourage community interaction by engaging different sections of the community in wholesome sporting activities, regardless of age, race, ethnicity, or gender. Participation can also help deter antisocial behavior, including vandalism, gang violence, and crime. Communities can benefit economically from well-planned and well-managed sport facilities. These economic benefits include direct and indirect employment in recreational sport programs, income from sales of recreational sporting goods and services, and the revenue generated from holding local, city, state, regional, or even national recreational sports tournaments and events. Tourism-related activities, through the promotion of recreational sport opportunities and the quality of sporting facilities, can contribute significantly to the local economy.

Agency, Organization, or Setting Benefits

Participation in recreational sport programs can have a direct effect on the agency, organization, or setting that provides the activities. The following are examples:

- The Employee Morale and Recreation Association (EMRA) suggests that "recreational sport leagues and special-interest clubs allow employees to develop a broader range of skills, learn to be leaders, and enjoy coming to work" (EMRA, 2012, par. 4). Recreational sport programs can deliver tangible benefits in terms of workplace safety and improved productivity from happier and healthier employees.

- Studies conducted by the National Intramural-Recreational Sports Association (NIRSA) report that in the collegiate setting, active engagement in recreational sport and fitness programs is a "key determinant of college satisfaction, success, recruitment, and retention" (Blumenthal, 2009, p. 60).

- Navy MWR fleet recreational sport programs and equipment support the quality of life of more than 200,000 men and women on land and at sea on board navy ships. These mission-essential MWR programs consist of voluntary fitness and recreational sport activities conducted for the purpose of promoting morale and physical and mental combat readiness (Navy Morale, Welfare and Recreation, n.d.).

- Through the YMCA mission of "putting Christian principles into practice," recreational sport, a mainstay of the YMCA offerings, emphasizes fun, teamwork, and friendly competition in a supportive

Participation in recreational sport can benefit the individual as well as the community. Individuals can boost self-esteem and decrease stress, and the community can see economic benefits from a large event as well as increase community cohesion.

community for all ages and skill levels (YMCA, 2012).

TRENDS IN RECREATIONAL SPORT MANAGEMENT

To be able to fully plan and make projections properly, it is essential to examine current issues and concerns. Examining current challenges and problems and forecasting their impact on the future are of great value to any profession, and recreational sport management is no exception. By identifying and studying future trends, professionals and practitioners in the field can prepare and explore many aspects of their current programs and activities. Although it is not possible to predict exactly what will occur, observing and identifying future trends might allow us to redefine the nature of what we do and how we do it.

Young and Ross (2000) conducted a research study with a panel of recreational sport management experts in order to identify possible trends affecting the delivery of recreational sport programs. Experts in the study identified 31 trends having the great-est potential for impact, with the majority of these trends emerging from funding, legal aspects, sport facilities, technology, personnel, and programming areas.

Funding

One of the top trends in administering recreational sport programs is income generation for sport programs and facilities. Most recreational sport administrators are not surprised by this trend because many programs have been forced to reduce budgets during the past few years because of the sluggish economy. The severe economic recession in 2009 had a major effect on many sport programs. Because of the lethargic economy, a significant decline occurred in recreational sport participation and sport spending. Over 25 percent of active participants in sport, fitness, and recreation indicated that they spent considerably less in 2009 (Physical Activity Council, 2010). Because of this decline in participant spending, additional revenue or sources of income must be generated. The challenge for the recreational sport administrator is to find creative ways to overcome these economic constraints.

Legal Aspects

It is imperative for recreational sport administrators to educate not only themselves in various legal aspects but also their staffs and participants. Recreational sport administrators must become responsible for developing sound risk management plans and programs that reduce the likelihood of accidents and injuries that might lead to participant lawsuits against the agency. Administrators should become familiar with the laws of their state that apply to recreational sport programs and facilities. Effective risk management planning is essential for reducing losses and avoiding lawsuits. Well-prepared risk management plans and thorough reporting, record keeping, facility inspections, training, event supervision, and emergency procedures will help reduce the potential for lawsuits.

Sport Facilities

Facility construction is a growth area in recreational sport management. Over the past few decades, recreational sport programs, in a variety of sectors, have witnessed tremendous growth in the number of new sport facilities being constructed. Collegiate recreational sport is leading the way in the number of new recreational sport complexes on campuses across the country. Experts believe that participants will continue to demand larger and more specialized recreational sport facilities resulting in even more new construction well into the 21st century. The sport industry continues to change and expand to meet the demands of current and future participants. Administrators will need to be prepared in many areas related to sport management, including securing funding for existing and new sport facilities.

Technology

In the past 15 years computing technology has significantly affected the way that sport businesses and agencies deliver sport and tournament programming. Selecting appropriate technology may have the biggest effect on improving the efficiency of a sport program. Although technology is not the panacea for a quality recreational sport program, using technology, including hardware and software components, is clearly an important trend and tool that can improve the quality and speed of daily operations. Software and web-based programs make it easy for sport administrators and programming staff to create round-robin and single-elimination schedules for single or multisport leagues, register teams and accept payments online, and manage websites and facilities. For sport facility managers, new computer-aided facility management technologies have been designed to help them do their jobs more effectively and efficiently. Technologically advanced exercise gadgets and equipment innovations ranging from the Wii and xBox 360 to sophisticated, cutting-edge fitness machines are transforming not only how participants exercise but also how they stay motivated to exercise. Once considered an enemy to physical activity among youth, "motion game experiences" are now engaging youth in physical activity while using technology.

Personnel

Because technology is ever changing and its use is growing, recreational sport managers must hire additional staff to maintain current computer applications to assist with registration, scheduling, facility use, and marketing efforts. The increase in the technological benefits of local area networks (LANs) and servers owned by recreational sport agencies will cause an increase in the number of part-time computer generalists and full-time LAN and network administrators on the traditional recreational sport programming staff. In addition, because of the popularity of the web, individuals knowledgeable of web programming will be critical to sport programs. Lastly, because of the power of the social networking revolution (e.g. Facebook, MySpace, Twitter, and so on) to reach the masses, sport agencies will use this medium to advertise their programs. Specialists will be needed to create and maintain this presence.

Due to the fact that recreational sport programs have become so diverse and are rapidly expanding in terms of programs and facilities to meet the growing needs of participants, marketing has become a core activity for recreational sport management. Recreational sport staffs now include marketing specialists with the skills, experience, and dedicated time to plan and implement marketing strategies to support the sport programs and services. These staff members have a significant impact on the success of the agency.

Parental Concerns

In recent years an alarming number of head injuries and related concussion issues have occurred, primarily in professional football but also in other sports and at the youth and collegiate levels. Parents and sport administrators are concerned. Many parents have chosen not to let their children participate in football, basketball, or other contact sports because of the increased risk of these types of head injuries. Sport administrators from the NFL down to the neighborhood youth sport association are now reviewing and updating sports rules, regulations, and standards for sports equipment, especially helmets used in football.

Paramount to recreational sport is staff education and the use of background checks among youth sport programs. Recreational sport agencies must ensure that all staff and volunteers are properly trained by providing educational sessions such as workshops, certification opportunities, educational materials, and routine supervision. In addition, screening staff and volunteers is no longer an option. The practice of yearly background checks for all staff and volunteers is a must for youth sport agencies. Costs for background checks can be a concern for youth sport agencies. Ways to offset these costs are to require the staff or volunteer to pay for the background check, have the agency pay part of the fee, use free sources (web, local and state agencies), or seek grants or private funding to assist with costs. Regardless, each youth sport agency must ensure the safety of its participants by requiring background checks.

Programming

Recreational sport and fitness programs are immensely popular and usually attract large numbers of participants. Countless millions of Americans partake in a variety of recreational sport and outdoor recreation activities throughout the year. *Sports, Fitness and Recreation Participation—Overview Report* (Physical Activity Council, 2010) measures participation in 117 sport, fitness, and recreation activities in the United States and describes a variety of participation trends in recreational sport programming. Among the many facts listed in the report are the following:

- The economy and the economic recession in 2009 had a major effect on spending in sport, fitness, and recreation.
- Technological advances in heavy cardio equipment accounted for a 2 to 4.9 percent increase in use of elliptical motion trainers, treadmills, and stationary cycles.
- Aerobics and other socially based exercise activities at health clubs increased 8.1 percent.
- Free weight training using dumbbells and other hand weights has increased over 30 percent since 2000.
- Golf remained one of the top individual sports in 2009 with 27.1 million participants even though the number of golfers dropped 5.1 percent.
- Participation in school physical education programs continues to be the key pathway to regular participation among youth during their school years as well as when they reach adulthood. Adults who were inactive during their school years are three times more likely to be inactive as adults (55.6 percent compared with 19.1 percent).

From a programming perspective, it is important that recreational sport programmers are aware of these trends when planning and developing sport activities for their agency. Knowing and understanding participant trends can provide a better understanding of participant needs and interests which can then enable agencies to better plan, design, and implement a comprehensive recreational sports program. Tables 14.1 and 14.2 provide the estimated number of participants in several recreational sport activities in 2007 as listed in the *Statistical Abstract of the United States* (U.S. Census Bureau, 2010).

As illustrated in table 14.1, exercise walking, camping, swimming, and exercising with equipment rank among the top series I recreational sport activities in which Americans participate. (Series I and II are categories used by the U.S. Census Bureau.) Table 14.2 reflects the top series II recreational sport activities in which Americans participate: working out at a club, boating, target shooting, and in-line skating.

INTERNATIONAL PARTICIPATION IN RECREATIONAL SPORT

Although participation in recreational sport is immensely popular in the United States, it is just as popular in other countries. In 2005 over one-half (51 percent) of Canadian children 5 to 14 years old, or an estimated 2.0 million youth, regularly took part in organized sport. In addition, 7.3 million adults, about 28 percent of the adult population, participated in some form of sport (Statistics Canada, 2005). Over 10 million Australians aged 15 years and over (66 percent) participated in recreational sport during 2005 and 2006. As was the case in the United States, walking was the most commonly reported activity among Australians (Australian Bureau of Statistics, 2007). In China approximately 37 percent of the 1.3 billion population actively participated in sport activities (China. org.cn, 2008). Approximately 2.7 million South African people participated in sport and recreation in 2007 and 2008 because of opportunities provided by the Syiadlala Mass Participation Program, which was launched to facilitate access to sport and recreation by as many South Africans as possible, especially those from historically disadvantaged communities (SouthAfricaWeb.co.za, 2010). Brazil reported approximately 10.8 million regular sport participants in 2005 (Blogamericas, 2007).

CAREER OPPORTUNITIES

Although a general core of sport management competencies is required to work in the sport management profession, the various career settings and venues will dictate specific competency areas (Barcelona & Ross, 2005). Those interested in working in professional sport management will need advanced knowledge of business and marketing principles and techniques, whereas recreational sport professionals will need more knowledge in sport programming including tournament scheduling, personnel (i.e., officials, supervisors, lifeguards, and so on) training and scheduling, and facility management. Regardless of the career path chosen, the growing popularity of sport programs will create significant demand for competent professionals, both full-time and part-time, who are capable of delivering and overseeing sport management programs and services in diverse employment settings. The number of positions and specific job responsibilities will vary depending on the sport setting.

Four Levels of Positions

With the growth and interest in recreational sport programs, there have been increased opportunities for employment ranging from leadership positions working face to face with participants to top administrative positions. Four general levels of

Table 14.1 Estimated Number of Participants in Top 10 Series I Recreational Sport Activities: 2007

Rank	Activity	Participants (million)
1	Exercise walking	89.7
2	Exercising with equipment	52.8
3	Swimming	52.3
4	Camping	47.5
5	Bowling	43.5
6	Bicycle riding	37.4
7	Fishing (net)	35.3
8	Weightlifting	33.1
9	Fishing (fresh water)	30.8
10	Running or jogging	30.4

Reprinted from U.S. Census Bureau, 2010.

Table 14.2 Estimated Number of Participants in Top 10 Series II Recreational Sport Activities: 2007

Rank	Activity	Participants (million)
1	Working out at a club	33.8
2	Boating (motor or power)	31.9
3	Target shooting	20.5
4	Hunting	19.5
5	In-line skating	10.7
6	Scooter riding	10.6
7	Skateboarding	10.1
8	Paintball games	7.4
9	Mountain biking (off road)	7.4
10	Target shooting	6.6

Reprinted from U.S. Census Bureau, 2010.

personnel are commonly found in settings providing recreational sport management: administrative staff, program administrative staff, program staff, and auxiliary staff (Mull, Bayless, & Jamieson, 2005).

• **Administrative staff.** The administrative staff personnel are the ultimate authority and provide the overall direction and leadership for the entire recreational sport program and its resources including staff, budget, facilities, and equipment. Specific duties of the administrator are to determine the nature, scope, and direction of the program; evaluate overall program efficiency in terms of goals and standards; provide guidelines, establish priorities, and determine schedules for the acquisition and construction of recreational sport facilities; and explain policy and major program changes to staff and the public. Typical job titles at this level are administrator, director, or executive director. Because of the wide range of recreational sport programs and the need for experience in decision making, top administrators usually hold a master's degree and have a minimum of 10 years of experience.

• **Program administrative staff.** The program administrative staff are full-time professionals who support the administrator. In addition, they help formulate and administer policies, guidelines, and resources while monitoring programs, facilities, and program staff. People in this role also serve as a liaison between the top administrator and the program staff in day-to-day decision making. Job titles are often specific to the sport setting, but general titles at this level include associate director, program director, fitness director, public relations director, operations director, facility manager, and sports coordinator or director. People in these positions usually hold a bachelor's degree and many hold a master's degree in recreation, sport management, or a related field and have a minimum of five years of programming-related experience.

• **Program staff.** Program staff member is the entry-level position in this field and refers to many positions within an organization. Work responsibilities require specialized skills and training in organizing and conducting various sport programs. People in this role may initiate publicity and promotion, purchase and inventory equipment, and implement policies for safety, participant control, and

governance. The program staff is also responsible for recruiting, hiring, training, and scheduling support staff including sport officials, lifeguards, and supervisors. Typical job titles are assistant director, marketing assistant, coordinator, building manager, personal trainer, pool operator, leader, and activity specialist. Many of these positions require a bachelor's degree, but many employers prefer candidates with a master's degree.

• **Auxiliary staff.** The auxiliary staff consists of part-time, hourly wage or volunteer positions that engage in face-to-face contact with the program participants. The auxiliary staff primarily consists of seasonal or part-time positions such as officials, scorekeepers, supervisors, aerobics and group exercise leaders, equipment room attendants, aquatics instructors, fitness consultants, facility entry attendants, lifeguards, maintenance crews, and youth sport coaches. Although this is the level at which many program staff members gain experience, people seeking employment at this level usually do not have a degree but may hold some type of specialized sport credential such as first aid, water safety instructor, CPR, sport official certification, or youth sport coaching certification.

Job Outlook

Finding a career in recreational sport management is a promising prospect for those willing to pursue it. There are various levels of recreational sport management positions in thousands of for-profit and nonprofit institutions throughout the United States. These institutions support recreational sport programs that serve millions of people of all ages. In many settings, the demand for qualified recreational sport management specialists far exceeds the supply, which provides great job opportunities for students interested in this field. Employment opportunities include the following:

• The Amateur Athletics Union (AAU), founded in 1888, has a philosophy of "sports for all, forever" that is shared by nearly 500,000 participants and more than 50,000 volunteers in the United States. The AAU is divided into 56 distinct associations that annually sanction more than 34 sport programs, 250 national championships, and over 30,000 age division events across the country. These activities and events provide employment opportunities involving sport facilities, programming, and operations.

• Armed forces recreation supports 215,000 full-time employees with 10 million users at more than 900 locations within the United States and 360 overseas locations. Sport programmers and sport directors provide various services to all branches of the U.S. military. PSP Division, or the Personnel Support Division of the Canadian Forces Personnel Support Agency, is the key provider of recreational services within the military environment.

• Boys and Girls Clubs of America serves more than 4.2 million youth in more than 4,000 chartered clubs in the United States. It is one of the fastest growing youth services agencies and has nearly 51,000 trained full-time professional staff members. The 102 Boys and Girls Clubs of Canada serve 200,000 children and youth in 700 community-based locations nationwide. The organization has more than 3,000 trained full-time and part-time staff.

• Association of Church Sports and Recreation Ministers (CSRM) serves a network of church recreation and sports ministry professionals.

• In Canada in 2003, about 161,000 nonprofit and voluntary organizations were operating across the country in a wide variety of areas. The largest group of organizations (21 percent) operates in the area of sports and recreation (Statistics Canada, 2005).

• The collegiate and campus setting offers a variety of recreational sports career opportunities across the United States.

• Commercial sports offer thousands of job opportunities in country clubs, bowling centers, theme parks, health and fitness spas, racket clubs, tennis centers, ski resorts, golf courses, aquatic centers, hotels, and natural settings for boating, rafting, and fishing.

• Correctional recreation programs are staffed by practitioners at the federal, state, and local levels, working in juvenile, medical, and community-based facilities. A growing emphasis in this specialty is on promoting inmate health and fitness and providing sport opportunities.

• Employee recreational sports provide career opportunities for sport programmers in business, commercial, and industrial employee recreational sport programs.

• Fitness club membership in the United States at the end of 2005 was estimated at approximately 42.7 million people in approximately 23,500 health clubs. Fitness is a $17.6 billion industry in the United States alone. The International Health, Racquet & Sportsclub Association is a global trade association that represents over 9,000 health and fitness facilities in 75 countries.

• Municipal parks and recreation departments in the United States staff approximately 3,000 positions in sports programming.

• State games festivals are organized by the State Games of America, a property of the National Congress of State Games (NCSG), which is a membership organization composed of 31 summer state games and 10 winter state games organizations. The NCSG is a community-based member of the United States Olympic Committee. Nearly 500,000 athletes of all ages, backgrounds, and skill levels participate nationwide. Job opportunities are available at the national and state levels for full-time sport directors and event management coordinators as well as thousands of volunteers needed to conduct these large, multisport events across the United States.

• The 2,600 YMCAs and 302 YWCAs in the United States (now known as just the Y) employ approximately 20,000 full-time professionals. Of these positions, 4,000 are related to recreational sport. The Y serves more than 4.5 million participants in 124 countries. YMCA Canada is a federation of all 53 YMCAs and YMCA-YWCAs in Canada and serves 1.8 million people in more than 250 communities. Each of the 53 clubs is independent, hires its own staff, and recruits its own volunteers. Over 14,000 people are employed in this setting.

• In the United States, Big Brothers Big Sisters serves more than 245,000 children ages 5 through 18 in 5,000 communities across all 50 states in after-school sport programs and other recreational activities. Big Brothers Big Sisters of Canada is the leading child- and youth-serving organization in Canada and has more than 128 local agencies.

Professional Associations and Organizations

Sport management professionals need to remain current in theoretical and practical concerns in the field. Many sport practitioners hold active memberships in a variety of professional associations and organizations that sponsor a wide range of continuing education courses, institutes, workshops, regional and national conferences, and other in-service training for people working in this field. The professional associations and organizations most closely associated with sport management are listed in the web resource. Professional associations and organizations provide practitioners and students with opportunities for conferences, workshops, seminars, and management schools that help them stay abreast of trends and practices and their implications for program delivery in the rapidly changing sport management field.

SUMMARY

The role of recreational sport as an integral part to human enjoyment and vitality is well established and recognized. Participation in sport for fun and fitness is a very popular leisure-time pursuit among Americans and Canadians. Active participation in recreational sports is an important part of day-to-day existence for many people and involves an individual's choice of participating in either structured sports (instruction, intramural, extramural, club) or self-directed sports (informal) at a multitude of sport settings. These settings, ranging from municipal parks and recreation, campus recreation, YMCA, and military installations to youth service organizations, offer recreational sport programs and events that provide mental, physical, social, and emotional benefits to all participants.

With the increasing interest in recreational sport participation and fitness activity for all age groups, there has arisen a need for broad-based recreational sport programming that reflects these needs and interests. In turn, this will continue to spur the growth of recreational sport management, providing a variety of exciting and fulfilling job opportunities in diverse settings.

For glossary terms, learning experiences, and more, please visit the web resource at
www.HumanKinetics.com/IntroductionToRecreationAndLeisure

CHAPTER 15

Health, Wellness, and Quality of Life

Terrance Robertson, Matthew Symonds,
Michael Muehlenbein, and Clifford Robertson

" The first wealth is health. **"**

Ralph Waldo Emerson,
American poet, lecturer, and
essayist, 1803-1882

LEARNING OUTCOMES

After reading this chapter, you should be able to do the following:

> Describe at least three current trends in health
> Explain at least four factors that affect health
> Identify five factors to consider when assessing your personal wellness status
> Describe at least three roles that parks, recreation, and allied professions play in developing and maintaining healthy lifestyles

INTRODUCTION

Future parks and recreation professionals will play leading roles in health, wellness, and quality of life globally; such areas of applied research are wide open for the motivated, academically prepared, and appropriately credentialed and committed person. Although people generally appreciate the benefits of health, many take for granted their good health until it is gone. Health experts have long advocated for the implementation of diverse behaviors to prevent disease and disability, a view that importantly goes beyond clinical treatment of signs and symptoms of illness. As long ago as 1947, the World Health Organization adopted the following definition of **health**: A "state of complete physical, mental, and social well-being and not merely the absence of disease and infirmity." Yet although for many populations education has improved, income levels have risen, and life expectancies have increased, many behavioral changes have led to an increasing incidence of lifestyle-related disease such as obesity and diabetes. In the United States, because people are living longer and the birth rate is decreasing, the population structure is aging rapidly. A significant proportion of this aging population is overweight or obese (Centers for Disease Control and Prevention, 2009). In Canada the proportion of obese children has nearly tripled over the last quarter century (Health Canada, 2006). These developments present a number of challenges and opportunities for people entering the parks and recreation and related professions. In this chapter, you will read about health, wellness, and quality of life. These three topical areas and their related trends, issues, programs, and services provide an important foundation for the future of parks and recreation professionals.

PERSONAL HEALTH

Individual or **personal health** is a specialized discipline. Those interested in this area professionally can find careers in everything from being a primary care physician to an aerobics instructor, from a dietician to an organic food producer. The options are broad, as is the related professional preparation. The careers in this area can also be specialized and thus so can be the professional preparation.

Personal health and wellness are often assessed by using a standard set of indicators, including blood pressure, body mass index, amount of physical activity, diet, alcohol and tobacco use, and access to health care, to name a few. Ultimately, the health of an individual affects both **community health** and **population health**.

Current State of Health in the United States and Canada

People in most locations globally are living longer than did previous generations. In its 2007 report, the U.S. Centers for Disease Control and Prevention noted a record life expectancy at birth in the United States of nearly 78 years, as well as historically low age-adjusted death rates (Xu et al., 2010). In contrast, the life expectancy in 1940 was 62.9 years, meaning that life expectancy has increased 15 years in less than seven decades. Similarly, Canada is experiencing changes in its population. By 2026 one in five Canadians will be age 65 or older (Health Canada, 2002).

Preterm and low-weight births along with child mortality rates also help us describe overall health (Behrman & Butler, 2007). Although the preterm birth rate declined for the second year in a row in 2008 in the United States, the rate for low birth weight did not change (National Center for Health Statistics, 2008). Health challenges still exist for infants, children, and mothers. In 2005 the United States ranked a surprising 30th in infant mortality (MacDorman & Mathews, 2009). In contrast, infant mortality in Canada is much lower—a reported 5.1 deaths per 1,000 live births in 2007 (Statistics Canada, 2011). Generally, lower infant and child mortality rates equate to healthier communities.

High-school-aged students in the United States also face health challenges. According to the 2009 Youth Risk Behavior Survey, many high school students engage in behaviors that can lead to compromised health. Moreover, some of these risky behaviors can have health implications lasting into adulthood. Such risky behaviors include not wearing a seat belt, riding in a car with a driver who had been drinking, using marijuana and alcohol, having unprotected sexual intercourse, and smoking cigarettes (Centers for Disease Control and Prevention, 2010). High school students' nutrition and physical activity practices are also of concern. More than

Parks, recreation, and allied professions can play a role in discouraging youth from engaging in risky behaviors.

77 percent had not eaten fruits and vegetables five or more times a day, less than 20 percent had not been physically active for 60 minutes per day, and 12 percent were obese (CDC, 2010).

These poor eating habits and low physical activity levels are associated with obesity, type 2 diabetes, and heart disease—all of which are increasing in children and young adults in the United States (U.S. Department of Health and Human Services, 2001). Data have indicated that obesity rates are on the rise and contribute to 4 of the top 10 leading causes of death (heart disease, cancer, stroke, and diabetes) (Hedley et al., 2004; National Institutes of Health, 1998; Ogden et al., 2002, 2008).

The potential economic impact of obesity is staggering. For example, costs may have reached as high as $90 billion in 2002 dollars (Finkelstein et al., 2003). Approximately 75 percent of the nation's total health care costs are incurred by treating lifestyle-related chronic diseases (Centers for Disease Control and Prevention, 2004). Despite all the current dialogue, proposed legislation, and debate, the problem is increasing. In addition, an increasing number of individuals and families are underinsured or uninsured. The problems illuminate the opportunities that exist for people, programs and services, and communities related to parks, recreation, and health promotion.

World Leisure and Health Promotion and Disease Prevention

To be clear, issues of health, wellness, and quality of life are of interest to professionals, educators, and individuals globally, not just at the **community** or national level. Similar health assessment and surveillance work as mentioned earlier has taken place for many years throughout the world. Similarly, parks and recreation professionals around the world are also becoming interested. In August 2010 at an international congress in Chuncheon, South Korea, a global meeting of the World Leisure Organization's new commission on health promotion and disease prevention was convened. The commission developed a global vision, seven essential tenets, and an approximate timeline that was adopted by the commission (World Leisure Organization, 2012):

1. Leisure is an essential element of the human experience.
2. Participation in leisure pursuits contributes to an individual's health capacity.
3. Leisure engagement contributes to the health capacity of a community.
4. A lack of access to or participation in health-based leisure adversely affects an individual's long-term health capacity.
5. A variety of factors influence the provision of leisure-related resources and opportunities for engagement.
6. The environment and human experiences are inextricably linked and significantly affect leisure experiences.
7. Governments, nongovernmental organizations, and private-sector entities must be engaged in the process of planning for, monitoring of, and advancing the roles of leisure, recreation, and play as deterrents to lifestyle-related illnesses and disease.

Using these tenets, the commission's work will continue to focus on the factors that affect health and well-being, including the physical, intellectual, social, emotional, environmental, and spiritual components of wellness.

Factors That Affect Health

The four major categories of factors that affect our health are (1) genetics, (2) healthy or unhealthy behaviors, (3) access to, and availability of health care, and (4) the environment. Although not an exhaustive list, table 15.1 outlines several important items in each of these categories. As you examine these factors, do you know how each factor influences your personal health? If not, do you know where to access more information about the effect of these factors on your health?

A positive change in health behaviors is an important part of developing a healthy population and economy (U.S. Department of Health and Human Services, 1996). Research has demonstrated that even moderate changes in health behaviors such as decreased smoking, increased fruit and vegetable consumption and physical activity, and decreased alcohol consumption have significant health benefits that can lead to lower morbidity and mortality (Kvaavik et al., 2010).

A Global Perspective

Many indicators of health are monitored globally by experts who look for triangulation of causes or indicators. Individual indicators are direct or leading indicators, whereas others are considered secondary or contributing indicators or factors. For example, as seen in figure 15.1, body mass index (BMI), which is an indicator of obesity, is mapped by the World Health Organization (2010b) and shared globally. Others may track the leading causes of death by county or region of the world. Often leading causes of death vary by geographic region and income level. However, lifestyle-related disease is responsible for nearly 40 percent of deaths, regardless of income level (WHO, 2009). These would be independent of genetic predisposition, aging-related causes, and acquired illnesses. Other analyses track causes of death attributable to environmental causes (natural or built), as shown in figure 15.2.

Table 15.1 Factors That Affect Health

Genetic and personal factors	Healthy and unhealthy behaviors	Health care factors	Environmental factors
• Age • Body mass index • Body type • Gender • Height • Race and ethnicity • Weight	• Alcohol consumption • Fruit and vegetable consumption • Hours of sleep • Physical activity • Seatbelt use • Stress management • Tobacco use	• Annual physical examinations • Blood pressure • Fasting glucose • High-density lipoproteins • Low-density lipoproteins • Preventative age- and gender-specific screenings • Total cholesterol	• Access to fitness facilities • Access to healthy food sources • Access to parks and trails • Access to public transportation • Living environment • Working environment

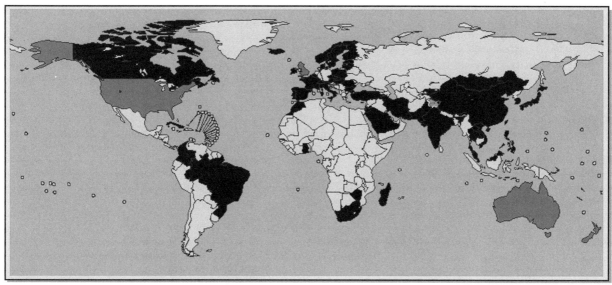

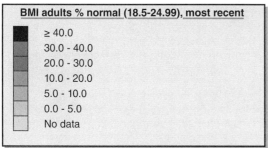

BMI adults % normal (18.5-24.99), most recent

≥ 40.0
30.0 - 40.0
20.0 - 30.0
10.0 - 20.0
5.0 - 10.0
0.0 - 5.0
No data

Figure 15.1 Global estimates of adult BMI as mapped by the World Health Organization.

Reprinted, by permission, from World Health Organization, 2012, *Global database on body mass index* (Geneva, Switzerland: WHO). Available: http://apps.who.int/bmi/index.jsp.

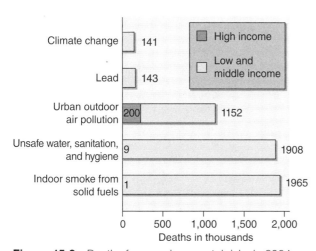

Climate change	141
Lead	143
Urban outdoor air pollution	200 · 1152
Unsafe water, sanitation, and hygiene	9 · 1908
Indoor smoke from solid fuels	1 · 1965

High income
Low and middle income

Deaths in thousands

Figure 15.2 Deaths from environmental risks in 2004.

Reprinted, by permission, from World Health Organization, 2010, *Global estimates of burden of disease caused by the environment and occupational risks* (Geneva, Switzerland: WHO). Available: www.who.int/quantifying_ehimpacts/global/envrf2004/en/index.html.

To understand the entire scope and sequence of events presented in figure 15.2 and to develop health promotion interventions to help address these implicit needs, a model can be utilized. It would include a minimum of three factors simultaneously, including person or human factors (P), environmental factors (E), and individual or situational factors (s) in a PE(s) model. We can better illustrate health from a multifaceted perspective. This model attempts to address the four major factors that affect our health: genetics, behaviors, health care, and the environment. Others have used communication and health logic models (one example of this is included in the web resource for your use and practice), and still others have used complex plotting and factoring models to understand these factors (relationships, timelines, causation, and so on). Ideally, model development would allow the prescription of services (assessment, monitoring, treatment, and so on) and the implementation of potential interventions to decrease morbidity and mortality.

Traditionally, the United States has focused on diagnosis and treatment of disease. Only recently has it moved to adopting a health promotion or prevention perspective that includes a holistic wellness approach. Other countries including Canada adopted the prevention or wellness model long ago. So in essence, service providers have either been trying to prevent illness and disease or trying to treat illness and disease, whereas other providers have been focused on doing both. Regardless of the treatment or prevention activity, service providers usually focus activities on people within prescribed geographic areas, eventually expanding based on patterns of individuals or diseases.

Assessment and monitoring of disease, however, is a collaborative global effort. The World Health Organization is generally considered the entity responsible for collection and dissemination of these data on a global level. In the United States the Centers for Disease Control and Prevention is the primary national collection and dissemination agency. Data collected from local public health departments are sent to respective individual state health departments and from there they are sent to the Centers for Disease Control and Prevention and then on to the World Health Organization.

THE WELLNESS PERSPECTIVE

Thinking back to the World Health Organization's early definition of health, the current state of health, and the factors that affect health, we begin to see that achieving optimal health is a multidimensional endeavor. This whole-person approach can be referred to as **wellness**. The wellness perspective includes examining health across several interrelated components or dimensions, including physical, intellectual, emotional, social, environmental, and spiritual wellness. This holistic approach helps us make a connection between our health, wellness, and quality of life. Figure 15.3 outlines key findings from the Centers for Disease Control and Prevention (2003) about health-related quality of life.

In our information age, the consumer has access to voluminous resources regarding health, but not everyone has the same level of health literacy. According to *Healthy People 2010* (U.S. Department of Health and Human Services, 2000), health literacy is defined as "the degree to which individuals have the capacity to obtain, process, and understand basic health information and services needed to make appropriate health decisions." The degree of health literacy affects every dimension of wellness and is an important consideration for those entering health-related professions. Here we explore each of these wellness dimensions.

HEALTH-RELATED QUALITY OF LIFE FINDINGS

- Americans felt physically or mentally unhealthy approximately 6 days per month.
- Americans felt "healthy and full of energy" about 19 days per month.
- Almost one-third of Americans said that they suffered from some mental or emotional problem every month.
- Ten percent said that their mental health was not good for 14 or more days per month.
- Adults aged 18 to 24 years reported the most mental health distress.
- Older adults suffered the greatest poor physical health and activity limitation.
- Native Americans and Alaska Natives reported the highest levels of unhealthy days among American racial and ethnic groups.
- Adults with the lowest income or education reported more unhealthy days than did those with higher income or education.
- Americans with chronic diseases or disabilities reported high levels of unhealthy days.

Figure 15.3 The key findings from the Centers for Disease Control and Prevention, Behavior Risk Factor Surveillance System, 2003, show the connection between health, wellness, and quality of life.

Source: www.cdc.gov/hrqol/key_findings.htm.

Physical Wellness

Nutrition and physical activity provide foundations for our overall wellness. Several components of physical wellness are in the control of the individual, including what we eat and how active we are. Let's explore some accepted guidelines in these areas as well as the roles that parks and recreation may play here.

Proper nutrition has many health benefits. Proper eating habits decrease the likelihood that a person will become overweight or obese and decrease the risks for some chronic diseases like high blood pressure, type 2 diabetes, and some cancers. According to the 2005 Dietary Guidelines for Americans (www.health.gov/dietaryguidelines/dga2005/document/), a healthy diet (1) emphasizes fruits, vegetables, whole grains, and low-fat or fat-free milk, (2) includes lean meats, poultry, fish, beans, eggs, and nuts, and (3) is low in certain fats, cholesterol, sodium, and added sugar. Although we understand the importance of proper nutrition, many people do not meet recommended dietary guidelines. You can learn more about proper nutrition, develop an individual nutrition plan, and track your progress at www.choosemyplate.gov.

Being physically active is not an all-or-nothing proposition. Rather, health benefits derive from what appear to be low levels of physical activity. How much physical activity is enough? According to the U.S. Department of Health and Human Services (2000), children and adolescents should be physically active for 1 hour or more per day. As adults, we should be moderately active for 2 hours and 30 minutes per week or vigorously active for 1 hour and 15 minutes per week. Both children and adults should also participate in strength-training activities. Evidence supporting the benefits of leading a physically active lifestyle is clear (www.cdc.gov/physicalactivity/everyone/health/). Benefits include the following:

- Lowered risk for
  - premature death,
  - heart disease,
  - stroke,
  - type 2 diabetes,
  - high blood pressure,
  - metabolic syndrome, and
  - colon and breast cancer
- Prevention of weight gain
- Promotion of weight loss
- Improvement in cardiovascular and muscular **fitness**
- Prevention of falls
- Reduction of depression
- Improvement in cognitive function
- Improvement in quality of sleep

Physical activity and nutrition programs are commonplace in all sectors of the parks and recreation profession. Ranging from worksite wellness programs to health clubs and public parks, hiking and biking trails, and aquatics facilities, programs and facilities managed by parks and recreation

Physical activity programs offered by recreation and leisure professionals specifically promote one of the seven dimensions of wellness—physical wellness.

professionals provide an outlet for physical activity for individuals, families, and communities. Moreover, nutrition and weight management programs are often deployed as a program or service. Physical activity and nutrition trends point toward a continued focus on these programs and services for parks and recreation professionals. In addition, emerging areas of recreation include nature, adventure, and medical tourism. People have visited and will continue to visit spas, national parks, and other destinations to improve personal health.

Intellectual Wellness

One of the many benefits of physical activity is improved cognitive function. Intellectual wellness focuses on learning throughout the lifespan. We live in a dynamic, changing, fast-paced world. To adapt, we need to continue to read, think, and reflect throughout our lives. Our minds require frequent stimulation. The adage "Use it or lose it" applies to both our bodies and our minds!

Although parks and recreation professionals may not consider intellectual development their primary goal, a number of programming and service opportunities for intellectual wellness development exist. Developing a book club in which people hold book discussions while walking on a community trail would contribute to the development of more than one component of wellness. Parks and recreation professionals can embrace facilities as centers for lifelong learning where individuals, families, and communities can gather to learn new skills and apply their knowledge and skills in recreation settings. The possibilities are limited only by our imagination.

Emotional Wellness

Nearly one-fourth of Americans have experienced a mental illness during the previous year, and as many as half will develop a mental illness during the lifespan (CDC, 2011). Over the course of a life, a person will encounter a number of challenges. The wellness perspective includes a component that encourages people to develop a skill set that will allow them to handle these emotional encounters effectively. New friendships, relationships, job challenges and opportunities, and the death of friends and family members are examples of events that present emotional challenges.

Abundant research supports the link between emotional health and overall health. Stress has been linked to the six leading causes of death. Moreover, positive emotional health has been shown to increase longevity and increase productivity at work (American Psychological Association, 2011). Emotional health and the ability to cope with stress are important parts of a healthy person's life. People can deal with events in a number of ways that elicit an emotional response. Whether by learning stress management techniques, participating in physical activity, eating a healthy diet, developing a support system of friends and family, or relying on religion or spiritual growth, individuals can address emotional situations in ways that reinforce the interconnectedness of the components of health and wellness.

Although an improved outlook and attitude may not seem like a primary goal of many parks and recreation programs, because of the interrelated nature of the wellness perspective, emotional benefits are, at a minimum, a secondary outcome of many parks and recreation programs. Because exercise, diet, relationships, and stress management affect mental and emotional well-being, we can easily see the influences that parks and recreation can have on this important component of wellness.

Social Wellness

Humans are, by nature, social creatures. Social interaction is an important part of leading a well-rounded, healthy lifestyle. Social wellness represents a person's ability to interact and participate effectively in a variety of environments and includes communication skills, meeting new people and building relationships, showing respect for self and others, and developing a supportive network of family and friends. Social wellness is also important in allowing people to participate effectively in the workplace, in communities, and in society.

Often, the concepts of compassion, volunteerism, fairness, inclusivity, and justice are viewed as parts of social wellness and exist in parks and recreation programs. As leisure professionals, we frequently take advantage of volunteers in our programs. In addition, fairness and programming for everyone is fundamental to our efforts. Finally, as parks and recreation professionals, we provide many opportunities for people to interact with one another while being active in leisure pursuits. Parks and recreation professionals and programs are leaders in providing social wellness opportunities across the lifespan.

Environmental Wellness

Environmental wellness has received increased attention over the past several years. As societies have begun to focus on green initiatives, the impact that our environment has on our health has become more evident. Ranging from access to parks, trails, and community fitness and recreation facilities to the products that we buy and the services that we use, each of us makes a measurable contribution to the state of our environment during our lifetimes. Conversely, environmental factors have an important effect on the wellness of people, communities, and regions. For example, consider two instances of obesity rates in the United States: Could the natural environment in a state like Colorado or the environmental conditions in a major metropolitan area like New York City influence or lead to different rates of obesity in those areas? If so, how can

parks and recreation leverage those environmental influences in other parts of the country?

In many cases, parks and recreation professionals do this all the time. Whether we take advantage of natural settings in developing parks and trails, campaign for a bond issue to build new facilities, or renovate parks and swimming pools, we often focus on the built environment to improve access to and the use of public areas. These contributions are important to developing an environment that can promote wellness.

The R&R model is helpful in understanding the relationships between a person's (or an organization's) behavior, the environment, and the resources available (see figure 15.4). The figure illustrates that a person who has high regard for her or his environment and resources will interact with the environment and thus exhibit healthier behavior. A person who has low regard for her or his environment and resources will be inactive and thus exhibit behaviors that are less healthy. Of course, a person could have

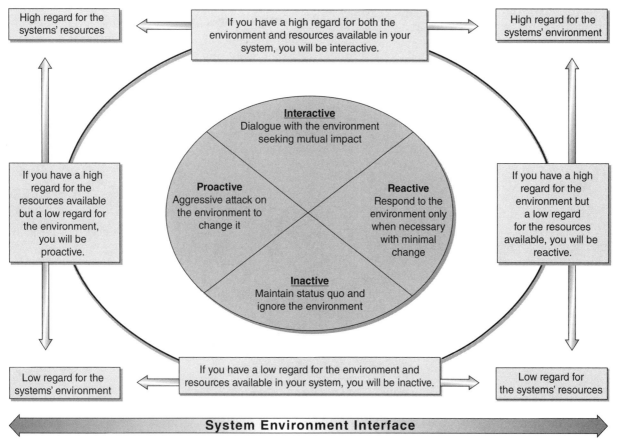

Figure 15.4   The R&R model of interaction between the environment and resources.

© Terry Robertson and Clifford Robertson.

high regard for the environment and low regard for available resources and thus be reactive in exhibiting healthy behaviors. Finally, a person could have high regard for her or his resources and low regard for the environment, in which case the person would be proactive in exhibiting healthy behaviors. To help someone move from one area to another (e.g., move from being inactive to proactive), a service provider would need to (*a*) help the person increase her or his regard for resources or (*b*) help improve or increase available resources. To help someone move from reactive to interactive, a service provider would also need to help the person increase or improve available resources (real or perceived).

Spiritual Wellness

The spiritual wellness component is different for each of us. This component of wellness involves our values, ideals, belief system, and ultimately our purpose in life. Often, spiritual wellness is viewed as the concept of balance between what we need as individuals and our interactions with the world in which we live. According to the National Wellness Institute, "You'll know you're becoming spiritually well when your actions become more consistent with your beliefs and values, resulting in a 'world view.'" Spiritual wellness follows these tenets:

- It is better to ponder the meaning of life for ourselves and to be tolerant of the beliefs of

others than to close our minds and become intolerant.
- It is better to live each day in a way that is consistent with our values and beliefs than to do otherwise and feel untrue to ourselves" (National Wellness Institute, 2011).

Each person may follow a different route to spiritual wellness. It may involve prayer, meditation, or other practices that support the person's progress toward a spiritual "place" or "connection." The role of parks and recreation professionals in spiritual wellness promotion may be more passive than their role in other areas. Although they may actively offer programs such as yoga, their role in the development of spiritual wellness may be about providing a safe place for people to practice developing this component of wellness at their own pace in their own way.

QUALITY OF LIFE, HEALTH, AND HEALTHY COMMUNITIES

The term *quality of life* is often used and overused (abused). Similarly, the term *healthy community* is familiar and often overused (abused). Combining these two terms when speaking of health can further confuse issues, purpose, and intent, so each topic is briefly discussed here.

Quality of life (QoL) is often considered the degree of well-being felt by a person or group of

By providing playgrounds and walking areas in residential areas, cities can improve the quality of life of their residents.

Measuring Health-Related Quality of Life

A growing field of research is concerned with developing, evaluating, and applying quality of life measures within health-related research (e.g., within randomized controlled trials), especially health services research. Many of these investigations focus on the measurement of health-related quality of life (HRQoL) rather than a more global conceptualization of quality of life. They also focus on measuring HRQoL from the perspective of the patient and thus take the form of self-completed questionnaires. The International Society for Quality of Life (www.isoqol.org) was founded in response to this research and is a useful source of information on the topic.

A number of groups and agencies around the world, including the United Nations and the World Health Organization, have tried to develop ways of assessing quality of life. Additionally, many disciplines and individual researchers have studied or are currently studying QoL. Few, however, are studying this for people who have disabilities. Why do you think this is so?

people. Unlike a standard of living (SoL) approach that primarily uses socioeconomic measures to determine relative health or **health status**, QoL examines broader constructs. As such, QoL is not a physically tangible concept, so it cannot be measured directly. Instead of using only a single type of measure (say economic only), an examination of QoL uses indicators that represent various aspects of health and wellness. QoL generally consists of two components: physical and psychological. The physical aspect includes such items as health, diet, and protection against pain and disease; the psychological aspect includes stress, worry, pleasure, and other positive or negative emotional states. Environmental quality of life includes air, water and soil quality, diet and nutrition, and diseases caused through environmental exposure. Holistic wellness, health, and health status are conceptually linked to QoL, and they have similar measures. Although these are all related, they are different in some key ways.

As mentioned earlier, another method of measuring differences in quality of life is to examine the difference in the standard of living (SoL) between individuals or groups based primarily on economic indicators. So, for example, income would be an indicator of health and a predictor of health status. Therefore, the more a person earns, the better his or her health and health status should be. Further, according to the technical application of that term, people in rural areas and small towns (who generally have lower income levels) might be reluctant to move to cities (larger urban areas), even if doing so would mean a substantial increase in their standard of living (income). Conversely, some people living in urban areas might prefer a higher SoL in exchange for a lower QoL. Thus, the quality of life experienced by living in a rural area may be of enough value to offset a lower standard of living. Similarly, people are sometime paid more to accept jobs that would lower their quality of life. Night jobs, jobs that require extensive travel, or jobs that are potentially hazardous might pay more, so the difference in salaries can also be a measure of the value of quality of life.

In summary, QoL and wellness are integrally related. The measures or indicators can be similar, if not the same. In both areas, an ecological or holistic approach is preferred. Professionals and participants (individuals, patients, folks with disabilities, organizations, and so on) all are interested in at least three things in order to make sustained change or improvement: the person (or organization), the environment, and any leading or causal situations (PE(s)). The R&R model (figure 15.4) is an informal model that a person or organization can use for self-examination in relation to resources, environment, and interactions with each.

Predicting the quality of life of a specific person is virtually impossible because the combination of attributes that leads one individual to be content is rarely the same for another. But we can presume with some confidence that a higher average level of diet, shelter, safety, freedoms, and rights in a general population will result in a better overall quality of life. As mentioned before, health literacy is the one of the primary predictors of health status, and both health status and its predictors can be measured directly. Further, those who teach or provide health and recreation or wellness services are not the only ones who are interested in it. For instance, the magazine *International Living* uses a variety of sources to create its quality of life index. According to its website, nine categories are analyzed: cost of living, culture and leisure, economy, environment, freedom, health, infrastructure, safety and risk, and climate (http://internationalliving.com/2010/02/quality-of-life-2010/). The magazine *The Economist* also has a quality of life index, which is based on a unique methodology that links the results of subjective life satisfaction surveys to the objective determinants of quality of life across countries (2005). The economist Robert Putnam's seminal work *Bowling Alone* (2000) looks at the economic and civic impact of changing trends within communities.

In his book Putnam presents evidence from over 500,000 interviews on how we have become increasingly disconnected from family, friends, neighbors, and our democratic structures. The issue of social capital (who we know) is also a major element of this book. Putnam warns that our stock of social capital has plummeted, impoverishing our lives and communities. As evidence, Putnam identifies that as a society we sign fewer petitions, belong to fewer organizations that regularly meet face to face, know our neighbors less well, meet with friends less frequently, and even socialize with our families less often. His evidence also indicates that we are even bowling alone. Although more Americans are bowling than ever before, they are not bowling in leagues. Changes in work, family structure, age, suburban life,

History in the Making: Healthy Communities

The term *healthy communities* owes its origins to a conference in Toronto, Ontario, held in 1984 and organized by Trevor Hancock, then in the city's department of public health. The conference was organized in part because of his assignment to create a plan for the city's public health, his remembering of an old book, *Hygeia: A City of Health* (Richardson, 1876), that he had read, and his reading of the works by Leonard Duhl (particularly *The Urban Condition*, 1962) of the University of California, Berkeley. The conference, Beyond Health Care, had one day set aside for discussion of the health of cities (seemingly a European term because a city was a relatively consistent legal entity in most countries). A speech by Leonard Duhl was on what he called healthy cities. His healthy cities thesis proposed the use of a comprehensive, community-based approach to improving public health. Also attending the conference was Ilona Kickbusch, a health promotion officer then with the World Health Organization's regional office for Europe in Copenhagen. As a result, Ilona Kickbusch began a healthy cities network in Europe. In 1987 the U.S. Public Health Service hired the National Civic League to facilitate a comprehensive nationwide examination for ways to improve the health of communities. The result was the start of the U.S. healthy communities movement.

From 1987 to 1997 two primary groups of actors seemed to appear and be active within the movement: (a) hospitals and health care providers and (b) related professionals and community problem solvers (volunteers, civic leaders, investors, entrepreneurs, and so on). In the early to mid-1990s a split in efforts occurred, a bit of fragmentation between medical and civic groups. Today this split has widened, but instead of disappearing it has spread into many areas of life. Businesses, governments, educational institutions, and organizations of all types have adopted the terminology and approach, sometimes as part of their approach to quality or customer service standards and other times as part of human resources or training efforts. The accession of the movement may result from just the connotation that the term brings to mind, or from the time in our life, but living or working in a healthy community is surely more desirable than living or working in an unhealthy community.

OUTSTANDING GRADUATES

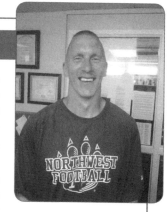

Background Information

Name: Joe Quinlin

Education: Bachelor of science from Northwest Missouri State University, Department of Health Physical Education, Recreation and Dance, in corporate and therapeutic recreation. Master of science from West Virginia University in physical education.

Credentials: CSCS, ACE.

Special awards: Academic Honor Roll, football, three years.

Affiliations: National Strength and Conditioning Association, College Strength and Conditioning Coaches Association.

Career Information

Position: Varsity strength and conditioning coach, Department of Athletics, at Northwest Missouri State University in Maryville, Missouri.

Organization: Originally established in 1905, Northwest Missouri State University is a state-assisted, four-year regional university that also offers graduate degree programs. Northwest currently has about 7,000 students. We have over 400 varsity athletes participating in 14 NCAA Division II athletics programs.

> " A wide variety of career opportunities are available, and many people do not have an appreciation for all parts of the field. There are many areas to be involved in, and the field is important because it helps people learn how to become and stay healthy. "

Organization's mission: Northwest Missouri State University focuses on student success—every student, every day.

Job description: Along with the two graduate assistants whom I supervise, we coordinate all strength and conditioning activities for the varsity athletics program.

Career path: I was a graduate assistant at WVU and started youth speed and agility camps. Also, I worked one on one with several college athletes. This job is long term and is my dream job.

Likes and dislikes about the job: I like seeing individuals and teams succeed and witnessing individual athletes grow. I dislike the long hours.

Advice for Undergraduates

Make as many contacts as possible. You never know who will call you or what positions might be available to you. Learn as much as possible in your field.

---

television, computers, women's roles, and other factors have contributed to this decline. Clearly, each of these factors is related to quality of life. Given that civic engagement is a major part of the original thought behind the healthy communities movement, it is logical to surmise that those interested in civic engagement could also have interest in quality of life.

More than having an interest in civic engagement, those interested in healthy communities are interested in health—the health of each individual, the health of specific groups, the health of the community, and, of course, the health of the general population.

So what is a healthy community? A healthy community is one in which people (volunteers or paid personnel) come together to make their community (a place where they live, work, or play) better for themselves, their families, their friends, their neighbors, and others now and in the future. It is a community where citizens purposefully work together to create a healthier, more livable, and more sustainable environment. Creating such an environment takes time and commitment. A healthy community creates

OUTSTANDING GRADUATES

Background Information

Name: Tyler Tapps

Education: Bachelor of science in corporate recreation and wellness and master of science in recreation, Northwest Missouri State University; doctor of philosophy in health, leisure, and human performance, Oklahoma State University at Stillwater.

Special awards: Northwest Missouri State University Outstanding Young Alumni Award 2012.

Affiliations: National Recreation and Park Association; vice president of special populations for Oklahoma Recreation and Parks Society; president of research for Oklahoma Association for Health, Physical Education, Recreation and Dance; Oklahoma Geriatric Council; Therapeutic Recreation Association of Oklahoma.

Career Information

Position: Assistant professor of recreation management and therapeutic recreation department, School of Applied Health and Educational Psychology.

Organization: Oklahoma State University at Stillwater is a land-grant institution with more than 26,000 students. The university offers 91 programs of study leading to a bachelor's degree, 70 master's programs, and 46 programs at the doctoral level.

Oklahoma State University College of Education is a community of scholars dedicated to research, teaching, and service. Our work involves basic and applied research that informs and improves education in schools and other settings. Excellence in teaching illustrates a commitment to continued learning, cultural diversity, and use of appropriate technology. The college maintains and promotes links with constituents who develop, disseminate, and apply knowledge.

The recreation management and therapeutic recreation program seeks to facilitate learn-

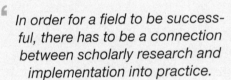 *In order for a field to be successful, there has to be a connection between scholarly research and implementation into practice.*

ers' personal and professional development through educational experiences guided by values, knowledge, and skills necessary for excellence in the recreation services profession. At the master's level we prepare future administrators for the various types of agencies and organizations associated with the field of parks, recreation, and recreation management. Doctoral studies at OSU are geared toward preparing well-rounded faculty members—higher education professionals who are committed to research, service, and teaching. The recreation management and therapeutic recreation program at Oklahoma State University has 105 to 130 undergraduate students and 35 to 50 graduate students at any given time.

Organization's mission: Oklahoma State University is a multicampus public land grant educational system that improves the lives of people in Oklahoma, the nation, and the world through integrated teaching, research, and outreach. The instructional mission includes undergraduate, graduate, technical, extension, and continuing education informed by scholarship and research. The research, scholarship, and creative activities promote human and economic development through the expansion of knowledge and its application.

Job description: My duties include teaching theory classes at the undergraduate, master's, and doctoral levels and supervising field experiences. I also mentor and advise master's and doctoral students. I am required to maintain a high level of scholarship and do research.

Career path: I was drawn to the field of recreation through community programs in my hometown. I always wondered how municipal government worked and was interested in the

Outstanding Graduates *(continued)*

idea of public service. While attending Northwest Missouri State University, I discovered that a lot of places were not like my hometown and had differing opinions about financial distribution related to parks and recreation. At that point I became interested in evaluation and analysis of city parks and recreation systems. This passion continued through my master's degree and led into a PhD program. I studied research design and statistical analysis extensively in college so that I would be prepared to do evaluations to see what works and what doesn't work for community programs. I am lucky to have a job where research is a major requirement. I also have the opportunity to take the knowledge gained from experiences in the field and present it in the classroom to better prepare future generations of parks and recreation professionals.

Likes and dislikes about the job: I enjoy seeing students grow from shy introverts during their first semester to very happy and outgoing young professionals. Nothing is better than watching students

discover what they want to do with their lives and watching how easy the academic portion becomes when students are passionate. The best part about my job is being able to implement practices in our community by studying programs, participants, and other aspects of recreation. Students who participate in the research portion are more aware of how they can affect their communities. These students are better educated when they enter the workforce, and they become assets to their employers.

Advice to Undergraduates

Learning is never completed. In a field that evolves, it is important to keep ahead of the game. Seek out certifications! In such a massive industry it is vital to find your niche. Certifications make you more of an asset. Finally, learn the financial aspects of managing recreation facilities, people, and programs. These managerial skills will make you more marketable.

---

open and ongoing dialogue, generates leadership opportunities for all, embraces diversity, connects people of all ages and backgrounds, and fosters a sense of community. More important, it shapes its future through a shared vision, shared work, and shared learning. Healthy communities are self-developed, self-guided, and self-directed. Most use common language and concepts, whereas others try to create unique terminology to help establish a specific identity or to brand themselves and their work.

Parks, recreation, and tourism professionals should recognize that a healthy community is about more than physical activity. Physical activity is a key, but clean, safe, and nurturing programs, services, and environments are essential. As a professional, you need to consider how your programs, services, and environments can contribute to the health of your community and its citizenry. Further, you should look at how you can do more than offer passive support. Instead, try to build the promotion of health and well-being into your place of work, the place where you live, and the leisure that you enjoy. Be a role model. Assess yourself, your family, and your environments and identify opportunities

to make a difference within the lives of others now and in the future.

CAREER OPPORTUNITIES

Career opportunities, continuing education opportunities, and research opportunities within the health and wellness area are too extensive to cover here in a comprehensive manner. So, in an attempt to be both brief and helpful, the listing of potential careers under the six components of wellness presented earlier in this chapter is listed in table 15.2. Within an area of interest, the reader can investigate opportunities specific to individual wellness component areas. The potential employment opportunities are diverse in terms of role expectations, potential political and fiscal support, mobility, and longevity.

Note that the current opportunities are just a beginning. As in every viable profession, the dynamic nature of the area combined with increased knowledge, changes in technology, population trends, and evolving public policy combine to create constant change in both the science and application of the profession. Continuing education, training, and

Table 15.2 Career Opportunities Categorized by Component of Wellness

Wellness area	Potential employers	Possible position titles
Physical	Municipalities, community center, health clubs, boys and girls clubs, YMCA and YWCA, health departments, schools, universities, private companies	Fitness instructor, group exercise leader, personal trainer, nutritionist, massage therapist, athletic trainer, researcher, community health professional
Intellectual	Schools, colleges, universities, federal government, state and local governments, private companies, nonprofit organizations, web designers, public relations firms, professional associations	Teacher, leader, researcher, writer, consultant, graphic designer, musician
Emotional	Home health, hospitals, community health care organizations, municipalities, nonprofit organizations, religious organizations, churches, synagogues	Therapist, counselor, religious worker, hospice, researcher, community worker, advocate
Social	Private companies, not-for-profits, cruise ship lines, travel organizations, tourism, hotels, municipalities, country clubs, amusement parks, specialty camps	Special event manager, tournament director, researcher, game designer, manufacturer, social media developer, public relations, social justice advocate, cruise ship director, activity director
Environmental	Health departments, federal government, state and local governments, parks, developers, private organizations, schools, universities	Emergency management officer, community health professional, public health professional, researcher, environmental health professional, resource manager, health officer, solid waste manager
Spiritual	Churches, synagogues, hospital, nonprofit organizations, private companies, military	Church or religious worker, life coach, personal advisor, pastor, youth leader, 12-step program director, motivational speaker, product developer, landscape architect, funeral service provider

research are essential. Opportunities will come and go, although not as quickly as in less robust and diverse professions.

SUMMARY

We have introduced a variety of concepts related to health, wellness, and quality of life. An understanding of the factors that affect health, the current health status and risks in our communities, the components of wellness, and other quality of life issues helps to provide a basis for many parks, recreation, and leisure programs and activities. Professionals have many opportunities to study, apply, or create new ways to contribute to the health and well-being of their communities. The time is right, the key elements are in place, and the future is not yet here, so the opportunities to explore, contribute, and provide services are wide open. But they are available only to those who are motivated to pursue a common vision: a healthy, sustainable, accessible, and livable community.

For glossary terms, learning experiences, and more, please visit the web resource at
www.HumanKinetics.com/IntroductionToRecreationAndLeisure

CHAPTER 16

Outdoor and Adventure Recreation

Alan Ewert and Franklin Vernon

" Without the instinct for adventure in young . . . any civilization, no matter how enlightened, any state, however well and ordered, must wilt and wither. "

George Trevelyan,
educational reformer,
philosopher, and visionary

LEARNING OUTCOMES

After reading this chapter, you should be able to do the following:

> Articulate the background and nomenclature associated with outdoor and adventure recreation

> Identify the major agencies, organizations, and resources commonly identified with outdoor and adventure recreation

> Describe some of the salient benefits and outcomes associated with participation and professional careers in outdoor and adventure recreation

INTRODUCTION

In 2009 over 137.8 million Americans participated in some form of outdoor or adventure recreation. During the same year over almost 12 million people visited a national park in Canada. In both cases, those visits might have included taking a quiet walk, scaling a forbidding peak, observing wildlife, or rafting down a raging river. Yet in many ways these extraordinary statistics fail to tell the complete story. What the statistics don't tell us is the immense sense of awe that these millions of people experienced, be it in quiet woods, at an open seashore, during a fun-filled picnic with family or friends, or at the top of a mountain. Moreover, these statistics don't tell us about the profound sense of accomplishment that many hundreds of people felt after reaching the top of the highest mountain in North America (Mt. McKinley, Alaska), or the connection to the sea and marine wildlife that thousands of sea kayakers experienced while pursuing their recreational interests along the Vancouver coast, or the varied emotions that countless other people experienced in unique recreational settings doing unique activities.

Another thing the statistics don't tell us is the connection that many Americans and Canadians draw between the types of activities they engage in while in the outdoors and the image they have of themselves, both as individuals and collectively as a nation. The psyche of both nations includes a sense of growing up within reach of outdoor spaces in which to test themselves, develop their belief systems, and assume the ability to function in times of adversity. Although incomplete, this explanation captures the essence of the outdoor recreation and adventure scene in Canada and the United States—heavily endowed in significant outdoor resources, having governments at all levels striving to provide suitable outdoor landscapes, and holding an unquenchable belief that being in these places is among the best ways to enjoy leisure time.

For example, in 2009 over 48.9 percent of Americans aged 6 and older participated in some form of outdoor recreation or adventure activity (Outdoor Foundation, 2010). This participation amounted to more than 10.1 billion outdoor outings and more than 161.6 million Americans participating in outdoor activities such as bicycling, fishing, hiking, camping, and trail running.

Finally, the statistics about the number of users fail to paint a complete picture of the impact that participation in outdoor and adventure recreation (OAR) has on economic growth. For example, in 2006 OAR contributed over $730 billion to the U.S. economy (Outdoor Industry Association, 2006). This level of participation resulted in nearly 6.5 million jobs being created or tied to the outdoor recreation delivery system and $88 billion of tax revenue being generated at the state and federal levels. Viewed from the perspective of sales, in 2006 over $289 billion were exchanged in retail sales and services related to OAR across the United States. This figure means that one in every eight dollars circulating in the United States is tied to outdoor recreation.

This chapter explores the outdoor and adventure recreation scene as it exists in the United States and Canada. To do so, we look at the definitions of some terms, a brief history of the growth of OAR within a North American context, the settings and delivery systems within OAR, some characteristics of the participants, professional careers, expected benefits and outcomes from participating in OAR, and some emerging trends and issues. To start, we examine some of the ways that these activities and experiences are defined.

CONCEPTS RELATED TO OUTDOOR AND ADVENTURE RECREATION

The fields of outdoor recreation and **adventure recreation** are similar and different in a number of ways. First, let's start with the set of definitions and meanings. **Outdoor recreation** implies an intrinsically rewarding experience that is voluntarily engaged in and typically occurs during nonobligated or leisure time and principally occurs in some type of outdoor setting (Driver & Tocher, 1970, p. 10). Moore and Driver (2005) provide a generic summary of these aspects of outdoor recreation in their definition: "Outdoor recreation is recreation experiences that result from recreation activities that occur in and depend on the natural environment" (p. 11).

Thus, another distinguishing characteristic of outdoor recreation is that it occurs in natural environments. Some activities that typically fall within the outdoor recreation definition are hiking, camping, hunting, fishing, horseback riding, bird watching, picnicking, sightseeing, skateboarding, jogging, trail running, sledding, and going to the beach, among many others. Paramount to this classification scheme is the importance of the natural environment as the place where outdoor recreation occurs.

Adventure recreation has a number of similarities to outdoor recreation but also some important differences. First, several definitional characteristics serve to separate the two terms. In this case, adventure recreation is defined in the following way: "A variety of self-initiated activities often utilizing an interaction with the natural environment that contains elements of real or apparent danger, in which the outcome, while uncertain, can be influenced by the participant and circumstance" (Ewert, 1989, p. 6).

As can be seen from this definition, just as with outdoor recreation, adventure recreation typically, but not always, occurs within a natural environment and is usually a self-initiated or voluntary activity. Unlike outdoor recreation, however, adventure

While adventure recreation occurs within a natural environment just like outdoor recreation, adventure recreation also involves real or apparent danger to the participant.

recreation involves elements of real or apparent danger that present an uncertain outcome to the participant. In turn, this outcome can be influenced by the participant and circumstance. Let's examine this definition in more detail.

First, what is meant by real or apparent danger? One way to distinguish between these two terms is to think about objective danger versus subjective danger. Objective danger refers to danger or hazards that exist whether the participant "sees" the danger or not, yet it can be identified and agreed upon by knowledgeable observers. Examples of objective danger would include rock fall, avalanches, or fast-moving cold water.

Subjective danger, however, implies that a participant has a feeling of being at risk, and this aspect is generally (but not always) coexistent with objective danger. For example, top-rope rock climbing may present the participant with a vision of extreme danger, but apart from rock fall or a misapplied belay, the activity is generally considered safe from an objective standpoint. Thus, top-roping may manifest a high degree of subjective danger, but it contains relatively low levels of objective danger. Second, this danger or risk is part of a larger context, namely, **uncertainty of outcome**. Within the adventure recreation context, uncertainty of outcome generally refers to questions such as "Will we make the summit?" or "Can we get through this cave?" Finally, the abilities of the participants and the circumstances of the experience interact in such a manner to shape the adventure process.

CONCEPTS RELATED TO OUTDOOR ADVENTURE EDUCATION

Often confused with outdoor adventure recreation is **outdoor adventure education**. Although similar in respect to using outdoor adventure as the venue for the experience, the content and intent of the experience is in fact quite different. Outdoor adventure education has been defined as "a type of education that utilizes specific risk-taking activities, such as ropes courses and mountaineering, to foster personal growth" (Wurdinger, 1997, p. xi). Given the popularity of ropes courses and adventure-based team building among school systems, therapeutic programs, and professional businesses, it would

make sense that not all people engaged in outdoor adventure education do so in a manner void of external obligations or motivations. Instead, outdoor adventure education programs organize lessons using outdoor adventure activities to facilitate learning, much of which is oriented toward psychosocial development (Hattie et al., 1997). Instructors and facilitators working in the outdoor adventure education industry are often employed by ropes courses or wilderness-based organizations, such as Project Adventure, **Outward Bound**, NOLS, or one of thousands of other programs in operation in North America and around the world. Similar to adventure guides, many outdoor educators are employed seasonally, although some make a year-round career of it. These concepts and definitions have a long history in the United States and Canada. The following section provides a brief overview of that history.

HISTORY OF OUTDOOR AND ADVENTURE RECREATION IN CANADA AND THE UNITED STATES

Discussing outdoor and adventure recreation is difficult without mention of cultural and historical foundations. These foundations are tied to the sociocultural, economic, religious, and political movements that have shaped North America's cultural and historical landscape. In this section we outline how outdoor adventure has transitioned from predominantly a form of labor to a form of leisure, as well as some of the historical key points that occurred throughout the process.

Adventure in Western Culture

Outdoor adventure as a form of leisure is a rather recent development in Western culture. Before further discussion, however, some differentiation is in order. When using the term *Western culture*, we seek to identify the cultural groups who have arisen primarily from individualistic ideals (Triandis et al., 1988). Individualism is the tendency to identify the self as primarily autonomous, self-determined, intrinsically motivated, and free from outside influence. If this notion sounds similar to the definition of leisure, it should, because one of the first cultural groups to adopt an individualist view of self is the same group that provided us with an early conceptualization of leisure—the ancient Greeks. The other cultural group thought to be one of the first to develop individualism was the Hebrews; individualism was brought to the Middle East, then Europe, and finally to North America through both Greco-Roman and Judeo-Christian cultures. Keeping this background in mind is useful when approaching a discussion of OAR.

The term *adventure*, from the Latin *adventura*, did not have the same meaning that we associate with the word in modern Western culture. Although the etymology of *adventura* is not fully known, by context it would appear to refer to unfortunate or surprising events wherein the consistent character traits of an individual allow successful passage. Michael Nerlich (1987), in his seminal two-part book *Ideology of Adventure: Studies in Modern Consciousness*, traces the development of adventure in Western civilization from feudal Europe through the dawn of Western modernism, arguing for the pivotal role that adventure played in shaping the cultural and historical movement to modern society. He argues that the construction of *adventure* throughout Western civilization is intimately linked with the development of Western societies.

The Age of Immigration

Much has been said elsewhere (e.g., the classic *Wilderness and the American Mind*) in regard to Europeans' perceptions of the North American wilderness and the communities already living here. Indeed, the perception of both *outdoor* and *adventure* is the focus of this chapter, so we will briefly state early Judeo-Christian influence on new European arrivals (generally regarded as the Puritans), who saw a stark change from the early religious perception of wilderness as a place of cleansing and spiritual growth. Where once the desert wilderness of the Middle East held a pious connotation, during the latter half of the millennium the mountains of Europe and deep forests of eastern North America took on sinister and frightening roles. Early writing from the first European immigrants colors the land they encountered as dark, harsh, and the home of ill spirits. Although more will be said in the next section on the transition from fear to an embrace of the outdoors as a healthy environment, note here

that although the outdoors had, for a time, fallen out of favor as a venue for adventure, this should not lead us to believe that adventure had also fallen out of favor within Western cultures in general.

Likewise, little has been mentioned thus far concerning the original North American nations. This omission is odd given the communities that for centuries had lived interdependently with the outdoors before the age of North American immigration. That the manners in which the first peoples to inhabit what is now referred to as North America were directly tied with the outdoors is a rather common aspect of cultural knowledge, as are the diverse interactions that have shaped their history—both among one another and with the Europeans who began to immigrate here beginning in the 1500s. The first peoples and European interactions did take on different forms to the north and south of the Canadian–United States border; the former was marked by relatively peaceful integration of cultures, whereas the latter was marked by violence.

Westerners, Adventure, and the Return to the Outdoors

That Western culture, upon arrival in North America, had little interest in the natural environment as a source of recreation or education may best be explained by taking a closer look at the cultural use of adventure during that historical period. Adventure, of course, has not always been directly linked with the outdoors, although many examples that involve human interaction with wilderness spring easily to mind. In this section we examine phenomena starting in Western culture through which we can trace the rise of outdoor recreation as a venue for the pursuit of adventure.

Adventure arose as a cultural artifact in the early parts of the first millennium as an individual undertaking by a member of the class of knights, who were members of the noble courts yet served only occasional use, such as during times of conflict. The notion of adventure as a quest (often for romantic, religious, or monetary gain) was a sort of occupational expectation, a way for knights to make a living, as the noble courts could not necessarily afford the full-time lifestyle yet sporadic usefulness of a warrior.

During the 15th century variations on *adventure* begin to appear not only in English and French writings but also in Spanish, Italian, and German (Nerlich, 1987). Most often, adventure dealt with the business of merchants and the rise of capitalism; this connection should not be a surprise because the individuals with whom we now associate with exploration and adventure were indeed engaged in mercantile occupations (e.g., Marco Polo, Cortez, Christopher Columbus). Furthermore, as Europeans immigrated en masse to North America, the people who adopted roles as outdoor adventurers did so through labor roles, such as the French-Canadian voyageurs of the northern Great Lakes or the fur trappers who pushed westward through the American West. The members of the Western community who followed caused dramatic changes to the North American landscape that had seen millennia of humans living interdependently with the ecosystems. The expanse of North America gave the impression of infinite possibility to the European immigrants.

As the continent became more settled and physical and social boundaries began to take shape, most notably in the eastern United States, public opinion also began to change. In many ways, the exploits of the outdoor adventurers such as the voyageurs or Lewis and Clark were similar to the activities of the knight–adventurers and merchant–adventurers of Europe. Outdoor adventurers served both economic and romantic roles as an idealized class of self-sufficient, autonomous people advancing (yet separate from) Western culture into the unknown. By the late 19th century the U.S. Census Bureau declared the disappearance of the frontier line, an occasion whose consequence should not be understated.

With the end of the frontier and rapid urbanization came both a crisis and an opportunity. On the one hand, the culture was losing an idealized class of adventurers because of industrial progress. The westward expansion and industrial revolution that brought North America great wealth and success during the 19th century and early 20th century left little space for outdoor adventurers as cultural icons; the outdoor adventurer (e.g., Davey Crockett or Daniel Boone) was replaced by the capitalist adventurer (e.g., Rockefeller, Vanderbilt, or Ford). On the other hand, advances in transportation, wealth, and communities centered on common interests allowed members of the upper classes to claim outdoor adventure as hobby. Although adventure had been reserved for a specific labor class throughout much of Western premodern and modern society, the move toward urbanized and globalized capitalism, built on the groundwork laid by merchant–adventurers and outdoor adventurers, brought about the opportunity for a tourist and armchair adventurer.

The year 1872 saw the world's first national park established, Yellowstone National Park, championed by naturalist and geologist Ferdinand V. Hayden. The following decades saw dramatic (although not without controversy) movements to set aside land for public use without industry takeover. Haphazard management was soon replaced. In 1911 Parks Canada became the world's first national park service, founded to manage the national and provincial park system in Canada, and in 1916 the National Park Service was founded to manage the growth and use of the national park system in the United States. The automobile boom, occurring at this same time and made possible by the new class of adventurer–laborers, brought the real possibility of outdoor adventure recreation to the public.

Because of the increase in accessibility and discretionary income and the romanticism of the outdoor adventurer fresh in North American psyche, the early 1900s saw an infatuation with outdoor recreation in the forms of hiking, camping, fishing, and hunting. Stymied by the Great Depression and World War II, it was not until the mid-1900s that the public began to return to the outdoors, only now a new generation with a new perspective. The hunter–fisher outdoor adventure recreationalist, left alone during those tumultuous years, was inundated by a new kind of outdoor adventurer. With the end of World War II came a new interest in the outdoors as a place to take up activities such as rock climbing, backpacking, white-water boating, and other physical-risk adventures; the focus on such activities was a sharp departure from the era of woodcraft.

James Morton Turner (2002) described the environmental change in the mid-1900s as a shift from a woodcraft ethic, in which people conceived of outdoor adventure as an interaction with the wilderness, to the minimum-impact ethic, in which people conceived of human–environment interaction as generally negative. As budding commercial businesses noticed the growing class of recreationalists, this new kind of outdoor adventurer used commercial stoves and tents instead of fires and hand-built shelters and began the movement toward the now-accepted norm in outdoor adventure of a "humans in, not humans of" wilderness. The development of educational materials such as the Leave No Trace principles provided access to these new values, allowing a much larger audience to explore the outdoor areas of North America with less situated, or immediately observable, environmental degradation, kicking off what is generally thought of today as outdoor adventure recreation.

The development of OAR is heavily contingent on a number of factors, such as acceptable settings, available programs, and the participants themselves. The next section discusses these factors from the perspective of how they influence and are influenced by OAR.

SETTINGS, DELIVERY SYSTEMS, AND PARTICIPANTS IN RECREATION

The organization of outdoor adventure recreation in North America is complex, made up of interdependent networks of structural, cultural, commercial, and community aspects. In this section we investigate some of the common settings for outdoor adventure recreation, the delivery systems through which adventure becomes accessible, and the participants engaged in such activities.

Natural Areas in North America

Thinking of outdoor adventure recreation occurring in a nonnatural environment is difficult, although some crossover has occurred for either fitness (e.g., rock-climbing gyms) or commercial (e.g., indoor skydiving) reasons. Aspects of outdoor adventure recreation may be amenable to nonnatural environments, but it would be difficult to argue that the full experience is captured or maintained. We briefly discuss here some of these special locations in North America, but for a more complete discussion refer to chapter 6.

The most common resources associated with outdoor adventure recreation are areas of land, water, or sky, as well as the specific management plan for those areas from both user-values and ecological, as well as economic perspectives. Although a good deal of outdoor adventure recreation takes place on public land, such as in a park or on a white-water river, a surprising amount also occurs in private or pay-to-play areas, such as at a ski resort.

Ski resorts provide a classic example of outdoor adventure recreation opportunities available for a fee.

Private Outdoor Recreation Resources

A long-standing example of a private and somewhat commercial outdoor adventure resource is the Appalachian Mountain Club (AMC) of the northeastern United States. The AMC was founded in 1876 to preserve the White Mountains of New Hampshire, and today it has close to 100,000 members, a number of backcountry huts, thousands of acres of land, and guided trips available year round in a number of outdoor adventure activities. Members' dues, sales of maps and guidebooks, and thousands of volunteers help keep the club in the business of facilitating outdoor adventure recreation and maintaining its lodges, huts, and educational goals.

Another example is the numerous ski resorts that provide outdoor adventure recreation opportunities in a private pay-to-play fashion. Whereas the woods, rivers, and mountains of the northeastern United States are largely accessible to outdoor adventure seekers without membership in a club, alpine skiing is logistically and physically complicated, perhaps too much so for many skiers, outside a managed ski area.

Despite the recent growth in low-impact winter sports (see table 16.1), backcountry skiing and snowboarding, that is, alpine skiing, snowboarding, or telemark skiing in wilderness environments removed from immediate services, requires abilities and skill sets beyond the scope of a casual downhill skier or snowboarder. A managed downhill or cross-country ski or snowboard area, by providing rental, education, transportation, safety, and comfort services, removes many of the obstacles that would otherwise discourage recreationalists from picking up the activity. Moreover, private lands on which outdoor adventure recreation occurs can provide substantial economic stimulus to local and regional economies. For example, North Carolina currently has six ski resorts in operation (RRC Associates, 2010) that directly employ roughly 1,600 people and provide a total economic value to the state of about $146 million. The winter playgrounds in British Columbia, the western American states, and the Canadian Rockies multiply this figure by many times, adding up to a significant part of local, regional, and cultural capital.

Public Outdoor Recreation Resources

Not all outdoor adventure recreation takes place on private land, of course. A brief look at local communities organized around the potentialities of adventure tourism, guiding, and indeed development and maintenance of a local adventure recreation culture such that in Banff, Alberta, or Jackson, Wyoming, is an indication of this orientation to public land. Unlike a ski resort or private bouldering park, the actual land or water in which outdoor adventure recreation activities are occurring is not managed for maximum economical

Table 16.1 Growth in Select Nature-Based Outdoor Activities

	2008 participants	2009 participants	One-year change
Adventure racing	920,000	1,089,000	18.4%
Snowshoeing	2,922,000	3,431,000	17.4%
Triathlon (nontraditional or off-road)	602,000	666,000	10.6%
Kayaking (white water)	1,242,000	1,369,000	10.2%
Skiing (cross-country)	3,848,000	4,157,000	8.0%
Camping (RV)	16,517,000	17,436,000	5.6%
Skiing (alpine or downhill)	10,346,000	10,919,000	5.5%
Bicycling (road or paved surface)	38,114,000	40,140,000	5.3%
Running or jogging	41,130,000	43,892,000	6.7%
Snowboarding	7,159,000	7,421,000	3.7%
Telemarking (downhill)	1,435,000	1,482,000	3.3%
Camping (within .25 mile [.4 km] of vehicle or home)	33,686,000	34,338,000	1.9%

potential. Instead, taxpayer dollars and nominal fees (to enter a national park or purchase a fishing license) provide access to recreational resources for a large number of people, many of whom may find for-profit outdoor adventure recreation prohibitively expensive.

Setting aside land and water areas in North America as public, instead of private, is an often-controversial (e.g., the Alaska National Wildlife Refuge) allocation of resources. Although both Canada and the United States are predominantly capitalist societies, both are foremost democratic societies, and the voices of actual and potential outdoor adventure recreationalists has dramatically helped secure public access to resources. Notable examples include the Access Fund, an organization that advocates for access to climbing areas in North America, and the Wilderness Society, which helped promote the development of the National Wilderness Preservation System and has been involved in many major public land decisions since its founding in 1935. As a natural result of public pressure to ensure access to wild environments, governments have both created public spaces and found the need to manage those spaces.

Participants and Usage

As illustrated in figure 16.1, participation in both outdoor recreation and adventure recreation constitutes a multidimensional interaction of people, settings, activities, and expected benefits.

One of the primary considerations regarding aspects of outdoor and adventure recreation is that of **motivation**. What motivates or impels a person to go into the outdoor environment is a question that

has received a great deal of research attention. Contemporary theories of motivation tend to focus on expectancies for success, values, or a combination of the two. Motivational theories that have direct connections to outdoor and adventure recreation and are most consistently seen in the literature are self-efficacy (Bandura, 1997), self-determination theory (Deci & Ryan, 1985), "flow" (Csikszentmihalyi, 1988), and attribution theory (Weiner, 1985). Figure 16.2 illustrates some of the salient characteristics attributed to each of the theories.

By their very definition, settings play a critical role in outdoor recreation and adventure contexts. In the case of outdoor recreation, settings have been classified along a number of continuums, mostly involving degree of development or specific activity. For example, one early classification system (Driver & Brown, 1978), termed the recreational opportunity spectrum (ROS), identified six classifications ranging from urban to primitive. Linked to each category was a somewhat specified range of activities that were most appropriate for that type of setting. For example, wilderness hiking was most closely aligned with a primitive type of setting, whereas urban landscapes would be candidate

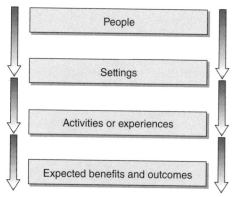

Figure 16.1 Outdoor recreation and adventure interaction.

IMPORTANT MOTIVATIONS IN OUTDOOR ADVENTURE AND RECREATION

- Sense of accomplishment and achievement
- Fun and restoration
- Self-confidence
- Being with family and friends
- Working as a team member
- Developing skills and competence
- Creativity
- Using specific equipment and techniques
- Image
- To be close to nature
- Personal testing
- Physical exercise
- Problem solving

Figure 16.2 What motivates a person to go outdoors has received a lot of research attention, specifically in the realm of motivational theories.

Table 16.2 Recreation Opportunity Spectrum

ROS classification	Attributes
Primitive	Unmodified natural environment (e.g., wilderness). No motorized use allowed.
Semiprimitive	Similar to primitive but often with more evidence of other users. Often less remote than primitive. No motorized use allowed.
Semiprimitive motorized	Similar to semiprimitive but with motorized use allowed.
Roaded natural	Moderate evidence of other users with conventional motorized use allowed.
Rural	Substantially modified with substantial presence of other users. Facility development is present.
Urban	Highly urbanized environment with predominance of human presence; often intense motorized use.

settings for activities such as picnicking or sports (e.g., baseball). See table 16.2.

The purpose of the ROS and other classification systems is to link the desired activity with the most appropriate setting. The expectation is that this matching would produce the highest probability of achieving specific benefits and desired outcomes. Inherent in this process is the use of indicators and standards to determine the linkage between the setting and the activity.

PROFESSIONAL CAREERS IN OUTDOOR AND ADVENTURE RECREATION

Multiple avenues exist for those interested in employment within the greater outdoor and adventure recreation industries. The employment options make up a spectrum of opportunity similar to those available in any large cultural practice, a few of which we highlight here.

Guiding Industry

Many styles of outdoor recreation, such as biking or hiking, are generally more accessible to the public than outdoor adventure recreation activities that require specialized equipment and training. The expenses, both in time and money, make a personal investment in an adventure recreation pursuit such as ice climbing or white-water rafting daunting if not out of reach for many. Whereas owning ice tools, crampons, rope, harness, ice screws, appropriate clothing and footwear, helmet, and the many other pieces of equipment necessary to take up ice climbing may cost upwards of $1,000 and the actual activity requires knowledge of anchors, ice

formation, and climbing technique, an individual or group may be able to hire a guide to provide an ice-climbing experience for a fraction of the cost.

Working in the outdoor **adventure guiding industry** is not, however, just "getting paid to play." Guides work long hours to manage the leisure experience of clients and to provide the education and safety necessary to ensure that the experiences are beneficial. Thus, guiding provides an opportunity to introduce a new set of possibilities to those who may otherwise not take up an outdoor adventure pursuit. Likewise, outdoor adventure guiding typically occurs in locations with multiple outdoor adventure venues, and a professional engagement in these areas may result in increased personal adventure opportunities through personal and community practice. Whereas weekends may be spent introducing clients to a local rock-climbing crag or popular stretch of river, a slow weekday may be an opportunity to explore a remote, difficult, or more personally rewarding outdoor adventure activity. Outdoor adventure guiding, therefore, is a professional service that provides valuable adventure experiences to clients and positions the guide in a location and community where she or he can balance pursuing personal adventure and providing introductory adventure to others.

Outdoor and Adventure Tourist Industry

The adventure guiding industry and the outdoor adventure tourism industry are often closely connected. Review chapter 9, which focuses on tourism, for an in-depth discussion of this industry. Adventure tourism, more specifically, is made up of organized adventure programming in a tourism experience.

Outdoor adventure guiding provides an opportunity for clients to pursue an activity they may not otherwise be able to and an opportunity for the guide to pursue personal adventure.

Destination tourism to the mountains and forests of the Appalachian, Rocky, and western mountain ranges of North America began in the mid-1930s. Although destination mountain resorts were already popular in Europe, the 1932 Winter Olympics in Lake Placid, New York, brought this type of opportunity to North America. For example, Idaho's Sun Valley was the first ski resort built as a tourist destination in America, and Quebec's Mont-Tremblant followed three years later. Today adventure tourism locations exist almost everywhere, and the employment possibilities are both numerous and varied. Larger mountain resorts offer year-round opportunities, because many draw visitors in every season. Likewise, locations in southern North America have a more consistent year-round draw than locations dependent on seasonal access. Many large tourist destinations hire people with experience and training in outdoor adventure to lead or manage in the adventure tourism side of their organizations, whereas others specifically capitalize on adventure tourism as the sole focus of their operation.

Land Management Industry

Both the adventure guiding industry and the adventure tourism industry often operate on public lands. Much as the private sector employs people with training and experience in outdoor adventure to distribute services, the public sector provides employment opportunities at national and local levels. As an example, the National Park Service (NPS) has historically employed park rangers and specialized staff to manage visitor experience from multiple facets, including outdoor recreation and interpretation. Increasingly the NPS permits commercial organizations to run outdoor adventure experiences, but the park ranger remains iconic in aiding the visitor's personal adventure pursuit by providing valued information and service. At the local level many communities have departments that manage recreational opportunities; oftentimes an outdoor adventure component exists in the form of running a summer camp or managing adventure recreation sites such as mountain bike parks or rock-climbing crags. Employment in this sector allows people the opportunity to oversee the larger community's access to outdoor adventure activities.

Whether private or public in employment, the outdoor adventure recreation industry appears to enjoy consistent growth, especially in adventure exercise activities available locally, such as trail running and cross-country skiing. The concerted effort of communities to establish and maintain

outdoor recreation resources, especially those uniquely adventure based in nature, may be the best way of both promoting local outdoor adventure and attracting adventure tourists, such as has been accomplished in locations like Ouray, Colorado, and Whistler, British Columbia.

BENEFITS AND OUTCOMES OF OUTDOOR RECREATION AND ADVENTURE

The history of outdoor recreation and adventure programs suggests that participants enjoy a number of benefits and program outcomes (e.g., Driver, Brown, & Peterson, 1991; Gibbons, 1999; Miles & Priest, 1999). These include hard-earned personal and physical victories, emotional and psychological development, sociological advantages of rehabilitation and assimilation, and a sense of restoration and spirituality. In particular, outdoor adventure education programs are generally developed around the promotion, acquisition, and realization of these types of benefits and outcomes.

A number of specific benefits and outcomes have been commonly associated with both outdoor recreation and adventure. These benefits can be categorized into four general areas: psychological, sociological, physiological, and spiritual. The following sections describe these benefits.

Psychological

The essence of many outdoor recreation and adventure programs is how an activity can effectuate change on a personal level. In fact, this possibility is often the primary motivator for participation in adventure and outdoor recreation. Comments such as, "I've always wanted to try that challenge," "I want to change my life," or "I need to find something in my life that's missing," often motivate a person to take on an adventure experience or activity. At its core, this type of thinking reflects the powerful psychological influence that is sought and associated with outdoor adventure.

In particular, outdoor recreation and adventure activities can have a considerable and often long-lasting influence on the psychological variables referred to as the self-systems. Examples of these self-systems include self-esteem, self-efficacy, self-

determination, self-empowerment, self-control, and so forth. Challenging or pushing oneself to extreme or untested personal levels can create significant alterations in self-perceptions. Outdoor recreation activities can provide the opportunity to change a person's psychological schemata, or ingrained coping mechanisms, from a past that may not have always been successful. When a person is able to change a preconceived thought process or schemata to cope better with life's future trials, the results can be profound.

Outdoor recreation and adventure programs offer the occasion to challenge and reflect on internalized norms and learned coping behaviors through a sequentially based progression and mastery of concrete tasks or skills. Opportunities for reflection during this process can allow alterations in perceptions of the perceived self versus the ideal self, which in turn may influence personal determination, resilience, and competence. Besides enhancing the self-systems, outdoor recreation and adventure activities can have a mediating effect on psychological issues associated with depression and anxiety. Moreover, educational tactics such as framing, debriefing, and skilled facilitation are thought to heighten the effectiveness of adventure activities.

Sociological

Outdoor adventure, much like any other lived experience, does not occur just within the individual, but also usually includes larger social structures, cultures, and social interactions that every person is embedded in. Outdoor adventure recreation has sociological roots and implications, because humans both shape and are shaped by social situations (House, 1981). In this section we briefly discuss two sociological aspects, although many more exist and are worth pursuing for further learning.

Alienation and Anomie

Two sociological concepts have been thought to give rise to people's search for adventure in leisure and recreation choices. First, and most commonly associated with adventure recreation, is the notion of social **alienation**. Social alienation, although a comprehensive term, refers here to a person's interactions with his or her everyday life that becomes numbingly routinized to the point of detachment or estrangement. People suffering from alienation feel isolated and unchallenged as social actors because the world feels too ordered and rule bound. This condition has been historically considered an outcome of modern labor. Although this notion may seem extreme, Mitchell (1983) explained how professionals engaged in highly routinized labor living near the Sierra Nevada sought out complex outdoor adventure recreation opportunities such as mountaineering to reintroduce uncertainty or risk. Other people, however, live surrounded by structures wherein they are not able to feel a sense of control or consistency. For these people society feels unpredictable and therefore oppressive. The feeling that everyday life lacks norms or predictable organization is an example of **anomie**, which may be thought of as a mismatch between an individual and his or her social environment. For example, many adventure enthusiasts have a home activity area, wherein they find comfort in returning time and again to climb, paddle, surf, or otherwise pursue a favored activity. People feeling the anomic qualities of life in modern society, then, may also engage in outdoor adventure, especially in familiar environments, as a way to regain a sense of control and stability in the same way that people who dislike the routinized aspects of modern society may seek outdoor adventure to regain a sense of unpredictability.

Adventure Experiences and Socialization

Although many people think of a camping trip as a way to get away from civilization and society, the social experience is often the most important variable linked to visitor satisfaction. Even a solitary hiker in Stein Valley Nlaka'pamux Heritage Park in southern British Columbia is engaged in social activity; the tools that she uses, such as boots, tent, camp stove, compass, and technical clothing, are all linked in a process of cultural and historical value (Engeström, 2001). Attempting to escape the social or cultural meaning of our outdoor activities is an exercise in futility, because the very existence of outdoor recreation is socially and culturally mediated.

Thus, although our hiker in Stein Valley is temporally by herself yet still engaged in social activity, a group of rock climbers in Tuolumne Meadows on the eastern side of Yosemite National Park may also be seen as constructing a "community of practice" (Lave & Wenger, 1991). People who claim membership in this community end up participating

in much more than climbing, although that is the primary focus of their activities. What they learn when participating in a community of practice is much more than how to rock climb; they also learn how to be a functioning member of a local culture. The group and its membership, and subsequent participation, directed toward a common activity offer space for growth and learning, not just about the specific activity but also about the social practices, culture, and structures that make up the experience.

Physiological

Although often overlooked, the physical benefits associated with outdoor recreation and adventure programs can provide important contributions to our holistic, overall health. In an era of increased health issues, obesity, and living longer as older adults, engaging in enjoyable and exciting outdoor recreation can provide a lifelong interest in maintaining fitness. Specifically, increases in strength, endurance, metabolic levels, catecholamine levels, agility, flexibility, cardiovascular and orthopedic fitness, as well as decreases in cholesterol, blood pressure, and sleep disturbances are a few of the physiological benefits derived from participating in outdoor recreation activities.

When outdoor recreation and adventure activities become inculcated as part of a person's lifestyle, they can provide a valid alternative, or addition, to exercising at fitness clubs or gyms. The arena for using nature as a means of maintaining or increasing physical and mental health is almost boundless and can range from less challenging activities such as walking and hiking on trails in city, state, or national parks and forests to more adventurous endeavors such as mountain biking; rock, ice, or mountain climbing; cross-country skiing; and snowboarding.

Spiritual

The spiritual draw to outdoor natural areas often eludes definition and remains an ineffable interface between an individual and nature's canvass. People feel a strong attraction, or need, to be a part of nature. But this need is not always easy to define, nor is it necessarily the same need that attracts people to be engaged in outdoor recreation. Regardless of the individual reasons for wanting to participate in

OUTSTANDING GRADUATES

Background Information

Name: Kim Collins

Education: Master of science degree in outdoor recreation from the School of Health, Physical Education, and Recreation at Indiana University.

Credentials: Certified outdoor leader, Wilderness Education Association.

Special awards: Voyageur Award (2010), Significant Contribution Award, IUOA (2005).

Affiliations: WEA Board of Trustees, American Whitewater lifetime member, Hoosier Canoe Club member.

Career Information

Position: Assistant program coordinator: adventure trips, custom experiences, leadership training.

Organization: Since 2007, I've worked for Indiana University Outdoor Adventures (IUOA), a student leadership development program that has existed in Bloomington, Indiana, since 1972. We employ 13 part-time shop staff, 50 part-time trip leaders, 10 adjunct instructors, one outreach coordinator, two graduate assistants, and three full-time administrators. IUOA serves around 6,000 participants each year through our trips, courses for credit, bouldering wall, and gear shop.

Organization's mission: IUOA is committed to providing unique, high-quality outdoor programs, services, and products that engage, encourage, and empower everyone we serve in the lifelong journey of self-discovery and development.

Job description: I coordinate and oversee student staff leading trips for IU student population and local community; create, staff, and coordinate custom experiences for IU students and the surrounding communities; identify and implement marketing strategies in conjunction with the Indiana Memorial Union; coordinate and organize internal and external staff training (leadership, winter skills, whitewater paddling); manage special projects and events on and off campus; train IUOA trip leaders through classes each fall; contact past, present, and future clientele to set up programs and events; supervise OA outreach coordinator; assist IUOA marketing staff with IUOA brochures and promotional materials; schedule consultation meetings (in and out of house); develop contracts with instructors, clients, and outside companies; foster partnerships with IU and non-IU organizations and companies; coordinate all custom experiences from 2 hours to multiple days in length; and coordinate and co-lead whitewater staff trainings according to ACA (American Canoe Association) and IUOA training manual.

> *Make time for yourself and your trips. Know that your first string of jobs will most likely be part time or seasonal, but if you work hard and make connections, the full-time career of your future will find you.*

Career path: My career began as a resident camp counselor with YMCA Camp Tecumseh in 1997. After a few years of being a resident counselor, I was invited to lead adventure trips for Camp Tecumseh. I led trips around the country (backpacking, rafting, sailing) for two summers and decided to head to the National Outdoor Leadership School (NOLS) in Alaska to receive more training. NOLS introduced me to my new passion, whitewater paddling. I spent 30 days backpacking, 30 days coastal kayaking, and 30 days whitewater canoeing and kayaking in the Arctic National Wildlife Refuge. It was life changing. From NOLS, I continued my education at IU, graduating in 2003 with a BS in outdoor recreation and resource management. After graduation, I worked for four seasons at Bradford Woods as an environmental educator and challenge facilitator. During my employment, I noticed outdoor recreation and adventure activities, certain attributes may provide an explanation about why so many people feel some type of connection to nature and outdoor places.

Being outdoors and experiencing the uniqueness of nature is often characterized as providing people with a sense of knowing something "bigger" than themselves, bringing them a greater appreciation and feeling of a higher being or spiritual connection. Indeed, a major outcome or benefit from outdoor recreation participation is that it may render a heightened awareness on a holistic level—the sense of belonging to, and being of, the world. These notions are often compelling reasons for people to seek outdoor recreation experiences.

OUTDOOR ADVENTURE EDUCATION PROGRAMMING AND PROFESSIONAL CAREERS

Many programs today focus on outdoor adventure learning as a function of small-group and individual interactions. Outdoor adventure education includes many genres, although two appear most prominent.

Adventure-Based Facilitation

Growing in popularity and social acknowledgement since being defined in the early 1970s is the use of ropes courses. Adventure-based facilitation developed as a way to consolidate the social and individual challenges met on the longer expeditions of adventure education programs into accessible and marketable short experiences. Facilitators use a range of props, constructions, and techniques to propel a group into situations of increasing challenge; each is designed, run, and debriefed to achieve educational outcomes such as improved communication, problem-solving skills, or group cohesion.

Today the adventure-based facilitation industry has grown into an in-demand service, working with such diverse groups as school systems, at-risk or therapeutic groups, corporations and businesses, and even birthday parties. Easily recognized activities such as zip lines, high-ropes courses, and trust falls, some of which are commonplace in media and television, may leave the impression that physical risk is the predominant contributor to the educational experience. Although physical risks are important in that they are thought to capture the challenges historically found in expedition-based programming, social and emotional interactions may form the bedrock of adventure-based facilitation (Seaman, 2007). Facilitators, therefore, must draw from a large repertoire of educational, sociological, psychological, and adventure-based practices in developing experiential lessons, especially because many adventure-based facilitation programs last only for a few hours or a day.

Outdoor Adventure Expeditions

Also falling under the umbrella of outdoor adventure education is the wilderness expedition or trip. These experiences remove people from what Kurt Hahn thought were the corrupting effects of society, providing an opportunity to engage in an intensive interdependent community while overcoming challenges in a complex environment—a mixture that under the tutelage of knowledgeable and skilled instructors can foster personal and social learning. Outdoor educators often work in shared-leadership teams and manage the lessons and experiences of the group, often for weeks or months at a time. The instructional team serves multiple purposes, such as risk management, providing multiple perspectives in the group's shared knowledge, and it tends to be an important part of each instructor's experience and growth as an educator and leader (Vernon, 2011).

Outdoor adventure education diverges from outdoor adventure recreation by its emphasis on the educational part of the experience. Despite the difference in programming and outcomes, the same activities (albeit organized and managed differently) can be used to achieve these diverse outcomes. It is not mountaineering, then, that gives rise to a recreational or educational experience, but the manner in which mountaineering is approached. People interested in outdoor adventure can gain access to both styles of experience as either a personal or professional pursuit.

The expedition or wilderness-based outdoor adventure education experience, therefore, is a

The wilderness expedition is one aspect of outdoor adventure education where the instructional team fosters personal and social learning.

prolonged encounter of a social group (made up of students and coinstructors) with and within an intentional wilderness experience. Oftentimes the instructors organize the expedition, both in scope and detail, to maximize learning oriented to outdoor abilities, leadership abilities, and psychosocial learning, in that students learn about self and others through interactions in an intensive community. The outdoor educators, much as the facilitator, must therefore draw from a wide range of practices to provide a successful educational expedition to a diverse group of students.

EMERGING TRENDS AND ISSUES

Within the fields of outdoor and adventure recreation are a number of trends and issues that are affecting both the users and the delivery of those experiences. For the purposes of this chapter, we discuss three of them:

- Impacts of technology on outdoor recreation and adventure activities
- Changing values associated with outdoor recreation and adventure, particularly on public and other undeveloped lands
- Consumerism

Impacts of Technology

Technology plays an increasingly influential role in outdoor recreation and adventure. The last 10 years in particular have seen an explosion of technological developments in the outdoors, ranging from clothing to specific equipment, signaling devices, and protective gear. Ewert and Shultis (1999) describe five areas in which technology has had a substantial impact in the realm of outdoor and adventure recreation. These areas include access and transportation, comfort, safety, communication, and information. In turn, each of these areas has resulted in greater use of the outdoors, differing expectations, and changes in public policy.

For example, technology has increased access and transportation through improvements in overland travel by snowmobiles and off-road vehicles (ORVs). These machines have allowed visitors to get farther into remote areas faster and with less effort. Likewise, comfort in the outdoors has been substantially improved through lighter weight and more effective clothing, tents, boots, and so on. This reduced weight and greater effectiveness have allowed more people, of greater age range and differing ability levels, to get into extremely remote or challenging areas.

Technology has affected outdoor recreation and adventure in two ways relative to safety. First, improved technology has increased the level of safety often available to both individuals and groups. By and large, equipment is both stronger and more versatile, but in some cases its use requires higher levels of knowledge and skill. For example, dive computers have essentially replaced dive tables for scuba diving. Although the devices are reliable and extremely useful, the diver must be competent in their use to capitalize on their safety features.

Communication may be the technology-related area that is experiencing the fastest growth. With the advent of GPS units, 36-mile (58 km) radios, and PLBs (personal locator beacons), among others, technology now gives outdoor enthusiasts the possibility of knowing their precise location, the speed and direction in which they are moving, and a way to signal for help—all with the press of a button. The potential danger of these technological advances lies in two areas. First, knowing what direction you need to go to reach a particular point doesn't ensure that you can get there. Ravines, canyons, mountains, steep slopes, avalanche areas, and other features may conspire to prevent you from getting where you want to go. Second, technology sometimes does not work. Just as helicopters cannot always fly to your location, the GPS or handheld radio might not be working, for a variety of reasons (e.g., dead batteries).

As alluded to in the previous paragraphs, increases in technology have often served to increase use. This increased use is not without a price, namely in visitors finding themselves in situations far more challenging than their skill or knowledge levels would warrant. That is, technology often creates a "bubble of safety." Skill in or knowledge of technology can create the illusion that the visitor is safe and can be provided assistance at the critical moment, when in fact no such safety mechanism exists. For example, using an avalanche beacon can be a life-saving behavior, but no beacon has ever prevented an avalanche from occurring.

If you are buried in one, your chances of survival automatically decrease by 50 percent. Thus, thinking that you are safe in going out in avalanche-prone areas during a period of high avalanche danger because you are carrying an avalanche beacon is a prime example of allowing technology to create the illusion of safety. This kind of behavior gets people into serious trouble.

In sum, technology has provided a number of positive aspects to outdoor recreation, adventure activities, and participants. As described earlier, technology has increased comfort and safety (depending on the situation), improved access, enhanced the ability to communicate, and increased the information base from which we make decisions. It has also served at times to create the illusion of safety, which can allow visitors, often by overdependence on technology, to get themselves in situations requiring search and rescue (SAR) or other forms of assistance from the managing agency. Within this context, technology serves to increase, rather than decrease, the demand on land and resource management and resources. Thus, although generally positive and certainly not going away, technology should be viewed as a phenomenon that can also create problems. An understanding of how technology works and sometimes doesn't work, coupled with an awareness that it should not be relied on exclusively, provides the proper perspective on using technology.

Changing Values

Cultural and historical values commonly associated with outdoor recreation and adventure activities include categories such as personal challenge, self-identity, teamwork, image, and setting (Ewert & Sibthorp, 2009); these values have expanded to include health and wellness issues. More specifically, awareness is growing that outdoor activities can be beneficial for a number of health-related problems, such as stress, obesity, balance, children's health, and attention deficit hyperactivity disorder (ADHD) (Godbey, 2009). A sample of these beneficial impacts is depicted in table 16.3.

Concomitant with the values associated with health enhancement is the need for public policy to consider the importance of providing space and resources for people to engage in outdoor recreation and adventure-based opportunities. Although much of the attention devoted to public outdoor recreation resources is directed to the national parks and forests, a study by Roper ASW (2004) indicated that only 32 percent and 28 percent of Americans have visited a national park and national forest, respectively. Thus, from the perspective of providing opportunities to enhance individual health, outdoor recreation and adventure will increasingly lie in the provision of municipal and regional locations.

Consumerism

Outdoor adventure recreationists underwent an impressive change in the years between World War II and the 1980s. Although at one time outdoor adventure was predominantly associated with hunting, fishing, and otherwise "living off the land" and outdoor adventures were thought to be associated with an ethic of woodcraft (Turner, 2002), the popularity of wilderness exploration, the development of equipment that facilitated new adventure-seeking behaviors, and a shift in public values concerning human interaction with nature brought about a

Table 16.3 Effect on Outdoor Recreation and Adventure on Selected Health-Related Disorders

Health-related disorders	Effects of outdoor recreation and adventure
Stress	• Rejuvenation from indoor environments • Reduction of negative moods • Reduction of self-reported levels of stress
Obesity	• Increased physical activity • Increased enjoyment through physical activity
Children's health	• Reduced incidence of type 2 diabetes
Attention deficit hyperactivity disorder	• Reduced symptoms of ADHD • Reduction in nonactive spectator activities such as TV • Reduced need for medication

new majority in outdoor adventure recreation. With the newfound interest in outdoor adventure came a surge of users who had little expertise regarding how to have a mutually beneficial encounter with a natural environment. To counteract potential degradation of our wilderness, in the 1970s many authors began to publish books and articles providing instruction on how to travel with as little impact as possible; oftentimes this approach required a shift away from the woodcraft ethic. Whereas lean-tos and canvas dominated in earlier times, nylon tents are now the norm; fires and spits have been replaced by small camping stoves; a snared or shot rabbit has been replaced by a package of dehydrated premade food or something else brought in from a store; wool has been replaced by fleece. Although it may not sound romantic, the minimal-impact movement in outdoor adventure recreation has historically gone hand in hand with consumerism.

Unfortunately, this new ethic comes with a paradoxical quandary. For example, camp stoves and nylon tents can be both extremely useful and reduce the immediate impact on a site, but both have some ecological and ethical issues associated with their use. Many camp stoves are made of metals that had to be mined, processed, molded, and assembled, more than likely at various points on the planet, and nylon is, of course, made from petroleum. Both were created in various labor markets, some of which may not be favorable to the people engaged in that particular labor, and so it would be foolhardy to expect a camp stove or nylon tent to exist without a trace on both planet and livelihood, albeit difficult to perceive while held in the user's hand. But these products allow a certain level of environmental interaction to occur without using the particular resources at the user's immediate disposal. Multiplied through many users, the use

of these items provides some security to a natural area.

Despite the complexity inherent in the equipment used for outdoor adventure pursuits, business is booming. Nearly half of all people in North America participate in outdoor adventure recreation in some form, and roughly one-quarter of those people anticipate annual increases in equipment and travel expenditures to continue pursuing adventure activities (Outdoor Foundation, 2010). Not taking into account the popularity of such brands as The North Face and Patagonia among nonoutdoor adventurers, we are still looking at a multibillion dollar industry. A new market for manufacturers is now developing as the relatively recent historical dependence on petroleum for technical clothing and fabric is shifting toward sustainable resources, such as wool, bamboo, and recycled material. Patagonia, for example, now recycles many of its own used products back into production.

SUMMARY

In this chapter we have discussed the concept of outdoor adventure recreation by tracing its roots in Western culture, exposing its current embedded structure within North American society, and discussing potential future directions. We believe that outdoor adventure recreation is a historically purposeful activity that has both personal and cultural implications, and its growing popularity, complexity, and potential benefits make it a particularly relevant avenue for both leisure and labor. After reading this chapter you should be able to discuss basic concepts of outdoor adventure recreation and education, including its historical context, its users and user areas, its importance to both leisure and labor in North America, and some individual and social aspects.

For glossary terms, learning experiences, and more, please visit the web resource at
www.HumanKinetics.com/IntroductionToRecreationAndLeisure

CHAPTER 17

Arts and Culture

Gaylene Carpenter

> " In recreation, experiences in the arts are one of the most sought after opportunities in which people may rediscover themselves and their relationships within a family and community. "
>
> Nellie D. Arnold, author,
> *The Interrelated Arts in Leisure*

LEARNING OUTCOMES

After reading this chapter, you should be able to do the following:

> Demonstrate an understanding and awareness of cultural experiences
> Explain the importance of providing arts and cultural experiences in North America
> Identify components in the arts and cultural program area
> Describe the meanings and benefits realized by organizations and individuals through arts and cultural experiences and programs
> Describe the evolution of arts and cultural programming in parks and recreation, public education, and private enterprise
> Compare the number, type, and breadth of arts and cultural experiences available
> Contrast programs provided by public agencies and nonprofit arts organizations that address contemporary needs and demonstrate contemporary practices

INTRODUCTION

In the first edition of this textbook, I shared that I was surprised by an unanticipated **arts** experience called PDX in Bloom (PDX is the acronym for the Portland International Airport). A baby grand piano sat in a busy central location in the airport near the security check-in area that led to the terminals. A pianist was replacing the white noise and hustle of the airport with delightful, relaxing melodies. As I began to board my flight, the airport public-address announcer mentioned that a dulcimer performance would be beginning shortly. Although airports have long been places to view visual art, the idea of airports as performing arts venues was new to me, yet in retrospect this experience was indicative of the rapid growth in arts and cultural programming opportunities across North America. It is no longer surprising to experience spontaneous acts of song and dance almost anywhere, anytime. Simply entering key words into a search engine will reveal a vast array of contemporary practices that people are doing and finding enjoyable. YouTube, the emerging remix culture, lip dubbing, and flash mobs are redefining the concept of arts participation and making creators and observers of us all.

Increased opportunities for arts and cultural experiences have grown in the public, nonprofit, and business or for-profit arts sectors. Reasons cited for the increased interest in arts and culture include the number and variety of experiences available, organizational initiative, arts education, inviting venues, and participant expectations (Carpenter, 2008). The provision for arts and cultural experiences has been a long tradition in recreation and leisure settings. Fifty years ago, Meyer and Brightbill (1956) advocated that arts and crafts, dancing, dramatics, literary activities, and music activities be standard in a comprehensive recreation program. Arts and cultural recreation opportunities continue to be both part of public agencies' responsibilities to their citizens and viable offerings in self-support programs.

Arts managers working in a variety of for-profit and nonprofit arts and cultural organizations provide a wide array of arts and cultural opportunities that offer benefits to individuals and societies. Participation in the arts occurs in a variety of contexts including museums, galleries, community arts centers, art fairs and festivals, and performance venues. Arts and cultural programs have become more visible in part because of administrative initiative to provide arts and cultural experiences and in part because arts managers have been responsive to the desires of people for more choices of things to do during their discretionary time. In addition, successful efforts to build arts participation have resulted from restructuring efforts undertaken by small nonprofit and community-based arts organizations and large nonprofit and commercial arts institutions (McCarthy & Jinnett, 2001). Economic impact studies show the importance of arts and cultural activities to communities throughout North America. Information generated by various studies shows that when community leaders invest in the arts, they also invest in the economic health of their local communities. Private-sector businesses and organizations also benefit from activity-related spending by arts and culture attendees.

Cultural activities attract tourists and spur the creation of ancillary facilities such as restaurants, hotels, and the services needed to support them. Cultural facilities and events enhance property values, tax values, tax resources, and overall profitability for communities. In doing so, the arts become a direct contributor to urban and rural revitalization (Americans for the Arts, 2002). The National Governors Association noted that audiences drawn to arts venues and cultural events also produce economic benefits for other businesses because a thriving cultural scene helps attract visitors who not only spend money on the events themselves but also contribute to local economies by dining in restaurants, lodging in hotels, and purchasing gifts and services in the community (NGA, 2009).

Americans for the Arts (2005, 2008) and Canadian Heritage (2007) report findings associated with the economic impact of arts and culture participation. Although government spending on culture varies in Canada, monies to support cultural-sector objectives are made available at the municipal, territorial, provincial, and federal levels. The United States also supports this sector at the regional, state, and national level. Arts and cultural organizations in both countries are now receiving minimal financial help in relationship to their needs. In spite of funding concerns, economic figures and participation patterns in arts and culture seem to be holding steady. The following examples describe the economic impact associated with arts and cultural participation for the United States and Canada.

- The total economic activity in the nonprofit arts industry in the United States was US$166.2 billion, which included the total spending by organizations (US$63.1 billion) and spending by arts audiences (US$103.1 billion).
- Sixty-five percent of adult American travelers included a cultural, arts, heritage, or historic activity or event while on a trip of 50 miles (80 km) or more, one-way. Cultural tourists spend more and stay longer than other types of U.S. tourists.
- Nonlocal U.S. arts patrons attending performances, festivals, and so on spend almost twice as much as local attendees do.
- The number of nonprofit performing arts companies (theater, music, dance, opera) across Canada has increased 22 percent in the last decade. Figures indicate that the total number of theater, music, dance, or opera companies exceeds 600.
- Over half of all U.S. adults (53 percent) participate in the arts through electronic and digital media. Forms include TV, radio, CDs and DVDs, and portable media devices to view or listen to an arts performance, a program about artists, artworks, a museum program or exhibit, or a program about books or writers.
- Canadian Heritage reported that cultural tourism spending was C$8.0 billion and represented 15 percent of the total tourist spending of C$53.5 billion in 2007.
- The Canadian Tourism Commission routinely gathers data that describe the demographics, market size, and cultural activities of festival tourism participants. These participants, referred to as festival tourism enthusiasts, exhibit a particular interest in festivals when they travel.

Arts and cultural activities not only provide recreation and leisure opportunities but also make solid contributions to the economic health of communities. Thinking about the value of providing arts and cultural opportunities for improving peoples' lives, livelihoods, and communities can be extended further. Many believe that the arts attract educated workers and the companies that seek to hire them to geographic regions, resulting in even greater positive economic benefits to communities, local governments, and business enterprises (Florida, 2002).

This chapter discusses arts and cultural leisure experiences and the organizations that offer them. The importance of providing arts and cultural experiences and gaining their inherent benefits is examined. Contemporary programs are provided throughout to highlight specific arts and cultural programs.

ARTS AND CULTURE AS PART OF RECREATION AND LEISURE

It is helpful for us to clarify terms that will be used throughout this chapter. As we've mentioned, those involved in the arts and culture sector represent nonprofit, for-profit, public, and private organizations. Broadly defined, arts and culture can be thought of as an identifiable sector present in every community and understandable in both economic and quality-of-life terms (Godfrey, 2002). The definition of arts and culture also lies in two contexts: social interaction and cultural anthropology. We explore both briefly.

Congdon and Blandy (2003) describe a direct relationship between arts and culture as everyday life that includes the myriad ways in which people assemble, work, and act together for a variety of political, aesthetic, economic, familial, religious, and educational purposes. The authors believe that participating in the culture of everyday life through art—broadly conceived of as *folklife*—is something all of us do. Within this context, then, the inclination to make and appreciate art is so ordinary that it is often overlooked for the extraordinary contribution it makes to such commonplace activities as cooking, fishing, keeping house, gardening, computing, and the multitude of other endeavors required in daily life (Congdon & Blandy, 2003, p. 177).

The **arts and cultural sector** in America is a large, heterogeneous set of individuals and organizations engaged in the creation, production, presentation, distribution, and preservation of and education about aesthetic, heritage, and entertainment activities, products, and artifacts (Wyszomirski, 2002). Some see the arts industry, or sector, at the very center of a circle of circles made up of cultural industries (Chartrand, 2000). Sixteen cultural industries make up Chartrand's well-regarded conceptualization of the arts industry and include parks and recreation, leisure, education, tourism, antiques and collectables, cosmetics, cuisine, funeral, furniture and fixtures, gaming, multiculturalism, native culture, official languages, physiotherapy and psychotherapy, sports, and religion. As can be seen, organizational contexts such as parks and recreation, leisure education, and tourism are all viewed as part of the arts and culture sector in America. Other components in the sector suggest leisure behaviors (antiques and collecting, cuisine) and pursuits (gaming, sports). As such, leisure organizations and behaviors are considered part of the contemporary arts and culture sector.

When it comes to tracking arts participation, how figures are reported becomes important in understanding how many are engaged in arts and cultural activity and exactly where such activity is taking place. Arts participation data are often obtained by accessing organizational records, thus leaving out other kinds of involvement. The National Endowment for the Arts (2010) reported that informal arts participation in urban and rural communities

A performing arts group shares their music and dance to bring people closer together.

is occurring under the watchful eye of what is typically reported by nonprofit or for-profit arts organizations. NEA calls for closer tracking of participation found in informal or unincorporated arts. Sunil Iyengar, research and analysis director for the National Endowment for the Arts, notes that informal arts is a phrase that denotes a range of personal and grassroots arts activity that typically lack national, reliable statistics.

Within the literature on recreation and leisure, the arts have been categorically identified. Traditionally, the arts consist of a variety of visual, performing, folk, and ethnic activities as well as specific sports, home economics, and horticultural practices (Arnold, 1976). Popular art, a term suggested by Arnold (1978) as a way to categorize arts experiences, includes 11 content areas. These areas are illustrated in table 17.1. Arnold's categories were the first definitions of the various popular arts experiences found in parks and recreation programs.

As depicted in table 17.1, the arts are often defined by activity descriptors. McCarthy and Jinnett (2001) remind us that defining what we mean by the arts can be challenging because many make a distinction between what has been called the classic arts (opera, ballet, dance, theater, classical music, painting, sculpture, literature), the more popular arts (rock and roll, hip-hop, graffiti murals), and entertainment enterprises (film, radio, television, computers). It seems reasonable, however, to conclude that the arts include notions associated with auditory, visual, movement, and experiential factors. Over the years, Arnold's categories have proven useful to recreation professionals.

MEANINGS OF ARTS AND CULTURE: ORGANIZATIONS AND PARTICIPANTS

Arts and culture is meaningful within the context of recreation and leisure in contemporary society. Some experts predict that changes related to time and subtle shifts in workplaces, leisure activities, communities, and peoples' everyday lives are developing creative class economies (Florida, 2002). According to Florida (2002), the creative class is made up of artists, engineers, architects, musicians, computer scientists, writers, entrepreneurs, entertainers, and creative professionals in business, finance, law, health care, and related fields.

Through the various program offerings, recreation organizations have contributed greatly to the general population's knowledge about arts and cultural opportunities. In doing so, not only have they assisted in educating the public about leisure options in the arts sector, but they have also played

Table 17.1 Categories for Popular Arts

Category	Description
Horticulture arts	Parks, gardens, houseplants, growing scenes
Home economic arts	Weaving, crafts, cooking, fabrics, decorating, design
Athletic arts	Martial arts, display arts of gymnastics, fencing, exhibitions
Folk arts	Participatory level of arts in fairs, festivals, and circus
Cultural arts	Arts participated in by people of various cultures, which are distinguishable by their geographic location
Ethnic arts	Performance or exhibition of cultural arts by performing groups
Fine arts	Visual arts expressions in painting, sculpting, photography, and architecture
Performing arts	Ballet, opera, theater, and symphonies performed on stage
Communication arts	Theater arts for television, radio, speech, some modern dance, children's theater, extemporaneous theater, and improvisational works
Sensual arts	Arts experiences designed to provide exploratory use of the senses: touch, taste, sight, smell, and hearing
Child art	Children's interpretation and experimentation with life

Adapted from N.D. Arnold, 1978, "Pop art: The human footprint in infinity," *Journal of Physical Education, Recreation and Dance* 49(8): 56-57.

a key role in defining and perhaps establishing social values that reinforce the idea that creative opportunities for all is a good thing.

State and provincial representatives from organizational settings such as folklife and heritage, historic preservation, visual and performing arts, and other culture-based groups have formed alliances and written position papers exalting the values of policies designed to enhance public support for arts and culture (Dwyer & Frankel, 2002). Recreation and leisure organizations are well positioned to be among those who advocate for, offer arts and cultural experiences to, and partner with organizations that make up the broader arts sector. Many recreation and leisure organizations already participate in these ways; examples are given later in this chapter.

The National Endowment for the Arts (2009) *Arts Participation 2008 Summary Report* reported that 81.3 million Americans visited an arts museum or gallery or attended at least one of the following types of events: theater; opera; ballet or other dance; or classical music, jazz, or Latin or salsa concert. This number represents one in every three adults. An earlier analysis found that 65 percent of adult Americans watched or listened to the arts primarily produced or presented by nonprofit arts organizations through the media by watching television or listening to the radio, 58 percent created or produced these arts themselves, and 43 percent experienced these arts in person. The report noted that electronic arts experiences, such as those experienced through the media, a computer, or a portable digital music player such as an iPod, had become the dominant form of participation in the arts. The media was the primary means of distribution for both for-profit and nonprofit agencies (American Assembly, 1997).

Participation in arts and culture must also be viewed outside organizational or agency contexts. As interest in arts and cultural participation has proliferated, ideas regarding who provides arts and cultural experiences have expanded (Carpenter, 2008). Many people experience art alone and in individually determined groups that occur in nonorganizational settings. The total arts industry consists of a much broader spectrum of activities than is normally considered (Taylor, 2008). As such, terms such as *informal arts* and *participatory arts* are sometimes used to describe contemporary arts

and cultural participation that takes place outside an organizational context. These forms of creative expression and experience are in part related to the popularity of DIY (do it yourself), access to electronic media, and social networking opportunities that are inviting many to participate in nontraditional, nonorganizational promoted experiences. The participatory culture has relatively low barriers to artistic expression and civic engagement, strong support for creating and sharing one's creations, and some type of informal mentorship whereby what is known by the most experienced is passed along to novices (Jenkins, Clinton, Purushotma, Robinson, & Weigel, 2006). Searching *treadmill dancing* online, for example, will enable the viewer to see numerous choreographed sequences done by performers on moving treadmills synchronized to music, thus showing participatory art in action. Remixing or creating alternative versions of a song, film, literature, or other art form is another example of participatory culture.

BENEFITS OF ARTS AND CULTURAL RECREATION OPPORTUNITIES

Next we explore benefits associated with arts and culture participation in recreation. In doing so, we rely on the wisdom of author and philosopher David Gray (Gray, 1984) who wrote a seminal paper titled "The Great Simplicities." Simply put, these are the workings of the human mind, moral imagination, and the value of people and their capacity for growth. In his paper, Gray challenged recreators to negotiate the maze of organizational complexity, budgets and bargaining woes, and bureaucratic channels in order to find these three great simplicities and the real meaning and value of the recreation experience for individuals, groups, and communities. Clearly, our understanding of the benefits of arts and cultural experiences can be examined within the contexts of individuals, groups, and communities. These benefits are examined next, and specific programs that highlight each benefit are presented.

Individuals

The ways in which people in a free society choose to spend their discretionary time has been of interest to professionals whose jobs are to develop and conduct arts and cultural programs. The benefits people realize from arts and cultural participation vary by individual and by actual type of experience. We know that leisure is characterized by feelings of individual freedom and choice. Central to the nature of creative activity is freedom (Kelly & Freysinger, 2000). We also know that repeat participation in certain leisure is, in part, because individuals receive unique benefits from participation. The same experience, such as singing in a choral group, will produce different benefits for different people. One person may find joy in the music, and another may find joy in the friendships that singing with others facilitates.

Research tells us a good deal about typical benefits people realize during leisure engagement, and this information is useful for parks and recreation professionals. Estes and Henderson (2003) remind us that parks and recreation professionals would do well to remember that the unique thing we do best is provide people with opportunities for enjoyment.

> Happiness . . . may . . . be found in full engagement in the present through involvement in creative endeavors, or may occur in repose or quiet peacefulness. To become happy, one needs to open oneself to the delights of pleasure and the many wonderful things to enjoy in the world, such as food, art, poetry, music, science, and adventure. (Estes & Henderson, 2003, p. 24)

The arts add excitement and joy to our lives, and arts-related experiences are said to create an understanding of and appreciation for the arts that will lead us to participate more as adults (Orend, 1989). Over the years, studies have shown that older people who have consistently participated in a core of leisure activities throughout their lives display positive attitudes toward their leisure over time and lead a more balanced life (Kelly, 1997; Kleiber, 1999).

Knowing oneself is another benefit of participation in arts and culture. Csikszentmihalyi (1990) reminds us that when involved in expressive activity, we feel in touch with our real self. Use of our creative abilities and potential is also reason to participate in arts and cultural experiences.

Groups

Activities that involve others can be beneficial in forming and validating friendships and relationships that revolve around shared passions for arts and cultural experiences. Shared experience is a common ingredient of many recreation events (Gray, 1984) and often brings people together who might not share other interests or relationships. Take, for example, the popular concert in the park programs that take place across North America. People from all walks of life converge in New York City's Central Park for free, open-air concerts or in Albany, Oregon, for their outdoor summer concert series in Monteith Riverpark just to sit together and enjoy the *same* musical performance at the *same* time.

Leisure is an ongoing learned behavior (Kelly, 1996). We not only learn how to engage in activities and interact with others in leisure settings, but we also learn culture-specific values and orientations for our leisure (p. 42). Family, schools, recreation and arts organizations, and peer groups and friendships provide contexts in which our early creative interests are developed. Our propensities for arts and cultural experiences are found and nourished within group situations.

The family unit typically presents people with their first group. This group is important because arts participation by adults can influence participation by their children. If parents enjoy playing music, for example, it is more likely that their children will find similar activities challenging (Csikszentmihalyi, 1990). We know that early exposure to recreation experiences will establish roots from which future recreation pursuits reemerge during adulthood (Iso-Ahola, 1980; Kleiber, 1999). Sharing arts experiences encourages intergenerational activity (Taylor, 2008) and in doing so creates family memories. Research shows that early arts experiences, arts learning, and the valuing of the arts by family members and peers dispose people toward arts participation as adults (Zakaras & Lowell, 2008).

The concept of *serious leisure* is often viewed as group activity and has relevance in understanding arts and cultural leisure experiences. Stebbins (1992) studied and wrote about serious leisure because of his personal avocation as an amateur musician. Stebbins found that serious leisure is the systematic and determined pursuit of an activity by an amateur, hobbyist, or volunteer that eventually

Example of a Program Benefitting Individuals

According to organizers of the Great Dickens Christmas Fair, the 2010 event was the jolliest and most well attended ever (www.dickensfair.com). Each year organizers and volunteers re-create Victorian London using 120,000 square feet (11,100 sq m) of San Francisco's Cow Palace Exhibition Halls. The fair features continuous performances of historically appropriate music, dance, visual arts, literary arts, and performing arts on several designated stage and performance areas and by characters wandering along the snow-dusted winding streets and lanes and located in the various shops, eating establishments, and businesses. Before the fair, hundreds of costumed players are required to spend their time and money creating their character, attending workshops and rehearsals, following guidelines related to dress and costume, and meeting onsite performance responsibilities. As an individual leisure experience, participating at this level requires ongoing commitment and involvement. Attending the fair, also an individual leisure experience, involves onsite participation. Both forms of leisure participation are indicative of how people seek benefits from this type of arts and cultural experience. To examine this form of arts and cultural participation further, consider other historically based arts and culture organizations that offer benefits to participants and observers, such as Civil War Reenactors, the Society for Creative Anachronism, and the many state- and provincial-wide Renaissance fairs and festivals.

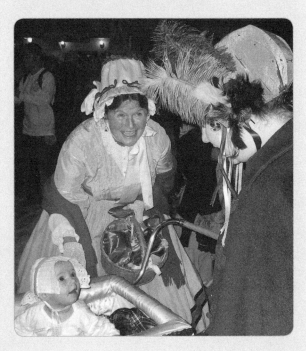

Re-enactor Miss La Creevy encounters other characters at the Great Dickens Christmas Fair held each year in San Francisco.

leads to a career in the activity (p. 3). Arts and cultural activities, whether participated in alone or in a group, easily lend themselves to the pursuit of serious leisure. When a person starts to earn money for the pursuit, it shifts from leisure to a vocation. Work for pay examples include professional musician or a person who gets hired after having "worked" as a volunteer.

Amateurs include musicians, dancers, and other performing artists. Hobbyists include collectors (rare books, violins, paintings), makers and tinkerers (furniture and toys, classic cars), and activity participants (social dancing, video games). Volunteering is a serious leisure pursuit that is gaining increased importance in arts and cultural agencies (Stebbins & Graham, 2004). Volunteering affects both participants and arts and cultural organizations because volunteers donate hours and expertise to advance an organization's missions and programs, and volunteering also serves as a leisure experience for the individual. Stebbins' (2005) exploration of **project-based leisure** contributes to an understanding of group behavior that may relate to shared arts and cultural activities. Many times, project-based leisure is experienced in a group. Examples include short-term projects that are beneficial to the larger community, which is explored next.

Communities

Arts and cultural recreational experiences are socially significant because these types of experiences, either when people participate in them or attend them, build communities. Researchers in the city of Philadelphia found that local **cultural activity** has a dramatic influence on neighborhoods (Stern & Seifert, 2002). Their findings showed that

- cultural activity draws new residents into communities, reducing poverty and increasing population;
- cultural participation and diverse communities are mutually reinforcing and tend to promote gradual growth rather than rapid gentrification;
- cultural activity creates a positive social environment resulting in greater civic participation, lower truancy rates, and lower delinquency rates; and
- cultural participation builds bridges across neighborhood, ethnic, and class divisions in ways that many other forms of civic engagement do not.

Shared recreational pursuits are based on kinship, work, and neighborhood (Gray, 1984) and friendship or special interest groups—contexts in which we build a sense of community with others. Pioneering work in the benefits of recreation and leisure was done in Canada during the early 1990s by a team of professionals and educators under the auspices of the Parks and Recreation Federation of Ontario and the Ontario Ministry of Tourism and Recreation. This work produced a catalog of benefits associated with personal, social, economic, and environmental leisure. The social benefits that contribute to building community follow:

- Leisure provides leadership opportunities that build strong communities.
- Community recreation reduces alienation, loneliness, and antisocial behaviors.
- Community recreation promotes ethnic and cultural harmony.
- Recreating together builds strong families, the foundation of a stronger society.
- Leisure provides opportunities for community involvement and shared management and ownership of resources.

Example of a Program Benefitting Groups

Programs such as those provided at the Charles M. Schultz Museum can have special appeal for families because parents and children share intergenerational interests. The opening of the museum served to commemorate the 50th anniversary of *Peanuts*, the popular comic strip that Schultz created. As both a museum and research center, program offerings include exhibits, workshops, educational programs, in addition to housing Schultz's strip collection, personal artifacts, and licensed *Peanuts* products. Special events and workshops have broad appeal for both adults and children, and some can even be attended together, thus enhancing the family experience. Volunteers play a key role in program facilitation, and volunteer opportunities abound at the Schultz Museum for teenagers and adults.

A volunteer welcomes family members to their visit to the Charles E. Schultz Museum, reflecting both individual and group benefits in arts and cultural participation.

Example of a Program Benefitting Communities

Two examples highlight how arts and cultural experiences enhance communities. Everyone Matters was an art exhibit that brought together community organizations, art therapists, and artists to share stories of personal growth in the Chicago Latina community. As part of Chicago's New Communities Program, the event included poetry performance, speakers, and a theatrical troupe. In the Fountain Valley School District in California, parent–teacher organizations fund Art Masters.

One of the recent programs introduced visual arts masters Picasso and O'Keeffe through multimedia educationally oriented assemblies, follow-up self-guided technique packets for students, and then a step-by-step teacher-guided journey to create an art project. This local program is affiliated with the national organization Meet the Masters, an interactive, multimedia art education program geared toward elementary school and homeschooled students.

- Integrated and accessible leisure services are critical to the quality of life of people with disabilities and disadvantaged people.
- Leisure opportunities, facilities, and the quality of the local environment form the foundation of community pride.
- Leisure services enrich and complement protective services for latchkey children through after-school and other recreational services.

Driver and Burns (1999) posited other benefits in a category called social and cultural benefits that add to our understanding of social benefits. Their view included cultural and historical awareness and appreciation; social support; understanding and tolerance of others; community integration; social bonding, cohesion, and cooperation; and reciprocity and sharing.

The social benefits of community festivals have become an area of interest to organizers and lend additional credence to the importance of the individual, group, and community in arts and culture (Delamere, Wankel, & Hinch, 2001). Parks and recreation agencies often produce large-scale public festivals, and many arts organizations hold art fairs and festivals in their major promotional and fundraising efforts. Agency staff motivated by their desire to be able to measure the social impact of community festivals can help arts and culture advocates bring intangibles associated with these kinds of leisure experiences into policy-driven discussions. Knowing the intangible benefits, along with eco-

nomic impact benefits, allows staff to bring more information to agency decision-making.

Delamere (2008) discusses the bigger picture that festival organizers need to be aware of—the effect that their festival has on the host community. A scale to measure residents' attitudes toward the positive and negative social impacts of community festivals has been used throughout Canada and the United States (Delamere, 2001). Because the scale provides substantial information in four categories—community benefits, cultural and educational benefits, quality-of-life concerns, and community resource concerns—organizers can identify and promulgate positive factors associated with their events and address and minimize negative factors. For example, participants' beliefs about the social benefits of a festival may include an enhanced image of the community, a sense of community well-being, or the ability to have a variety of cultural experiences. These positive effects can be weighed against social costs such as reduced community privacy, overcrowding, and increased noise levels during the festival.

EVOLUTION OF ARTS AND CULTURAL PROGRAMMING

To examine how arts and cultural programming has evolved, it is helpful to look at roles played by parks and recreation, public schools, arts and cultural organizations, and private enterprise. Parks and recreation agencies have traditionally provided a number and variety of arts and cultural opportunities for people of all ages. The public schools have also traditionally contributed by providing children and youth with learning opportunities in a range of arts and cultural experiences as part of the school curriculum. Private businesses have created arts and cultural options based on public demand for these experiences. Because institutional constraints on businesses are often less confining than those on public organizations, businesses are often able to offer experiences more quickly, and these endeavors become cost effective as patrons demonstrate their willingness to pay for experiences. We examine recreation, schools, arts organizations, and business contributions next.

Role of Parks and Recreation in Arts and Culture

Since the early beginnings of recreation programs at Hull House, we can trace the attention paid to arts and cultural programming through textbooks on program theory published in leisure studies. This review shows the developing emphasis placed on providing arts and cultural programs during the preparation of recreation and parks professionals.

Historically, parks and recreation agencies have made significant contributions to arts and culture over time. In responding to their missions, which emphasize providing recreation opportunity for all, arts and cultural activities have been part of comprehensive recreation programs offered to the public at community, state, regional, and national and provincial levels. Meyer and Brightbill (1956) discussed what they called the field of activities in recreation: arts and crafts, dancing, dramatics, literary activities, and music. Later, Butler (1976) devoted entire chapters of introductory textbooks to arts and crafts, music, and drama. He also introduced the idea of cultural activities in which recreation agencies cooperated with several community organizations, for example, the Oakland Education Association. Tillman (1973) included arts and crafts, dance, music, and drama in a category that he called cultural programming.

Kraus (1966, 1979, 1985) was a prolific author in parks and recreation. His textbooks in programming, administration, and leadership extensively cover programming for the arts. His early texts devote entire chapters to performing arts and to recreational arts and crafts and include specific examples about how to develop and lead arts experiences. Although Kraus' how-to approach has been followed by other authors, new lines of thinking about arts and cultural programming have emerged. For example, Farrell and Lundegren (1978, 1983, 1991) presented art, crafts, dance, drama, and music along with four other categories—environmental activities, sports and games, volunteering, and social recreation—in a chapter identified as program areas. Corbin and Williams (1987) included individual chapters on drama, arts and crafts, dance, and music; they also included mental and linguistics as its own type of art.

Although not strictly a program theory text, Arnold's 1976 book, *The Interrelated Arts in Leisure*, provides an in-depth examination of arts and culture in parks and recreation. Referred to earlier in this chapter, Arnold's categorization of arts and cultural activities continues to guide recreation professionals producing arts and cultural programs. As an artist, arts manager, and professor of leisure studies, Arnold provides an informed overview of arts programming in public recreation settings.

Changes in textbooks on program theory were seen in the mid-1980s and early 1990s. Carpenter and Howe (1985) broke from the tradition of in-depth discussions of specific program areas and instead presented a program theory that emphasizes procedures associated with needs assessment, program development, implementation, evaluation, and modification. Up to that time, the idea of cultural programs had not been addressed in detail. Kraus (1966) mentioned cultural activities briefly in discussing arts and crafts, music, dance, and drama. One of the patterns in leisure programs that Carpenter and Howe identified and discussed was the cultural program pattern. This type of programming included festivals and celebrations, excursions to see musical or theatrical performances, culinary events, multicultural activities, and historic reenactments.

Rossman (1995; Rossman & Schlatter, 2009) also broke from the tradition of examining specific program areas. Instead, they focused on program theory with the underlying assumption that whatever the program was (music or sports), the programmer's task was to facilitate individuals' engagement in leisure experiences based on their understanding of how leisure was experienced, how best to structure programs to facilitate leisure realization, and the purpose of their particular organizational context.

The notion of culturally based programs designed to address the needs of diverse groups through arts and crafts, festivals, and special events that reflect participants' cultural backgrounds was briefly mentioned by Edginton, Hanson, Edginton, and Hudson (1998). Later, Edginton, Hudson, Dieser, and Edginton (2004) delineated arts and cultural programs in detail, including the performing arts (dance, music, drama, visual arts), new arts (photography, computer-generated animation), and literary activities along with other programming areas (self-improvement and education activities; sport, games, and athletics; aquatics; outdoor recreation; wellness hobbies; social recreation; volunteer services; and travel and tourism).

Role of Public Education in Arts and Culture

Schools have traditionally contributed greatly to citizens' knowledge of arts and culture and appreciation for and aptitudes in the many forms of artistic and cultural expression. Arts education in the schools dates back to the late 1800s and typically included music, dance, theater, and visual arts at the elementary and secondary levels. Arts education was based on the desire to pass on the cultural achievements of a civilization to new generations, and the arts represented these achievements (Webster, 2003). But some are finding that American public schools are no longer adequately preparing students to participate in a rich cultural life (Zakaras & Lowell, 2008).

Over the years, efforts in arts education have varied and included cycles of interest and neglect, often depending on budget constraints. Webster (2003) noted that these cycles have spawned school and community interest in the arts.

As these cycles evolved, partners outside of the school setting emerged alternately to support, stimulate, or restore the loss of school arts programs. This has resulted in the expansion of the field of arts education to include school as well as community-based efforts, and those working in it to comprise arts specialists, generalists, artist, and arts groups. (p. 154)

Nonprofit and public organizations can provide education for children that is no longer provided for in their schools.

Noting that arts education has been a low priority in the schools for 30 years, Bodily and Augustine (2008) report that much of the difficulty in keeping arts education in urban schools is associated with general education reforms that influence curriculum decisions.

As a result, many schools have had to reduce or eliminate music, dance, theater, and visual arts experiences from their curriculums. For many elementary schools, arts specialists are a thing of the past (Dreeszen, 2003). Increasingly, public educators must look outside the schools to community-based arts organization programs and services for specialists. More and more, school districts must rely on the efforts of nonprofit and public organizations and regional arts councils and associations to send staff, artists, and volunteers to schools to teach the various arts. Larger arts and cultural organizations frequently employ staff designated to conduct arts learning. Other times, students are invited to attend agencies' rehearsals or previews. These arts experiences give students an opportunity to view performance art and to interact with some of the artists and performers. The budgetary challenges that schools face in offering arts experiences to students add to the challenge of arts managers and program specialists who are highly motivated to share the arts with young audiences but often don't have the financial resources to do all they want to do.

Role of Arts Organizations in Arts and Culture

As budget restrictions in public parks and recreation and public school districts have limited or minimized arts and cultural programs, we have seen nonprofit arts organizations offer more arts programs. Organizational uniqueness typically dictates the type of program that will be provided. As such, we are likely to see a community theater organization offering acting classes and camps, a symphony orchestra organization offering music experiences, and an arts center offering classes in the visual arts for all ages and all levels of expertise. But just as frequently we will see an arts fair or festival offered by one or more arts organization collaborating with other organizations to produce an experience that contains several arts and cultural components. Collaborative programming efforts initiated by arts managers and other community-based professionals who are committed to providing arts and cultural opportunities contribute to positive community development (Carpenter & Blandy, 2008).

Many programs are provided in partnership with park and recreation agencies and with public school teachers and administrators. Organizational missions have been extended to include a provision for continuing and expanding educational and introductory activities. A community arts organization may provide grant assistance for a visual or performing artist to facilitate school-based experiences during school time. Artist groups and collectives are figuring out new ways to provide arts experiences and earn a living (De Michiel, 2010). As this occurs, more sharing between artists and the public will occur. Performing arts organizations frequently host school-aged youngsters at their venues for free concerts during school days. These exchanges typically include interaction between students and musicians.

A wide range of programs is provided for youngsters who are just learning about the arts and cultural experiences. Community arts centers, performing arts organizations, and museums are creating experiences in response to their organizational goals and the willingness of artists to facilitate programs. Many of these programs feature activities designed to introduce children to arts experiences for the first time; other programs are designed to enable children to move further along in their art interest or pursuit.

Still other programs focus on youth and young adults, and many of these feature groundbreaking arts experiences. Technology is influencing creative programming options for arts managers. Media arts in particular are increasingly popular given the influence of electronic media and social networking on the arts and culture. Film, digital or video, and other moving-image media would seem to be particularly appealing to youth who have grown up using computers. A recent program offered by the Brooklyn Art Museum that featured rapper Jay-Z discussing his art and new book brought much acclaim and awareness about the museum to new audiences. Programmers must use innovative and attractive ways to engage the participation of youth.

Arts and cultural organizations have also become proactive by providing a variety of experiences for adults that go beyond selling seats at performances or space in classes. In the past, compulsory public

A youngster finds an interactive exhibit in a local museum engaging.

education afforded most people the opportunity to learn and even practice the visual arts, music, dance, and theater through school curricula. Adults with such experiences can draw on the many creative pursuits they learned in school when making leisure choices during adulthood. Many arts managers are recognizing this particular demographic group by providing arts and culture leisure experiences for adults at their organizations. Such programs not only meet adults' interests but also become revenue sources for nonprofit arts organizations. Even non-arts organizations such as Road Scholar, formerly known as Elderhostel, promote and publicize arts and cultural experiences and travel opportunities for active adults.

Role of Private Enterprise in Arts and Culture

Businesses and industries also add to the number and variety of art and cultural opportunities for people of all ages. From Disneyland to Las Vegas, from a children's birthday gathering at a local pizza parlor to a specially prepared culinary event for adults seeking a unique dining experience, private enterprises can take risks to pursue new markets and new arts and cultural experiences. Entrepreneurs have devised many ways for people to spend their discretionary money during their free time.

Entertainment choices abound, particularly in large urban areas, and in part because of the initiative of entrepreneurs. Through private exchange, the cost of participating in certain arts and cultural experiences is passed on to the consumer. Historically, those who could afford it, could buy it; others did without. Today, we see more of what is called democratization in arts and culture where certain experiences are theoretically accessible to everybody. This democratization occurred in part because of the commercialization of leisure experiences. So as more arts-related leisure experiences become accessible to more people, the choices and opportunities multiply and in turn, more people are able to participate in more experiences.

The growth of the middle class, commercialization of leisure, and cultural assimilation have spawned new entertainment choices along with new concepts we associate with arts and cultural experiences. Ideas linked to popular culture, high culture, and mass culture also add entertainment choices. Even though these terms are related, there are subtle distinctions. Popular culture is the commercialized everyday pastimes of a majority of people in a social group (Russell, 2009). An example is the Deadheads, thousands of fans who followed the Grateful Dead around the country attending their concerts. High culture generally refers to classical music, theater, poetry, and the fine arts (Kando, 1975). And the culture that is widely disseminated through the mass media is known as mass culture.

Commercial recreation organizations function within the business and industry sector operating leisure experiences that people are willing to purchase. Commercial organizations offering arts and cultural experiences include operations that directly sell entertainment and others that use entertainment in attracting or keeping patrons (music halls, casinos, movie theaters); organizations that disperse popular culture and media-based forms of entertainment including computers, television, and magazines; theme parks and amusement centers and businesses that sell food and drink; and operations that provide shopping opportunities such as malls and estate sales.

Another role played by private-sector businesses is that of supporting public and nonprofit organizations through sponsorships. Seen as positive advertising strategies, businesses provide money to organizations that in turn help to support arts or cultural offerings. Sponsorships are a way for businesses to support the arts and to align themselves with respected arts organizations in the community. Arts managers and recreation and public school professionals have become more and more skilled in securing sponsorships and therefore are able to plan and implement a wider variety of arts experiences for the general public. And businesses have learned that it is good for business to contribute to their communities in this way.

TYPES OF ARTS AND CULTURAL ORGANIZATIONS

The American Assembly (2006) places arts and cultural organizations into nonprofit, for-profit, and informal or unincorporated categories. The vast majority of these arts and cultural organizations are nonprofit or quasi-public organizations, each having its own mission and resources for meeting its goals. These organizations include community arts centers, art museums, performing arts organizations, art commissions and councils, historic sites, museums and reenactments, folklore associations, libraries and literary organizations, arts and cultural festivals, and youth organizations that offer special arts and cultural programs. These organizations typically have both professional and volunteer staff. In addition, they work with professional and amateur performers, artists, crafters, teachers, and facilitators to offer arts and cultural experiences.

To illustrate the types of arts and cultural organizations operating in North America today, table 17.2 lists jobs most of which were recently acquired by graduates of the University of Oregon's master's program in arts and administration. Jobs are categorized by type (i.e., museums, performing arts, community arts, events, and media). Most of these positions are in arts and cultural organizations, not parks and recreation agencies. These professionals work in a variety of museum, galleries, performing arts settings, visual arts organizations, and arts and cultural fairs and festivals. The positions depicted are typical of options available to a graduate of a master's program that emphasizes arts and culture. The diversity of positions further illustrates the growth that is taking place in arts and culture programming.

CONTEMPORARY PRACTICES IN ARTS AND CULTURE

Next we examine contemporary practices for providing arts and cultural experiences and programs in the parks and recreation setting. Each example demonstrates comprehensive arts and cultural programs. After reviewing current practices, we examine contemporary management practices associated with the delivery of arts and cultural programs. These examples not only cross many organizational boundaries in order to show the various ways organizations work and plan together, but they also show programs that address the unique interests of various user and lifestyle groups.

Table 17.2 Examples of Professional Positions in Arts and Cultural Organizations

Museums	Performing arts	Community arts	Events	Media
Manager of School and Education Programs, Seattle Art Museum	Program manager, Hult Center for the Performing Arts, Eugene, Oregon	Development associate, Southwestern Association for Indian Arts, New Mexico	Assistant event manager, Mondavi Center for the Performing Arts, UC Davis, California	Video documentarian, Portland, Oregon
Arts program coordinator, Asian Art Museum of San Francisco, California	Executive director, Altoona Symphony Orchestra, Pennsylvania	Public art manager, Clackamas County Arts Alliance, Oregon	Managing director, Portland Jazz Festival, Oregon	Graphic designer, World Forestry Center, Portland, Oregon
Project coordinator, University of Oregon Museum of Natural and Cultural History	Audience services manager, UC Berkeley Cal Performances	Associate director, Maude Kerns Art Center, Eugene, Oregon	Executive director, AIA, Memphis, Tennessee	Denver production coordinator, KGNU Community Radio, Boulder, Colorado
Exhibit evaluator, Museum of Nature and Science, Denver, Colorado	Director of information systems, Oregon Ballet Theatre	Director, community development, Idaho Commission on the Arts	Cultural arts programmer, Hillsboro, Oregon	Independent computer consultant, Portland, Oregon
Program coordinator, Van of Enchantment, Museum of New Mexico	General manager, Lord Leebrick Theatre, Eugene, Oregon	Cultural affairs coordinator, Minneapolis, Minnesota	Recreation program supervisor, Eugene, Oregon	Instructional technology specialist, University of Oregon School of Architecture and Allied Arts
Director of education, Frederic Remington Museum, New York	Director of development and major gifts, Oregon Festival of American Music	Executive director, Norris Square Neighborhood Project, Philadelphia, Pennsylvania	Special projects, Pacific Northwest College of Art, Portland, Oregon	Director of information technology services, Oregon Shakespeare Festival, Ashland, Oregon

Arts and Cultural Programs in Parks and Recreation: Best Practices

In the last few years, and in spite of challenging economic times, Oregon is experiencing growth in the number and type of opportunities for citizens to participate in arts and cultural programs. In this state of less than 4 million residents, an increasing number of nonprofit and for-profit organizations have been producing a wide variety of cultural and arts experiences including dance, theater, visual and performing arts, and culinary and literary arts. In addition, the public sector plans and implements programs. Recreation professionals have long been aware that the social and psychological benefits derived from recreation participation include those associated with arts participation. Therefore, as public organizations with a mission to provide recreation opportunities for all citizens in their service areas (cities, counties, special districts, regions), public agencies are in a unique position to provide arts opportunities to a wide range of people. A look at the arts opportunities offered by one state, one city, and the national park system in the United States follows.

To document the extent to which Oregon public recreation agencies were providing arts and cultural programs, selected members of the Oregon Recreation and Park Association (ORPA) were invited to participate in a study designed to identify the number and types of arts and cultural summer programs taking place throughout the state (Carpenter, 2004). A brief overview of the findings follows.

- Most agencies provided arts opportunities for both youth and adults throughout the summer months. The majority of these offerings were visual arts programs, followed by performing arts programs. The most popular visual arts programs were a wide variety of arts and crafts experiences. Performing arts programs included dance, movement, music, and theater experiences.

- Special events that included arts and cultural experiences were offered in nine cities, five districts, and two regional organizations.

- In three of the cities, programs took place in visual or performing arts centers. Eight of the cities conducted visual or performing arts camps that ran for at least one week throughout the summer months. Proportionately more cities than special districts held summer concert series (9 of the 12 cities, 1 of the 6 special districts).

- Nontraditional program offerings included literary and culinary arts experiences and culturally based touring opportunities. Three of the cities, two of the districts, and both of the regional organizations offered literary arts programs. Five of the cities and two of the districts offered culinary arts programs. Five of the cities and three of the districts offered culturally based touring opportunities with those serving adults far more often than youth.

The city of Philadelphia offers a wide array of arts and cultural experiences for its nearly 1.5 million citizens. The Philadelphia Department of Recreation was organized at the turn of the 19th century. The department has a long-standing and well-developed arts and cultural program that includes historic buildings, such as the Philadelphia History Museum at the Atwater Kent, Betsy Ross House, the Carousel House, and Olde Fort Mifflin, and a wide range of recreation programs that include cultural programs, after-school programs, aquatics programs, camps, visual arts programs, sport athletics, ice rinks, teen centers, programs for people with physical or mental disabilities, activities for senior citizens, and creative resolution. Arts and cultural programs include dance classes and dance festivals; music classes and neighborhood concerts; theater camps for young performers; and visual arts programs in crafts, ceramics, painting, and pottery and events such as art shows and art camps. Although the Philadelphia Department of Recreation offers arts and cultural experiences that most people expect to see, these programs include several innovative features:

- After-school programs include the arts at 100 sites, five days a week, and serve 2,800 children per week.

- Four cultural camps are offered including Art Camp (painting, drawing, sculpture, and printmaking for ages 6 to 17); Young Performers Theater Camp (ages 9 to 18 with an interest in theater, dance, or musical theater); Intro to the Performing Arts Camp (combines acting, singing, and creative movement for ages 6 to 10); and Youth Environmental Stewardship Program (employment and learning opportunity for teens interested in nature and the ecology of their urban communities).

- The Teen Center Program includes cultural activities, educational programs, photography, ceramics, jewelry making, movie nights, social events, sports, and special events.

Arts and crafts are vital to the growth of youth and is one of the most popular visual arts programs.

- The Performing Arts Program offers programs in dance, musical theater, conflict resolution theater, performing arts workshops, intensive acting workshops, and vocal lessons.

In addition to providing traditional activities, the department offers several unique programs. One of these is the Creative Resolution Theatre Program, which uses interactive theater to help children and adults move from conflict to creative resolution in a fun, safe, and supportive environment. The Mural Arts Program has created more than 3,000 indoor and outdoor murals throughout the city including the newly established Mural Mile available in cell phone or downloadable podcast formats. The program involves city residents in the creative process by offering art education programs at recreation centers, homeless shelters, and other sites around the city. The Mummers Parade that takes place on New Year's Day each year is one of America's oldest folk art traditions. More than 15,000 Philadelphia Mummers strut their stuff up Broad Street dressed as comics, fancies, string bands, and fancy brigades.

Many do not realize the extent to which the National Park Service (NPS) is involved in arts and culture in the United States. Although most of its 84 million acres located on 394 areas are prized natural and scenic lands, many NPS sites are historical or cultural in nature. NPS frequently contracts with organizations that offer onsite arts and cultural experiences. Yellowstone National Park, for example, is the site where a number of workshops take place for people interested in drawing, sketching, writing, photography, painting, and the like. The outdoor environment provides a special place for beginning and advanced artists to hone their craft under the watchful eye of renowned artists who facilitate the workshops.

The Wolf Trap National Park for the Performing Arts in Virginia has evolved into a showcase of both parks and arts in one locale. The park is one of the best examples of arts and cultural programming in the United States. Wolf Trap's comprehensive programs and services in arts and culture mirror the best practices of what most local recreation agencies and arts organizations are able to offer only in smaller segments. Wolf Trap manages two performance venues, an opera company, and an education program, all of which produce a variety of arts and cultural activities in addition to public performances. The mission is to present and create excellent and innovative performing arts programs for the enrichment, education, and enjoyment of diverse audiences and participants.

Contemporary Management Strategies That Enhance Arts and Cultural Opportunities

Contemporary management practices in arts and culture include using high-profile events to promote awareness and entertain the public, collaborating and forging partnerships, planning cultural events, addressing youth interests, associating with tourism initiatives, responding to lifestyle shifts, and creating art experiences in public places. In this last portion of the chapter, we present several best practices that emphasize these contemporary management strategies in providing arts and cultural experiences.

High-Profile Events

High-profile arts and cultural events are popular strategies for promoting ongoing programs, entertaining the public, and generating income. By high profile, we are referring to large public events that are promoted to wide markets outside of the regional area in which the promoting organization resides. Fringe festivals are a good example because their uniqueness draws arts-friendly attendees from all around North America to see nonjuried performers and emerging artists in a festival-like environment, usually lasting several days. During its run, the Winnipeg Fringe Theatre Festival, member of the Canadian Association of Fringe Festivals, boasts 23 venues, 134 performing companies, 1,168 shows, 800 volunteers, two full-time staff members, and another 50 hired during the festival (C. Couldwell, personal communication, July 29, 2004). The following are examples of other high-profile events that draw hundreds even thousands of attendees regionally:

- Cities from Belmar, New Jersey, to Portland, Oregon, have hundreds of cubic yards of sand delivered so that all ages can engage in sand sculpting.
- Mega arts events take place throughout North America, including the Cherry Creek Arts

Festival in Denver, Colorado, and Burning Man, held 120 miles (193 km) north of Reno, Nevada, and attended by up to 50,000.

- The Charlottetown Festival on Prince Edward Island is recognized as the top event in Canada by the American Bus Association.
- Plate and pitchfork events featuring gourmet meals and fine wines are held in agricultural fields or inside venues to promote organic and locally produced food and beverage.
- Classic car collectors and enthusiasts travel to towns across North America to participate in events such as the Concours d'Elegance or hot rod cruises.
- The Hemingway Days Festival takes place in Key West, Florida, and the Wizard of Oz Festival is held in Chesterton, Indiana.

Collaboration and Partnerships

We are seeing more and more collaborative efforts and partnerships among public and nonprofit agencies to offer arts and cultural programs. Partnering with organizations that have similar missions in order to accomplish goals for the greater good is increasing throughout North America. Ninety-one percent of local arts agencies have formed a partnership with at least one other public or community agency such as a school district, parks and recreation department, social service, economic development organization, or chamber of commerce, and 78 percent participate in three or more ongoing collaborations (Americans for the Arts, 2004). Collaborating not only makes sense in terms of using limited human resources, but it also enables organizations to provide arts and cultural experiences. Several examples illustrate this growing strategy.

The state of New York's innovative Urban Cultural Park/Heritage Area program is a joint venture between the New York State Office of Parks, Recreation and Historic Preservation and 22 historically significant communities around the state. Kingston is one of these areas and has benefited from this partnership by creating a series of outreach history and educational programs, local history exhibits created with school-age youngsters, celebrations and festivals, band concerts on the waterfront, and even a reenactment of the story of the British trying to rid Kingston of rebels during the Revolutionary War.

Collaborations between universities and arts organizations can create learning opportunities for college students and provide arts opportunities for the public. The Kamloops Art Gallery and the University College of the Cariboo in Kamloops, British Columbia, supported by a Community–University Research Alliance grant, are involved in a collaborative effort to find out how cultural and arts organizations work together in a small city setting. ArtsBridge America is a national network of universities that work in partnership with public schools in their communities. Their efforts have brought arts education back to many public schools. The ArtsBridge America program demonstrates that having the arts in education is valuable, promoting interdisciplinary knowledge while enhancing students' appreciation of and contributions to **culture** (ArtsBridge, n.d.). In Los Angeles, the housing authority police, city and county recreation and parks departments, and California State University at Dominguez Hills partnered to offer a comprehensive program that emphasizes the development of self-confidence, cultural awareness, and constructive social interactions of young girls through personal exploration and guided group activities.

Government grant support can encourage arts organizations to engage in collaborative efforts. For example, the Canada Council for the Arts was created by Parliament over 50 years ago to foster and promote the study and enjoyment of and the production of works in the arts. One of these programs, Artists and Community Collaboration Fund, offers grants in support of diverse artistic activities.

Emphasis on Cultural Planning

Local arts agencies typically lead efforts for community cultural planning, and in communities with a cultural plan, local government arts funding grows at a significantly faster rate than communities without a plan (Americans for the Arts, 2004). The city of Edmonds, Washington, is located about 15 miles (24 m) from Seattle. You would expect residents to access arts and culture in that large, metropolitan city, but through cultural planning, arts-related organizations in Edmonds have found ways to meet residents' interests locally. This pattern may well become the norm as more and more professionals with interest in the arts and the desire to live and work in less urban areas look around at the cultural

Background Information

Name: Sabrina Hershey

Education: Bachelor of arts cum laude in art (studio) and English (double major) from Franklin and Marshall College. Master of science in arts and administration with a concentration in museum studies from the University of Oregon, 2005.

Credentials: University of Oregon, Not-for-Profit Management Certificate, 2005; Pennsylvania College of Art and Design, Desktop Publishing Certificate, 2003.

Special awards: Student Travel Grant for Masters Research, 2005; John Marshall Scholar (Academic Merit), 1999.

Career Information

Position: I am currently working as the associate director for Maude Kerns Art Center (MKAC), located in Eugene, Oregon.

Organization: Maude Kerns Art Center is Eugene's oldest visual arts nonprofit organization and has been serving the community for over 60 years. During the year, between 500 and 550 youth, young adults, and adults take classes at the art center and between 8 and 10 exhibits are on display in the art center's gallery. MKAC has a membership of over 400 people, and more than 10,000 people attend the art center's annual fund-raising event, Art and the Vineyard. Currently, the art center has two full-time employees, namely, the executive director and me, and three part-time employees, including a publicity coordinator, exhibits designer, and administrative assistant.

Organization's mission: The mission of the art center is "to nurture artistic expression and creativity in the individual and to cultivate an appreciation and understanding of art and culture in our community." The art center serves the community in a number of ways by providing art classes and workshops; exhibiting the work of local, national, and international artists; providing studio spaces for artists; and presenting an annual arts festival, Art and the Vineyard.

Job description: As the associate director, I oversee all educational activities at the art center, including youth, young adult, and adult classes; outreach activities and events for the community and local schools; and the center's exhibits education program, including the gallery guide (docent) program and artists' services programs. On average, the center offers between 15 and 20 quarterly classes and serves between 500 and 550 students per term. Working within this organization, I have taken on several roles outside the Education Department, which include designing and creating materials used to market, promote, and advertise the center's exhibits programs. In addition, I have taken on a key role in planning and marketing the center's annual fund-raiser, Art and the Vineyard, which serves over 10,000 people.

Career path: Upon receiving my master's degree in arts management from the University of Oregon, I accepted the position of arts program manager at Maude Kerns Art Center. In January 2008 I was promoted to associate director of the art center. I believe that my current position has given me an excellent foundation on which to build my career and one day to become the executive director of an arts organization.

Likes and dislikes about the job: In my current position I enjoy working with all the people who come into the art center, from students taking classes to long-time artists and art center members. Because the art center has been operating for more than 60 years, it has become a permanent fixture in the community and is treasured by the people who use it. I also enjoy that I am continually learning at the art center. Being part of a small staff has given me the opportunity to be involved in all facets of the art center, and I have learned a lot about how this organization functions. The challenges of my position include the continual struggle to obtain funding for the arts. In these difficult economic times, finding funding for the art center's programs is hard. We have to be amenities in their own backyard. The Edmonds Community Cultural Plan includes goals related to increasing the visibility of the arts; positioning the arts as a focus for economic development; creating links with arts, business, education, heritage, tourism, city beautification, and recreation; broadening community involvement in the arts; and developing work, performance, exhibition, and retail space for artists and gathering places for the public. Cultural planners represented arts organizations, the city of Edmonds, the state, private businesses, local nonprofit organizations, and local festivals and museums. Recreation professionals should be involved when community-wide cultural planning takes place and may even want to initiate such efforts if they are not already being undertaken.

Addressing Youth Interests

Youth and young adults often have special interests in arts and cultural activities that occur outside the typical organizational contexts. It is important to keep in mind that many youth and young adults are attracted to community arts experiences, but it is also important to recognize that many others are not. Two innovative, nonagency-based practices that many youth and young adults find interesting are the DIY movement and creating and reading zines. DIY refers to doing it yourself: making and promoting music without major record label backing and without a great level of "selling out." Zines are low-volume, periodic publications distributed to satisfy the publisher's whim rather than to produce profit. Two additional examples that address youth and young adult interests in arts and culture that do occur within an organizational context are discussed next.

Filling a desire of girls who had an interest in rock music but few opportunities to engage, Rock 'N' Roll Camp for Girls (RRCG) took hold in Portland, Oregon in the early 2000s. Designed for girls and young women, RRCG is a weeklong day camp that includes musical education, technical instruction, forums to discuss and explore creativity and self-expression, and role models and examples for promoting motivation, self-reliance, and empowerment through music. Camp culminates with a public showcase on the last night. It has spawned similar camps in other cities and offers institutes fall, winter, and spring along with summer camps, private lessons, and coaching.

Totally Cool Totally Art (TCTA) is a program for youth run by the Austin (Texas) Parks and Recreation Department. Austin, known for its comprehensive parks and recreation arts and cultural programs, which include outdoor sculpture, murals, public art, and museum and cultural heritage, responded to a city council initiative to help the community deal with teen issues. TCTA objectives include promoting arts education, a sense of belonging, new experiences, teamwork and communication, and respect and trust for youth during high risk, after-school hours by creating alternative activities. TCTA is modeled as a free, after-school, arts education program that maintains a strong mentoring compliment both before the classes with recreation center staff, and during the classes where teens work alongside professional artists (www.austintexas.gov/department/totally-cool-totally-art).

Associating With Tourism Initiatives

Recreation agencies and arts organizations offering arts and cultural programs should routinely associate with their local convention and visitors bureaus (CVB). CVBs can assist programmers by including the arts and cultural opportunities in tourism initiatives. They also have tools and systems in place to help professionals conduct economic impact studies to determine when arts programs bring visitors to a region. And because CVBs are part of strategic tourism planning, they recognize ways that organizations can partner to offer better and more inclusive and exciting arts and cultural programs.

The city of Hamilton, Ontario, for example, designed and offers walking tours that go beyond the traditional historic overview to include topics with clear cultural connections related to the evolution of the city. Tours like "The Man Who Knew Lincoln" and "Pardon My Lunch Bucket Industrial Heritage Tour" are available to tourists. And the European Festival Network created and markets a FestPass Guide to help tourists not only find and get to the various festivals but also to encourage them to stay in the area for a few days at a time, thus boosting visitor spending in local regions. Arts organizers can also lobby with their local CVBs to create a familiarization tour. "Fam" tours help organizations publicize their programs and services to others in the city or region. Arts and cultural organizations, whether public and nonprofit agencies or private businesses, should nurture public awareness whenever possible.

Responding to Lifestyle Shifts

Those creating and promoting arts and cultural experiences are better served when paying close attention to lifestyle and popular culture changes. The idea that one size does *not* fit all is one that arts organizers must continue to embrace. Peoples' contemporary lifestyles influence what they do with their free time and discretionary money, and their choices represent their values. Many times, these values emerge in expressions associated with arts and culture and therefore have relationships to management strategies. Take, for example, recent research on the informal arts.

Researchers are intrigued by what they call the intersection between arts and everyday life (Wali, Marcheschi, Severson, & Longoni, 2001; Taylor, 2008). Their discoveries not only have implications for cultural planning, but they also address lifestyle issues because they are finding that vast numbers of people experience the arts in an informal manner.

The researchers have found that the **informal arts** are characterized and distinguished by their overall accessibility as vehicles for artistic expression, by the self-determining nature of people's participation, and by the generally noncommercial nature of the activities (Wali et al., 2001). They describe their motivation to start their inquiry from observing the following activities.

On any given evening around the city of Chicago, you are likely to encounter people singing, dancing, rehearsing lines of a play, working on a painting, or writing poems. A sense of intense engagement, of dedication, and of enjoyment permeates the spaces in which these activities take place. At a drumming circle in the park, a young man rises and moves into a fluid dance, an expression of ecstasy on his face. In a church basement, a director painstakingly rehearses the actors in their lines, while the stage crew works late into the evening painting the set. At a weekly rehearsal of a south Asian music ensemble, a chemist, a computer engineer, an executive secretary, and a music student lead the group through a composition. Everyone is intensely concentrating on everyone else's playing, trying to stay on beat. (p. 215)

Informal arts were found to be taking place in park district facilities (painting and folk dancing classes), branch libraries (poetry workshops and readings), in neighborhoods (storefront theater and performance-related groups), and faith-based institutions (choral groups). Next we present lifestyle-related factors that have the potential to continue to define new forms of informal arts.

- As people continue to move from older, industrial cities, places such as Detroit, Pittsburgh, and Baltimore have focused on recent revitalization, and new projects are creating trendy areas that attract young professionals wanting to be close to work and nightlife.

- Sundays are days that programs can be, and increasingly are, offered to the public.

- As time scarcity continues to be challenging for so many people, what has been called **leisure episodes** will remain relevant. Fairs, festivals, and special events in particular have

Fairs, festivals, and special events appeal to people with limited time by creating a leisure episode.

properties that appeal to people with limited time (Carpenter, 1995). Other arts and cultural experiences may need to be designed with leisure episodes in mind.

- As the baby boomers grow older, they may develop interest in reengaging in activities they participated in as children, and if so, many activities are likely to be related to the arts. Many in this population are moving to downtowns, drawn to urban cultural attractions such as performing arts, museums, and gourmet food.

Creating Arts Experiences in Public Places

Making arts available in public places is a long-standing practice. Parks and recreation organizations often coordinate public arts design, selection, and placement. Although these types of programs emphasize visual arts, this discussion also includes performance arts. Places for public arts and culture can include certain sections of our towns and cities that temporarily become arts places, such as increasingly popular arts walks in busy sections of towns. Space can be set aside for arts and cultural events in settings designed for something else: for example, bringing musicians or magicians into shopping malls, using public parks to turn soccer fields into arts festivals, or creating rose gardens in outdoor movie theaters during the summer. Businesses can support the arts by offering late-night poetry slams to small groups in clubs after the larger groups have left or letting musicians practice in a neighborhood restaurant after it closes.

Another way to create public spaces for arts experiences is to renovate rather than bulldoze abandoned buildings. The Dia Art Foundation renovated an abandoned Nabisco carton-making plant along the Hudson River in Beacon, New York, to create the Dia:Beacon museum that houses its contemporary art collection. Reexamining decisions that would allow for the development of public spaces to serve as appropriate venues or centers for a variety of arts and cultural experiences, instead of practices that favor demolition of unused private buildings, could be cost effective ways to increase the number of program sites and offerings. Those with an interest in arts and culture must continually remain open to new ways of bringing these experiences to unanticipated public places, for example, finding a pianist in PDX as I did and described earlier in the chapter.

SUMMARY

Opportunities in arts and cultural recreation represent a multifaceted area of recreation programming. Ample evidence indicates its importance throughout the history of the parks and recreation movement. Our professional literature offers numerous examples of how professionals can provide arts and cultural leisure experiences to the public. Many people have not only enjoyed the arts through recreation services over the years but have also developed an appreciation for and skill in leisure pursuits that have lasted a lifetime. It is important for recreation professionals with an interest in promulgating arts and cultural experiences not only to be aware of the many arts and cultural programs provided today but to find ways to associate with and partner with other arts enthusiasts in their communities. The benefits derived from arts and cultural experiences contribute not only to individual growth and the development of leisure interests but also to building our communities through shared experiences. There is every reason to believe that arts and cultural experiences will continue to be vital experiences that define our time and communicate our social values.

For glossary terms, learning experiences, and more, please visit the web resource at **www.HumanKinetics.com/IntroductionToRecreationAndLeisure**

CHAPTER 18

The Nature
of Recreation and Leisure
as a Profession

Denise M. Anderson

We don't build bridges; we build the
people who build bridges.

Fran McGuire, professor,
Clemson University

LEARNING OUTCOMES

After reading this chapter, you should be able to do the following:

❯ Describe the benefits of the profession to both society and the individual practitioner

❯ Outline the six criteria of a profession

❯ Define what is meant by a human services profession

❯ Explain career planning and the nine steps of career positioning

❯ List seven current trends in the recreation and leisure services profession

INTRODUCTION

Let's be honest. How often have you had a conversation with your parents, aunts and uncles, or roommate about your career choice in recreation and leisure services only to have them respond, "Well, that sounds like fun"? Or have you ever tried to explain to your grandmother what recreation and leisure service management is only to have her stare at you blankly and ask why you aren't studying something meaningful like medicine or engineering? Although these comments may be well intentioned, they shed a great deal of light on the misperceptions associated with the recreation and leisure services profession. This chapter provides you with not only the answers to your friends' and family members' questions but also a framework with which to move toward a successful career in the recreation and leisure services profession.

VALUE OF THE PROFESSION AND BENEFITS TO THE PROFESSIONAL

Recreation and leisure services have long provided a great deal of benefit to all sectors of society. Because it contributes to the quality of life and enhances communities, the field is identified as a core value within the United States, Canada, and other countries. Those who work in the field enjoy a career with numerous benefits.

Working within a profession that can provide an array of benefits to society would undoubtedly provide a great deal of satisfaction to the professional. But the benefits to the professional go beyond self-satisfaction. For many, the desire to work in the field stems from a love of recreation and leisure. Those professionals have chosen a career path that allows them to combine their passion with their paycheck. For the park ranger, a love of being outside and spending time in some of the most beautiful places on earth lends itself to working to protect those areas. A student with a passion for travel may end up using that knowledge and interest to help ensure that others develop the same passion. Whatever branch of the profession you choose to enter, you will have the opportunity to live your passion. Certainly, the workplace itself can be a benefit. State and national parks, sports arenas, cruise ships, golf courses, and other leisure spaces are settings that can be beautiful, exhilarating, and just plain fun.

Professionals in the field of parks and leisure services also find themselves drawn to the profession by their love of working with the public. When you are working with the public, no two days are the same. Boredom tends to be nonexistent because a job in the field provides constant challenges and opportunities for growth as well as interaction with a diverse set of people.

CHARACTERISTICS OF THE RECREATION AND LEISURE SERVICES PROFESSION

Remember that conversation you had with your parents or grandparents about your chosen career path? Part of their concern may have stemmed from the all-too-common confusion about working as a professional in the field. But a strong case can be made that recreation and leisure services is indeed a noble profession. Six commonly accepted markers explain what makes a job not just a job but a profession, and recreation and leisure services appears to measure up (McLean & Hurd, 2012).

Social Value and Purpose

The first criterion recognizes that a profession must have a social value and purpose. That is, the field in question must contribute to the greater good of society. With its emphasis on health, wellness, youth development, quality of life, community and economic development, the environment, and sustainability, recreation and leisure services easily meets this requirement (McLean & Hurd, 2012).

Public Recognition

The second standard is that the field has public recognition. That is, the public acknowledges the importance of recreation and leisure and, perhaps more important, is willing to pay for it. Certainly, the acknowledgement differs among the various sectors of the field. Spending patterns related to travel and tourism and other forms of commercial recreation differ from those of government-sponsored, or public, recreation. Of course, the means of funding each are also different. The private sector, or commercial recreation, depends entirely on the willingness of people to choose one product over another (e.g., Disney World versus Six Flags), whereas public-sector organizations such as local parks and recreation agencies get at least a portion of their funding through appropriated government funding such as property and hospitality taxes (McLean & Hurd, 2012).

Specialized Professional Preparation

Another necessary component of a profession is specialized professional preparation, which refers to the degree to which the profession has requirements that those working in the field must meet before they can practice, or the degree of professional authority that a practitioner must possess. In recreation and leisure services, three areas are related to this criterion: professional preparation in recreation and parks, specialized body of knowledge, and **accreditation** in higher education (McLean, Hurd, & Rogers, 2008).

Professional preparation refers to the college and university curricula that have been developed, including the two-year degree level (associate degree), four-year degree level (bachelor's degree), and the graduate degree (master's degree and doctoral degree). The four-year bachelor's degree is the most common requirement for entry into a full-time position within the field, although the degree specifications can vary from program to program depending on a student's specific area of interest. For example, in many recreation and leisure service university programs, students have a choice of concentration areas that may include community recreation management, sport management, camp management, travel and tourism, therapeutic recreation, recreation resource management, and professional golf management, among others. Therefore, although most programs develop their core curricula around accreditation standards, which are discussed next, course requirements following completion of the core delve more specifically into the concentration area requirements.

Specialized body of knowledge as a criterion is concerned with whether the field has a unique knowledge base that a practitioner must have to be effective. A cursory look at any recreation and leisure services curriculum may suggest that the field has simply absconded and claimed as its own knowledge from a variety of areas including communications, management, marketing, and finance while adding a parks and recreation spin on the content. On closer look, however, it becomes apparent that this spin, as well as an increasingly specialized research base that contributes to the overall body of knowledge in the field, has assisted the recreation and leisure services field in developing its own specialized body of knowledge. In fact, an examination of our growing base of literature, exemplified by both books about recreation and leisure services and journals focused on the field of leisure research, illustrates the advancements that have been made in understanding how the field is unique. Further enhancing this body of knowledge are practical, defined internship experiences that are required of recreation and leisure services students. These internships allow students to put this knowledge into action. This hands-on experience, combined with our growing understanding of the nature of recreation and leisure services as a

Students who major in recreation and leisure services often get a large amount of hands-on learning in skills such as programming.

human services profession, provides students and practitioners with the confidence to identify recreation and leisure services as a profession that has a specialized body of knowledge.

Finally, this specialized professional preparation is enhanced through a commitment to accreditation in higher education. Accreditation requires academic programs to meet standards set by a governing body that has identified the critical skills and knowledge needed to work in a profession, in this case recreation and leisure services. Although not all recreation and leisure programs are accredited, those that are have demonstrated to the governing body that their curriculum is not only designed to teach those skills and knowledge but also been successful at doing so, as verified by outcome measurement. Recreation and leisure services has enhanced its standing as a legitimate area of scholarship concern through the development and approval of standards by the Council on Postsecondary Accreditation in 1982. Today, the Council on Accreditation of Parks, Recreation, Tourism and Related Professions (COAPRT) is the accrediting body for recreation and leisure services curriculums and is recognized by the Council for Higher Education Accreditation (CHEA), which provides oversight to COAPRT.

Existence of a Professional Culture

The existence of a professional culture and related professional associations is another indication that a field is recognized as a profession (McLean & Hurd, 2012). Professional associations are membership organizations that provide a variety of services related to the development and advancement of the field. Professional associations can serve as advocates for the goals of the profession and provide opportunities for networking and continuing education of their members to advance the profession. For instance, the National Recreation and Park Association advocates conservation, preservation, and recreation and leisure issues nationally and internationally through interaction with government officials and partnerships with public- and private-sector agencies. Eight primary activities of professional associations have been identified (Edginton, DeGraaf, Dieser, & Edginton, 2006):

1. Advocacy for the professions ideals
2. Educational opportunities for members
3. Written and electronic community with and among members

4. Networking opportunities that are both face to face and electronic

5. Promoting standards of practice

6. Recognition of best practices and exemplary performance by individuals and agencies

7. Conducting research and fact finding that will advance the profession

8. Providing liability, health, or retirement benefits

All these activities contribute to the growth of both individual members as well as the profession as a whole. See the web resource for a partial list of professional associations in the field.

Credentialing and Standards

True professions will also recognize **credentialing**, certification, and agency accreditation as key indicators of quality within the field. Credentialing refers to qualifications that professionals must meet before they can practice in a given field. Although recreation and leisure services, as a diverse field, has no unified credentialing system, various arms of the field have certification processes designed to set standards for practice. Numerous certifications exist for a variety of specific areas of our field ranging from tourism (e.g., event planning) to sport management (e.g. coaching certifications) to park services (e.g., interpretive guides). Two of the most well known certifications are the certified park and recreation professional (CPRP) and the certified therapeutic recreation specialist (CTRS). Certification ensures that a practitioner in the field has attained a certain level of skill and knowledge as measured by a standardized exam. Practitioners must not only meet certain education or experience guidelines to sit for the certification exam but also, upon successful completion of the exam, earn a predetermined number of continuing education units over a specified time to retain certification, thereby ensuring that their knowledge remains current. Detailed information on the certification processes can be found for the CPRP at www.nrpa.org/cprp or for the CTRS at www.nctrc.org. Like academic programs, public parks and recreation agencies can also undergo an accreditation process to ensure that they are practicing at a high level with respect to the services they offer to their audience. This type of accreditation process also ensures higher levels of professionalism in the recreation and leisure services field (McLean & Hurd, 2012).

Code of Ethical Practice

The final criterion for a profession is that it has developed a **code of ethical practice**. This code outlines the responsibilities of the field to the public and the manner in which professionals will carry out services in the field. Although the recreation and leisure services profession does not have an overarching code of ethical practice like that found in the medical field, individual agencies typically develop their own codes or, more commonly, professional associations for the various sectors of the field develop codes of ethical practices that individual agencies then follow (McLean & Hurd, 2012). For instance, the Code of Ethics for the America Therapeutic Recreation Association addresses such issues as autonomy, justice, fairness, and confidentiality (www.atra-online.com). Figure 18.1 illustrates the Code of Ethics for the Commonwealth of Virginia's Department of Conservation and Recreation. See the web resource for the NRPA code of ethics.

NATURE OF THE PROFESSION

The recreation and leisure services field is associated with enhancing the quality of life for participants. The goals and outcomes associated with programs, facilities, and services are designed to improve individuals' lives as well as enhance communities in a variety of ways. For these reasons, a career in recreation and leisure services is a career in a human services profession.

Human Services Profession

Parks and recreation services is a **human services profession**. The human services field has the objective of meeting human needs through an interdisciplinary knowledge base, focusing on prevention and remediation of problems and maintaining a commitment to improving the overall quality of life of those they serve. Human services professions are also seen as promoting improved service delivery systems not only by addressing the quality of direct services but also by seeking to improve accessibility, accountability, and coordination among professionals and agencies in service delivery

---

COMMONWEALTH OF VIRGINIA DEPARTMENT OF CONSERVATION AND RECREATION

AGENCY MISSION STATEMENT AND CODE OF ETHICS

Agency Mission Statement: The Department of Conservation and Recreation works with Virginians to conserve, protect, and enhance their lands and improve the quality of the Chesapeake Bay and our rivers and streams, promotes the stewardship and enjoyment of natural, cultural, and outdoor recreational resources, and ensures the safety of Virginia's dams.

Agency Code of Ethics: As employees of the Commonwealth of Virginia and its Department of Conservation and Recreation, we will

- conduct ourselves with integrity, dignity, and respect for others;
- transmit or use confidential agency information only for the purpose intended;
- adhere to the relevant Virginia Standards of Conduct for Employees (DHRM Policy 1.60) and standards of any professional associations or organizations of which we may individually be a member;
- strive to perform the duties of our position and supervise the work of our subordinates with the highest degree of professionalism;
- exercise diligence, objectivity, and honesty in our professional activities, and be aware of our responsibility to disclose improprieties that come to our attention to the appropriate parties without fear of retribution;
- commit to the highest ideals in the stewardship of the Commonwealth's natural resources;
- exercise prudence and integrity in managing public funds and property;
- strive for professional excellence by maintaining and enhancing professional knowledge, skills, and abilities;
- maintain and promote nonpartisanship in our professional dealings;
- cooperate with all governmental entities to promote the greater good of the Commonwealth; and
- hold ourselves accountable, as employees, for adhering to this Code of Ethics.

Figure 18.1 The Commonwealth of Virginia's Department of Conservation and Recreation's Code of Ethics outlines the agency's expectations for employee behavior.
Reprinted from The Commonwealth of Virginia's Department of Conservation and Recreation.

(National Organization for Human Services, n.d.). Recreation and leisure services agencies certainly fit this profile. Whether the service population is interested in youth programs, a cruise around the world, a game of tennis, camping, or rehabilitation services, our field is about improving people's lives through recreation and leisure. So, what does that mean for you?

Recreation and leisure services professionals provide numerous services to the public in a variety of ways. Professionals may be **direct service providers**, information providers, or advocates, or they may take on more of a facilitator or educator role in the provision of services (Henderson, Bialeschki, et al., 2001). A direct provider of services is a professional who is responsible for a program from start to finish and leads the participants through the program. In other words, the direct provider controls the program, and participants are responsible for little more than participating in the program. An example would be a youth soccer league.

A professional who is serving as an **information provider** focuses on facilitating engagement in recreation by serving as a conduit through which information about opportunities available in the community can flow. In addition, this service delivery method may include making direct referrals to specific programs or people so that the agency can meet the needs of community members, both recreational and otherwise. No single person or agency can provide everything that a community wishes to receive in terms of recreation. Therefore, an agency that is committed to providing information about other services not provided by its own staff is providing a needed service to the community, although it is not engaged in direct service provision.

A third way that professionals serve their publics is by taking on the role of an **advocate**. An advocate is a professional who recognizes an injustice that prevents community members from engaging in recreation and leisure services. For example, advocating for people with disabilities is just one role that professionals in recreation and leisure may play. Although the information referral approach would provide people with disabilities information about activities available to them, it may not recognize the significant barriers to participation beyond lack of knowledge about available opportunities. The advocate would work to gain a better understanding of these barriers and try to help that group overcome the barriers. Therefore, if the barrier to participation in wheelchair sport was the cost of a wheelchair sport chair, an advocate might work with local agencies or funders to provide those chairs for people with disabilities so that they could increase their participation in recreation and leisure programs.

The final type of service provision is that of a **facilitator** or educator. This type of professional facilitates participants' engagement in leisure in such a way that they are responsible for many of their own leisure experiences. The provision of leisure education is an excellent example of this type of service delivery. A practitioner who can improve the public's attitudes, knowledge, skills, and awareness toward leisure provides the necessary components for community members to meet their leisure needs on their own outside the context of programs offered by direct service providers (Henderson et al., 2001).

All four of these types of services can be found in the numerous sectors of service provision in the recreation and leisure services profession. From travel and tourism to outdoor recreation to therapeutic recreation, all recreation agencies will likely incorporate direct service provision, information referral, advocacy, and enabling services (Murphy, Niepoth, Jamieson, & Williams, 1991). For example, the nonprofit sector of the field, which includes agencies like the YMCA, is well known for its direct service provision, in which professionals such as afterschool program directors and youth sports coordinators work directly with participants. But the same sports coordinator may also serve as an information provider if someone is looking for a youth swim team and the agency itself does not offer one. The sports coordinator may be able to provide parents with information about the swim team that the parks and recreation department offers down the road. The result is the same whether the YMCA or the parks and recreation agency offers a swim team—the child gets to swim. The role played by the professional, however, differs based on circumstances. Likewise, a front-desk manager at a hotel may serve the role of information referral provider when she or he directs guests to restaurants in town. On the other hand, a hotel staff member may play the role of an advocate if she or he, after learning from guests that a local attraction is not easily accessible for people in wheelchairs, tries to persuade the attraction to make changes. Making the necessary changes would likely be in the best business interest of the attraction and would provide increased leisure opportunities for people who use wheelchairs. A wide variety of employment opportunities is available in the recreation and leisure services profession. Regardless of the type of position that a new professional is interested in, he or she should be prepared to serve the public in many ways to provide leisure and recreation opportunities.

A Day in the Life of a Human Services Professional

There is no typical day for a human services professional. The two critical words are *human services*. Professionals who deal with people are in many ways engaged in professions that never sleep. Don't worry—I didn't say, "Professionals who never sleep." But dealing with the public, a public that is often passionate about its recreation and leisure pursuits, is indeed a full-time job. The profession works to facilitate the public's quality of life. Let's look at one day in the life of a professional in the field—a front-desk manager at a resort. Although at first glance this type of position may not seem to qualify as a career in a human services profession, it takes numerous people, doing a variety of tasks, to provide services that contribute to increasing quality of life, in this case for those who may be trying to get away from it all on vacation.

A Day in the Life of a Front-Desk Manager

Working at a resort can be highly rewarding and exciting, but no two days are the same. The following is an example of the type of work that a professional in the area of resort management may encounter in one day's time:

9:00 a.m.   Have a morning meeting with other departmental managers. Discuss topics like occupancy and revenue per available room. Review any security incidents or guest complaints. Look at arrivals for VIPs and address any special needs for groups.

9:30 a.m.   Conduct a lineup meeting with the front-desk staff to report any issues that may affect the daily operation. Review guest complaints and VIPs. Discuss any group arrivals or departures and any special concerns for billing or room assignments.

10:00 a.m. Analyze the arrivals report. Block all guaranteed requests into correct room type based on bed type, view, available upgrades, and so on. Pay special attention to VIPs or repeat guests. Change the availability in the reservations system so that it accurately matches the room types that are still open.

10:30 a.m. Call any guest who reported a complaint from the night before. Determine whether the issue is resolved or whether the guest needs further compensation. Communicate with the head of the department in which the complaint occurred.

11:00 a.m. Interact with the front-desk staff. See whether any billing issues need resolution during the shift. Conduct audits to monitor that the checkout process is meeting the standards.

11:30 a.m. Meet one on one with the direct manager. Review financial progress on weekly, monthly, and yearly goals. Discuss any significant challenges with guests or employees. Discuss upcoming events and issues. Get approval on any upcoming expenses.

12:00 p.m. Eat lunch.

12:30 p.m. Analyze the departure report and determine whether all guests who are meant to check out have left. This task may require sending a staff member to check the room if the guest did not officially check out. Process transactions for accounts that are still active and close out charges to the credit card on file.

1:00 p.m.   Conduct an interview for an open front-desk position. Consider the candidate's punctuality, professionalism, and preparedness. Look for experience in the service industry, a genuine interest in helping others, and a pleasant and outgoing disposition. Contact references if the candidate meets the initial qualifications.

2:00 p.m.   Analyze the room status report in preparation for arrivals. Communicate to housekeeping management to prioritize which rooms to clean and inspect for VIPs or repeat guests.

Resort management requires a great deal of job flexibility, multitasking, and organization.

CAREER PLANNING

Many professionals' first glimpse of working in recreation and leisure services as a professional option does not occur until they reach college. Others, after working as a lifeguard for a summer, attending camp as a child, or serving as a volunteer for a special event, knew that providing leisure for others was the career path for them. For many, the opportunity to work in recreation and leisure services seems almost too good to be true. People can be paid for providing fun? A major in recreation and leisure services, regardless of area of interest, is often seen as a "discovery" major. But discovery of the field as a profession is just the first step. Planning for a career in the profession requires taking some specific steps to ensure success.

Your Education

The education component is critical because it really starts a student toward a path of success. Students may choose to begin with a two-year degree, but a four-year degree is often what both students and employers are looking for at minimum. Specifically, employers usually look for degrees from accredited programs in recreation and leisure services. The accreditation process, described earlier in this chapter, helps to ensure that students in a specific academic program are gaining the necessary education to be competent professionals in the field. Program requirements include the education level of faculty members, available facilities including library and technological resources, and administrative requirements. Accreditation is the hallmark of a quality degree program that has been vetted by an objective outside group.

Networking and Mentoring

Beyond education, networking can be crucial to getting your foot in the door. **Networking** is the process of developing a list of professional contacts who can assist with your career development. Networking can take place formally or informally. Formal networking may occur through a professional conference where, perhaps with the help of a faculty member, you can gain opportunities to meet professionals in the field whose contact information may be helpful when you start looking for an intern-

ship or job. Even if those you meet do not have either position available, they may know other professionals in the field who are hiring. Informal networking is less structured but may be less intimidating and more productive. At a professional conference, job seekers often inundate practitioners, looking to make their acquaintance, so you may get lost in the crowd. On the other hand, informal networking opportunities may be a good way to build your list of contacts. Informal networking opportunities can include introducing yourself to staff members at a recreation event that you are attending or volunteering with or talking with a guest speaker outside of class if the opportunity presents itself. Regardless of the situation, presenting yourself professionally through your words and actions will go a long way in enhancing your network.

Mentoring is another way to advance your career, and it too can be formal or informal, early career or late career. In a formal mentoring program, an agency assigns you to an experienced person who can help you navigate the hiring process (e.g., a graduate of an academic program, a faculty member). The same type of mentoring can take place informally when you identify on your own someone whom you feel comfortable going to with questions and who can help provide insight into the hiring process. Formal and informal mentoring is more common in the workplace after you are hired. Professional mentoring focuses on how to navigate the process of career advancement, especially the politics of career advancement. Because mentoring can enhance employee satisfaction and commitment, agencies sometimes develop a formal mentoring program. Research has shown, however, that informal mentoring in which both the mentor and the mentee are involved in the selection process can be more effective because the parties have a higher comfort level. Either way, a mentor can be an invaluable tool at all stages of your career.

Getting Your Feet Wet

Finally, in the field of recreation and leisure services, gaining experience is the most effective way to further your career. The recreation and leisure services field is incredibly hands on. Without that hands-on experience, students will not have success navigating the hiring process. In fact, the hands-on nature of the field is the rationale behind the requirement in academic programs for an internship. The fact that a typical internship is a 10-week, 40-hours-per-week experience suggests how important it is. Beyond the internship, other ways to gain experience include part-time work and volunteering. Both are excellent ways to increase your experience as well as make additional contacts in the field. Faculty members recognize how important this hands-on experience is and typically want students to do more than meet the internship requirement, so they build a variety of volunteer experiences into the curriculum. Any future employer will want to see commitment to the profession in the form of related work experience that goes beyond the internship. Although paying your way through school is admirable, doing it in a position that is relevant to the field is both admirable and smart.

Professional Certifications and Continuing Education

As mentioned earlier, one hallmark of a profession is recognition of the importance of certifications and continuing education. Certifications are a good way to indicate to a potential employer that you have the skills and knowledge base needed to be an effective employee. The certified parks and recreation professional (CPRP) is one of the most widely known professional certifications in the field. A person can take a number of routes to become eligible to sit for the CPRP, as illustrated in the sidebar.

The National Recreation and Park Association has identified five reasons why professional certifications are important:

1. Greater career opportunities and advancement
2. Demonstration of your commitment to the parks and recreation profession
3. Enhanced quality of parks and recreation services nationwide
4. Recognition of your accomplishments and ability to meet national standards
5. Expansion of your skills and knowledge through continuing professional development

Continuing education is typically required to maintain certification. This continuing education often takes the form of continuing education units (CEUs) earned at professional conferences or graduate education. Continuing education demonstrates that a professional has made a commitment to keeping his or her knowledge, abilities, and skills at a high level.

Membership in Professional Associations

Membership in professional associations can be an effective way to address all the points made

---

Routes to Eligibility for Sitting for the Certified Parks and Recreation Professionals Examination

To qualify to take the CPRP examination, applicants must

- have just received, or be about to receive, a bachelor's degree from a program accredited by the Council on Accreditation; or
- have a bachelor's degree from an institution in recreation, park resources, or leisure services and have no less than one year of full-time experience in the field; or
- have a bachelor's degree in a major other than recreation, park resources, or leisure services

and have no less than three years of full-time experience in the field; or

- have a high school degree or equivalent and have five years of full-time experience in the field.

For purposes of measuring years of experience, one year of part-time work experience in the field (20 or more hours per week) is equivalent to six months of full-time work experience in the field (NRPA, 2009).

previously. For this reason, students should begin their membership while still in school. Professional associations are committed to engaging future professionals early, so they often offer significantly reduced membership fees to students. Professional associations offer numerous opportunities for networking as well as continuing education through their sponsorship of annual meetings, schools, and conferences designed to bring together professionals with common interests. For example, the International Festivals and Events Association offers an annual convention where practitioners from around the world meet to share ideas related to careers in festival and event planning. Another example is the National Association of Interpreters, whose annual workshop brings together more than 1,000 interpreters to train, network, share ideas, and enjoy a different part of the country as the conference moves from region to region.

CAREER POSITIONING: A NINE-STEP PROCESS

Although planning is an important first step in the road to a career in the field of recreation and leisure services, you may need a systematic plan known as career positioning to put yourself in the best launch point for the specific career path that you hope to embark upon. Kauffman (2010) outlined nine steps that students can take to position themselves for a career in the recreation and leisure services profession.

Proximity

First, proximity is everything. A student needs to determine a career path and "locate" himself or herself in various ways to secure that career path. Proximity does not always mean physical proximity; it is an alignment that puts the person "close" to a position. Four main types of proximity are relevant to developing a career. The first type of proximity concerns people. Identifying the people who can help you find a position that you desire can be key to your success. These people can include faculty members, mentors, and internship and volunteer supervisors. The second type of proximity variable is place. A student needs to figure out where he or she wants to work. This preference can be influenced by a number of factors including significant others, family, and desire. A person may want a job

Attendance at professional conferences can help practitioners learn about the latest trends in the field as well as provide networking opportunities with other professional association members.

that will require a move or may have to move for other reasons before looking for a job. Often the student who does not restrict his or her job search by location (and is not forced to by extenuating circumstances) has the most success in finding an appealing job because more options are available. A third issue related to proximity is proximity by organization. A person may be interested in working for a specific organization. His or her willingness to gain experience with that organization through part-time or volunteer experience may allow greater access to a full-time job because the person has gotten a foot in the door. Finally, proximity by knowledge, skills, abilities, and other characteristics (KSAOCs) that the student possesses is another point to consider. A student with a strong set of KSAOCs will often be at the top of the applicant pool if the KSAOCs align with what the agency needs. The applicant is "close" to the ideal candidate. Therefore, students should identify areas of career interest, examine how their current KSAOCs line up with a desired position, and work to gain additional experience in areas in which they are deficient.

Being Proactive

Step 2 involves beings proactive rather than reactive. People who wait for jobs to come to them typically find themselves without a job. Whether by seeking additional credentials, identifying new career opportunities, or doing whatever it takes to advance her or his career, a proactive person will be in a stronger position to meet her or his career goals.

Thinking Evaluation

The third step in positioning oneself for a successful career is "thinking evaluation." In other words, you ask yourself, "Why should they hire me?" This self-evaluation can help you determine your strengths and weaknesses and position yourself for the job in which you are interested. If you have identified a specific job of interest, you can compare the KSAOCs that you currently possess with those outlined in job announcements for the type of position that you are interested in, either immediately or in the future. A table can provide a visual representation of where you stand in relation to what employers are seeking. For instance, if you are interested in a position involving youth sport and every job announcement lists a requirement for first aid and CPR training, then you would want to gain those certifications. After examining the completed table, you can start to identify which KSAOCs you need to start working on to position yourself for the type of position that you desire.

Bridging

Step 4 involves **bridging**—preparing for the job you seek. Vertical bridging involves acquiring the KSAOCs that you need to move up in an organization or advance your career. Horizontal bridging entails obtaining the KSAOCs necessary to make a lateral move into a new discipline or career. Academic preparation is one form of bridging. Students need to consider a number of variables to determine whether a program will provide the necessary bridge to their desired career. These variables include the academic content of a program or department, including whether it is accredited. A second variable is the networking ability of faculty. Is the faculty able and willing to help you make connections with practitioners in the field who can facilitate your career development? Another area to look at is the availability of service learning opportunities within the department. Do class projects or other academic opportunities lend themselves to getting real-world, hands-on experience that will build your resume? Academic opportunities such as internships, practica, volunteer experiences, and continuing education for bridging can help with both vertical and horizontal bridging. Other nonacademic experiences such as part-time jobs, volunteer experiences outside class requirements, and other professional development opportunities can also go a long way, whether you are trying to advance your career or change career paths.

Professional Networking

Professional networking, the fifth step to positioning your career, is similar to proximity. Professional networking is all about meeting the people who will either hire you or introduce you to other professionals who will. Networking can take many forms, some more effective than others. Asking faculty, mentors, or other practitioners which avenues can be the most effective for networking is a good starting point. Attending networking events such

OUTSTANDING GRADUATES

Background Information

Name: Sean Flanagan

Education: Bachelor of science in parks, recreation, and tourism management from Clemson University.

Special awards: Community Recreation Awards.

Affiliations: South Carolina Recreation and Parks Association.

Career Information

Position: Senior program director for the Caine Halter Family Branch.

Organization: The YMCA of Greenville is a nonprofit community service organization in the upstate of South Carolina. YMCA of Greenville is a YMCA association made up of four family branches, two community centers, Camp Greenville Resident Camp, and a teen services branch. With close to 500 employees throughout the association, the YMCA serves thousands of people through member services, youth and adult programs, and special events.

Organization's mission: "The YMCA of Greenville, following the example of Christ, builds healthy spirit, mind and body for all." The YMCA serves the people of Greenville County.

Job description: As the senior program director for the Caine Halter Family Branch, I lead our child care, youth and adult sports, and aquatics programs. My job functions include leading three full-time staff in those departments and directly running our summer camps.

My day-to-day responsibilities span a wide range. Here are some specific examples: budget tracking and approval such as payroll approval for staff, snack purchasing for our after-school program and chemical and equipment purchases for aquatics; staff development and evaluation including recruit-ing, hiring, training, observing, and evaluating; program planning, implementation, and evaluation through meeting with staff from other branches to assure quality; leading or supporting any program from preschool sports to Senior Olympics; and conducting parent and participant surveys.

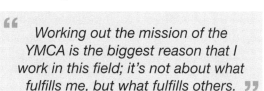

Working out the mission of the YMCA is the biggest reason that I work in this field; it's not about what fulfills me, but what fulfills others.

Likes and dislikes about the job: Working for the YMCA demands flexibility and passion. My job is a great example of that because I spend time as a program director during the summer and I supervise three program directors. My leadership style requires staff who are able to work well independently while seeing themselves as teammates to others. When a staff person needs help, we need to be there in support. That is what I love about my job and what can be most difficult.

During my seven years with the YMCA, I have continually been reminded that I believe in the mission. Working out the mission of the YMCA is the biggest reason that I work in this field; it's not about what fulfills me, but what fulfills others. Whether things are difficult or easy, the plan is still the same. Many of us can achieve it in different ways, but we are like-minded in our reason for working for the YMCA.

Career path: Since my graduation from Clemson five years ago, I have moved from an assistant childcare director to youth sports director. Then I changed YMCAs when I accepted my current position. As senior program director I am gaining valuable experience that will one day help me move into an executive director position. That is the next step within the YMCA structure, but it is not necessarily right around the corner.

(continued)

Outstanding Graduates *(continued)*

Advice for Undergraduates

Working for the YMCA while I was in school helped me gain valuable experience and develop my resume. New college graduates are joining a huge pool of qualified job seekers, so a successful resume will distinguish itself from others with something more than just an internship.

Early in my career I heard someone say, "We stand on the shoulders of giants." I am inspired by the work of those who have come before me with the YMCA. Each employee and volunteer at the YMCA has a connection to George Williams, who started a bible study for young men in London in 1844. He laid a foundation that has been built upon by people like me for many years. My hope for new graduates is that they will begin a career that is fulfilling because of how it fulfills others.

---

as professional conferences, professional meetings, and job fairs can provide the right environment for meeting a wide variety of professionals. In addition, activities such as volunteering will not only build your skill set but also introduce you to professionals who are running the event or program for which you volunteered. Kauffman (2010) recommends developing a professional family. A professional family will grow over time as your career grows. If you have nurtured the family, it can provide you with a wide-ranging net of potential opportunities.

Casing the Joint

Step 6—"casing the joint"—sounds less than professional. Casing the joint forces you to examine what you know about a job that you are seeking or the organization for which you want to work. You can use a number of approaches to find out more about the job market, in reference to both jobs in general and specific positions in which you have an interest. Casing the joint may start with casing the field, which involves identifying trends and major issues in the field. Gathering this type of information can help you determine growth and hiring trends, as well as give you a better picture of necessary KSAOCs for working in the field, both now and in the future. Other ways to learn more about the big picture of the field include becoming a member of a professional organization, reviewing major publications in the field to familiarize yourself with current research and trends, attending conferences and other educational sessions, and identifying major players in the field.

Casing an organization gets more specific. In this case, you work to gain a thorough understanding of the purpose of the organization and its structure, including the organizational chain of command. If possible, you may want to try to get a feel for the corporate culture and discern the strengths and weaknesses of the organization. This type of information can help you gain perspective on whether you really want to work for that organization. You likely also want to find out more about the specific type of position that you are looking for. Obviously, the first step is identifying the position. The next step is to determine the career track of the position and evaluate the match between your KSAOCs and those required of the position. Finally, you should case the people. Identify the people who will hire for the position. Researching key people can give you insight into both the type of people who work for the agency as well as whether you would want to work for them.

One-on-One Interview

Step 7 is the one-on-one interview. You start by identifying the person in the organization who you are interested in working for and who might hire you. Kauffman (2010) recommends a seven-step sales model to position yourself for a job in the organization:

1. Identify the organization that you want to work for, your prospect.

2. Engage the decision maker, the person who will do the hiring.

3. Survey the organization to see how you might fit in.

4. If you are meeting with someone but the agency isn't sure what they are hiring for, design a job description and job announcement to use in convincing the person that you would be a good fit for the agency.

5. Propose—the employer agrees that the agency needs someone for the job that you are seeking and offers the position.

6. Close the deal—negotiate and accept the position.

7. Follow up—if you are not hired, a thank-you note or an open-ended note along the lines of "even if you can't hire now, remember me" can go a long way in leaving a positive impression.

Formal Interview

The formal interview, step 8, differs from the one-on-one interview in that it is not a positioning technique used to convince an organization that they need you when they have not announced any job openings. Instead, it is a necessary step in response to a posted job announcement. The formal interview can give you the opportunity to move beyond your application or resume. Talking to your strengths and turning weaknesses into strengths as you position yourself as the strongest candidate for a job allows an organization to see how you might fit beyond what they see on your resume. Your resume may get you in the door; the formal interview may allow you to shut that door on all other applicants.

Communication Tools

Finally, developing communication tools is a vital piece of positioning. If you are not able to communicate with the people whom you hope to work for or with, all other aspects of positioning become irrelevant. Communication tools include resumes, portfolios, cover letters, phone skills, and electronic tools such as e-mail. These communication skills will be invaluable when it comes to preparing for the job search, entering the job search, and securing and retaining the position. Good verbal skills in networking can go a long way toward impressing a decision maker and securing yourself at worst a good contact and at best a foot in the door for a job. These same skills, along with a well-written resume and cover letter, will be instrumental in a one-on-one interview for a specific position. If you are unable to communicate your fit for a position, you are not likely to secure one. Basic skills such as how to answer a phone, speak on the phone professionally, and make appropriate use of technology such as e-mail need to be refined if you expect to be seen as a worthy job candidate and employee. On-campus resources such as career centers or contacts that you have made in the field including volunteer and internship supervisors can provide constructive feedback on communication tools such as your resume and cover letter. Students (and professionals) should keep a few points in mind with respect to e-mail and social networking sites like Facebook. Many students have personal e-mail accounts outside their university accounts on which they have less-than-professional user names. A potential internship supervisor or employer will not react kindly to a resume or e-mail note from someone with a user name like "cutiepatootie" or "studmeister." Although social networking sites are a great way to connect with friends, remember that what ends up on the Internet is forever. Future employers will often run background checks on applicants by simply searching a person's name online. Incriminating pictures or stories can cause a lot of damage to your professional reputation. Therefore, students and professionals alike, regardless of what type of communication tools they use, need to be sensitive to the messages that they convey.

CHANGES IN THE FIELD: TASTE THE EXCITEMENT

As you get ready to embark on a career path in recreation and leisure services, a working knowledge of current trends in the field is instrumental to having a broad perspective of where the field is and where it is heading. Professionals in the field are working in numerous areas to increase the relevance of recreation and leisure services at all levels, from the individual to the community. Certainly all the trends are centered on the profession's overarching mission of increasing happiness and quality of life for all. From the individual micro level to the community and global macro levels, recreation and leisure services improve lives.

Vision, Insight, and Planning

California is a trendsetter in developing a vision that promotes the influence that parks and leisure services can have on individuals and communities. The Vision, Insight and Planning (VIP) Action Plan—Creating Community in the 21st Century is about positioning public recreation and leisure services agencies as providers of essential community services. The California Parks and Recreation Society (CPRS), the state of California's parks and recreation professional association, has worked tirelessly to enhance the role of recreation in the lives of state residents. Members provide recreational experiences to individuals, families, and communities that foster human development, promote health and wellness, increase cultural unity, facilitate community problem solving, protect natural resources, strengthen safety and security, strengthen community image and sense of place, and support economic development (California Parks and Recreation Society, n.d.). This VIP movement has spread across the country. Agencies in states such as South Carolina, Illinois, and Michigan have embraced the goal of "creating communities through people, parks, and programs."

Environmental Sustainability and Stewardship

A second emerging trend in the field is environmental sustainability and environmental stewardship. Sustainability focuses on meeting our current needs for resources such as food and water without compromising the ability of future generations to meet those same needs. Environmental stewardship, as a related concept, is the ethic focused on cooperative planning and management that allows for the protection of environmental resources. Although these topics are not unique to recreation and leisure services, putting a focus on the trend is a priority for the profession. Numerous big cities including Seattle, Portland, San Francisco, Chicago, and Sacramento are taking steps to measure and control their carbon footprints. Eugene, Oregon, offers a fantastic example of the unique ways that a parks and recreation agency can incorporate sustainable planning in its efforts to provide services to the community.

Environmental stewardship is critical to sustainability and conservation. Partnerships, often between public and private agencies, go a long way in assisting the conservation and preservation of resources. Examples such as the North Cumberlands Conservation Acquisition initiative illustrate how partners can work together to protect open space for years to come. Without the cooperation of the state of Tennessee, the Nature Conservancy, and two timber companies, Conservation Forestry and Lyme Timber, it would have been difficult if not impossible to protect 127,000 acres (51,000 ha) of land that had been identified as among the most important temperate hardwoods in the world and that served as home to countless unique species (Fyke, 2009).

Also tied to sustainability and environmental stewardship is the trend of ecotourism. The International Ecotourism Society (n.d.) defines ecotourism as "responsible tourism to natural areas that conserves the environment and improves the well-being of local people." With a focus on both introducing tourists to remote sections of the world and providing opportunities for native peoples to enhance their standing through tourism, ecotourism is seen by many as a responsible form of tourism. But ecotourism providers must meet certain guidelines to ensure that ecotourism is indeed a positive experience for both sides. National Geographic has identified Brazil, Dubai, Canada, Belize, and Kenya as the current top five destinations.

How One Parks Department Is Going Green

Eugene's Parks and Open Space Department exemplifies the concept of "going green." Park workers eschew the use of motorized vehicles and instead ride bicycles with trailers behind them as they work on trails and landscape beds. In addition, Eugene uses no chemical pesticides in six neighborhood parks and has plans to use herds of goats to control invasive plants in park spaces in summer. Other examples of going green include using vegetable oil rather than diesel fuel in chainsaws and planting trees that shed fewer leaves in the fall to reduce leaf blowing (Lyman, 2009).

Health and Wellness

Other programming directions in the field emphasize health and wellness. Today's obesity crisis has agencies scrambling to find new (and hopefully more successful) ways of helping people get on a better path to health and longevity at all ages. With strong respect for the power of recreation and the outdoors, professionals are dedicated to the cause of increasing the amount of time that children are outdoors and physically active. Initiatives such as "no child left inside," which focuses on environmental education and participation in the outdoors, have made a statement that children and adults alike need to develop a meaningful relationship with the out of doors. These programs recognize the numerous benefits associated with outdoor play including cognitive enhancement, creativity, social enhancement, and physical and psychological well-being. Related programming has and will continue to be an area of emphasis for recreation and leisure providers.

The National Physical Activity Plan is an excellent example of efforts being taken by representatives from all sectors of society including health care, education, business, media, government, and nonprofits to encourage physical activity. In fact, the overarching goal of the plan is that one day all Americans will be physically active and will live, work, and play in environments that facilitate physical activity. Parks, recreation, fitness, and sports is one of eight sectors that have been identified as playing fundamental roles in the plan. Within this sector, the plan outlines six strategies for improving levels of physical activity (figure 18.2).

Leisure, Aging, and the Baby Boomers

Today's seniors look significantly different from their counterparts of 50 years ago, and leisure opportunities need to reflect this difference. People are living longer than ever before. In 1900 less than 4 percent of the population was 65 or older; by 2005 the number was 12.5 percent (McGuire et al., 2009). About 76 million baby boomers are either entering retirement or gearing up for it. Although the economic woes that began with the housing market crash of 2007 have prevented some older Americans from retiring "on time," many are find-

Improving participants' levels of physical activity is an important role for recreation and leisure service professionals in the fight against obesity.

ing themselves with a lot of free time to fill. Other demographics of note include where the aging population is living. More than half (52 percent) reside in nine states: Florida, New York, California, Texas, Ohio, Michigan, New Jersey, Pennsylvania, and Illinois, and the majority live in family settings. Because they have a longer lifespan than males do, more female seniors find themselves single.

Today's senior population is more educated than ever before, and advancements in medicine have improved their health. By having an increasingly better understanding of this audience (and its size), recreation professionals can embrace the notion of "Ulyssean living," a philosophy held by seniors who are seeking new adventures and opportunities in later life, much as Ulysses did in later life. These activities may be designed to increase health, such as programs like the Senior Games. Seniors are looking for activities that challenge them and help them further develop their mental and physical skills. Volunteering and participating in hobbies are two ways that seniors stay involved (McGuire et al., 2009). Volunteering can be an important leisure activity for seniors because research has shown that it can help people feel needed. This need is often unmet for new retirees. Both recreation and leisure services agencies and individual volunteers can benefit.

As seniors express a desire to expand their horizons within an intergenerational learning

---

PARKS, RECREATION, FITNESS AND SPORTS STRATEGIES TO IMPROVE LEVELS OF PHYSICAL ACTIVITY

Strategy 1

Promote programs and facilities where people work, learn, live, play, and worship to provide easy access to safe and affordable physical activity opportunities.

Strategy 2

Enhance the existing parks, recreation, fitness, and sports infrastructure to build capacity to disseminate policy and environmental interventions that promote physical activity.

Strategy 3

Use existing professional, amateur (Amateur Athletics Union, Olympics), and college (National Collegiate Athletics Association) athletics and sports infrastructures and programs to enhance physical activity opportunities in communities.

Strategy 4

Increase funding and resources for parks, recreation, fitness, and sports programs, and facilities in areas of high need.

Strategy 5

Improve physical activity monitoring and surveillance capacity to gauge program effectiveness in parks, recreation, fitness, and sports settings based on geographic population representation and physical activity levels, not merely numbers served.

Strategy 6

Increase social marketing efforts to maximize use of recreations programs and facilities and promote co-benefits with environmental and other related approaches.

Figure 18.2   These strategies represent the parks, recreation, fitness, and sports sector in the National Physical Activity Plan.

Reprinted from the National Physical Activity Plan. Available: www.physicalactivityplan.org/parks.php.

environment, demand is growing for engagement with college and university campuses. Numerous universities now offer education courses that would fit the profile of recreation through Osher Lifelong Learning Institutes, designed to offer older adults opportunities to engage in lifelong learning centered on activities as diverse as hiking to webpage development to learning a foreign language. Catering to the demands of baby boomers and other seniors is both good service and good business.

Technology

As with all parts of today's world, the use of technology has taken hold on recreation and leisure services. From the use of Facebook pages to contact participants to virtual reality to entice visitors to new destinations, technology is now a tool that recreation professionals cannot ignore. Today you can visit Dresden's world-class art gallery through Second Life by "walking" from room to room to take in the artwork on the walls without leaving the comfort of your home. Planning, providing, and evaluating recreation and leisure today is largely dependent on technologies that did not exist even 10 years ago. In these exciting times we can reimagine a world where programming takes on completely different forms (and realities).

Growth of Sport

Sport continues to be a growth industry at all levels—recreational, amateur, and professional—as sports of all types expand throughout the world. Certainly, the economic impact of sport and sport tourism plays a role in this expansion as communities and countries recognize the money that can pour into a local economy because of both team participation and fan loyalty. For example, the 2010 NSA Girls Fastpitch World Series in Rock Hill, South Carolina, attracted 200 teams and resulted in an economic boost of $3.5 million. Sport tourism is also a growth industry in the field as travelers plan their vacations around a sporting event that they will either watch or participate in, such as the New York City Marathon.

Inclusion

Inclusive programming continues to grow. Inclusive programming does not refer only to programming for people with disabilities, the "differently abled," although that important sector certainly needs continued attention. The populations in both the United States and Canada continue to become increasingly diverse. In some cases that diversity is easily identifiable with respect to race and some disabilities. In others the diversity is less marked, but people are becoming more willing to share their diversity, and they expect programs that are sensitive to characteristics such as religion and sexual orientation. For instance, defining a traditional family is difficult today. Trends related to single-parent families (by choice or not), same-sex couples with children, and grandparents raising grandchildren all represent opportunities for adjustments in programs, services, or facilities.

SUMMARY

The field of recreation and leisure services provides exciting opportunities for those who choose to make it their career path. The field offers a great deal of value to both individuals and communities. These benefits are economic, physical, psychological, social, and many others. The professional also benefits in that he or she gets to enjoy a fulfilling career. Let's face it; those employed in recreation and leisure services work long hours, but they gain a great deal of personal satisfaction and have

fun providing services that improve participants' quality of life.

Working in recreation and leisure services means that you are working in a field replete with possibilities and have the opportunity to enhance the field as a profession through your service. Recreation and leisure services has proved its worth as a human services profession dedicated to the betterment of people. As a human services profession, the field is constantly changing. Demands for services, changing interests, enhancements in technology, and generational shifts have all contributed to a field that is evolving over time. To reach their full potential, both the profession and the practitioners working in it need to challenge themselves constantly to meet the changing needs of society. Becoming part of this dynamic profession will take hard work and perseverance. Clear career planning and positioning, as described earlier in this chapter, will go a long way in setting the stage for an illustrious career in the field. From networking to improving communication skills, the best and brightest students and professionals set their course for success early in their careers. It's never too early to make a good impression.

This chapter started with the quote "We don't build bridges; we build the people who build bridges." Certainly, building bridges is important; getting to certain places would be tough without the engineers who are responsible for those bridges. The bridges are tangible representations of the hard work of engineering professionals, and the public respects that. An engineering major never has to justify her or his choice of profession. But what does the recreation and leisure services professional build? She or he builds people—happier, healthier, more confident people. Those people are likely to be engineers, schoolteachers, doctors, and students. The list could go on. Seeing what recreation and leisure services professionals build is difficult. What the recreation and leisure services professional does is ensure that all those people are better because of what our field does to build them.

For glossary terms, learning experiences, and more, please visit the web resource at
www.HumanKinetics.com/IntroductionToRecreationAndLeisure

CHAPTER 19

International Perspectives on Recreation and Leisure

Holly Donohoe, Arianne C. Reis, Alcyane Marinho,
Jinyang Deng, and Huimei Liu

" The bow cannot always stand bent, nor can human frailty subsist without some lawful recreation. "

Miguel de Cervantes, Spanish novelist, poet, and playwright

LEARNING OUTCOMES

After reading this chapter, you should be able to do the following:

> Describe how the Internet has transformed leisure and recreation on a global scale

> Explain how nongovernmental and governmental organizations are working to enhance individual and community quality of life through leisure development

> Describe the role of youth leadership in leisure and recreation policy and program development

> Describe the effects of social and economic issues on leisure pursuits

> List different ways of socializing and enjoying leisure time in different societies

> Describe the similarities and differences between developed and developing countries' leisure pursuits

> Explain how historical events, be they political, cultural, economic, or social, contribute to current leisure practices

> Describe the scope and importance of recreation and leisure in China

> Identify the characteristics of recreation and leisure pursuits among people of different walks of life

> Explain the influence of modernization and globalization on the pursuits of leisure and recreation of Chinese people

International Overview

Holly Donohoe

" Life is seemingly a journey of transformation. Leisure is a powerful medium that can assist individuals, communities and nations in the process of transformation, providing time and space to rethink, renew and reinvent oneself. **"**

Christopher Edginton, secretary general of the World Leisure Organization

In your community and in communities around the world, leisure is undergoing a significant transformation. Historically, changes in the organization and experience of leisure have been driven by technological developments as well as economic and social priorities. In the last 25 years, three noteworthy developments have contributed to the seemingly accelerated changes occurring in the leisure field. First, the growth of the Internet has had an impact on nearly all areas of life. For leisure and recreation, the Internet has revolutionized how we engage in leisure activities and how we share information about leisure programs and policy. Second, the realization that leisure is integral to individual and community **quality of life** has changed the way that leisure is understood and prioritized by governments at all scales, from the global to the local. Third, youth participation in decision making is emerging as a key priority area in many fields, including leisure. Although other developments have certainly contributed to the **transformation** of leisure in the last few decades, the three explored here have particular relevance on the world stage where most of the change has taken place.

LEISURE AND THE INTERNET

The availability and adoption of Internet technology has increased exponentially since its introduction in the 1960s. From its earliest conception as a galactic network of globally connected computers, the Internet has moved beyond the realm of science fiction to become the primary global communication medium. The United Nations Telecommunications Agency reported that by the end of 2010 the number of Internet users worldwide had mushroomed to over 2 billion, doubling in number since 2005 (see figure 19.1). Although the United States has historically maintained the most users on a per capita basis, the spatial reach and the **Internet penetration rate** continue to grow within developing countries where 1.2 billion users are located. China, now the largest Internet market in the world, has over 420 million users. In developing countries, rapid improvements to Internet infrastructure are expected to provide accessibility to a growing number of users. A number of countries, including Estonia, Finland, and Spain, have declared access to the Internet a legal right for citizens. Until now, no other communication device has been so readily adopted with such widespread sociocultural and economic implications.

How does the Internet influence contemporary leisure meanings, activities, and spaces? Today, traditional leisure activities and spaces such as sport fields, parks, cinemas, restaurants, and amusement parks exist alongside virtual ones (see the sidebar). Traditional leisure spaces and activities may be reproduced in online role-playing games (e.g., Star Wars Galaxies, World of Warcraft), which attract over 20 million players worldwide and contribute billions of dollars to the world economy (Castronova, 2005). The Internet has also provided a new public realm for the development of community. No longer is geography the primary mechanism. **Virtual communities** are bringing people together who share ideas, interests, and lifestyles. These virtual communities represent a space where many people spend their leisure time. For example, Facebook has over 750 million active users who spend 700 billion minutes per month on the website. Fifty percent of users log on to Facebook on a daily basis to communicate with their friends, family, coworkers, and communities. Individuals can share photographs and videos, update a personalized news feed, join groups of interest, and communicate through live chat and personal messages. Since its creation in 2004, Facebook has evolved into one of the most trafficked websites in the world. More than 70 percent of users live outside the United States.

Online shopping, while considered primarily a commercial transaction, is also a popular leisure activity. People are now turning to the Internet as the primary medium through which to plan leisure activities and purchase hotel rooms and airline travel. Others are using the Internet to buy books, video games, and movies. In America, Amazon.com is the number one Internet retailer. In 2009 a deep recession caused a drop in consumer spending worldwide, but in 2010 the online market recovered as consumer confidence to spend improved and people spent more of their time and money online. Online sales of the top 500 global retailers grew 18 percent to $150 billion in 2010 (from $127 billion in 2009). The U.S. Department of Commerce reported that e-commerce sales increased by 15 percent (to $165.4 billion) in 2010. Statistics Canada, the government agency equivalent to the U.S. Census Bureau, reported that online retail grew by 8 percent over 2009 sales. The magnitude of online shopping has transformed the retail landscape and the way that people engage in recreational retail.

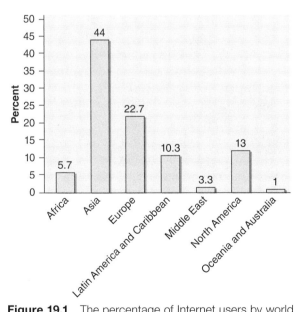

Figure 19.1   The percentage of Internet users by world region, 2011, has doubled since 2005.

Data from Internet World Stats, 2011, *Users and population statistics.* Available: www.internetworldstats.com/stats.htm.

Virtual Child's Play

Traditional toys such as building blocks are said to enhance motor skills, creativity, and the problem-solving abilities of children. But the sale of hands-on constructive toys has declined in recent years as the number of children who use the Internet has risen. To mitigate profit loss, toy manufacturers have invaded the virtual world with interactive websites and games that engage children of all ages. For example, Lego has been a favorite toy for generations of children in over 130 countries. This little plastic brick is available in every color of the rainbow, and its constructive configurations are seemingly limitless. Lego has emerged as a leader in the global toy market because the Danish company has taken their products digital with the release of Lego-inspired video games, websites, and interactive online design features. For example, Lego offers free software that allows people to design their own creations and order the bricks necessary to start building it at home. Online club membership and a series of free games and movie downloads are also available from the manufacturers' website. Because of its efforts to keep up with the changing nature of children's play, Lego has recovered from a near collapse to become the world's fourth largest toymaker. In 2010 sales in America surpassed $1 billion for the first time, and worldwide sales and net profits were up 37 percent and 69 percent, respectively (www.Lego.com).

Deviant leisure has also manifested in the virtual landscape. Like "normal" leisure, deviant leisure has been identified as a source of fun and enjoyment for some people. But the anonymity of the Internet together with the availability of shared-interest virtual communities provides opportunities for information exchange and behavior that may be in conflict with the social and moral values of Internet users and society in general. Concerns have also been raised about the sedentary nature of Internet use and its potential to affect health negatively. A recent study published in the *Journal of Medical Internet Research* reports that leisure-time Internet and computer use was significantly associated with weight gain and obesity. Compared with those who do not use the Internet and computers, people with low Internet and computer use were 1.3 times more likely to be overweight and 1.4 times more likely to be obese, and people with high Internet and computer use were 1.5 times more likely to be overweight and 2.5 times more likely to be obese. So although Internet-based leisure activities fulfill positive functions (escape, relaxation, social interaction, sensory stimulation, active entertainment, and the development of self-identity), the reality is that negative functions may also be realized (Bryce, 2001).

The Internet has been responsible for the transformation of leisure and the rise of "**e-leisure**." This significant transformation can't be compared with the magnitude of change associated with previous technological influences on leisure and recreation (e.g., trains, commercial flights, and television). Leisure is an important component of people's lives, and now more than ever, people have an abundance of leisure choices and venues—both physical and virtual. The challenge is that Internet access is limited in developing countries and rural areas where dial-up and broadband Internet penetration rates are low (though improving) and Internet service prices are high. But the falling cost of mobile services and smart phones will make Internet access through the cellular network an on-the-go reality for more people in more locations. The UN News Centre (2010) indicates that among the 5.3 billion mobile subscriptions in 2010, 3.8 billion were in the developing world. Growing numbers of people have access to mobile technologies, and the distribution of people with Internet access will certainly change across time and space in the near future. It will be fascinating to observe how smart phones transform the leisure landscape in the decades ahead.

LEISURE DEVELOPMENT AND ADVOCACY

The availability of the Internet and the knowledge sharing that it enables has transformed the way that leisure is planned and managed. Leisure managers tasked with developing or enhancing programs often turn to the Internet to communicate with colleagues and experts and to seek out information and best practices from other communities to inform their own projects. In the past, leisure managers did not have access to the breadth of information that is now available, almost immediately, through the Internet. Translation features of Google or other search engines also make it possible to access information in other languages and in other countries where leisure may be conceived and practiced in different ways. This sharing of information across geographical and cultural borders is enriching the way that leisure is evolving in North America and beyond.

In the context of technological developments as well as changing political, economic, and social conditions, leisure policy and practice has also undergone a transformation. The value of leisure as an income generator and as a stimulus to other forms of economic and social development is a significant and continuing rationale for government involvement. It has also been the impetus for the **commodification** of leisure programs, products, and services by private business, a phenomenon that is rapidly changing the global leisure landscape. Consequently, leisure policy and practice has changed subtly over time, and in some countries the change has been significant. Take, for example, China and Brazil, two countries whose economic presence in world markets has grown quickly in recent years. Both countries successfully won bids to host the Olympics, an international sporting event that is known to raise the international profile of the host country, attract tourists and foreign investment, and leave a leisure legacy for the host communities (e.g., new leisure facilities). Both China and Brazil have made political commitments to invest in leisure infrastructure and programming to enhance the quality of life of their citizens.

In China significant investment has been made to improve the leisure lives of individuals and communities, and nowhere is this investment more visible than in Hangzhou. Known as the Oriental Leisure Capital, Hangzhou has transformed from a quiet lakeside town to a popular leisure destination that attracts more than 20 million domestic and international travelers annually. Nestled beside historic West Lake, Hangzhou is home to 4 million people who are benefiting from the government's commitment to leisure development within the city's boundaries. The city has strengthened its international ties with partners so that information can be shared and foreign interest attracted in the coming years. One of the most significant leisure investments has been the city's hosting of the World Leisure Expo. In partnership with the World Leisure Organization, a nongovernmental organization dedicated to leisure advocacy (see the sidebar), Hangzhou hosted the first World Leisure Expo in 2006. The purpose of the event was to advance leisure concepts, services, and products that promote leisure best practices in China and abroad. The event attracted 18 million visitors who participated in hundreds of events, festivals, performances, workshops, and conferences. In 2011 the second World Leisure Expo was developed around the theme "Leisure—enhancing quality of life." Again the event attracted millions of visitors who enjoyed dragon boat races on West Lake, marveled at the puppet performances on Hefang Street in the cultural district, and viewed the latest leisure technologies at the Expo Garden. Unique to this event was an interactive online portal that was created to enable visitors, regardless of their geographic location, to contribute to and benefit from the event through access to Expo presentations, training, and leisure industry representatives and experts (http://en.wl-expo.com). For people around the world, the legacy of the event is a greater awareness of the importance of leisure for enhancing quality of life. For the people of Hangzhou, the event's legacy is the many leisure spaces that were developed to host the event and that now provide a place for leisure in the community (e.g., the World Leisure Expo Garden, the Oriental Cultural Park, and the West Lake Digital Recreation Industry Garden).

LEISURE AND YOUTH LEADERSHIP

Regardless of the virtual or physical landscape, advocacy plays a critical role in the way that leisure is being shaped today and for tomorrow. Organizations such as World Leisure work tirelessly to ensure that leisure is a priority in communities around the world. Looking forward, the leisure field is certainly

World Leisure Organization

Founded in 1952 World Leisure is a worldwide, nongovernmental association of people and organizations dedicated to discovering and fostering the conditions that best permit leisure to serve as a force for human growth, development, and well-being. The need for access to meaningful leisure experiences is no less than the need for shelter, education, employment, and fundamental health care. Yet improving the quality of life does not occur by chance. Rather, it happens through the joint efforts of our policy makers, our leisure professionals, and our public- and private-sector program providers.

Internationally, World Leisure works to foster inquiry to discover the personal and social potentialities of leisure experiences through research and scholarship. The organization disseminates knowledge and information through face-to-face forums such as world congresses, regional conferences, and workshops as well as through print and electronic media such as *World Leisure Journal*, newsletters, and the World Leisure website. For students, the organization offers scholarships and funding to attend the world congress, provides hands-on international training through the World Leisure Future Leaders Program, and cooperates with leading educational institutions to offer postgraduate education. Perhaps most important is that World Leisure engages in informed advocacy by promoting conditions that optimize leisure experiences: legislation, infrastructure, leadership, and programming. To do so, World Leisure has partnered with the United Nations and its agencies as well as international, regional, and national nongovernmental organizations.

Members, both collective (educational institutions and government agencies) and individual, are from all parts of the world. They come from diverse occupations such as tourism, parks and recreation services, arts and culture, sport and exercise, theme and entertainment centers, and children's play. They include researchers and scholars, managers and policy makers, leisure educators, and concerned members of the community.

For more information, visit www.worldleisure.org.

---

going to require a new generation of strong leaders and skilled professionals. As future leaders, students have an important role to play in their own communities and on the world stage (see figure 19.2).

Participation in decision making is one of the key priority areas of the United Nations (UN) agenda on youth. The UN defines youth as people between the ages of 15 and 24, although the organization is sensitive to the fact that the experience of being young varies enormously across regions and within countries. On August 12, 2010, the UN International Year of Youth was launched to provide a framework for bringing youth to the forefront of global debates. The year consisted of events and programs throughout the world, all designed to advocate for increased investments in and strengthened commitments to youth. Beyond the International Year of Youth, young people can become involved in the activities of the United Nations in many ways. One way is through the inclusion of youth delegates in a country's official delegation to the United Nations General Assembly and various functional commissions of the Economic and Social Council. The youth delegate program is coordinated by the UN Programme on Youth at the global level, but each member country is responsible for establishing a youth delegate program and deciding who will represent its young people. The role of a youth representative varies from country to country, but it may include attending meetings and informal negotiations and providing input on issues related to youth. Youth delegates may also participate in intergovernmental meetings at the United Nations.

The United Nations Educational, Scientific, and Cultural Organization (UNESCO) also encourages the participation of young men and women. UNESCO fosters partnerships with youth networks and organizations to collaborate and integrate their views and priorities into the development of projects and programs in a variety of areas including leisure and recreation. Representative examples include the International Union of Students, the African Youth Network, the Caribbean Federation of Youth, the Asian Youth Council, the Arab Youth Union, the World Organization of the Scout Movement, and the World Association of Girl Guides and Girl Scouts.

Figure 19.2 World Leisure Future Leaders Program: Students from around the world receive hands-on event management training at the World Leisure Games in Chuncheon, Korea. Information about the program is available at www.worldleisure.org.

The integration of youth concerns and issues into the policy agendas of member countries in education, the sciences, culture, and communication is meant to create spaces and opportunities for empowering young people and giving recognition, visibility, and credibility to their contributions. In the area of leisure, the Section for Youth, Sport, and Physical Education of the Social and Human Sciences Sector of UNESCO also promotes the integration of youth perspectives into their activities. With a mission to advance knowledge in order to facilitate social transformations that reflect the universal values of justice, freedom, and human dignity, this UNESCO sector works with youth to improve the conditions necessary for youth, sport, and physical education development.

In your own communities, opportunities to become involved abound. The local YMCA offers leadership training, volunteer, and employment opportunities. Community and recreation centers are also places where youth leadership is not only needed but also greatly appreciated. Municipal and state or provincial governments often have youth advisory groups for those interested in political issues, and national nongovernmental organizations offer ways to get involved on the national stage. The Association of Outdoor Recreation and Education, the American Therapeutic Recreation Association, the National Recreation and Parks Association, and the Canadian Parks and Recreation Association are representative North American examples.

As a future leader you would be remiss to embark on a career in the leisure and recreation field without an awareness of the changing global leisure landscape. The transformation of leisure in the Americas and around the world is evidence that leisure is a force of social, economic, and political change at local, regional, and global scales. The following chapter sections provide further evidence of these changes and offer important lessons about sharing knowledge and learning from the experiences of other leisure professionals around the world.

Recreation and Leisure in Brazil

Arianne C. Reis and Alcyane Marinho

" All persons have a need to celebrate and share our diversity in leisure. **"**

São Paulo Declaration, World Leisure Association

OVERVIEW

Brazil is an exciting and diverse country. Who has not heard of at least one of these typical Brazilian trademarks: *carnaval*, **samba**, the **Amazon**, "The Girl From Ipanema," **bossa nova**, or *caipirinha*? But these are far from what this country is all about. A nation as large and populous as Brazil cannot possibly be summarized in a few words. This chapter intends to briefly present the **cultural diversity**, contrasting worlds, and rich history of Brazil that may be better understood if experienced firsthand. Therefore, the chapter provides only a glimpse of what Brazil is and what its people do to have fun, relax, enjoy their friends and family, and seize the day. In summary, it describes what they do for leisure and recreation.

With a total area of 8,514,877 square kilometers, Brazil is the fifth largest country in the world and the largest in the Southern Hemisphere. It is also the fifth most populous country, containing more than 190 million people within its borders (IBGE, 2011). These numbers mean that Brazil is too large to be considered a unitary whole that displays a uniform pattern of leisure and recreation. To complicate matters further, Brazil has a colonial history that created the ideal environment for the development of regions as "silos," which enabled cultural developments that were distinct from each other in several ways. As discussed in previous chapters, culture plays a vital role in producing leisure patterns and behaviors. Therefore, Brazil has distinct leisure practices in different parts of the country, although a few commonalities are seen across the nation. In the following sections these leisure patterns and behaviors will be explored in more detail. Before that, however, general information about the

country is provided to build a better understanding of leisure practices and traditions in Brazil.

Brazil has an extensive coastline, which has also been the place where most of its development occurred since the early days of colonialism. Approximately 90 percent of its territory sits between the equator and the Tropic of Capricorn (IBGE, 2011). From this information we can conclude a few things that will have a considerable influence on some general aspects of Brazilian leisure choices:

- Brazil has a significant beach culture, based on large white sandy beaches blessed with tropical weather.
- Because most of its population resides along the coast, free coastal recreation pursuits are in high demand, by both tourists and locals.
- The warm weather is conducive to a variety of outdoor cultural experiences and activities all year long, which in Brazil have been dominated by **folklore festivals**, popular parties (religious and pagan), and unregulated sport and physical activities (**football** played on the beach or in any open area, walking and jogging, *capoeira*, skateboarding, and so on).

Brazil's colonial history contributes significantly to its diversity. For more than 300 years, the labor force in Brazil was composed almost entirely of African slaves, particularly along the eastern coastline and hinterland, where sugar cane and coffee plantations predominated. This region was therefore significantly exposed to African culture, and today African cultural expressions are still predominant in music, religion, dance, and food along the coastline. In the Amazon region, where colonialism was not so present, indigenous peoples have left a stronger mark on the local culture, and leisure practices have been significantly influenced by their customs.

After slavery was abolished in 1888, the Brazilian government encouraged European immigration to the country. Germans, Italians, Japanese, Turkish, and others were attracted to various regions of the country, particularly to the southern regions. Therefore, in the southeast and south of Brazil the visitor will most feel the European and Asian influence in food, dance, festivities, and general customs.

Another major aspect affecting leisure and recreation practices is the social and economic condition of a given population. Those without financial resources will obviously have limited access to some forms of paid leisure opportunities, such as cinemas, theme parks, theater, and concerts. Also, some recreation practices require the purchase of specific equipment, such as climbing gear, sailboats, and kayaks, or entrance to private spaces, such as golf clubs and gyms. In addition, some leisure and recreation practices are in part determined by the local physical environment, such as easy access to green parks, open public spaces, and bars and restaurants, among others. Brazil holds great differences in terms of its social class structure and economic distribution of wealth, and these disparities help determine the leisure and recreation patterns of its diverse population (Mascarenhas, 2003).

For the past 30 years Brazil has consistently been among the 15 most powerful economies in the world. In more recent years, it has climbed to the top 10 tier, and in 2011 it was classified as the 6th strongest global economy. But Brazil is ranked 73rd in the United Nations **Human Development Index** (HDI) (UNDP, 2010), indicating that a rich country can exhibit extreme inequality, excluding many of its inhabitants from access to their most basic needs, including leisure opportunities. When the HDI is adjusted for social inequality discrepancies, Brazil loses 15 places and ranks 88th in the world list.

In the last 10 years the level of poverty has fallen dramatically, and consumer power has increased in all levels of society (Cetelem, 2011; Beghin, 2008; Neri, 2011), producing a significant improvement in social programs for the poor and marginalized. But approximately 25 percent of the population, or more than 40 million people, remain in poverty. In contrast, 25 percent of the population has a stan-dard of living, including access to and enjoyment of leisure and recreation opportunities, at levels similar to that in the developed nations of North America and Europe. This contrast is clearly apparent in leisure choices and behaviors, as we will discuss later. A clear difference is present between the leisure choices and opportunities of those who have economic power and those who do not, between those who live in the exclusive neighborhoods and those who live in the shantytowns, or *favelas*, as they are called in Brazil.

HISTORICAL DEVELOPMENT OF RECREATION AND LEISURE IN BRAZIL

Brazilian modern history is commonly divided into three main periods: colonial (1500-1824), imperial (1824-1888), and republican (1889-). Highlighting some significant aspects of these historical moments in Brazilian life can aid in understanding how some leisure practices and traditions have evolved.

Both the colonial and imperial periods were characterized by slave labor and colonial regions that were independent from each other. Moreover, being a colony of a conservative European Catholic power at the time, Portugal, the Catholic Church played a significant role in Brazil's cultural development. This context fostered the suppression of expansive manifestations of leisure, particularly physical recreation. In addition to Catholics' negative views on leisure participation in general, physical recreation was associated with slave labor and was therefore avoided by all free residents (De Jesus, 1999). Moreover, any joyful activity engaged in by slaves, such as dancing, singing, and playing, was immediately suppressed by landowners who viewed these activities as distractions from work (Gebara, 1997). Slave leisure practices were therefore clandestine, but fortunately they have survived and are expressed today by the hugely popular dance–fight of *capoeira*, by the *congado*, an annual sacred and pagan festivity, and the extensive use of African drums in music (*batucadas*), among many other forms.

The republican era, which started in the last decade of the 19th century, also has been divided into various periods. In the first half of the 20th century Brazil became a predominantly urban society, and the government pushed for industrialization

Capoeira is a Brazilian martial art that combines dance and music and developed as part of slave leisure practices.

and economic development. This context favored the creation of social clubs that heavily promoted the practice of sport, a late phenomenon compared with the European context (De Jesus, 1999). The explanation for this was the abovementioned rejection of any physical activity by the Brazilian elite until some decades after the abolishment of slavery in the country. The general feeling was one of optimism and civic pride, which was translated into value being given to unique expressions of Brazilian culture in music, dance, theater, and other arts, and access to these being extended to the working class through the public presentation of arts and the construction of open leisure spaces in the urban environment (Almeida & Gutierrez, 2005; Melo, 2003).

In 1964 a military coup changed the cultural environment of the country again and, as a consequence, its leisure practices. Repression and censorship curtailed spontaneity, and fear led people to spend more of their free time at home. Mass communication networks developed during this period, and television became one of the most important forms of leisure in the country, a legacy carried forward until this day (Mascarenhas, 2003).

Soap operas were used for political propaganda and therefore were highly supported by the government. Nevertheless, they became increasingly popular. The dictatorial government also reduced dramatically the possibility of artistic expression being accessible to the working class, which in turn increased even more the significance of television as a pastime for this group. The elite, on the other hand, were starting to go to the cinemas, new shopping centers, and their second homes, phenomena that increased substantially during this period. Because of the economic development experienced during this time, the Brazilian elite also started to travel more, particularly to overseas destinations, and their leisure choices became increasingly more influenced by the international trends in recreation and leisure (Almeida & Gutierrez, 2005).

The rapid development of the cities together with a political regime that was clearly repressive for most forms of leisure and recreation practices led to a decrease in public open spaces where the working class, increasingly marginalized economically, could freely recreate. Traditional folklore phenomena began to fade away, and sport became the major form of recreational pursuit. In fact, sport practices were encouraged by the government, who used them as political propaganda, as did several other dictatorial regimes across the world (for some recent examples see Brady, 2009; Lee & Bairner, 2009).

With the fall of military power in the mid- to late 1980s, Brazil rapidly opened up to the international market. But because of the historical contingencies mentioned earlier, urban areas became extremely crowded and open spaces were not appropriately planned and developed. With the rise of poverty, violence became a problem in most urban centers, which caused people to curtail their exploration of streets, parks, and other open areas of the city. Therefore, visits to shopping centers, concerts in closed spaces, parties, restaurants, cinema, and television started to rank higher as choices of leisure activities. The poor and working class, who cannot afford to go to the same places as the elite do, improvise and create their own parties, like the *baile funk* in Rio de Janeiro, or they go to bars in their neighborhoods where problem drinking and illegal gambling are a constant presence (Mascarenhas, 2003). Such a scenario is still a reality today.

This historical background helps contextualize the contemporary leisure and recreation programs and services provided for the population by various agencies in Brazil today and is therefore crucial to a better understanding of the current leisure practices of its citizens. In the following section we further explore the common activities, programs, and services available and popular across the nation.

TYPES OF PROGRAMS, SERVICES, AND POPULATIONS

As in developed nations, the growth of leisure services in Brazil has been concentrated in metropolitan areas and in some tourist areas. The larger cities contain the largest public recreational facilities, such as the main facilities of the Serviço Social do Comércio (Social Service for Commerce, SESC), one of the most significant providers for leisure and recreation in the country; sports clubs with the best infrastructure; the main concert venues; the major hotel chains; and modern shopping malls.

SESC, a public–private institution whose main aim is to provide quality of life to the working class, was established in 1946 and is present in all Brazilian state capitals, as well as in several mid-sized cities and even small towns. SESC owns and operates several activity centers with large facilities and extensive infrastructure, including hotels, theaters, sport complexes, cinemas, spas, schools, and environmental protection areas. SESC policies follow Dumazedier's (1980) understanding of leisure practices as divided into five main realms: artistic, intellectual, sportive or physical, manual, and social. Programs therefore range from permanent sport programs with weekly classes to theater groups, open cinema showings, technical courses in hospitality, camping trips, and nature walks.

In Brazil the framework proposed by Dumazedier to classify leisure pursuits has been influential and has been interpreted as a set of strategies to be implemented in programs and projects for leisure at the national level in government initiatives such as the *Recreio nas Férias* (Holiday Playtime).

The *Recreio nas Férias* is part of *Segundo Tempo* (Second Half), a program created and implemented by the Ministry of Sports to increase participation in sport and recreation activities (Oliveira e Pimentel, 2009). This program is based on the premise that sport and recreation help the holistic development of children, adolescents, and youth; provide for the exercise of citizenship; and improve quality of life. This program is targeted at communities with lower socioeconomic status, servicing children and youth in public schools across the nation. The main goal of *Recreio nas Férias* is to bring leisure and recreational practices to the *Segundo Tempo* program in its activities during the Brazilian school holidays.

Clubs in contemporary Brazil play an important role as recreation providers, particularly with their holiday camps. The holiday camps target school-aged children and youth and are open to all members of a particular club or community. YMCAs across the country were influential in developing holiday camps as alternative leisure activities for children during their holidays and are particularly common in the southeast region of the country (Stoppa, 1999).

Sport programs are also commonly associated with clubs in Brazil, and sports such as volleyball, gymnastics, futsal, tennis, swimming, handball, and basketball are among the most popular provided in clubs and engaged in by youth. But the most popular organized sport in Brazil is undoubtedly football (called soccer in North America). Although it is popular in clubs, football is played, usually in an informal way, by everyone and everywhere there is a small area of dirt, grass, or pavement. Poles for the goals are made with anything available, from cans filled with small rocks to coconuts, bricks, or stones. Every kid has a football, even if it is made only of old socks. Going to football games, in big stadia in the major cities or in open grass areas with iron stands in rural areas, is an important form of leisure in Brazil. Watching games in the stadium or on television at home, in a bar, or restaurant, or just listening to the radio broadcast, is almost a ritual in every corner of the country. Most significantly, it is a ritual enjoyed by rich and poor alike, although the type of engagement—watching the game on a flat screen with friends in a private function, watching the game live in a public stand or in the VIP seating, or sharing a radio in an open bar with neighbors—may vary considerably.

The hotel industry is also active in the provision of leisure opportunities in Brazil. Active leisure providers in the hotel industry are usually **farm-stays**, hotel spas, particularly in thermal spring areas, resorts, and **eco-lodges** (Ribeiro, 2004). Club Mediterranée on Itaparica Island, Bahia, was the first resort to implement organized leisure activities for their clients in the early 1970s, run by so-called gentle organizers, trained staff whose main job is to entertain guests by providing various leisure and recreation activities. Leisure-focused hotels can be found across the country. Luxury resorts are usually found along the coast, and farm-stays are located in the hinterlands and mountain regions.

As in North America and elsewhere around the world, shopping centers in Brazil are significant spaces of leisure where a number of entertainment options are available, such as shops, cinemas, theaters, amusement parks, skating rinks, and go-carting. The highest concentration of shopping centers is found in São Paulo. In 2003 Brazil ranked 10th in the world in number of malls built (Ferreira, 2004). Shopping malls have grown to become part of the urban fabric for Brazilian urban dwellers. Middle-class families have exchanged traditional places of recreation, such as public squares and parks, for the alleys of the malls, increasingly because of the security and convenience offered by these spaces (Ferreira, 2004). In Rio de Janeiro, a city surrounded by free leisure opportunities (e.g., forest parks and beaches), the proliferation of malls is oddly intense. Barra da Tijuca, a large middle-class neighborhood in the city, has the most malls per square mile in the country. Some argue that the building of malls is a

Football is the most popular organized sport in Brazil and it is also played informally anywhere there is space and a ball.

result of the violence and criminality found in large Brazilian urban centers and is a means of separating the lower and poor classes, who are confined to the few open and free leisure spaces of the city, from the middle and high classes, who increasingly "hide" in private and paid leisure spaces.

In one place, however, the two worlds collide harmoniously—the beach. As mentioned earlier, Brazil has a significant beach culture. Along the long coast of Brazil the beach is one of the central spaces for leisure and recreation. From north to south the poor and the rich share this space, and several recreation practices were born, or have thrived, on sandy Brazilian beaches. *Futvôlei* (an interesting mix of soccer and volleyball played on the sand) and *frescobol* (a beach paddle ball game) were created on Brazilian beaches and now have been exported to beaches across the world, from California to Australia. Surfing and body boarding are also extensively practiced along the Brazilian coast, and poor kids may start their adventures in the ocean with only a wooden board and later gain worldwide recognition.

Another popular leisure practice in Brazil is the engagement in folk festivals, as active participants or simply as spectators. These festivals range from large folkloric parties and festivities, some of national and even international reach, to small local traditional festivals performed in small towns and *vilarejos*. What they hold in common is their significance to a community's identity and history.

One of the main folkloric festivities in Brazil is the *Boi-Bumbá*, a performance influenced by the country's Portuguese culture blended with African traditions. The performance is a play in which an ox dances, dies, and is resurrected to the sound of drums and singing by all participants. The title and interpretation of the colorful play (e.g., *Bumba-meu-boi*, *Boi-calemba*, *Bumba-de-reis*, *Reis-de-boi*, *Boi-pintadinho*, and *Boi-de-mamão*) vary across the country (Cavalcanti, 2006), but it is always dramatic and spectacular, involving hundreds of people in the main public squares of small towns or large cities.

Another important Brazilian folk festival is the *Festa Junina*. These festivals, among the most significant Catholic festivals around the country, take place in June in honor of St. Peter, St. Anthony, and St. John. Dances around big bonfires, crafting, the launching of colorful hot air balloons, sale of typical foods in rustic stalls, and the staging of a forced-marriage play are central aspects of these festivities. Music is a main theme, and the genres played are genuinely Brazilian, like the *forró*, *xaxado*, and *baião*, all played with violas, accordions, triangles, and other traditional instruments.

The most popular Brazilian festival, however, is certainly the *carnaval*, a blend of European traditions adapted to a tropical country and a society with a large population of African descent. *Carnaval* is eagerly awaited by most of the population, rich and poor, all year round, and it is certainly part of the country's international imagery as well as its local identity. *Carnaval* parties in clubs have developed from the European masked balls of years past, the parades of floats (*escolas de samba*) from similar European traditions, and the street music with lots of drums and percussion from the African influence. *Carnaval* is celebrated annually, 46 days before Easter, officially for 4 days (national public holiday) but usually going on for an entire week, and it is present in every town of the country. *Carnaval* is celebrated during the country's summer in various forms across the nation. The cheerful and lively atmosphere is the commonality between all of them.

DEMAND AND FUTURE GROWTH

Besides the examples already mentioned in relation to supply and demand for recreation and leisure, another expanding segment in Brazil that has been the focus of interventions at various levels and is proving to be promising is adventure activities, whether in green parks, wilderness areas, or artificial built environments.

Outdoor education has become increasingly popular in schools, and adventure activities in the natural environment are commonly used as part of an educational program that aims not only to teach issues about nature but also to develop leadership and teamwork skills. Such an approach has also increased in popularity among large businesses. Employees might spend a day in the outdoors experiencing challenges that can later be transposed to the competitive working environment. The success of these programs shows how adventure and nature-based leisure and recreation activities are becoming more popular in the country, a trend currently occurring in other countries in the West.

The diversity of natural resources in all Brazilian regions facilitates outdoor pursuits, and activities such as climbing, rafting, caving, diving, and paragliding have become popular in some parts of the country. Not incidentally, the segment of adventure and ecotourism is one of the fastest growing in recent years, and numerous agencies and businesses have emerged (Marinho, 2008). Following this trend, large urban centers also are catering to the adventure market by establishing skate parks for skateboarding, in-line skating and scooters, and indoor climbing gyms for sport climbing. These innovative approaches to recreation follow international trends and represent the social dynamics experienced in the cities, enabling participants to take on new behaviors and create new lifestyles (Marinho, 2005). These activities, however, are still enjoyed mainly by the middle and upper classes because the gear required can be too expensive for the less affluent.

TRENDS AND ISSUES

As discussed earlier, Brazil is a fast-growing economy and the demographics of its population are changing rapidly (IBGE, 2011). Because of the increase in consumer power in the last 10 years and the likelihood that the trend will continue, more Brazilians will start enjoying the benefits of disposable income to be spent on leisure activities. In addition, because levels of education are also increasing, what today are considered pastimes of the intellectual elite, such as visit to museums, outings to the theater or to arts exhibitions, and attendance at classical music concerts or ballets might become experiences more widely enjoyed. According to Mascarenhas (2003), 46 percent of the population has never been to a theater play, 52 percent has never been to a museum, 88 percent has never been to a ballet, and, surprisingly, 49 percent has never gone to a football stadium to watch Brazil's number one game live. These statistics are likely to change in the next few years.

The rapid demographic change in Brazil is reflected also in the increase of the urban popula-

tion. Towns that were previously considered small or medium-sized have moved to city status, and with this change have come the associated problems of space. Urban planning has never been a strong focus of Brazilian urban development, and less open land is available for the public. In this context, virtual reality games, participation in social networks on the Internet, and general Internet surfing have experienced exponential growth. According to a recent study by the Fundação Getúlio Vargas, one of the largest research institutes in the country, Brazil will have one personal computer for every two inhabitants by the first trimester of 2012 (Istoé, 2011). In the last three years the number of computers in the country has doubled, and the number of Brazilian *Facebook* users has increased exponentially and is now considered the fastest growing user group by country of origin. This trend in behavior directly affects how people spend their free time. The use of electronic games, electronic devices, and social media is becoming an important leisure-time experience in Brazil, following trends in more developed nations.

SUMMARY

The Brazilian elite today enjoy the leisure opportunities and practices available in any developed country in the world, and they engage in similar pursuits. The working class and the poor, as is commonly the case, have had their leisure options increasingly restricted by the unplanned and unsustainable development of the cities. These limited options include public open spaces, such as beaches and some urban parks, which are usually underfunded and therefore not always suitable for some leisure practices. Along the coast, beaches are an exception, and all groups of society value them highly. The situation, however, is changing slowly as poverty rates decrease and purchasing power increases. We hope that the creativity expressed by the marginalized groups in overcoming some of the barriers encountered throughout the years will remain, and that along with it we will witness a fairer distribution of leisure and recreation opportunities across all segments of society.

Recreation and Leisure in China

Jinyang Deng and Huimei Liu

“ Play is one of the essential needs for people. We need to have the culture of play, do academic research in play, and master skills in and develop the arts for play. ”

Guangyuan Yu, renowned economist and contributor to leisure development in China

OVERVIEW

Although leisure, recreation, and tourism are conceptually different, they are inherently interdisciplinary and practically interrelated (Smith & Godbey, 1991). A recreationalist and a leisure pursuer often share the same resources, use the same facilities, and generate similar social and psychological outcomes (McKercher, 1996). Thus, as far as the scope of leisure, recreation, and tourism is concerned, drawing a distinct line between the three is difficult. In fact, recreation and leisure are usually discussed under the rubric of leisure in Western literature. This line of thought has also been followed by most Chinese tourism and leisure researchers and scholars. That is, all leisurely activities or anything made to be enjoyed (i.e., entertainment, recreation, tourism) during free time falls into the category of the leisure industry. In this sense, the development of recreation and leisure as an industry and particularly as an academic field in China is a recent phenomenon, although the Chinese words for leisure 休闲 (*xiu xian*) can be traced back at least three millennia (Liu, Yeh, Chick, & Zinn, 2008) and leisure has been pursued in many forms (e.g., practice of tai chi, play of mahjong) by people of different walks of life for thousands of years in China.

The contemporary leisure industry in the country covers many sectors that can be classified into 11 categories (You & Zhen, 2007):

1. Entertainment leisure (singing halls, dance halls, discotheques, concert halls, tea houses, cafes, chess houses, bars, cinemas, theaters, resorts, performing art centers, karaoke bars, KTVs)

2. Sporting leisure (all kinds of sports and adventurous outdoor activities)

3. Health leisure (springs, forest recuperation, flower recuperation, water therapy, mud therapy, salt therapy, spas, bath, sun bath, beauty, hairdressing, massage, oxygen bars, and so on)

4. Tourism leisure (natural and historical sites, theme parks, zoos and botanic gardens, and urban scenic spots and belts)

5. Rural leisure (happy farmer inns, happy fisher inns, happy ranch inns, folk villages, rural historical towns)

6. Educational leisure (libraries, memorial halls, galleries, all types of museums, martyr cemeteries, religious temples, college campuses, industrial parks, bookstores, and so on)

7. Food leisure (restaurants, hotels, guesthouses, flavor snack bars, food courts)

8. Shopping leisure (shopping malls, exhibitions, wholesale markets, pedestrian streets, specialty shops, auctions, pawns, and so on)

9. Hobby leisure (pets, image design, gardening, stamp collecting, collecting of antique and other items, sculpture, calligraphy, painting, knitting, flower arranging, pubs, making ceramics for fun, and phone bars)

10. Social leisure (charity, volunteering, social media and Internet cafes, festivals and events, making friends, cell phone messages, parties, and so on)

11. Leisure products manufacturing (leisure foods and beverages, leisure clothing, leisure health care, leisure books and materials, leisure equipment, and leisure facilities)

You and Zhen's classification of China's leisure industry demonstrates that China's leisure industry encompasses a wide range of sectors, many of which have emerged in the past two decades or so because of the influence of modernization and globalization. These sectors have begun to play an increasingly important role in the country's economic growth and "the Construction of a Harmonious Society," a national goal proposed by President Jintao Hu in 2004 when he suggested, in an address to a high-level seminar at the Party School of the Central Committee of the Communist Party of China, that a high priority be placed on social harmony. This came at a time when the country was confronted with a series of social problems such as disparity in development and distribution, inequality, injustice, and corruption, despite rapid economic growth.

In recent years the leisure industry in China has played an important role in generating revenues and jobs. For example, there were 1.9 billion domestic visitors in 2009, an increase of 4.6 times over 1993. Domestic tourism revenue was US$147.5 billion, an increase of 11.8 times over 1993 (National Tourism Administration of China, 2009). In the same year, 76 million people were directly (11 million people) or indirectly (65 million people) employed in the tourism industry, accounting for 9.6 percent of the total employment of the country. In addition, the total consumption in cultural entertainment was estimated at US$46.2 billion (Zhang, Hu, & Zhang, 2010). Overall, domestic consumption in leisure industry in 2009 was approximately 1,700 billion RMB (US$258.4 billion), accounting for 5.07 percent of total GDP (Liu, Gao, & Song, 2010, p. 5).

Currently, China's leisure industry is concentrated in urban areas, particularly in large and middle-sized cities where the leisure industry has grown fast on a large scale and has generated considerable benefits. For example, Changsha, dubbed the Culture and Leisure Capital of the People as well as the Capital of Foot Message, received revenue of RMB 26 billion (US$3.3 billion) in 2005 (You & Zhen, 2007). Hangzhou, another city in eastern China, famous as the Oriental Leisure Capital, City of Quality of Life, is among the first in China to position the leisure industry as the leading industry of the city. In 2009 the city had approximately 90,000 leisure-related businesses in the top 10 promising leisure industry sectors (i.e., food, tea houses, entertainment, spa resorts, health care, makeup, female clothing, sports leisure, baby care, and arts and crafts). These businesses provided 725,000 jobs and generated revenue of RMB $95.8 billion (US$13.7 billion) for the city (Weng, 2010).

Tai chi is a traditional healthy exercise, which has been practiced by people of different walks of life for thousands of years in China.

Parallel to the rapid development of leisure industry in the county is the continuing growth of leisure education at various levels. For example, in 2006 there were 1,703 tourism education institutions, including 762 higher institutions that enrolled 730,000 students. In addition, 18 forestry and agriculture universities offer outdoor recreation education, a remarkable change since 1993 when the first forest recreation department was established in the Central South University of Forestry and Technology, Hunan Province. Recently, as the term *leisure* has become a buzzword among the public, 14 sport universities or schools and several other universities with tourism programs have begun to offer four-year undergraduate education in leisure studies. Furthermore, a doctoral degree program in leisure studies, the first and the only one in China, was approved in 2007 for Zhejiang University. Finally, several leisure research centers have been established since 2003 when the Centre for Leisure Culture Study, the first leisure research center in China, was created by the Chinese Academy of Arts.

A BRIEF HISTORY OF CHINA'S LEISURE DEVELOPMENT

Recreation and leisure began to emerge as an important sector in China in the early 1980s when China began to adopt an open-door policy and make major economic reforms, resulting in impressive economic development in the following decades. As in advanced economies, the increase of discretionary income and free time has stimulated increasing demand for leisure pursuits in China. The central government played an important role in formulating national policies for leisure industry development. For example, in 1995 China adopted a 40-hour week, and in 1999 the State Council approved three Golden Weeks (i.e., the Spring Festival Golden Week, the National Day Golden Week, and the May Day Golden Week) as national holidays, which, along with the two-day weekends and other holidays, increased the free time of the country's working class to 115 days per year. In addition, the 11th National Five-Year Plan placed higher priority on industry structure transformation by focusing on the tertiary sectors, or service industry. The 12th National Five-Year Plan will implement national tourism and leisure

strategies that aim to increase awareness of leisure among the public and to promote leisure industry development to a higher level. Finally, in terms of leisure research, topics on leisure research were for the first time included in the application guidelines of the National Social Science Fund in 2009.

Several key people have played an essential role in promoting leisure development and leisure studies and education in the country. Among the most important is the late leader Xiaoping Deng, who pointed out on many occasions that more emphasis should be placed on tourism development as a means to increase national income. Other important figures include Professor Guangyuan Yu and Huidi Ma, who have made great contributions to leisure development and leisure education and research in the country. Besides their own writings and talks on leisure, another contribution that they made to the field of leisure studies was the translation and publication of five books written by renowned leisure scholars in North America. Other key people include Professor Chucai Wu, proclaimed a National Level Expert by the State Council, who founded the country's first four-year outdoor recreation program in 1993, and Professor Xuequan Pang, Director of the Asian Pacific Centre for the Education and Study of Leisure, Zhejiang University, who has played an essential role in promoting leisure studies within and beyond the university.

In recent years China has organized several international leisure conferences (i.e., the Ninth World Leisure Congress and 2006 World Leisure Expo, an annual international leisure development forum held in Hangzhou since 2003) and national leisure forums (i.e., 2007, 2008, 2009, and 2010 National Leisure Industry Economics Forums), which have increased public awareness of leisure and facilitated collaboration and cooperation between Chinese leisure scholars and their international counterparts.

RECREATION OPPORTUNITIES IN CHINA

China is abundant with natural and cultural resources that offer great opportunities for leisure and outdoor recreation pursuits. This section introduces the settings, organizations, and structures as they relate to the provision of leisure and recreation opportunities in the country. A brief description of popular recreation and leisure activities pursued by the public follows.

Settings, Organizations, and Structures

The most popular outdoor recreation settings in China are scenic areas, nature reserves, and forest parks. As of 2009 China had 2,458 forest parks including 731 at the national level, having a total area of 16.53 million hectares; 2,541 nature reserves including 319 national ones, comprising 147 million hectares; and 906 scenic areas including 208 at the national level, having a total area of 1.10 million hectares. In addition, numerous urban parks, farmlands, and forest areas provide outdoor recreation opportunities for urban dwellers.

Although the aforementioned settings provide the public with opportunities to pursue outdoor recreational activities, Chinese people also enjoy leisure activities in indoor settings such as tea houses, mahjong houses, spas, foot massage houses, and bars of all kinds, among others.

Most outdoor recreational opportunities are provided by public agencies, including (1) the State Forestry Administration, which manages all forest parks at all levels; (2) the Ministry of Housing and Urban-Rural Development, which manages all scenic areas at all levels; (3) the Ministry of Agriculture, State Marine Bureau, Geological and Mineral Bureau, Ministry of Environmental Protection, and Ministry of Water Resources, which, along with the two agencies listed earlier, manage nature reserves across the country; and (4) the Ministry of Culture, which manages world heritage sites and thousands of cultural and historical sites across the country.

Popular Recreation and Leisure Pursuits

China is made up of 56 ethnic nationalities that are distinctively different from one another, culturally and historically, resulting in a distinct pattern of leisure pursuits from group to group. Obviously, the scope of this chapter precludes detailed description

Forest parks such as Zhangjiajie National Forest Park (original model for Hallelujah Mountain in the movie *Avatar*) are popular outdoor recreation settings in China.

of the leisure patterns of every nationality. Because the Han nationality accounts for 98 percent of the country's population and represents the mainstream culture of the country, the following discussion of recreation and leisure pursuits of Chinese people refers primarily to the Han nationality.

In comparison with North Americans, Chinese people tend to prefer quiet or passive leisure pursuits. For example, a comparative cross-cultural study (Jackson & Walker, 2006) found that the most frequent or most enjoyable leisure activities were passive for 84 percent of Mainland Chinese university students versus 64 percent for Canadian students, who reported that their most frequent or most enjoyable leisure activities were active. This finding was endorsed by a survey study on leisure activities pursued by urban residents in China, which found that watching TV, reading books or newspapers, listening to the radio, playing mahjong, and chatting with family members were the most popular leisure activities. Playing golf was the least popular because of its high cost, and tennis, billiards, ice-skating, fishing, hunting, and playing bridge were also less popular (Yin, 2005). A more recent study (Jim & Chen, 2009) about leisure activity patterns in Zhuhai, a newly developed city situated on the south coast of Guangdong province on the banks of the Pearl River estuary and close to Macau and Hong Kong, found that residents in the city reported participating in activities in the home more frequently than they did in activities outside the home. Moreover, they were more likely to participate in passive activities than active ones. In-home physical exercise and sport games outside the home accounted for 10 percent of all reported leisure participation.

Indeed, leisure is so highly related to culture that culture is often viewed as a synonym of leisure in the country (Ma, 1999). Leisure in China is closely related to "philosophy, aesthetics, literature and the arts, and practices of health and wellness" (Gong, 1998, as cited in Wang & Stringer, 2000, p. 35). Pursuit of such leisure activities is justified by Confucianism, which encourages a scholar or student to excel at playing the harp and chess and doing painting and calligraphy. In this way, leisure pursuits involving learning and culture could be regarded as high leisure, whereas leisure pursuits such as mahjong can be viewed as popular leisure.

China is at a crossroads of social, economic, and political transformation. During this transformation, the traditional Chinese cultural values formed in a traditional agrarian society could be changed in the process of modernization. Economic globalization could accelerate this change. In fact, globalization has already had great influence on the daily life of Chinese people. For instance, attitudes toward miss contests, fashion shows, sexual behavior, consumption behavior, dress, hairstyles, celebration of Western festivals, and leisure have been largely changed in the past two decades because of modernization and globalization. In recent years, Western leisure pursuits and sports that are active and adventurous have been introduced to China (e.g., rock climbing, mountaineering, camping, picnic and barbecue, recreational vehicles, water rafting, tennis, golfing). These activities are becoming increasingly popular among Chinese people, especially the youth. Another example is that cultural leisure pursuits among Chinese people have been fundamentally influenced. For instance, American movies are much more popular than local movies. Watching American movies and playing board games are rated as top leisure activities by current college students. Another cultural leisure pursuit greatly influenced by globalization is the celebration of Western festivals and holidays, which have become more popular than Chinese ones, especially among the youth. For instance, many people celebrate the Western style of Valentine's day; *qi xi*, the traditional Chinese version of its kind, is almost unknown among most Chinese people. Christmas is another holiday celebrated with great passion by Chinese people. A recent survey study of leisure pursuits of the Chinese middle class found that the leisure patterns pursued by the youth fall into one of four leisure types, the tag type (fashion followers) (Zhou, 2008). The other three types are entertainment and relaxation, function (utilitarianism), and free.

Of numerous leisure activities pursued by Chinese people, tai chi and mahjong are arguably the favorite traditional ones, particularly among middle-aged and older people. Tai chi is taught in physical education class to college students, but because of its slow tempo, few young Chinese like it. When people grow old, however, they realize the importance of being healthy, and they learn to practice tai chi. Although the Chinese government has favored tai chi as a healthy exercise, mahjong was once banned as a gambling activity and is not endorsed by the government even today, although people of all classes, occupations, and ages are obsessed with the table game.

Another leisure activity that has recently become popular among residents in almost every city in China is public dance, or square dance, in which dozens to hundreds of people dance together for several hours, usually in the evening in an urban open space (public square or plaza). Most of these dancers spontaneously stand in formation and follow one or two dancers in front of them, who lead the dance featured by simple moves and a relatively slow tempo. A recent survey study conducted in Chongqing, a northwest city, found that 45 percent of the city's residents reported having participated in this group activity (Li, Zhou, & Chen, 2009). The significance of public square dance has also attracted the attention of researchers (Peng, 2010).

CHALLENGES AND TRENDS FOR THE FUTURE

Although the leisure industry in China has experienced rapid growth in recent years, there is no sign to indicate that this growth will stop if the country's economy continues to grow. That being said, the leisure industry in the country faces a number of challenges.

First, attitudes toward leisure among Chinese people are generally negative. Traditionally, leisure conveys a derogatory connotation from the perspective of traditional Chinese culture. As recently as the 1970s, leisure (*xiu xian*) was a bad word and a symbol of pursuing the lifestyle of capitalist societies. Wang and Stringer (2000) observed that Chinese people are less likely to view leisure as an important component of their lives compared with North Americans because Chinese, in general, tend to have a stronger work ethic (see also, Ap, 2002; Xiao, 1997). Potentially, this view of leisure reflects the traditional values that Chinese place on hard work and achievement. But this negative attitude toward leisure has changed considerably in recent years because of the rapid economic development, increasing living standards in mainland China, and the influence of globalization. In recognition of the global trends in leisure and its importance to enhancing the quality of life of Chinese people, a number of scholars have recently called for devoting more attention to leisure and leisure research in China, which, we contend, has led greater awareness of leisure among the public. With that said, many Chinese people still consider leisure as something similar to being lazy.

Second, leisure education is lacking among Chinese. Chinese education is fundamentally examination and score oriented, which deprives students of time for leisure. The education system is extremely competitive, which put students under heavy pressure. As a result, leisure awareness is not well nurtured among Chinese (Deng, 2002; Liu, 2007).

Third, China is experiencing rapid urbanization. Open spaces are shrinking, and limited facilities are available for leisure. For example, a survey study (Lu & Yu, 2005) found that 37 percent of residential areas in Beijing had no sport facilities. In addition, Beijing had only 1.96 community sports centers per 10,000 people in 2003 as compared with 9.08 centers per 10,000 people in Germany in 1976 (Lu & Yu, 2005). Therefore, in the inner city, facilities are rare for the residents. Godbey and Shim (2008, p. 28) observed that

> one obvious issue here is the lack of consideration for the leisure lives of urban dwellers that are moving into the high-rise apartment buildings being built by entrepreneurs. Government plays little role in requiring that such buildings be designed with an understanding of the play needs of children, the leisure needs of young couples or elderly grandparents, who live with their children. Where will children play? Where will there be opportunity for contact with nature?

Finally, inequality is present in leisure pursuits. Although China has experienced rapid economic development in the past two decades and has become world's second largest economy after the United States, the country is confronted by a number of issues including unequal economic development across regions and a growing gap in income between the wealthy and the poor, resulting in leisure opportunities not being equally available to the public. For example, in 2010 China had an estimated 230 million migrant workers who emi-

OUTSTANDING GRADUATES

Background Information

Name: Peiling Zhong

Education: Bachelor's degree in management in the Department of Forest Recreation from Central South Forestry College (renamed the School of Tourism, Central South University of Forestry and Technology).

Credentials: National certificate of middle-level tourist guide (Chinese), national certificate of entry-level tourist guide (English), national certificate of outbound tour leader.

Special awards: Best Seller of Shenzhen Branch of China International Travel Service, 2010; Outstanding Employee of China International Travel Service (Shenzhen Branch); and Experts in Australia Tourism, Switzerland Tourism, Canada Tourism, and Austria Tourism.

Career Information

Position: Manager of the Department of Business Package Tours, China International Travel Service (Shenzhen Branch).

Organization: China International Travel Service (Shenzhen Branch), located in Shenzhen City, Guangdong Province, was established in 1954. It is the first and largest travel agency in the Shenzhen region. Since 1979 the agency has accommodated more than 2 million foreign tourists, 500,000 domestic tourists, and 300,000 outbound tourists. The agency has 625 full-time employees and 800 part-time tourist guides and outbound tourism leaders. Annual revenues in 2009 were RMB 710 million (approximately US$100 million).

Organization's mission: To provide customers with happy and valuable experience and remain China's largest wholesale agency for the Hong Kong and Macau markets; increase Internet sales; place priority on outbound tourism, commercial tourism, domestic high-end tourism, and inbound tourism of Hong Kong and Macau; develop the wholesale center for Hong Kong and Macau into a national one; and enhance the competitiveness of the agency.

Job description: I am responsible for the organization and arrangement of meetings; incentive tourism; conventions and exhibitions; and outbound tours for study, cultural exchanges, and other activities.

Career path: After graduation in 2000 from Central South Forestry University, I have worked in several travel agencies as a tourist guide and tour package leader and have done study tours in 28 provinces and 30 countries.

---

grated from the countryside to cities looking for better paying work in construction sites and manufacturing factories. Most of these migrant workers do not pursue leisure activities because their pay is low and they have to work long hours.

Even some middle-class people do not have time for leisure because they are busy with work and cannot experience leisure with real relaxation. According to Zhou's (2008) study, 58.6 percent of participants were not satisfied with their leisure and only 5 percent reported being very satisfied. The survey also showed that over 65 percent of the middle class had less than 20 hours per week of leisure time, 80 percent reported that their leisure was constrained by work, 80 percent felt heavy work pressure, and 28 percent believed that their work pressure reached a point that they cannot stand. Their salaries are lower than expected for the high pressure that they are under, which further affected their leisure quality because of their low pay.

Although China's leisure industry faces significant challenges, it will likely continue to grow because of several trends. First, although domestic travels continue to grow, more Chinese can afford to travel to other countries. In 2009 the ratios of domestic, inbound, and outbound tours were 90.8:6.5:2.7 (Liu, Gao & Song, 2010, p. 13). It is safe to say that most Chinese will enjoy travel as a leisure activity in their lives. Second, unlike traditional package tours, various kinds of independent tours are thriving because of the rapid development of highway and railway systems and the increasing ownership of cars. Third, the development of technology makes it possible to accomplish many things online. More leisure activities such as online reading and gaming will be realized through Internet use. In the meantime, online selling and purchase of leisure services will grow tremendously. Finally, with increasing globalization and modernization, Western culture will continue to affect the leisure pursuits of Chinese people, which may cause the loss of local cultural traits.

SUMMARY

Traditionally, Chinese people placed less value on leisure and instead emphasized hard work and education. This view of leisure has changed in recent years because of modernization and globalization. More people have come to realize that leisure is an essential part of daily life. Under such circumstances, the leisure industry has seen steady development over the past two decades, causing tremendous economic and social impacts in the country.

The central government played an essential role in promoting and guiding leisure pursuits of Chinese people. In the meantime, people's leisure attitudes and behaviors have been shaped by leisure researchers, particularly those who have actively promoted leisure participation of the public through conferences, forums, mass media, magazines, and academic publications.

Although a number of public agencies provide a wide array of outdoor recreational opportunities for the public, Chinese people tend to enjoy indoor passive leisure activities more than they do outdoor activities. Some of those indoor passive leisure activities are deeply rooted in traditional Chinese culture.

The leisure pursuits of Chinese people, particularly the youth, have been considerably influenced by Western culture because of globalization. Leisure pursuits in China have traditionally been different from those in Western society. But both cultural distance and the distinction in leisure pursuits between China and Western society have diminished under the pressure of cultural diffusion resulting from economic and cultural globalization. Although cultural diffusion may bring with it some negative impacts, the concept of harmony, which is strongly rooted in Chinese culture, plays an essential role in the absorption of elements of other cultures. Moreover, the proactive policies of the Chinese government help to maintain traditional Chinese culture. Thus, the negative influence of globalization on the leisure pursuits of Chinese people may be cushioned by the compatible nature of Chinese culture and preemptive measures taken by the Chinese government.

For glossary terms, learning experiences, and more, please visit the web resource at
www.HumanKinetics.com/IntroductionToRecreationAndLeisure

Bibliography

CHAPTER 1

Barton, J., Griffin, M., & Pretty, J. (2011, April). Exercise, nature and socially interactive based initiatives improve mood and self-esteem in the clinical population. *Perspectives in Public Health*. doi:10.1177/1757913910393862

Buchholz, A.C., Ginis Martin, K.A., Bray, S.R., et al. (2009). Greater daily leisure time physical activity is associated with lower chronic disease risk in adults with spinal cord injury. *Applied Physiology Nutrition & Metabolism, 34*, 640-647.

Carmichael, D. (2008). *Youth sport vs. youth crime—Evidence that youth engaged in organized sport are not likely to participate in criminal activities*. Brockville, ON: Active Healthy Links.

City of Lethbridge. (2011). *The environmental benefits of Lethbridge trees: Press release*. Lethbridge, AB: Author.

Corwin, M.R. (2001, September). Guess who I am? *Parks & Recreation*, 168.

Csikszentmihalyi, M. (1991). *Flow: The psychology of the optimal experience*. New York: Harper Perennial.

Driver, B. (1998, February). The benefits are endless . . . but why? *Parks & Recreation*, 26.

Enigma Research Corporation. (2010). *The economic impact of Canada's largest festivals and events*. Canadian Festivals Coalition.

Flusche, D. (2009). *The economic benefits of bicycle infrastructure investments*. Washington, DC: League of American Bicyclists.

Gies, E. (2006). *The health benefits of parks: How parks help keep Americans and their communities fit and healthy*. San Francisco: The Trust for Public Land.

Harris Interactive. (2011). *Playgrounds increase sense of family well-being*. Washington, DC. Foresters.

Millward, A.A., & Sabir, S. (2011). Benefits of a forested urban park: What is the value of Allan Gardens to the city of Toronto, Canada? (2011). *Landscape and Urban Planning, 100*(3), 177-188. doi:10.1016/j.landurbplan.2010.11.01

New York City Department of Environmental Protection. (2011). NYC to acquire 1,655 acres of land for watershed protection. www.nyc.gov/html/dep/html/press_releases/11-75pr.shtml

Potwarka, L.R., Kaczynski, A.T., & Flack, A.L. (2008). Places to play: Association of park space and facilities with healthy weight status among children. *Journal of Community Health, 33*(5), 344-50.

Stern, M.J., & Seifert, S.C. (2008). *From creative economy to creative society*. Philadelphia: The Reinvestment Fund and the Social Impact of the Arts Project (University of Pennsylvania, School of Social Policy and Practice).

CHAPTER 2

American Alliance for Health, Physical Education, Recreation and Dance. (n.d.a). *About*. Retrieved August 9, 2004, from www.aahperd.org/about/

American Alliance for Health, Physical Education, Recreation and Dance. (n.d.b). *Mission*. Retrieved August 9, 2004, from www.aahperd.org/aahperd/template.cfm?template=mission_statement.html

Canadian Association of Health, Physical Education, Recreation and Dance. (n.d.). *Canadian Association of Health, Physical Education, Recreation and Dance*. Retrieved June 30, 2004, from www.cahperd.ca/e/cahperd/index.htm

Canadian Broadcasting Corporation. (2000). *ParticipACTION packing it in?* Retrieved January 30, 2012, from http://archives.cbc.ca/lifestyle/fitness/clips/3312/

Canadian Parks and Recreation Association. (n.d.a). *About CPRA*. Retrieved June 30, 2004, from www.cpra.ca

Canadian Parks and Recreation Association. (n.d.b). *CPRA history*. Retrieved June 30, 2004, from www.cpra.ca

Canadian Public Health Association. (2004). *ParticipACTION: The mouse that roared: A marketing and health communications success story*. Retrieved January 30, 2012, from www.cpha.ca/en/about/media/media2004/participaction.aspx

Cross, G. (1990). *A social history of leisure since 1600*. State College, PA: Venture.

Dare, B., Welton, G., & Coe, W. (1987). *Concepts of leisure in Western thought: A critical and historical analysis*. Dubuque, IA: Kendall/Hunt.

DeGraff, J., Wann, D., & Naylor, T.H. (2001). *Affluenza: The all-consuming epidemic*. San Francisco: Berrett-Koehler.

Edgington, C., Jordan, D., DeGraff, D., & Edgington, S. (1998). *Leisure and life satisfaction: Foundational perspectives*. Boston: WCB/McGraw Hill.

Francis, R.D., Jones, R., & Smith, D. (1988). *Origins: Canadian history to confederation*. Toronto, ON: Holt, Rinehart and Winston of Canada.

Goodale, T., & Godbey, G. (1988). *The evolution of leisure*. State College, PA: Venture.

Harrington, M. (1996). Women's leisure and the family in Canada. In N. Samuel (Ed.), *Women, leisure and the family in contemporary society: A multinational perspective* (pp. 35-48). Wellingford, UK: CAB International.

Horna, J. (1994). *The study of leisure: An introduction*. Toronto, ON: Oxford University Press.

Ibrahim, H. (1979). Leisure in the ancient world. In H. Ibrahim & J. Shivers (Eds.), *Leisure: emergence and expansion* (pp. 45-78). Los Alamitos, CA: Hwong.

Ibrahim, H. (1991). *Leisure and society: A comparative approach*. Dubuque, IA: Brown.

Illinois State Museum. (2000). *The Illinois Society Recreation*. Retrieved January 15, 2000, from www.museum.state.il.us/muslink/nat_amer/post/htmls/soc_rec.html

Interprovincial Sport and Recreation Council. (1987). *National recreation statement*. Retrieved June 30, 2004, from www.lin.ca/resource/html/statemen.htm

Karlis, G. (2004). *Leisure and recreation in Canadian society: An introduction*. Toronto, ON: Thompson.

Kraus, R. (1971). *Recreation and leisure in modern society*. Glenview, IL: Scott, Foresman.

Kraus, R. (1990). *Recreation and leisure in modern society* (4th ed.). Glenview, IL: Scott, Forseman.

Kraus, R. (2001). *Recreation and leisure in modern society* (6th ed.). Sudbury, MA: Jones and Bartlett.

LaPierre, L. (1992). *Canada, my Canada: What happened?* Toronto, ON: McLelland & Stewart.

Markham, S. (1992). Our leaders speak up. *Recreation Canada, 50*(2), 15-19.

Markham, S. (1995). The early years: 1944 to 1951. *Recreation Canada, 53*(3), 6-16.

Markham-Starr, S. (2005). Early efforts to professionalize leisure services in Canada. *Avante, 11*(1), 15-26.

McFarland, E.M. (1970). *The development of public recreation in Canada*. Ottawa, ON: Canadian Parks and Recreation Association.

McLean, A.D., Hurd, A.R., & Rogers, N.B. (2005). *Kraus' recreation and leisure in modern society*. Sudbury, MA: Jones and Bartlett.

Mendelsohn, D. (2004, August 8). What Olympic ideal? *New York Times Magazine*, pp. 11-13.

Missouri State Parks and Historic Sites. (2005). *The history of Missouri's state park system*. Retrieved February 10, 2012, from http://mostateparks.com/page/59044/history-missouris-state-park-system

National Recreation and Park Association. (n.d.). *About us*. Retrieved July 21, 2004, from www.nrpa.org

Parks and Recreation Ontario. (n.d.). *Parks and Recreation Ontario*. http://216.13.76.142/PROntario/about.html

Parks Canada. (n.d.). *Parks Canada Agency*. www.pc.gc.ca

Parks Canada. (2002). *Parks Canada Mandate*. www.pc.gc.ca/agen/index_E.asp

ParticipACTION. (n.d.). *The early years: TV, radio and print media*. Retrieved January 30, 2012, from www.usask.ca/archives/participaction/english/motivate/theearlyyears.html

Poliakoff, M. (1993). Stadium and arena: Reflections on Greek, Roman and contemporary social history. *Olympika: The International Journal of Olympic Studies, 2*, 67-78.

Rainwater, C. (1992). *The play movement in the United States*. Chicago: University of Chicago Press.

Recreation Nova Scotia. (n.d.). *Recreation Nova Scotia*. Retrieved June 30, 2004, from www.recreationns.ns.ca

Saskatchewan Parks and Recreation Association. (n.d.a). *What is the SPRA?* www.spra.sk.ca/about.htm

Saskatchewan Parks and Recreation Association. (n.d.b). *SPRA history*. www.spra.sk.ca/history

Searle, M., & Brayley, R. (1993). *Leisure services in Canada: An introduction*. State College, PA: Venture.

Shivers, J., & deLisle, L. (1997). *The story of leisure: Context, concepts and current controversy*. Champaign, IL: Human Kinetics.

Veblen, T. (1998). *The theory of the leisure class*. Amherst, NY: Prometheus Books. (Original work published 1899).

Vennum, T., Jr. (2005). *Native American history of lacrosse*. www.laxlinks.com/history/vennuum.htm

Virginia State Parks. (2005). *History of Virginia state parks*. www.dcr.state.va.us/parks/his_parx.htm

Westland, C. (1979). *Fitness and amateur sport in Canada—government's programme: An historical perspective*. Ottawa, ON: Canadian Parks/Recreation Association.

Wetherell, D.G., & Kmet, I. (1990). *Useful pleasures: The shaping of Alberta 1896-1945*. Regina, SK: Canadian Plains Research Centre.

Wright, J.R. (1983). *Urban parks in Ontario, Part I: Origins to 1860*. Ministry of Tourism and Recreation.

CHAPTER 3

Borgmann, A. (1984). *Technology and the character of contemporary life: A philosophical inquiry*. Chicago: University of Chicago Press.

de Grazia, S. (1963). *Of time, work and leisure*. Garden City, NJ: Doubleday.

Gerbner, G. (1999, March). The stories we tell. *Peace Review, 11*(1).

Groarke, L. (2008). Informal logic. In Edward N. Zalta (Ed.), *Stanford encyclopedia of philosophy*. http://plato.stanford.edu/archives/fall2008/entries/logic-informal/

Hamilton, E., & Huntington, C. (Eds.). (1961). *The collected dialogues of Plato*. Princeton, NJ: Princeton University Press.

Hemingway, J. (1988). Leisure and civility: Reflections on a Greek ideal. *Leisure Sciences, 10*, 179-191.

Hemingway, J. (1996). Emancipating leisure: The recovery of freedom in leisure. *Journal of Leisure Research, 28*(1), 27-43.

Hunnicutt, B. (1990). Leisure and play in Plato's teaching and philosophy of learning. *Leisure Sciences, 12*, 211-227.

Jackson, A., Fawcett, G., Milan, A., Roberts, P., Schetagne, S., Scott, K., & Tsoukalas, S. (2000, November). *Social cohesion in Canada: Possible indicators—highlights*. Ottawa, ON: Canadian Council on Social Development.

Johnson, R., & McLean, D. (1994). Leisure and the development of ethical character: Changing views of the North American ideal. *Journal of Applied Recreation Research, 19*(2), 117-130.

Kubey, R., & Csikzentmihalyi, M. (1990). *Television and the quality of life: How viewing shapes everyday experience*. Hillsdale, NJ: Lawrence Erlbaum.

McKeon, R. (Ed.). (1941). *The basic works of Aristotle*. New York: Random House.

Nash, R. (1982). *Wilderness and the American mind* (3rd ed.). New Haven, CT: Yale University Press.

Neulinger, J. (1974). *The psychology of leisure: Research approaches to the study of leisure.* Springfield, IL: Charles C Thomas.

Pieper, J. (1998). *Leisure: The basis of culture* [R. Scruton, Trans.]. South Bend, IN: St. Augustine's Press.

Plato. (1930). *The republic* [P. Shorey, Trans.]. Cambridge, MA: Harvard University Press.

Putnam, R. (2000). *Bowling alone.* New York: Simon & Schuster.

Russell, B. (1960). *In praise of idleness: And other essays.* London: George Allen & Unwin.

Schor, J. (1998). *The overspent American.* New York: Basic Books.

Sylvester, C. (1991). Recovering a good idea for the sake of goodness: An interpretive critique of subjective leisure. In *Recreation and leisure: Issues in an era of change* (pp. 441-454). State College, PA: Venture.

Veblen, T. (1998). *The theory of the leisure class.* Amherst, NY: Prometheus Books (Original work published 1899).

Weber, M. (1958). *The Protestant ethic and the spirit of capitalism.* [T. Parson, Trans.] New York: Scribner's (Original work published 1930).

CHAPTER 4

Beaubier, D. (2004). Athletic gender equity policy in Canadian universities: Issues and possibilities. *Canadian Journal of Educational Administration and Policy, 34,* 49-59.

Beauregard, A. (1996). Running feet. *Ultra legends.* www.ultralegends.com/tarahumara-indians/

Bell, C.M., & Hurd, A.R. (2006). Research update: Recreation across ethnicity: People of different races often seek contrasting recreation opportunities. *Parks & Recreation, 41*(10), 27-36.

Byrne, J.A. (2007). *The role of race in configuring park use: A political ecology perspective.* Dissertation and thesis, 1-129.

Central Intelligence Agency. (2004). *World factbook.* www.cia.gov/cia/publications/factbook/rankorder/2172rank.html

Clark, W. (2008). Kids' sports. *Canadian Social Trends, 85*(3), 54-61.

Countries and Their Cultures. (n.d.). *Pakistan.* www.everyculture.com/No-Sa/Pakistan.html

Crawford, D., Jackson E., & Godbey, G. (1991). A hierarchical model of leisure constraints. *Leisure Sciences, 9,* 119-127.

Curtis, J. (1979). *Recreation: Theory and practice.* St. Louis, MO: Mosby.

Edwards, H. (1973). *Sociology of sport.* Homewood, IL: Dorsey Press.

Eschleman, J., Cashion, B., & Basirico, L. (1993). *Sociology: An introduction* (4th ed.). New York: Harper Collins College.

Floyd, M. (1998). Getting beyond marginality and ethnicity: The challenge for race and ethnic studies in leisure research. *Journal of Leisure Research, 30*(1), 3-22.

Gruneau, R. (1999). *Class, sports, and social development.* Champaign, IL: Human Kinetics.

Henderson. (1997). A critique of constraints theory: A response. *Journal of Leisure Research, 29*(4), 453-458.

Henderson. (2010). Leisure studies in the 21st century: The sky is falling? *Leisure Sciences, 32*(4), 391-400.

Henslin, J.M. (1993). *Sociology: A down-to-earth approach.* Boston: Allyn & Bacon.

Kelly, J.R. (1987). *Freedom to be: A new sociology of leisure.* New York: Macmillan.

Kelly, J.R. (1996). *Leisure* (3rd ed.). Boston: Allyn & Bacon.

Lenski, G., & Lenski, J. (1987). *Human societies: An introduction to macrosociology* (5th ed.). New York: McGraw-Hill.

Lenski, G., Nolan, P., & Lenski, J. (1995). *Human societies: An introduction to macrosociology* (7th ed.). New York: McGraw-Hill.

McChesney, J., Gerken, M., & McDonald, K. (2005). Reaching out to Hispanics. *Parks & Recreation, 40*(3), 74-78.

Mill, R. (1986). Tourist characteristics and trends. *Literature review: The President's Commission on Americans Outdoors.* Washington, DC: Government Printing Office.

Nash, J. (1953). *Philosophy of recreation and leisure.* Dubuque, IA: Brown.

NCAA. (2006). *NCAA gender-equity survey results 2005-2006.* www.ncaa.org/wps/wcm/connect/0462e7804e0d4e469171f11ad6fc8b25/GenderEquityRept-Final.pdf?MOD=AJPERES&CACHEID=0462e7804e0d4e469171f11ad6fc8b25/GenderEquityRept-Final.pdf

Newman, D. (1999). *Sociology of families.* Thousand Oaks, CA: Pine Forge Press.

Online Newshour. (1997, May 19). *Gender parity in sports: The pros and cons of Title IX.* Retrieved June 16, 2005, from www.pbs.org/newshour/forum/may97/title9_5-19.html

Phillip, S. (2000). Race and the pursuit of happiness. *Journal of Leisure Research, 32*(1), 121-124.

Prebish, C. (1993). *Religion and sport: The meeting of sacred and profane.* Westport, CT: Greenwood Press.

Roberts, K. (2010). *Sociology of leisure.* ISA (sociopedia.isa), pp. 1-13.

Robinson, J.P., & Godbey, G. (1997). *Time for life: The surprising ways Americans use their time.* University Park, PA: Penn State University Press.

Russell, R.V. (2002). *Pastimes: The context of contemporary culture* (2nd ed.), pp. 308-309. Champaign, IL: Sagamore.

Shinew, K.J., Floyd, M.E., & Parry, D. (2004). Understanding the relationship between race and leisure activities and constraints: Exploring an alternative framework. *Leisure Sciences, 26,* 181-199.

U.S. Census Bureau. (2010). www.census.gov/

U.S. Department of Labor. (2010). *Women's employment during the recovery.* www.dol.gov/_sec/media/reports/femalelaborforce/

Veblen, T. (1998). *The theory of the leisure class.* Amherst, NY: Prometheus Books. (Original work published 1899).

CHAPTER 5

Advisory Commission on Intergovernmental Relations. (1964). *The problem with special districts in America*. Washington, DC: U.S. Government Printing Office.

Babcock, R.F., & Larsen, W.U. (1990). *Special districts—The ultimate in neighborhood zoning*. Cambridge, MA: Lincoln Institute of Land Policy.

Bannon, J., & McKinney, W. (1980). *White paper: A study and analysis of Illinois Park Districts*. Champaign, IL: University of Illinois Press.

Barlow, E. (1977). *Frederick Law Olmsted's New York*. New York: Praeger.

Blinn, S.R. (1977). *The professional preparation of municipal recreation and park executives*. Boston: Boston University.

Bollens, J.C. (1957). *Special districts in the United States*. Berkeley, CA: University of California Press.

Bollens, J.C., & Schmandt, H.J. (1975). *The metropolis: Its people, politics and economics*. New York: Harper & Row.

Botkin, R., & Kanters, M.A. (1990). *Benefits of Illinois Park District leisure services*. Macomb, IL: Western Illinois University Printing.

Brinberg, D., & McGrath, J.E. (1997). *Validity and the research process*. Beverly Hills, CA: Sage.

Bromage, A.W. (1962). *Political representation in metropolitan agencies*. Ann Arbor, MI: Institute of Public Administration, University of Michigan.

Brown, D. (1980). *A presentation of the oral testimony received at hearings of the special district subcommittee*. Springfield, IL: League of Women Voters.

Burton, T.L. (1971). *Experiments in recreation research*. Totowa, NJ: Rowman & Littlefield.

Butler, G.D. (1976). *Introduction to community recreation*. New York: McGraw-Hill.

Cairns, M. (1997). The history of Illinois Park Districts. *Illinois Parks and Recreation* (July/August), 23-27.

Cape, W.H., Graves, L.B., & Michaels, B.M. (1969). *Government by special districts*. Manhattan, KS: Government Research Center Press.

Chadwick, B.A., Bahr, H., & Albrecht, S. (1984). *Social science research methods*. Englewood Cliffs, NJ: Prentice-Hall.

Collins, M.F., & Cooper, I.S. (1998). *Leisure management issues and application*. London: Wallingford.

Cook, C. (1972). *A description of the New York Central Park*. New York: Blom.

Dickason, J.G. (1983). The origin of the playground: The role of the Boston Women's Clubs, 1885-1890. *Leisure Sciences, 6*, 83-98.

Dickinson, M.M. (1978). *The history of the Illinois Association of Park Districts, May 1928-October, 1978*. Springfield, IL: Illinois Association of Park Districts.

Driver, B.L., Brown, P.J., & Peterson, G.L. (1991). *Benefits of leisure*. State College, PA: Venture.

Edginton, C.R., Jordan, D.J., DeGraaf, D.G., & Edginton, S.R. (2002). *Leisure and life satisfaction*. Boston: McGraw-Hill.

Edginton, C.R., & Williams, J.G. (1978). *Productive management of leisure service organizations*. New York: Wiley.

Elazar, D.J. (1970). *Cities of the prairie*. New York: Basic Books.

Emanuelson, D.N. (2002). *A comparative analysis of Illinois Park Districts and Illinois Municipal Parks and Recreation Departments*. DeKalb, IL: Northern Illinois University.

Fahrion, K.A. (1984). *Development and powers of Illinois Park Districts*. Springfield, IL: Illinois Legislative Council.

Finkler, S.A. (2009). *Financial management for public, health, and not-for-profit organizations* (3rd ed.). Upper Saddle River, NJ: Prentice Hall.

Flickinger, T.B., & Murphy, P. (2004). *The park district code*. Springfield, IL: Illinois Association of Park Districts.

Foster, K.A. (1997). *The political economy of special purpose government*. Washington, DC: Georgetown University Press.

Halsey, E. (1940). *The development of public recreation in metropolitan Chicago*. Chicago: Chicago Recreation Commission.

Hendon, W.S. (1981). *Evaluating urban parks and recreation*. New York: Praeger.

Henry, N. (2001). *Public administration and public affairs*. Upper Saddle River, NJ: Prentice-Hall.

Howard, D.R., & Crompton, J.L. (1980). *Financing, managing and marketing recreation and park resources*. Dubuque, IA: Brown.

Human Kinetics. (Ed.). (2006). *Introduction to recreation and leisure*. Champaign, IL: Human Kinetics.

Hurd, A.R., Barcelona, R.J., & Meldrum, J.T. (2008). *Leisure services management*. Champaign, IL: Human Kinetics.

Ibrahim, H. (1991). *Leisure and society: A comparative approach*. Dubuque, IA: Brown.

Illinois Association of Park Districts. (2001). *The park district advantage*. Springfield, IL: IAPD.

Illinois Municipal League. (2000). *Illinois municipal directory*. Springfield, IL: Illinois Municipal League.

Kaszak, N.L. (1993). *Handbook of Illinois Park District law*. Springfield, IL: Illinois Association of Park Districts.

Lutzin, S.G. (1979). *Managing municipal leisure services*. Washington, DC: ICMA Press.

Mitchell, J. (1999). *The American experiment with government corporations*. Armonk, NJ: Sharpe.

Milakovich, M.E., & Gordon, G.J. (2004). *Public administration in America*. Belmont, CA: Wadsworth.

Mobley, T.A., & Newport, D. (1996). *Parks and recreation in the 21st century*. Myrtle Beach, SC: Springs.

Nalbandian, J. (1991). *Professionalism in local government*. San Francisco: Jossey-Bass.

National Recreation and Park Association. (1997) *The legends of parks and recreation administration*. [Video]. Arlington, VA: Author.

Olmsted, F.L., & Kimball, T. (1973). *Frederick Law Olmsted: Landscape architect*. New York: Blom.

Rainwater, C.E. (1922). *The play movement in the United States*. Chicago: University of Chicago Press.

Riess, S.A. (1996). *City games: The evolution of American urban society and the rise of sports*. Champaign, IL: University of Illinois Press.

Rosenweig, R., & Blackmar, E. (1992). *The park and the people: A history of Central Park*. Ithaca, NY: Cornell University Press.

Searle, G.A.C. (1975). *Recreation economics and analysis*. New York: Longman.

Sessoms, H.D. (1993). *Eight decades of leadership development*. Arlington, VA: National Recreation and Park Association.

Shivers, J.S. (1967). *Principles and practices of recreational service*. New York: Macmillan.

Shivers, J.S., & Halper, J.W. (1981). *The crisis in urban recreation*. East Brunswick, NJ: Associated University Press.

Smith, S. (1975). Similarities between urban recreation systems. *Journal of Leisure Research* (July), 270-281.

Stetzer, D.F. (1975). *Special districts in Cook County*. Chicago: University of Chicago.

Sullivan, A., & Sheffrin, S.M. (2003). *Economics: Principles in action*. Upper Saddle River, NJ: Pearson Prentice Hall.

van der Smissen, B., Moiseichik, M., Hartenburg, V.J., & Twardzik, L.F. (2000). *Management of park and recreation agencies*. Ashburn, VA: National Recreation and Park Association.

CHAPTER 6

Adirondack State Park Agency. (2011). *The Adirondack Park*. Retrieved February 10, 2011, from www.apa.state.ny.us/about_park/index.html

Alabama State Parks. (2012). *Alabama State Park resorts*. Retrieved February 24, 2012, from www.alapark.com/Resorts/

American Planning Association. (2003). *How cities use parks to help children learn*. Retrieved June 4, 2005, from www.planning.org/cityparks/briefingpapers/helpchildrenlearn.htm

Balmford, A., Beresford, J., Green, J., Naidoo, R., Walpole, M., et al. (2009). *A global perspective on trends in nature-based tourism*. PLoS Biology, 7(6): e1000144. doi:10.1371/journal.pbio.1000144

Belasco, W.J. (1979). *Americans on the road: From autocamp to motel 1910-1945*. Baltimore: Johns Hopkins Press.

Brown, D. (1970). *Bury my heart at Wounded Knee: An Indian history of the American West*. New York: Henry Holt.

Bureau of Land Management. (n.d.). *The Bureau of Land Management's outdoor recreation and visitor services accomplishments report 2006-2008*. Retrieved February 10, 2011, from www.blm.gov/wo/st/en/prog/Recreation.html

Bureau of Land Management. (2011). *About the BLM*. Retrieved February 10, 2011, from www.blm.gov/wo/st/en/info/About_BLM.html

Bureau of Reclamation. (2011). *Bureau of Reclamation quickfacts*. www.usbr.gov/facts.html

Cavallo, D. (1981). *Muscles and morals: Organized playgrounds and urban reform, 1880–1920*. Philadelphia: University of Pennsylvania Press.

Chape, S., Blyth, S., Fish, L., Fox, P., & Spalding, M. (compilers). (2003). *2003 United Nations list of protected areas*. Gland, Switzerland, and Cambridge, UK: IUCN and Cambridge, UK: UNEP-WCMC.

Chavez, D.J. (2002). Adaptive management in outdoor recreation: Serving Hispanics in southern California. *Western Journal of Applied Forestry*, 17(3), 129-133.

Cordell, H.K., Betz, C.J., Green, G., & Owens, M. (2005). *Off-highway vehicle recreation in the United States, regions and states: A national report from the national survey on recreation and the environment (NSRE)*. U.S. Forest Service Southern Research Station. Retrieved November 17, 2011, from www.fs.fed.us/recreation/programs/ohv/OHV_final_report.pdf

Eagles, P.F.J. (2005). *Ontario provincial park budgets 1982-2003*. Guelph, ON: Canada Parks Research Forum of Ontario.

Eagles, P.F J., McLean, D., & Stabler, M.J. (2000). Estimating the tourism volume and value in parks and protected areas in Canada and the USA. *George Wright Forum*, 17(3): 62-76.

Ehrlich, G. (2000). *John Muir: Nature's visionary*. Washington, DC: National Geographic.

Foster, J. (1978). *Working for wildlife: The beginning of preservation in Canada*. Toronto, ON: University of Toronto Press.

Glendening, J. (1997). *The High Road: Romantic tourism, Scotland, and literature, 1720-1820*. New York: St. Martin's Press.

Harnick, P. (2000). *Inside city parks*. Washington, DC: Urban Land Institute.

Hudson, B.J. (2001). *Wild ways and paths of pleasure: Access to British waterfalls, 1500-2000. Landscape Research*, 26(4), 285-303.

Johnson, C.Y., Bowker, J.M., English, D.B.K., & Worthen, D. (1997). *Theoretical perspectives of ethnicity and outdoor recreation: A review and synthesis of African-American and European-American participation*. General Technical Report SRS-11. Asheville, NC: USDA Forest Service, Southern Research Station.

Jones, K.R., & J. Wills. (2005). *The invention of the park*. Cambridge, UK: Polity Press.

Keene, A. (1994). *Earthkeepers: Observers and protectors of nature*. New York: Oxford University Press.

Kentucky State Parks. (2005). *The Lake Barkley State Resort Park*. Retrieved June 6, 2005, from http://parks.ky.gov/parks/resortparks/lake-barkley/default.aspx

Killan, G. (1993). *Protected places: A history of Ontario's provincial park system*. Toronto, ON: Dundurn Press.

Landrum, N.C. (2004). *The state park movement in America: A critical review.* Columbia, MO: University of Columbia Press.

Leduc, J. (2009). *The Canadian Heritage Rivers System.* Hull, PQ: Canadian Heritage Rivers Board.

Lysenko, I., Besançon, C., & Savy, C. (2007). *2007 UNEP-WCMC global list of transboundary protected areas.* Retrieved February 10, 2011, from www.tbpa.net/docs/78_Transboundary_PAs_database_2007_WCMC_tbpa.net.pdf

Manning, R. (2007). *Parks and carrying capacity: Commons without tragedy.* Washington, DC: Island Press.

Marty, S. (1984). *A grand and fabulous notion: The first century of Canada's parks.* Toronto, ON: NC Press.

McFarland, E. (1982). The beginning of municipal park systems. In G. Wall & J. Marsh (Eds.), *Recreational land use: Perspectives on its evolution in Canada.* Ottawa, ON: Carleton University Press.

McWilliam, W., Eagles, P., Seasons, M., & Brown, R. (2010). Assessing the degradation effects of local residents on urban forests in Ontario, Canada. *Journal of Arboriculture and Urban Forestry, 36*(6): 253-260.

Miller, C. (2004). *Gifford Pinchot and the making of modern environmentalism.* Washington, DC: Island Press.

Nash, R. (1982). *Wilderness and the American mind* (3rd ed.). New Haven, CT: Yale University Press.

National Association of State Park Directors. (2011). Retrieved November 17, 2011, from www.naspd.org/

National Geographic News. (2004). Retrieved November 17, 2011, from http://news.nationalgeographic.com/news/2004/03/0319_040319_parks.html

National Marine Sanctuaries. (2011). *National marine sanctuaries.* Retrieved February 10, 2011, from http://sanctuaries.noaa.gov/about/faqs/welcome.html

National Park Conservation Association. (2006). *The U.S. national park system: An economic asset at risk.* Washington, DC.

National Park Service. (2003). *A brief history of the National Park Service: National Park Service created.* Retrieved June 12, 2005, from www.cr.nps.gov/history/online_books/kieley/kieley4.htm

National Park Service. (2004). *Careers: Park rangers.* Retrieved June 13, 2005, from www.nps.gov/personnel/rangers.htm

National Park Service. (2005). *State Land and Water Conservation Fund.* Retrieved June 4, 2005, from www.nps.gov/lwcf/

National Park Service, Office of International Affairs. (2005). *Office of International Affairs.* Retrieved June 4, 2005, from www.nps.gov/oia

Nature Canada. (2011). *National wildlife areas and migratory bird sanctuaries.* Retrieved February 11, 2011, from www.naturecanada.ca/parks_nwa.asp

Nebraska Game and Parks Commission. (2011). *Eugene T. Mahoney State Park.* Retrieved February 11, 2011, from http://nebraskastateparks.reserveamerica.com/campgroundDetails.do?topTableIndex=CampingSpot&contractCode=ne&parkCode=0273

Parks Canada. (2011a). *National parks list.* Retrieved February 10, 2011, www.pc.gc.ca/progs/np-pn/recherche-search_e.asp?p=1

Parks Canada. (2011b). *Canada's existing World Heritage sites.* Retrieved February 10, 2011, from www.pc.gc.ca/progs/spm-whs/itm2.aspx

Pergams, O.R.W., Czech, B., Haney, J.C., & Nyberg, D. (2004). Linkage of conservation activity to trends in the U.S. economy. *Conservation Biology, 18*(6), 1617-1623.

Pergams, O.R.W., & Zaradic, P.A. (2006). Is love of nature in the US becoming love of electronic media? 16-year downtrend in national park visits explained by watching movies, playing video games, Internet use, and oil prices. *Journal of Environmental Management, 80,* 387-393.

Ramsar. (2011). *The list of wetlands of international importance.* Retrieved February 11, 2011, from www.ramsar.org/cda/en/ramsar-documents-list/main/ramsar/1-31-218_4000_0__

Ritvo, H. (2003). Fighting for Thirlmere: The roots of environmentalism. *Science, 300*(5625), 1510-1511.

Runte, A. (2010). *National parks: The American experience* (4th ed.). Lincoln: University of Nebraska Press.

Rybczynski, W. (1999). *A clearing in the distance: Frederick Law Olmsted and America in the nineteenth century.* New York: Scribner.

Saunders, A. (1998). *Algonquin story* (3rd ed.). Whitney, ON: Friends of Algonquin Park.

Sears, J. (1980). *Sacred places: American tourist attractions in the nineteenth century.* Amherst: University of Massachusetts Press.

Seibel, G.A. (1995). *Ontario's Niagara Parks, Niagara Falls.* Niagara Falls, ON: Niagara Parks Commission.

Sellars, R.W. (1999). *Preserving nature in the national parks.* New Haven, CT: Yale University Press.

Shaffer, M.S. (2001). *See America first: Tourism and national identity, 1880-1940.* Washington, DC: Smithsonian Institution Press.

Sheail, J. (2010). *Nature's spectacle: The world's first national parks and protected areas.* London: Earthscan.

Tate, A. (2001). *Great city parks.* New York: Routledge.

Taylor, A.F., Kuo, F.E., & Sullivan, W.C. (2001). Views of nature and self-discipline: Evidence from inner city children. *Journal of Environmental Psychology, 22,* 49-63.

Tennessee Valley Authority. (n.d.). *Recreation.* Retrieved June 6, 2005, from www.tva.gov/river/recreation/index.htm

Trans Canada Trail. (2011). *Trans Canada Trail year-end review 2009-2010.* Montreal, PQ: Trans Canada Trail.

UNESCO. (2011a). *World Heritage list.* Retrieved February 11, 2011 from http://whc.unesco.org/en/list

UNESCO. (2011b). *United States of America.* Retrieved February 10, 2011, from http://whc.unesco.org/en/statesparties/us

U.S. Army Corps of Engineers. (2011). Recreation brochure. Retrieved November 17, 2011, from www.usace.army.mil/CECW/Operations/Pages/Recreation.aspx

U.S. Department of the Interior. (n.d.). *Bureau of Indian Affairs.* Retrieved February 10, 2012, from www.bia.gov/

U.S. Fish and Wildlife Service. (2011). *Welcome to the national wildlife refuge system*. Retrieved February 19, 2011, from www.fws.gov/refuges/index.html

USDA Forest Service. (2011). *National Forest system statistics FY 2010*. Retrieved February 10, 2011, from www.fs.fed.us/publications/

Virden, R.J., & Walker, C.J. (1999). Ethnic/racial and gender variations among meanings given to, and preferences for, the natural environment. *Leisure Sciences, 21*(3), 219-239.

Wals, A.E.J. (1994). Nobody planted it, it just grew! Young adolescents' perceptions and experiences of nature in the context of urban environmental education. *Childrens Environment, 11*(3), 1-27.

West Virginia Division of Natural Resources. (2005). *Pipestem Resort State Park*. Retrieved June 4, 2005, from www.pipestemresort.com/

Wetlands International. (2005). *Introduction to Ramsar Sites Information Service*. Retrieved February 10, 2012, from www.wetlands.org/RSIS/Introduction.htm

Young, T. (2004). *Building San Francisco's parks, 1850–1930*. Baltimore: Johns Hopkins University Press.

Zaslowsky, D., & Watkins, T.H. (1994). *These American lands: Parks, wilderness and the public lands*. Washington, DC: Island Press.

Zinser, C.I. (1995). *Outdoor recreation: United States national parks, forests and public lands*. New York: Wiley.

CHAPTER 7

Burton, T.L., & Glover, T.D. (1999). Back to the future: Leisure services and the reemergence of the enabling authority of the state. In E.L. Jackson & T.L. Burton (Eds.), *Leisure studies: Prospects for the twenty-first century*. State College, PA: Venture.

Canada. (1938). *Final report of the National Employment Commission*. Ottawa, ON: King's Printer.

Canada. (1943). *The National Physical Fitness Act*. Ottawa, ON: King's Printer.

Canada. (1961). *Fitness and Amateur Sport Act*. Ottawa, ON: Queen's Printer.

Canada. (1982). *Constitution Act*. Retrieved September 27, 2011, from http://laws-lois.justice.gc.ca/eng/Const/page-11.htm

Canada. (2003). *Physical Activity and Sport Act*. Retrieved September 27, 2011, from http://laws-lois.justice.gc.ca/eng/acts/P-13.4/FullText.html

Canada. (2011). *Ministers of Amateur Sport in Canada*. Retrieved September 28, 2011, from www.parl.gc.ca/

Canadian Heritage. (2010). *Welcome*. Retrieved September 27, 2011, from www.canadianheritage.gc.ca/

Cuff, G. (1990). First on the agenda: Last on the budget. *Recreation Canada, 48*(2), 32-34.

Foot, D.K. (1998). *Boom, bust and echo 2000*. Toronto, ON: Macfarlane Walter & Ross.

Foot, D.K. (2002, March 21). Boomers blow up census. *Globe and Mail*, p. A17.

Godbey, G. (1997). *Leisure and leisure services in the 21st century*. State College, PA: Venture.

Interprovincial Sport and Recreation Council. (1987). *National recreation statement*. Retrieved September 27, 2011, from http://lin.ca/resource-details/4467

MacIntosh, D., Bedecki, T., & Franks, C.E.S. (1988). *Sport and politics in Canada: Federal government involvement since 1961*. Kingston, ON: McGill-Queen's University Press.

Martin, P., & Midgley, E. (2010). *Population Bulletin Update: Immigration in America 2010* (p. 3). Washington, DC: Population Reference Bureau.

McFarland, E.M. (1970). *The development of public recreation in Canada*. Ottawa, ON: Canadian Parks and Recreation Association.

National Benefits Hub. (2011). *Home*. Retrieved September 28, 2011, from http://benefitshub.ca/

National Recreation Summit. (2011). Retrieved May 3, 2012, from http://lin.ca/national-recreation-summit

Parks and Recreation Association of Canada. (1947). *Charter*. Toronto, ON: Author.

Peters, M. (1913). Annual report of the committee on vacation schools and supervised playgrounds. In National Council of Women of Canada (Ed.), *The yearbook containing the report of the twentieth annual meeting of the National Council of Women of Canada* (pp. 43-48). Toronto: National Council of Women of Canada.

Rutherford, P. (Ed.). (1974). *Saving the Canadian city: The first phase, 1880-1920*. Toronto, ON: University of Toronto Press.

Schrodt, B. (1979). *A history of Pro-Rec: The British Columbia provincial recreation programme: 1934-1953*. Unpublished dissertation, University of Alberta, Edmonton.

Statistics Canada. (2007). *Immigration in Canada: A portrait of the foreign-born population, 2006 census*. Retrieved February 18, 2011, from www12.statcan.ca/english/census06/analysis/immcit/pdf/97-557-XIE2006001.pdf

Statistics Canada. (2008). *Aboriginal peoples in Canada in 2006: Inuit, Métis and First Nations, 2006 census*. Retrieved from www12.statcan.ca/census-recensement/2006/as-sa/97-558/pdf/97-558-XIE2006001.pdf

Statistics Canada. (2012). *The Canadian population in 2011: Age and sex*. Retrieved May 30, 2012, from www12.statcan.gc.ca/census-recensement/2011/as-sa/98-311-x/98-311-x2011001-eng.pdf

Strong-Boag, V.J. (1976). *The parliament of women of Canada, 1893-1929*. Ottawa, ON: National Museums of Canada.

Vancouver Profile. (2011). *Sunset Community Centre*. Retrieved February 18, 2011, from www.vancouverprofile.com/recreation/content.php/id/1089

Westland, C. (1979). *Fitness and amateur sport in Canada: The federal government's programme: An historical perspective*. Ottawa, ON: Canadian Parks and Recreation Association.

CHAPTER 8

American Society of Association Executives. (2004). *Association FAQ*. Retrieved September 1, 2011, from www.asaecenter.org/AboutUs/content.cfm?ItemNumber=16309

BoardSource. (2011). *What is the nonprofit sector?* Retrieved September 1, 2011, from www.boardsource.org/Knowledge.asp?ID=3.377

Bureau of Labor Statistics. (2009). *U.S. Department of Labor, wages in the nonprofit sector: Management, professional, and administrative support occupations*. Retrieved September 1, 2011, from www.bls.gov/opub/cwc/cm20081022ar01p1.htm

Corporation for National and Community Service. (2011). *Corporation for National and Community Service, volunteering in America*. Retrieved September 1, 2011, from www.volunteeringinamerica.gov

Hall, M., & Banting, K.G. (2000). *The nonprofit sector in Canada: An introduction*. Kingston, ON: McGill-Queen's University Press.

Hall, M.H., de Wit, M.L., Lasby, D., McIver, D., Evers, T., Johnston, C., et al. (June 2005). *Cornerstones of community: Highlights of the National Survey of Nonprofit and Voluntary Organizations*. (Catalogue no. 61-533-XPE, Rev. ed.). Ottawa, ON: Statistics Canada.

Hansmann, H. (1987). Economic theories of non-profit organizations. In W.W. Powell (Ed.), *The nonprofit sector: A research handbook*. London: Yale University Press.

Mason, D. (1999, November 5). [Address on accepting ARNOVA's Award for Distinguished Lifetime Achievement]. Speech presented to the Association for Research on Nonprofit Organizations and Voluntary Action, Washington, DC.

Nanus, B., & Dobbs, S.M. (1999). *Leaders who make a difference: Essential strategies for meeting the nonprofit challenge*. San Francisco: Jossey-Bass.

National Center for Charitable Statistics. (2009). *Number of nonprofit organizations in the United States, 1999-2009*. Retrieved October 1, 2011, from http://nccsdataweb.urban.org/PubApps/profile1.php

O'Neill, M. (2002). *Nonprofit nation: A new look at the third America*. San Francisco: Jossey-Bass.

Payton, R.L. (1988). *Philanthropy: Voluntary action for the public good*. New York: American Council on Education and Macmillan.

Revenue Canada. (2011). *Definition of a nonprofit organization*. Retrieved October 1, 2011, from www.cra-arc.gc.ca/E/pub/tp/it496r/it496r-e.html

Salamon, L. (1999). *America's nonprofit sector* (2nd ed.). New York: Foundation Center.

Salamon, L.M., & Anheier, H.K. (1996). The international classification of nonprofit organizations: ICNPO-revision 1. *Working Papers of the Johns Hopkins Comparative Nonprofit Sector Project*, no. 19. Baltimore: Johns Hopkins Institute for Policy Studies.

Statistics Canada. (2009). *Highlights from the 2007 Canada survey on giving, volunteering and participating*. Retrieved September 1, 2011 from www.givingandvolunteering.ca/files/giving/en/csgvp_highlights_2007.pdf

CHAPTER 9

Branson, R. (2006). *Screw it, let's do it: Lessons in life*. London: Virgin Books.

Brown, J. (2008). Avoiding high gas prices with a staycation. www.msnbc.msn.com/id/24859538/

Covey, S.R. (1992). *Principle-centered leadership*. New York: Simon and Schuster.

Gunn, C.A., & Var, T. (2002). *Tourism planning: Basics, concepts, cases* (4th ed.). London and New York: Routledge.

Hotelier.com. (2010). Don't use the R word: Hotels find trick to business bookings. http://hotelier.typepad.com/hotelier/2010/01/dont-use-the-rword-hotels-find-trick-to-business-bookings-.html

Kotter, J.P. (1996). *Leading change*. Boston: Harvard Business School Press.

Kotter, J.P. (1999). *What leaders really do*. Boston: Harvard Business School Press.

Nahavandi, A. (2009). *The art and science of leadership*. Upper Saddle River, NJ: Pearson Education.

Pinchot, G., & Pellman, R. (1999). *Intrapreneuring in action: A handbook for business innovation*. San Francisco: Berrett-Koehler.

Ramsey, D. (2011). *EntreLeadership: 20 years of practical business wisdom from the trenches*. New York: Howard Books.

Rickards, T., & Clark, M. (2006). *Dilemmas of leadership*. London and New York: Routledge.

Tierney, P., Hunt, M., and Latkova, P. (2011). Do travelers support green practices and sustainable development? *Journal of Tourism Insights*, 1-2.

CHAPTER 10

Austin, D. (1998). The health protection/health promotion model. *Therapeutic Recreation Journal*, *32*(2), 109-117.

Austin, D., & Crawford, M. (2001). *Therapeutic recreation: An introduction* (3rd ed.). Needham Heights, MA: Allyn & Bacon.

Bullock, C., & Mahon, M. (2000). *Introduction to recreation services for people with disabilities: A person-centered approach* (2nd ed.). Champaign, IL: Sagamore.

Bullock, C. & Mahon, M., & Killingsworth, C. (2010). *Introduction to recreation services for people with disabilities: A person-centered approach* (3rd ed.). Champaign, IL: Sagamore.

Bureau of Labor Statistics, U.S. Department of Labor. (2010). Recreational therapists in *Occupational outlook handbook, 2010-11 edition*. www.bls.gov/oco/ocos082.htm

Carter, M., Van Andel, G., & Robb, G. (1996). *Therapeutic recreation: A practical approach* (2nd ed.). Prospect Heights, IL: Waveland Press.

Dattilo, J., Kleiber, D., & Williams, R. (1998). Self-determination and enjoyment enhancement: A psychologically-based service delivery model for therapeutic recreation. *Therapeutic Recreation Journal, 32*(4), 258-271.

Dieser, R. (2002). A cross-cultural critique of newer therapeutic recreation practice models: The self-determination and enjoyment enhancement, Aristotelian good life model, and the optimizing lifelong health through therapeutic recreation. *Therapeutic Recreation Journal, 36*(4), 352-368.

Frye, V., & Peters, M. (1972). *Therapeutic recreation: Its theory, philosophy, and practice.* Harrisburg, PA: Stackpole Books.

Heintzman, P. (2008). Leisure-spiritual coping: A model for therapeutic recreation and leisure services. *Therapeutic Recreation Journal, 42*(1), 56-73.

Hood, C., & Carruthers, C. (2007). Enhancing leisure experience and developing resources: The leisure and well-being model, part II. *Therapeutic Recreation Journal, 41*(4), 298-325.

Kunstler, R., & Stavola Daly, F. (2010). *Therapeutic recreation leadership and programming.* Champaign, IL: Human Kinetics.

NCTRC. (2009). *CTRS profile.* New City: National Council for Therapeutic Recreation Certification.

Negley, S. (2010). Therapeutic recreation. In C. Bullock, M. Mahon, & C. Killingsworth, *Introduction to recreation services for people with disabilities: A person-centered approach* (3rd ed.) (pp. 335-377). Champaign, IL: Sagamore.

Ross, J., & Ashton-Shaeffer, C. (2003). Selecting and designing intervention programs for outcomes. In N. Stumbo (Ed.), *Client outcomes in therapeutic recreation services* (pp. 127-148). State College, PA: Venture.

Stumbo, N., & Peterson, C. (2009). *Therapeutic recreation program design: Principles and procedures* (5th ed.). San Francisco: Benjamin Cummings.

Sylvester, C., Voelkl, J., & Ellis, G. (2001). *Therapeutic recreation: Theory and practice.* State College, PA: Venture.

Wilhite, B., Keller, M.J., & Caldwell, L. (1999). Optimizing lifelong health and well-being: A health enhancing model of therapeutic recreation. *Therapeutic Recreation Journal, 33*(2), 98-108.

CHAPTER 11

Addams, J. (1909). *The spirit of youth and the city streets.* New York: Macmillan.

Anahar, H., Becker, U., & Messing, M. (1992). Scholastic sport in the context of an Islamic country. *International Journal of Physical Education, 29*(4), 32-36.

Beattie, J.M. (1977). *Attitudes toward crime and punishment in upper Canada, 1830-1850: A documentary study.* Toronto, ON: Centre of Criminology, University of Toronto Press.

Benn, T. (1996). Muslim women and physical education in initial teacher training. *Sport, Education and Society, 1*, 5-21.

Borish, L. (1999, Summer). Athletic activities of various kinds: Physical health and sports programs for Jewish American women. *Journal of Sport History, 26*(2), 240-270.

Bucher, C., & Bucher, R. (1974). *Recreation for today's society.* Englewood Cliffs, NJ: Prentice-Hall.

Byl, J. (1999). Calvinists and Mennonites: A pilot study on shepherding Christianity and sport in Canada. In J. Byl & T. Visker (Eds.), *Physical education, sport, and wellness: Looking to God as we look at ourselves* (pp. 311-326). Sioux Center, IA: Dordt College Press.

Bynum, M. (2003). The little flock. *Athletic Business, 27*(5), 36-40.

Carrington, B., Chivers, T., & Williams, T. (1987). Gender, leisure and sport: A case-study of young people of South Asian descent. *Leisure Studies, 6*, 265-279.

Chenoweth, D.H. (2007). *Worksite health promotion* (2nd ed.). Champaign, IL: Human Kinetics.

Correctional Services of Canada. (2004). *Organization.* Retrieved June 28, 2005, from www.csc-scc.gc.ca/text/organi/organe01_e.shtml

Cross, G. (1990). *A social history of leisure since 1600.* State College, PA: Venture.

Dean, L.A. (Ed.). (2009). *CAS standards and guidelines for higher education* (7th ed.). Washington, DC: Council for the Advancement of Standards in Higher Education.

De Knop, P., Theeboom, M., Wittock, H., & De Martelaer, K. (1996). Implications of Islam on Muslim girls' sport participation in Western Europe: Literature review and policy recommendations for sport promotion. *Sport, Education and Society, 1*, 147-164.

Dungy, G.J. (2006). Learning reconsidered: Where have we come? Where are we going? In R.P. Keeling (Ed.), *Learning reconsidered 2: A practical guide to implementing a campus-wide focus on the student experience* (pp. 1-2). Washington, DC: American College Personnel Association.

Ekstedt, J.W., & Griffiths, C.T. (1988). *Corrections in Canada: Policy and practice* (2nd ed.). Toronto, ON: Butter-worths.

Elkins, D.J., Beggs, B.A., & Choutka, E. (2007). The contribution of constraint negotiation to the leisure satisfaction of college students in campus recreational sports. *Recreational Sports Journal, 31*(2), 107-118.

Emard, M. (1990). Religion and leisure: A case study of the role of the church as a provider of recreation in small Ontario communities. Unpublished master's thesis, University of Waterloo.

Federal Bureau of Prisons. (n.d.). *Mission and vision.* Retrieved June 28, 2005, from www.bop.gov

Fleming, S. (1993). Schooling, sport and ethnicity: A case study. *Sociology Review, 3*, 29-33.

Fleming, S., & Khan, N. (1994). Islam, sport and masculinity: Some observations on the experiences of Pakistanis in Pakistan and Bangladeshis in Britain. In P. Duffy & L. Dugdale (Eds.), *HPER: Moving toward the 21st century* (pp. 119-128). Champaign, IL: Human Kinetics.

Franklin, D.S., & Hardin, S.E. (2008). Philosophical and theoretical foundations of campus recreation: Crossroads of theory. In NIRSA, *Campus recreation: Essentials for the professional.* Champaign, IL: Human Kinetics.

Godbey, G. (1978). *Recreation, park and leisure services: Foundations, organization, and administration.* Philadelphia: Saunders.

Goss, H.B., Cuddihy, T.F., & Michaud-Tomson, L.L. (2010). Wellness in higher education: A transformative framework for health related disciplines. *Asia-Pacific Journal of Health, Sport & Physical Education, 1*(2), 29-36.

Haines, D.J. (2001). Undergraduate student benefits from university recreation. *NIRSA Journal, 25,* 25-33.

Howard, K. (2007, March). *Fitness certifications and trends.* Presented at the 2007 Missouri Parks and Recreation Association Conference, Springfield, MO.

International Centre for Prison Studies. Retrieved September 22, 2011, from www.prisonstudies.org/info/worldbrief/wpb_country.php?country=190

Jalili, G. (1994). Moslem students and physical education. *Active and Healthy, 1*(1), 9-10.

Jewish Community Centers Maccabi Games. (2005). www.jccmaccabi.org/index_home.php [June 28, 2005].

Jones, T.R. (1999). Programming facilities. In S.C Brown and L. Schoonmaker, *Managing the collegiate recreational facility.* Corvallis, OR: NIRSA.

Kahan, D. (2003a). Islam and physical activity: Implications for American sport and physical educators. *Journal of Physical Education, Recreation and Dance, 74*(3), 48-54.

Kahan, D. (2003b). Law review: Religious boundaries in public school physical activity settings. *Journal of Physical Education, Recreation and Dance, 74*(1), 11-12, 14.

Kamiyole, O. (1993). Physical educators' albatross in African Muslim societies. *International Journal of Physical Education, 30*(2), 29-31.

Keeling, R.P. (Ed.). (2006). *Learning reconsidered 2: A practical guide to implementing a campus-wide focus on the student experience.* Washington, DC: American College Personnel Association.

Kosmin, B., Mayer, E., & Keysar, A. (2001, December). *American religious identification survey: Profile of the U.S. Muslim population.* Retrieved March 15, 2012, from www.gc.cuny.edu/Faculty/GC-Faculty-Activities/ARIS--American-Religious-Identification-Survey/ARIS-Report-2

Kraus, R. (1984). *Recreation and leisure in modern society* (3rd ed.). Dallas, TX: Scott Foresman.

Lindsey, R., & Sessoms, E. (2006). Assessment of a campus recreation program on student recruitment, retention and frequency of participation across certain demographic variables. *Recreational Sports Journal, 30*(1), 30-39.

Lussier, R., & Kimball, D. (2009). *Applied sport management skills.* Champaign, IL: Human Kinetics.

Maccabi Canada. (2005). www.maccabicanada.com [June 28, 2005].

MacLean, J., Peterson, J., and Martin, W.D. (1985). *Recreation and leisure: The changing scene* (4th ed.). New York: Macmillan.

Mittelstaedt, R. (2006). Unique groups. In Human Kinetics, *Introduction to recreation and leisure.* Champaign, IL: Human Kinetics.

Mittelstaedt, R., Robertson, B., Russell, K., Byl, J., Temple, J., & Ogilvie, L. (2006). Unique groups. In Human Kinetics (Eds.), *Introduction to recreation and leisure* (pp. 216-219). Champaign, IL: Human Kinetics.

Moffitt, J. (2010). Recreating retention. *Recreational Sports Journal, 34,* 24-33.

National Intramural-Recreational Sports Association. (2004). *The value of recreational sports in higher education: Impact on student enrollment, success, and buying power.* Champaign, IL: Human Kinetics.

National Intramural-Recreational Sports Association. (2008). *Campus recreation: Essentials for the professional.* Champaign, IL: Human Kinetics.

National Intramural-Recreational Sports Association. (2010). *Facility construction report (2010-2015).* www.nirsa.org/AM/Template.cfm?Section=Search&CONTENTID=13520&TEMPLATE=/CM/HTMLDisplay.cfm

National Intramural-Recreational Sports Association. (2011). *NIRSA's rich history.* www.nirsa.org

National Wellness Institute. (2011). *The six dimensions of wellness model.* Retrieved October 10, 2011, from www.nationalwellness.org/index.php?id_tier=2&id_c=25

Popke, M. (2001a). Spread the word. *Athletic Business, 25*(10), 55-61.

Popke, M. (2001b). Spiritual profit. *Athletic Business, 25*(10), 58.

Recreation Management. (2010). *State of the industry report: Our 2010 report on the state of the managed recreation industry.* www.recmanagement.com/features.php?fid=201006fe01&ch=1

Robertson, B.J. (1993). The roots of at risk behaviour. *Recreation Canada, 41*(4), 21-27.

Robertson, B. (1998). Issues in leisure education for persons in correctional systems. In J. Mundy (Ed.), *Leisure education theory and practice.* Champaign, IL: Sagamore.

Robertson, T., & Long, T. (2008). *Foundations of therapeutic recreation.* Champaign, IL: Human Kinetics.

Rodgers, R.F. (1990). Recent theories and research underlying student development. In D.G. Creamer & Associates, *College student development: Theory and practice for the 1990s* (pp. 27-79). Alexandria, VA: American College Personnel Association.

Rothman, D.J. (1971). *The discovery of the asylum.* Toronto, ON: Little, Brown.

Sessoms, H.D., Meyer, H., & Brightbill, C.K. (1975). *Leisure services: The organized recreation and park system* (5th ed.). Englewood Cliffs, NJ: Prentice-Hall.

Shaull, S., & Gramann, J. (1998). The effect of cultural assimilation on the importance of family-related and nature-related recreation among Hispanic Americans. *Journal of Leisure Research, 30*(1), 47-63.

Taylor, T., & Toohey, K. (2001/2002). Behind the veil: Exploring the recreation needs of Muslim women. *Leisure/Loisir, 26*(1-2), 85-105.

Thompson, W.R. (2010). Worldwide survey of fitness trends for 2011. *Health and Fitness Journal, 14*(6), 8-17.

Todd, M., Czyszczon, G., Wallace Carr, J., & Pratt, C. (2009). Comparison of health and academic indices between campus recreation facility users and nonusers. *Recreational Sports Journal, 33*(1), 43-53.

U.S. Department of Health and Human Services. (2000). *Healthy people 2010* (2nd ed.). *Understanding and improving health and objectives for improving health.* 2 vols. Washington, DC: U.S. Government Printing Office.

Wilson, P.E. (2008). History and evolution of campus recreation. In NIRSA, *Campus recreation: Essentials for the professional.* Champaign, IL: Human Kinetics.

CHAPTER 12

Anderson, D.R., Lorch, E.P., Field, D.E., Collins, P.A., & Nathan, J.G. (1985, April). Television viewing at home: Age trends in visual attention and time with TV. Paper presented at the biennial meeting of the Society for Research in Child Development, Toronto.

Antonucci, T.C. (1990). Social supports and relationships. In R.H. Binstock & L.K. George (Eds.), *Handbook of aging and the social sciences.* San Diego: Academic Press.

Arnett, J. (2000). Emerging adulthood: A theory of development from the late teens through the twenties. *American Psychologist, 55,* 469-480.

Baltes, P.B. (2003). On the incomplete architecture of human ontogeny: Selection, optimization, and compensation as a foundation of developmental theory. In U.M. Staudinger and U. Lindenberger (Eds.), *Understanding human development.* Boston: Kulwer.

Baltes, P.B., Lindenberger, U., & Staudinger, U. (2006). Lifespan theory in developmental psychology. In W. Damon & R. Lerner (Eds.), *Handbook of child psychology* (6th ed.). New York: Wiley.

Bandura, A. (2000). Self-efficacy. In A. Kazdin (Ed.), *Encyclopedia of psychology.* Washington, DC: American Psychological Association.

Barnett, L.A. (1991). The developmental benefits of play for children. In B.L. Driver, P.J. Brown, & G.L. Peterson (Eds.), *The benefits of leisure.* State College, PA: Venture.

Berndt, T.J. (2002). Friendship quality and social development. *Current Directions in Psychological Science, 11,* 7-10.

Bertrand, R.M., & Lachman, M.E. (2003). Personality development in adulthood and old age. In I.B. Weiner (Ed.), *Handbook of psychology, vol. VI.* New York: Wiley.

Bosma, H.A., & Kunnen, E.S. (2001). *Identity and emotion.* New York: Cambridge University Press.

Bowlby, J. (1989). *Secure and insecure attachment.* New York: Basic Books.

Butler, R.N. (1996). Global aging: Challenges and opportunities of the next century. *Aging International, 21,* 12-32.

Coccheri, S. (2010). Antiplatelet drugs—do we need new options? With a reappraisal of direct thromboxane inhibitors. *Drugs, 70,* 887-908.

Cully, J.A., LaVoie, D., & Gfeller, J.D. (2001). Reminiscence, personality, and psychological functioning in older adults. *The Gerontologist, 41*(1), 89-95.

Doherty, M. (2008). *Theory of mind.* Philadelphia: Psychology Press.

Dunbar, L., Leventhal, H., & Leventhal, E.A. (2007). Self-regulation, health, and behavior. In J.E. Birren (Ed.), *Encyclopedia of gerontology* (2nd ed.). San Diego, CA: Academic Press.

Erikson, E.H. (1968). *Identity: Youth and crisis.* New York: Norton.

Gardner, H. (1983). *Frames of mind.* New York: Basic Books.

Gardner, H. (1993). *Multiple intelligences.* New York: Basic Books.

Gardner, H. (2002). The pursuit of excellence through education. In M. Ferrari (Ed.), *Learning from extraordinary minds.* Mahwah, NJ: Lawrence Erlbaum.

Gottman, J.M., & Parker, J.G. (1987). *Conversations of friends.* New York: Cambridge University Press.

House, J.S., Landis, K.R., & Umberson, D. (1988). Social relationships and health. *Science, 241,* 540-545.

Hyde, J.S., & DeLamater, J.D. (2003). *Understanding human sexuality* (8th ed.). New York: McGraw-Hill.

Joiner, T.E. (2000). Depression: Current developments and controversies. In S.H. Qualls & N. Abeles (Eds.), *Psychology and the aging revolution.* Washington, DC: American Psychological Association.

Jopp, D., & Rott, C. (2006). Adaptation in very old age: Exploring the role of resources and attitudes for contenarians' happiness. *Psychology and Aging, 21,* 266-280.

Jung, Y., Gruenewald, T.L., Seeman, T.E., & Sarkisian, C.A. (2010). Productive activities and development of frailty in older adults. *Journals of Gerontology B: Psychological Sciences and Social Sciences, 65B,* 256-261.

Kagan, J. (2002). Behavioral inhibition as a temperamental category. In R.J. Davidson, K.R. Scherer, & H.H. Goldsmith (Eds.), *Handbook of affective sciences.* New York: Oxford University Press.

Kagan, J. (2008). Fear and wariness. In M.M. Haith & J.B. Benson (Eds.), *Encyclopedia of infant and early childhood development.* Oxford, UK: Elsevier.

Kagan, J. (2010). Emotions and temperament. In M.H. Burnstein (Ed.), *Handbook of cultural developmental science.* New York: Psychology Press.

Keating, D.P. (1990). Adolescent thinking. In S.S. Feldman & G.R. Elliott (Eds.), *At the threshold: The developing adolescent.* Cambridge, MA: Harvard University Press.

Larson, R.W., & Verma, S. (1999). How children and adolescents spend their time across the world: Work, play, and developmental opportunities. *Psychological Bulletin, 125,* 701-736.

Lee, I.M., Manson, J.E., Hennekens, C.H., & Paffenbarger, R.S. (1993). Body-weight and mortality: A 27-year follow-up. *Journal of the American Medical Association, 270,* 2823-2828.

Lewis, S.J. (2009). Prevention and treatment of atherosclerosis: A practitioner's guide for 2008. *American Journal of Medicine, 122* (Suppl. 1), S38-S50.

Mahoney, J.L., Larson, R.W., & Eccles, J.S. (Eds.) (2005). *Organized activities as contexts of development.* Mahwah, NJ: Lawrence Erlbaum.

Mannell, R.C. (2000). Older adults, leisure, and wellness. *Journal of Leisurability, 26,* 3-10.

Mannell, R.C., & Dupuis, S. (1996). Life satisfaction. In J.E. Birren (Ed.), *Encyclopedia of gerontology (Vol. 2).* San Diego: Academic Press.

National Association for Sport and Physical Education. (2012). *Active start: A statement of physical education guidelines for children birth to five years.* Reston, VA: National Association for Sport and Physical Education Publications.

Olsho, L.W., Harkins, S.W., & Lenhardt, M.L. (1985). Aging and the auditory system. In J.E. Birren & K.W. Schaie (Eds.), *Handbook of the psychology of aging* (2nd ed., pp. 332-377). New York: Van Nostrand Reinhold.

Peplau, L.A., & Beals, K.P. (2002). Lesbians, gays, and bisexuals in relationships. In J. Worell (Ed.), *Encyclopedia of women and gender.* San Diego: Academic Press.

Pruchno, R., & Rosenbaum, J. (2003). Social relationships in adulthood and old age. In I.B. Weiner (Ed.), *Handbook of psychology, Vol. VI.* New York: Wiley.

Robins, R.W., Trzesniewski, K.H., Tracey, J.L., Potter, J., & Gosling, S.D. (2002). Age differences in self-esteem from 9 to 90. *Psychology and Aging, 17,* 423-434.

Schaie, K.W. (2005). *Developmental influences on adult intelligence: The Seattle Longitudinal Study.* New York: Oxford University Press.

Schaie, K.W. (2010). *Developmental influences on adult intellectual development.* New York: Oxford University Press.

Singh, M.A.F. (2002). Exercise comes of age: Rationale and recommendations for a geriatric exercise prescription. *Journal of Gerontology: Medical Sciences, 57A,* M262-M282.

Sorte, J., Daeschel, I., & Amador, C. (2011). *Nutrition, health, and wellness.* Upper Saddle River, NJ: Merrill.

Tab, E.D. (2006). *National household education survey: Before- and after-school programs and activities: 2001-2005.* Washington, DC: National Center for Education Statistics, U.S. Department of Education.

Tucker, J.S., Schwartz, J.E., Clark, K.M., & Friedman, H.S. (1999). Age-related changes in the associations of social network ties with mortality risk. *Psychology and Aging, 14,* 564-571.

Vernberg, E.M., & Biggs, B.K. (2010). Preventing and treating bullying and victimization: An evidence based approach. In E.M. Verberg & B.K. Biggs (Eds.), *Preventing and treating bullying and victimization.* New York: Oxford University Press.

Wellman, H.M., & Woolley, J.D. (1990). From simple desires to ordinary beliefs: The early development of everyday psychology. *Cognition, 35,* 245-275.

Yin, Y., Buhrmester, D., & Hibbard, D. (1996, March). *Are there developmental changes in the influence of relationships with parents and friends on adjustment during early adolescence?* Paper presented at the meeting of the Society for Research on Adolescence, Boston.

CHAPTER 13

DeGraff, D., DeGraff, K., & Jordan, D. (2010). *Programming for parks and leisure services: A servant leadership approach* (3rd ed.). State College, PA: Venture.

Harenburg, V., Moiseichik, M., & van der Smissen, B. (Eds.). (2005). *Management of parks and recreation agencies.* Ashburn, VA: National Recreation and Park Association.

Human Kinetics (Ed.). (2006). *Introduction to recreation and leisure.* Champaign, IL: Human Kinetics.

Rossman, J.R., & Schlatter, B. (2011). *Recreation programming* (6th ed.). Urbana, IL: Sagamore.

CHAPTER 14

Australian Bureau of Statistics. (2007). *Australian social trends 2007: Participation in sports and physical recreation.* Retrieved November 18, 2010, from www.ausstats.abs.gov.au/ausstats/subscriber.nsf/0/1CE05AE897BAD438CA25732F001CA62F/$File/41020_Participation%20in%20sports%20and%20physical%20recreation_2007.pdf

Barcelona, R.J., & Ross, C.M. (2005). An analysis of the perceived competencies of recreational sport administrators. *Journal of Park and Recreation Administration, 22*(4), 25-42.

Blogamericas. (2007). *Sport participation in Brazil.* Retrieved November 15, 2010, from www.blogamericas.com/2007/11/16/sports-participation-in-brazil-2/

Blumenthal, K.J. (2009). Collegiate recreational sports: Pivotal players in student success. *Planning for Higher Education, 37*(2), 52-62.

China.org.cn. (2008). *China wants its people fighting fit for 2008.* Retrieved November 14, 2010, from www.china.org.cn/english/MATERIAL/200339.htm

Cordes, K.A., & Ibrahim, H.M. (2003). *Application in recreation and leisure for today and the future.* Boston: McGraw-Hill.

Edginton, C.R., Jordan, D.J., DeGraaf, D.G., & Edginton, S.R. (2002). *Leisure and life satisfaction: Foundational perspectives* (3rd ed.). Boston: McGraw-Hill.

Eitzen, D.S. (2009). *Fair and foul: Beyond the myths and paradoxes of sport.* Lanham, MD: Rowman & Littlefield.

Employee Morale and Recreation Association. (2012). *Employee morale & recreation programs.* Retrieved on January 26, 2012, from www.esmassn.org/Default.aspx?pageId=372979

Ghafouri, F., Mirzaei, B., Hums, M.A., & Honarvar, A. (2009). Effects of globalization on sport strategies. *Brazilian Journal of Biomotricity, 3*(3), 261-270.

Henderson, K.A. (2009). A paradox of sport management and physical activity interventions. *Sport Management Review, 12,* 57-65.

Kelly, J.R. (1996). *Leisure* (3rd ed.). Boston: Allyn and Bacon.

Kelly, J.R., & Freysinger, V.J. (2000). *21st century leisure: Current issues.* Boston: Allyn and Bacon.

Kidd, B. (2008). A new social movement: Sport for development and peace. *Sport in Society, 11*(4), 370-380.

Kraus, R. (2000). *Leisure in a changing America: Trends and issues for the 21st century.* Boston: Allyn and Bacon.

Mull, R.F., Bayless, K.G., & Jamieson, L.M. (2005). *Recreational sport management* (4th ed.). Champaign, IL: Human Kinetics.

Navy MWR. (n.d.). *Navy MWR fleet recreation.* Retrieved on January 24, 2012, from http://navymwr.org/mwrprgms/fleetrec.htm

North American Society of Sport Management. (2010). *NASSM home.* Retrieved on November 28, 2010, from www.nassm.com

Physical Activity Council. (2010). *Sports, fitness and recreation participation-overview report.* Retrieved November 28, 2010, from www.physicalactivitycouncil.com/pages/scactivecoalition/pdfs/PACToplineReport2010.pdf

Price, J.L. (2005). *From season to season: Sports as American religion.* Macon, GA: Mercer University Press.

Robinson, J.P., and Godbey, G. (1997). *Time for life: The surprising ways Americans use their time.* University Park, PA: Pennsylvania State University.

SouthAfricaWeb.co.za. (2010). *Recreational sports in South Africa.* Retrieved November 14, 2010, from http://southafricaweb.co.za/page/recreational-sports-south-africa

Sporting Goods Manufacturers Association. (2004). *Sports participation in America: Participation trends in fitness, sports and outdoor activities.* North Palm Beach, FL: SGMA.

Statistics Canada. (2005). *Sport participation in Canada, 2005.* Retrieved November 14, 2010, from www.statcan.gc.ca/pub/81-595-m/81-595-m2008060-eng.pdf

Stier, W.F. (2001). The current status of sport management and athletic (sport) administration programs in the 21st century at the undergraduate and graduate levels. *International Journal of Sport Management, 2*(1), 60-97.

U.S. Census Bureau. (2010). *Statistical abstract of the United States.* Washington, DC: U.S. Government Printing Office.

YMCA. (2012). *The YMCA: Belong and support.* Retrieved on January 26, 2012, from www.ymca.net/health-wb-fitness/

Young, S.J., & Ross, C.M. (2000). Recreational sports trends for the 21st century: Results of a Delphi study. *NIRSA Journal, 24*(2), 25-38.

CHAPTER 15

American Psychological Association. (2011). *Mind/body health: Did you know?* Retrieved January 2011 from www.apa.org/helpcenter/mind-body.aspx

Behrman, R.E., & Butler, A.S. (2007). *Preterm birth: Causes, consequences, and prevention.* Washington, DC: National Academies Press.

Centers for Disease Control and Prevention. (2003). *Health related quality of life.* Retrieved January 2011 from www.cdc.gov/hrqol/key_findings.htm

Centers for Disease Control and Prevention. (2004). *The burden of chronic diseases and their risk factors—national and state perspectives.* Atlanta, GA: U.S. Department of Health and Human Services, Centers for Disease Control and Prevention.

Centers for Disease Control and Prevention. (2009). *Behavioral risk factor surveillance system survey data.* Atlanta, GA: U.S. Department of Health and Human Services, Centers for Disease Control and Prevention.

Centers for Disease Control and Prevention. (2010). Youth risk behavior surveillance—United States, 2009. *Morbidity and Mortality Weekly Report, 59,* 1-142.

Centers for Disease Control and Prevention. (2011). Mental illness surveillance among adults in the United States. *Morbidity and Mortality Weekly Report, 60,* 1-32.

Duhl, L.J. (Ed.). (1962). *The urban condition.* New York: Basic Books.

Finkelstein, E.A., Fiebelkorn, I.C., & Wang, G. (2003). National medical spending attributable to overweight and obesity: How much, and who's paying? *Health Affairs, W3,* 219-226.

Health Canada. (2002). *Canada's aging population.* Retrieved October 2011 from www.phac-aspc.gc.ca/seniors-aines/alt-formats/pdf/publications/public/various-variee/papier-fed-paper/fedpager_e.pdf

Health Canada. (2006). *It's your health.* Retrieved October 2011 from www.hc-sc.gc.ca/hl-vs/alt_formats/pacrb-dgapcr/pdf/iyh-vsv/life-vie/obes-eng.pdf

Hedley, A.A., Ogden, C.L., Johnson, C.L., Carroll, M.D., Curtin, L.R., & Flegal, K.M. (2004). Prevalence of overweight and obesity among US children, adolescents, and adults, 1999–2002. *Journal of the American Medical Association, 291,* 2847-2850.

Kvaavik, E., Baty, G.D., Ursin, G., Huxley, R., & Gale, C.R. (2010). Influence of individual and combined health behaviors on total and cause-specific mortality in men and women. *Archives of Internal Medicine, 170,* 711-718.

MacDorman, M.F., & Mathews, T.J. (2009). *Behind international rankings of infant mortality: How the United States compares with Europe.* National Center for Health Statistics data brief, no. 23. Hyattsville, MD: National Center for Health Statistics.

National Center for Health Statistics. (2008). *Natality detailed data sheet, 2006.* Hyattsville, MD: National Center for Health Statistics. Retrieved October 2011 from ftp://ftp.cdc.gov/pub/Health_Statistics/NCHS/Dataset_Documentation/DVS/natality/UserGuide2006.pdf

National Institutes of Health. (1998). *Obesity education initiative: Clinical guidelines on the identification, evaluation, and treatment of overweight and obesity in adults. The evidence report.* NIH publication no. 98-4083.

National Wellness Institute. (2011). *A definition of spiritual wellness.* Retrieved January 2011 from www.nationalwellness.org/general.php?id_tier=2%20&%20id=684

Ogden, C.L., Carroll M.D., & Flegal, K.M. (2008). High body mass index for age among U.S. children and adolescents, 2003–2006. *Journal of the American Medical Association, 299*, 2401-2405.

Ogden, C.L., Flegal, K.M., Carroll, M.D., & Johnson, C.L. (2002). Prevalence and trends in overweight among U.S. children and adolescents, 1999–2000. *Journal of the American Medical Association, 288*, 1728-1732.

Putnam, R.D. (2000). *Bowling alone: The collapse and revival of American community.* New York: Simon & Schuster.

Richardson, B.W. (1876). *Hygeia: A city of health.* London. MacMillan.

Statistics Canada. (2011). *Infant mortality, by sex and birth weight, Canada, provinces and territories, annual* (CANSIM Table 102-0030). Ottawa, ON: Statistics Canada.

U.S. Department of Health and Human Services. (1996). *Physical activity and health: A report of the surgeon general.* Atlanta, GA: U.S. Department of Health and Human Services, Centers for Disease Control and Prevention, National Center for Chronic Disease Prevention and Health Promotion.

U.S. Department of Health and Human Services. (2000). *Healthy people 2010: Understanding and improving health.* Washington, DC: U.S. Government Printing Office.

U.S. Department of Health and Human Services. (2001). *The surgeon general's call to action to prevent and decrease overweight and obesity.* Rockville, MD: U.S. Department of Health and Human Services, Public Health Service, Office of the Surgeon General.

World Health Organization. (2009). *Global health risks: Mortality and burden of disease attributable to selected major risks.* Retrieved January 31, 2012, from www.who.int/healthinfo/global_burden_disease/GlobalHealthRisks_report_full.pdf

World Health Organization. (2010a). *Global estimates of burden of disease caused by the environment and occupational risks.* Retrieved October 2011 from www.who.int/quantifying_ehimpacts/global/en/index.html

World Health Organization. (2010b). *WHO Global Infobase: Data for saving lives.* Retrieved October 2011 from https://apps.who.int/infobase/

World Health Organization. (2012). *Burden of disease attributable to the modifiable environment, 2002.* Retrieved October 2011 from www.who.int/quantifying_ehimpacts/national/countryprofile/mapenv/en/index.html

World Leisure Organization. (2012). *Commission on health prevention and disease prevention.* Retrieved January 2012 from http://worldleisure.org/template.php?id=144&Health+Prevention+and+Disease+Prevention

Xu, J., Kochanek, K.D., Murphy, S.L., & Tejada-Vera, B. (2010). Deaths: Final data for 2007. *National Vital Statistics Reports, 58*, 1-72.

CHAPTER 16

Bandura, A. (1977). Self-efficacy: Toward a unifying theory of behavioral change. *Psychological Review, 84*(2), 191-215.

Csikszentmihalyi, M. (1988). *Optimal experience.* New York: Cambridge University Press.

Deci, E.L., & Ryan, R.M. (1985). *Intrinsic motivation and self-determination in human behavior.* New York: Plenum Press.

Driver, B.L., & Brown, P.J. (1978). The opportunity spectrum concept and behavioral information in outdoor recreation resource supply inventories: A rationale. In *Integrated inventories and renewable natural resources: Proceedings of the workshop.* United States Department of Agriculture (USDA) Forest Service General Technical Report RM-55, 23-31. Fort Collins, CO: Rocky Mountain Forest Range Experiment Station.

Driver, B.L., Brown, P.J., & Peterson, G.L. (1991). *Benefits of leisure.* State College, PA: Venture.

Driver, B.L., & Tocher, S.R. (1970). *Elements of outdoor recreation planning.* Ann Arbor: University of Michigan.

Engeström, Y. (2001). Expansive learning at work: Toward an activity theoretical reconceptualization. *Journal of Education and Work, 14*(1), 133-156.

Ewert, A. (1989). Managing fear in the outdoor experiential setting. *Journal of Experiential Education, 12*(1), 19-25.

Ewert, A., & Shultis, J. (1999). Technology and backcountry recreation: Boon to recreation or bust for management? *JOPERD, 70*(8), 23-31.

Ewert, A., & Sibthorp, J. (2009). Creating outcomes through experiential education: The challenge of confounding variables. *Journal of Experiential Education, 31*(3), 376-389.

Gibbons, S.L. (1999). Team building through physical challenges. *Connections '99: Proceedings of a faculty conference* (5th, Victoria, BC, Canada, May 1999).

Godbey, G. (2009). *Outdoor recreation, health, and wellness: Understanding and enhancing the relationship.* (RFF DP 09-21). Washington, DC: Resources for the Future.

Hattie, J., Marsh, H.W., Neill, J.T., & Richards, G.E. (1997). Adventure education and Outward Bound: Out-of-class experiences that make a lasting difference. *Review of Educational Research, 67*(1), 43-87.

House, J.S. (1981). Social structure and personality. In M. Rosenberg & R.H. Turner (Eds.), *Social psychology: Sociological perspectives* (pp. 525-561). New York: Basic Books.

Lave, J., & Wenger, E. (1991). *Situated learning: Legitimate peripheral participation.* New York: Cambridge University Press.

Miles, J.C., & Priest, S. (1999). *Adventure programming.* State College, PA: Venture.

Mitchell, R. (1983). *Mountain experience: The psychology and sociology of adventure.* Chicago: University of Chicago Press.

Moore, R.L., & Driver, B.L. (2005). *Introduction to outdoor recreation: Providing and managing natural resource based opportunities.* State College, PA: Venture.

Nerlich, M. (1987). *Ideology of adventure: Studies in modern consciousness, 1100-1750.* Minneapolis: University of Minnesota Press.

Outdoor Foundation. (2010). *Outdoor recreation participation report, 2010.* Boulder, CO: Outdoor Foundation.

Outdoor Industry Association. (2006). *State of the industry report 2006*. Boulder, CO: Outdoor Industry Association.

Roper ASW. (2004). *Outdoor recreation in America 2003: Recreation's benefits to society challenged by trends*. Washington, DC: Recreation Roundtable.

RRC Associates. (2010). *North Carolina ski areas association economic value analysis: Final results*. Boulder, CO: RRC Associates.

Seaman, J. (2007). Taking *things* into account: Learning as kinaesthetically-mediated collaboration. *Journal of Adventure Education and Outdoor Learning*, 7(1), 3-20.

Shultis, J., & More, T. (2011). American and Canadian national park agency responses to declining visitation. *Journal of Leisure Research*, 43(1), 110-133.

Triandis, H.C., Bontempo, R., Villareal, M.J., Asai, M., & Lucca, N. (1988). Individualism and collectivism: Cross-cultural perspectives on self-ingroup relationships. *Journal of Personality and Social Psychology*, 54(2), 323-338.

Turner, J.M. (2002). From woodcraft to "leave no trace": Wilderness, consumerism, and environmentalism in twentieth-century America. *Environmental History*, 7(3), 462-484.

Vernon, F. (2011). The experience of co-instructing on extended wilderness trips. *Journal of Experiential Education*, 33(4), 374-378.

Weiner, B. (1985). The attributional theory of achievement motivation and emotion. *Psychological Review*, 92(4), 548-573.

Wurdinger, S.D. (1997). *Philosophical issues in adventure education* (3rd ed.). Dubuque, IA: Kendall-Hunt.

CHAPTER 17

American Assembly. (1997). The arts and the public purpose. http://americanassembly.org/project/arts-and-public-purpose

American Assembly. (2006). The arts and the public purpose. Retrieved January 10, 2011, from www.americanassembly.org/

Americans for the Arts. (2002). *Arts & economic prosperity*. New York. www.AmericansForTheArts.org

Americans for the Arts. (2004). *Arts facts: Local arts agencies*. www.AmericansForTheArts.org

Americans for the Arts. (2005). *Arts facts: Local arts agencies*. www.AmericansForTheArts.org

Americans for the Arts. (2008). *Arts & economic prosperity III: The economic impact of nonprofit arts and culture organizations and their audiences*. Retrieved January 8, 2011, from www.artsusa.org/information_services/research/services/economic_impact/default.asp

Arnold, N.D. (1976). *The interrelated arts in leisure*. St. Louis, MO: Mosby.

Arnold, N.D. (1978). Pop art: The human footprint infinity, *Leisure Today*, 24-25.

ArtsBridge. (n.d.). *ArtsBridge America*. Retrieved February 8, 2012, from www.artsbridgeamerica.com

Bodilly, S.J., & Augustine, C.H. (2008). *Revitalizing arts education through community-wide coordination*. Santa Monica, CA: Rand.

Butler, G.D. (1976). *Introduction to community recreation*. New York: McGraw-Hill.

Canadian Heritage. (2007). Retrieved January 8, 2011, from www.pch.gc.ca/

Carpenter, G. (1995). The appeal of fairs, festivals, and special events to adult populations. *World Leisure & Recreation*, 37(1), 14-15.

Carpenter, G. (2004). Assessing arts and cultural programming in Oregon's recreation organizatons. *CultureWork*, 8(4), 1-6. http://aad.uoregon.edu/culturework/culturework.html

Carpenter, G. (2008). Overview of arts and cultural programming. In G. Carpenter & D. Blandy (Eds.), *Arts and cultural programming: A leisure perspective*. Champaign, IL: Human Kinetics.

Carpenter, G., & Blandy, D. (2008). Imagining the future of arts and cultural programming. In G. Carpenter & D. Blandy (Eds.), *Arts and cultural programming: A leisure perspective*. Champaign, IL: Human Kinetics.

Carpenter, G.M., & Howe, C.Z. (1985). *Programming leisure experiences: A cyclical approach*. Englewood Cliffs, NJ: Prentice-Hall.

Chartrand, H.H. (2000). Toward an American arts industry. In J.M. Cherbo & M.J. Wyszomirski (Eds.), *The public life of the arts in America* (pp. 22-49). New Brunswick, NJ: Rutgers University Press.

Congdon, K.G., & Blandy, D. (2003). Administering the culture of everyday life: Imagining the future of arts sector administration. In V.B. Morris & D.B. Pankrantz (Eds.), *The arts in a new millennium* (pp. 177-188). Westport, CT: Praeger.

Corbin, H.D., & Williams, E. (1987). *Recreation: Programming and leadership* (4th ed.). Englewood Cliffs, NJ: Prentice-Hall.

Csikszentmihalyi, M. (1990). *Flow: The psychology of optimal experience*. NY: Harper & Row.

Delamere, T.A. (2001). Development of a scale to measure resident attitudes toward the social impacts of community festivals, part II: Verification of the scale. *Event Management*, 7, 25-38.

Delamere, T.A. (2008). Festivals. In G. Carpenter & D. Blandy (Eds.), *Arts and cultural programming: A leisure perspective*. Champaign, IL: Human Kinetics.

Delamere, T.A., Wankel, L.M., and Hinch, T.D. (2001). Measuring resident attitudes toward the social impact of community festivals: Pretesting and purification of the scale. *Festival Management and Event Tourism*, 7(1), 11-24.

De Michiel, H. (2010). Hacking the policy space. *CultureWork*, 14(3). https://scholarsbank.uoregon.edu/xmlui/bitstream/handle/1794/10598/culturework_jun2010_vol_14_no_3.pdf?sequence=1

Dreeszen, C. (2003). Program evaluation. In C. Dreeszen & P. Korza (Eds.), *Fundamentals of arts management*. Amherst, MA: Arts Extension Service.

Driver, B.L., & Burns, D.H. (1999). Concepts and uses of the benefits approach to leisure. In E.L. Jackson & T.L. Burton (eds.), *Leisure studies: Prospects for the twenty-first century* (pp. 349-369). State College, PA: Venture.

Dwyer, M.C., & Frankel, S. (2002). *Policy partners: Making the case for state investments in culture*. RPM Research Corporation. Funded by the Pew Charitable Trusts.

Edginton, C.R., Hanson, C., Edginton, S.R., & Hudson, S.D. (1998). *Leisure programming: A service-centered and benefits approach* (3rd ed.). New York: McGraw-Hill.

Edginton, C.R., Hudson, S.D., Dieser, R.B., & Edginton, S.R. (2004). *Leisure programming: A service-centered and benefits approach* (4th ed.). New York: McGraw-Hill.

Estes, C., & Henderson, K. (2003). Enjoyment and the good life. *Parks & Recreation*, pp. 22-31.

Farrell, P., and Lundegren, H. (1978). *The process of recreation programming: Theory and technique*. New York: Wiley.

Farrell, P., and Lundegren, H. (1983). *The process of recreation programming: Theory and technique* (2nd ed.). New York: Wiley.

Farrell, P., and Lundegren, H. (1991). *The process of recreation programming: Theory and technique* (3rd ed.). New York: Wiley.

Florida, R. (2002). *The rise of the creative class*. New York: Basic Books.

Godfrey, M.A. (2002). National and local profiles of cultural support executive preface. Americans for the Arts, Ohio State University Arts Policy & Administration Program, with support from the Pew Charitable Trusts. Online paper. https://arted.osu.edu/files/arted/paper26.pdf

Gray, D. (1984). The great simplicities. J.B. Nash Scholar Lecture, Anaheim, CA, April.

Iso-Ahola, S.E. (1980). *The social psychology of leisure and recreation*. Dubuque, IA: Brown.

Jenkins, H., Clinton, K, Purushotma, R., Robinson, A.J., & Weigel, M. (2006). *Confronting the challenges of participatory culture: Media education for the 21st century*. John D. and Catherine T. MacArthur Foundation. Retrieved January 8, 2011, from www.digitallearning.macfound.org

Kando, T.M. (1975). *Leisure and popular culture in transition*. St. Louis, MO: Mosby.

Kelly, J.R. (1996). *Leisure* (3rd ed.). Boston: Allyn and Bacon.

Kelly, J.R. (1997). Activity and aging: Challenge in retirement. In J.T. Haworth (Ed.), *Work, leisure and well-being* (pp. 165-179). London: Routledge.

Kelly, J.R., & Freysinger, V.J. (2000). *Twentieth century leisure: Current issues*. Needham Heights, MA: Allyn & Bacon.

Kleiber, D.A. (1999). *Leisure experience and human development*. New York: Basic Books.

Kraus, R. (1966). *Recreation today: Program planning and leadership*. New York: Appleton-Century-Crofts.

Kraus, R. (1979). *Social recreation: A group dynamics approach*. St. Louis, MO: Mosby.

Kraus, R.G. (1985). *Recreation program planning today*. Glenview, IL: Scott, Foresman.

McCarthy, K.F., & Jinnett, K. (2001). *A new framework for building participation in the arts*. Santa Monica, CA: Rand.

Meyer, H.D., & Brightbill, C.K. (1956). *Community recreation: A guide to its organization*. Englewood Cliffs, NJ: Prentice-Hall.

National Endowment for the Arts. (2009). *Arts participation 2008 summary report*.

National Endowment for the Arts. (2010, March). *Come as you are: Informal arts participation in urban and rural communities*. NEA Research Note #100. Retrieved January 11, 2011, from www.nea.gov/research/Notes/100.pdf

National Governors Association. (2009). *Using arts and culture to stimulate state economic development*. Retrieved January 8, 2011, from www.nga.org/files/live/sites/NGA/files/pdf/0901ARTSANDECONOMY.PDF

Orend, R.J. (1989). *Socialization and participating in the arts*. Princeton, NJ: Princeton University Press.

Rossman, J.R. (1995). *Recreation programming: Designing leisure experiences* (2nd ed.). Champaign, IL: Sagamore.

Rossman, J.R., & Schlatter, B.E. (2009). *Recreation programming: Designing leisure experiences* (5th ed.). Urbana, IL: Sagamore.

Russell, R.V. (2009). *Pastimes: The context of contemporary leisure* (4th ed.). Urbana, IL: Sagamore.

Stebbins, R.A. (1992). *Amateurs, professionals, and serious leisure*. Montreal, QC: McGill-Queen's University Press.

Stebbins, R.A. (2005). Project-based leisure: Theoretical neglect of a common use of free time. *Leisure Studies*, 24(1).

Stebbins, R.A., & Graham, M. (2004). *Volunteering as leisure/leisure as volunteering: An international assessment*. Cambridge, MA: CABI.

Stern, M.J., & Seifert, S.C. (2002). *Culture builds community evaluation summary report*. Philadelphia: University of Pennsylvania School of Social Work. Online paper retrieved January 10, 2011, from www.sp2.upenn.edu/siap/docs/culture_builds_community/summary_report.pdf

Taylor, D.G. (2008). *Magnetizing neighborhoods through amateur arts performance*. Urban Institute's Arts and Culture Indicators Project, Rockefeller Foundation. Online paper retrieved January 10, 2011, from www.oac.state.oh.us/MakingtheCase/

Tillman, A. (1973). *The program book for recreation professionals*. Palo Alto, CA: Mayfield.

Wali, A., Marcheschi, E., Severson, R., & Longoni, M. (2001). More than a hobby: Adult participation in the informal arts. *Journal of Arts Management, Law, and Society*, 31(3), 212-230.

Webster, M. (2003). Arts education: Defining, developing, and implementing a successful program. In C. Dreeszen (Ed.), *Fundamentals of arts management*. Amherst, MA: Arts Extension Service.

Wyszomirski, M.J. (2002). Arts and culture. In L.M. Salamon (Ed.), *The state of nonprofit America* (pp. 187-218). Washington, DC: Brookings Institution Press.

Zakaras, L., & Lowell, J.F. (2008). *Cultivating demand for the arts: Arts learning, arts engagement, and state arts policy.* Santa Monica, CA: Rand.

CHAPTER 18

California Parks and Recreation Society. (n.d.). *VIP—Positioning your agency.* Retrieved November 9, 2010, from www.cprs.org/index.php?option=com_content&view=section&id=12&Itemid=59

Edginton, C.R., DeGraaf, D.G., Dieser, R.B., & Edgington, S.R. (2006). *Leisure and life satisfaction* (4th ed.). Boston: McGraw-Hill.

Fyke, J. (2009). Connecting the Cumberlands: A public lands success story in Tennessee reveals the benefits of cooperative partnering. *Parks & Recreation.*

Henderson, K.A., Bialeschki, M.D., Hemingway, J.L., Hodges, J.S., Kivel, B.D., & Sessons, H.G. (2001). *Introduction to recreation and leisure services* (8th ed.). State College, PA: Venture.

Industry Canada. (n.d.). *Tourism.* Retrieved November 9, 2010, from www.ic.gc.ca/eic/site/dsib-tour.nsf/eng/home

International Ecotourism Society. (n.d.). *What is ecotourism?* Retrieved November 14, 2010, from www.ecotourism.org/what-is-ecotourism

Kauffman, R.B. (2010). *Career development in recreation, parks, and tourism.* Champaign, IL: Human Kinetics.

Lyman, F. (2009). Parks unplugged: Getting greener by the day. *Parks & Recreation.* Retrieved March 15, 2012, from http://findarticles.com/p/articles/mi_m1145/is_2_44/ai_n31415607/

McGuire, F.A., Boyd, R.K., & Tedrick, R.E. (2009). *Leisure and aging: Ulyssean living in later life* (4th ed.). Champaign, IL: Sagamore.

McLean, D.D., & Hurd, A.R. (2012). *Recreation and leisure in modern society* (9th ed.). Sudbury, MA: Jones & Bartlett Learning.

McLean, D.D., Hurd, A.R., & Rogers, N.B. (2008). *Kraus' recreation and leisure in modern society* (8th ed.). Boston: Jones and Bartlett.

Murphy, J.F., Niepoth, E.W., Jamieson, L.M., & Williams, J.G. (1991). *Leisure systems: Critical concepts and applications.* Champaign, IL: Sagamore.

National Organization for Human Services. (n.d.). Retrieved November 14, 2010, from www.nationalhumanservices.org/mc/page.do?sitePageId=89926&

National Recreation and Park Association. (2009). *Certification programs.* Retrieved October 6, 2010, from www.nrpa.org/Content.aspx?id=410

CHAPTER 19

Almeida, M.A.B., & Gutierrez, G.L. (2005). O lazer no Brasil: Do nacional-desenvolvimentismo à globalização. *Conexões,* 3(1), 36-57.

Ap, J. (2002). *Inter-cultural behavior: Some glimpses of leisure from an Asian perspective.* Invited paper presented at the Leisure Futures Conference, April 11-13, 2002, Innsbruck, Austria.

Beghin, N. (2008). Notes on inequality and poverty in Brazil: Current situation and challenges. In Oxfam (Ed.), *From poverty to power: How active citizens and effective states can change the world.* Available at www.fp2p.org

Brady, A-M. (2009). The Beijing Olympics as a campaign of mass distraction. *China Quarterly, 197,* 1-24.

Bryce, J. (2001). The technological transformation of leisure. *Social Science Computer Review, 19*(1), 7-16.

Castronova, E. (2005). *Synthetic worlds: The business and culture of online games.* Chicago: University of Chicago Press.

Cavalcanti, M.L.V.C. (2006). Tema e variantes do mito: Sobre a morte e a ressurreição do boi. *Mana, 12*(1), 69-104.

Cetelem. (2011). *O Observador.* www.cetelem.com.br/portal/Sobre_Cetelem/Observador.shtml

Chen, L. (2004). *On leisure for the people.* Beijing, China: Chinese Economy Press.

De Jesus, G.M. (1999). Do espaço colonial ao espaço da modernidade: Os esportes na vida urbana do Rio de Janeiro. *Scripta Nova, 45*(7). www.ub.edu/geocrit/sn-45-7.htm

Deng, R. (2002). Leisure education and the strategy of Chinese higher education. *Studies in Dialectics in Nature, 18*(6), 46-48.

Downey, G. (2005). *Learning capoeira: Lessons in cunning from an Afro-Brazilian art.* Oxford: Oxford University Press.

Dumazedier, J. (1980). *Valores e conteúdos culturais do lazer.* São Paulo, Brazil: SESC.

Feng, S., & Sha, R. (2009). Study on self-driving tours in China and tourism gentrification. *Human Geography, 24*(3), 61-65.

Ferreira, R.F. (2004). Shopping center. In C.L. Gomes (Org.), *Dicionário crítico do lazer* (pp. 211-213). Belo Horizonte, Brazil: Autêntica.

Gebara, A. (1997). Considerações para a história do lazer no Brasil. In H.T. Bruhns (Ed.), *Introdução aos estudos do lazer* (pp. 61-81). Campinas, Brazil: Unicamp.

Godbey, G., & Shim, J. (2008). The development of leisure studies in North America: Implications for China. *Journal of Zhejiang University (Humanities and Social Science), 38*(4), 21-29.

IBGE. (2011). *Sinopse do Censo Demográfico 2010.* Rio de Janeiro, Brazil: IBGE.

Istoé. (2011). *País terá 1 PC para cada 2 pessoas no início de 2012.* www.istoe.com.br/reportagens/133834_PAIS+TERA+1+PC+PARA+CADA+2+PESSOAS+NO+INICIO+DE+2012

Internet World Stats. (2011). *Users and population statistics.* Retrieved October 1, 2011, from www.internetworldstats.com/stats.htm

Jackson, E.L., & Walker, G.J. (2006). *A cross cultural comparison of leisure styles and constraints experienced by Chinese and Canadian university students.* Abstracts of the 9th World Leisure Congress, Hangzhou, China.

Jim, C.Y., & Chen, W.Y. (2009). Leisure participation pattern of residents in a new Chinese city. *Annals of the Association of American Geographers, 99*(4), 657-673.

Lee, J.W., & Bairner, A. (2009). The difficult dialogue: Communism, nationalism, and political propaganda in North Korean sport. *Journal of Sport & Social Issues, 33*(4), 390-410.

Lego. (2011). *About us.* http://aboutus.lego.com/en-us/lego-group/

Li, S., Zhou, Z., & Chen, Y. (2009). The functions, problems and strategies of group dance in squares in the establishment of community culture. *Science & Technology Information, 19,* 491.

Liu, D., Gao, X., & Song, R. (2010). *Green book of China's leisure No.1.* Beijing, China: Social Sciences Academic Press.

Liu, H. (2007). The education of leisure loses the position, the dislocation and turns over to the position (Note: This is the original title of the paper, which is not a good translation. It means "The losing position, dislocation and relocation of leisure education.") *Studies in Dialectics in Nature, 23*(4), 67-70.

Liu, H., Yeh, C.K., Chick, G.E., & Zinn, H.C. (2008). An exploration of meanings of leisure: A Chinese perspective. *Leisure Sciences, 30*(5), 482-488.

Lu, Y., & Yu, Y. (2005). Investigation on sport facilities in Beijing residential areas. *Sport Science Research, 26*(5), 20-24.

Ma, H. (1999). *Call for leisure studies in China.* Retrieved November 15, 2010, from www.chineseleisure.org/onatheory.htm

Ma, H. (2004a). *Leisure: The making of beautiful home for the human spirit.* Beijing, China: Chinese Economy Press.

Ma, H. (2004b). *Toward a leisure economy with humanistic concerns.* Beijing, China: Chinese Economy Press.

Ma, H., & Zhang, J. (2004). *Survey studies of the state of leisure life among the Chinese public.* Beijing, China: Chinese Economy Press.

Marinho, A. (2005). Atividades de aventura em ambientes artificiais. In R.R. Uvinha (Org.), *Turismo de aventura: Reflexões e tendências* (pp. 247-268). São Paulo, Brazil: Aleph.

Marinho, A. (2008). Lazer, aventura e risco: Reflexões sobre atividades realizadas na natureza. *Movimento, 14*(2), 181-206.

Mascarenhas, F. (2003). O pedaço sitiado: Cidade, cultura e lazer em tempos de globalização. *Revista Brasileira de Ciências do Esporte, 24*(3), 121-143.

McKercher, B. (1996). Differences between tourism and recreation in parks. *Annals of Tourism Research, 23*(3), 563-575.

Melo, V.A. (2003). Lazer e educação física: Problemas historicamente contruídos, saídas possíveis—um enfoque na questão da formação. In C.L.G. Werneck & H. F. Isayama (Eds.), *Lazer, recreação e educação física* (pp. 57-80). Belo Horizonte, Brazil: Autêntica.

National Tourism Administration of China. (2009). *The People's Republic of China national tourism industry statistics official gazette.* Retrieved October 17, 2011, from www.cnta.gov.cn/html/2010-10/2010-10-20-10-43-69972.html

Neri, M.C. (2011). *Desigualdade de renda na década.* Rio de Janeiro, Brazil: FGV/CPS.

Oliveira, A.A.B., & Pimentel, G.G.A. (Eds.). (2009). *Recreio nas férias: Reconhecimento do direito ao lazer.* Maringá, Brazil: Eduem.

Peng, W. (2010). Square leisure culture and the construction of a harmonious, healthy and civilized lifestyle. *Proceedings of the 11th World Leisure Congress* (pp. 189-190), Chuncheon, Korea.

Ribeiro, O.C.F. (2004). Hotéis de lazer. In C.L. Gomes (Org.), *Dicionário crítico do lazer* (pp. 107-112). Belo Horizonte, Brazil: Autêntica.

Smith, S.L.J., & Godbey, G.C. (1991). Leisure, recreation and tourism. *Annals of Tourism Research, 18,* 85-100.

Stoppa, E.A. (1999). *Acampamentos de férias.* Campinas, Brazil: Papirus.

UN News Centre. (2010). *Number of internet users to surpass 2 billion by end of year, UN agency reports.* Retrieved October 1, 2011, from www.un.org/apps/news/story.asp?NewsID=36492&Cr=internet&Cr1

United Nations Development Programme. (2010). *Human development report 2010.*

Vandelanotte, C., Sugiyama, T., Gardiner, P., & Owen, N. (2009). Associations of leisure-time Internet and computer use with overweight and obesity, physical activity and sedentary behaviors: Cross-sectional study. *Journal of Medical Internet Research, 11*(3), e28.

Wang, J., & Stringer, L.A. (2000). The impact of Taoism on Chinese leisure. *World Leisure, 42*(3), 33-41.

Weng, J. (2010). *Rapid development of leisure industry in Hangzhou.* Retrieved October 17, 2011, from www.zj.xinhuanet.com/photo/2010-11/15/content_21393221.htm

Xiao, H. (1997). Tourism and leisure in China: A tale of two cities. *Annals of Tourism Research, 24*(2), 357-370.

Yin, X. (2005). New trends of leisure consumption in China. *Journal of Family and Economic Issues, 26*(1), 175-182.

You, B., & Zhen, X. (2007). *On the leisure society and the leisure industry of China.* Retrieved October 17, 2011, from www.gogoplay.cn/html/xiuxianlilun/200711/20071110164526733.html

Yu, G. (2004). *On the society of universal leisure.* Beijing, China: Chinese Economy Press.

Zhang, X., Hu, H., & Zhang, J. (2010). *Annual report on development of China's cultural industries.* Beijing, China: Social Sciences Academic Press.

Zhou, X. (2008). *Survey of Chinese middle class.* Beijing, China: Social Science Academic Press.

Index

Note: The italicized *f* and *t* following page numbers refer to figures and tables, respectively.

About the Contributors

Denise M. Anderson, PhD, is an associate professor and coordinator of graduate studies in the department of parks, recreation, and tourism management at Clemson University. Anderson's professional experience includes working in campus recreation and as a program coordinator for the Champaign Park District in Champaign, Illinois. Her research interests include community recreation management, youth development, gender equity, and student development through leisure. Anderson teaches courses in evaluation, finance, programming, and management and she is a core instructor in Clemson University's innovative PRTM immersion semester experience, EDGE (Engaging in Diverse, Guided Experiences).

Robert F. Ashcraft, PhD, is executive director of the Lodestar Center for Philanthropy and Nonprofit Innovation and an associate professor in the School of Community Resources and Development at Arizona State University. He has over 30 years of experience working in nonprofit leadership and management roles and teaching students the theory and practice behind that work. Ashcraft served for 10 years on the national board of the YMCA of the USA and served as the youngest executive director of a local chapter in the American Red Cross. Ashcraft serves on the board of trustees of the National Recreation and Park Association (NRPA), among other leadership roles, and is past president of the Nonprofit Academic Centers Council. He has served as director and in many other capacities for the Nonprofit Leadership Alliance, an undergraduate nonprofit management education program based in Kansas City.

Lynn A. Barnett, PhD, is an associate professor in the department of recreation, sport, and tourism at the University of Illinois at Urbana-Champaign, where her research has focused on the play of children and young adults and the contribution of play to development. Barnett is the author of numerous theoretical and empirical chapters and articles about play as an essential quality of human experience, learning, and development. She has translated this research into the design of toys and play structures and programs. For many years she has been teaching an upper-division course called Leisure and Human Development, which chronicles the course of play and leisure across the life span. She is a member of the Academy of Leisure Sciences, Play Research International, and the National Recreation and Park Association.

Joel A. Blanco, MS, is a doctoral candidate in recreation, sport, and tourism at the University of Illinois at Urbana-Champaign. He received his master's degree from Pennsylvania State University in University Park. During work on his master's degree, his focus was investigating the impact of human development and family studies on leisure behavior. His current research interests explore the interrelationships between leisure behavior and mental health.

Diane C. Blankenship, EdD, is an associate professor at Frostburg State University in Frostburg, Maryland, where she teaches freshmen orientation, a diversity class, recreation leadership, and senior seminar. Blankenship has used her skills in developing program delivery systems to meet the needs of people with disabilities, military service personnel and their family members, the Boy Scout community, and public communities in the Washington DC area. She is a member of the Maryland Recreation and Parks Association (MRPA) and has served numerous times on the conference committee to assist with the program development and mentor program for students. In addition, she serves as a site visitor for the Commission for Accreditation of Park and Recreation Agencies (CAPRA) and is a member of two CAPRA certification committees for the National Recreation and Park Association.

John Byl, PhD, is the president of Canadian Intramural Recreation Association (CIRA) Ontario and a professor of physical education at Redeemer University College in Ancaster, Ontario. Dr. Byl has authored or coauthored 20 books, including *101 Fun Warm-Up and Cool-Down Games* and *Organizing Successful Tournaments*, and has coauthored several books, including *Chicken and Noodle Games* and *Christian Paths to Health and Wellness*. He is the winner of several professional awards and a regular workshop leader. He has a special interest in promoting fun, active participation for all children and developing and maintaining personal wellness.

Gaylene Carpenter, EdD, is associate professor emerita and former director of the arts and administration program at the University of Oregon. She has 45 years of professional and academic experience in leisure programming and 37 years of teaching in both recreation and leisure studies and in arts management academic units at five universities in the United States. She has published numerous articles on arts and cultural programs, festivals and events, and leadership and supervision. She is coauthor of *Arts & Cultural Programming: A Leisure Perspective*. In her role as principal investigator for *A Study of Leisure During Adulthood*, she has published many journal articles and given frequent presentations on adult leisure, life perceptions, and values, including at NRPA's Leisure Research Symposium and the Canadian Congress for Leisure Research. An advocate of arts and cultural programs, Carpenter initiated the festival and event management certificate program at the University of Oregon between 1998 and 2007. She received the Ovation Award for Lifetime Achievement from the Oregon Festivals and Events Association and the Teaching Innovation Award and the Excellence in Teaching Award from the Society of Park & Recreation Educators.

Jinyang Deng, PhD, is associate professor in the recreation, parks, and tourism resources program at West Virginia University. He was born and raised in a rural village in central China. He earned a BS in forestry from the Central South Forestry College (renamed Central South University of Forestry and Technology) in China (1987), an MS in forest recreation from the same university (1990), and a PhD in recreation and leisure studies from the University of Alberta, Canada (2004). From 1997 to 1998, he was visiting scholar in the department of hospitality, tourism, and marketing at Victoria University, Melbourne, Australia. His current teaching activities and research interests are focused on ecotourism, GIS application in tourism and recreation, and cross-cultural comparison of leisure.

Holly Donohoe, PhD, is an assistant professor in the department of tourism, recreation, and sport management at the University of Florida. She has collaborated on research projects and provided consultant support to organizations and agencies worldwide, including the World Leisure Organization, Canadian Parks and Recreation Association, National Capital Commission, Canadian Index of Wellbeing, and Quebec Counsel on Leisure. Her current research interests include the geography of tourism and recreation, indigenous tourism, heritage tourism marketing, outdoor recreation management, e-tourism, and e-leisure.

Paul F.J. Eagles, PhD, is a professor specializing in environmental planning at the University of Waterloo in Canada. His primary appointment is in the department of recreation and leisure studies. He is also cross-appointed to the School of Planning. Over the last 40 years Eagles has worked on a variety of planning projects with an emphasis on the planning and management of parks and protected areas. He has undertaken work in nature-based tourism in more than 25 countries. Professor Eagles has authored more than 350 publications in tourism, planning, management, and related areas. He coauthored the book *Sustainable Tourism in Protected Areas: Guidelines for Planning and Management* (2002).

David N. Emanuelson, PhD, is president and CEO of Impact Planning and a partner at the Public Research Group. Impact Planning provides planning and financial analysis to parks and recreation agencies, and Public Research Group conducts community needs assessment surveys, studies, and political polls to help parks and recreation agencies provide better services. He served as a parks and recreation professional for over 30 years. He received his PhD in political science from Northern Illinois University. David also served 7 years as an assistant professor in recreation administration at George Williams College of Aurora University in Williams Bay, Wisconsin. He has received the Gold Medal Award for Excellence in Park and Recreation Management, nine Certificates of Achievement for Financial Reporting, three literary awards from *Illinois Parks and Recreation Magazine* and one from *Wisconsin Park and Recreation Magazine*, and the Distinguished Scholar and Distinguished Manuscript Awards from Northern Illinois University.

Dr. Alan Ewert, PhD, is a distinguished and titled professor at Indiana University. He is the holder of the Patricia and Joel Meier Endowed Chair in Outdoor Leadership and serves as the director of the Leisure Research Institute in the department of recreation, park, and tourism studies. Dr. Ewert's research publications include articles in the *Journal of Leisure Research, Leisure Sciences, Environment and Behavior, Journal of Park and Recreation Administration, Journal of Experiential Education*, and *Society and Natural Resources*. He has published four books: *Outdoor Adventure Pursuits: Foundations, Models, and Theories* (1989); *Culture, Conflict, and Communication in the Wildland-Urban Interface* (1993); *Natural Resource Management: The Human Dimension* (1996); and *Integrated Resource and Environmental Management* (2004). He has authored over 200 articles and research presentations as well as 14 book chapters. He has instructed in a variety of programs, including Outward Bound, NOLS, and Wilderness Inquiry, and has been a survival instructor for the U.S. Air Force.

Jeffrey Ferguson, EdD, is an associate professor at Northwest Missouri State University, where he has served as the recreation curriculum coordinator for the past 25 years. He established the degree program in corporate recreation and wellness at Northwest in 1990. Jeff has served on the advisory group for the Northwest Fitness Center for two decades. Before coming to Northwest, Jeff held recreation positions with the City of Berkeley in Missouri and the King Faisal Specialist Hospital and Research Centre in Riyadh, Saudi Arabia, and as a campus recreation director and instructor at Bethany College in Kansas. He received his formal education from Southwest Missouri State University, University of Missouri at Columbia, University of Oregon, and Oklahoma State University.

M. Rebecca Genoe, PhD, is an assistant professor in the faculty of kinesiology and health studies at the University of Regina, where she teaches in the therapeutic recreation program. Rebecca completed her PhD at the University of Waterloo in recreation and leisure studies with a specialization in aging, health, and well-being. Her research focuses on the meaning and experience of leisure among older adults.

H. Joey Gray, PhD, is an associate professor in the department of health and human performance and program manager of leisure, sport, and tourism studies at Middle Tennessee State University. She has received several prestigious teaching awards and published several articles related to pedagogy in recreation. Gray has many years of professional experience in sport management and special-event planning both in the public and private sectors. She has also served as the athletic director of the National Youth Sports Program. Gray has given presentations at the local, state, and national levels in recreational sport management and pedagogical aspects of recreation.

Dr. Jeffrey C. Hallo, PhD, is an assistant professor in the department of parks, recreation, and tourism management at Clemson University. He focuses his research on understanding, planning for, and managing recreational visitor use in parks, forests, and other protected areas. Dr. Hallo conducts research and writes on topics that include provision of high-quality visitor experiences, park transportation, motorized recreation, and park and recreation carrying capacities. Dr. Hallo teaches graduate and undergraduate courses in management of parks and protected areas.

Jane Hodgkinson, MS, was the executive director of the Western DuPage Special Recreation Association (WDSRA) for 30 years until her retirement in 2011. WDSRA won two National Gold Medal Awards for its special recreation programs. She spent more than 40 years in special recreation settings in Illinois. She was named the 2011 Outstanding Nonprofit Leader in DuPage County and a Legend by the American Academy of Park and Recreation Administration (AAPRA) in 2010. She received the 1999 Robert Artz Award, the 1989 Illinois Park and Recreation Association's Professional of the Year Award, and the Outstanding Woman Leader Award from DuPage County. Hodgkinson is a founding board member of the Illinois Special Olympics and past president of the Illinois Park and Recreation Association (IPRA). She is a member of the IPRA, the NRPA, and the AAPRA.

Douglas Kennedy, EdD, CPRP, is a professor in the department of recreation and leisure studies at Virginia Wesleyan College in Norfolk, Virginia. He has taught a course on history, philosophy, trends, and cultural dimensions of recreation and leisure for over two decades. He has spoken at numerous professional events nationally and internationally, addressing critical events in the development of the recreation profession. Kennedy is a past chair of the Council on Accreditation, a past president of the Virginia Recreation and Park Society, an instructor for the National Camping School, and a delegation leader of the Uzbekistan National Youth Democracy Education Project. As part of that project, Kennedy wrote a series of documents that facilitated democracy education in Uzbekistan through work with local teachers on integrating principles of democracy in grade-school curricula. He is also a member of the board of directors of the YMCA of South Hampton Roads and chair of the board of directors of Camp Silver Beach. His current research focuses on examining the measurement of high-altitude decision making in recreation environments.

Robin Kunstler, ReD, CTRS, is a professor in the department of health sciences and the director of the recreation education and therapeutic recreation programs at Lehman College of the City University of New York. She is coauthor of the text *Therapeutic Recreation Leadership and Programming.* With over 35 years of experience in the field of therapeutic recreation as both a practitioner and a professor, she has presented at many state and national conferences, authored numerous articles and book chapters on therapeutic recreation, and served as editor and reviewer for the leading journals in the field. A member of numerous committees and boards of national and state professional organizations, she is a recipient of the Lifetime Achievement Award from the New York State Therapeutic Recreation Association and the New York State Recreation and Park Society Literary and Research Awards.

Rebecca Lesnik, MS, CTRS, is a practicing recreation therapist currently working for the Department of Veterans Affairs Palo Alto Health Care System and is assigned to the Homeless Veterans Rehabilitation Program. Before assuming her current position, she worked for a decade as a recreation therapist for the Vermont Department of Corrections serving those actively incarcerated at both the Caledonia Community Work Camp and the Northeast Regional Correctional Facility. In addition, Rebecca completed an extensive internship at Oregon State Hospital, where she was assigned to a maximum-security mental health treatment unit. After receiving her BS in recreation therapy from Temple University in Philadelphia, she went on to earn an MS in counseling and psychology from Springfield College of Human Services. With a strong foundation in cognitive behavioral therapy, Rebecca maintains a keen focus on motivating positive change with those having a history of incarceration as well as challenges involving substance use disorders and mental health concerns.

Huimei Liu, PhD, is an associate professor in the School of International Studies at Zhejiang University in China. She is also a researcher in the Asia Pacific Centre for the Education and Study of Leisure at Zhejiang University. She earned her BA and MA in English in 1993 and 1996 from Xiangtan Normal University (now named Hunan University of Science and Technology) and Changsha Railway University (now named Central South University), respectively. She earned her PhD in 2008 from Zhejiang University. Her strong interest in leisure studies, which is still a new subject in China, led her to work as a volunteer for the organizing committee of the 2006 Hangzhou World Leisure Expo from 2003 to 2006. She spent a year at Penn State University on a Fulbright Scholarship for a U.S.-Sino joint PhD program. She currently teaches a leisure and culture course. Her research interests are cross-cultural studies of leisure and leisure policy.

Alcyane Marinho, PhD, is a lecturer in the physical education department at Santa Catarina State University (Udesc) in Brazil. She completed her bachelor's degree in physical education at Sao Paulo State University (Unesp) in 1995 and her master's degree in 2001 and PhD in 2006 at Campinas State University (Unicamp) in Brazil. Her research interests include leisure and tourism, adventure tourism, and outdoor education. Some of her more recent publications (in Portuguese) are *Leisure, Sport, Tourism and Adventure: Nature in Focus* (2009); *Travels, Leisure and Sport: The Space of Nature* (2006); and *Tourism, Leisure and Nature* (2003).

Susan Markham-Starr, PhD, is professor emerita in the School of Recreation Management and Kinesiology at Acadia University in Wolfville, Nova Scotia. She has experience as a researcher of the history of the development of recreation and parks services in Canada and as a practitioner and consultant in recreation and parks planning. She is the former president of the Canadian Association for Leisure Studies (CALS) and served as chair for the Canadian Parks and Recreation Association (CPRA) editorial committee and Integrated Research Dissemination Project and the Wolfville Recreation Commission. Markham-Starr wrote the CPRA research policy and coedited its 50th-anniversary publication. She also wrote the first City of Halifax recreation master plan and is a member of CALS and World Leisure.

Donald J. McLean, PhD, is a professor and coordinator in the department of recreation, park, and tourism administration at Western Illinois University–Quad Cities in Moline, Illinois. He holds advanced degrees in both philosophy and recreation and leisure studies and has presented papers on applied ethics at national conferences and served as guest editor for a special issue on applied ethics in the *Journal of Applied Recreation Research* (now known as *Leisure/Loisir*). In his leisure time, he enjoys downhill skiing, walking, and golfing (which, as Samuel Clemens says, simply "is a good walk spoiled").

Michael Muehlenbein, PhD, MsPH, MPhil, is an assistant professor of anthropology at Indiana University. He is also affiliated with Indiana's program in international studies, the Center for Research in Environmental Sciences, and the Anthropological Center for Training and Research on Global Environmental Change. His research interests include global health, epidemiology of infectious disease, and travel medicine. He is coeditor of the educational workbook *Health Communities: Repositioning Public Park and Recreation Agencies as Catalysts for Healthy People.* He is the author of more than 30 peer-reviewed articles or chapters; is an associate editor for 5 journals; has taught more than 1,300 students; and is a reviewer for 35 journals, 10 publishing houses, and 8 granting agencies. He has spent more than 2 years in the field outside the United States conducting research on health of tourists and the wildlife and indigenous populations that the tourists visit.

Laurie Ogilvie, MA, is a national manager in policy and program development with the Canadian Forces personnel and family support services of the Department of National Defence. She has been primarily involved in the development of national policies and programs for the morale and welfare of Canadian Forces personnel and their families. She is currently involved in the enhancement of services for families of Canadian Forces personnel, focusing on programs that mitigate the unique challenges families face as a result of the military lifestyle.

Ellen O'Sullivan, PhD, serves as the chair of the Center for Public Recreation and Parks, a nonprofit organization focused on providing information and data leading to the long-term sustainability of the movement. She is the author of two marketing books for the field as well as two of the original benefit-based publications for NRPA. She completed a guide for NRPA on rejuvenating neighborhoods and communities through parks. She is an NRPA National Distinguished Professional and a member of the American Academy for Park and Recreation Administration. She also served as lead trainer for Hearts N' Parks, a project that she helped develop in North Carolina that led to a nationwide program for the National Institutes of Health that established the groundwork for further initiatives into health and wellness by the park and recreation movement.

Robert E. Pfister, PhD, is a retired professor with the department of recreation and tourism management at Vancouver Island University (VIU) in Nanaimo, British Columbia, Canada, where he currently serves as an adjunct faculty member. For over 35 years, Pfister instructed courses in entrepreneurial recreation and tourism to students in the United States and Canada. He held full-time tenured faculty appointments at California State University at Pomona, University of Northern British Columbia, and East Carolina University (ECU). In 2010, the ECU College of Health and Human Performance bestowed on Dr. Pfister the Meritorious and Emeritus Service Award for his contribution during his time there. In 2011, he was recognized again at the VIU commencement ceremony for his teaching, scholarship, and leadership in creating a new graduate program focused on sustainability in recreation and tourism. Pfister is a member of the Association of American Geographers and served as chairperson of the recreation, tourism, and sports specialty group. He is a member of the Society of Park and Recreation Educators, Canadian Council for Small Business and Entrepreneurship, and World Leisure Organization. He served on the editorial board of *Tourism Geographies* and on the board of directors for Tourism Vancouver Island and Tourism Prince George, both regional tourism destination marketing organizations.

Carol J. Potter, BS, is a senior program analyst in the Morale, Welfare, and Recreation (MWR) Policy Directorate in the Office of the Deputy Assistant Secretary of Defense for Military Community and Family Policy. Ms. Potter is an authority for military MWR programs and is responsible for developing policies, strategic planning, program analysis, evaluation, and program oversight. She developed the Return and Recreate program initiative that promotes high-adventure recreation for returning deployed service members and their families to reduce stress, promote reintegration, and build resilience. Ms. Potter conducts the biennial MWR Customer Satisfaction Survey that measures current trends of service members and prioritizes program improvements and funding. The survey results provide empirical data that validate the relationship between MWR, mission readiness, and unit cohesion. She directors the effort to expand inclusion in recreation by training military installation recreation staff, enabling them to program and execute MWR activities for people with all abilities such as wounded warriors and families with special needs. Ms. Potter manages a research project that measures resilience when service members and families participate in MWR activities, since resilience is a major contributor to mission readiness. She is an advisor to the Armed Forces Recreation Network for the National Recreation and Park Association.

Arianne C. Reis, PhD, is a research fellow with the School of Tourism and Hospitality Management at Southern Cross University, Australia. Reis is originally from Brazil, where she completed her undergraduate and master's studies in physical education. Before completing her PhD work at the University of Otago, New Zealand, Reis worked for several years for public and private institutions in Brazil in the fields of nature-based recreation and sport management. Her research interests have developed from these professional experiences and have focused on outdoor recreation and the sustainability issues of sport events. Reis has presented her work in local, national, and international conferences, and her research has been published in sport, tourism, and recreation journals and books over the past decade.

Brenda Robertson, PhD, is a professor in the School of Recreation Management and Kinesiology at Acadia University in Wolfville, Nova Scotia. She has studied youth crime and correctional recreation for the past two decades and focused her PhD research on why youths commit crime for fun. Her research and teaching focus on leisure behavior, disenfranchised populations, and leisure education. She has presented her work on youth crime throughout Canada and the United States as well as in Europe and Africa, and she has produced over 30 publications on leisure, youth crime, and related topics. Among her publications is a report titled *The Interface Between Leisure Education Delivery Models and Youth Justice Renewal*, which examines the role of leisure education in correctional settings. She has served on numerous boards and committees, including the board of the National Correctional Recreation Association and the Canadian Association of Leisure Studies, chair of the Citizens Advisory Committee for Correctional Services of Canada, director of the Recreation Resource Centre of Nova Scotia, and program manager for commissions of the World Leisure Organization.

Clifford Robertson, BA, earned his degree in kinesiology exercise science from Cornell College. While at Cornell, Clifford was commissioner of the intramurals program for two years. He helped design two disc golf courses, one for the city of Mount Vernon and the other for Cornell's campus. He competed in four varsity sports: soccer, tennis, golf, and wrestling. Currently Clifford is working on his master's degree in applied health science at Northwest Missouri State University.

Dr. Terrance Robertson, PhD, is a professor and chair of the department of health and human services at Northwest Missouri State University. Dr. Robertson worked in various areas of health for several years (i.e., director of special services for Clark County Parks and Recreation Department in Las Vegas, Nevada, consultant to long-term care and managed care organizations, substance abuse counselor, case manager, and assistant director of rehab services for a small hospital). As an educator, Dr. Robertson has continued his contact with the field through consulting and through special university-related programs and research projects. Current research projects are focused on at-risk and adjudicated youth as well as the development of regional health care cooperatives. He has consulted for a variety of municipalities, including the cities of Las Vegas, Reno, and San Jose; the North Suburban Special Recreation District; the Nevada and Florida Developmental Disabilities Councils; and a host of not-for-profit agencies and health care agencies. He is a past president of the National Therapeutic Recreation Society and of the Midland Empire Independent Living Center Board of Directors (currently serving nine counties). He is also the president (his second publicly elected four-year term) of the Nodaway County Health Department with emergency response planning responsibilities for 10 counties and special responsibility for people who have disabilities and other health concerns.

Craig M. Ross, ReD, is a professor in the department of recreation, park, and tourism studies at Indiana University. He has written over 75 professional articles, many of them published in the *Recreational Sports Journal*. He has received nearly two dozen awards for his writing, teaching, research, and service. In addition, he has coauthored three editions of *Recreational Sport Management* for Human Kinetics and has served as associate director at Indiana University Campus Recreational Sports with primary responsibilities in the campus intramural sports program. Ross has delivered over 150 presentations at the local, state, national, and international levels in recreational sport management.

Jerome F. Singleton, PhD, CTRS, is a professor in the recreation and leisure studies department in the School of Health and Human Performance at Dalhousie University. He is also cross-appointed to the school of nursing, the sociology and anthropology departments, and faculty of management at Dalhousie. Dr. Singleton's research is focused on leisure and aging. He graduated from the University of Waterloo with a bachelor's degree in recreation with honors, completed his master of science degree in recreation at Pennsylvania State University, and received his PhD in leisure studies at the University of Maryland. He also completed the academic requirements for a doctorate certificate in gerontology at the University of Maryland. Currently Dr. Singleton teaches courses in therapeutic recreation and aging, therapeutic recreation techniques, and introduction to recreation and leisure and aging at Dalhousie University. He was made a fellow of the World Demographic Association in 2006 and was named Professional of the Year by the Canadian Therapeutic Recreation Association in 2007. He was recognized by the recreation and leisure studies program at the University of Waterloo as a distinguished alumni in 2008 and is the founding member of the Leisure and Aging Research Group, which was established in 2008. Dr. Singleton received the Dr. Gonzaga da Gama Memorial Award from the Canadian Therapeutic Recreation Association in 2011 and was made a fellow of the Academy of Leisure Science by the Society of Park and Recreation Educators in 2011. Dr. Singleton is currently a research associate with the Dalhousie European Center of Excellence. He has advised 25 graduate students who have investigated questions related to leisure and aging and has published over 80 journal articles during his career and made local, national, and international presentations related to the area of leisure and aging. He has served on the editorial boards for *Therapeutic Recreation Journal*, *American Therapeutic Recreation Annual*, *Topics in Geriatric Rehabilitation*, and *Recreation and Society in Africa, Asia, and Latin America*. He has reviewed articles for *Loisir*, *Leisure Science*, and *Topics in Geriatric Rehabilitation*.

Tod Stanton, MS, has two decades of professional experience in the field of recreation, including working for an Illinois park district. He holds a master's degree in recreation administration from George Williams College of Aurora University. He is a founding partner of Public Research Group, a consultant firm that specializes in community surveying for park and recreation agencies. Tod has given numerous education sessions at the state level surrounding recreation programming, comprehensive planning, and leadership. He has worked with various agencies in creating comprehensive park and recreation master plans, and through those efforts he has gained insight into the trends facing recreation professionals.

Frances Stavola Daly, EdD, CTRS, CPRP, is an associate professor and the recreation administration program coordinator in the department of physical education, recreation, and health at Kean University in New Jersey. She is coauthor of the text *Therapeutic Recreation Leadership and Programming*. She has over 35 years of experience in the recreation field as both a practitioner and a professor and as a consultant to numerous agencies and is a frequent speaker at state, regional, and national conferences. Stavola Daly has served as the president of the National Therapeutic Recreation Society (NTRS) and as a member of the board of trustees of the National Recreation and Park Association (NRPA). She is a recipient of the Presidential Citation from the NTRS in 2007 and the Lifetime Achievement Award from the New York State Therapeutic Recreation Association in 2004. In 2010, she received the Presidential Distinguished Service Award from Kean University.

Dr. Matthew Symonds, EdD, is an assistant professor in the department of health and human services at Northwest Missouri State University. He currently serves as co-coordinator of the department's graduate programs and basic instruction program. Dr. Symonds also coordinated the university's faculty and staff wellness program for eight years. While his primary teaching responsibilities are in the health and physical education teacher preparation program, he has research interests in a variety of areas related to health and physical activity. Dr. Symonds has served as board president and is in his fourth term on the Maryville Parks and Recreation Board of Directors. Dr. Symonds is also a past president and former health division chair of the Missouri Association for Health, Physical Education, Recreation, and Dance.

Patrick T. Tierney, PhD, is a professor in the department of recreation, parks, and tourism at San Francisco State University. As a business owner, instructor, and researcher, Tierney has more than 30 years of experience in theories and applications of the recreation, event, and tourism industry.

For 25 years, Tierney was co-owner and operator of Adrift Adventures, Inc., a successful adventure recreation business nominated for the Conde Nast International Ecotourism Award. Tierney is past chairperson of the Colorado River Outfitters Association and a member of the board of directors of the California Tourism Industry Association. He is a licensed whitewater guide instructor and former U.S. Forest Service and National Park Service ranger.

In 1997, Tierney was co-recipient of the Best Tourism Research Award from the California Division of Tourism. He also received the 1991 Excellence in Research Award from the Resort and Commercial Recreation Association.

Juan Tortosa Martínez, PhD, is an assistant professor in physical activity and sport science at the University of Alicante, Spain. He earned his undergraduate degree from the University of Valencia. He lived several years in Illinois, where he earned a master's degree in recreation, park, and tourism administration at Western Illinois University. During this time, Dr. Tortosa Martínez worked in various recreation settings from the small rural community of Virginia, Illinois, to the city of Elgin, Illinois. He has been interested in comparing the leisure and recreation fields in the United States and Spain, publishing three papers about the topic. His research also encompasses leisure and aging as well as recreation for special populations. He has publications in the *Annual in Therapeutic Recreation* and the *International Journal on Disability and Human Development*. He currently runs various therapeutic recreation programs for people with mental health problems and people with mild cognitive impairment and Alzheimer's disease.

Franklin Vernon, MS, is currently a doctoral student at Indiana University, where he focuses his teaching and research on experiential learning and adventure education. He has been an outdoor and adventure educator for 13 years, most recently as a lead instructor for Northwest Outward Bound School and North Carolina Outward Bound School, as well as an instructor trainer for Indiana University Outdoor Adventures. His research and writing focus on philosophical, educational, and sociological aspects of outdoor adventure education, such as critical and pragmatic approaches to experiential learning and the role of co-instructor relationships in shaping expedition experiences. When he can sneak away from outdoor adventure as a labor arrangement, he can be found climbing rock, ice, and mountains or paddling rivers with his partner Katie and their North American dingo Nootka.

Julia Wallace Carr, EdD, is a senior associate director at University Recreation and associate professor in sport and recreation management at James Madison University. She has 20 years of experience in campus recreation. Wallace Carr has served as a trainer and consultant nationwide for campus recreation programs on using the principles of LR2, developing learning outcomes, and staff development. She has also been a frequent speaker at the NIRSA national conference on learning outcomes and program planning. Wallace Carr coauthored (with Dr. Sarah Hardin of DePaul University) "Writing Measureable Learning Outcomes" (2010) for the *Recreational Sports Journal*. In 2010, she received the NIRSA Region II Award of Merit and NIRSA's President's Award for Outstanding Writing. She received her doctorate of education from The George Washington University.

Daniel G. Yoder, PhD, is a professor in the recreation, park, and tourism department at Western Illinois University in Macomb. His research and teaching are focused on leisure and sociology. In his position as a parks and recreation director in Colorado, he observed and organized activities for a diverse group of people and faced practical leisure and sociological issues on a daily basis. He coauthored *Issues in Recreation and Leisure: Ethical Decision Making* (2005) with Don McLean for Human Kinetics. Yoder is a member of the NRPA and the Illinois Park and Recreation Association, having served in a number of positions with the IPRA. He is also involved in a variety of nonprofit organizations dealing with recreation and youth in his community. Yoder has served on various university committees and boards. Besides his teaching and community involvement, he is a husband, father, part-time farmer, full-time conservationist, and avid beekeeper. Because optimal experiences have profoundly affected Yoder's life, he is committed to the exploration of this life-enriching phenomenon for himself and others.